Praise for Closed Communion

"No" can be a positive word. If a toddler wants to touch a hot burner, "No" is the right directive to give. Admitting communicants to the Lord's Table carries the responsibility to invite to the Banquet those confessing the real presence of the Lord but also to withhold the elements from those who do not. Given Americans' esteem for their autonomy and their sacrament-free approach to spirituality, closed Communion is countercultural. This book empowers pastors and other church leaders to implement or maintain the ancient church's practices in Communion fellowship.

—Mark Mattes,
Grand View University,
Des Moines, Iowa

This book fills a definite void. Pastors and laypeople from churches who practice closed Communion will find here support for the practice from a variety of sources and angles, in a thoughtful manner that is neither parochial nor pedantic. Those whose churches do not practice closed Communion but who want to better understand the practice, both as it was treated in the past and as it is taught by Christians today, will likewise find a very helpful array of arguments to consider. *Closed Communion* deserves a place on the shelves of pastors' studies and church libraries and, even more, deserves to be read.

—Wade Johnston, PhD
Assistant Professor of Theology
Wisconsin Lutheran College,
Milwaukee, Wisconsin

What a splendid way to honor a faithful Lutheran theologian! What a fantastic collection of articles regarding the faithful administration of the Lord's Supper! To lose the proper administration of the Sacrament is to eventually lose justification by grace through faith in Christ (Augsburg IV). This book is a must read for anyone who values the Sacrament. Thanks to CPH for taking up this important project! This is a thorough exposition regarding why we in the Lutheran Church practice "closed Communion." An easy read, yet essential to our Lutheran confession and identity!

—Rev. John C. Wille, President,
South Wisconsin District LCMS

Praise for Closed Communion

Pastors and congregations need strength, comfort, and wisdom to practice closed Communion. Pastors are stewards of God's mysteries (1 Cor. 4:1), entrusted with the administration of the Lord's body and blood. Yet so often they feel uneasy, even guilty, about denying anyone from the altar, having experienced conflict or frustration from the congregation in the past. Now, more than ever, pastors need a greater cloud of witnesses to believe, teach, and confess that the loving practice of closed Communion is, in fact, loving. *Closed Communion* is that great cloud of witnesses. Congregations need resources to understand theologically the pressures facing their pastor every Sunday. The very best of these resources are found here. God grant that our pastors and churches study this volume to find comfort and strength!

—Jason D. Lane
Assistant Professor of Theology
Concordia University Wisconsin,
Mequon, Wisconsin

The essays in this book provide a wonderfully broad perspective on the necessity and challenges of a faithful practice of closed Communion. The editors have gathered a variety of voices from the present and the past and thus shed a light on the long tradition the practice has in the Lutheran Church. The witness given thereby to the fact that the difficult challenges that go along with closed Communion are nothing new only further serves to whet the reader's appetite.

—Rev. Jacob Corzine
Lutheran Campus Minister of the Free Evangelical Lutheran Synod in South Africa
Arcadia Lutheran Ministries, Pretoria, South Africa

This comprehensive volume gives a cloud of witnesses to faithful practice of closed Communion across history. It also includes practical essays addressing today's ministry context and will guide contemporary pastors to shepherd precious souls with integrity and love in delivering the gifts of Christ. In nearly three decades of ministry, I saw the compassionate application of these principles yield fruit in bringing comfort to believers and creating anticipation for receiving Christ's gifts in those not yet catechized. This served mission outreach and cultivated growth in new member classes.

—Rev. Dr. W. Mart Thompson,
Associate Professor,
Concordia Seminary, St. Louis, Missouri
long-time parish pastor

The dogma of inclusiveness poses a serious and sometimes overwhelming challenge to the catholic Lutheran principle of closed Communion and the implied rejection of unionism. It is therefore highly recommended to equip the worldwide confessional Lutheran churches of our time with a multitude of exegetical, dogmatic, historical, and pastoral resources as can be found in this volume. Parishes and pastors will be encouraged to continue or return to a Communion practice in which the highest priority is the faithfulness to the Lord Jesus Christ and His divine institution of the Sacrament of the Altar.

—Rev. Dr. Armin Wenz,
Halle (Saale), Germany

Promiscuous admission to Communion is when the Lord's body and blood are given to or taken by those who do not share the Church's confession of faith, or do not repent, or sometimes even when they deny that it truly is the Lord Jesus' body and blood. Confessional admission to Communion recognizes that Communion has not just a vertical but also a horizontal aspect; it takes into account the confession of the Church and of the individual in words and deeds; rather than covering over division and differences at the Lord's Table, it seeks first to remove those differences before celebrating the Supper of unity. This book, therefore, is most welcome as a resource to enable pastors and parishioners more faithfully to seek unity and avoid promiscuity in Communion practices.

—Benjamin T. G. Mayes
Assistant Professor of Historical Theology
Concordia Theological Seminary, Fort Wayne, Indiana
co-general editor, Luther's Works, American Edition (CPH)

CLOSED COMMUNION?

Admission to the Lord's Supper in Biblical Lutheran Perspective

GENERAL EDITORS
Matthew C. Harrison
and John T. Pless

CONCORDIA PUBLISHING HOUSE · SAINT LOUIS

3558 S. Jefferson Ave., St. Louis, MO 63118-3968
1-800-325-3040 • www.cph.org

Manufactured in the United States of America

LIBRARY OF CONGRESS CATALOGING-IN-PUBLICATION DATA

Names: Harrison, Matthew C., editor.
Title: Closed communion : admission to the Lord's Supper in biblical Lutheran perspective / general editors, Matthew C. Harrison and John T. Pless.
Description: St. Louis : Concordia Publishing House, 2017. | Includes bibliographic references and index.
Identifiers: LCCN 2017034616 (print) | LCCN 2017037885 (ebook) | ISBN 9780758658616 | ISBN 9780758658586 (alk. paper)
Subjects: LCSH: Lord's Supper—Lutheran Church. | Close and open communion.
Classification: LCC BX8073 (ebook) | LCC BX8073.C56 2017 (print) | DDC 264/.041036—dc2 3
LC record available at https://lccn.loc.gov/2017034616

4 5 6 7 8 9 10 11 27 26 25 24 23 22 21 20 19 18

Contents

Abbreviations

AC	Augsburg Confession
AE	*Luther's Works: American Edition.* Volumes 1–30: Edited by Jaroslav Pelikan. St. Louis: Concordia, 1955–76. Volumes 31–55: Edited by Helmut Lehmann. Philadelphia/Minneapolis: Muhlenberg/Fortress, 1957–86. Volumes 57–60, 67–69, 75–79: Edited by Christopher Boyd Brown and Benjamin T. G. Mayes. St. Louis: Concordia, 2009–.
Aland	Kurt Aland. *Hilfsbuch zum Lutherstudium.* 4th ed. Bielefeld: Luther-Verlag, 1996. Cited by main catalog number, sermon number (Pr), or letter number (Br).
ANF	*The Ante-Nicene Fathers: Translations of the Writings of the Fathers down to A.D. 325.* Edited by Alexander Roberts and James Donaldson. Revised by A. Cleveland Coxe. 10 volumes. Buffalo: Christian Literature Publishing Co., 1885–96. Reprint, Peabody, MA: Hendrickson, 1994.
Ap	Apology of the Augsburg Confession
BDAG	Walter Bauer, William Arndt, Fredrick Danker, and F. Wilbur Gingrich. *Greek-English Lexicon of the New Testament and Other Early Christian Literature.* Chicago: University of Chicago Press, 2000.
BKS/BSLK	*Die Bekenntnisschriften der evangelisch-lutherischen Kirche*
BLP	*Briefe an lutherische Pastoren*
CSEL	*Corpus scriptorum ecclesiasticorum Latinorum.* Vienna: Verlag der Österreichischen Akademie der Wissenschaften, 1866–.
Ep / FC Ep	Epitome of the Formula of Concord
FC	Formula of Concord
Kolb-Wengert	Robert Kolb and Timothy J. Wengert, eds. *The Book of Concord: The Confessions of the Evangelical Lutheran Church.* Minneapolis: Fortress, 2000.
LC	Large Catechism
LCMS	The Lutheran Church—Missouri Synod
LD	Kurt Aland, ed. *Die Werke Martin Luthers in neuer Auswahl für die Gegenwart.* Göttingen: Vandenhoeck & Ruprecht, 1959–83.

NPNF[2]	Schaff, Philip, and Henry Wace, ed. *A Select Library of Nicene and Post-Nicene Fathers of the Christian Church*, series 2. 14 vols. New York: The Christian Literature Series, 1890–99.
MH	Matthew C. Harrison
ODCC	*Oxford Dictionary of the Christian Church*
PG	*Patrologiae cursus completus: Series Graeca*. Edited by J.-P. Migne. 161 volumes in 167. Petit-Montrouge: Apud J. P. Migne, 1857–66.
RE	*Realenzyklopädie für Theologie und Kirche*
SA	Smalcald Articles
SC	Small Catechism
SD / FC SD	Solid Declaration of the Formula of Concord
StL	Johann Georg Walch, ed. *Dr. Martin Luthers sämmtliche Schriften: Neue revidirte Stereotypausgabe*. 23 volumes in 25. St. Louis: Concordia, 1880–1910.
Tappert	Theodore G. Tappert, ed. and trans. *The Book of Concord: The Confessions of the Evangelical Lutheran Church*. Minneapolis: Fortress, 1959.
TDNT	Gerhard Kittel and G. Friedrich eds. *Theological Dictionary of the New Testament*. Transalated by Geoffrey W. Bromiley. 10 volumes. Grand Rapids: Eerdmans, 1964–76.
Tr	Treatise on the Power and Primacy of the Pope
Triglotta / Concordia Triglotta	*Triglot Concordia: The Symbolical Books of the Ev.-Lutheran Church*. Edited by G. Friedrich Bente and William H. T. Dau. St. Louis: Concordia, 1921.
WA	*D. Martin Luthers Werke: Kritische Gesamtausgabe*. 73 volumes in 85. Weimar: H. Böhlau, 1883–.
WA Br	*D. Martin Luthers Werke: Briefwechsel*. 18 volumes. Weimar: H. Böhlau, 1930–.
WA DB	*D. Martin Luthers Werke: Deutsche Bibel*. 12 volumes in 15. Weimar: H. Böhlau, 1906–.
Walch, Walch[1], or W[1]	*D. Martin Luthers sowol in Deutscher als Lateinischer Sprache verfertigte und aus der letztern in die erstere übersetzte Sämmtliche Schriften*. Edited by Johann G. Walch. 24 volumes. Halle: Gebauer, 1740–53.
W[2]	*Dr. Martin Luthers Sämmtliche Schriften*. Edited by Albrecht F. Hoppe. 23 volumes. St. Louis: Concordia, 1880–1910.

INTRODUCTION

WRITING IN THE MIDST OF INCREASING PRESSURES for a more relaxed approach to altar and pulpit fellowship in 1957, Hermann Sasse observed: " 'Open Communion' is not Communion at all; it may be a fascinating rite, a religious experience, but it is not the Sacrament of the NT."[1] Biblically and historically, admission to the Lord's Table was on the basis of confession.[2] In American Lutheranism, this is expressed in the so-called "Galesburg Rule." It was a position advocated by no less than Franklin Clark Fry, then president of the United Lutheran Church in America, who stated in 1956: "Insistence upon agreement in doctrine as a precondition for church fellowship is a distinguishing mark of Lutherans among all Protestants and should never be relaxed."[3] This is not a Missouri Synod idiosyncrasy but a catholic practice. Indeed, the Lutheran Confessions cite John Chrysostom as an example: "Chrysostom says that the priest stands daily at the altar, inviting some to Communion and keeping others away."[4] Clearly, for the Lutheran Confessions, the apostolic exhortation for self-examination (1 Corinthians 11:27) does not relieve the pastor of his responsibility as a steward of the mysteries of God (1 Corinthians 4:12).

The issue of admission to the Lord's Supper entails questions regarding both the nature of the Sacrament and the character of the Church. Werner Elert sets Schleiermacher in contrast with Luther. Schleiermacher argued that: "The Christian Church takes shape through the coming together of regenerate individuals to form a system of mutual interaction and cooperation."[5] With Schleiermacher the doctrine of the Church is derived from a concept of fellowship: "The concept of fellowship which is here said to characterize the church does

---

1 Hermann Sasse, "Selective Fellowship" in *The Lonely Way*, vol. 2: *1940–1976*, ed. Matthew C. Harrison (St. Louis: Concordia, 2002), 262.

2 Here see the magisterial study of Werner Elert, *Eucharist and Church Fellowship in the First Four Centuries*, trans. Norman E. Nagel (St. Louis: Concordia, 1966).

3 Franklin Clark Fry, "Presentation of United Lutheran Attitude," in *Documents of Lutheran Unity in America*, ed. Richard C. Wolf (Philadelphia: Fortress, 1966), 225.

4 AC XXIV 36.

5 Friedrich Schleiermacher, *The Christian Faith,* trans. H. R. Macintosh and J. S. Stewart (Berkeley: Apocryphile Press, 2011), 532.

not derive from the nature of the church, but the nature of the church is derived from the concept of fellowship."[6] This means for Schleiermacher that the Church can continue to exist by the voluntary actions of human beings. The conclusion then for Schleiermacher and those who follow him is that "fellowship is a matter about which men are free to make their own arrangements."[7] Luther on the other hand sees *koinonia/communio* not as something having to do with a person but as having a part in a common thing. Hence Luther "first asked what is the church, and what is the Sacrament, and sought to determine what way each might be called a *communio*."[8]

The implication of the Lutheran teaching is well-stated by Sasse: "Altar fellowship is only possible, where a real church fellowship already exists. . . . Thus, Christianity has the duty to strictly avoid every church and altar fellowship with heresy, to examine individual believers, to instruct the erring in love, and most strenuously advance church and altar fellowship within orthodox Christianity."[9]

The Lord's Supper does not create church fellowship but presupposes that there is already a unity in the pure preaching of the Gospel and the administration of the Sacrament in accord with this divine word. Sasse critiques the modern ecumenical assertion that "baptismal fellowship" equals "altar fellowship."[10] Such a notion can only occur when the Sacraments become interchangeable. Participation in the Lord's Supper presupposes Baptism, but Baptism alone does not constitute admission to the Supper: "Even though a man must first be baptized before he may partake of the Holy Communion, this does not mean that all the baptized may without distinction partake of the Eucharist together."[11] Elert cites the Early Church apologist Justin: "Only those are permitted to partake of it (Lord's Supper) who believe the truth of our doctrine, who have been washed in the laver of the forgiveness of sins and regeneration, and who live accordingly, even as Christ has bidden us."[12]

Admission to the Lord's Supper is not based on notions of being a welcoming and affirming church but on a common confession of the faith embodied in one's attachment to a particular altar. "The unity of faith is not merely some shared sentiment. Paul had already made it clear not only that there is no faith without

6 Elert, *Eucharist and Church Fellowship*, 2.

7 Elert, *Eucharist and Church Fellowship*, 3.

8 Elert, *Eucharist and Church Fellowship*, 5.

9 Hermann Sasse, "Theses on the Question of Church and Altar Fellowship," in *The Lonely Way*, Vol. 1: *1927–1939*, ed. Matthew C. Harrison (St. Louis: Concordia, 2001), 333.

10 See Hermann Sasse, "Word and Sacrament: Preaching and the Lord's Supper," in *We Confess: The Sacraments*, trans. Norman E. Nagel (St. Louis: Concordia, 1985), 21.

11 Elert, *Eucharist and Church Fellowship*, 80.

12 Elert, *Eucharist and Church Fellowship*, 115.

kerygma, but also that believing with the heart is coupled with confessing with the mouth (Rom. 10:8ff). . . . Fellowship is possible only on the basis of the confessed faith."[13]

Historically there is no question of the relationship between a person's confession of faith and participation in the Lord's Supper: "The early church was never in doubt that unity in doctrine is a prerequisite of altar fellowship. No one who taught false doctrine might receive Holy Communion in an orthodox congregation."[14] One cannot with integrity move from altar to altar where contradictory confessions are made. "Since a man cannot at the same time hold two differing confessions, he cannot communicate in two churches of differing confessions. If anyone does this nevertheless, he denies his own confession or has none at all."[15] The practice of the Early Church was continued in the Lutheran Reformation and affirmed by C. F. W Walther and those who with him would organize what today is The Lutheran Church—Missouri Synod.

The faithful practice of closed Communion is challenged in our day both culturally and ecclesiastically. As Western culture careens down a path of radical individualism and autonomy, the privatization of faith leads many to regard participation in the Sacrament as a matter of personal entitlement. Ecclesiastically, the novel ecumenical concept of "reconciled diversity" is the institutional form of Christianity without dogmatic moorings. The essays brought together in this volume are both old and new. Taken together they bear testimony to a common Lutheran conviction that has increasingly come under attack in even conservative Lutheran churches. It is the hope of the editors that these essays will serve to assist both pastors and laity in understanding the biblical and confessional basis for closed Communion. We are grateful for our fathers in the faith who faced this challenge with conviction and clarity as well as brothers who are still with us who have labored to articulate the unity of this practice with the Church's confession in our own time. We note with gratitude the assistance of Pastor Aaron Hambleton of Redeemer Lutheran Church in Lisbon, North Dakota, who assisted the editors in preparing the manuscripts for publication.

Finally, we wish to dedicate this book to the memory of The Rev. Dr. Ronald Feuerhahn (1937–2015) whose life and teaching was a testimony to the unity of doctrine and practice for the sake of Christ and His Gospel.

Matthew C. Harrison
John T. Pless
Ash Wednesday 2016

13 Elert, *Eucharist and Church Fellowship*, 71.

14 Elert, *Eucharist and Church Fellowship*, 109.

15 Elert, *Eucharist and Church Fellowship*, 182.

CHAPTER ONE

AN OPEN LETTER TO THOSE IN FRANKFURT ON THE MAIN, 1533

MARTIN LUTHER
TRANSLATED BY JON D. VIEKER

INTRODUCTION

With the Marburg Colloquy of 1529, the controversy between Luther and Zwingli concerning the Lord's Supper had reached a watershed moment. Although Luther had made a further effort toward agreement and agreement was finally reached on fourteen of the articles, it was not reached on the fifteenth, regarding the Lord's Supper. In this final article, it was stated that "although at present we are not agreed as to whether the true body and blood are bodily present in the bread and wine, nevertheless each party should show Christian love to the other."[1] Lack of agreement on this article concerning the Lord's Supper was to produce further controversy in the years which followed, and it is within this period that Luther's letter to the people of Frankfurt has its setting.

The situation in Frankfurt during the period after the Marburg Colloquy and before the appearance of Luther's letter had run a disintegrating course with respect to the doctrine of the Lord's Supper. This was surprising in light of the fact that in 1528 Luther's *Confession Concerning Christ's Supper*, his foremost response to Zwingli's understanding of the Lord's Supper, appeared first at the annual book-fair in Frankfurt.[2] Nevertheless, it came to Luther "by way of many who have come from your Frankfurt fair" that the Zwinglian teaching concerning the Lord's

1 Hermann Sasse, *This Is My Body* (Adelaide: Lutheran Publishing House, 1977), 219. Sasse gives the best account in English of the Colloquy, pp. 151–279.

2 Walther Köhler, *Zwingli und Luther: Ihr Streit über das Abendmahl nach seinen politischen und religiösen Beziehungen*, 2 vols., *Quelle und Forschungen zur Reformationsgeschichte* 6–7 (Leipzig: M. Heinsius, 1924), 1:561, notes that Luther mentions this in a letter of February 25, 1528, to Wenceslaus Link, found in Ernst Ludwig Enders, ed., *D. Martin Luthers Briefwechsel*, 8 vols. (Calw & Stuttgart: Vereinsbuchhandlung, 1884–98), no. 1289.

Supper was being taught as if it were "completely one and the same thing" with Luther's confession [§ 1].

Some of the preachers responsible for this pretense were known, although Luther either did not wish to name them in this letter or did not himself know their names [§ 2]. We do know, however, of Johann Cellarius, who since August of 1529 had taught the Lutheran doctrine in Frankfurt but was compelled by a Zwinglian-minded colleague, Dionysius Melander, to leave Frankfurt on account of it. Cellarius then went to Wittenberg, and so Luther learned of the happenings in Frankfurt. Confirmation came from merchants traveling between the two cities. At this point, somewhere toward the end of 1532, Luther wrote his "Open Letter." It was sent in the first part of January 1533, and by the end of the month, the pastors in Frankfurt had already begun to concern themselves with it. By March of that same year they issued an "Apology" that by and large followed an ambiguous position originally conceived by Martin Bucer.[3] Indeed, Bucer stood behind the Frankfurters' Zwinglian understanding from the beginning. At Marburg, he had been prepared to accept Luther's confession of the real presence of the body and blood of the Lord, yet more for the sake of his own ability as a mediator than for resolving[4] theological differences.[5] Likewise, his role in the composition of the Frankfurters' "Apology" was more than advisory. Although the document was signed by four pastors, among them Dionysius Melander, this response was in fact written by Bucer, as the original manuscript attests.[6]

The following translation has been prepared from *D. Martin Luthers Werke: Kritische Gesamtausgabe* [WA] (Weimar: Hermann Boehlaus Nachfolger, 1883–), 30/3:558–71; as compared with Johann Georg Walch, ed., *Dr. Martin Luthers Sämmtliche Schriften* [StL], 2nd ed. (St. Louis: Concordia, 1880–1910), 17:2007–24; and Kurt Aland, ed., *Die Werke Martin Luthers in neuer Auswahl für die Gegenwart* [*LD*] (Göttingen: Vandenhoeck & Ruprecht, 1959–83), 4:214–223.7. For the sake of convenient reference, the paragraphs here are numbered and divided as found in StL. They were not numbered in the original, nor are they in WA.[7]

---

3 Martin Brecht, *Martin Luther*, 3 vols. (Stuttgart: Calwer Verlag, 1981–87), 3:49. According to Brecht, this position stated that not the substance but rather the true body and blood of Christ were given in the Lord's Supper, and that for this reason it was not only "*eitel Brot*" ["bread alone"].

4 Sasse, *This Is My Body*, 231.

5 Sasse, *This Is My Body*, 246.

6 Martin Bucer, *Martin Bucers Deutsche Schriften* (Gütersloh, 1970) 4:507–14, 312–19. StL 17/3:2024 notes that the original manuscript in Bucer's hand is in the archives of St. Thomas' Church in Strasbourg.

7 The translator is humbly grateful to Dr. Norman Nagel for giving considerable time and effort to reviewing this translation.

AN OPEN LETTER TO THOSE IN FRANKFURT ON THE MAIN

To the honorable and prudent, to the Council and parishioners of the city of Frankfurt on the Main, to my gracious gentlemen and friends. Grace and peace to you in Christ our Lord and Savior.

Honorable, prudent, dear gentleman and friends:

§ 1. It has come to me by way of many who have come from your Frankfurt fair that the Holy Sacrament is taught among you in your city according to the Zwinglian way, yet this is done under the appearance and with such words as if it were completely one and the same thing as with us and with our own teaching. And I have often heard it said that this is so artfully done that no one is certain as to what or how it is meant or believed. All this I have left alone for what it is worth. I have not tackled it since I have not been given responsibility for it. I know well enough that it is not I who must answer for it but rather your preachers and all of you together in Christ.

§ 2. However, since I have been so sincerely requested to register my counsel, I am moved to put out this open letter for you all. I want to be of service to those among you who are unsure as to what is what, and so are standing in uncertainty between the two ways, and to those who may be quite certain that your preachers neither believe nor teach that the body and blood are truly in the bread and wine, and therefore ask themselves whether they should go with the crowd to the Sacrament or whether there is cause enough for them not to, and so do without it. For I do not know the names of those who are unsure nor do I wish to know. My business is not with your preachers and their followers. They have heard and seen enough concerning what I and our own teach and believe concerning the Sacrament. And no matter how hard they denounce us and hold us at a distance, let them go at it. They do it so well that they ought to be satisfied![8]

§ 3. Therefore, I kindly ask you to receive graciously this necessary letter, which should at the same time be a witness before God and the world.[9] If there are some among you who stand in the delusion that your preachers are at one with us and teach the same thing concerning the Holy Sacrament, they should know by this letter that we are not at all at one, and that no one should consequently count on hearing our teaching from them. At so many points they deride and discard it (as does all the world), and this is the unanimous report of all who come from Frankfurt. We do not doubt what they say, and so take this to be the situation.

§ 4. Now there are many places (I am assured) where they continue to teach as we do. But there are some others who now see that their previous clamoring

8 *Machen sie es gut, so werden sie es wol finden.*

9 *Fur Got und der Welt*; cf. FC SD VII 29; also *BKS* 981.23. See below, § 19 and § 21.

about there being nothing but bread and wine in the Sacrament is no longer well received. That cart has been driven too far and too deep into the mud.[10] Instead, they have adjusted their mouths[11] and bent their words another way, holding, however, their original meaning in sense and practice. With their mouths they say, "Christ's body and blood are truly present in the Sacrament." When an unsuspecting person hears this, he thinks, of course, that they teach the same as we do, and he goes to the Sacrament and consequently receives nothing but bread and wine, for his teacher neither gives nor means anything more. The hidden gloss and understanding are just as before—that the true body and blood of Christ are truly present in the Sacrament, yet only spiritually and not bodily, and are received only in the heart by faith and not bodily with the mouth which receives only bread and wine, as before.[12]

§ 5. Look! Is this not a devilish juggling act being pushed on the very words of Christ, and by it are not simple hearts shamefully deceived and robbed concerning their Sacrament? Indeed, it is the same as Jerome wrote concerning the Arians.[13] Their bishops preached in such a way that the Christians understood something other than what the preachers' words actually meant. The Arians, too, had pushed the cart so far into the mud[14] that their clamoring was no longer well received: namely, that Christ was only creature and not God. But then the Arians also adjusted their mouths,[15] remaining silent about the creature part and calling Christ "God," even "true God." But their hidden understanding was this: Christ was a God *nuncupative*,[16] that is, He had the name of God and was *called* "God." That Christ was called "God" [by the Arians], this was true, but for them He was certainly not by nature God, eternal and one with the Father; just as John the Baptist was called an "angel" (and it is true that he was called an "angel" [Matthew 11:10])[17] he was nevertheless a man by nature and not an angel. In this way the Arians

10 *das der karren zu fern und tieff jnn schlam gefürt ist.*

11 This sarcastic phrase, *wisschen sie das maul*, or literally, "they wipe their mouths," is used elsewhere by Luther to indicate duplicity (e.g., § 5).

12 *Das der warhafftige leib und blut Christi sey wol gegenwertig im Sacrament, Aber doch nur geistlich und nicht leiblich, wird auch allein im hertzen mit dem glauben empfangen und nicht leiblich mit dem munde, welcher empfehet eitel brod und wein, wie vorhin.* This was one of the fundamental principles of the Zwinglian teaching on the doctrine of the Lord's Supper from the beginning, as in Köhler, *Zwingli und Luther*, 1:472ff.; also Cristof Gestrich, *Zwingli als Theologe* (Zürich: Zwingli Verlag, 1967), 66ff.

13 "Epistola ad Damasum," CSEL XV, 3–5 (Vienna: 1866ff.), 54:64–67.

14 See above, § 4.

15 *da wisschten sie auch das maul.* See above, § 4.

16 Literally, "called by name."

17 In Greek, *angelos*, which in English has usually been translated "messenger" in this context. Luther, however, translates it *Engel* ("angel") in the *Deutsche Bibel* [WA DB 6:53].

maintained the hidden sense that Christ was only a creature, yet with their mouths they said that He was God.

§ 6. So also our papists now do the very same thing.[18] When they perceived that their abominable abomination was seen too clearly in the light of day—when they taught and almost screamed that Christ the Savior and His faith ought to be utterly damned and that we are to build upon our own works—now they also have changed their tune.[19] They have taken hold of that word "faith," preaching concerning faith *and* good works. Yet concealed under the word "faith," they remain with their old abomination. For they say: "It is true that one must through faith become righteous—but only insofar as works accompany it. For before works and without works, faith is nothing." With these words they speak of faith as that which makes righteous, but they give the righteousness part to works and give absolutely nothing to faith. They then spruce it up by saying that faith makes righteous when it is accompanied by works, otherwise it is nothing. But this is just talking out of both sides of the mouth[20] if I say: "Faith makes righteous . . . but without works it is nothing." For if faith is nothing, alone and without works, then works must be everything, if already that same "nothing" (that is, faith) comes from works. Thus their hidden meaning and the old, former abomination is brought forward under new words—an old doll dressed in a new coat.[21]

§ 7. Thus our double-tongued sectarians also do the same thing. They say: "Christ's body and blood are truly in the Sacrament, but of course spiritually and not bodily." They stay with their previous error, that there are only wine and bread in the Sacrament. It follows from this that it is not necessary that the ordinary Christian know how Christ's body may be in the Sacrament, but it is enough that he believe that it is the body which Christ meant.[22] Now if you believe according to this doctrine, that Christ's body is bodily in heaven and spiritually in the

---

18 Here Luther refers to the Roman criticism of Article 20 of the Augsburg Confession, as contained in the *Confutation*, Art. 20, found in M. Reu, *The Augsburg Confession: A Collection of Sources with an Historical Introduction* (Chicago: Wartburg Publishing House, 1930), 359.

19 *zihen sie nu die pfeiffen ein*. Literally, "Now they draw in the pipes."

20 *Das heisst warm und kalt aus einem maul blasen*. Literally, "That's just blowing warm and cold out of the same mouth."

21 *Und dem alten Götzen ein newer rock angezogen*. Literally, "An old idol dressed in a new coat."

22 This seems to be a reference to Bucer's perception concerning the *manducatio oralis* and *manducatio impiorum*. See Köhler, *Luther und Zwingli*, 2:299.

Sacrament,[23] then in spirit and faith you have the body which Christ meant, even though in the bread and wine you receive nothing but bread and wine.

§ 8. In this way, they lay waste to the Lord's Supper and accustom the people to go their way without it and die without it. People can then say: "What is the Sacrament to me (that is, only bread and wine)? Don't I have Christ's body and blood spiritually in my heart?" What kind of false duplicity and lies is this, where they not only deny the truth, but they do not even dare to confess freely what they themselves believe? What kind of Christians are these that behave so underhandedly and are afraid to confess their teaching freely, but rather sell it under a false pretense and disguise? From this, two things are quite clear: first, they lie against God's Word; and second, they deny and do not freely confess their own teaching, which they boast of as God's Word.

§ 9. Now what do you make of this? When a faithful heart has knowledge of such wickedness and falsity in his pastor, or suspects him of it, what should he do? Do you really think that it is possible for his heart to be set at peace trusting such outrageously false words as: "Believe in the body, which Christ meant, and ask no further"? No, dear friend! He believed as much as that already before he came, even if he does not go to the Sacrament. The reason he comes and asks this question is because he wants to know whether he receives with his mouth only bread and wine. He does not ask what he should believe in his heart concerning Christ and His body, but only what is given to him by the hands [of the pastor]. Here, there is no use in rolling mush around the mouth and saying, "Mmmm, mmmm."[24] One must not teach him, "Believe in the body, as Christ meant." The mush must be spat out and the "mmmming" quit! Freely and plainly he must be told whether with his mouth he receives only bread and wine. How he should believe the body Christ meant should be left for the pulpit or some other time. Rather, here he should be told what bread and wine are in the Sacrament and not be sold something hidden in a sack.[25] Here there is no use for playing tricks under a hat or rummaging about in the dark![26]

---

23 Sasse, *This Is My Body*, 100, notes that with regard to this view, Zwingli seems to have been influenced by Karlstadt. Luther, too, seems to have held this to be the case since he so often lumped together Karlstadt, Müntzer, and Zwingli as "Enthusiasts."

24 *Hie gilts nicht den brey im maul weltzen und Mum, Mum sagen*, that is, to speak unclearly or guardedly as if one is not sure what it is he is eating. Sasse, *This Is My Body*, 229, describes this passage as "untranslatable" and quotes it to show "that for Luther 'Zwinglians' were not only people who held Zwingli's view of the Sacrament as a memorial feast, but also those who spoke of a Real Presence in an ambiguous way."

25 Cf. § 18 below.

26 *Denn es gilt hie nicht, so unter dem hütlin spielen und im finstern mausen.*

§ 10. Therefore, this is my honest advice, for which before God I am held accountable both to you in Frankfurt and wherever else:[27] whoever has public knowledge that his pastor teaches in a Zwinglian way, he should avoid him and rather go without the Sacrament all his life long rather than receive it from him—yes, even be ready to die on this account and suffer everything before that. If his pastor is one of the double-tongued sort who mouths it out that in the Sacrament the body and blood of Christ are present and true, and yet who prompts an uneasiness that he is selling something in a sack[28] and means something other than what the words say, you should go to him, be free to inquire of him, and have him say quite plainly what it is he gives out to you with his hands and what you receive with your mouth. What one believes or does not believe in the heart can wait for another time. One should put to him the straight question: "What is held here in hand and mouth?"

§ 11. It is an honest Enthusiast [*Schwermer*] who will deal with you straightforwardly and say: "He gives to you mere bread and wine, and while he is doing this you should think about and believe in the body and blood of Christ, etc." If, however, he is a circus juggler who plays tricks under a hat and says, "Mmmm, mmmm," he will toss the mush about in his mouth and drivel: "Ah yes, it is enough that you believe the body Christ meant." What a fine way, then, of giving an answer and the testimony of the faith that is in you, as St. Peter teaches [1 Peter 3:15].

§ 12. And so according to the art of such lofty spirits I would like to have a go at playing with all of the articles of faith, saying: "It is not necessary that I believe that three persons are one divine being, and yet each one true God,[29] but it is enough that you believe in the Holy Trinity which Christ meant—that is, what I, Arius, meant (who means, however, no Trinity). Furthermore, it is not necessary that you believe that Christ is true God,[30] but it is enough that you simply believe the God which Christ meant—that is, what I, Arius, Sabellius, Mohammed, etc. mean (who mean no such thing). Furthermore, it is not necessary that you believe that Mary was a proper mother and virgin, but it is enough that you believe the virgin[31] which the evangelist meant. That may be, then, what Caiaphas and the Jews meant (who meant, however, nothing but a loose whore).[32]

---

27 See above, § 3.

28 See below, § 18.

29 Athanasian Creed 3–4; *BKS* 28.10–12; 29.1ff.

30 Tappert, *Book of Concord*, Nicene Creed, 18; *BKS* 26.9ff.

31 Tappert, *Book of Concord*, Apostles' Creed, 18; *BKS* 21.11.

32 Here, Luther refers to the report spread by Celsus concerning the alleged adultery of Mary with a Roman soldier named Panthera. See Origen, *Contra Celsum*, J. P. Migne, ed., *Patrologia Graeca* (Paris, 1857), 11:720ff.

§ 13. Such preachers, if they want to play around like this, should busy themselves with something else and leave divine matters in peace, lest thunder strike them down. If you are earnest about this, then with such earnestness should they be removed from the public office [*Amt*] and pulpit and banished from the country.[33] For what is this fearful juggling act with which they would teach the people yet say absolutely nothing to them? Instead, they guide them into a dark hole and say: "Believe what Christ meant." But what Christ meant they are unwilling to say, for they fear that if they should say what they think He meant, the whole world would declare: "Christ did not mean that; that is your 'meaning,' and your father's, the devil, with you" [John 8:44]. Both of you use the name of Christ as an infamous cover for your lies, with which you would mislead and destroy us.

§ 14. Wherever there are such preachers who have got it so good and have discovered such an easy way to preach, they have no more need for Scripture and its studying. For with every part of it they can say to the people: "Dear people, you do not have to be bothered with this; believe what Christ meant, that is quite enough."[34] Is there anyone who could not preach in this way? Who would not gladly want to be a pupil here, if we would not have to bother with the toil of preaching and teaching and instead give both jobs over to Christ? Then we could say: "I believe what Christ believes," or what would be even better, "I let Christ believe for me and let him worry about what I should believe." Oh, wouldn't that kind of a Christian be the very finest and the most splendid of fellows! So also the papists![35] They still say nowadays that they believe what the church believes. And there is what people say of the Poles. They say: "I believe what my king believes." Why not? What could be a better faith than this, which would have so much less toil and care?

§ 15. Thus there is the story of a learned doctor who met a coal miner on the bridge in Prague. Out of sympathy over the poor layman he asked: "My good man, what do you believe?" The coal miner replied: "What the church believes." The doctor said: "But what then does the church believe?" And the coal miner answered: "What I believe." Later on, when the doctor was about to die, he was sorely troubled in the faith by the devil, so that there was nothing sure for him on which to stand nor rest until he declared: "I believe what the coal miner believes."[36]

33 In *Sendschreiben an Herzog Albrecht von Preußen* (1532), WA 30/3:552, Luther also proposes only exile for heretics, rather than the traditional execution.

34 One often encounters this sort of formulation in Bucer. Luther intentionally exaggerates here on account of Bucer's attempt at union.

35 Concerning the *intentio* of the priest upon the consecration of the Mass, see Gabriel Biel, *Canonis misse expositio*, ed. Heiko A. Oberman and William J. Courtenay, 4 vols. (Wiesbaden: Franz Steiner Verlag, 1963–67), 1:46ff.

36 This common story of the Reformation period is told in Nr. 234 of Johannes Agricola, *Die Sprichwörtersammlungen*, ed. Sander L. Gilman, 2 vols. (Berlin: de Gruyter, 1971), 1:180.

Then there is also the story of the great Thomas Aquinas.[37] At the end of his life he had no sure ground against the devil until he declared: "I believe what is in this book." He had the Bible in his arms. May God not grant us too much of that sort of faith. Indeed, if they had only such a faith as their story tells us, then both doctor and the coal miner believed themselves into the very pit of hell. Such spirits also believe themselves into the same place who say: "Believe in the body Christ meant. That is enough." Oh, yes, what a nice, fine faith that is! Such a faith does the devil no harm.

§ 16. Could there ever be a finer way for keeping people in error than with such talk? For wherever they become certain that they do not need to be bothered, whether they have been taught rightly or wrongly, they sleep and snore quite securely, naturally asking no more questions concerning teaching or preaching. Once they have learned that it is enough that they know and believe that Christ believes for them, why should they want to have more than this? What more could they ask for, these free, happy, and secure Christians? Unless, of course, one wanted to learn in addition that it is not necessary to do good works and suffer wrong, that it is enough that Christ does and suffers. Let Him also be pious for you and do it all. Then you have no need to believe or to do what is good. And for whatever is bad, you would consequently have to let the devil be an unbeliever and do evil, for then he would have to go to hell for you just as Christ must go to heaven for you. We good fellows, however, would remain here on earth to eat and drink, confident that we need go neither to heaven nor hell. Now there's a church fit to be praised—built in a pigsty!

§ 17. I hope, however, that such Christians and preachers do not boast or pretend that it was Luther who first advised and taught this. For where I could see and be certain that they suck such a poison from my books and lay all the blame on me, I would have to spare no pains to scrub each one a little around the eyes and set their spectacles on their noses and bid them not to read my books through colored glass. For I know well enough to give the devil and his apostles credit, that wherever they turn my words upside down and afterward are able to lead the people astray with my name, there they do not let it lack persuasion. This is something these same sectarians have often done to me, pulling my words into their own meaning. Just recently, a sermon (which I preached before the Sacramentarians were even heard of, thought of, or named) they recently had republished,[38] and because they found the words "bread and wine" in it, they supposed that Luther

37 See Ernst Schäfer, *Luther als Kirchenhistoriker* (Gütersloh: C. Bertelsmann, 1897), 447.

38 Here Luther could well mean the reaction of the Zwinglians at the printing of three sermons in 1526, one of which was *The Sacrament of the Body and Blood of Christ Against the Fanatics* (1526), AE 36:329–61; WA 19:482–523. A certain Johann Landsberger compared the content of this sermon with *Luthers Sermon auf das Euangeli Johannis vj* (1523), WA 12:580–84, and tried to establish inconsistencies between them. Any actual *re*printing

had gone off with their evil enthusiasm. All this was irrespective of the fact that the sermon itself was well enough defensed against such a notion.

§ 18. Therefore, I have advised and taught in a little book against the Enthusiasts[39] that if a Christian is troubled by those who represent the Words of Institution in symbolic language,[40] then he should remain firm and solid with the words of Christ and believe (as the words by themselves declare) that the body and blood of Christ are in the bread and wine, confidently staking it all on Christ. If Christ were to be leading him astray (which is impossible), then He is the one who will answer well enough for it on Judgment Day. In this way, the Christian may remain unshaken in his faith, sticking to the words and knowing with his faith that it is the body, which the words themselves give and declare. See, this is no true doctrine: "Believe in the body Christ meant." For with this kind of talk the words of Christ are put out of sight, and faith flies free in the air following one's own thoughts. I, however, will have the words with faith founded on them (as they themselves declare). Thus I will not believe the body which *Christ* means outside of and apart from His word, but rather the body which His *words* mean as they stand there and declare. That is His true meaning, and He has said and shown for us His true meaning in the words and through the words. Outside of His word and without His word we know of no Christ, much less about Christ's "meaning." For the Christ who pretends to have a meaning without Christ's words—that is the accursed devil from hell, who takes Christ's holy name and under it markets his own hellish poison.[41]

§ 19. That is what I now want to say out of a concern to warn everyone who may desire it, and it may be that someone has been troubled by my books or my name. For although I do not know of someone actually doing this, and I am also neither able nor do I desire to accuse anybody of it, I must, nevertheless, be careful myself in the presence of the crafty dragon [Job 41:6ff.] and his disciples of wickedness and malice, as I have so warned, that he would well like to try such a thing. Although I would have certainly hoped that no one could be so impudent and

---

of the 1526 sermon has been difficult to establish, however. See Köhler, *Zwingli und Luther*, 1:383–96.

39 Here Luther is most likely referring to either *That These Words of Christ, "This Is My Body," etc., Still Stand Firm Against the Fanatics* (1527), AE 37:3–150; WA 23:64–283; or *Confession Concerning Christ's Supper* (1528), AE 37:151–372; WA 26:261–509.

40 *von den Tropisten und Figuristen*, i.e., the Zwinglians who did not allow the literal meaning in the Words of Institution, but, in effect, returned to a type of medieval *Quadriga*, where a tropological or figurative sense was used instead of the literal sense.

41 Here Luther drives home the point made in §§ 8–10 above with the marketing of [*verkeuffen*] false goods. See also LC III 41; *BKS* 671.23ff.: "In the first place, then, it is profaned when men preach, teach, and speak in God's name anything that is false and deceptive, using his name to cloak lies and make them acceptable [*verkeuffen*]; this is the worst profanation and dishonor of the divine name."

shameless, the dragon's error has done nothing but to strengthen and uphold me, because my Confession[42] stands there today publicly before all the world[43] and my books' witness are evidence enough to show with what great earnestness I have battled against this error, so that even an Enthusiast should be ashamed in his heart to cite or to need a single letter of Luther as the grounding of his error. Moreover, before all the world there came the splendid Confession and the Apology[44] which were freely confessed and maintained before his Emperor's Majesty at Augsburg and before many of the highest estates of the Roman Empire, in which also the papists, although they are doubtlessly hostile to us about the Mass, nevertheless cannot blame us for any Enthusiast articles. We were not the ones to say, "Mmmm, mmmm," or to play tricks under a hat, but rather, there stands our clear, plain, and free words, without any rummaging about in the dark![45]

§ 20. *In summa,*[46] it is appalling to hear[47] that in one and the same church or at one and the same altar both sides should come for and receive of one and the same Sacrament, yet with the one side believing that it receives only bread and wine while the other is believing that it receives the true body and blood of Christ. And I often doubt whether it is possible to believe that a preacher or pastor could be so hardened and malicious (and moreover remain silent) as to let both sides go, each one in their delusion that they receive one and the same Sacrament, each one according to his faith, etc.[48] If there is that kind of a pastor, he must have a heart harder than any rock, steel, or even a diamond. He must certainly be an apostle of wrath; the Turks and Jews are much better. They deny our Sacrament and confess this plainly. Thus we are not deceived by them, and we fall into no ungodliness. But these fellows must be the right high archdevil, who would give me only bread and wine and would let me mistake it for the body and blood of Christ and so miserably deceive me. Too hot and too hard, that is simply going too far; God will strike there before long. Therefore, whoever has such preachers or is deceived by them, let this be a warning for them as before the devil incarnate himself.

42 Cf. note 39 above, *Confession Concerning Christ's Supper.*

43 See above, § 3; see below, §§ 21ff.

44 Apology of the Augsburg Confession.

45 See above, § 9, note 26.

46 "To summarize and conclude this point."

47 Here Luther may have had Bucer in mind since several letters were exchanged between them in 1531. Cf. WA Br 6:25.27ff.; 31.50ff.

48 Cf. Werner Elert, *The Structure of Lutheranism*, trans. Walter A. Hansen (St. Louis: Concordia, 1962), 280ff.

§ 21. Furthermore, I am also asked for advice regarding Confession and Absolution,[49] and how good and faithful hearts should conduct themselves in this since your preachers have utterly condemned and ridiculed it, particularly the way it is put in our catechism[50] where we teach the young people to say to the pastor or priest: "Worthy sir, etc."[51] Now we would let our teaching, catechism, and the whole thing be condemned and profaned by whoever wants nothing of it, but we have this to comfort us before God and all the world:[52] that our high-flown judges and condemners so far have not brought forward or done anything better (not even in one document). Quite the opposite. They have done so much and such great damage, if only it would come to a stop. That we would indeed like to see. They are bad masters indeed who can only condemn what others do and then do nothing better themselves. That's what you could call a real Mr. Know-It-All, "who can bridle the horse on its hind, then ride it backward as if blind"; "his own bagpipes' peals make the best-sounding squeals."[53]

§ 22. Certainly we *force* no one to Confession,[54] as all of our writings bear witness. Whoever does not want to have it, he can let it go, just as we do not press those who do not want to have our catechism and teaching. Here, no one binds another! For we (praise God!) are abundantly taught that Christ our Lord wants to tolerate no haughty, obstinate heads in His kingdom. Why should we then compel such arrogant spirits by force into His kingdom? Just let them go the way of the chaff which the wind blows away [Psalm 1:4]; their fire will surely find them. Our teaching, however, is for those who are in earnest for the sake of salvation and seek something higher of the Gospel than fleshly freedom to eat meat, eggs, and butter, not to fast, not to pray, etc. This is the Enthusiasts' loftiest art and spirit,

---

49 Here Luther uses the word *Beicht*, which entails and is here translated "Confession and Absolution," but which in the following will be translated simply "Confession."

50 Zwingli and his disciples were against Luther on this matter from the beginning, as documented in Erich Roth, *Die Privatbeichte und Schlüsselgewalt in der Theologie der Reformatoren* (Gütersloh: C. Bertelsmann, 1952), 102ff.

51 Here the original *Wirdiger, lieber Herr*, as found also in *BKS*, 518.7, has been translated "Worthy sir." It comes out as "Dear Pastor" in Tappert, *Book of Concord* (Small Catechism V 21), 350, and *Lutheran Worship* (St. Louis: Concordia, 1982), 310ff., and is omitted completely in *Lutheran Book of Worship* (Minneapolis: Augsburg Publishing House, 1978), 196.

52 See above, § 3 and § 19.

53 *das ross im hindern zeumen kan und rücklings reit seine ban, Seiner sackpfeiffen hall ist der aller beste schall.* Although these two verses are not found together in this form elsewhere, Luther probably compiled them from disparate sayings of his time. The translator has endeavored to retain the poetic meter of the German while at the same time maintaining the original sense.

54 Already in *The Babylonian Captivity of the Church* (1520), AE 36:88ff.; WA 6:546.17ff., Luther protested against the Roman Church's confession by coercion. He later expanded this protest in *Von der Beicht ob die der Bapst macht habe zu gepieten* (1521), WA 8:138–85.

even though they were not the first to discover it nor was their spirit its source.[55] They have, in addition, not even properly understood it and so can give no proof for even a praise of it, nor do they know how to defend it. All they can manage to do is to make a row, scream, tear apart, and desolate the church and create a frenzied mob which learns to understand neither this nor that, as St. Paul writes: "They are always learning, yet cannot come to a right knowledge of the truth" [2 Timothy 3:7].

§ 23. Now this is what we have to say to those who desire our advice in this matter. In Confession there are two parts. The first part is the telling of sins. In this part we have by God's grace rescued consciences (before the Enthusiasts ever dreamed up anything about it) and freed them from the intolerable burden and impossible obedience to the pope's law which demanded that every sin must be recounted.[56] To the distressed conscience this gave such anxiety and misery that it was driven to despair. He [the pope] had no better name for it than a work of obedience by way of which they were to earn forgiveness and satisfaction for sin.[57] It was, however, nothing but a great torture without end because such a work was impossible. That is the way he comforted distressed consciences. Such a great and glorious freedom should so fill us that we give forth thanks to God unceasingly for such a vast and unspeakably comforting gift. If only the pope had known such freedom, and accordingly set up his annual fair with this (as elsewhere he has everything for sale), would it not rain thousands of gulden from the kings and princes, a hundred gulden from the counts and nobility, and from townsmen and farmers a gulden and a groschen each![58] He would have taken in three worlds of gold and silver in one year. Now we, however, have it all for free, and yet our thanks to God are only such as are fit for Him to strike down with hellfire on Judgment Day.

§ 24. Along with this freedom we maintain the practice that a penitent is to tell those sins which press most heavily on him. And we do this not merely for the sake of understanding; for those who have a good understanding, such as our pastor, chaplain, Magister Philip and such people who know well what sin is, we do not need to instruct. But because our dear youth grow daily away from it and because among the people there is so little understanding, we maintain such a

---

55 Perhaps Luther is referring to Zwingli's early writing at the beginning of the Swiss Reformation, *Von erkiesen und fryheit der spysen*, as found in *Corpus Reformatorum* (Berlin: C. A. Schwetschke & Sohn, 1905), 88:88–136.

56 The practice of confessing all of one's sins was first officially articulated by Pope Innocent III at the Fourth Lateran Council in 1215, as found in Heinrich J. D. Denzinger, ed., *Enchiridion Symbolorum*, 23rd ed. (Freiburg in Breisgau: Herder, 1965), nos. 312–14.

57 This is articulated in Gabriel Biel, *Collectorium circa quattuor libros Sententiarum*, ed. Wilfridus Werbeck and Udo Hofmann, 2 vols. (Tübingen: J. C. B. Mohr [Paul Siebeck], 1977), 4:499.

58 These were the traditional amounts.

practice for their sakes, that they may be well brought up through this Christian training and understanding. For such Confession does not go on only for their recounting of sins, but also one should listen to them concerning whether or not they understand the Lord's Prayer, the Creed, the Ten Commandments, and whatever else the catechism gives them. For we have come to know quite well how little the common crowd and the youth learn from the sermon, unless they are individually questioned or examined. Where better would one want to do this and where is it more needed than for those who should go to the Sacrament?

§ 25. It is quite true that wherever the preacher administers only bread and wine for the Sacrament, he is not very concerned about to whom he gives it, what they know or believe, or what they receive. There one sow feeds with the others, and such preachers simply see themselves above such caring. They would rather have uninstructed, ecstatic saints than have the care of nurturing Christians. Rather, they want to do things in such a way that after three years everything would be laid waste, and neither God nor Christ nor Sacrament nor Christians would remain anymore. However, because we are concerned about nurturing Christians who will still be here after we are gone, and because it is Christ's body and blood that are given out in the Sacrament, we will not and cannot give such a Sacrament to anyone unless he is first examined regarding what he has learned from the catechism and whether he intends to forsake the sins which he has again committed.[59] For we do not want to make Christ's Church into a pigpen [Matthew 7:6], letting each one come unexamined to the Sacrament as a pig to its trough. Such a church we leave to the Enthusiasts!

§ 26. And all of this we have received from the beginning of Christendom.[60] For there we see and grasp the way in which the Creed, the Our Father, and the Ten Commandments were put together as a short summary and doctrine for the young and for those in need of instruction. From early on this was what was called a "catechism." For "catechism" (say the Greeks) is a way of teaching with questions and answers, just as a schoolmaster has his pupils recite their lesson to see if they know it or not. In this way, those in need of instruction are to be examined and by their answers show that they know the parts of the catechism, that they recognize the sin they again have done, and are willing to learn more and desire to do better. If they will not do this, they may not come to the Sacrament. The pastor is there as Christ's faithful servant, and as far as it is possible for him, he may never cast the Sacrament to swine or dogs [Matthew 7:6]. He is to hear the people out and how it

59 Cf. LC V 2; *BKS*, 708.7ff. Also *An Order of Mass and Communion for the Church at Wittenberg*, AE 53:34; WA 12:206.

60 Regarding the Creed, see Werner Elert, *Eucharist and Church Fellowship in the First Four Centuries*, trans. N. E. Nagel (St. Louis: Concordia, 1966), 90ff. Regarding the Lord's Prayer, see Joachim Jeremias, *The Lord's Prayer*, (Philadelphia: Fortress Press, 1964), 2.

is with them. If they deceive him and do not speak honestly, then he is exonerated. They have deceived themselves.

§ 27. And such is also the case with the old German word *Bejicht.*[61] This was used when the holy bishops were called *confessores,* i.e., *Bejichter,* or "confessors."[62] For the verb *bejichten* means "to confess," as the word is also still used in court where we hear of *Urjicht* or "testimony." There one says: "*das jicht er, das hat er bejicht,*" that "he confesses" or "has confessed."[63] And there are two distinct "js" in the word *Bejicht,*[64] which in time were changed to a single "j," and by misuse it was written and spoken as *Beicht* with one "j." Many other old German words were spoiled in this way. So then, a *Bejichter* or "one who confesses" does this not only by telling his sins but also by testifying to what he has learned of the Creed and of Christ and what is contrary to them.[65] To confess [*Bejichten*], then, is something we are to grow in doing, whether it be before parents, teachers, or pastors. It may even come to this: that we are brought before a judge and there make a confession [*Bejichten*] that could cost us our lives. It is because this did indeed happen that St. Cyprian calls the martyrs "confessors," that is, *Bejichter.*[66]

§ 28. Because such a practice is an ancient, praiseworthy, Christian and necessary training, in which one is exercised and prepared for right living, for learning of Christ, and for confessing before the world, one can consequently well observe what unlearned and inept teachers they are who condemn the practice as something which God has not given us to do—as if they had such supreme knowledge of what is God's bidding. What doubt can there be that God would have us teach and learn His Word, both together and individually and in the best possible way that we can? We will not quibble and talk about specified places, persons, ways, and times for teaching and learning His Word. Such unqualified teachers should be instructed, for it is quite clear that He would have His Word going on in all sorts of ways, every day, and in all places. We have this from God in the Law of Moses. They should think on His commandment as they go, as they stand and as they sit, and should write it on all places [Deuteronomy 6:7–9]. A pastor cannot push the Word of God at every time, place, and person, and so he takes this time,

---

61 This is Luther's Middle High German spelling of the modern German word *Beichte*, or "confession."

62 Cf. *Sermon vom Sakrament des Leibes und Blutes Christi* (1526), WA 19:513.

63 See Jacob and Wilhelm Grimm, eds., *Deutsches Wörterbuch*, 16 vols. (Leipzig: W. Hirzel, 1854–1954), for the backgrounds and meanings of *urgicht* [11:2425ff.] and *gichten* [4:7293ff.].

64 Luther counts the "i" as a "j." A further complication in spelling is the fact that the actual Middle High German spelling was probably *begichten* with a "g." Luther possibly substituted a "j" due to regional pronunciation differences.

65 Cf. Elert, *Eucharist and Church Fellowship*, 57ff.

66 Cf. Cyprian, *De catholicae ecclesiae unitate*, CSEL 3/1:228.

this place, and this person as they are in Confession. You devil, show me how he is then acting without and against God's bidding! And how utterly "holy" are these Enthusiasts who stand in the way of teaching God's Word at this place and at this time, when we are indeed responsible for teaching it at all places and times (as we are able). All their screaming amounts to nothing; their ignorance is displayed in what they say and in what they print. Therefore, let every pious heart beware of them. They will teach no one nothing because they themselves know nothing.

§ 29. Take a look at how the papists have completely damned this priceless part of Confession! They have utterly suppressed it, except for that false, intolerable torture of recounting sins. And then they gussied it up as a good work by which God is reconciled and satisfaction is rendered for sin. This brought in so much gold and goods that it became an idol for all the world. And yet here there was no teaching, no instruction in the faith, no training in the way of Confession nor of confessing Christ. Now that we have brought it into use again, the devil and his apostles want to strike it down. But that doesn't bother me! Whoever does not want to have it for himself, so let him be; but let him not on that account take it away from us and make it nothing for us and other pious folk (who understand their need for it and its benefit). As they say: "Leave the ignoramus to his ignorance."[67] Were a thousand worlds mine, and another thousand, I would gladly lose them all before I would let the least little part of such Confession be lost to the Church. Yes, I would much rather put up with the pope's tyranny of fasts, feast days, vestments, holy places, tonsures, cowls, and whatever else I could bear without injury of faith, than that Christians be robbed of Confession. For Christians, it is the primary, the most necessary, and the most profitable school, in which they learn to understand and use God's Word and exercise their faith. This cannot be done so deeply in the public teaching and preaching.

§ 30. The other part of Confession is the Absolution, which the priest speaks in God's place, and which therefore is nothing other than God's word with which He comforts and strengthens our hearts against the sinful conscience. This we are to believe and trust as we believe and trust God Himself. But whoever is so blind that he does not see this or is so deaf that he does not hear it, he certainly knows nothing of what God's Word and Christian faith and comfort are. What good thing can such a one teach? But if he does see it and hear it, and then knowingly condemns this part of Confession, he is nothing but a devil and not a human being. Such a one knowingly sets himself against God and forbids God's Word to be taught to the people, for their hearts to be comforted and their faith strengthened. Let such a one be regarded as an enemy of God and all people and in particular of all those who are Christians. And wherever there are such preachers, then truly

---

67 *Qui ignorat, ignoret.* Literally, "Whoever is ignorant, let him be ignorant," a common phrase used by Luther, perhaps a paraphrase of 1 Corinthians 14:38. Cf. AE 53:34; WA 12:206.

let all pious Christians beware of them as of the devil incarnate. For God's Word should be free and go forth both publicly and for each one individually, for the teaching and comfort of all.

§ 31. This part of Confession [Absolution] is not only for the young and for people in general, it is for everyone's use and need. No one may scorn it, no matter how learned and holy he may think himself to be. Is there anyone so superior that he has no need of God's Word and would even look down upon it from above. And it is for the sake of this part of Confession most of all that I myself go to Confession and will not and cannot do without it. It often gives me great comfort, and day by day when I am cast down and troubled. The Enthusiasts, on the other hand, because they are so sure of themselves and know nothing about such wretchedness and temptations, make light of and scorn this medicine and comfort. And on top of that, they would take it away or block it from those who need it and cannot do without it. If they are so full, then they should yet let the hungry have some food to eat; if they are so holy, then they should yet let sinners become holy; if they have no further need of God and His Word anymore, then they should yet let it be there for those who still have need of it. However (as I said earlier),[68] raving around in their blindness and folly, they show that they have not learned what God's Word, faith, comfort, Christ, and conscience are. One blind man leads another, and both fall into the pit [Luke 6:39]. Let them travel on as they will, they will fall in as they always do. Be on your guard against them!

§ 32. Therefore, we use Confession as a Christian exercise. In the first part the Law does its work on us; in the second part, the Gospel. For in the first part we learn to use the Law rightly (as St. Paul tells us [1 Timothy 1:8]), namely, to recognize sin and hate it. In the second part we learn in the way of the Gospel to hold fast to God's promise and comfort. Thus is brought into action what is preached from the pulpit. Even though a preacher may teach Law and Gospel from the pulpit, if he leaves it at that and does not work it through, put forth questions, and inquire of one as to how that preaching has been understood, then he cannot see where his preaching is lacking or when he should further comfort or rebuke because he has no particular person in front of him with whom he may work things through. And even though the hearer hears them both [Law and Gospel] in the sermon, he will grasp it even more strongly and surely if it is spoken to him in particular as an individual person. Concerning this other part, then, we have extended our exposition plenty and enough.

§ 33. Now what of their scoffing and turning what we say upside down? We have taught the children in our catechism to say to the father confessor, "Worthy sir, etc."[69] If they object, we can put up with it. Whoever does not want to say

---

68 See above, § 30.

69 See above, § 21, note 51.

"Worthy sir" may say instead "Dear sir" or "Dear Father."[70] We force or condemn no one with such words. We have God's commandment, which bids us to teach the young how to behave properly and show respect to their elders, and especially to show honor to the priests and be respectful toward them [1 Timothy 5:17]. God said to the Levites through Moses: *Ut faciant filios Israel reverentes.* That is: "You shall teach the children of Israel to show honor, etc."[71] For such conduct is expected even in the world, that the young and people in general are to behave with modesty and deference toward the elderly and toward their teachers. But because the Enthusiasts deride such a necessary behavior, one can well observe that their lofty spirit is nothing other than one full of hatred and envy, malicious and contriving, not only against our doctrine and God's Word but also against all decency and honor in the secular realm. They are so full of a rebellious spirit that the stink of it belches forth from their mouths. They would like to equate everybody—obliterate what makes us different—yet only so far that ultimately they alone end up being called, "Worthy sir," and no one else. Remember Müntzer who wanted to kill everyone called "sir" and himself alone be "lord"?[72]

§ 34. I would like to see the young and people in general accustomed not only to say, "Worthy sir," but also "Holy sir" and "Holy father." For clearly Confession is to be called "holy," Absolution "holy," preaching "holy," and everything that belongs to the Word [of God] "holy." So it was with St. Augustine and St. Jerome and other Fathers who called one another "holy."[73] I would hope that no one thinks this is breaking bones[74] or establishing a great heresy, inasmuch as such honor should come not to the person but to the office [*Amt*] and to the Word of God. If there were nothing else wrong in the papacy than that the pope were called "Most holy," then I would gladly call him three times over "Most holy."

§ 35. The trouble is that we have leaders who are blind [Matthew 15:14]. They mix up together what is inside and what is outside. They have seen the smoke, but they do not know where the fire is burning. From us they have heard[75] (where else did they get it from?) that we are all in spirit the same before God. This they pull around to mean what is on the outside and would make all of it the same. What a splendid job the devil does through these blind leaders, training the young and

70 Luther makes even more intolerable suggestions for his opponents.

71 This verse is not to be found in the Latin Vulgate, but may be an allusion to Leviticus 21:8.

72 In this sentence Luther uses the word "Herr," which may be translated both "sir" and "lord." Concerning Müntzer, see below, § 36.

73 Several letters were exchanged between Jerome and Augustine, as found in CSEL 34/2:67.2; 240.2; 248.2; 255.7; 380.2.

74 *Ich hoffe, Es solte jn kein bein brechen*, or literally, "I would hope that it would break no leg of yours."

75 In this paragraph Luther refers to the Peasants' Revolt of 1525; cf. *Luther's Antwort auf den dritten der oberdeutschen Zwölf Artikel*, WA 18:326.13ff.

people in general in such a way that the young tread on the throats of their elders and the mob tramples underfoot the government and obedience to it! There is already more than enough mischievousness in the young and in people in general, yet their leaders think it a good idea to put even more fleas into the hide and go about tying up hens' tails to make them stand up straight.[76] They are as men driven by their father, the liar and murderer [John 8:44].

§ 36. And because I see such scoundrels popping up, I plead and exhort you all, together and individually, both council and community, that my instruction and sincere advice would be received favorably; I mean it for your good. I am now so often taught by experience that I have to be concerned about all sorts of things. "Keep a keen eye on the game"; "don't shove your eyes in a bag." That will keep you from having such preachers among you or coming to you. The devil is a trickster. Before the uprising, I warned those in Mühlhausen, and also against Müntzer, just as I sent printed copies of the same to you and all the cities as a warning.[77] However, whether the council was unable to do anything at that time, or how it all went, I do not know. What followed afterward is sadly known only too well. I am no great hand at prophecy, but in my heart I fear the worst from these impudent spirits. Up until now they have done nothing good, but have produced much evil. May God scatter them, and may He preserve you and all pious hearts in His pure Word and right faith in Christ our Lord. To Him be praise and honor forever and ever. Amen.

Your willing servant, Doctor Martinus Luther.

---

76 *Darumb denken sie vollend leufe jnn den peltz zu setzen und den hünern den schwantz auff zu binden*. The point of this saying is that they act foolishly and irresponsibly: hides already have fleas and hens already have tails that stand up straight.

77 Cf. *Ein Sendbrieff an die ersamen vnd weysen Herrn Burgermeyster, Rhatt vnd gantze Gemeyn der stadt Mülhausen* (1524), WA 15:230–40. This document was reprinted and attached to Luther's letter to Frankfurt.

CHAPTER TWO

Theses on Communion Fellowship with Those Who Believe Differently

C. F. W. Walther
Translated by Laurence White
Edited by Paul T. McCain

Translator's Preface

In his classic *The Two Natures in Christ*, Martin Chemnitz compares his theological relationship with the Fathers of the Early Church to that of a pygmy standing on the shoulders of a giant. This admirable sense of humility and historical perspective is a quality often lacking among theologians of our day. All too often we reverse the image and think of ourselves as theological giants who understand theology more fully and interpret the Bible more correctly than anyone who has come before. I am hopeful that Dr. Walther's essay on the question of Communion fellowship will help to dispel this dangerous delusion. Contemporary discussions of this issue seldom get past the point of semantic wrangling over terminology ("close" vs. "closed," etc.). Walther, on the other hand, penetrates directly to the heart of the matter. Beginning with the biblical doctrine of the Church, he argues decisively that Communion fellowship without agreement in doctrine is contrary to a scriptural understanding of the Sacrament and totally inconsistent with the historic practice of the Lutheran Church.

A bit of historical background will be helpful in understanding the approach and the emphasis of the essay. In 1866 the Pennsylvania Ministerium severed its connections with the General Synod and issued a call to all Lutheran synods in the United States and Canada, "which confessed the Unaltered Augsburg Confession," to unite for the purpose of forming a union of Lutheran synods. Thirteen bodies, including the Missouri Synod, reacted favorably to the summons. The constituting convention of this new group, called the General Council, was held in Fort Wayne,

Indiana, in 1867. At this time the Missouri Synod, along with the Ohio and Iowa Synods, declined to join the new body because they did not believe that theological unanimity had been reached among the constituent synods. Shortly thereafter the Ohio Synod requested a position paper from the General Council on four specific theological points. They included: (1) chiliasm, (2) altar fellowship, (3) pulpit fellowship, and (4) secret societies. These issues became known as "the Four Points" and continued to generate a considerable amount of discussion among conservative Lutherans for many years. After much discussion and dissension within the General Council, which resulted in the withdrawal of the Wisconsin, Illinois, and Minnesota Synods, the so-called "Akron Rule," stating the Council's position on altar and pulpit fellowship, was adopted in 1872. The rule states:

> Lutheran pulpits are for Lutheran ministers only. Lutheran altars are for Lutheran communicants only. The exceptions to the rule belong to the sphere of privilege, not of right. The determination of the exceptions is to be made in consonance with these principles, by the conscientious judgment of pastors, as the cases arise.[1]

While this position expressed the conviction of the majority of the Council and its able leader Charles Porterfield Krauth, and was reaffirmed as the "Galesburg Rule" in 1875, it was never consistently supported by all of the constituent synods. In 1877, Krauth prepared a series of 105 theses to explain and defend this principle, but even that did not settle the argument. Clifford Nelson describes the situation which prevailed in the General Council as follows:

> Thus, while the General Council's practice regarding pulpit and altar fellowship was tighter than that of the General Synod, there was internal disagreement regarding the issue, with the result that the Galesburg Rule was interpreted and applied strictly by some and loosely by others. Uniformity could not be expected under such circumstances, particularly since the General Council's approach was educational and persuasive rather than disciplinary.[2]

It is in the context of this ongoing controversy that Dr. Walther's essay must be understood. The more liberal faction within the Council was highly critical of the Missouri Synod's practice on altar fellowship. This criticism was no doubt heightened by the fact that many of the more conservative Midwestern synods which left the General Council went on to join the Synodical Conference in which Missouri played a dominant role. The "Church Council" to which Walther refers repeatedly in the essay is in fact the General Council, and the positions and practices criticized in the essay are those which were tolerated by some within the General Council.

---

1 Clifford Nelson, *The Lutherans in North America* (Philadelphia: Fortress, 1975), 237.

2 Nelson, *Lutherans in North America*, 312.

While this translation lacks the "roll and thunder" of Walther's German, it is a conscientious attempt to convey the sense of the original in contemporary idiom. Where this goal has not been fully accomplished, the translator begs your indulgence.

L. White

THESES ON COMMUNION FELLOWSHIP WITH THOSE WHO BELIEVE DIFFERENTLY

THESIS I

The true visible Church in an absolute sense, or part of the same, is that Church in which the Word of God is preached purely and the Holy Sacraments are administered according to Christ's institution.

THESIS II

A fellowship in which the Word of God is fundamentally denied, or in which a fundamental denial of the Word of God is tolerated, is not a true orthodox Church, but a false heterodox church or sect.

THESIS III

Every man is obligated to recognize the true visible Church and, if he has the opportunity, to join it.

THESIS IV

Every man is obligated to avoid heterodox churches, and in the event that he has belonged to a heterodox church, his obligation is to renounce it and separate himself from it.

THESIS V

True Christians are also found in heterodox fellowships as a result of their lack of knowledge.

THESIS VI

Those who are aware of the partial apostasy of the church fellowship to which they belong and yet continue to remain within that fellowship are not to be considered among the weak but are either the lukewarm whom the Lord will spit out of His mouth or epicurean religious skeptics who within their hearts would ask with Pilate, "What is truth?"

THESIS VII

The main purpose of the Holy Sacrament is to be a tool and a means through which the promises of grace are offered, communicated, and appropriated, as with a seal, guarantee, and pledge through which these promises are confirmed. However, within this major purpose, as a secondary goal, the Sacrament is to be a distinguishing sign of confession and a bond of fellowship in worship. Therefore Communion fellowship is church fellowship.

THESIS VIII

Holy Communion was not instituted to make people Christians. It was instituted to strengthen the faith of those who already are true Christians. Therefore Communion should be administered to no one who has been revealed as a false Christian.

THESIS IX

In Holy Communion the body and blood of Christ are actually present, distributed, and received by every communicant. Therefore Communion cannot be administered to anyone who does not confess a belief in this mystery, without grievous sin.

THESIS X

Holy Communion is a mark of confession of faith and doctrine among those who celebrate together. Therefore the admission of members of heterodox fellowships to the celebration of Communion within the Lutheran Church is in conflict with:

1. Christ's institution;
2. The commanded unity of the Church in faith and accordingly in confession;
3. Our love for those to whom the Sacrament is administered;
4. Our love for our own fellow believers, especially the weak who by this action would be given serious offense;
5. The command not to become participants in the sin and error of others.

THESIS XI

We do not place members of heterodox fellowships under excommunication or declare them to be heretics or damned by our refusal to allow them to participate in the celebration of Communion within the fellowship of the Lutheran Church. Instead, they are merely suspended until such time as by their separation from the false fellowship they are reconciled with the orthodox Church.

THESIS XII

The heterodox themselves regard and declare it improper for them to commune with those who are orthodox. Would it not then be disgraceful for those who are last in regard to Christ's own institution and administration of the Sacrament to expose those who have been first?

THESIS XIII

The more unionism and syncretism is the sin and corruption of our time, the more the loyalty of the orthodox Church now demands that the Lord's Supper not be misused as a means of external union without internal unity of faith.

THESIS I

The true visible Church in an absolute sense, or part of the same, is that Church in which the Word of God is preached purely and the Holy Sacraments are administered according to Christ's institution.

It is important to understand why the doctrine of the true visible Church is established here as a foundation for what is to follow. Why do we not admit to Holy Communion those who believe differently? This is a burning question of our time. It is also the basis for most bitter accusations against us from our would-be counselors within the multitude of the gross, undisguised union of a modern, new-believing Lutheranism. I admit that our Lutheran accusers do not want to have anything to do with the wretched theory which holds that everyone should be admitted to Communion just as they are to preaching. This is based on a false appeal to the words of Christ: "Come to Me, all who labor and are heavy laden, and I will give you rest" (Matthew 11:28). They, too, would label this theory as a vile sin and a distortion of the Word of God and indignantly cry out: "One should not cast pearls before the swine nor throw down that which is holy before the dogs." But nevertheless they are still willing to admit anyone to Holy Communion who is not openly unchristian regardless of his particular confessional position. This unionistic error is defended by the spokesmen of the so called "Church Council," among others, who wrongly appeal to a passage from our Symbols.[3] They say that we must admit all those who are proven to be dear Christians to Holy Communion. This basic principle of unionism originates in a perverted doctrine of the Church. Our opponents do not really believe that there is one true visible Church on earth

3 That is, namely, in the Preface to the Book of Concord, paragraph 20: "For we have no doubt whatever that even in those churches which have hitherto not agreed with us in all things many godly and by no means wicked men are found who follow their own simplicity, and do not understand aright the matter itself but in no way approve the blasphemies which are cast forth against the Holy Supper as it is administered in our churches, according to Christ's institution, and, with the unanimous approval of all good men, is taught in accordance with the words of the testament itself."

in an absolute sense. Therefore, it is all the more important that this doctrine be clearly understood in order to justify our doctrine and practice on Communion. If the opinion of the leaders of the "Church Council" and their spiritual comrades were divine truth, then we Lutherans would have committed a grievous sin with our churchly separation from all other Christian fellowships. If this were true, then those who believe differently would belong at our Communion. In fact, they would really also belong in our Church, for the Sacrament is the Church's mark of confession and band of unity. If this were the case, then we would also necessarily have to unite with them in all other churchly things. But our thesis provides us with the correct explanation of the true visible Church. It speaks of such a Church in an absolute sense. One can also speak of a true visible Church in a relative sense, just as one can speak of a deformed man as a real, actual human being. One is designated as a man only insofar as in all his parts he is a normal healthy human being—a man as he should be. In the same way, when we speak here of a true visible Church in an absolute sense, it is understood that we are referring to the Church as it actually should be according to the will and institution of God, a model. However, it is good to note that we are not speaking here of the Church in general [*überhaupt*], but of a visible Church. A true visible Church in an absolute sense is a group of Christians, in which there are certainly always evil men and hypocrites intermingled, but among whom the pure, unadulterated Word of God and Sacraments are found.

On the other hand, we can likewise call a mixed group in which the Word of God and the Sacraments are only generally or fundamentally present a true visible Church in a relative sense. One such church, for example, is the Reformed. That is to say, they are a fellowship that is organized in the goal of promoting the Word of God and the Sacraments among themselves. It is only because they do not have these Means of Grace purely, in accordance with the institution, that they cannot be called a true visible Church in an absolute sense. But praise God that there is still one such Church! That Church is the evangelical Lutheran Church. We confess joyfully and in steadfast certainty of faith that our beloved Church is the Church founded by Christ and His apostles more than 1,800 years ago. We make this statement because our faith, doctrine, and confession, in all of its parts, agree precisely with Scripture, the Word of Christ, and the apostles. The Lutheran Church is actually not only "a" but "the" true visible Church of God on earth, insofar as "true" means nothing other than "as it should be according to the Word of God." We neither can nor do we want to boast before other churches about our pious behavior. But we can and must boast about the pure doctrine which, by God's grace to us poor sinners, shines among us like the clear bright light of the sun. But the leaders of the "Church Council" deny this. To them our Church is merely the best among many goods, not the orthodox next to the heterodox, not the true visible Church in an absolute sense. To these theologians, the distinction between our Church and others is a matter of degree, not substance. Therefore, they consistently speak only of "denominations" and believe that those who in their arrogance claim to be the best must appear totally ridiculous and prove themselves to be a sect. This label "denomination" or "evangelical denomination" for all Protestant groups, except perhaps the Unitarians, serves our opponents in the "Church Council" as a substitute for the more vulgar expression "union." It implies that all Christians who are not either papists or gross rationalists are to be considered orthodox and that all these various orthodox groups must cultivate church fellowship with one another. But this label is just as distorted as the concept it implies. Then one cannot, for example, call the Reformed Church an evangelical Reformed Church because they have not been reformed through the pure Gospel. The adjective *evangelical* applies to our Church alone. We place the name *evangelical* before the name *Lutheran* because we do not believe in Luther but in the pure Gospel which Luther taught. We are not followers of Luther. Our opponents know this full well, and hence the doctrine of our orthodox Lutheran Church is basically a horror to them. If we Lutherans maintain that we alone possess the truth, they discard it as arrogant, intolerable presumption. One can see that their unionistic Communion practice originates in the wretched theory of open questions. For if within the Lutheran Church itself there were doctrines of the faith which Lutherans could either accept or reject, then why not also practice Communion fellowship with non-Lutherans who hold to this or that particular doctrine? Our theologians of uncertainty wish only to seek endlessly the truth but have never found it, and they even study those heathen methods which also endlessly seek the truth without finding it, and they therefore style themselves philosophers, that is, lovers of the truth. But since Christ and His Gospel have appeared on earth, the eternal, complete, sanctifying truth is on earth for every man. He who denies this and does not have the truth is truly a miserable, lamentable creature, and certainly no Christian. The doctrines of Baptism, Communion, and the eternal, universal gracious will of God, for example, are contained in God's Word clearly, plainly, and understandably enough for a child. Anyone who will hold his reason captive to the obedience of faith and not petulantly resist, can and must become certain of divine truth and convinced that the contrary doctrine is from the devil. Would our opponents dare to describe the apostolic congregation as arrogant and presumptuous when they refused the hand of brotherhood and Communion fellowship to the erring spirits who were creeping in? The holy apostles warned against their soul-poison by word and letter with this explanation: "We have the truth, but you do not. Yours is the doctrine of the devil." They would not. But they will not concede to us that which they will concede to the apostolic congregation. Why not? They explain their reason this way: "We do not have the apostles but only Luther as our teacher." But what a foolish objection which reveals to us their lack of faith in the Word of God! Do not we Lutherans still today have the holy

Word of God "pure, as well as one may, written down through His power in Holy Scripture"? Does not St. Paul still speak to us in the Bible in just the same way that he preached and wrote to his congregation? Do we not therefore still today have the eternal, complete, inerrant truth? And would it not be a totally false, miserable sham stirred up by the devil to think that it would be arrogant and presumptuous to say: "I have the truth, and therefore I stand on the rock of the Word of God and reject the contrary doctrine as the lies of Satan!" May God in His grace preserve us from such a sense of shame and all admiration for the spirit of unionism.

Moreover, many fear holding fast to the Word of God and pure doctrine so much because the true holding of a life that is in strict conformity with Scripture can be disclosed from it, rightfully and easily, and such a lifestyle is basically just as hateful to them as pure doctrine. On the other hand, an orthodox Christian, who rightly understands the doctrine of original sin and the Word of God in general has admiration only for that piety which agrees with the Word.

We perceive that the great power for temptation within the church at this time is, on the one hand, the pope who considers himself alone to be infallible and, on the other hand, unionism, which can find no infallible truth. We Lutherans firmly maintain against both of them that there certainly is infallible truth, but only in the Word of God. We possess that truth with certainty as long as we stand on the Word. Or is that an overstatement, the assertion of which makes us comparable to the Roman Antichrist, who claims for himself alone infallibility in matters of faith, practice, and discipline? No, not at all! For there in Rome one asserts an outward infallibility at the prompting of the devil without—and, in fact, contrary—to the Word of God. But we confess that with all of our personal fallibility we are nonetheless infallible because and so long as we speak that which God speaks in His infallible [*unfehlbaren*] Word. That is a major difference! Our spirit, praise God, is a different spirit than that of the pope, and at the same time it is also different than that of the Methodists. For while they slander and condemn us for our doctrine of the only orthodox Lutheran Church, they meanwhile assert that they alone are the true Church of God because they alone live devoutly. They therefore fall into what Paul writes about in 2 Timothy 3:1–9 in regard to the boastful, arrogant, conceited, and hypocritical people of the last evil times. It says to us that which is written in verse 14: "But as for you, continue in what you have learned and have firmly believed, knowing from whom you learned it."

Let us hear what Luther says about the form of the true visible Church and the infallible truth of its doctrine:

> The children's faith[4] also says that the church is holy and Christian. And St. Paul says in 1 Corinthians 3 [:17], "For God's temple is holy, and that temple you are. If anyone destroys God's temple, God will destroy him."

4 Luther frequently refers to the Apostles' Creed as "the children's creed." Ed.

> Therefore the holy church cannot and may not lie or suffer false doctrine, but must teach nothing except what is holy and true, that is, God's word alone; and where it teaches a lie it is idolatrous and the whore-church of the devil. . . . Now a kindhearted man (as they say) might ask, "What harm is there if one holds to the word of God and yet lets all these matters, or at least those that are bearable, remain as well?" I answer, "They may be called kindhearted, but they are wronghearted and misled, for you have heard that it is impossible to teach any word other than God's word, to serve anyone other than God, to light any light other than that which has been placed by God in the darkness" [Matt. 6:24]. It is indeed an error and a will-o'-the-wisp thing, even if it were only one single thing, for the church ought not and cannot teach lies and error. If it teaches one lie, then it is wholly false, as Christ says in Luke 11 [:35–36],"Be careful lest the light in you be darkness. If then your whole body is full of light, having no dark part, it will be wholly bright." That is to say, it must be all light, without any darkness in it. The church must teach God's Word and truth alone, and not error or falsehood. And how could it be otherwise? For God's mouth is the mouth of the church and vice versa. God cannot lie, nor can the church. . . . Now the purpose of all this is to show that the church must teach God's word alone, and must be sure of it. The church is the pillar and bulwark of the truth, built on the rock, and called holy and irreproachable [Eph. 2:21]. Thus one rightly and truly says, "The church cannot err, for God's word which it teaches cannot err." But whatever else is taught or whatever is not with certainty God's word, cannot be the doctrine of the church. . . . Even Duke George, of unhappy memory, said that he knew perfectly well many abuses had spread within the church; but that one single monk from some obscure place should attempt a reformation, that he could not endure. Now then, he confesses (and undoubtedly not he alone) that your church is full of abuses—which means that it is not the true, pure church, for the church must be pure and holy, without any additions, not to mention abuses.[5]

In these words, Luther is certainly not saying that there will be no poor, weak, or erring Christians in the orthodox Church. But as soon as such people have been convinced of their error from the Word of God, they should abandon it, conform with the Word of God, and confess the truth. In the Lutheran Church, however, whoever stubbornly maintains his error must finally be removed. It is different in the Reformed Church. Their specialty is to stand for error and listen to their foolish reason instead of the clear Word. Their doctrine of Holy Communion is a good example of this. The man who holds fast to the Word of God is infallible and free of error in all things. As sure as the Bible is the Word of God, given by the Holy Spirit, and as sure as Christ is the Son of God and the source of eternal truth, so certain is it also that we cannot err, if we hold to the Word of Holy Scripture!

---

5 *Against Hanswurst (1541)*, AE 41:214–22.

He who does not believe this has neither power nor victory in the temptations of the devil nor comfort in the terror of death and must be miserably lost. His faith is nothing but a phantom. For the true believer, as Luther said, has died a thousand times that he might have the truth. He makes us infallible. We are not saying that a Lutheran Christian cannot err in anything that is contained in Holy Scripture. We only maintain that he has the full truth in all of the articles of faith, which are revealed for everyone clearly and plainly in Scripture, so that thereupon he may joyfully live and die. Another evil delusion of the erring spirits is their assertion that only this or that doctrine of faith (as, for example, the divinity of Christ) is clearly and plainly revealed in Holy Scripture. But others (like the distinctive doctrines of other churches) have not been clearly revealed, and therefore one cannot attain the infallible truth in such doctrines. To this we say no! Every doctrine of the faith is revealed in Holy Scripture with complete clarity and unmistakability, and as our Church confesses these doctrines, it is the infallible mouth of God. This is an assertion which is, as we have said, a scandal to our opponents. But to us it is a great comfort. That which we have confessed in the thesis we will now prove with the following Scripture passages. John 8:31–32: "So Jesus said to the Jews who had believed in Him, 'If you abide in My word, you are truly My disciples, and you will know the truth, and the truth will set you free." The first part of this passage actually says, according to the original text, "If you abide in My word (λόγος), then you are truly My disciples," and so one can plainly see that the Lord Jesus defines those who are His true disciples, that is, those who are the true Church, as those who hold fast to His Word, that is, to the simple understanding of it. The Lutheran Church now does that.

Yes, this also applies to the living children of God in false churches, for though they may err here and there, they do so unconsciously. But as soon as they perceive their error, let them depart and remain with the words of Christ. Also, in their hearts they do not cling to their error but to Christ their Lord alone. So also the same Lord also says of those who remain in His Word: "and you will know the truth, and the truth will set you free" [John 8:32]. He who would not make Christ Himself a liar must, according to this, confess that the true visible Church of God on earth—that is, the evangelical Lutheran Church, and every Christian who remains in the Word—has found and attained to the infallible truth. The next passage, John 10:4–5, says: "The sheep follow him, for they know his voice. A stranger they will not follow, but they will flee from him, for they do not know the voice of strangers."

Now, according to this, what is the Church? The gathering of the sheep or the disciples of Christ. That which applies to them applies also to the Church. A sheep hears the voice of his shepherd and follows after him. So it is also with Lutheran Christians and their Shepherd, Christ. They believe His Word, even if their reason makes it appear to be unbelievable. Further, a sheep does not recognize the voice of a stranger, but flees from him. A Lutheran Christian does the same thing with the false spirits and their false doctrine even though their own reason may cling to it as so sweet and acceptable.

The text of Revelation 3:7–11 presents a part of the letter to the bishop of the church in Philadelphia. Christ does not say to him through the mouth of John, "Because you have lived so piously." Instead, He says, "Because you have kept My word about patient endurance, I will keep you from the hour of trial that is coming on the whole world." This holding to the pure doctrine was also their crown which no one could take away. In fact, the text previously said, "I know your works," and nothing else is meant here than faithful holding fast to the Word of truth, just as with the bishop of Laodicea, nothing other than his lukewarmness and apostasy from a good confession is meant. In the same way Christ gave a promise to the congregation at Philadelphia which has been kept to this very day, that a group of Christians would always live in that city. The Laodicean congregation has vanished, and their city has become a heap of rubble. If we want the above-mentioned promise to be kept for us and for our children, then it is truly important that we, in these last days of temptation, hold faithfully to the Word. One also notices that here in this letter Christ does not call those who have fallen away "dear brothers who have another equally valid viewpoint," but He calls them "the liars." First Corinthians 1:10 says: "I appeal to you, brothers, by the name of our Lord Jesus Christ, that all of you agree, and that there be no divisions among you, but that you be united in the same mind and the same judgment."

Here divine judgment is spoken over the spirit of this time, and unionism is condemned by the Holy Spirit Himself. In the same way the Lord says to them, "You are not My church!" It is well-known that to the unionist, being of one voice, mind, and understanding is a horror which in their opinion has produced the division and splintering of the Church. They would abandon this unity to us "old Lutherans." But at the same time do they not therefore themselves show that their much-praised unity in the union is nothing more than a whitewashed grave and a hypocritical comedy? How can one in truth speak of unity in the Church where its members are only (as also in the papacy) outwardly pasted together and carry on with their various beliefs and doctrines? The reproach of "splintering the Church" does not apply to us but to the unionists, for to them one might as well say, "You have as many divisions as there are men." In the same way God the Holy Spirit here condemns the spokesmen of the "Church Council" with the words "united in the same mind and the same judgment." I admit that they would like there to be a united voice in the Church. That is why they require subscription to the collected confessional writings of the evangelical Lutheran Church. Nonetheless, over "the same mind" and "the same judgment" they do not wish to spend a long time arguing and fighting. Thus in the eyes of the Holy Spirit this is nothing less than a hypocritical and abominable tactic of unionism. For how can the words of the mouth or the writing of the hand produce unity where the heart is split and divided by various understandings and meanings?

The text of Ephesians 4:3–6 also strikes the human effort of union down to the ground: "eager to maintain the unity" (not of the body, but) "of the Spirit in the bond of peace." And wherin does this consist? "One body" (namely, implanted together in one spiritual body in Christ) so that Christians might have "one Lord, one faith, one baptism, one God and Father of all." This is the true inner unity in which Christians should live within the Church. And where it thus exists now, there one ought to work diligently to preserve it and take care that envy and pride do not set one Christian against the other. One can also see how this passage, which is so often and eagerly produced by unionists as a motto and a favorite saying, contains precisely their destroying judgment.

THESIS II

A fellowship in which the Word of God is fundamentally denied, or in which a fundamental denial of the Word of God is tolerated, is not a true orthodox Church, but a false heterodox church or sect.

This is the clear conclusion of this text from John 10:26–27: "But you do not believe because you are not among My sheep. My sheep hear My voice, and I know them, and they follow Me." In the same way also according to this (cf. also above the text of John 10:4–5), only those are the sheep of Christ or the right, true Church who hear His voice, that is, His Word, and follow Him. Therefore, on the other hand, those who do not hear His voice, that is, those who do not believe His Word, are not His sheep but a false church. It says further (14:23–24): "If anyone loves Me, he will keep My worrd, and My Father will love him, and We will come to him and make Our home with him. Whoever does not love Me does not keep My words."

Thus Jesus also in these words clearly indicates the marks of the true and the false church. Those who hold to the words of Christ are the true Church in which God Himself makes His dwelling. They are the house of God and the true temple. The Lord of heaven and earth lives among them not only as He does everywhere according to His essence but also according to His gracious presence. These are the marks of the true Church. One can therefore recognize a false church in this, that it does not fundamentally hold to the Word of God but denies it. Therefore, God cannot dwell in it. It is a sect—with which we will have no fellowship. I admit that within the evangelical Lutheran Church it sometimes happens that one will deviate in this or that from the Word of God. But because this happens out of weakness or in ignorance, our Church still does not through it become a sect. But whoever fundamentally and persistently falls away from the Word of God belongs to the false church.

However, the point made in this thesis is also very important: a church in which a fundamental denial of the Word of God is tolerated is also a false church. This is the case, for example, in the Union. We do not deny that there may still be some within the Union who in general teach the Word of God purely. But this circumstance makes the Union church neither pure nor a true visible Church of God. Much more, we must testify to them that they are worse off than any other Protestant sect. For with the other Protestant sects there exists true Christians in their midst who in their ignorance believe, and are convinced in their hearts, that their error is the truth. One can openly and honestly struggle with them, as we Lutherans also have done with honest Reformed on the doctrines of Communion, Baptism, the person of Christ, etc. But in the Union church one can falsify the Word of God with impunity. Here the lie is reckoned to be as good as the truth and error is wickedly tolerated. Pure doctrine is generally interpreted to be an indifferent thing while a life which evidences good works is of major importance. Truly this miserable principle of unionism would have been condemned by the heathen Cicero himself. In a speech which he made on the various teachings of individual philosophers Cicero once added: "I do not know which of these beliefs is correct. But this I do know, that only one of them can be correct." The fearful judgment of Christ upon the bishop of Laodicea also applies to the Union: "Would that you were either cold or hot. So, because you are lukewarm, and neither hot nor cold, I will spit you out of My mouth" (Revelation 3:15–16).

In the same way, when a person who is eager for a refreshing drink of water instead receives lukewarm water in his mouth, he is so disgusted that he immediately spits it out. So also our holy God is disgusted with those who consider His revealed Word to be an indifferent thing and equate error with the truth. He is so disgusted that He will cast them out of His sight. The theory invented and maintained by the followers of the Union and unionistic, false Lutherans which states that different directions may lead to the same goal is absurd. Just as little as it is possible for a multitude of travelers to reach the same city when they follow roads that lead in different directions, just as little in the spiritual area can one and the same goal be reached by following different directions. Where different directions are followed, different goals are always attained. The orthodox Lutheran Church knows full well that it bears in its midst those who are erring out of weakness in order that through admonition and reproof from the Word of God they might be moved to repentance. However, when these efforts fail and one is revealed as a stubborn errorist, our Church will then no longer recognize him as a brother but will separate itself from him. The orthodox Church can never tolerate or authorize false doctrine. It can never make a union with the lie. If, for example, a pastor were to propose false doctrine and his hearer were to allow this without protest or struggle, or did not withdraw from him, so must we consider them also to be erring and, under the circumstances, even heretical. One may with justification judge a member of the congregation by his pastor, just as one may judge a church by its confession. We also freely admit, for example, that there are many just souls in the Reformed Church, who with more precise knowledge we must consider as dear Christians and brothers. But our churches could never unite. The Union church, on the other hand, is that in which false doctrines and also teachers are tolerated and considered as brothers. In fact, the unionists would retort that they, too, are going by the Word of God and that they have adopted the confessions of both churches—the Lutheran and the Reformed—where they agree; and where this is not the case, the decision is made by God's Word according to the principle of evangelical freedom in doctrine. But this is in fact nothing other than a hypocritical excuse and deliberate ungodliness. A third position is not confessed as correct in regard to the divergent doctrines in question, but instead those who are of a Lutheran disposition hold and define it to be correct while those who are Reformed do the same with the Reformed doctrine. Now we will also hear from the fathers. First of all Luther:

> For the holy church sins and stumbles or can even err, as the Lord's Prayer teaches. However, it does not defend or excuse itself, but humbly asks for forgiveness and improves itself as it is able. Thus it is forgiven so that its sin is no longer reckoned as sin. Now if I do not know or distinguish the true church from the false one on the basis of obedience and obdurate disobedience, then I am unable to speak of a church any longer. Then one might accordingly also with due deference call all heretics, all factions and sects that are wantonly disobedient to Christ, the holy church; for they are in no way worse than the pope's church, if indeed wanton disobedience against God does no harm. On the other hand, the papal church is no better because it is just as stubbornly disobedient to God and wickedly perverts his word and, besides, it is more insistent on being right than any other faction and heretic.[6]

Further W. Baier says:

> The unity of the church is also opposed by syncretism, or the unifying of discordant parts in religion despite the difference, in a fraternal, ecclesiastical union so that either the teachers of error in those parts which do not agree or at least the erring persons themselves are allowed within the church fellowship as brothers in Christ and joint heirs of eternal life; which toleration is also improper if the latter are seen as those who are weak and erring but still as brothers who are to participate in the same communion. In so doing it is indeed certain that the weak who from invincible ignorance have submitted to certain errors, but who nevertheless hold to sanctifying faith, may be tolerated as weak brethren if they were known to us. But here the comment in regard to the discordant parts is in view of the public preaching

6 *A Letter of Dr. Martin Luther Concerning His Book on the Private Mass* (1534), AE 38:229.

office, and the doctrine of faith and life, as it is publicly proclaimed, as also in view of the Sacraments as they are publicly administered, namely falsely, so that members of such a visible communion are regarded per se, inasmuch as they are a member of the same, but not in view of that which happens incidentally. All toleration of false teachers is in conflict with (1) the expressions of Scripture which require that the whole of Christian doctrine be maintained pure from all falsification (2 Thessalonians 2:15); to beware of additions, taken in its entirety, unabridged, and unadulterated (2 Timothy 1:14); and to remain in what one has learned and trusted. This would not be purely preserved if the contrary falsifications were to be tolerated at the same time, and if man were allowed to mix them together. All toleration is in conflict with (2) the office of judgment which God has imposed on true teachers through which false doctrine is to be corrected and condemned. Titus 1:9, 13; 2 Timothy 4:2, 3, 16; the example of Christ, Matthew 5:12ff.; and Paul, Galatians 1:6. It is (3) because every errorist and falsification, if it is not controlled, opposed, and condemned, will always spread further, making the truth of doctrine doubtful and suspect; or will be seen as an indifferent opinion, and the errorist himself will finally be confirmed in his error and the temptation will be given an opportunity to contaminate others. But the toleration of errorists, extended not only to the innocent but also to entire fellowships and therefore at the same time to the public preaching office [*öffentliche Predigtamt*] itself, and false teachers, is in conflict with the command to convict, punish, and avoid disseminators of error. Romans 16:17; 2 Corinthians 6:14–17; Galatians 1:8; Galatians 5:12; 2 Thessalonians 3:6; 1 Timothy 6:3; Titus 3:10.[7]

THESIS III

Every man is obligated to recognize the true visible Church and, if he has the opportunity, to join it.

This thesis is obviously important for our purpose. He who is convinced that there can be, should be, and is a true visible Church, as stated above, must also add that every man has the duty to join it. The belief that one has the freedom to join this or that church flows from unbelief that there actually can be a true visible Church of God. Note what David said long ago in the words of Psalm 26:6–8: "I wash my hands in innocence and go around Your altar, O LORD, proclaiming thanksgiving aloud, and telling all Your wonderous deeds. O LORD, I love the habitation of Your house and the place where Your glory dwells."

The prophet is also thinking here of the true Church. For the glory of God dwells in this Church alone because (1) here alone His Word is decisive, and (2) because only here is taught that which alone justifies by grace through faith

7 Jena 1712, p. 917.

in the Gospel, which resounds here in preaching, Absolution, Baptism, and Communion. In false-believing churches, works-righteousness has been accepted contrary to the glory of God.[8] It is as absurd as it is godless to say, "I have contributed something to my own physical life or to my creation out of my own works and service." But it is still more terrible and godless to assert, "I have contributed something, if only the least bit, to the attainment of spiritual and eternal life." He who thinks this way is a robber of God's glory and is damned. And this is exactly what happens in the false church. Here one does not thank and honor God, but himself. But the orthodox Church is the Church of thanksgiving, and in it all the wonder of the Lord is proclaimed. That is why David loves this Church and belongs to it.

Matthew 10:32–33 is also a major passage which demonstrates that one should belong to the true visible Church: "So everyone who acknowledges Me before men, I also will acknowledge before My Father in heaven, but whoever denies Me before men, I also will deny before My Father who is in heaven." This is because profession is a duty. The papists wrongly assert that membership in the visible Church is the primary way one becomes Christian and is made holy. Such membership is important not for God's sake, but for ourselves and for the sake of our lost world. For it is God's will that all men would be saved through the Gospel. Christians should preach it to and confess it before the world, not because everyone should or must be public servants of the Church, but so that they might join the true visible Church in which they hear the pure Gospel. In this way the Church is a saving leaven in the world. Christ the Lord says in Luke 9:26: "For whoever is ashamed of Me and of My words, of him will the Son of Man be ashamed when He comes in His glory and the glory of the Father and of the holy angels." All those who do not confess the Church of the pure Word, but hang on to false doctrine—the Reformed, for example—are ashamed of the Word of Christ. The first Christians in Jerusalem are an excellent example of faithful profession and holding to the true visible Church.

Acts 2:41–42 declares of them that they remained steadfast not only in the apostles' doctrine but also in fellowship—that is, they acknowledged the orthodox congregation, although there was great danger to life and limb connected with this. For they understood that it is not enough for you yourself to believe the pure truth but that you are also responsible to confess this truth openly. If, therefore, Nicodemus had remained as he was at first when he came to Jesus by night, in woeful timidity of profession, he would not have been a Christian and would not have been saved. Indeed, precisely because of this approach, the Lord Jesus said to him, "Truly, truly, I say to you, unless one is born again he cannot see the kingdom of God" (John 3:3). Hebrews 10:24–25 says: "And let us consider how to stir up one another to love and good works, not neglecting to meet together, as is

8 *welches hier in Predigt Absolution, Taufe und im Abendmahle erschallt.*

the habit of some, but encouraging one another, and all the more as you see the Day drawing near."

The "neglecting" does not so much mean a withdrawal from congregational gatherings or divine worship services as much as it means a keeping away from the fellowship of the orthodox Church generally, although it is certain that he who first neglects Divine Services and gatherings of the congregation has therefore already separated himself from the Church. The Lord says in Matthew 18:17: "If he refuses to listen to them (to the witnesses), tell it to the church. And if he refuses to listen even to the church, let him be to you as a Gentile and a tax collector." One should bear this word in mind against the enthusiasts, who allege that Christ has, as it were, thrown the truth into the world and anyone who has the desire to receive it may do so. But that is perverted. Christ has established a kingdom through which to save the world, and according to His Word and will, there actually should be a true visible Church whose voice one can hear and which one should acknowledge. First John 2:19 says: "They went out from us, but they were not of us; for if they had been of us, they would have continued with us. But they went out, that it might become plain that they all are not of us." One should hold up this passage before those who believe differently, who perhaps come to us and speak of us and our confession in a praiseworthy way but who then desire to remain quietly in their faith and their church, in which, as they believe, they can also just as well be saved without coming over to us. To such people one should say: "If you really belonged to us you would also come to us. Either your praise is only hypocrisy, or you are acting contrary to your own conscience." In 2 Timothy 1:8 the apostle writes to Timothy: "Therefore do not be ashamed of the testimony about our Lord, nor of me His prisoner."

This passage demonstrates why we should also be called Lutherans. Paul asks Timothy not only to confess the Word of Jesus but also to confess to him, to Paul. He who confesses Jesus should also acknowledge those who properly preach Jesus. Some who acknowledge our Lutheran confession as correct still deny it before our enemies in that they deny the name Lutheran. We can find consolation in the face of such a denial because these people are hypocrites to whom Christ will one day say: "You have betrayed Me in that you have betrayed My faithful witnesses. Or have you never read, 'What you have done to My brothers and My servants you have done to Me'?" Of course we are only speaking here of those who deliberately deny the true Church. It could very well be possible that someone might leave the evangelical Lutheran Church and still remain a true Christian. It could be, for example, that an awakened but ignorant Christian from Germany who had previously belonged to a Lutheran congregation, bewitched by the appearance of the Methodists, could conclude that only in that fellowship is true, living Christianity to be found, and that therefore he could go over to them without losing his Christianity. But from all this we can see that it is not enough to believe the pure doctrine, but that one should also publicly acknowledge orthodox believers.

Luther also writes on this topic most excellently:

> Finally, I see that I must add a good word of admonition to those whom Satan has now begun to persecute. For there are some among them who think that when they are attacked they can escape the danger by saying: I do not hold with Luther or with anyone else, but only with the holy gospel and the holy church, or with the Roman church. For saying so they think they will be left in peace. Yet in their hearts they regard my teaching as the teaching of the gospel and stand by it. In reality this kind of statement does not help them, and it is in effect a denial of Christ. Therefore, I beg such people to be very careful. True, by any consideration of body or soul you should never say: I am a Lutheran, or papist. For neither of them died for you, or is your master. Christ alone died for you, he alone is your master, and you should confess yourself a Christian. But if you are convinced that Luther's teaching is in accord with the gospel and that the pope's is not, then you should not discard Luther so completely, lest with him you discard also his teaching, which you nevertheless recognize as Christ's teaching. You should rather say: Whether Luther is a rascal or a saint I do not care; his teaching is not his, but Christ's. For you will observe that the tyrants are not out merely to destroy Luther, but to wipe out the teaching. It is on account of the teaching that they attack you and ask you whether you are Lutheran. Here you must be sure not to speak with slippery or evasive words but frankly to confess Christ, no matter who did the preaching—Luther, or Tom, Dick, or Harry. The person you can forget; but the teaching you must confess. Paul also writes thus to Timothy in 2 Tim. 1 [:8]: "Do not be ashamed then of testifying to our Lord, nor of me, a prisoner for his sake." If it had been enough here for Timothy to confess the gospel, Paul would not have commanded him not to be ashamed also of Paul—not of Paul as a person but of Paul as a prisoner for the sake of the gospel. Now if Timothy had said, I do not hold with Paul or with Peter, but with Christ . . . then he would actually thereby have denied Christ himself. For Christ says in Matt. 10 concerning those who preach him: "He who receives you receives me, and he who rejects you rejects me." Why this? Because holding thus with his messengers, those who bring his word, is the same as holding with Christ himself and with his word.[9]

THESIS IV

Every man is obligated to avoid heterodox churches, and in the event that he has belonged to a heterodox church, his obligation is to renounce it and separate himself from it.

---

9 *Receiving Both Kinds in the Sacrament* (1522), AE 36:265–66.

This is taught by Psalm 26:4–5: "I do not sit with men of falsehood, nor do I consort with hypocrites. I hate the assembly of evildoers, and I will not sit with the wicked." The vain people from whom David separates himself are the erring spirits, who stand on their own vain wisdom and righteousness and not on the Word of God. Furthermore, it says in Psalm 94:20 [KJV]: "Shall the throne of iniquity have fellowship with Thee, which frameth mischief by a law?" "Throne" here means the seat of a teacher or a pulpit. God will never be united with those who from this position use the law—that is, the Word of God in general—wrongly, that is, falsely. He is always their enemy. But if God is their enemy, how can we have friendship and oneness with them? Therefore, we should and must be separate not only from those who as unbelievers wish to know nothing from the Word of God in general but also from those who use the Word wrongly or pervert it into false doctrine.

The following text from Jeremiah 15:19 says exactly the same thing: "If you return, I will restore you, and you shall stand before Me. If you utter what is precious, and not what is worthless, you shall be as My mouth. They shall turn to you, but you shall not turn to them." Here separation from the ungodly is also commanded. One might object: Are all the members of heterodox churches ungodly? We can only reply: Certainly not all. There are Christians among them. Only the ungodly, namely, false teachers and stubborn defenders of error, are to blame for the fact that such heterodox fellowships exist and are maintained. Therefore, we must withdraw and be separate from them. "I appeal to you, brothers, to watch out for those who cause divisions and create obstacles contrary to the doctrine that you have been taught; avoid them" (Romans 16:17). We have been falsely blamed for destroying and splintering the unity of the Church because we divide and separate from the heterodox. Here we see this is not true. Instead, everyone who causes division and offense contrary to the pure, sound doctrine of the Word of God is responsible for the division. St. Paul says in 1 Corinthians 11:19: "For there must be factions among you in order that those who are genuine among you may be recognized."

Divisions, according to the original text, αἵρεσις, here means a fellowship of people who hold to erring doctrine contrary to one or more of the articles of faith, thus a sect. Orthodox Christians will be revealed if they separate themselves from such sects. The Christians who unknowingly remain among them may also remain Christians through the wonderful gracious preservation of God, but they are not revealed to us as such.

Among other things 1 Corinthians 10:18 says: "Are not those who eat the sacrifices participants in the altar?" This text indicates an important element of our separation from the false church, namely, that we include all Communion fellowship with them. Because in the same way as that Corinthian who ate from the heathen idol offerings had fellowship with the heathen, so still today a Christian who takes part in a false Communion service practices fellowship with the heterodox church.

Matthew 7:15 is the well-known but, sadly, little heeded warning of Christ: "Beware of false prophets, who come to you in sheep's clothing but inwardly are ravenous wolves." I admit that some who would listen to false teachers say, "We take out for ourselves the best of that which they preach." But we would ask, "Is that what it means to beware of the wolf, or are you running into the jaws of the wolf?" Christ says, "Do not listen to them." And in fact if one were not to listen, the preaching would have to stop. Yet, for the most part, such people are also belly-servers who only want to preach for good wages. Luther could say, "All that is lacking in order to overthrow the papacy is a great sack of money." First Timothy 6:3–5 is also a major proof-text for our thesis: "If anyone teaches a different doctrine and does not agree with the sound words of our Lord Jesus Christ and the teaching that accords with godliness, he is puffed up with conceit and understands nothing. He has an unhealthy craving for controversy and for quarrels about words, which produce envy, dissension, slander, evil suspicions, and constant friction among people who are depraved in mind and deprived of the truth, imagining that godliness is a means of gain." Titus 3:10: "As for a person who stirs up division, after warning him once and then twice, have nothing more to do with him." A heretic is a man who even stubbornly errs in an article of faith. Acts 20:30–31: "And from among your own selves will arise men speaking twisted things, to draw away the disciples after them. Therefore be alert, remembering that for three years I did not cease night or day to admonish every one with tears."

Unionists are willing to repudiate obvious unbelievers. But they are not willing to repudiate the heterodox. This is, however, in conflict with this passage in which the congregation is warned against those who carry on perverted or false doctrine. Second John 10–11 says: "If anyone comes to you and does not bring this teaching, do not receive him into your house or give him any greeting, for whoever greets him takes part in his wicked works." This is a major text. John is called the beloved disciple, but if he were to preach this text in the world today, they would stone him. But he speaks divine truth. He has also previously said, "Everyone who goes on ahead and does not abide in the teaching of Christ, does not have God." Therefore, one should not greet such people. This does not mean that one should avoid secular courtesy and necessary communication. Instead, it means that over against the heterodox one should avoid all that communication which could open up our sympathy for them, because that would mean a denial of Christ. Therefore, marriage with those who believe differently is dangerous, particularly if the man is the erring partner. What a difficult cross the orthodox partner then has to bear, and how many often succumb and therefore lose faith and good conscience totally. Business associations with the heterodox are also not recommended. The apostle says of such, "Do not take him into your house." That means that one should, except in cases of actual destitution, not extend cordial hospitality and in no way provide support for their religious goals. Finally, 2 Corinthians 6:14 says: "Do not be unequally yoked with unbelievers. For what partnership has righteousness with lawlessness? Or what fellowship has light with darkness?"

Many think that this text does not apply to erring believers but is only speaking of unbelievers. But they are wrong. Unionism is based on nothing but unbelief, in that it receives, justifies, and tolerates erring believers and those who openly teach contrary to the Word of God. For that reason it is actually unbelievers who build the temple of unionism. He who takes part in unionism also therewith takes part in the evil and unbelief that is basic to it. An orthodox Christian should and must earnestly flee from that kind of fellowship and would rather never receive Communion or die than partake of a Zwinglian Communion. We know well that the false believers charge that conflict and quarreling over pure doctrine and disunity in the Church are our chief delights. Little do they suspect that they are heavy crosses for us. But God's Word unites us. The Savior says, "Whoever loves father or mother more than Me is not worthy of Me, and whoever loves son or daughter more than Me is not worthy of Me" (Matthew 10:37). Indeed, He says: "If anyone comes to Me and does not hate his own father and mother and wife and children and brothers and sisters, yes, even his own life, he cannot be My disciple" (Luke 14:26).

In these latter words the Lord wants to say that he who is not resolved to do something out of love for me, and also does that which may be viewed by his own parents or other relatives as something hateful, cannot be a true Christian. So perhaps a true Lutheran may have a tender, loving father who is erring and deluded in faith, who comes to him with many moving words and pleas—yes, with threats and oaths that he not belong to the Lutherans, this (in his view) stubborn, obnoxious sect, that he would not by the reception and defense of the Lutheran name and confession cover his grey head with disgrace and bring him down to his grave in grief. But even then, in this situation, he cannot retreat and give way, nor consider his own father's grief and crying, but only the Word of God. But how will the blind world interpret this obedience to the Scriptures? They will interpret his action as disgraceful hatred and evil against his beloved father. To endure that is not easy, but it is important. The Appendix [*Treatise on the Power and Primacy of the Pope*] to the Smalcald Articles says:

> This being the case, all Christians ought to beware of becoming partakers of the godless doctrine, blasphemies, and unjust cruelty of the Pope. On this account they ought to desert and execrate the Pope with his adherents as the kingdom of Antichrist; just as Christ has commanded, Matt. 7:15: "Beware of false prophets." And Paul commands that godless teachers should be avoided and execrated as cursed, Gal. 1:8; Titus 3:10. And 2 Cor. 6:14 he says, "Be ye not unequally yoked together with unbelievers;

for what communion hath light with darkness?" To dissent from the agreement of so many nations and to be called schismatics is a grave matter. But divine authority commands all not to be allies and defenders of impiety and unjust cruelty.[10]

Luther:

Because so many of God's great warnings and admonitions have simply had no effect on them[11] . . . therefore, I must leave them to their devices and avoid them as the self-condemned [αὐτοκατακρίτος, Titus 3:11] who knowingly and intentionally want to be condemned. I must not have any kind of fellowship with any of them, neither by letters, writings, and words, nor in works, as the Lord commands in Matthew 18 [:17], whether he is called Stenckefeld, Zwingli, or whatever he is called. I regard them all as being cut from the same piece of cloth, as indeed they are. For they do not want to believe that the Lord's bread in the Supper is his true, natural body which the godless person or Judas receives orally just as well as St. Peter and all the saints. Whoever (I say) does not want to believe that, let him not trouble me with letters, writings, or words and let him not expect to have fellowship with me. This is final.[12]

THESIS V

True Christians are also found in heterodox fellowships as a result of their lack of knowledge.

One reads in Galatians 1:2 that the holy apostle Paul still calls the Galatians a Church (Greek: ἐκκλησία, German: *Kirche*), although in chapter 3 he must refer to them as foolish people who have not obeyed the truth and have become a sect. But he nonetheless calls them a Church because there are still true Christians among them. Furthermore, Revelation 2:24: "But to the rest of you in Thyatira, who do not hold this teaching, who have not learned what some call the deep things of Satan, to you I say, I do not lay on you any other burden." The Son of God had previously said to the same congregation (v. 20): "But I have this against you." That is sanctified satire. That which you consider minor, Christ wants to say is really something of major importance, a terrible sin, "that you tolerate that woman Jezebel, who calls herself a prophetess and is teaching and seducing My servants to practice sexual immorality and to eat food sacrificed to idols." The congregation at Thyatira was also openly sectarian. Nevertheless, this text provides definite proof that there remain in the sects those who have not taken false doctrine to heart, but they remain in the sect because they have not recognized the deep things of Satan.

---

10 Tr 42.

11 The Sacramentarians. Ed.

12 *Brief Confession Concerning the Holy Sacrament* (1544), AE 38:304.

First Kings 19:14, 18 is the complaint of Elijah over an Israel that is faithless and apostate from the Lord, and the comfort which God offers the prophet. False believers so totally dominated the Jewish Church that the dear prophet in his despondency could believe that he alone remained. But God revealed to him that there still remained seven thousand in Israel who along with him had not bowed the knee to Baal. Generally speaking, where the Word of God is still essentially present, there the Church is still present. There are always sincere Christian souls hidden in the sects.

The story of 2 Samuel 15:11 also shows this: "With Absalom went two hundred men from Jerusalem who were invited guests, and they went in their innocence and knew nothing." As is well-known, the infamous Absalom secretly prepared a rebellion against David, his father and king, in that he enticed and captivated his subjects with all kinds of deceptive words. Now some good men, who did not perceive his evil purpose, believed that as the king's son and by the will of the king Absalom was gathering the people around himself, and so their legs followed him though their hearts remained loyal to David. This is an appropriate picture of Christians in the sects. Absalom represents the false prophets who rebel against the king—that is, Christ. But they do so under a pious facade. For that reason sincere Christians often do not perceive their evil and outwardly follow them while in their hearts they depend on Christ. Our confessional writings also witness to the truth expressed here.

> As to the condemnations, censures, and rejections of godless doctrines, and especially of that which has arisen concerning the Lord's Supper, these indeed had to be expressly set forth in this our declaration and thorough explanation and decision of controverted articles (in the Formula of Concord), not only that all should guard against these condemned doctrines, but also for certain other reasons that could in no way have been passed by. Thus as it is no way our design and purpose to condemn those men who err from a certain simplicity of mind but are not blasphemers against the truth of the heavenly doctrine, much less, indeed, entire churches, which are either under the Roman Empire of the German Nation or elsewhere; nay, rather has it been our intention and disposition in this manner openly to censure and condemn only the fanatical opinions and their obstinate and blasphemous teachers. . . . For we have no doubt whatever that even in those churches which have hitherto not agreed with us in all things many godly and by no means wicked men are found.[13]

None of our confessional writings are decried as intolerable by our opponents more than the Formula of Concord. Yet it is the Formula more than any of the others which asserts, as does the passage we have cited, that though our Church is the only Church which stands on the Word of God and not the doctrines of men,

13 Preface to the Book of Concord, *Concordia Triglotta*, 20.

it is not be considered as the only saving Church, outside of which there can be no salvation. There are also Christians in other churches. We do not condemn them, but only the false doctrine and its stubborn teachers and defenders. This passage is all the more significant in this discussion because from it, as noted above, the spokesmen of the "Church Council" wish to conclude that one can rightfully admit heterodox, simple, dear Christians and their preachers from other church fellowships to altar and pulpit fellowship.[14] They contend that we are guilty of un-Lutheran practice because we exclude these people from our altars and pulpits. But we will hear later how false that conclusion is from this passage.

THESIS VI

> *Those who are aware of the partial apostasy of the church fellowship to which they belong and yet continue to remain within that fellowship are not to be considered among the weak but are either the lukewarm whom the Lord will spit out of His mouth or epicurean religious skeptics who within their hearts would ask with Pilate, "What is truth?"*

It is certainly true that there are Christians in false-believing churches. But they are weak Christians who unknowingly labor under a delusion. But it is hypocrisy if they are convinced of their error and still remain in the sect, still desiring to be considered as the weak. They are either the lukewarm or epicurean religious skeptics. Then what does the Lord say? He says: "Whoever is not with Me is against Me, and whoever does not gather with Me scatters" (Luke 11:23). He who hears the truth and pretends to believe it but will not also publicly confess it does not honestly believe his Christianity. Neutrality in the kingdom of God is condemned. He who is not openly for the truth is against it. As far as in him lies, he does not gather, but scatters the congregation of God. Christ says further: "Do not think that I have come to bring peace to the earth. I have not come to bring peace, but a sword. For I have come to set a man against his father, and a daughter against her mother, and a daughter-in-law against her mother-in-law. And a person's enemies will be those of his own household" (Matthew 10:34–37).

Some who recognize the errors of their sect still remain in them because of timidity, fear of conflict, cross, and all kinds of earthly trouble. They have misgivings about publicly separating themselves and joining the orthodox Church. They should take particular note of this text. But the struggle in the kingdom of God for the sake of God's Word is truly a holy, sanctifying struggle, a struggle against the devil. It is ordained for all true Christians that the Church here will always be the Church in conflict. Those who think that a quiet, comfortable, outward peace is more edifying and conducive to the growth of the Church are fools. No, nothing is more dangerous or more evil than if a so-called "graveyard peace" prevails in the

14 *Abendmahls = oder Kanzelgemeinschaft.*

Church. The Savior says: "I came to cast fire on the earth, and would that it were already kindled." Luther, his servant, experienced and tested in holy war, often pointed out the great blessings which follow where the spirits burst in spiritual conflict with one another. Conflicts, crosses, and hardship appeared in the household of Job, as in a synagogue of Satan, and yet it was still a true house of God. Unionists hate conflict for the sake of God's Word. At most they would perhaps fight against the unbelievers, but not against the heterodox and false doctrine. They do not want to understand that false doctrine is much more dangerous to the Church than open unbelief.

"I know your works: you are neither cold nor hot. Would that you were either cold or hot! So, because you are lukewarm, and neither hot nor cold, I will spit you out of My mouth" (Revelation 3:15–16). This passage, which we mentioned before, condemns as lukewarm those who believe that it is absolutely improper to change their religion. It is true that he who has the true Christian religion may not exchange it for another so that he may have a certain hope of salvation. But woe to him who recognizes that his faith, doctrine, and church are not correct and still will not move to join the true orthodox Church. Adam would never have become a Christian, or Luther a man of the Gospel, if both of them had not penitently abandoned their false religions; in the case of the former, his service of the devil, and with the latter, his papism. Whosoever, therefore, pronounces our evangelical Lutheran doctrine and Church to be correct but nonetheless remains in the false church and does not come over to us burdens himself with a serious condemnation. He then knows full well the way of the truth, but that does not change him; as Christ says: "And that servant who knew his master's will but did not get ready or act according to his will, will receive a severe beating. But the one who did not know, and did what deserved a beating, will receive a light beating" (Luke 12:47–48).

Therefore, so that no one who, because of his own infidelity and laziness is guilty of ignorance, might use that as a defense for remaining in a false church, our Lord Jesus also says: "For to the one who has, more will be given, and he will have an abundance, but from the one who has not, even what he has will be taken away" (Matthew 13:12). Our gracious God will allow His gifts (knowledge, for example) to an individual to increase and grow if the person to whom God has given any measure of spiritual gifts uses them faithfully for honest searching of God's Word. On the other hand, the gift of knowledge is gradually reduced in him who does not faithfully use it, until it is totally lost. For example, if a Reformed person perhaps perceives through the grace of God that a particular point of his doctrine is false, and he faithfully uses this light and searches further, God will also help him to be convinced little by little of all the errors of the Reformed Church and then to settle on the Lutheran Church and its doctrines. On the other hand, if he does not use the first gift correctly, all the light of knowledge will once again be extinguished in him and he will be all the more deeply mired in error. According to Romans 14:23: "But whoever has doubts" (namely, whether the eating of meat is proper) "is condemned if he eats, because the eating is not from faith." Those also are committing a damnable sin who are in doubt over the orthodoxy of their church and still remain in it, for thereby they demonstrate that sin in general is an indifferent thing to them. One should also listen to Luther, who in his conversation with George Major said, among other things:

> Whoever really regards his doctrine, faith, and confession as true, right, and certain cannot remain in the same stall with such as teach, or adhere to, false doctrine; nor can he keep on giving friendly words to Satan and his minions. A teacher who remains silent when errors are taught, and nevertheless pretends to be a true teacher, is worse than an open fanatic and by his hypocrisy does greater damage than a heretic. Nor can he be trusted. He is a wolf and a fox, a hireling and a servant of his belly, and ready to despise and sacrifice doctrine, Word, faith, Sacrament, churches, and schools. He is either a secret bedfellow of the enemies, or a skeptic and a weathervane, waiting to see whether Christ or the devil will prove victorious; or he has no convictions of his own whatever, and is not worthy to be called a pupil, let alone a teacher; nor does he want to offend anybody, or say a word in favor of Christ, or hurt the devil and the world.[15]

It is also very significant to note what J. Spener, the mildest of all the Lutheran theologians in the seventeenth century, who has often been called the grandfather of unionists, says in this regard:

> Since in God's providence Christendom has been divided into many parts because of infiltrating false doctrine, I can call no one my brother other than those who acknowledge the Lutheran Church.[16]

> As relates to outward brotherhood which is based on the fellowship of the faith, that which one believes, or religion, all Lutherans are my brothers since they confess and hold to one faith; but no Reformed, as long as he remains such, is my brother, because he confesses another religion, a religion whose doctrine I recognize as dangerous error.[17]

How grievously sin also those who pursue their devotion in heterodox churches, especially here where full religious freedom prevails and they only have to put up with the cost and discomfort of a trip in order to hear God's pure Word in a Lutheran Church!

---

15 Quoted in F. Bente, *Historical Introductions to the Symbolical Books of the Evangelical Lutheran Church* (St. Louis: Concordia, 1921), 94.

16 *Ubereinstimmung mit der Augsb. Conf.*, 226.

17 *Letzte theol. Bedenken*, Cap. II, 605.

THESIS VII

The main purpose of the Holy Sacrament is to be a tool and a means through which the promises of grace are offered, communicated, and appropriated, as with a seal, guarantee, and pledge through which these promises are confirmed. However, within this major purpose, as a secondary goal, the Sacrament is to be a distinguishing sign of confession and a bond of fellowship in worship. Therefore Communion fellowship is church fellowship.

This thesis is particularly important because our opponents say: If you Lutherans acknowledge that there are also Christians in other churches, then you must admit that they also should have a part in your Sacraments, which are signs and seals of the gracious goodwill of God which belongs to all Christians. Against this we now say: It is true that the Sacraments are this and indeed primarily and principally this, and it would have also been proper if they had been nothing other than this. But they are also distinguishing marks of confession and bonds of fellowship in the Divine Service.[18] Surely we allow the Catholics or even the heathen to hear the Word of God with us; but if one is to be permitted to participate in the Sacraments, he must be recognized as a person who stands in proper Christian faith, for by his participation he is marked with a seal of brotherly fellowship in the faith. This applies equally to Holy Baptism and Holy Communion. And for that reason Christ has also ordained both Sacraments. For the Gospel is not a philosophical system but a productive power of God. It is preached so that there is a Church in which believers find unity together. And the Sacraments are, so to speak,the holy bonds and fences within which Christians stand over against the world. This was already the case in the Old Testament with circumcision. "You shall be circumcised in the flesh of your foreskins, and it shall be a sign of the covenant between Me and you" (Genesis 17:11). "He [Abraham] received the sign of circumcision as a seal of the righteousness that he had by faith while he was still uncircumcised" (Romans 4:11).

From this we see that it was not the outward hearing of the Word of God in Israel, but circumcision by which one was to be recognized as belonging to the people of God. He who would belong to God's people had to allow himself to be circumcised. And if he stood then in justifying faith in the promised Messiah, then was this circumcision a holy binding mark and a sign of the acquired righteousness of faith. Exactly the same thing is true of the Passover: "And the LORD said to Moses and Aaron,'This is the statute of the Passover: no foreigner shall eat of it. . . . If a stranger shall sojourn with you and would keep the Passover to the LORD, let all his males be circumcised. Then he may come near and keep it; he shall be as a native of the land'" (Exodus 12:43, 48). The Passover was also in the same way a sign of unity within Israel, separating them from the heathen. The heathen could

18 *Bänder gottesdienstlicher Gemainschaft.*

and indeed should be allowed to hear the proclamation of the Word of God, but no Gentile could be allowed at the Passover meal who was not himself a believing proselyte. Only circumcised Israelites participated. The same also holds true now for the Sacraments of the New Testament. First Corinthians 12:13 says of Holy Baptism: "For in one Spirit we were all baptized into one body."

He who is baptized will therefore be declared as a member of that mystical Body, the Body to which I, too, belong as a Christian, and through Baptism I give the baptized this witness: you are my dear fellow Christian, my brother in Christ. Exactly the same thing is also the case with Holy Communion. First Corinthians 10:17 says this: "Because there is one bread, we who are many are one body, for we all partake of the one bread."

In that Christians eat of the one bread of the Sacrament, all of them become mystically, that is spiritually—morally or figuratively—one Body; and by the one action of eating together a person is declared to be one in Christ with all Christians. Then in the same way as the bread consists of a vast multitude of tiny kernels of grain which have been baked, and just as it is impossible to separate these kernels again from one another, in the same way through Communion all Christians are one in Christ, and many thousands are inwardly bound together, as body and soul themselves, to form one organism. They are actually one. One God dwells within them. One Spirit rules within them. They all have one Savior, and one Lord Jesus Christ speaks from them. And now consider what a grievous sin those commit who administer Communion to those who are of another faith and confession, and thereby recognize them as being one and brothers: "When you come together, it is not the Lord's supper that you eat" (1 Corinthians 11:20).

Here the apostle rebukes the fact that the Corinthians celebrated Communion without showing in practice the brotherhood in faith and fellowship in love which is therewith declared. One can also see here that Communion should be a bond of fellowship in worship. All should come to preaching, but only Christians should come to Communion who have confessed the proper Christian faith with their mouths. Whoever, therefore, goes to Holy Communion in a Lutheran Church declares openly before the world: "I belong to this church, to the doctrine which is preached here, to the faith which is confessed here, and to all the confessors who belong here." The pastor who administers the Sacrament to him declares exactly the same thing.

In Acts 2:42, 46 and 20:7, the Holy Spirit mentions with praise how the Christians in Jerusalem and at Troas in Asia Minor demonstrated their oneness in the faith and their brotherhood in the breaking of bread, that is, in the celebration of Holy Communion. If heterodox Christians come to our Communion, with our knowledge, then both we and they are hypocrites. They appear to be Lutherans but are not.

Thus all of these passages from Scripture corroborate the truth of our thesis. If the leaders of the "Church Council" were to accept them, they would have to give up their false principles and practices; but they will not soon accept them until they recognize that there actually is a true visible Church of God in an absolute sense on earth. They do not say to their communicants who believe differently that they, through their partaking of Communion with us, are confessing our doctrine and our Church. Instead, they allow them to remain stuck in their error and plunge them and themselves into the sin of hypocrisy. So it is still necessary and important to testify before all over against the Reformed and the unionists that the Sacraments actually are Means of Grace and guarantees of our faith. The time has now also come when we must confess over against unionistic Lutherans that the Sacraments are also marks and bonds of liturgical and brotherly fellowship in the faith. Our Church also confesses this in its symbols. The Augsburg Confession says:

> Of the use of the Sacraments they teach that the Sacraments were ordained, not only to be marks of profession among men, but rather to be signs and testimonies of the will of God toward us.[19]

The Apology adds in the corresponding article:

> The Christian Church consists not alone in fellowship of outward signs, but it consists especially in inward communion of eternal blessings in the heart, as of the Holy Spirit, of faith, of the fear and love of God; which fellowship nevertheless has outward marks so that it can be recognized, namely, the pure doctrine of the Gospel and the administration of the Sacraments in accordance with the Gospel of Christ. And this Church alone is called the body of Christ in Scripture. . . . Neither have we said anything new. Paul has defined the Church precisely in the same way, Ephesians 5:25f., that it should be cleansed in order to be holy. And he adds the outward marks, the Word and Sacraments. For he says thus: Christ also loved the Church, and gave Himself for it, that He might sanctify and cleanse it with the washing of water by the Word.[20]

Luther:

> When Christ adds the mention of Baptism to the first point, "whoever believes," this applies to His command about the external office in Christendom, as He combines both points in Matthew 28 [:19–20]: "Teach all the heathen and baptize them," etc. He points out first that the faith about which this Gospel preaches must nevertheless not remain secret and hidden, as if it were enough for each one to go away when he hears the Gospel, believe for himself alone, and have no need to confess his faith before others. Rather, so that it may become obvious not only where the Gospel is preached but also where it is accepted and believed—that is,

19 AC XIII 1.

20 Ap VII/VIII 5–7.

where the Church and Christ's kingdom are in the world—He wants to bring and keep us together through this divine sign of Baptism. If we were without it, and scattered without any external assembly and sign, then Christendom could not be spread or preserved to the end. Now, however, He wants us tied together through this divine assembly so that the Gospel goes further and further and others are brought to it through our confession. Thus Baptism is a public testimony to the doctrine of the Gospel and of our faith before all the world, by which people can see where and among whom this Lord rules.[21]

Luther:

To promote and use such doctrine among Christians He has ordained that they should come together and hold to two ceremonies, that is Baptism and the Sacrament of His body and blood, and this has been sufficiently revealed in the Gospels and the Epistles of St. Paul; so that such doctrine, faith, and grace may not only be received and daily increased but also so that it may be known publicly before the world, as with an action, who is a Christian and who is not and whether he will freely and fearlessly confess such doctrine and honor God and provide his neighbor with an encouraging example; as He Himself says: "Do this in memory of Me" (1 Corinthians 11:24–25), which is nothing other than publicly to remember, confess, praise, and thank; as St. Paul interprets and says, "Do this that you may proclaim the death of our Lord" (1 Corinthians 11:26). That is all a part of that which we should do for God, namely, preach His Word and believe and receive the Sacraments as distinctive marks and confession. Hence it follows that the cross is over those who confess such doctrine.[22]

Luther:

The Sacrament is a public confession and should have public servants because thereby it happens, as Christ said, that one should do in remembrance of Him, that is, as St. Paul says, to proclaim or preach the Lord's death until He comes.[23]

Luther:

Although also under the papacy there have been such abuses that some have had a particle in the home for individual Masses, but for the sake of this instance and other reasons, I will and cannot judge. Then for a time someone could want to use it in this way so that the public church and

21 [From *Church Postil* (1540–44), sermon for Ascension on Mark 16:14–20, AE 77:283, paragraph 57.]

22 *Unterricht und Beweis, daß die Ev. Lehre mit dem Munde und mit der That zu bekennen. An Graf Albrecht von Mansfeld* (1523), StL 10:2211–12.

23 *Briefe an Wolfgang Brauer von der Hauscommunion* (1536), StL 10:2225.

gathering would be abandoned and deserted; even so it still should be a public and common confession.[24]

Luther:

> Now we shall speak of the proper manner of communicating the people .... Here one should follow the same usage as with baptism, namely, that the bishop be informed of those who want to commune. They should request in person to receive the Lord's Supper so that he may be able to know both their names and manner of life. And let him not admit the applicants unless they can give a reason for their faith and can answer questions about what the Lord's Supper is, what its benefits are, and what they expect to derive from it. ... Those, therefore, who are not able to answer in the manner described above should be completely excluded and banished from the communion of the Supper, since they are without the wedding garment [Matt. 22:11–12]. ... For participation in the Supper is part of the confession by which they confess before God, angels, and men that they are Christians. Care must therefore be taken lest any, as it were, take the Supper on the sly and disappear in the crowd.[25]

Luther:

> Third, God's people, or Christian holy people, are recognized by the holy sacrament of the altar, wherever it is rightly administered, believed, and received, according to Christ's institution. This too is a public sign and a precious, holy possession left behind by Christ by which his people are sanctified so that they also exercise themselves in faith and openly confess that they are Christian, just as they do with the word and with baptism.[26]

Johann Gerhard lists among the purposes of the Holy Sacraments which do not belong to its major purpose:

> That we testify that we consent to the doctrine which resounds in the particular church in which we, along with others, eat the same bread of holy Communion and drink from one and the same cup, according to 1 Corinthians 10:17: "There is one bread, and so we many become one body in that we share in the one bread."[27]

Gerhard:

> Just as the church is distinguished from worldly fellowships which are outside the church by the preaching of the Word and the administration of the Sacraments, so it also distinguished itself through pure preaching and

---

24 *Bedenken, ob man das hochw. Sacrament beider Gestalt in geheim zu Hause sich möge reichen lassen* (1535), StL 10:2226–27.

25 *An Order of Mass and Communion for the Church at Wittenberg* (1523), AE 53:32–34.

26 *On the Councils and the Church* (1539), AE 41:152.

27 *Loci Theologici: Locus de s. coena*, 214.

> legitimate administration of the Sacraments from the sectarian fellowships which are within the church.[28]

The theological faculty of the University of Leipzig writes in the year 1620:

> So the Sacrament is also a distinguishing mark of the Christian Church. Then because we cannot acknowledge consistent Calvinists as righteous members of our church because of their unbelief, so also we cannot permit them to participate in the distinguishing marks of our church because there could not be a greater scandal than when religions are mixed together.[29]

Then Christians should demonstrate that they are the Church and the people of God, not only through good works but also and especially through the Holy Sacraments. The Sacraments should gather the Church and mark its members. A communicant comes forward as a preacher in that he confesses the true Church to be there where he eats the Sacrament. The spokesmen of the "Church Council" would also admit that Baptism and Holy Communion are the distinguishing marks of the orthodox Church. This being the case it is a most grievous fraud and a deception in the name of God to impress the seal of orthodoxy upon those who believe differently, in that they are received at Holy Communion. In an attempt to justify themselves the spokesmen of the "Church Council" accuse us of treating those Christians who believe differently the same as those who are excommunicated and banned. But this charge is thoroughly false. We have often said, and we say it now again, that there are still true Christians in heterodox churches. But they stand under a false banner and label. Now we cannot and will not give them the true spiritual banner until they also confess to it from their hearts with us. In fact, our opponents object that the Sacrament and even the mutilated Sacrament of the sects is to be a distinguishing mark of confession of Christianity generally over against the heathen, the Jews, and the Turks, and therefore Christians should very well cultivate Communion fellowship among one another. But this is also in error. If the Sacrament is a mark of confession, as it is, then it is a mark of pure confession. If anyone comes to our altar, we must first ask him: "Do you believe and confess what we Lutherans believe and confess?" And if someone would answer, "Whether the Lutheran or Reformed faith is correct I do not know and I will not judge," it should be known that he is either an unworthy hypocrite or an epicurean skeptic. We for our part know that we Lutherans alone have the correctly administered Communion. But if we were to suppose that there might also be others, it would still always be valid that wherever anyone participates in Communion he thereby confesses as his own the doctrine which prevails there. Our Communion is our banner.[30] He who in his heart does not stand with us Lutherans should also

---

28 *Loci Theologici: Locus de s. coena*, 131.

29 *Dedekennus Thesaur.*, vol. 1, P.II, fol. 313.

30 *Unser Abendmahl ist unser Banner.*

not stand under this banner, and he who does this nevertheless we declare to be a traitor.

THESIS VIII

> *Holy Communion was not instituted to make people Christians. It was instituted to strengthen the faith of those who already are true Christians. Therefore Communion should be administered to no one who has been revealed as a false Christian.*

This is clearly asserted by this passage: "Whoever, therefore, eats the bread or drinks the cup of the Lord in an unworthy manner will be guilty of the body and blood of the Lord. Let a person examine himself, then, and so eat of the bread and drink of the cup. For anyone who eats and drinks without discerning the body eats and drinks judgment on himself" (1 Corinthians 11:27–29).

If the external use of Holy Communion itself were saving, then it would not matter so much if one misuses it. But the Sacrament does not work *ex opera operato*, that is, for the sake of the mere performance of the act. Unbelieving, mere so-called "calendar-goers" are unworthy. Unworthy users bring down the judgment of God upon themselves, often, as already in Corinth, in all kinds of temporal punishments: "You cannot drink the cup of the Lord and the cup of demons. You cannot partake of the table of the Lord and the table of demons" (1 Corinthians 10:21). Certainly this is possible on a physical or bodily level, and unfortunately it happens all too often; but morally and spiritually it is impossible. Matthew 7:6 also applies here: "Do not give dogs what is holy, and do not throw your pearls before pigs, lest they trample them uderfoot and turn to attack you."

From this it follows that a preacher does not have the obligation to give Holy Communion to everyone. He should not administer it to heretics, to the heterodox, to openly fleshly people, but only to those of whom he cannot publicly prove unchristian behavior. Luther also writes about this.

> Although indeed until now, according to the old custom, everyone has been admitted to the Sacrament who comes to it, this should not continue from now on, but instead it should be established that he who would take the Sacrament should henceforth be asked what the Sacrament is and what it is he seeks there, and if he answer that . . . he cannot do that, then he would not be given the Sacrament. . . . The Sacrament also should not be cast out among people in their homes as has been done under the pope. If I preach the Gospel, I don't know whom it strikes; but here I should have the opinion that it has struck those who come to the Sacrament; I must have no doubt but be certain that those to whom I give the Sacrament have laid hold of the Gospel and sincerely believe.[31]

31 Cf. *Sermon on the Reception of the Holy Sacrament*, Lenker 2:230.

Luther:

No one should be allowed to go to communion who has not been individually examined by his pastor to see if he is prepared to go to the holy sacrament. For Paul says in 1 Cor. 11 [:27], that they are guilty of profaning the body and blood of Christ who receive it unworthily. Not only do they who receive it unworthily dishonor the sacrament, but also those who carelessly give it to the unworthy.[32]

Dannhauer:

The teachers should do and go as far as they can. If they are unable to do more, they should still prevent wicked sinners from coming to Communion. For whoever admits an obstinate sinner, for whose iniquity there is sufficient evidence, and gives him the pledge of the forgiveness of sins, sins against him in a threefold way: with a false witness in which he takes part, with an increase of condemnation, and with a betrayal of the body and blood of Christ.[33]

George König:

Can an acknowledged papist or Calvinist be admitted to Communion in good conscience by a minister of the Lutheran Church? Some believe that these certainly ought to be admitted for two basic reasons. First, because the Church and its spiritual blessings should be open to all and closed to no one. And here perhaps the word of Christ also applies: "Come to Me . . . all who labor and are heavy laden, and I will give you rest," Matthew 11:28. Second, because the true and proper Sacraments are found in the Lutheran Church which they are missing in their own fellowships. However, in their desire to accomplish such a great blessing they reveal a foolish envy. But these are fables. We then put no one off of the way to the Church and its blessings, but we do encourage this, that everyone follow the right way. If, then, a shaking reed seeks a street which is riddled with invisible barriers and proceeds in the wrong way, is it any wonder that they then wander about, lost in the open fields, and can positively not find the door? The voice of Holy Scripture itself acknowledges: Such people "forsake the paths of uprightness to walk in the ways of darkness" (Proverbs 2:13). Also Christ does not call everyone without distinction to Himself, and does not promise the unworthy rest as well as the worthy, but those who are weary and heavy laden, that is, as it is interpreted by Theophylact, those who are weary from the working of the Law and heavy laden with the burden of their sins. These He calls to come to Himself, not with their bodies but with their hearts, and if they do so, He promises to them, and not to the others, His willing aid, namely, spiritual and eternal rest. As regards the other reason, we neither can nor want to deny that everyone receives the

32 *Instructions for the Visitors of Parish Pastors*, AE 40:296.

33 *Catechismus—Milch.*, 10:489.

> true Supper from our people. Therefore, because we are the true Church which correctly believes in the Sacrament of Holy Communion according to Christ's institution, they also administer it according to Christ's will in His place. It does not therefore follow that whoever knows where the true celebration of Communion is should at once therefore be admitted to it. In this regard it is also important that he be a true member of the true Church and wear the wedding garment. The guest of Matthew 22:11 is an example of this. This one desired the heavenly wedding; in fact, he appeared at it, and what's more, he took his place among the guests; nevertheless he was thrown out and in fact by his own fault, because he lacked the wedding garment. Therefore, also that one who does not wish to be refused admittance should previously provide himself with a wedding garment, namely, preparing himself through conversion and joining our Church, through a genuine recognition and confession of sin, through true trust in Christ and His servants, and therefore properly examining himself, etc. Then he will be accepted at this heavenly meal with joy as a person who hurries after the blessings of the Church.[34]

In his famous work *Institutes of the Christian Religion*, Calvin himself writes:

> And here also we must preserve the order of the Lord's Supper that it may not be profaned by being administered indiscriminately. For it is very true that he to whom its distribution has been committed, if he knowingly and willingly admits an unworthy person whom he could rightfully turn away, is as guilty of sacrilege as if he had cast the Lord's body to the dogs. . . . Therefore, lest this most hallowed mystery be disgraced, discretion is very much needed in its distribution.[35]

This indicates the continuing importance of personal announcement before Holy Communion in our churches. Those pastors who do not continue these announcements practice shamefully, faithlessly, and unscrupulously and do not exercise the utmost care toward the salvation of the members of their congregations. The thought of the most holy body and blood of Christ being eaten by false Christians is even more dreadful than the thought of throwing them down into the mud! A false Christian is one who will not give up either false doctrine or a godless life. However, even one who still has love for Christ may not automatically receive Holy Communion in all circumstances. For example, Holy Communion should not be received in situations where offense has been given or taken and there has been no Christian reconciliation. In the same way, those who believe differently should not receive Holy Communion as long as they have not renounced their error or their heterodox fellowship and in this way reconcile themselves with the orthodox Church. If, however, one does not give the Sacrament to a Christian in this kind of

34 *Casus conscientiae*. Altdorf, 1654, 592ff.

35 *Institutes of the Christian Religion*, IV.xii.5.

individual situation, one has not thereby excommunicated him but only suspended him. Someone may ask: If we suspend the Reformed from Lutheran Communion, how can we tolerate receiving a lodge brother to the same who has not yet decided to give up his evil association? We answer: The former is a sin in doctrine, and the latter is a sin in life. That is a major distinction. Now we Lutherans who eat of this Holy Communion are all poor miserable sinners, but in doctrine we are pure despite the devil who wants us to wander off. We can admit a penitent fellow sinner with us, as in the case of a lodge brother, so long as he does not openly sin wantonly and does not intend his association to have any religious character—or as long as he does not participate in a single religious act of the lodge. But from the pure doctrine and confession, because it is God's, we can abandon nothing, not even one letter. He who does not hold to it with us totally and completely cannot go with us to Holy Communion, as has been previously stated.

We would be sinning dreadfully if we held ourselves separate from all other fellowships only out of mere blind preference or taste. But this division and standing alone is the command of God and therefore necessary. We may not invite the heterodox as such into our fellowship as our opponents in the "Church Council" have done and want to justify. For thereby they have become guilty of a severe sin. And we for our part will endure our standing alone as a cross, inseparably united with the slanders of our enemies and the unjustified accusations of our erring fellow Christians. We are all the more encouraged by this as by faith we remember the high and holy goal which God has revealed to us in His Word for the divisions of His New Testament Church before the world. God in His merciful love has given the world a great host of preachers and living witnesses to Christ in the Church. They should work in the world as a saving leaven. They should be heralds who through their faithful holding fast to a pure confession, through their listening to preaching and going to Communion, are calling out to the world, as it were, "Come also with us! Believe as we believe! Be reconciled as we are and therefore take part also in the guarantee of your reconciliation as we do!" And certainly more of God's pleasure and blessing rests upon this decreed and enduring witness and preaching of the Church than on all experiments in church politics and unscriptural unionism. What would have happened to the Lutheran Church in America without the orthodox Lutheran synods? If twenty-five or thirty years ago a few Lutherans had sat in the corner with their faith, there would hardly be an orthodox Lutheran Church in our land today. But there are now thousands upon thousands of Lutherans here who have come to life in Christ, who circulate confessionally faithful church publications, and who have founded Lutheran Church institutions for education and charity which are now in full bloom. Our gracious God had accomplished all these through the faithful witness to and confession of the truth from the mouths of orthodox Lutheran Christians. And if this is already the fruit in so small an ecclesiastical circle such as ours, how much richer could it be in the greater Church at large. This is also the blessing of the Church coming together and its separation from the world. And furthermore, just as our Lord Christ at one time for eternity separated us from the fellowship of the ungodly, so must we already here be separated from the world.

THESIS IX

In Holy Communion the body and blood of Christ are actually present, distributed, and received by every communicant. Therefore Communion cannot be administered to anyone who does not confess a belief in this mystery without grievous sin.

First Corinthians 11:29 says: "For anyone who eats and drinks without discerning the body eats and drinks judgment on himself." "This is how one should regard us, as servants of Christ and stewards of the mysteries of God" (1 Corinthians 4:1). Accordingly pastors are not only distributors of the divine mysteries of grace but also their stewards. God, the heavenly landlord, has bound them to definite instructions according to which they are to administer His mysteries, as treasures entrusted to the Church. And from this flow the shepherd's responsibilities for the administration of the Holy Sacrament which have already been mentioned in our thesis and the earlier theses and their explanations. In this regard let us now hear our public Confessions and the voice of our Fathers.

In his "Questions for those who wish to go to the Sacrament" (Number 13), Luther poses the question: "Do you believe the true body and blood of Christ to be present in the Sacrament?" and instructs that the response be, "Yes, I believe it."

Luther:

> For it is not our intention to admit to it and to administer it to those who know not what they seek, or why they come.[36]

Augsburg Confession:

> Our churches are falsely accused of abolishing the Mass. But it is obvious without boasting that the Mass is celebrated among us with more devotion and seriousness than by our opponents. And so our people are frequently instructed on the Holy Sacrament with the utmost diligence as to how it was established and is to be used. . . . And in that regard there is also instruction against other impure doctrines on the Sacrament.[37]

Luther:

> It is very well true that where preachers administer mere bread and wine as the Sacrament there is no more concern about to whom it is administered; or what they understand or believe; or how they perceive it. . . .

---

36 LC V 2.

37 AC XXIV.

> But we intend to educate Christians and to leave some behind us; for in the Sacrament we administer the body and blood of Christ. We cannot and will not give such a Sacrament to anyone who has not been previously examined as to what he has learned from the Catechism and whether he is willing to abandon the sins which he has done to the contrary.[38]

THESIS X

Holy Communion is a mark of confession of faith and doctrine among those who celebrate together. Therefore the admission of members of heterodox fellowships to the celebration of Communion within the Lutheran Church is in conflict with: (1) Christ's institution; (2) the commanded unity of the Church in faith and accordingly in confession; (3) our love for those to whom the Sacrament is administered; (4) our love for our own fellow believers, especially the weak who by this action would be given serious offense; and (5) the command not to become participants in the sin and error of others.

The premise of this thesis has already been demonstrated in Thesis VII. Therefore, only the conclusions cited on the basis of the thesis still remain to be proven. And so, first of all, we give an account of number one. "For as often as you eat this bread and drink this cup, you proclaim the Lord's death until He comes" (1 Corinthians 11:26).

The holy apostle explains here with the solemn Words of Institution themselves which the Lord quoted twice: "Do this in rememberance of Me" (vv. 24–25). The entire doctrine of the redemption won through the blood and death of Christ is included in this "telling how the Lord died." Therefore, when anyone eats of Holy Communion, he is confessing for himself the whole doctrine of the redemptive work of Christ. A Reformed person, naturally, confesses the false doctrine and only a Lutheran confesses the one, pure doctrine. It is impossible for anyone to go to Communion with a person like this without grievous sin against the testament of Christ. Listen to Hülsemann on this topic:

> There is controversy between us and the Socinians, Arminians, and some of the Calvinists as to whether the outward purpose of Holy Communion consists only in this, to distinguish all those who are called Christians from the heathen (this is what Osterodt in his catechism and the Arminians in their Apology assert); or to distinguish from idolaters all those who actually agree with the foundation of the Christian religion but are mutually separated from one another on their articles by an outward division. This is what the new unionists among the Calvinists (G. Hotten, Moses Anniwald, and Thomas Morton) teach. Our conviction is this: according to the institution of its Founder, no one is to be admitted to Communion

38 *Warnungsschrift an die zu Frankfurt a. M., sich vor Zwinglischer Lehre und Lehrern zu Hüten*, StL 17:2018.

fellowship who has been separated from the household by an open confession of faith or by entrance into another, evidently schismatic, house, for if he were to be admitted to Communion fellowship, he would still be considered orthodox and would desire to participate in this table with them. We prove this our position from the institution itself and in the following ways. (1) That external goal which the Founder has bound together with Communion fellowship is not to be separated from Communion fellowship. Now the Founder has bound this outward purpose with Communion fellowship that the communicants by their joining together become one spiritual body and testify that through this fellowship they are one mystical body. Also this purpose is not to be separated from Communion fellowship. This conclusion is proven by 1 Corinthians 10:17–18: "Because there is one bread, we who are many are one body, for we all partake of the one bread." Look at Israel according to the flesh. Don't those who share the sacrifices share the altar? But now, those who confess various contrasting articles of faith through various contrasting public confessions in various contrasting groups are not one mystical body. Also, then, according to the institution of the Founder they may not receive part of the one mystical bread. (2) The understanding among all people, the Jews as well as the heathen, is that eating from the sacrifices of the Jews or the heathen had the same meaning as eating the bread of Holy Communion. This is according to verses 18 and 21: "Are not those who eat the sacrifices participants in the altar? . . . You cannot drink the cup of the Lord and the cup of demons. You cannot partake of the table of the Lord and the table of demons." Now all people, the Jews as well as the heathen, held that this was the significance of the eating of the sacrifice, that those who ate together were to be considered as fellow members of that particular religion, whose members could be distinguished by their sacrificing at this or that altar. The eating of the bread of Communion has the same significance according to its institution, namely, that those who eat of this bread are fellow members of the same faith. Therefore, on the other hand, those who are not members of the same faith should not receive one and the same Communion bread. (3) It is not permitted to do that which the Founder has forbidden. Now the Founder has forbidden that those who confess the faith at various altars should take part in one and the same Communion bread. It is then also not permitted for us to do this. This conclusion is proven by verse 21: "You cannot drink the cup of the Lord and the cup of demons. You cannot partake of the table of the Lord and the table of demons." We here understand "you can't" in a moral sense as "you may not." As the legal maxim says: "One can do that which one may do in an honorable way, that which one can do rightly." The Calvinist interpreters themselves also acknowledge that in the New Testament the term "can't" may very often be taken as "impermissible" or "improper," as in Matthew 9:15: "Can the wedding guests mourn as long as the bridegroom is with them?"[39]

For the past two hundred years the enemies of a correct doctrine and practice on Communion have asserted that the use of the Sacrament should distinguish Christians from the heathen, not the orthodox from the heterodox. But that is false. All unbelief and all false doctrine is a part of heathenism. Communion fellowship with all those who believe differently is forbidden in the institution of Christ. We do not consider the Reformed orthodox, and they do not consider us orthodox. Therefore, it is a crass contradiction and vile mockery of the institution of Christ if both parts celebrate one Communion in fellowship with one another. Communion is also a sacrificial meal. Christ, offered for us once on the cross, would here be eaten by us. This was prefigured in the Levitical sacrifices which were not totally burned but in part also were to be eaten and in fact also to this end, that those who ate also by this action declared themselves to be participants of the same holy religion and congregation.

The theological faculty of the University of Wittenberg wrote the following in 1656 in response to a question as to whether Calvinists ought to be admitted to Holy Communion:

> Because this Sacrament is a public witness and confession of the Church, of the faith, doctrine, and religion which an individual confesses, and also holds to be the immutable truth, so the Sacrament is also to be used so that faith may be increased, the faith which believes in the promises that are given in the Sacrament, as Article XIII of the Augsburg Confession reminds us. Such a faith, however, one does not find among those who cannot believe in Christ's Words of Institution and promise in regard to the oral eating and physical presence. Paul says in 1 Corinthians 10:17, "Because there is one bread, we who are many are one body, for we all partake of the one bread." But now the kind of Calvinists that we have described are not one body with our Church; therefore, they do not also belong to the eating of the bread and Holy Communion. If we are not to take into our homes those who do not bring the doctrine of Christ nor greet them, according to St. John's reminder (2 John 10–11), so that we do not therefore become participants in the evil things they do, much less can we admit one to Holy Communion who cannot believe in the oral eating and physical presence which Christ has instituted and promised.[40]

George König:

> If David did not allow false people in his house (Psalm 101:7), how should a minister in the house of God, which the true Church is, allow those, and receive as guests at the heavenly banquet those, who deal falsely in their

39 *Vindiciae S. Scripturae etc. Lips.*, 1679, 660.

40 *Consilia Witteberg*, II, 131.

works and with shameless impudence are as easily inclined to the true and to the false church. Others are inclined to act as Elijah the Tishbite once did. This one, clad in heroism, did not flee from his concern for religion, but openly stepping forth among the people he said, "How long halt ye between two opinions?" so, namely, that they practiced diverse divine services and wanted partially to serve both God and Baal. God wants nothing to do with the kind of mixed religion which desires to be a third thing from the combination of the pure and the corrupt. "If the Lord is God, then turn to Him"; that is, if the divine worship prescribed by God through Moses is the true divine worship, then they should satisfy Him through this alone. "But if Baal, then turn to him," that is, but if they believe the worship of Baal to be true, why do they hesitate to practice Baal worship alone and totally abandon the Mosaic worship of God with all of its holy places and ceremonies? (1 Kings 18:21). It is undoubtedly certain that God demands not only a part of divine worship but all of it without exception, and those who want to worship Him partially through true and partially through false religion neither worship God properly nor hold to the true religion. Every altar on which Holy Communion will be celebrated should have the following dictum inscribed on it:

Cui non mens eadem, cui non confessio simplex,
Hanc mensam vetitam noverit esse sibi!

That is, "Those who do not have one and the same faith and confession, let them know that this table is forbidden to them."[41]

A rumor once circulated that Count Frederick of Württemberg and Montbéliard permitted French Reformed refugees to participate in a Lutheran Communion. The count clarified the matter with the following denial:

> By God's grace we have attained such knowledge of spiritual things in regard to the salvation of our souls that we know well that among many other purposes our Lord's Communion was established for this purpose, that as with a standard or marker it can be recognized to which faith an individual belongs. Then he who takes part in Communion with a particular church, which presently exists, no matter what it is called, therefore gives it to be understood that he is also a follower of the doctrine of that church. Thus Communion should not be held with those who follow another doctrine, but we should openly separate ourselves from them. . . . Therefore, we have always held, and still do, that the reception of the Lord's Holy Communion should not be trifled with in that a person would be willing to confess one doctrine by a public reception of the Sacrament while holding to another doctrine in his heart.[42]

41 *Casus consc.*, pp. 594ff.

42 *Colluquium Mopergartensae*, translated from Latin into German, Tübingen, 1587, Preface, ii.

In support of number two we cite 1 Corinthians 1:10 and Ephesians 4:3–6 (cf. the explanation of Thesis I for comment on both texts). First of all, unity in the faith is also demonstrated in Holy Communion. Second, the Church should be one in faith and doctrine. From those it follows that only those who confess the pure doctrine with us may be admitted to Holy Communion. He who communes with us Lutherans gives the public appearance that he belongs to our household. But would we not be misrepresenting the unity of our Church if we were to allow a Reformed person to display this certificate of citizenship and family origin? Who in our own country would confer citizenship on an immigrant who still declared himself to be a subject of the king of Prussia or some other monarch? Truly a preacher who is willing to admit people who believe whatever they choose to Communion is treacherous, deceptive, and, yes, even devilish. How Luther, that true man of God, would be amazed if he could see what goes on in the Lutheran Church today! In his own time he wrote:

> The significance or effect of this Sacrament is fellowship of all the saints. From this it derives its common name *synaxis* [Greek] or *communio* [Latin], that is, fellowship. And the Latin *communicare* [commune or communicate], or as we say in German, *zum sacrament gehen* [go to the sacrament], means to take part in this fellowship. Hence it is that Christ and all the saints are one spiritual body .... On the other hand *excommunicare* [excommunicate] means to put out of the community and to sever a member from this body .... To receive this sacrament in bread and wine, then, is nothing else than to receive a sure sign of this fellowship and incorporation with Christ and all saints. It is as if a citizen were given a sign, a document, or some other token to assure him that he is a citizen of the city, a member of that particular community. St. Paul says this very thing in 1 Corinthians 10[:17], "We are all one bread and one body, for we all partake of one bread and of one cup."[43]

> If we were to allow ourselves to take such unity, then we would have to consent to both parts, namely, that where our people would perhaps come to them and desire to receive the Sacrament, or, on the other hand, their people would come to us, and this would involve the intolerable error, that our people would receive mere bread and wine and still believe that it was the body and blood of Christ and their people with us would receive the body and blood of Christ and still believe that it was mere bread and wine, and the outrage much more.[44]

> And, in summary, I come to this matter. It is horrible for me to hear that in some churches or at some altars both parts may get and receive the same

43 *The Blessed Sacrament of the Holy and True Body of Christ, and the Brotherhoods* (1519), AE 35:50–51.

44 *Schrift wider König Heinrich in England*, StL 19:430.

> Sacrament and one part believes that they are receiving the true body and blood of Christ. And I often wonder whether it can be believed that such a preacher or pastor could be so impenitent and spiteful, and in addition to this be silent, and allow both parts to come in, each in their own delusion, that they are receiving one and the same Sacrament, each according to their own belief. If perhaps there is such a one, he must have a heart that is harder than any stone or steel or even a diamond, who must certainly be an apostle of wrath. Then Turks and Jews are much better, for they openly confess that they deny our Sacrament, and we therefore remain separate from them and do not fall into apostasy. But these comrades must be the true high archdevils, who give to me mere bread and wine and allow me to consider it the body and blood of Christ, and so I am wretchedly cheated. That would be too devilish and too difficult; then God will shortly break all that in pieces. Therefore, he who has such a preacher, or who would be inclined to excuse such a thing, let him be warned about this as against the devil incarnate himself.[45]

Of course some of our opponents object that a Lutheran certainly cannot go to Communion with a Zwinglian but he can very well do so with a Calvinist because they still teach that the body of Christ is present in the Sacrament, though only spiritually. But this pretext is invalid because the Calvinists are deceptive with their confession. If the body of Christ is in Communion only spiritually, it is really not there at all. One should not rely on the fine-sounding words of the Calvinists because, especially in reference to the doctrine of Communion, they use their words to disguise their beliefs and conceal their errors. With such people, through questions like: "Is the body of Christ in Communion?" "Is He truly present?" "Is He essentially present?"—the fox, as Luther said, has not yet appeared. They will respond to all of them with "yes," but they will always mean only a spiritual body of Christ. Therefore, one must go further and ask whether also Judas and all the godless receive the true body of Christ orally. That they will deny and will recoil from it with the greatest horror. And in this way they prove that they make the presence of the body of Christ in the Holy Sacrament dependent on faith and deny the presence of the true body of Christ. But it is wicked and as hypocritical as perjury that the men of the "Church Council," who still subscribe to the Confessions which included the indicated words of Luther, will nonetheless admit those who believe differently to the Sacrament. Although their consciences may take comfort in the position of the Iowa Synod that by subscription to the Symbols one does not subscribe to everything, not to the incidentals.

Moreover it should be noted that the Church, through Holy Communion, is divided not only from heretics and errorists but also from so-called schismatics. A schismatic is particularly one who would separate from the Church not because of

45 *Warnungschrift an die zu Frankfurt*, StL 17:2446.

a fundamental article, but because of a teaching or certain adiaphora. In the same way this kind of person may not be admitted to the Sacrament. Hülsemann also certifies this:

> The fourth proof is taken from the established practice of the Church that fellowship, which from the beginning of the Church has distinguished heretics and schismatics from the orthodox and pure believers, has not been abolished. But from the beginning of the Church, Communion fellowship has distinguished heretics and schismatics from the orthodox and pure believers so that under the punishment of the ban it was not allowed to admit an open schismatic to Communion fellowship if he persisted in his separation. The *Magdeburg Centuries* demonstrates this with great unanimity from Justin, Irenaeus, Tertullian—Flacius in his catalog, from the letter of Ignatius to the Smyrneans, Augustine from the practice of his time in the second book of *On Christian Doctrine*, and Chrysostom in his twenty-eighth sermon from Matthew, chapter 26, among others.[46]

Our doctrine and practice in regard to Communion fellowship is that of the apostolic Church until the time of St. Ignatius.[47] And even today in this regard all other churches teach as we do with the single exception of the Congregationalists, to whom unfortunately the defenders of the "Church Council" compare themselves. The former declare in the conclusion of their confession:

> The members of churches which have been gathered and converted according to Christ's will, and may be regarded as true churches, although they are less pure, may on occasion be received into fellowship if they have the faith-worthy marks of piety and lead a life without scandal.[48]

And, finally, as regards the members of secret societies—the Freemasons, the Oddfellows, the Druids, and whatever other titles they may confer upon themselves—we repeat that we in reference to their reception at our Communion make a distinction between those who remain in this bulwark of the devil stubbornly and against better conviction, and those who stay in such an "order" or "lodge" to pursue some religious tendency, or who also participate in one or more of the religious acts within the lodge, on the one hand, and those for whom neither one nor the other of the situations described applies; while we would hold the former far from our altar like other impenitents or heterodox, for the latter, however, as weak and erring in life, we cannot refuse Communion fellowship with us. This proper principle can only find its correct use where one has analyzed and considered the

---

46 *Vindicia*, etc., p. 660.

47 For further evidence on this point, see W. Elert, *Eucharist and Church Fellowship in the First Four Centuries*, trans. Norman Nagel (St. Louis: Concordia, 1966).

48 *Declaratio Fidei atque ordinis ecclesiarum congregationalium*, 1658. Cf. J. Hoombeek, *De Independentismo*, Ultrajecti, 1661, p. 443.

individual situation in the light of the manifold forms and colors of the secret societies here in this land. Now we continue to the proof for number 3.

We cite here Leviticus 19:17: "You shall not hate your brother in your heart, but you shall reason frankly with your neighbor, lest you incur sin because of him." This is a noteworthy text. Reprimanding is so often presented as lovelessness, but unjustly, as we hear here. If you do not love someone, you will not reprimand him. To warn your fellow man away from a false or destructive way is certainly true love. A Reformed, for example, follows such a way if he desires our Communion. He does not believe in this most holy mystery. Therefore, he is unworthy to eat it. An unworthy participant eats and drinks judgment unto himself as 1 Corinthians 11:29 proves (cf. Thesis VIII). To refuse admittance to a Reformed to our Communion table is certainly a work of true love, and woe to those who will not perform it. For the Lord says: "If I say to the wicked, 'You shall surely die,' and you give him no warning, nor speak to warn the wicked from his wicked way, in order to save his life, that wicked person shall die for his iniquity, but his blood I will require at your hand" (Ezekiel 3:18).

Here also belong the words of Luther:

> For you people can easily understand that, if unity were established between us, some of your people would commune in our congregations, and also some of ours in your congregations. Those who would commune with a different faith and with a different attitude of conscience would necessarily on both sides receive something different than that which they believe [they are receiving]. Thus it would be unavoidable that through the ministry [of the sacrament] and our consciences either their faith would be made a mockery through hidden deceit and lies if the communicants were unaware of this difference, or, if they were aware of the difference, then their faith would be destroyed through a public sacrilege. You can see how devout and Christian this would be. For this reason let us select rather the lesser of two evils, if one of the two must be endured at all. Let us therefore rather put up with this smaller disagreement, together with a limited peace.[49]

George Dedekenn:

> As little as an orthodox Christian who confesses Luther's doctrine with mouth and heart can desire Communion with a clear conscience from a Zwinglian and suspicious teacher (according to Luther's advice one would withdraw from such throughout his life), just as little can also a Reformed who understands the work and is properly serious about his religion even desire our Communion without the highest burden on his conscience.[50]

George König:

49 *A Letter to Martin Bucer* (1531), AE 50:8–9.

50 *Thesaur.* 1:2.316.

> If a Calvinist wants a Lutheran preacher to give him Communion whether he is a layman or a pastor, is either informed or uninformed. If he is uninformed, he is perhaps unaware of the distinction which exists between us and the Calvinists on this part of doctrine, particularly because such an action would also give the appearance, as they teach, that the body and blood of Christ is truly present in the Sacrament. Therefore, one must guard with the greatest diligence that one does not admit anyone to Communion who does not understand the matter and is still filled up with his error. Much more, he must previously be clearly taught how far apart from one another we are in this part of doctrine and clearly instructed as to why one part cannot commune with the other, namely, because also among other purposes the Lord's Supper also has this: to be a mark and a sign of the religion which an individual confesses. Then he who takes part in the fellowship of their Sacrament within a particular church in this way publicly confesses that he accepts the doctrine of the church and rejects that which is contrary, and that he will follow this way separated from the others. It is therefore important that he first accepts our confession, reject Calvinism as erring, and therefore separate himself from it, if he desires to participate in our Communion.[51]

These texts belong to number 4: Romans 14:1, 15: "As for the one who is weak in faith, welcome him, but not to quarrel over opinions. . . . For if your brother is grieved by what you eat, you are no longer walking in love. By what you eat, do not destroy the one for whom Christ died." Matthew 18:6: "But whoever causes one of these little ones who believe in Me to sin, it would be better for him to have a great millstone fastened around his neck and to be drowned in the depth of the sea."

In the year 1568, the theological faculty of the University of Wittenberg gave the following as the first reason why a persistent Calvinist may not be admitted to Communion in a Lutheran Church:

> First of all, it is undoubtedly true that this command binds all men, but especially ministers and pastors: "Don't share in the sins of others." Now it is certain, and will be forever maintained throughout our Church, that the belief of the Sacramentarians is a severe and most criminal error and sin from many sources which are unnecessary to mention. Then here again it is certain and undoubtable that such people with this belief and error are finally and irretrievably burdened and bewitched, as it were; so the minister and pastor cannot allow them to Communion and the eating of the Sacrament without sin and burdening his conscience. And how without a doubt all the Sacramentarians would allow no one who was attached and related to the confession and faith of our Church to come to their Communion for the same reasons. Also, pious and reasonable ministers or pastors cannot, without noticeable impiety and burdening of

51 *Casus consc.*, p. 597.

their consciences, receive other people who through unbelief and a false understanding of Communion's Words of Institution, which are so clear and bright, are exactly where they want to be, sinning against God and the Lord Christ, musing and dreaming. Then those eat and drink Communion to judgment and, according to the words of St. Paul, become guilty of the body and blood of Christ who eat it unworthily; how much more must those become participants in also the same judgment and severe sins who administer it to them, knowing of the unbelieving and perverted convictions and therefore the judgment and guilt which will follow and burden their consciences.[52]

Luther:

They desired from us the brotherhood which we had refused them in Marburg and could not accept. For if we had received them as brothers and sisters, we would also have had to consent to their doctrine. Although they did not gladly accept this refusal, they asserted that one should nurture love over against them until God brings us together again, because we should also love our enemies. Now whoever wants to construe this badly, let him do so.[53]

And, finally, George Dedekenn:

And the second reason why Lutherans do not admit Calvinists to Communion is the office and the character of a faithful preacher. Because (1) the Sacraments are not only the preachers' but gifts to the whole Church. On account of which he must not administer them according to his own pleasure, but because the Sacraments are a common treasure of the whole Church, so also these must in every way have knowledge about who takes part with them in the unity of the Sacrament and who does not. (2) Moreover, we preachers are only stewards of the mysteries of God. Now nothing more is required of a steward than that he be found faithful. This faithfulness does not only involve his teaching office in proclaiming the divine truth and reproving the errorists but also the administration of the Sacraments, that he therein uses good caution and discretion, and does not allow everyone without distinction, but taking heed over the whole flock, and distinguishing between the pure and the impure, and holy and the unholy. Therefore, he should not make himself responsible as regards administration for various people, for giving the Sacrament merely on his own responsibility. To such a degree one would be either papist or Photinian. Also those whom one knows to be willfully receiving it to judgment can justly be refused since one is not allowed to joke with divine things. And a preacher is appointed to the end that he will be on his guard,

52 *Dedekennus Thesaurus*, 1:1309ii.

53 *Erzählung von der Canzel, seine Reise gen Marburg und das Gespräch, daselbst mit den Sacramentirem gehalten, belangend in Auslegung des 5 B. Mose III*, StL 3:1770.

> and should watch and warn against eternal shame so that he may not have to give an account with a heavy conscience for the lives he neglected.[54]

Our tenth thesis is also directed against the union, that grave of the Lutheran Church, and specifically also against its adherents and defenders within our Church. It is directed against unionistic, syncretistic preachers. We label them all as shameful, unscrupulous belly-servers, who abandon the consciences of their Communion guests, whether and what they believe in and confess about this Sacrament, and thereby falsely invoking the words, "Let a man then examine himself," etc., as if this text not only applied to the laymen but also to the preachers. "This is how one should regard us, as . . . stewards of the mysteries of God. Moreover, it is required of stewards that they be found faithful" (1 Corinthians 4:1–2).

THESIS XI

> *We do not place members of heterodox fellowships under excommunication or declare them to be heretics or damned by our refusal to allow them to participate in the celebration of Communion within the fellowship of the Lutheran Church. Instead, they are merely suspended until such time as by their separation from the false fellowship they are reconciled with the orthodox Church.*

This is a plausible and powerful charge by our opponents against our doctrine and practice on Communion. They say, "How can you be so bold as to excommunicate a child of God from another church through your rejection of him at your Communion? You declare him to be heretical and cut off from the Body of Christ! Jesus Himself would be astonished!" That sounds horrible, and if it were true it would truly be horrible. But this accusation is nothing more than an empty, hollow, false alarm. For, as has already been mentioned above, we do not place those Lutheran Christians under the ban (be he the offended or the offending party) if we, according to Christ's own words, separate them from Holy Communion as long as they have not been reconciled with their neighbor. Matthew 5:23–24: "So if you are offering your gift at the altar and there remember that your brother has something against you, leave your gift there before the altar and go. First be reconciled to your brother, and then come and offer your gift." Luke 17:3: "Pay attention to yourselves! If your brother sins, rebuke him, and if he repents, forgive him."

As long as he has been kept away from the Lord's Supper, he has not reconciled himself with his neighbor, although he could very well be worthy to receive the Sacrament throughout. Just as little do we excommunicate, disown, declare as heretics, or condemn those Christians erring in faith if we say to them, "We would be glad to allow you to come to Holy Communion with us. But there is still

54 *Thesaursus*, I:II:315.

a barrier in the way. That is, the sin of your error in doctrine which you have not recognized up to now. This you must acknowledge and abandon first and become a member of the orthodox Church. Then you will be to us a dear, welcome guest at Communion." It is, of course, an entirely different matter with openly impenitent sinners, mockers, and obstinate errorists. We call only the latter heretics. Such people, by the explicit command of Christ, are to be excommunicated. And in this matter we also agree with our orthodox Fathers.

The theological faculty of the University of Wittenberg wrote in an opinion in the year 1638:

> It is indeed a clear distinction between *indignitate intrinseca* ("inner unworthiness"), which originates in unrecognized moral sin, and *indignitate extrinsecqa* or *accidentali* ("outward or incidental unworthiness"), as is offense against the neighbor, which the penitent frequently does not know.[55]

> Luther:

> With God as my witness! I would, if it were possible, buy off this disunity with my own body and blood (if I also had more than one body). But how shall I deal with them? They have perhaps in good conscience been captivated by another understanding. Therefore, I will gladly patiently bear with them. But if they wish to remain with their conviction on the presence of the body of Christ with the bread and would ask that we still bear patiently with one another, so I would very happily be patient in the hope that we shortly might come into one fellowship.[56]

> St. Augustine:

> In fact the apostle Paul has said, "A heretic warn once and a second time and then avoid him. . . . He is a sinner who has condemned himself." but those who maintain their own opinion, however false and perverted, without obstinate ill will, especially those who have not originated their own error by bold presumption but received it from parents who had been led astray and had lapsed; those who seek truth with careful industry, ready to be corrected when they have found it are not to be rated among heretics. If I did not believe that they (the Donatists) were such, I would have indeed sent no letter to you. Yes, we are not opposed to seeking the improvement of the heretic himself in every possible way, who has been blown up in hateful arrogance and rages in stubborn contentiousness; but we are moreover admonished to avoid this kind of person so that he will not lead the weak and the children astray.[57]

---

55 *Consel. Witebergens*, 2:128.

56 *Rathschlag und Bedenken über die von den Zwinglianern gesuchte Vereinigung* (1534), StL 17:2051–52.

57 Ep. 162.

THESIS XII

The heterodox themselves regard and declare it improper for them to commune with those who are orthodox. Would it not then be disgraceful for those who are last in regard to Christ's own institution and administration of the Sacrament to expose those who have been first?

So the Reformed, for example, have often forbidden their own members to receive Holy Communion with us. The Reformed in Zürich, in the year 1539, forbade those studying at the University of Strasbourg to go to Communion, and in order to justify themselves wrote to the Strasbourg Church Council:

> Those who practice fellowship with us through the Sacrament, confess through that fellowship that they share with us a common faith in the Sacrament; but our youth do not now have the same faith with you.[58]

Calvin:

> If you ask my advice, as to whether you are allowed to take the Holy Communion of Christ from the hands of those who consider us to be heretical because we deny that the flesh of Christ is torn apart by the teeth: I perceive full well that it gives a bad example if anyone were to refrain from Holy Communion. Nevertheless it would be granting an improper—yes, a hypocritical—pretense (a false and absurd dream) through the reception of the symbol of unity which, even if only implied, subverts the foundation of the faith through pernicious delusion. A clear and public confession of the doctrine under consideration goes out. I therefore consider it best that you clearly and openly witness that you will refrain from your duty to participate in the Sacrament because you will not abandon the pure and proper doctrine of Christ.[59]

Also in the Wittenberg Conference, it said:

> Herewith our evangelical theologians and preachers certainly agree, thus far, that according to their belief such a preacher must be either a hypocrite or a crypto-Calvinist who would knowingly admit Calvinists to our Supper. It is also the case that one of the Calvinists, named Zacharias Ursinus, in his letter to Andraeas Dudithius in which he deals with unity or fellowship between the orthodox and the erring, specifically advises that no Calvinist can in good conscience go to the Supper with the Lutherans. The Calvinists themselves with their consciences, which fundamentally reject our doctrine, witness that they should not desire to use the Supper with us Lutherans But how much less could a Lutheran preacher in good conscience administer the Holy Supper to the Calvinists? Then, though there are also some to be found among the Calvinists who are of the conviction

58 Löscher, *Historia Motuim zwichen den Ev. Lutherischen und Reformirten*, 1:254.

59 Calvin, *Epistol. et respons*, editio secunda, Lausannae, 1576, Ep. 292. p. 478.

> that the articles still in contention between us and them are not those upon which the foundation of salvation depends, there is nevertheless no one among all the honest evangelical preachers who agrees with them in this matter. Yes, everyone who really has the advancement of the glory of God and our Savior in his heart is responsible to disabuse all those who have been falsely persuaded of this their error. For this it should be very evident that in no way could a Calvinist be immediately admitted to Holy Communion with us if he were willing to comply with our ceremonies and usages. As, for example, if he would not perhaps be offended by our round hosts and not insist upon the breaking of the bread. Meanwhile, these on account of the erring doctrine of the Calvinists in which they take part are rightfully to be excluded from the fellowship of our Church. In no way, only because of the fact that they are willing to consent to our ceremonies, can they be admitted and accepted again. Also the mere use and acceptance of such adiaphora cannot make them immediately fit for or worthy of this action, which their unbelief in the most important chief articles of faith and the resulting division and separation of inner spiritual unity has already made them objectionable and unworthy. Now to admit those whom we have described would prove them to be nothing other than hypocrites and lukewarm Christians in religion who consider the points remaining in conflict between us and the Reformed to be of poor basis and worth. . . . When Henry Alting, a Calvinist doctor from Heidelberg and Gröningen, diligently investigated whether a Reformed could in good conscience go to the Holy Supper with Lutherans, he specifically required this, that in cases where one would answer yes to this question, a clear and specific confession of the pure doctrine (which he as a Calvinist also called his own doctrine) should come first from the preachers from whose hands one would be receiving the Holy Supper as well as from the others (*Problematica theologica*, II, 10, 11). And therefore Alting was very doubtful whether this could happen for everyone (even then without burdening consciences). For how could Lutheran preachers be responsible to their own consciences when they did not require such a confession from their own penitents, especially when they know full well that those who would come to the Holy Supper are not of the same doctrine with us, and also would deliberately be allowed to come without inquiry or examination? They would thereby indicate with such an unscrupulous and questionable admission sufficiently and openly that they are anything but sincere Lutherans.[60]

But what should we really call such people? Without a doubt open hypocrites, syncretists, and Samaritans who hold as much to one religion as to another. The early Christians were accustomed to close the doors of the church whenever the Holy Supper was held, so that no one could come in who was a part of another

60 *Consil. Witeberg.* I, 1044. f.

foreign religion; how much less, then, would they have knowingly and deliberately admitted such people who have belittled this great divine mystery and condemned those within the Christian Church who believe this high mystery properly and well? They were not such hypocrites.

THESIS XIII

The more unionism and syncretism is the sin and corruption of our time, the more the loyalty of the orthodox Church now demands that the Lord's Supper not be misused as a means of external union without internal unity of faith.

The holy prophet Jeremiah called to faithless Israel: "Cross to the coasts of Cyprus and see, or send to Kedar and examine with care; see if there has been such a thing. Has a nation changed its gods, even though they are no gods? But My people have changed their glory for that which does not profit. Be appalled, O heavens, at this; be shocked, be utterly desolate, declares the LORD" (Jeremiah 2:10–12).

If the blind heathen themselves will not change their false religion, is it not truly terrible if this would happen to Christians today if they, as it clearly happens at the Communion practice of the unionists, were to unite the truth of the Christian religion with the lie, and would justify this as much as that within the Church? We, for our part, would hold fast to that which the Formula of Concord says over against this unionistic abomination:

> Namely, when under the title and pretext of external adiaphora such things are proposed as are in principle contrary to God's Word (though painted another color), these are not to be regarded as adiaphora . . . but must be avoided as things prohibited by God. In like manner, too, such ceremonies should not be reckoned among the genuine free adiaphora, or matters of indifference, as make a show or feign the appearance, as though our religion and that of the papists (or the Calvinists)[61] were not far apart, thus to avoid persecution, or as though the latter were not at least highly offensive to us; or when such ceremonies are designed for the purpose, and required and received in this sense, as though by and through them both contrary religions were reconciled and become one body. . . . We believe, teach, and confess also that at the time of confession, when the enemies of God's Word desire to suppress the pure doctrine of the holy Gospel, the entire

61 Editor's note: Walther, quoting the FC, provides a fascinating gloss with his little addition *oder Calvinischen*, "or Calvinists." In our American environment, the Lutheran Church faces a far greater danger from a generalized "Protestantism," with roots in Calvinism and Reformed theology, than it does from the type of Romanism against which FC X was written. It is obvious from the Walther gloss that he, too, recognized this danger. American Lutheran churches which embrace Calvinist or Reformed forms of worship or polity or practice, in any area of church life, are on very shaky ground. Liturgical worship, in the form the Church has used for thousands of years, becomes far more than adiaphoristic in a context of confession, as Walther notes above.

> congregation of God, yea, every Christian, but especially the ministers of the Word, as the leaders of the congregation of God, are bound by God's Word to confess freely and openly the doctrine and what belongs to the whole religion, not only in words but also with works and with deeds.[62]

J. C. Daunhauer encourages us to this confessional faithfulness and vigilance against the evil foe. He writes:

> Sleepy security is the mother of carelessness. If one would therefore be on his guard against this enemy, there is nothing more evil about which one could be concerned. Quintus Curtius has correctly said, "No one can despise his enemy without danger, for if one is not careful, his enemy is strengthened through his own carelessness." Through exactly this carelessness the Antichrist was first born, and while the people slept he was allowed to sow his weeds. This same carelessness, looking on with lazy, dim eyes that were not suspicious enough, has allowed the machinations of the syncretistic spirits (the mixers of religion) which has raised its head in our time, and some in fact feel that it already rules. Perhaps the world will shortly be surprised at how quickly it has become syncretistic and, consequently, atheistic.[63]

The Antichrist first succeeded in seating himself in the midst of God's temple through security and carelessness in the Church. Later on, through the security and carelessness of the Church, false unionism also crept in. Now it is up to us to light against this enemy and to disentangle ourselves from the webs and the bindings of the syncretistic spirit of the time. May the faithful and merciful God aid us and fill our hearts with a hatred for the lying spirit and an inner true love for the Word of God and the truth.

62 FC SD X 5, 10: *Of Church Rites.*

63 *Liber consc.*, 1:139.

CHAPTER THREE

CLOSED COMMUNION

IN THE WAY OF THE GOSPEL; IN THE WAY OF THE LAW

NORMAN NAGEL

"THE HOLY THINGS FOR THE HOLY ONES" (τὰ ἅγια τοῖς ἁγίοις).[1] Thus the deacon calls to the faithful who are thus invited to be given the body and blood of our Lord. They are invited, others are not: closed Communion. A line is drawn: inside it the joy of the gifts, the holy things, the body and blood of our Lord; outside it the Law toward repentance.[2] So it was in the Church from as early as we know. When we learn of the catechumens not being invited, there is no hint of condemnation, nor is there of those in Corinth who did not belong to the congregation, but who were there during the Service of the Word. When the not-yet-invited were invited, then the full joy of "the holy things."[3]

1 *Prayers of the Eucharist: Early and Reformed*, ed. R. C. D. Jasper and G. J. Cuming, 3rd ed. (New York: Pueblo, 1987), 44, 50, 66, 73, 86, 99, 112, 123, 134, 137. For a discussion of this and much which follows, see Werner Elert, *Eucharist and Church Fellowship* (St. Louis: Concordia, 1966). Also, Hermann Sasse, *We Confess the Sacraments* (St. Louis: Concordia, 1985), *This Is My Body* (Adelaide: Lutheran Publishing House 1959), F. E. Brightman, *Liturgies Eastern and Western* (London: Oxford, 1896), and J. Jungmann, *The Mass of the Roman Rite* (New York: Benziger, 1951).

2 *Apostolic Constitutions* (c. 380), 2, 7; Funk 43, 21. "Unless they repent (κατακριθήσεται)." Cf. 1 Cor. 11:32. Note here κρίμα, κρίνω, διακρίνω, κατακρίνω. There is a judgment which if accepted (repentance) is not final. Then our Lord's judgment is His way of dealing with us as His children (παιδευόμεθα). The apostle has spoken of the judgment upon those who eat and drink as if eating and drinking ordinary bread and wine. This is not commensurate with (ἀναξίως) the fact of eating and drinking the body and blood of our Lord. From such eating and drinking the apostle would rescue them, lest they come to the judgment which is final (κατακρίθωμεν). See the Liturgy of St. Basil and St. Chrysostom, Brightman, *Liturgies Eastern and Western*, 330, 17; Jasper, *Prayers of the Eucharist*, 120,133. Chrysostom, *Homily on 1 Cor. 11:28ff.*, *LF V*, 384–86: "not estimating the weight of the gift."

3 *Apostolic Tradition* (c. 380), 26–27. In 1 Cor. 14:24, we are told of unbelievers and of those who did not belong to the congregation: ἄπιστοι and ἰδιῶται. In *Apostolic Constitutions*

The deacon's call is not in Scripture. We must ask whether what it says is. Nothing might have a place in the liturgy that was not supplied by Scripture, and in Scripture there are things liturgical.[4] When we begin to have evidence of the liturgy we find it to be almost all Scripture. That we have no documented liturgy for two hundred years may not only be accounted for by evidence lost, but also by the fact that it was done by heart. What was done is indicated in the New Testament, and this is evidenced by the evidence which we have. There never was a Church without the Means of Grace. Where the Means of Grace, there the holy, the Divine Service.[5]

What was read in Church was from the Old Testament and then there were apostolic letters and gospels.[6] What was read in Church settled into the apostolic canon. What was given here was received and extolled in the liturgy; there were the psalms and then Christian psalms (Philippians 2:6–11; Pliny's first letter to Trajan c. 112: *carmen invicem*). So of everything in the liturgy we may ask what was the Scripture that gave it. We are helped in this by the earliest accounts we have of the liturgy. They are not full accounts. Stahlin has called the *Didache* more a catechism for the laity than an agenda.[7] Some accounts draw evidence from the liturgy to support some particular point. As an apologist, Justin wrote to allay suspicions aroused by the Christians' closed Communion. Christians are not subversive of the government, not idolaters, not cannibals.[8] Or, as in our first major account (*Apostolic Tradition*, c. 215), they set down the way of doing things beyond the ordinary for a particular occasion (at the making of a bishop, Communion of the newly baptized). Everyone knew what happened every Sunday (Revelation 1:3, 10; 1 Thessalonians 5:12–28; Sasse, *This Is My Body*, 324ff.; 1 Corinthians 11:16–33). There never was a Christian Church without Holy Communion. The Words of Institution betray their use in the liturgy. The bread and wine were "holied" to

---

(c. 380), 2, 57, 21, unbelievers and the uninitiated (ἀμύητοι). In Chrysostom, the uninitiated, the imperfectly prepared. See n. 11. Horn. 3 on Eph. (3rd last paragraph): catechumens. Christians in Elvira Canons 39, 45, 59. C. J. Hefele, *A History of the Christian Councils* (Edinburgh: Clark, 1894). 1:153, 156, 163. Also 2:368.

4 For closed Communion here see Günther Bomkamm, *Das Ende des Gesetzes* (München: Kaiser, 1952), 123–32. *Einladung und Abweisung*. N.B. 1 Cor. 16:22; *Didache*, 10, 6. *Aufforderung zum Bekenntnis*. Rev. 22:16–20; *Didache* 9,2; 11–13. *Die Warnung vor Irrlehrern häufig im nächsten Umkreis von Abendmahlstexten begegnet*. Rom. 16:16f. 1 Cor. 11:27f. "In the 29 lines of the anaphora [St. Basil] as far as the sanctus, Brightman has identified 44 scriptural quotations" (*Prayers of the Eucharist*, 115).

5 Leonhard Fendt, *Einführung in die Liturgiewissenschaft* (Berlin: Töpelmann, 1958), 1–3.

6 Justin Martyr, *Apology I*, 67, 3.

7 Leiturgia I, 16.

8 Justin Martyr, *Apology I*, 26, 8; 66,1–3; *Dialogue* 10ff. Eusebius *HE V*, 1,14. Sasse, *Sacraments*, 80.

their use in the Lord's Supper. Beyond doubt "the holy things" are the body and blood of our Lord, but who then are "the holy ones"?

What Scriptures supplied "The holy things for the holy ones" into the liturgy is then our quest. "Holy" rings in from all over the place—of God, from God, His own. The holy ones are the saints, the ones the Lord has made His own, the baptized. They are holy with a received holiness, those upon whom the light of His grace has shined (the enlightened ones are the baptized, Justin Martyr, *Apology I*, 61, 12), the faithful who say "Amen" to the gifts given them. What cannot be said "Amen" to in this way has no place in the liturgy, "in church."[9] The response to "The holy things for the holy ones" confesses "holy" as only of and from the Lord. "One only is holy." What is the Lord's is holy and may not be affronted with any denial or compromise of this (1 Corinthians 10:14–22; 3:17). Those guilty of this would be unholy, and so not among those invited. "If anyone is holy, let him come! If anyone is not, let him repent" (*Didache* 10, 6; 1 Corinthians 16:22).

Thus in the *Didache* from the first century, sins are first confessed (14,1; 4,14). To bring them along would bring defilement. "That which was spoken by the Lord" is drawn in to substantiate the point: "to offer to Me a pure sacrifice, because I am a great king says the Lord, and My name is to be wondered at among the nations" (Malachi 1:11–14). Nothing may infringe His name. His holy name and what is going on here in His name. "We give thanks to you holy Father for your holy name which you have made to dwell in our hearts" (*Didache* 10,2; Nehemiah 1:9; 1 Kings 8:29; 1 Corinthians 3:16ff.). The prayer evokes Baptism and so identifies those who pray it. The text from Malachi has "sacrifice," but we cannot now pursue the history of this term into its problematical use.[10] Here the point of the quotation is to warn against unrepented sin in those who would be given the body and blood of our Lord. Defilement is by sins still held onto, both before God and one's neighbor. Sins against God, refusal of His gifts, what undermines the Means

9 1 Corinthians 14:16, 19. *Didache* 4,14; 14,1. *Apology I*, 65,3; 67, 5. *Apostolic Constitutions* 8, 13, 15. In Coptic liturgies: "Amen this I believe" (Brighton, *Liturgies Eastern and Western*, 186, 8). "Amen" is interchangeable with "we believe." Anaphora of Cyril of Alexandria in *Prex Eucharistica*, ed. A. Hanggi and I. Pahl (Freiburg: EVFS, 1968), 136. Ambrose, *De sacramentis* V, 25: *Ergo non otiose dicis tu: "Amen," iam in spiritu confitens, quod accipias corpus Christi. Dicit tibi sacerdos: "Corpus Christi," et tu dicis: Amen hoc est verum.* (Jasper, *Prayers of the Eucharist*, 145. With *hoc est enim corpus meum* homologised with Amen/*verum*, it is not surprising to find true body and true blood appearing in the Communion liturgy, e.g., the Coptic Jacobites (Brighton, *Liturgies Eastern and Western*, 184). Amen, (Luke 9:27; 12:44; 21:3). Verily, verily. In pidgin: *Itru.* Eusebius *HE VU*, 9, 4. LC 3,119. *BKS* 991ff.

10 Willy Rordorf, *The Eucharist of the Early Christians* (New York: Pueblo, 1978), 17. Sasse, *Sacraments*, 125–28. Rordorf gives a helpful discussion of the contents of the parts of the *Didache* and their relationship (pp. 3–7).

of Grace, false doctrine, are the most grievous.[11] There is reference to the latter and to lesser sins, and where there is refusal of reconciliation then also the sacrifice is defiled (*Didache* 14, 2). The text evoked here is Matthew 5:23ff. This is from the Sermon on the Mount whence also comes, "Do not give dogs what is holy" (τὸ ἅγιον 7:6). This is said of any who might presume to come unbaptized. Only those baptized in the name of the Lord may eat and drink of the Eucharist (*Didache* 9, 5).

Drawn in also were the passages which speak of keys and doors, and from both we have what is either open or what is closed. In the *Didache* we saw those toward whom the Eucharist was open and those to whom it was closed. There is no evidence that it was ever otherwise from the beginning. What is called "open communion" is a quite recent notion whose origin then calls for diagnosis.

With the Confession of sins such as we saw in the *Didache* goes their Absolution, and so the Keys. There are two Keys: one opens, the other closes. What is opened or closed is a door. Hence the deacon's call "the doors, the doors."[12]

---

11 Hebrews 3; 6:6; 13:9ff. Bornkamm, *Das Ende des Gesetzes*, 130. Elert, *Eucharist and Church Fellowship*, 108–24: "An understanding of the church according to which orthodox doctrine is an essential criterion of the church. Heretical doctrine is apostasy and the worst of all sins." J. N. Bakhrizen van den Brink, "Sakrament und Ethik in der frühen Kirche." *Kyriakon* ed. P. Granfield & J. Jungmann (Münster: Aschendorf, 1970), I:61: "Ketzerei war die schwerste Sunde." 60: "Die Reihe: lehren, taufen und die Lehre und die Gebote halten stand ja seit Matth. 28,19.20 fest." The explanation of the First Petition in SC III, 5. LC I, 64; m, 39f., 46–8. The two tables. Ap 2 14,16; 4 35,130. SA II IV 9.

12 The Liturgy of St. Basil and the Liturgy of St. John Chrysostom, Brightman, *Liturgies Eastern and Western*, 321, 3. In the *Didascalia* (II, 56, 6) a deacon is responsible at the door for those who come in (*Apostolic Constitutions* II, 57.21; VIC, 11, 11). Canon 22 of the Council of Laodicea. The one responsible for the doors being closed was in Latin *ostiarius*, still listed by Trent as the seventh sort of clergy. Denzinger, 1765. Luke 13:25: *clauserit ostium*. John 10:3. Clement of Alexandria, *Quis dives salvetur* 39, 2. Psalm 118:20.

Whence also in the liturgy comes entrance. In discussing the *Didache* Rordorf asks, "Was the eucharist celebrated in another room? Father Audet thinks that it was, on the basis of archeological discoveries at Dura Europos" (p. 8).

For keys see Strack Billerbeck I, 736–41, 792ff. Quoted by K. Hein, *Eucharist and Excommunication* (Bern & Frankfurt: Lang, 1973), 76. There is doctrine which is "loosed," and false doctrine which is "bound." "It is important to notice that Paul asks that the ban be imposed in view of the 'teaching' he has given." 1 Thessalonians 3:6; 2 Timothy 4:15. Justin Martyr, *Apology I*, 66,1: "This food we call eucharist, and no one may receive it unless he believes that our teaching is true, and has been washed with the washing for forgiveness of sins into regeneration, and lives as Christ handed down to us. For we do not receive these things as though they were common bread or common drink . . . as we have been taught they (the consecrated bread and wine) are the flesh and blood of the incarnate Jesus." Smyrnians 7, 1: "They keep away from the eucharist and place of prayer because they do not confess that the eucharist is the flesh of our Savior Jesus Christ, which suffered for our sins, and which the Father in his goodness raised. They speak against the gift of God; they perish while they dispute." Trallians 8,1; Romans 8:1; Philadelphians 4. Chrysostom, Horn, on Matthew, 23:3: "The holy things are profaned by them, not knowing what they are. . . . The Mysteries we also therefore celebrate with closed doors, and keep out the uninitiated,

Since in the Lord's Supper we are at table with the Lord already celebrating the Messianic banquet, the marriage feast of the Lamb, the parable of the wise and foolish virgins supplied ways for confessing this. As with the Eucharist some are included while others are excluded. "The door was shut" (ἐκλείσθη Matthew 25:10). In Latin, *clausa est ianua*, whence *communio clausa*, *geschlossene Kommunion,* and in English, closed Communion. The freight of the term *closed Communion* is there from the start. The history of the term is another story and one needing to be told.[13]

---

not for any weakness of which we have convicted our rites, but because the many are as yet imperfectly prepared for them."

13 Our neighboring Orthodox priest said that they do not speak of closed Communion. They never needed to; everybody always knew. "The doors" in the liturgy are expression enough. The Vincentian Canon does save a lot of bother.

The term "close Communion" was put into our use this century by the *American Lutheran*; it came from Baptist sources, and is in danger of blurring the primary reference by slipping into lateral and anthropocentric ways of thinking. The muddle is evinced by the antonyms. "Close" is capable of degrees; the Gospel is unfractionable. One day a retired pastor came hot-foot from his researches in the library and announced he had come upon the *American Lutheran in flagrante delicto*. Contact has been lost with him and his research. "Close" does appear in the *American Lutheran* of November 1941, p. 16. Does anyone know earlier instances?

Webster knows "close communion" as a usage peculiar to the Baptists, *New Unabridged Dictionary* (New York: Simon & Schuster, 1979), 367.

The likely place the *American Lutheran* got it from (if he is in fact the culprit) is *Cyclopedia of Biblical, Theological and Ecclesiastical Literature*, ed. John McClintock and James Strong (Grand Rapids: Baker, 1968 reprint; first published 1868), 443. Or perhaps *Bibliotheca Sacra* (Jan. 1895): 97–112 and (April 1895): 297–322.

And what are we to make of Krauth's usage/translation and quotation marks? *First Free Lutheran Diet in America*, ed. H. E. Jacobs (Philadelphia: Smith, 1878), 64ff.

In the official documents of Missouri "close" does not appear. *The Worthy Communicant* (St. Louis: Printing House of the German Evangelical Lutheran Synod of Missouri, Ohio and Other States, 1878). Nor when the English Synod became the English District of the Missouri Synod in 1911. They brought the *Lutheran Witness* with them. C. S. Meyer, *Moving Frontiers* (St. Louis: Concordia, 1964), 266ff., 349 n. 22. The first hypothesis was that they were some loose Lutherans out East, and when this did not survive the evidence, I transferred the prejudice to the *American Lutheran* and the ALPB. It has proven difficult to pin the perpetration of "close" on them. *American Lutheran* becomes a code word for those making the move out of German into English. The evidence prior to 1911 (witnessed to by S. Bartelt [Research Paper, 1970] and Nafzger to Council ofPresidents, 1989) points to the *Lutheran Witness* (Feb. 21, 1900): 138 (responding to its use in the *Lutheran Evangelist*); March 26, 1903, p. 50; Aug. 8, 1907, p. 121 (these two responding to its use in the *Lutheran World*). After 1911, it does seem to have lain fairly dormant until quite recently.

In 1920, Pieper wrote: *Auch die apostolische Kirche praktizierte nicht "open," sondern "closed communion." Christliche Dogmatik* (St. Louis: Concordia, 1920), 3:444: The edition of 1953 excised "closed communion." *Christian Dogmatics* (St. Louis: Concordia, 1953), 3:381. What villainy!

Luke 13:25–30 also rings in. There are those excluded and there are those who sit at table in the kingdom of God. "From east and west, and from north and south" finds expression in the *Didache*: "so let your church be brought together from the ends of the earth into your kingdom" (9, 4; also the Proper Prefaces). The comprehensive joy of this is extolled by Chrysostom. The Lord's Supper rings with the joy of the Bridegroom's coming and his marriage feast. So also Philip Nicolai:

> We follow all to the joy-filled hall.
> And join to celebrate the Abendmahl.[14]

Who the holy ones are to whom the holy things are to be given is made quite clear by the kiss of peace. The kiss of peace is in the conclusion of 1 and

---

Fritz speaks of "close communion" in *Pastoral Theology* (St. Louis: Concordia, 1932), 130. Fritz pushed the movement into English and would have known similarly motivated Frederick Kuegele's tract entitled *Why Must Lutherans Practice Close Communion* (Pittsburgh: American Lutheran Publication Board, 1912). This is No. 8 of Lutheran Witness Tracts. It states, as also does Fritz, the traditional doctrine and practice. The problem lies in the sensitive weighing of the English word to be used, hence we ought not to be too exacting with the first generation involved in doing this.

In 1938, George Luecke used the term "close" in *Distinctive Doctrines and Customs of the Lutheran Church* (St. Louis: Concordia), 43. In 1955, Deffner commended it for its lateral reference: "the close spirit and unity of faith which exists in the Christian congregation" in *Why Close Communion* (Berkeley: University Lutheran Chapel, 1955), 3.

The first use in an official document seems to be in a resolution of the 1967 convention where it appears in quotation marks (Res. 2, 19).

The LCMS story of "close" would seem then to have three parts: (1) Moving with some uncertainty into English, a problem of language and not of doctrine and practice; (2) submergence of "close" when the *Lutheran Witness* became an official organ of the Missouri Synod. During this period some use of "close" continuing from the first period. High-water mark for "closed communion" is in Pieper's use of the term; low-water mark his translator's suppression of the term; (3) recrudescence of "close" no longer as a translation but as an English word favored by some because of its accommodation of lateral degrees and fractions or levels, and defended by some who hold that "close" and "closed" are identical. Degrees, fractions, and levels are impossible ways of speaking if one is speaking in the way of the doctrine of justification and the proper distinction between Law and Gospel.

Apart from some Baptists and some in the LCMS the rest of the world speaks of closed communion. Where the apostolic and catholic usage is observed, the term serves with reference to those on their way to the Holy Communion and to those outside. It disavows the irresponsibilities and lovelessness of open Communion. Thus it runs in the way of keys and door—in the way of the Gospel and in the way of the Law.

14 Homily 27, 7 on 1 Cor. 11:17. TDNT 3, 178: door into the festive hall. Trillhaas on Matt. 25:10: "Leichte Anklange an die Eucharistie der alten Kirche wollen nicht uberhort werden: Die Tur wird verschlossen, wie beim Beginn der Feier des Herrenmahls, wo die 'Ostiarier' darüber wachen, dasz nur noch zum Sakrament zugelassene Christen zugegen sind." *Die altkirchlichen Evangelien*, ed. H. Iwand (Göttingen: Vandenhoeck & Ruprecht, 1966), 310. *LW* (*Lutheran Worship*) 177, *LBW* (*Lutheran Book of Worship*) 31, (also 25), *LH* (Australia) 487. Here as elsewhere Winkworth excises the sacramental reference. Won't someone please supply an adequate translation?

2 Corinthians, 1 and 2 Thessalonians, Romans, and 1 Peter. This fact has suggested that the epistle was read as sermon, and that the Pax indicated the transition to the Holy Communion. Only those who receive and give the kiss of peace are welcomed to the Lord's Table. (Hence letters of peace.)[15] The *Didascalia* (II, 54) evokes the vivid scene of the kiss of peace, which comes from the altar, coming to a sullen halt as it is being given and received all the way round. The celebrant leaves the altar and goes to where the kiss of peace is blocked. Only after he has worked reconciliation (*pacem facere inter eos* Matthew 5:24; 6:15; 7:6) does the kiss of peace continue on its way all the way round, and only then does the liturgy continue. We may regret the loss of the kiss of peace. We can imagine some reasons why. Yet whether by kiss or handshake or words, the Pax is given and received. It comes from the Lord, and we receive and embrace it together with our "Amen." It is His gift, not something we set going. Lamentable is the disintegration of the liturgy at this point into lots of separate heartinesses. The one Pax, from the Lord, was beautifully expressed by the usage with a piece of wood, metal, or ivory upon which a Calvary was often carved. It was called a pax. It came from the altar. It was kissed by the celebrant and then in turn by all the communicants.[16]

Those who did not receive the kiss of peace, and so were not given the body and blood of our Lord, were those who were not yet baptized and had not yet made confession of the faith or been absolved. The division is evidenced in the *Formula Missae* by the communicants gathering around the altar, while others remain in their places (AE 53:33f.).

In the ancient liturgies all who received and gave the kiss of peace received the "holy things," the body and blood of Christ. The kiss of peace then came at the beginning of the Service of Holy Communion. That it comes after the consecration and before the distribution is a consequence of following the Roman usage, which, along with much else, had here the Lord's Prayer. Then the Pax was close to "as we forgive," to coming to the altar (Matthew 5:23), and to the "holy things," and so "holy kiss" and "holy ones" and Holy Communion.[17]

The way it was from the beginning has continued until today, but there have been departures. In his letter to Frankfurt, Luther diagnosed the cause for the departure there from closed Communion. All depends on the body and blood of our Lord under the bread and wine given us to eat and to drink according to His institution. There were those in Frankfurt who were unwilling to confess this. They spoke rather of what the heart does and whatever it was that Christ meant. Luther advised that if your pastor speaks ambiguously then ask him what is it that he holds in his hand and gives into your mouth. If he does not confess the body

15 Elert, *Eucharist and Church Fellowship*, 131; Justin Martyr, *Apology I*, 65.

16 Jungmann, *The Mass of the Roman Rite*, 2, 328ff.

17 Jungmann, *The Mass of the Roman Rite*, 2, 321ff.

and the blood, then have nothing more to do with him. It is unthinkable that at the same altar there should be those who confess that into their mouths the pastor gives the body and blood of Christ and also those who do not confess this, who think they are receiving bread and wine and work at their heart's devotions and its eating and drinking the body and blood only spiritually. Where a pastor is indifferent to this, where a pastor teaches the latter, then he is relieved of his care for the Lord's body and blood, and for the people who are not eating and drinking them except in some spiritual way with their hearts.

> Now it must be said that this (closed communion) is not taken all that seriously when for the Sacrament preachers give out only bread and wine. Who they are to whom these are given, no matter what they know and believe, is then no great concern. . . . Since it is Christ's body and blood that are given out in the Sacrament we neither will nor can give such Sacrament to any unless he is first examined. What has he learned from the Catechism, and does he intend to forsake the sins which he has again committed? We would not make Christ's church into a pigpen (Matt. 7:6) letting anybody come unexamined to the Sacrament as a pig to its trough. Such a church we leave to the Enthusiasts.
>
> This is the practice then which comes to us from when there were first Christians. . . . A pastor is there as Christ's faithful servant and as much as he is able may never cast the Sacrament to swine and dogs. He is to hear the people out, how it is with them. If they deceive him and do not speak the truth, he bears no blame; they have done the deceit upon themselves.[18]

The catholic practice of closed Communion is confessed in the Large Catechism V, 2: "We have no intention to admit to it and give it out to those who do not know what they seek there or why they come" (also Preface II, 2). The Lord's Supper is not ours to do with as we please. It is not "something we do" (LC V, 7 *ein Ding, das wir tuen*) "not invented or devised by any man" (LC V, 4). "It is as he says" (LC V, 11). "Here we take our stand and see who dares to instruct Christ and alter what he has spoken" (LC V, 13). "For as we have it from the lips of Christ, so it is; he cannot lie or deceive" (LC V, 14).

---

18 WA 30/3:567.3; StL 17:2018. A writing not selected for inclusion in the American edition; a part of it is in *Luther Deutsch* 4:214–23. Here we find the page headings: Ambiguous doctrines of the Lord's Supper, A clear answer is what is needed. Ambiguous preachers. Holding fast to the words of Christ, Be watchful. See Vieker's translation in *Concordia Journal* 16, 4 (October, 1990): 333–47 [see also above, pp. 1–19, in this book].

One of Luther's conclusions, from loose practice to loose doctrine, is given the other way by Struckmann. He points to closed Communion in the ante-Nicene Church as proof of its confession of eating and drinking the body and blood of our Lord. *Die Gegenwart Christi in der heiligen Eucharistie nach den schriftlichen Quellen der vornizanischen Zeit* (Vienna: Mayer, 1905), 8, 50, 60.

For a millennium and a half the doctrine of the body and blood of our Lord in the Lord's Supper was as confessed in the liturgy. They are there as the Lord's words tell us. Theologians might lean one way or another, but none denied what every Sunday was there. Nor was there a case made against closed Communion, the correlate of such confession. This continued through the Reformation in the Lutheran tradition. What we saw at Frankfurt came to have an increasing place among Protestants who did not confess the Means of Grace and among whom there was confessional indifference. In America the Galesburg Rule became a sort of banner for the apostolic and catholic and Lutheran confession of the Lord's Supper and what went with that: closed Communion. In 1956, Franklin Clark Fry spoke respectfully of the Galesburg Rule, or some part of it.[19] What has happened more recently is another story.

Closed Communion goes with what is first confessed of the Lord's Supper in the Small Catechism. "It is the true body and blood of our Lord Jesus Christ under the bread and wine, for us Christians to eat and to drink, instituted by Christ himself," and then the Words of Institution just confessed (ὁμολογεῖν). From the Words of Institution the *Lutheran Book of Worship* excises a reference to drinking (1 Cointhians. 11:25). Some have inserted the word "sacrament" into the Small Catechism's first answer. This answer is sometimes difficult to find in some Lutheran documents which speak of Christ giving Himself rather than repeating first what He said: His body and blood for us to eat and to drink. A weakening in this confession naturally brings with it a weakening in the care exercised in closed Communion, as Luther saw so clearly.

Closed Communion is then a consequence of the Doctrine of the Lord's Supper and holds only as that doctrine does. Luther said that if we repeat what our Lord said, and are then wrong, then it is His fault. "See him. I only work here," was how a faithful seminarian put it. Stance of faith.

Günther Bornkamm has observed St. Paul turning the words of warning and exclusion addressed to unbelievers against some in the congregation at Corinth who regarded themselves as of course (self-evidently, *selbstverständlich*) having every right to partake of the Lord's Supper.[20] Is there any one of us who does not have some such *Selbstverständlichkeit* to repent of regarding the Lord's Supper? Does it not still some times cause us to tremble?

---

19 *Minutes of the Twentieth Biennial Convention of the United Lutheran Church in America* (Philadelphia: USPH, 1956), 30ff. He speaks of Christ being in us and of the *corpus mysticum*, but not of the *corpus verum* and the *sanguis verus*, "the holy things," and the *koinonia* they do. R. C. Wolf, *Documents of Lutheran Unity in America* (Philadelphia: Fortress 1966), 225. In "The Liturgy of the Eucharistic Meal" the body and blood of our Lord only receive mention in the trimmed formula of distribution; otherwise the talk is of meal and bread and cup, and liturgy is a work we do. *LBW Manual on the Liturgy* (Minneapolis: Augsburg, 1979), 226–47; 9.

20 Bornkamm, *Das Ende des Gesetzes*, 129.

CHAPTER FOUR

The Churchly Norms for Legitimate Altar Fellowship

In Refutation of Rietschel's "Fellowship in the Lord's Supper"[1]

Dr. Theol. C. A. G. von Zezschwitz,[2] Leipzig, 1870[3]
Translated by Shawn Barnett,
with Matthew C. Harrison

The question of altar fellowship with members of the United Church and with the Reformed is not one that someone undertakes with a great deal

1 Georg Rietschel, *Die Gewährung der Abendmahlsgemeinschaft an Reformirte und Unirte in ihrem Rechte und in ihrere Pflicht nach dem Bekenntnisse der lutherischen Kirche in besonderer Rücksicht auf die sächsische Landeskirche* (Leipzig: Roßberg, 1869). [Georg Christian Rietschel studied theology in Erlangen and Leipzig, 1860–63. His first pastorate was in Rüdigsdorf. In 1874, he became head pastor, second director of the Preacher Seminary, and superintendent in Wittenberg in 1878. He became head of the seminary in 1884. From 1887 on, he was pastor at St. Matthew's in Leipzig, where he became professor of practical theology, chief university preacher, and head of the Preacher College of St. Paul's, all of which he retained until retiring in 1911. That a man trained in Erlangen and Leipzig should support communing the Reformed and Union Christians in Lutheran Saxony demonstrates that by the time of his education the confessional revival in Germany was seriously waning. This is further confirmed by the fact that he became superintendent in Wittenberg (the Church of the Old Prussian Union), and then easily returned to Saxon Leipzig, where the Lutheran confession was still nominally intact. MH]

2 [Carl Adolf Gerhard von Zezschwitz (1825–86) was a Saxon. He studied theology in Leipzig and became a pastor in 1852 in Großzschocher near Leipzig, where he continued his studies and became professor of theology. After 1861, he lived for a time in Neuendettelsau (Loehe's home) and lectured on apologetics in various places. In 1865, he became a full professor at Giessen and then returned as professor in Erlangen the next year. MH]

3 *Die kirchlichen Normen berechtigter Abendmahlsgemeinschaft. Zur Widerlegung der Rietschel'schen Schrift über "Abendmahlsgemeinschaft" von Dr. th. C. A. G. Zezschwitz, ord. Professer der Theologie und Universitätsprediger zu Erlangen* (Leipzig, 1870. J. C. Hinrichs'sche Buchhandlung).

of relish. These days, someone who believes that, out of faithfulness to his confessing Church, he generally has to answer the question in the negative according to the jurisprudence [*Recht*] of this fellowship can hardly expect to meet with acclaim and success. It is a matter of necessity and as a result of a direct challenge that I am once again speaking out on this issue.

A Saxon divine, Pastor [Georg Christian] Rietschel [1842–1914], has made "the granting of altar fellowship to the Reformed and United in its right and duty" an object of a particular paper,[4] and his polemics refer specifically to a presentation that I gave at the Leipzig Pentecost Conference in 1868 on a topic that was assigned to me.[5]

We will leave the unmistakable bias of this booklet which has misled the author both to distort my ecclesiastical position,[6] distortions that are often beyond juvenile and poorly veiled accusations born of political animosity (cf. p. 4), to the judgment of those who are able to weigh the significance of this booklet. Aside from that, we must thank the author for taking pains with a calm approach to trace the question back to its foundational principles. Likewise, the least of my concerns is refuting personal attacks. However, it is all the more regrettable that Rietschel's writing, which gives the appearance of objective scientific investigation, proceeds with an often unbelievable lack of reserve and a contemptuous certainty in the assessment of historical facts and dogmatic conclusions, so that any reference to the booklet can only be made in the form of a running criticism. It is to be hoped that the bold accusation of an "un-Lutheran and unevangelical nature" which Mr. Rietschel dares to throw in the face of all who still permit themselves to advocate for a practice that was legitimated by the Saxon Church Order of 1580 will put in motion more adept pens from Saxony and elsewhere. As quickly as I had to throw the following together in the face of the other tasks of my vocation, I thought a response to something addressed so directly to me was unavoidable, particularly at the present time. I will lay out in more detail my personal stance on the question in the third section.

The first two sections examine the positions of Rietschel's writing on two fundamental principles of the Lutheran Church. The first treats the conditions for admittance, which the Lutheran Church in her normative time makes valid for the admittance to the Holy Supper. The second concerns the question of whether, according to the named entities, the reception of the Supper at a confessional Church is rightly characterized as an act of confession. Herein, I will essentially follow the course of Rietschel's document.

---

4 Leipzig, published by the Rossberg Buchverhandlung, 1869.

5 *Die Aufgaben, welche die Selbständigkeit der lutherischen Kirche auf Grund der Ereignisse der letzten Jahre stellt* (Leipzig: Hinrichs, 1868).

6 Cf. especially pp. 29ff.

I. The Conditions for Admittance to the Holy Supper According to Lutheran Principle

Pastor Rietschel has aptly chosen the principal starting point. We can only agree with the author when he characterizes it as an incorrect and unevangelical standpoint for the judgment of the entire question to speak of a defilement of the altar by admitting adherents of other confessions to the Holy Supper, since the content and gift of the Sacrament is *per se* independent of both the faith of the administrator as well as of the receiver. To be sure, the Church of all times knows and speaks of a profanation of the Holy Supper, but this applies to those who receive it in as much as "the Sacrament is negligently given to the unworthy," as the *Instructions for the Visitors of Parish Pastors in Electoral Saxony* of 1528 puts it [*Unterricht der Visitoren*; AE 40:269ff.; WA 26:175ff.; Aland 751].

Rietschel answers this question to the effect that, according to the Confessions, nothing is demanded for worthiness except repentant faith in the forgiveness of sins as the exclusive content of the blessing of the Supper. Because the body and blood are also received from and by those who are unworthy, the corresponding examination of worthiness cannot refer to the real presence of the body and blood of Christ in the Sacrament. It is, therefore, no mere coincidence that the Confessions do not explicitly touch upon this requirement—and this is determinative for all consequent conclusions of the author—"it is completely, consistently Lutheran that the Confessions in no way stipulate faith in the administration of the body and blood of the Lord as worthy preparation" (p. 16).

This major premise suffers from three essential defects. First, it is historically untrue. There is documentary proof that the Confessions presuppose—indeed, explicitly mention—the examination of right doctrine and faith as a requirement of worthiness. Second, this premise is based upon presuppositions which lack conceptual clarity. The author provides for himself and his reader no account at all for the distinction between the concepts "worthy" and "unworthy," on the one hand, with respect to the grace of the Sacrament and, on the other, with respect to the Lord's institution of the Supper. The latter is plainly the closest sense, in which these words are taken with respect to their specific use concerning the consumption of the Supper (1 Corinthians 11:28ff.). Chemnitz, an author of the Formula of Concord as is well-known, defines the concept thus: "*Digne manducare est eucharistia uti eo modo et in eum finem, sicut ab ipso filio Dei institute est*" ["To eat worthily is to use the Eucharist in that way and to that end according to which it has been instituted by the Son of God Himself"] (see below). Not passing over this distinction of concepts would suggest itself all the more since the most notable Lutheran dogmaticians (e.g., Johann Gerhard [1582–1637], see below) have indicated in which sense and for what reason Luther, and respectively the Lutheran Confessions, were accustomed to use these words.

Third, that premise speaks with a daring attribution of a "consistency" of the Lutheran Confessions that stands in blatant contradiction to the demonstrable consistency of the reformers in practice. We will prove our antitheses according to this sequence.

To begin with, it should already be apparent that for deciding this question Pastor Rietschel at no point discusses the demands explicitly established for the examination of communicants in the church orders of the sixteenth century. Yet these are certainly the closest sources for demonstrating how the reformers actually determined worthy and unworthy. Our astonishment over such a reticence increases substantially when we hear the Lutheran Confessions affirming over and again that no one is admitted to the Supper *nisi exploratus* ["unless he has been examined"]. Thus one simply cannot omit investigating the nature of this "examination," since that expression of the Symbols is itself dependent upon older prescriptions regarding this procedure. Thus the next step of our investigation is already laid out for us.

The first and most well-known document in which Luther himself sets forth more extensively the principle he considered normative for the administration of the Holy Supper is the Latin Mass of 1523 [*Formula missae et communionis pro ecclesia*; WA 12:205–20; AE 53:19–40; Aland 510], which [Rietschel] cites only once.

At a time when the opposition to the Swiss [i.e., Zwingli et al.] still was not a factor, simply in the interest of holding sacred the blessed use of the Sacrament, Luther demanded that no one be admitted to the Sacrament who had not been previously examined as to whether he knew and rightly understood the Words of Institution. And this examination is distinguished clearly enough from an examination of one's confidence of faith and repentance. Here we present the translation prepared by Paul Speratus [1484–1551] for those evangelically-minded Christians in Iglau. Because this translation deviates here and there from the original, we have provided the Latin text below.[7]

---

7 Latin Mass. Richter, *Kirchenordnungen,* 1:5ff. [WA 12:215ff.; AE 53:32–33]: "Hic autum servandum est ritus, qui in baptismo servatur. Nempe ut episcopo primum significetur, qui futuri sint communicantes petantque ipsi caena domini communicari, ut eorum et nomina et vitam cognoscere queat. Deinde petentes not admittat, nisi rationem fidei suae rediderint et interrogati responderint, an intelligant, quid sit caena domini, quid preastet, quo usu illa velint potiri. Scilicet si poterint verba benedictionis memoriter recitare et exponere, sese ideo venire, quod conscientia peccati . . . vexati esuriant et sitiant verbum et signum gratiae . . . Arbitror autem hanc interrogationem seu explorationem sufficere, si semel in anno fiat cum eo qui petit communicari. Quin poterit tam intelligens esse qui petit ut vol semel in tota vita, vel prorsus nunquam interrogetur. Nam hoc ritu illud cavere volumus, ne irruant ad caenam domini digni et indigni sicut hactenus vidimus fierei sub Romana

> But herein one should follow precisely that manner or order as is maintained for Baptism, namely, that those who want to receive the Sacrament are first presented to the bishop or pastors. They should request that he administer the Holy Sacrament to them. If they ask to receive it, he should, however, not permit them until they have given an answer regarding **their faith** and especially regarding the question as to whether they understand what the Sacrament is, what it benefits and gives, and to what end they want to use it, namely, whether they are able to recite by heart the words of the Sacrament along with its interpretation.

Only then should the next question follow as to whether they desire it on behalf of their sins and hunger and thirst for the word of grace.

Precisely in connection, however, with the "understanding" that someone has concerning the Sacrament, it continues:

> I, however, consider it to be enough that whoever desires the Sacrament be questioned and examined once a year in this way. In fact, it may be that this same person is so understanding that he would only need to be asked once in his entire life, or not at all. For with this order we want to prevent the **worthy** and the unworthy from going to the Lord's Supper at the same time. . . . But we want to have those who are unable to answer the above-mentioned questions **excluded and separated from the fellowship of this Sacrament** as those who lack the wedding garment.

Since especially at that time the reception of the Sacrament under one kind was an issue, there can be no doubt that examination in doctrine referred not merely to the blessing effected by the Sacrament, but rather, as it was later formulated, to the nature (*de substantia*) of the Sacrament and its reception.

Since Rietschel goes on to declare that the understanding of the celebration of the Supper as an act of confession [*Bekenntnissactes*] is essentially un-Lutheran and predominantly Reformed, it will be of interest right here to point out that this oldest document on Lutheran practice regarding the Supper at the same time gives indubitable testimony to this principle. "For the consumption of this Sacrament in the congregation," so it reads, "is a part of Christian **confession** [***Bekenntniss***], whereby those who go confess before God, angels, and men that they are Christians."[8] Of course, we still have to deal with the sense in which "act of confession" is used here (see below).

---

ecclesia. (Concerning the practice of this, it is said elsewhere explicitly: Quin et ipsa verba benedictionis scilicet ipsum panem vitae absconderunt.)"

"Nos autem eos, qui prespondere non poterint juxta preadicta, prorsus exclusos et alienos volumus ab istius caenae communione tanquam veste nuptiali carentes."

8 l.l. Nam huius communio caenae est pars confessionis, qua coram Deo angelis et hominibus sese confitentur esse Christianos [WA 12:216.25; AE 53:34]. [See also Luther's similar statements in WA 12:481.10ff: "It is also very necessary to do for this reason. The Sacraments are

This document introduces a train of witnesses from the Lutheran church orders and later casuistic decisions, which extend as far as the Saxon Church Order of 1580 and deep into the seventeenth, even the eighteenth century, which with many voices testify to the same principle.

The *Visitation Instruction* from 1528 [*Unterrricht der Visitatoren*; WA 26:195–240; AE 40:269–320; Aland 751] first takes up again that requirement of the Latin Mass almost verbatim and with a nice juxtaposition of examination of the faith and pastoral counsel: "Second, no one should be admitted to the Sacrament, unless he has previously met with the pastor. The pastor should listen as to whether he has been correctly instructed concerning the Sacrament, whether he requires any other counsel, etc." [WA 26:216.23; cf. AE 40:292]. Further below:[9] "No one should be admitted to the Sacrament, unless he has been examined by his pastor especially as to whether he is competent to go to the Holy Sacrament. For Paul says (1 Corinthians 11) that they are guilty of the body and blood of Christ who take it unworthily. Not only those who take it unworthily dishonor the Sacrament but also those who, lacking diligence, give it to the unworthy."[10]

Already before this Luther, in a sermon which was added to the winter portion of the *Church Postil* (appearing first in 1525) among the Easter sermons, had expressed the same principles anew before his congregation in Wittenberg.

We will return below to the more detailed explanation of the examination for the Supper that is found there. Here it will suffice to show what he says at the conclusion [of this sermon], among other places:[11]

> Therefore, I say once again: According to what was until now the old custom, everyone was allowed to go to the Sacrament who had come. Nevertheless, from here on out it should not remain that way, but rather be so ordered that whoever wants to receive the Sacrament should be questioned as to what the Sacrament is and what he seeks there. And he should answer as we have shown above: first, that the words of Christ and the sign of Christ's body and blood is the Sacrament; second, that he seeks to

externally instituted that one confess and demonstrate the faith openly before the world. Before God it is enough that we believe the Gospel. But on earth He wills that we serve people and that we with certain signs, which are Baptism and this Sacrament, confess this faith which we have in our hearts." MH]

9 Richter, *Kirchenordnungen*, 1:91.

10 Richter, *Kirchenordnungen*, 1:92 [WA 26:220.7ff.; cf. AE 40:296].

11 W[1] 11:840ff. [*Ein Sermon D.M. Lutheri am Gründonnerstag*, April 2, 1523; WA 12:476–93; Aland 262]. We cite according to Walch because a list of historical documents from the Reformation which we cannot do without are to be found only there. Cross-referencing has been made easy for anyone who possesses the Erlangen edition. [This sermon appears under the title "All Become One Cake," trans. Matthew C. Harrison, in *Mercy in Action: Essays on Mercy, Human Care and Disaster Response*, ed. Rev. Ross Edward Johnson, introduction by Rev. Dr. Matthew C. Harrison (St. Louis: LCMS, 2015), 219ff. MH]

> strengthen his faith thereby and to comfort his conscience, that we step out of ourselves and come to Christ. Therefore, you must become competent so that you know how you should use the Sacrament. If you cannot do that, you should not go to the Sacrament.
>
> . . . The Sacrament should not be tossed among mobs of people as the pope has done. When I preach the Gospel, I do not know whom it affects. Here, however, I should consider that it has affected the one who comes to the Sacrament. I should not take a shot in the dark [*es in Zweifel schlagen*], but should be certain that whomever I give the Sacrament has grasped the Gospel and believes rightly.

Already before 1530, those who were evangelically-minded in various provinces had appropriated these principles, often with Luther's own words. Thus the Augsburg Confession could speak of a custom common among the evangelicals (AC XXV):[12] "This custom is maintained among us: not to give the Sacrament to those who have not previously been examined and absolved (*nisi antea exploratis et absolutis*)." The significance which the Lutheran Confessions ascribe to this fact is illuminated by the constant references to it.[13] Here we are not dealing with an unspoken presupposition or a peripheral matter. Luther in the Large Catechism also provides the content of the examination in the entirely customary manner:

> . . . what it is, what it benefits, and who should receive it. And all of this is founded upon the words with which Christ instituted the Sacrament, which everyone ought to know who wants to be a Christian and go to the Sacrament. For we are not of a mind to allow and hand it to those who do not know what they seek there or why they come. [LC V 1]

The twenty-fourth article of the Augsburg Confession reveals that a connection is made specifically to the correct doctrinal understanding of the Sacrament in this examination [*Exploration*] in the instruction associated with it. Admittedly, the Latin text reads only: "Assuevit populus, ut una utuntur sacramento, si qui sunt idonei . . . Nulli enim admittuntur nisi ante explorati" ["The people are accustomed to using the Sacrament together, if any such are worthy. . . . For none are admitted unless previously examined"]. In the German text, however, along with the usual content of the instruction,[14] the following is explicitly added: ". . . thereby also instruction against incorrect doctrine concerning the Sacrament" (AC XXIV 5ff.).

---

12 Cf. the territorial Order of the Dukedom of Prussia from 1525 in Richter, *Kirchenordnungen*, 1:30, and Bugenhagen's Church Order for Braunschweig from 1528, *Kirchenordnungen*, 1:111.

13 Cf. Ap XXIV 1, 49; AC XXIV 7, *Of the Mass*; AC XXV 1, *Of Confession*; SA VIII 1; LC V 1; etc.

14 "Thus the people are instructed often and with the greatest diligence concerning the Holy Sacrament, to what end it was instituted and how it is to be use, namely, to comfort terrified consciences, whereby the people are drawn to Communion."

Why does Mr. Rietschel pass over these words of the Symbols in silence? In this passage these words signify without a doubt that in the examination [*Exploration*] anyone found to be in doctrinal error who refused correction would be treated as *idoneus*, that is, unworthy for admittance to the Sacrament, in the specific reference. And the entire practice that followed confirms precisely this to be the common understanding of examination [*Exploration*].

The later symbols, although they almost universally presuppose this procedure, as the above citations attest, do not go into the more detailed content of the examination, with the exception of the Apology. The Formula of Concord does not mention the examination at all. Nevertheless, from the outset anyone who is unbiased can have no doubt that precisely this confession which so sharply and clearly formulates its *damnamus* ["we condemn"] against the Calvinists could not, on the other hand, consider them worthy guests at the Supper. The concluding sentence of Article X, on ceremonies (*de ceremoniis*), of the Solid Declaration may be regarded as a summary explanation of the corresponding practice: "In such a way, the churches will not condemn each other on account of dissimilarity of ceremonies since in Christian freedom one has more or less of the same, if they are otherwise united in doctrine and all other articles, also in the correct use of the Holy Sacraments" (FC Ep X 5; cf. FC SD X 31). It must, therefore, have this meaning, since *vera fides* ["true faith"] is mentioned as a characteristic of the *digni convivae* ["worthy guests"] by itself or as *viva* ["living"] [faith] (FC Ep VII 19, 30, 39; FC SD VII 123, 125; cf. FC SD VII 68). The proof that the Formula of Concord itself makes this distinction is given in the first three citations, especially FC Ep VII 19, where *vera* and *viva fides* ["true" and "living faith"] are distinguished from each other and the first requirement is, in the German version, explicitly referred to with the term: "the orthodox" [*die Rechtgläubigen*]. This can only be ignored or interpreted otherwise with determined caprice. Especially as "Sacramentarians" are spoken of, "a number of whom shamelessly infiltrate into the Church under the name of the Augsburg Confession" (FC SD VII 111). Finally, the Confession also appropriates Luther's words: "I count them all as one lot, that is as sacramentarians and enthusiasts, as they also are, who do not want to believe that the Lord's bread in the Supper is His true natural body. . . . Whoever does not want to believe that should just leave me in peace and hope for no fellowship with me" (FC SD VII 33).

Therefore, if the symbolical books upon which Mr. Rietschel depends as the decisive, principle point of view only name repentance and faith as signs of worthiness, as the Epitome formulates it in such concise brevity: "We also believe, teach, and confess that there is only one type of unworthy guest, namely, those who do not believe"(FC Ep VII 18), then the above citations nevertheless leave no doubt that the symbolical books include orthodoxy [*die Rechtgläubigkeit*] in the Sacraments in this "faith." Directly after this thesis from the Epitome follows another statement used above: "We believe, teach, and confess that no one who is orthodox takes the Sacrament to his judgment as long as he maintains the living faith, as weak as he may be" (FC Ep VII 19).[15]

First of all, this does not determine whether this were a consequence of the major premise of justifying faith as general worthiness. It does, however, determine what the principle is on the part of the symbolical books. No one has a right to use this to contradict the commentary which they themselves give. Accordingly, the major premise from which Mr. Rietschel derives everything else exists so little that we must characterize it as a historical fiction and a distortion of documented facts. We therefore believe we have proven our first antithesis with this information.

Before we continue with a more detailed assessment of the terms, it is worth pursuing the further development of the principles which we first found established in Luther's Latin Mass [1523], especially in its direct application to the Reformed. We will also provide an overview of the general consensus of the Lutheran church orders regarding examination [*Exploration*] in the sense of the symbolical books. At first, we will limit ourselves to the evidence from the Lutheran church orders up to the advent of the conclusion of the Confessions with the Formula of Concord [1580], that is, up to the great Saxon Church Order of 1580. In doing this we will explicitly emphasize individual characteristics and forms of expression as they relate to the general maxims. The following references from Richter's collection [of church orders] will suffice [to demonstrate] the extent of their authority.[16]

An entire series of church orders characterizes as the object of the doctrinal examination all of the chief parts of the catechism with particular emphasis upon "the words of the Supper." And on this article one should "confess his faith" regarding "what he seeks and receives there." We note especially the following church orders:[17] Goslar [Amsdorf 1531] (p. 155); Brandenburg-Nürnberg [Osiander, Brenz] (p. 203) ("whether they know and rightly regard the Holy Sacrament,"

15 [Unfortunately the *Triglotta* and Tappert translate the German word for "orthodox" (*Rechtgläubige*) with "true" in these passages. "True" has more the sense of "genuine" or "sincere" (i.e., subjective) rather than "right," "correct," or what the German says, "orthodox." And "orthodox faith" is both subjectively genuine and sincere, *and* objectively correct and true. MH]

16 Göttingen 1530 I. p. 143 [Heinrich Winkel, student of Melanchthon]. Riga 1530 II. p. 488. Goslar [Amsdorf] 1531 I p. 155. Cleve 1532 p. 162. Hesse 1532 p. 164. Brandenburg-Nürnberg 1533 pp. 202ff. Saxon Visitation 1533 p. 228. Bremen 1534 p. 244. Hannover 1536 p. 274. Lippe 1538 II p. 496. Mecklenburg 1540 I p. 322. Brandenburg 1540 p. 326. Schleswig-Holstein 1542 p. 356. Schweinfurt 1543 II p. 22. Preussen 1544 p. 69. Ritzebüttel 1544 p. 79. Mansfeld 1554 p. 142. Waldeck 1556 p. 170. Hesse 1557 p. 505. Württemberg 1559 [Brenz] p. 206. Pommerania 1563 [Paul v. Rhoda, Benediger, Runge] p. 237. Hessen 1566 p. 295. Hoya 1573 p. 355; cf. 1581 p. 457. Brandenburg Visitation and Consistorial Order 1573 p. 360. Braunschweig-Grubenhagen 1581 p. 453. [Where Richter notes the author(s) of the order, the names have been added for reference. MH]

17 [Where Richter notes the author(s) of the order, the names have been added for reference. MH]

cf. p. 204); Bremen [based on Bugenhagen's Braunschweig Order 1528] (p. 244); Ritzebüttel II [based on Aepinus's Bergendorf Order] (p. 79); Waldeck [based on earlier orders by Jonas and Brenz] (p. 244); Pommerania [Bugenhagen] (p. 237); Hoya (pp. 355, 457); Braunschweig [Chemnitz, Andreae 1569] (p. 453).

The first reference regarding this announcement and investigation with respect to "enthusiasts and other faithless people who know nothing of the Sacrament" is already found in the Brandenburg-Nürnberg Church Order of 1533 [Osiander, Brenz]. Others demand explicitly the dismissal of all "foreign parishioners" (Mecklenberg 322 [based on earlier work by Osiander and Brenz]; Schleswig 350 [Bugenhagen]) "who stubbornly remain in open heresy." The Prussian Church Order protests explicitly against any fellowship with the "Sacramentarians" and with all those who do not "stand with them before God and men in one word, faith, doctrine, and confession" (II, 66). In the Württemberg Summary [*W. Summsarishcher Begriff*] recourse is made to the territory-wide expulsion of Sacramentarians (p. 205) which applied to all who during the visitation refused better instruction (p. 214). The Hessian Church Order (1566, p. 289) is similar, where an extensive confession of faith is required in advance. The Lippe Church Order of 1571 [Exter] wants to see all "convinced heretics and falsifiers of the truth" refused (p. 337). The Hoya Church Order emphasizes particular vigilance in this examination against the heterodox. The Brandenburg Visitation Order requires inquiry into "whether someone adheres to false doctrine and sects" (p. 360; cf. the Hessian Agenda from 1574, p. 394). In Lüneburg (1575, p. 399) "those who are not correct in doctrine" are immediately subjected to discipline. The Hanau Visitation Order expressly questions the presence of Zwinglians and others (p. 507).

Finally, the Bremen Church Order offers more extensive questions about the Supper itself (p. 244). The Hannover Church Order requires that everyone be investigated as to "whether he might test himself according to the doctrine of St. Paul, so that he might know what to believe regarding the Sacrament and what he should do."

We conclude with a somewhat more thorough treatment of the Saxon Church Order of 1580 [Jakob Andreae], which, aside from its general historical significance for all Saxon pastors, forms the basis for church law in Saxony as it is still valid today.[18]

The following question already has its particular place during the visitation: "Whether the pastor knows of anyone in his parish who adheres to false, errant doctrine or gives protection to such people" (2:410). Then the more detailed instructions are given for the required examination before the reception of the Supper about how to proceed with such people and who is included therein (438ff.). The

18 Cf. Weber, *Sächsisches Kirchenrecht*, 12, and (Richter), *Codex des im Königreich Sachsen geldenden Kirchen- und Schulrechtes*, 1ff. We cite the text, as previously, according to A. L. Richter's collection of evangelical church orders.

sources are recognizable from the wording: "Whoever does not know what the Sacrament is" (so it reads, in general), "appropriately should not be admitted to the Holy Supper until sufficiently instructed. For not only those who unworthily receive this Sacrament dishonor it but also those who, lacking diligence, dispense it unworthily." "For this and other reasons, the pastors should individually interview every person who wants to go to Communion and after instruction, admonition, and comfort, according to the person's situation, pronounce private Absolution." All of this clearly presupposes, as noted above, the reference to the heterodox. Finally, this is expressed in consideration of the doctrinal uncertainty in the territory that had broken out as a result of crypto-Calvinism. In order to confront this, every year the entire congregation should be instructed and strengthened in the correct doctrine of the Supper. Among individuals, then, the doctrinal interview before admittance to the Supper serves as a test.

"But those who err in the faith concerning the Holy Supper should be thoroughly instructed by the pastors with the spirit of gentleness from God's Word and the grades of admonition [*gradus admonitionem*] with those who hold otherwise, when they have been instructed from God's Word as necessary." Compare this with the teaching on excommunication (p. 442), whereby it was, of course, expressed that whoever upon reproach did not confess adherence to the Lutheran faith concerning the Sacrament would be refused.

Given the known relationship in which this church order [i.e., the Saxon Church Order of 1580] stood to the Book of Concord, as is expressly emphasized in the introduction of the former (p. 402), the one may be viewed as the official commentary on the other. However, the clear picture is that the principal term "worthiness for the Sacrament," as the symbolical books express it, intends to be understood in no other way than in connection with the practice derived therefrom. And it provides an overview of the entire development from the Latin Mass [Luther, 1523] up to these documents from 1580. And this development is both consistent and transparent.

The examination of the situation up to this point produces the simple historical result that anyone who demonstrably held to the Reformed view of the Holy Supper would not only not be allowed to go to the Sacrament in a Lutheran congregation but also would be treated as one who had lapsed into discipline. And this deviation from the correct belief concerning the Supper—in diametric opposition to Rietschel's assertion—would justifiably be viewed as unworthiness.

According to the above evidence from the symbolical books themselves, no one can assert a contradiction between what these books teach about the requirements of orthodoxy and the contemporary practice with any historical justification.

On the basis of our evidence, Rietschel's suggested remedy of "an unspoken presupposition" (p. 16) falls apart of its own accord. The only recourse that remains is to charge the symbolical books themselves with a small internal inconsistency, but more particularly, to accuse the practice [here documented] of contradicting the abundantly expressed principles of the Confessions, according to which "there is only one kind of unworthy guests, namely, those who do not believe." On the other hand, one would have to except entirely what the author derives from the Apology as a universal explanation for this "faith." That is, "whoever believes the divine promise and receives the promised grace, which is offered by the Sacrament and the Word" (R. 203, 19 [Ap XIII 20; *BKS* 295]). However, this refers first of all to the forgiveness of sins with which the Sacrament seals us. The conclusion, then, seems to be suggested that according to this principle those Reformed persons who believe, who seek this [forgiveness] in the Sacrament, must be given it, because they satisfy the main condition. Furthermore, one may question what right there is to mix the Lutheran doctrinal concept of the Sacrament [i.e., actual body and blood] with such salvific faith? If another practice is found to be set forth in the church orders, then by the necessary extension of this principle, this must be viewed as [the implementation of] mere maxims, which serve to police the Church [*Kirchenpolizei*]. If, however, the symbolical books demonstratively speak expressly in individual passages of a doctrinal examination and in other passages assume the same and its result, namely orthodoxy, then it only remains to treat this as a negligible factor over against those clear principles which are brought forth in preponderant abundance and in the more prominent passages. Such theorizing may be done and the matter may be put thusly according to the general rationale with which we tend to summarize the evangelical-Reformed principle. However, no one would so easily dare to claim that a historian, who is accustomed to grasp and objectively portray the factual state of affairs and the factual import of principles within the time period, without arguing *ad absurdum* [*Konzequenzmacherei*], could with a good conscience commit to haggling between one principle and another and, on the other hand, between such a dominant practice and such an allegedly deviant main principle. Whoever studies the religious character of that time simply as a historian, would, on the contrary, have to determine that the dominate maxims in practice point back to the actual effective principle [at work from the beginning]. Such study would find sufficient indication of this when this principle is found to be expressed explicitly in the church orders and even in the Symbols.

[The Reformed Practice]

According to the view of that era, errant belief about the Sacrament (this is the conclusion of historical inquiry) made one unworthy to receive the Sacrament. The historian will feel all the more strengthened in this position when he sees the same exact principle applied on the Reformed side. For example, the *Acta de Wesaliensis* (1568, Richter 2:316) in complete accord with the common requirement among the Lutherans, stipulate: "*Nemo autem ad coenam dominicam admitttur nisi qui fidei confessionem ante ediderit et se disciplinae ecclesiae subjecerit*" ["However, no one is admitted to the Lord's Supper unless he has first made a confession of faith and submitted himself to the discipline of the Church"]. The model for this is provided by the [Johann von] Lasky [1499–1560], Church Order of the Dutch in London from 1550 (Richter 2:107): "Therefore, we allow none to the use of the Supper other than those who have publicly made a confession of their faith before the congregation or before the ministers and elders and who have willingly submitted themselves to Christian discipline."[19]

The practice of the Reformed corresponds to Lutheran altar practice and over against Lutheran communicants. After 1539, those in Zurich fell out with [Martin] Bucer [1491–1561] on account of his rapprochement with Luther. They finally forbade their youth who studied in Strasbourg from going to the Supper there. What they wrote to the church consistory there is a clear expression of how both sides viewed altar fellowship as an expression of confessional fellowship: "*Qui sacramentis nobis communicant, ispa communicatione profitentur, eandam habere nobiscum de sacramentis fidem. Atqui juvenes nostrum eandem voscum fidem non habent*"[20] ["Those who commune with us in the sacraments profess by this Communion that they have the same belief as we about the Sacrament. And our youth do not have the same belief as you"]. The Oldenburg General Superintendent, [Herman] Hamelmann [1526–95], known by his participation in the Synod at Jever in 1576, recounts that Reformed preachers in several places demanded from communicants the verbal and public confession that they did not believe that the body and blood of Christ were truly present in the Holy Sacrament before receiving the Supper. Those on the Lutheran side were also aware of this and, in certain cases, even appealed to this.

Thus the Wittenberg faculty in an opinion from 1568 stated: "And as the Sacramentarians as a whole doubtless allow no one to come to Communion who is devoted and allied to this confession of our Church for this very reason, therefore pious and understanding parsons can," etc. For this purpose, appeal was made to [John] Calvin's own declaration (*Instit.* IV:12, 5): "Profanatur s. coena promiscua exhibitione" ["the Holy Supper is profaned by indiscriminate administration"]. Cf. Beza (*Op.* ed. 1582 II. fol. 364, Quaestionum pars. II. de sacramentis quaestio 245): "*Num quosvis admiseris? Hoc ne domi suae quisquam facit, ut quosvis pro domesticis venditantes ad mensuam suam admittat.—Deus severe prohibuit, ne ignem alienum sacris suis inferrent. Quia pastor ovium suarum rationem redditurus est coram Domino, ideo bona conscientia extraneos et sibi incognitos non admittat*" ["Whom should you not admit? God severely prohibits them from bringing forth

19 Cf. also the *Synodus gen. Herborn* of 1586. Richter 2:475.

20 Loescher, *Ausführliche Historia motuum* 1:235, according to the letters that are preserved in the Strasbourg archives. Cf. revised Strasbourg Church Order.

a strange fire to His holy things. Because a pastor must render an account before the Lord, he should not with good conscience admit outsiders and those unknown to him"].

This was the general practice of the time, essentially no different than that of the seventeenth century. Practice and principles meet here in evident agreement.

If this remains the immediate conclusion, then the other question can only be treated as a second and special question as to how this fact relates to the otherwise abundantly expressed principle of repentance and saving faith as the only condition of worthiness according to which a greater breadth in practice and principles might seem to be indicated. And this question is, in fact, not difficult to answer and in complete agreement with the main factual conclusion. In most cases, the context of the relevant passage provides the key. We will proceed to a more detailed justification of our second antithesis since what we have discussed thus far has already shed much light on our third antithesis.

[The General and Strict Sense of "Worthy"]

In the question of "worthy" and "unworthy," in that time [i.e., when the struggle was against the medieval view of the Sacrament as a meritorious work] when combatting the *meritum proprium* was the first goal, it was natural to expand that concept which, of course, most immediately signifies *idoneus* ["worthiness"] for the special celebration and gift in the Sacrament. Following this line of thought, it was understood finally that no one is worthy. Pastor Rietschel should not have avoided the fact that the concrete question was not so much treated as it was presented in the light of the fundamental principle of justification, as is entirely appropriate for the fundamental confessions [namely, the Augsburg Confession and its Apology]. At that time, the expressions "worthy" and "unworthy" pushed toward this line of thought. Clearly, however, the conclusion that further explanations of worthiness and unworthiness, which concern justification, for example, were unwarranted is entirely false. These same symbolical books establish these explanations as we have demonstrated. This should have led Rietschel to the fact that there is a double meaning of worthiness, a general and a strict sense. We will prove this with statements from the Lutheran witnesses most readily invoked.

The Confessions speak expressly mostly about the first kind [i.e., a general sense of worthiness] and mention additionally aspects of worthiness which result from this first kind, without giving a reason for the distinction. They could save themselves doing that especially because they could refer to the process of examination as a commonly known fact.

Had Pastor Rietschel consulted a Lutheran teacher about this rather than drawing his own hastily drawn conclusion about what is "Lutheran" and "un-Lutheran," then Johann Gerhard would have been able to instruct him, Martin Chemnitz [1522–86] even more thoroughly. In reference to Luther's manner of expression, from which Robert Bellarmine [1542–1621] had drawn other, false conclusions, Gerhard says:[21] "He thus rejects that vain faith which the hypocrites establish with their dispositions, preparations, and satisfactions, and he consoles anxious consciences which are terrified by the perception of sin and which realize it does not suffice to approach with [an alleged] worthy disposition. He rejects the view that the remission of sins is to be sought in the perfection of our contrition, in the full enumeration of sins, and in proper satisfaction. . . ." The conclusion that he comes to at the end suits our case *mutatis mutandis*.[22]

For those who understand, it is hardly necessary to provide evidence from the Lutheran Symbols to confirm this solution to the matter. The very passages that Rietschel cites contain the solution in part. Nevertheless, we want expressly to provide a few instructive words from Luther and the Symbols.[23]

---

21 *Loci theol.* ed. Cotta, X, 373.

22 [That is, comparing two or more things, making the necessary changes for application but not affecting the main point at issue. MH]

23 In the sermon cited here (W[1] 11:836 [*Ein Sermon D.M. Lutheri am Gruendonnerstag*, April 2, 1523; WA 12:476–93; Aland 262]), the question comes in a second passage: "What good are these words that Christ speaks here and on which He hangs so many important things? Answer: They are good to the end that I should believe in this and not that I should do a good work in this." Luther then compares (pp. 838ff.) the use of the Sacrament in the Roman Church with the superficial faith of the children of Israel (1 Samuel 4) that they had the ark of the covenant among them, whereby they were, nevertheless, defeated. "What was missing? Was not the ark present there, where God was most certainly present as in the Sacrament? Why did He not want to help them? Because they wanted to make a work out of it. . . . We do the same. We stand on our work that we have received the Sacrament, and this without faith." [In another sermon Luther states] (W[1] 12:1752, Epistle sermon [*Sermo de digna praeparatione cordis pro suscipiendo sacramento eucharistiae*, April 1, 1518; WA 1:329–34; Aland 209]): "Therefore, faith alone is the greatest and most imminent preparation; and this also makes people truly pure and worthy. **For faith does not depend upon and drive at our works or ability**, but upon the most pure, most kind, and strongest word of Christ (Matthew 11:28; 5:6; etc.) Therefore, **the best worthiness** is when a person is **least worthy**, and a person is never more unworthy of the most worthy Sacrament than when he is **most worthy**. This should be understood in this way: When a person senses that he is unholy, poor, and needs grace, in this he is receptive to the grace of God and most worthy of it. . . . For just as of old He did not come to call righteous men to repentance, so now He does not come to call the righteous but rather the unrighteous and sinners to repentance" (W[1] 12:1750ff. [WA 1:329–34; Aland 209]). "But you say: What about when I feel that I am not worthy? Answer: This is my affliction, too, especially from the old nature under the pope, when one agonized over whether he were entirely pure and whether God might find nothing at all reproachable in us. We became so timid because of this that everyone immediately was horrified and said: **O woe, you are not worthy! For nature and reason rise up to reckon our unworthiness against that great, precious good** (LC V 55). Therefore, such people ought to learn that the highest art is to know that **our Sacrament does not depend upon our worthiness** . . ." (LC V 61). The splendid Communion prayer developed from this view, cf. the *Sermon on the Worthy Reception of the Holy, True Body*, Maundy Thursday, 1521, W[1] 12:1766 [*Ein Sermon vom würdigen Empfang des heiligen*

First, we have to deal with generalization of the term. Positively formulated the same statement reads: only he who in repentance acknowledges his unworthiness and trusts God's grace deserves the predicate "worthy." This formulation directly addresses the specialization of the grace of the Supper in the forgiveness of sins.

However, whoever wants to pursue this principle unilaterally and without any regard for the evidence that the Church has to seek regarding the correct faith would necessarily come to the conclusion that the Holy Supper could only be administered to those who prove themselves to be living, believing Christians. Thus we occasionally find this conclusion clearly expressed by Luther. In the sermon, which has already been cited numerous times, we find among other things:

> There must be a faith which God creates, so that you step away from yourself and come to true faith. Then you would see how few Christians there are and how few of them would go to the Sacrament. But then someone could bring it about, as I would like to do, that all those who believe rightly could be set apart in one place and recognized before others. I would like to have done this [and here in the same breath Luther breaks off and returns to a more sober perception of reality], but it would not be allowed; for it has not yet been preached and urged enough. (W[1] 11:841 [*Ein Sermon D.M. Luthers am Gruendonnerstag*, April 2, 1523; WA 12:476–93; W[2] 11:608–21; Aland 262])

---

wahren Leichnams Christi, March 28, 1521; WA 7:692ff.; W[2] 12:1354ff.; Aland 407]: "Lord, it is true that I am not worthy that You should go under my roof. Yet I thirst for and desire Your help and grace, that I might become holy. I come with no other confidence than that I have now heard sweet words with which You have invited me to Your table and say to me, one who is unworthy . . . ." Before that it reads (p. 1765): "Now if a person hungers for and has prepared for the Sacrament: he should make sure that he go to it not upon **his worthiness** . . . ." In a sermon from 1518 [*Sermo de digna praeparatione cordis pro suscipiendo sacramento eucharistiae*, 1 Cor. 11:23, April 1, 1518; WA 1:329ff.; W[2] 12:1342ff.; Aland 209], Luther can go as far in comforting the timid that he advises them, if there is no other way, to go upon the faith of another or of the Church (W[2] 12:1757ff.).

"And this is the proper use of the Sacrament, which quickens **terrified consciences** through faith in the divine promise. And this is the true divine service in the New Testament; for in the New Testament the heart renders its highest service to God inwardly, in the heart, so that **we mortify the old Adam and are reborn through the Holy Spirit**. For this, Christ instituted the Sacrament. . . . **Now, that faith** which recognizes the superabundant grace of God **makes alive. And this is the chief use of the Sacrament, well to be noted, which makes one well prepared for the Sacrament, namely, the terrified consciences, which feel their sins, are terrified at God's anger and judgment, and long for consolation. . . . And the faith, which there recognizes such mercy, makes alive, and that is the right use of the Sacrament**" (Ap XXIV 71ff.). "**Worthiness** does not consist in greater or less weakness and strength of faith, but rather in the **merit of Christ** which we appropriate through true faith and of which we are assured by the Sacrament, not at all in **our actions** and inner and external **preparations**" (FC Ep VII 20).

"*Non judicat ecclesia de internis*" ["The Church does not judge the heart"] and "The Lord knows those who are His" [2 Timothy 2:19]. Even for repentance and faith the Church has to hold itself to the communicant's oral testimony of repentance and trust in grace. That principle then results in pastoral care and instruction that edifies anxious and despairing consciences with particular comfort. And, as Luther so often repeats, it makes clear to them that precisely this despair is true worthiness. On the other hand, every support of self-confidence, even orthodoxy, must be taken away from the person. This explains why the *viva fides* ["living faith"] is emphasized more than the *vera fides* ["true faith"]. The latter is not mentioned at all, or it is even juxtaposed to the former. Luther offers particularly clear evidence for this in the same context. Just before this he had spoken concerning the value of true knowledge. To the question "What is the Sacrament," the communicant should answer: "the Sacrament is the words of Christ and the sign of the body and blood of Christ." Whoever is unable to give such an answer should not be given the Sacrament. Thereafter he continues: "I hold that you do not render your faith false if you believe that Christ is given here and is yours. Where faith is only a human thought of your own making, then keep away from the Sacrament." And earlier, when he speaks about testing through satanic affliction: "When you say, 'I have received the Sacrament; I believe that it is truly the flesh and blood of Christ,' then the devil will respond: 'Yes, I believe that too. So your faith helps you in no way at all' " (W[1] 11:840, 837).

If, however, even repentance and faith only make themselves known to the office of the Church [i.e., the Office of the Ministry] in oral confession, then it follows as a matter of course that the Church establishes and requires certain forms and measures of oral expression. These represent the average character of that which is necessary and, at the same time, the minimum requirement. But, on the other hand, since such confession seeks indication of that which is *per se* internal, the examination is directed at how the publicly known, actual behavior of the communicant corresponds to his oral proclamation of repentance and faith. No one would dispute that public, moral conduct is to be taken into consideration here. But how could anyone escape the accusation of one-sidedness and ecclesiastical laxity while disputing that same right from the side of the Church's faith and conduct in accord with the Confessions? And no one will dispute that when it comes to a denial of the fundamental doctrines of the Christian faith, the same right applies to declaring the confession of faith to be untrue as the confession of a repentant attitude proves itself to be untrue when persistence in conscious sin is obvious. This, however, would grant the main principle and leave only the specific question as to whether misbelief concerning the Holy Supper has a fundamental significance in general or at least gains this significance for the examination for the Sacrament and admission thereto. Once again, however, we are not investigating this question theologically, but rather determining historically the answer that was given at that time.

The main statement remains constant: "Worthy communicants are exclusively those who are truly repentant and believe." But the investigation of this status, to which the Church is obligated, is relegated to open testimonies and signs, which are to be sought both in the area of faith and in life. We have seen that this is the principle from which the Lutheran Church has arranged an *exploratio fidei* and *vitae* ["examination of faith and life"] from the beginning.

The fact is that according to the Confessions and Reformation practice both were united. The general principle was held firmly. Those who during the examination [*Exploration*] turned out to be errant in doctrine were rejected as unworthy of the Sacrament. The requirements of the church orders would still not be absolutely conclusive to establish that this examination treated life and practice. Although some love to characterize the situation as if the examination did not become so rigorous until the seventeenth century as a consequence of the crypto-Calvinist movement, it can be documented with a whole series of facts to prove that this was not the case. We will limit ourselves, first of all, to Luther's practice.

[Luther's Practice]

Regarding Luther, Rietschel is satisfied to dismiss the much-cited letter to the Frankfurters from 1533 as unrelated to the matter, since Luther does not talk about the admission of the heterodox but rather concerning the deception experienced by those who go to the Supper among the Zwinglians, because there they do not receive the body and blood of the Lord at all. It is rightly remarked that Luther would have said nothing less of the celebration of the Supper in congregations of a Calvinist confession, and the fact that many Lutherans no longer share Luther's conclusion does not contradict this. Nevertheless, it must be remembered that the Lutheran Confessions have also directly appropriated Luther's statement on this point (FC SD VII 32).[24]

The testimony of this letter to the Frankfurters, however, cannot be so easily dismissed as was attempted. It will always remain that the main question that Luther expressly poses reads thus: "whether they should go with the crowd to

24 ["After this protestation, Doctor Luther, of blessed memory, presents, among other articles, this also: In the same manner I also speak and confess (he says) concerning the Sacrament of the Altar, that there the body and blood of Christ are in truth orally eaten and drunk in the bread and wine, even though the priests [ministers] who administer it [the Lord's Supper], or those who receive it, should not believe or otherwise misuse it. For it does not depend upon the faith or unbelief of men, but upon God's Word and ordinance, **unless they first change God's Word and ordinance and interpret it otherwise, as the enemies of the Sacrament do at the present day, who, of course, have nothing but bread and wine**; for they also do not have the words and appointed ordinance of God, but have perverted and changed them according to their own [false] notion. Fol. 245" (FC SD VII 32). MH]

the Sacrament" where the preacher "does not teach nor believe that the body and blood are truly in the bread and wine . . . or should for this **reason** avoid it and **do without**" (W[1] 17:2436 [*Ein Brief an die zu Frankfurt am Main. D.M. Luther*, 1533; WA 30/3:558–71; Aland 225]). Here it does not come down to Luther's rationale, but only to the fact that Luther agrees with those who "for this reason" have misgivings about going. On the contrary, the remark that Rietschel occasionally makes against [Franz] Delitzsch [1813–90] comes back on him: it is a matter of a *questio facti* and not a *questio juris* [a "question of facts," not a "question of rules"].

Besides this, much more important things have been overlooked. This writing [of Luther] indicates in the most definitive way what is required of a communicant, namely, that he does not merely have a faith in general and the spiritual participation which one can find outside of the Sacrament, but that he also must believe in the real presence of the body and blood in Christ in the Lutheran sense. "If the pastor is duplicitous [*ein Zweizuengiger*], then go freely to him or send to him and let him tell you what it is that he gives you with his hands and what you receive with your mouth" (W[1] 17:2440 [WA 30/3:558–71; Aland 225]). And further below: "Look, it is not academic to believe in the body which Christ means" (W[1] 17:2444 [WA 30/3:558–71; Aland 225]). And all of this is supported by a reference to the **examination** before the Supper to which another can hardly compare in terms of the emphasis and particular order of the content. "Indeed, it is true that wherever the preacher administers nothing other than bread and wine for the Sacrament, it does not matter to whom he hands it or **what** they know and **believe** who receive it. . . . But because we intend to raise up Christians and to leave such to posterity and to administer **body and blood** in the Sacrament, **we want to and can give such a Sacrament to no one, unless he has been previously interviewed** as to what he has learned from the Catechism" (W[1] 17:2449f. [WA 30/3:558–71; Aland 225]). Only the greatest caprice could interpret the content of this interview as something else than this: that the body and blood of Christ are received in the Sacrament. How, then, should we characterize a historical investigation which, with such a superficially justified excuse that this writing does not have to do with our question, avoids the authority of a witness, the significance of which has been acknowledged since the beginning?

And further, why keep silent about all of the other testimonies to **Luther's** practice? Admittedly, a case would likely not have presented itself in which Luther would have to refuse Calvinists from the altar in Wittenberg. Only after his death did the deviant doctrine of the Sacrament dare show itself in the heart of the Lutheran Reformation, and even then only in a clandestine and hidden way. However, Luther's parish was not confined to the municipal limits of the city of Wittenberg. His practice is recognizable in his manner of treating those who asserted the opposing doctrine. One may call it rigidness and gruffness when Luther refused to call [Huldrich] Zwingli [1484–1531] and the Reformed at

Marburg [1529] and elsewhere "brother"—of course, we will see [Philipp Jakob] Spener [1635–1705] do the same thing. But, in fact, no one can doubt what Luther said about his altar fellowship practice. It also does not change the situation if someone wanted to say that Luther set up such requirements for church unity, but they did not have any validity for Lutheran practice toward individuals who desired admittance to the Lutheran Supper. On the contrary, the reasons for the practice demonstrated in the last case may be found in Luther's judgment of the general stance of both fellowships [Lutheran and Reformed] to each other.

Is what **Luther** himself so clearly and consciously expressed "**un-Lutheran**"? Does it run contrary to the symbolical books, a main portion of which stems from Luther's hand? Call it what you will, but to call this "un-Lutheran" is ludicrous in the face of the judgment of history. Up to now anyone who was unsatisfied with this course of action confined himself to saying that the times of this rigorism were over. But Pastor Rietschel has attempted to prove that Luther advocated principles and practice that were not Lutheran.

It is, nevertheless, valuable for our question to describe in more detail Luther's course of action and his pronouncements regarding the unification attempts of that time. First of all, there is the fact of the **denial of the name "brother."** The importance of this pronouncement and its motive are expressed just as clearly. **It is precisely the denial of spiritual and church fellowship** that is intended by this. "**Wherever unity is sought in worldly things, this does not prevent the dissimilarity of faith**. As we know that acts of marriage and other worldly things can exist among those of dissimilar religions, according to 1 Corinthians 6:4." Luther gave this advice to Melanchthon on the way to the Cassel Religious Colloquy [1534] in reference to the proceedings at Marburg (W[1] 17:2489 [*Glossae D.M. Lutheri super sententias partum de controversia coenae, exhibitias ipsi a D. Phil. Melanchthone*, 1534; WA 38:302–10; Aland 129]). Before his congregation in Wittenberg, however, he expresses the same thought in the most well-meaning way on the occasion of an interpretation of Deuteronomy 7: "I am not saying that it is a brotherly unity, but rather a **kind, friendly unity** whereby they seek among us what they lack, and we serve them. Now if you diligently request it, they will also become brotherly" (W[1] 3:2618 [*5 Mose 7*, 11–7–29; WA 28:670–83; Aland Pr 1100]). Finally, Luther had already pronounced in writing: "That these words are firm: This is what we want to do. We want to be one with them in worldly things, i.e., maintain physical and temporal peace. **But we want to avoid them spiritually**" (W[1] 20:967 [*Dass diese Worte Christi (Das ist mein Leib etc) noch fest stehen wider die Schwarmgeister*, 1527; WA 23:64–283; Aland 679]). In this sense he has no misgivings about applying 2 John 1:10 ["If anyone comes to you and does not bring this teaching, do not receive him into your house or give him any greeting"] to their reciprocal relationship (W[1] 20:2202 [*Kurzes Bekenntnis vom heiligen Sakrament*, 1544; WA 54:141–67; Aland 661]) and dissolving any sort of fellowship, most of all fellowship in the Holy Supper (W[1] 20:2213 [WA 54:141–67]), as the latter is explicitly expressed elsewhere (W[1] 17:2429ff. [*Brief 2-1-31 an Herz Ernst v. Braunschweig-Lüneburg*; WA Br 6:27; 12:133; Aland Br 1778]; cf. *Tischreden v. Förstemann* 2:317 [*D.M. Luthers Tischreden oder Colloquia v. K. E. Förstemann.* 1–4 Abth. Leipzig (Berlin), 1844–48]).[25]

The negotiations between [Philip] the Duke of Hesse [1504–67] and the Lutheran theologians, which are found in their complete form in [David] **Chytraeus's** [1530–1600] *History of the Augsburg Confession*, are very instructive regarding the import of the requirement and refusal of brotherhood. The former demands that the Reformed "be recognized and considered as fellows of one faith . . . and as brothers regardless of the different opinion and division regarding the Sacrament" (p. 157). The opponents, [Philip] Melanchthon [1497–1560] and [Johann] Brenz [1499–1570], as well as Luther, maintain that one cannot grant this name and church fellowship without unity in doctrine, especially in such a chief part as the Sacrament. We give the justification with **Luther's** words: "They have desired brotherhood from us, which we had to refuse this time and not accept. **For, if we accept them as brothers and sisters, then we must approve their doctrine**" (W[1] 3:2617 [*5. Mose 6.7*, 10-24-29; WA 28:658–69; Aland Pr 1099]). ". . . Then we would also have to cherish and be pleased with their doctrine and conduct or at least tolerate it. Whoever wants to may do so; I will not. For Christian unity exists in the Spirit, since we are of one faith, one Spirit, one mind. Ephesians 4:6" (W[1] 20:967 [*Dass diese Worte Christi (Das ist mein Leib etc) noch fest stehen wider die Schwarmgeister*, 1527; WA 23:64–283; Aland 679]). "But now they emphasize love alone and Christian unity, which should not be separated. Conversely, **they make light of the article of the Supper, as if it were of little importance that we consider the Supper of the Lord as we want. We cannot tolerate this. Rather, as much as they emphasize the unity of life, so much do we emphasize the unity of doctrine and faith**. If they would leave this to us unharmed, we would lift up and praise the unity of love as do they, but without any harm to unity of faith and of the spirit" [*In epistolam Pauli ad Galatas M. Lutheri commentaries*, 1519; WA 2:443–618; W[1] 9:1–379; Aland 228].

Luther's anger and pain can be perceived when he writes in 1527 (W[1] 20:963 [*Dass diese Worte Christi (Das ist mein Leib etc) noch fest stehen wider die*

25 [From the *Table Talk* noted: 38. "Another question, asked of Dr. M.L. in the year 1542. 'May one take the Sacrament from a minister who publicly holds and teaches that the true body and blood of Christ are not in the Sacrament, rather that Christ is there spiritually, as He is in all places with His grace?' Some grant this and let it happen, for one should not look to the person or the dignity, worthiness or unworthiness of the same, who administers the Sacrament. But D.M.L. said a very definite 'No' to this question, 'for in that case it is not the worthiness of the person that ceases, but the matter itself, *res ipsa*, there is no Sacrament there. Again, if he does not rightly administer the Sacrament [*nicht recht haelt*], you may not act against Christ [i.e., by going to such a supper], who has shed His blood for you.'" MH]

Schwarmgeister; WA 23:64–283; Aland 679]): "May such love and unity be cursed to the abyss of hell, since such unity not only tears apart Christianity, but it mocks and derides it in a devilish way to its misery." And in the *Brief Confession* from 1544 (W[1] 20:2201ff. [WA 54:141ff.]): "For how we had to hear that we did not have Christian love, despised the servants of Christ, and troubled and confused the Church, etc., and that there were no other sinners on earth other than we and no saints except for the enthusiasts. Among them there was nothing but **a pure fire of love and among us nothing but the ice of ungraciousness**. . . . However, how has such a superabundant love and humility helped us now? Except that thereby everything has become worse and our hope was sadly missing."

"A stalemate in battle was praised. Since the opposing party seemed only to take offense at the *manducatio oralis* ["oral eating" of the body of Christ], they were borne in patience. They gave in and admitted that they do not deny that the true body and blood of Christ are there, which sounds like they consider it in the same way as do we. They do not want to admit a bodily consumption. We pushed this upon their consciences, because we have God's Word and the text in our favor, which they do not have. Thus there is much to be hoped for in this matter" (W[1] 3:2617ff. [*5. Mose 6:7*, 10–24–29; WA 28:658–69; Aland Pr 1099]). The last of the articles which was discussed in Marburg concludes with the explanation: "And though we have not at this time agreed as to whether the true body and blood of Christ are bodily in the bread and wine, nevertheless both parties should show Christian love to the other and diligently pray to God, the Almighty, that He would confirm us in the right understanding through His Spirit. Amen" (Giesel. III, 1, 238). As is known, Luther himself composed this article.

Just how serious Luther was about maintaining this basis of understanding despite bitter experiences in the meantime (W[1] 16:282ff. [*6-1-30 an Propst*; WA Br 5:338; Aland Br 1577]) is demonstrated in his instruction to **Melanchthon** for the meeting [*Vergleichgungsversuch*] at Cassel (1534/35): "If they want to stay with their opinion in the point of the presence of the body and blood and would request that we nevertheless tolerate one another, **I would gladly tolerate them in the hope that in the future we might come into one fellowship**" (W[1] 17:2489 [*Glossae D.M. Lutheri super sentientias partum de controversia coenae, exhibitas ipsi a D. Phil. Melanchthone*, 1534; WA 38:302–10; Aland 129]).

This appeared to be achieved with [Martin] Bucer in the Concord of 1536, and it is here in this place that we should remember the joy with which this unification was greeted in good faith by even the most unreliable among all the opponents. [Friedrich] Myconius's [1490–1546] report reads: "Since they have now confessed the real issue in the matter, namely, that the bread is the body of Christ by the power of Christ, who instituted and thus promised it out of divine majesty, that it is **misused by the unworthy**, etc., **peace and unity** has been made among us who were together. [Wolfgang] Capito [1478–1541] and [Martin] Bucer began to cry, and both parties have thanked God with folded hands" (W[1] 17:2541ff.). As a seal of the fellowship of faith that had now been gained, they celebrated together the Holy Supper.[26]

Whoever wanted to make the effort could easily demonstrate from these examples that according to Luther altar fellowship is church fellowship, and vice versa. This is precisely what Rietschel rejects outright as un-Lutheran. But we do not have any particular interest in demonstrating that here. Even the proof, that it is an act of confession, which we will present in the second section, still does not coincide exactly with the concept of "church fellowship."

It is enough to have established that it is impossible that Luther could have understood the expression about worthiness through repentance and saving faith alone, such that even those who think about the Supper as do the Calvinists, but who nevertheless fulfilled those requirements, should be administered the Supper. Our third thesis about the insinuated consequence has had sufficient light shed upon it. And now we return to the completion of the second point, namely, how on the Lutheran side the apparent contradiction between the two concepts of "worthy" is mediated and how the two concepts coincide.

[THE TWO MEANINGS OF "WORTHY"]

We are used to proceeding from the fact that truly pious and upright Christians could in good faith assert that the Reformed interpretation of Christ's Words of Institution is the correct and scriptural interpretation. And it would be an injustice to Luther to think that he rejected this outright. Although he does not draw any consequences from this, he wrote in his instruction to Melanchthon (W[1] 17:2489 [*Glossae D.M. Lutheri super sentientias partum de controversia coenae, exhibitas ipsi a D. Phil. Melanchthone*, 1534; WA 38:302–10; Aland 129]): "They are perhaps captivated by this other understanding **out of a good conscience**; therefore, we should gladly tolerate them. If they are pure, then Christ the Lord will indeed rescue them." But Luther adds, "**I, however, am truly captive to the other understanding with a good conscience.**" However he justified it, Luther considered this distinction to be too consequential regarding the essence of the Holy Supper, and the blessing one might receive from it, to be able to maintain altar and church fellowship with them.

A series of factors doubtless contributed to the more detailed justification of this view. The general justification for it could not be allowed under any circumstances. These were only peripheral factors compared with the dogmatic basis. According to the nature of the matter, the essential factor must lie in the concept of faith.

26 Loescher, *Historia motuum* 1:214.

Among these peripheral factors is what was mentioned above in passing, that the actual content of the sacraments was made dependent upon the denial of that content in confession. This argument could really only be used against the assertion that Lutherans should not go to the Supper among the Reformed.

It was the view at that time that there was a second important factor, namely, the **unrepentance** which caused those who, as often and convincingly as they were instructed to the contrary, to continue to hold fast to the Reformed understanding of the Supper. This argument is not only encountered in the opinions cited by Rietschel but also is emphasized strongly and often by Luther himself. From the outset, we will forgo adopting this argument. For here the possibility, occasionally recognized by Luther himself, that the Reformed could "with a good conscience" stand by their understanding as scriptural is not taken into account. It has to be recognized that in the penetrating manner with which this controversy was carried out at the time, the idea suggested itself to both parties, and especially to the Lutherans with their insistence upon the wording of the institution, that the other party could only blind itself to the better insight out of stubbornness and that it would be difficult for someone to remain unaware of the significance of the antithesis [i.e., opposing view]. Besides, the distinction is made here by Luther, as in the church orders and many faculty opinions, between the simple people and the teachers, and among the former between such that are hardened in their opinion.[27] Finally, the Lutherans could rightly point out that the opposition had more and more come to know their view, especially that of the *manducatio oralis* [i.e., that the body and blood of Christ are eaten by the mouth]. Luther asked more than once with outrage whether it could be expected of him to maintain fellowship with those who spoke so blasphemously about his belief concerning the Supper.[28] These are reasons from that time that have to be honored, given the historical context of this controversy. However, it would be wrong to use these reasons to explain the apparent difference in practice. For this, one must take into account two decisive reasons which have to do with the matter itself and with Reformed understanding, not with the persons and their spiritual condition.

The first of these reasons is the consequence of understanding of fellowship in sacraments as confessional fellowship [*Sacramentsgemeinschaft als Bekenntnissgemeinschaft*]. We will treat this separately later. However, the opposing viewpoint is connected to this as a fundamental presupposition.

---

27 Cf. besides the Saxon Church Order of 1580 the opinion in Dedekenn 1:635.

28 In the opinion which Brenz and Melanchthon wrote to Duke Philip on the offer of peace by those in the Palatinate, it reads, for example "We are amazed along with Luther how these people could come to this thought that they desire brotherhood with us since year after year they have shouted and called us horrid and dreadful heretics" (Dedekenn, *Consil.* I, 308. 84. Cf. FC Ep VII 41; FC SD VII 67).

It is rightly denied [by Rietschel] that "according to the Lutheran teaching the body and blood of Christ are an end in themselves as in the Catholic Church. They are means" (p. 11). However, they are particular means, established by a particular endowment of grace **in such a way and in no other way**, and **intended for this and for nothing else**. The forgiveness of sins is also given in the Word and in Baptism. In the Supper, however, according to Christ's bequest, forgiveness is received with the reception of His body and blood and in no other way. If the unworthy also receive the body and blood of Christ, then this is the result of the immutability and autonomy of the gift. If, however, the worthy seek forgiveness in the Supper, then they are to seek it according to Christ's institution, namely, in the reception of the true body and blood of Christ. Luther would answer anyone who would say that he seeks the forgiveness of sins but that he does not believe that the body and blood are truly received: "It is received precisely with the body and the blood and otherwise not at all." Herein lies the consequence of his teaching that the Zwinglians receive nothing at all in the Sacrament since according to their own denial they could not receive the body and blood. According to this view, orthodoxy is not a condition for the grace of the Sacrament. We have already cited relevant witnesses against this. Rather, what is a condition is a faith that seeks grace in the form in which it is offered in the Sacrament. To think of the *promissio* in the Sacrament, that is, the forgiveness of sins, as floating in the air or merely attached to the words "for you" and not, at the same time, to the preceding, namely, "My body—My blood, given for you," is a thought that is completely foreign to Luther and the old Lutheran teachers. The body, which is received for the forgiveness of sins, constitutes in one the *promissio* [i.e., the essence of body and blood for forgiveness] of the Sacrament. To conclude, we will substantiate this with the irrevocably clear treatment by one of the authors of the Formula of Concord.

The symbolical books themselves, however, contain the clearest witnesses that this was simply the most natural, common understanding. Thus the Apology says: "*Certo enim debent statuere corda . . . quum vescimur corpere Domini, quod ignoscat nobis Deus propter Christum*" ["For hearts should be assured when we consume the body of the Lord that God forgives for Christ's sake"] (Ap XIII 4). It does not state, as one could perhaps understand it according to the German text, that the Word effects this and that thereby "the external signs move the heart," because it continues in complete correspondence to the Latin text: "namely, through the word and the external signs at the same time." And it also does not prove anything [to assert] that here only the visibility of the rite is addressed. If, however, this [presence of Christ's body and blood in the Sacrament] is emphasized less in general than the belief in the promise of forgiveness as the grace unique to the New Testament, then this is similar to what we saw above regarding the generalization of the concept "worthy." There was no dispute with the Romanists on the reality of the gift of the Sacrament; but there was a dispute about the *opus operatum*. Compare the introduction on the *usus sacramentorum* ["use of the sacraments"] (Ap XIII 18): "It is nothing more than a Jewish error when they maintain that we should be made righteous through a work and external ceremonies even when faith in the heart is not present." All of the passages that Rietschel tries to use for his proof that the opposite statement [regarding the substance of Christ's body and blood in the Sacrament] is lacking revolve around this (cf. especially p. 8). He would be correct, if he were only trying to prove the predominant emphasis upon faith and forgiveness. But it just so happened that he entirely overlooked the other witnesses. For these other statements only very occasionally appear in the form of a presupposition. But the Small Catechism itself—like the first principle for any examination—offers the clear answer to the question "What is the Sacrament?"—namely, "The true body and the true blood under the bread and wine instituted for us Christians to eat and drink." Thus it consequently answers the fourth question: "Which words, **next to** the bodily eating and drinking, are the main part in the Sacrament?" And the Latin translation presents this innocuously enough: "*Quae verba sunt una cum corporali manducatione caput et summa hujus sacramenti*" ["Which words, together with the consumption of the body, are the height and summit of this Sacrament"]. To be consistent, Pastor Rietschel has to say that this is in no way a symbolic expression of the matter.

In the Large Catechism, Luther applies the words of his interpretation of Baptism to the Supper and calls it: "God's Word contained in bread and wine and bound to it." This is also the case for the indissoluble connection of both promises: that it is body and blood and that it is consumed for the forgiveness of sins. Right after this Luther expresses this more definitively (LC V 22): "*Ideo ad sacramentum accedimus, ut ejusmodi thesaurum (corpus et sanguis) accipiamus, per quem et in quo peccatorum remissionem consequamur*" ["Therefore, let us come to this Sacrament that we might enjoy its treasure (body and blood) **through which and in which** we obtain the forgiveness of sins"]. And just after this he goes into still more detail (LC V 28ff.): "Now our clever spirits contort themselves with their great art and cleverness, which cry out and clammer: 'How can bread and wine forgive sins (!) or strengthen faith?' Yet they hear and know that we are not saying this about bread and wine *per se*, but rather about **such bread and wine which is Christ's body and blood and which has the Word with it**. We call this and nothing else our treasure **through which** forgiveness is acquired. Now, this is brought and appropriated to us in no other way than in the word (given and shed for me), **for here you have both that it is Christ's body and blood and that it is yours** as a treasure and gift." I think that is clear enough. Pastor Rietschel is hung up on the word "the treasure" (p. 9), which Luther calls the body and blood. Why did he not immerse himself a little more deeply in this matter so he might realize from this single passage just how frail his entire argument is? Luther establishes the effect of forgiveness here with the sentence: "Now, Christ's body (naturally, that which is received in the Sacrament) cannot be a fruitless, idle thing that does nothing or has no benefit. Yet as great as the treasure is by itself, it must be apprehended and administered in the Word." This is the second thing. Consequently, in response to the objection that Christ's body and blood is, in fact, not given for us in the Sacrament—though, indeed, the "forgiveness of sins" has come to us through the Word—it reads "inserted **by the Word in this Sacrament and presented (*propositus*)** to us (namely, in the Sacrament)." To deny this would be as foolish as to assert: "The entire Gospel is useless apart from the Sacrament." Only then (LC V 33) does the catechism move on to the personal conditions for the Sacrament. Everything that preceded spoke concerning that "which the Sacrament is *per se* and what it brings and benefits." (Cf. also LC V 64, 66, 70.)

The Formula of Concord also expresses this, like the Apology, in a more immediate form: "*Sicut idem corpus una cum omnibus beneficiis suis* ***exhibetur***" ["Just as the body is presented together with all of its benefits"], for it is stated here of the opponents that they conform themselves to our way of speaking (FC SD VII 18). And what is written in FC SD VII 63 is simply a popular expression for the identity of the *promissio*: "*Ac pii quidem corpus et sanguinem Christi in certum pignus et confimationem accipiunt, quod peccata ipsis sint remissa et quod Chrisus in ipsis habitet*" ["And the pious do indeed receive the body and blood of Christ as a certain pledge and confirmation that their sins are forgiven and that Christ dwells in them"]. The opposite is namely the Reformed antithesis of assurance through the *signa tanquam* ["such signs"] which are *pignus externum* ["an external pledge"] (FC SD VII 116): "*Et quod hoc modo fides nostra in sacra coena tantummodo per externa symbola, non autem per verum praesens et nobis exhibitum corpus et sanguinem Christi obsignetur et confirmetur*" ["And that in this way our faith is sealed and confirmed in the Holy Supper as through external symbols, **but not through the true presence and administration of Christ's body and blood to us**"]. (Cf. FC Ep VII 30.) For just this reason all of the passages wherein the effects of both grace and judgment are exercised by the Christ, who is present in Christians through the Sacrament, belong here. (Cf. FC SD VII 105; FC Ep VII 17.) The passage cited above concerning the necessity of the words of consecration and their effect for true faith (FC SD VII 79) should be considered together with this.

Nevertheless, the confession is not a dogmatics [text], and one cannot demand from it the mediating dogmatic links between the uninterpreted statements of the Confessions, which are placed one next to the other. It suffices to demonstrate that both [what is present in the Sacrament and its benefits] are, in fact, present. We will present this with the words of an interpreter who is beyond suspicion and next in line. Below we provide **Chemnitz's** account of the entire point of doctrine in his *Examination of the Council of Trent* according to its principles.[29]

Luther in his early phase rarely expresses this side of the doctrine [namely, the substance of Christ's body and blood in the Sacrament]. Instead, at that time, opposition to the Romanist position predominated. Already in 1526, however, we find the clearest witnesses for this understanding, which achieved symbolical expression in both catechisms. We can best conclude the entire account we have provided up to now with a few passages from Luther's *Sermon on the Sacrament of the Body and Blood of Christ Against the Enthusiasts* from 1526 (W[1] 20:915ff. [*Sermon von dem Sakrament des Leibes und Blutes Christi wider die Schwarmgeister*, 1526; WA 19:482–523; AE 36:329–61; Aland 658]): "There are two parts to believe. [First,] the (body and blood) is truly there, which the papists also believe. Second, that it is imparted to us, which they do not believe" . . . (W[1] [20:]933). Here he is describing in general the object of faith. The first point indicates the antithesis against Zwingli, who emphasized the remembrance of Christ. "Therefore, we also preach Christ's death . . . but there is a difference here; when I preach His death, that is a public sermon in the congregation. I do not give anyone anything in particular. Whoever grasps it, grasps it. But when I distribute the Sacrament, I appropriate it specifically to whomever takes it. I give him Christ's body and blood, **so that** he might have the forgiveness of sins" (W[1] [20:]984). "Everyone should be able to answer thus: . . . I understand the words in such a way that His body and blood are given to me for the forgiveness of sins. Therefore, a Christian must know these words to the letter" (W[1] [20:]936). The commentary which Luther himself

---

29 Chemnitz exhaustively treats this question in the section *De praeparatione quae adhibenda est ut digne quis sancam Eucharistiam percipiat.* Pars II cap. VII fol. 291ff., ed. Francof., 1609. Starting with the exploration of communicants by the parson, which was common among and required by the Lutherans, he formulates the concept of dignity in contrast to any merit in a way that corresponds entirely with the proof we presented above.

For this reason, Paul immediately follows his reprimand of the Corinthians' use of the Supper with the Words of Institution themselves. To correct the understanding of 1 Corinthians 11:27 (Rietschel, pp. 17ff.), we here add Luther's words on the subject from his writing *Against the Heavenly Prophets* (W[1] 20:185ff. [StL 20:132ff.; WA 18:62ff.; AE 40:73ff.]): "How is it a **sin against the body of the Lord** in the eating of it, if He is not in the eating or bread? . . . If he did not intend this, he would also have had to say: he who eats this bread unworthily is guilty of the **bread of the Lord**. Or he would have had to say: . . . he who sins against the Lord's Supper or against God or against the command or against **the institution of the Lord**." Furthermore, Chemnitz describes . . . [Editor's Note: At this point in the original footnote, Dr. Zezschwitz provides an extensive citation from Chemnitz. We have deleted this text because it appears in this volume as chapter 25: see below, pp. 491–501.]

Cf. *de ratione institutionis hujus sancti Sacramenti* cap. II. p. 265. In an opinion from 1594, Chemnitz even declares himself in favor of the territorial expulsion of the Calvinists for the protection of the Lutheran Church—which was unfortunately at that time an all-too-common practice.

provides demands that all communicants know the Words of Institution and must be capable of giving an account for them, and cannot be overlooked. He continues: "Here my Lord has given me His body and blood in bread and wine that I should eat and drink it and it should be mine, **so that I may be certain** that my sins are forgiven. Therefore, I go to the Sacrament to seek this." Luther, who bases everything on the words "given for you," goes as far as to say, "Even if the words were not written there, as Paul leaves them out, nevertheless **you have the body** which died for your sins and **the blood** that is poured out for them. But **when Christ is given to you**, the forgiveness of sins is **also** given and everything that has been purchased with this treasure. If you have grasped it with the heart, as it cannot be grasped any other way, and if you believe, then you must say: no work, no deed can help me with sin. But **I have** another treasure, **my Lord's body and blood**, given for me for the forgiveness of sins" (W¹ [20:]937). "Would Christ institute such a great thing for nothing, without any benefit and holiness?" (W¹ [20:]938).[30]

We have come to the end of this part of our proof and can briefly summarize the results. First of all, the term *worthiness* is to be distinguished between worthiness before God and His gift of the Sacrament as a pure gift of grace; and between that worthiness which has as its rule the institution of Christ [regarding His body and blood]. The latter worthiness underlies the examination of the Church as an attested faith in the real presence of the body and blood. The faith of the Lutheran Church, however, combines the forgiveness of sins offered in the Sacrament with the specific gift of the Sacrament, namely, the body and blood of Christ offered for eating and drinking. It therefore declares all those unworthy who deny the reality of the latter. This explains the practice of the sixteenth century.

Simply in order to give a more complete picture of this practice, we will provide a couple of characteristic examples. Most cases that Dedekenn and the casuists offer refer to the practice of the seventeenth century. The examples that we have from a still earlier time are all the more valuable. One case found in Dedekenn (1:632ff.) is from the year 1568 and offers an abundance of instructive material. Within the Meissner bishopric [Hesse], which was administered by commissars, there was a nobleman esteemed for his piety who was deterred from the Supper by his pastor and respectively by the commissars themselves because he made no secret of that fact that he did not believe in "the true and substantial presence of the body and blood of the Lord in the bodily consumption." His complaint about this was the occasion for obtaining an opinion from the theological faculties of Leipzig and Wittenberg. Both opinions unconditionally recognize the correctness of this procedure, because the faith of the nobleman did not correspond to the public Confessions of the Lutheran Church. The Leipzig faculty explains this,

---

30 Cf. Thomasius's enlightening presentation on the stages of development in Luther's doctrine of the Sacrament, *Christi Person und Werk* III, 2, pp. 87ff.

quoting Luther and Chemnitz and the Formula of Concord almost verbatim: "For no one may establish his own thoughts as a foundation of faith, but rather has the word, order, command, and institution of God for himself. It is certainly true that whoever thinks and believes something other than the word, order, command, and institution of God does not have a true, correct, living . . . faith." The Wittenberg faculty agrees with one caveat, namely, that an attempt be made to better instruct the one concerned. We will return to their opinion when we deal with the question of the act of confession in the consumption of the Supper.

Still more interesting are the proceedings in Württemberg in connection with the Montbéliard Religious Dialogue [March 14–27, 1586]. Duke Friedrich of Württemberg [I, 1557–1608] and Montbéliard summoned [Jakob] Andreae [1528–90] and Beza [1519–1605] to a dialogue at Montbéliard castle in the interest of reconciling the disputing parties. French refugees to whom Montbéliard had been opened as a place of refuge had given occasion for this colloquy. An anonymous letter, which appeared soon after these proceedings, depicted the situation in such a way as though the prince had become more favorable toward the Reformed as a result of the dialogue, since from then on he allowed the French refugees to participate in the Lutheran Supper. This news did not fail to cause a stir and moved the prince to publish his own views with respect to the colloquium.[31] In the preface (ii) and afterword (978ff.), the prince denounced the letter as slander. His explanation can likewise help us with the transition to the second question as to what extent the Supper is an act of confession regarding church affiliation. He opens his defense with these words: "By God's grace we have arrived at such a knowledge in spiritual matters which regard the salvation of our souls that we know that the Lord's Supper has been instituted and ordained among other things to this end: that one may recognize as by battle flags and markers to which faith each person is devoted. For whoever holds the Supper with a church, whatever it may be or however it may be called, makes it thereby understood that he also adheres to the doctrine of that church and does not hold the Supper with those who teach another doctrine, but publicly separates himself from that church. . . . Therefore, we have always maintained and continue to do so that no joke is to be made of the reception of the Holy Supper of the Lord such that one confesses one thing with public reception of the Supper and has another thing in his heart."

After this it is further reported that "if they recognize and hold our doctrine, faith, and confession to be correct, true and Christian, then they may receive with us the Holy Supper." For the sake of the truth, no secret can be made of the fact that this was only the conclusion of very long, drawn-out discussion.

The first negotiations regarding admittance took place already before the colloquium whereby the Reformed had received explanations to the effect that,

31 *Colloquium Mompelgartense*, etc.—translated into German from Latin. Tübingen, 1587.

although they had repeatedly requested to do so, they could not celebrate the Supper together at Christmas.[32] By contrast, we do see them take part in Communion at Easter and Pentecost. The prince justified this in that it was assumed they were convinced of the correctness of the Lutheran doctrine so there were now no concerns regarding the earlier reasons for deterring them. The report, however, lacks clarity here. Thus some princely connivance may be assumed which someone did not want mentioned later.

However, already during the colloquium there was a genuine attempt made even by Beza and his party to have brotherhood in the Sacrament through a reciprocal approval and recognition of each other's doctrine. The answer given by the prince initially after the conclusion of the colloquium (March 29, 1586) seems somewhat noncommittal and is, in any case, not as decisive as the explanations from the foreword cited above.[33] All the same, what is reported from the negotiations between the clergy and the refugees (982ff.) does not indicate that the final blame should be placed on the refugees as if they had accepted things that had not been previously expressed in the notarized document which they immediately allowed to be drafted. On the other hand, at most the only complaint could be that this document was drafted after the departure of the clergy, as the prince himself excused the entire proceeding with his absence. The Reformed had also concealed the document from both parties. But enough. When matters became known, the vacillations came to an end, and the prince took the position demonstrated by the words cited above from the foreword.

Similarly, the proceedings against the crypto-Calvinists demonstrate the general understanding of the admittance to the Supper as an act of confession over against foreign doctrine. Upon the advice of the theologians at Dresden, [Casper] Peucer [1525–1602] was denied the Supper because he would not subscribe to the Book of Concord. It was granted to the court preacher [David] Steinbach only after he publicly recanted, and, finally, the court preacher [Christian] Schütz was harshly reprimanded for his negligence in this matter.[34] Now we turn our attention to the second principle question.

---

32 The answer from December 17, 1585, is reproduced in *Colloquium Mompelgartense*, 979.

33 It reads: "The said confession and church order in public print is well-known. If they now want to go to the Holy Lord's Supper by virtue of the same confession and order and their opinion is declared to the church servants at Montbéliard, then they should not be refused" (p. 980).

34 Cf. Gleich, *Annales Ecclesiastici*, 1:51, 461ff.

II. The Consumption of the Holy Supper according to the Lutheran Doctrinal Understanding: An Act of Confession

Pastor Rietschel bases his second main proof that the practice we have documented is "un-Lutheran" upon the claim that it is not justified to conceive of the reception of the Supper as an act of confession. Supposedly, the view of participation in the Supper as a confession is not taught but denied by the Lutheran Confessions, precisely because it has the characteristics of the Reformed view. The author goes as far as to accuse me of "Zwinglian" principles and to declare that I could call upon men of such ecclesiastical rank as [Friedrich] Schleiermacher [1768–1834] and [Karl Immanuel] Nitzsch [1787–1868] as witnesses. As much as we want to believe that insufficient insight into the doctrine of the Lutheran Confessions and teachers, and confusion concerning the actual intention of the Reformed views, could have made it possible for him to distort the historical facts in such an incredible way even in this point, as concerns the above-mentioned assertions, Pastor Rietschel could hardly be said to have a clean conscience.

Rietschel admits this much: the symbolical books do not absolutely deny the act of confession in the Holy Supper. He himself acknowledges that there are relevant passages from the Confessions—however, only very few (p. 27). The negative thesis in the Solid Declaration reads "that bread and wine should be nothing other than (*nihil aliud nisi*) signs by which Christians recognize each other."[35] Who as a Lutheran would claim such a thing, and who cannot see that we understand something entirely different by "act of confession" than what is asserted here? When the affirmative statement of the Augsburg Confession reads "that the Sacraments are instituted not only (*non modo*) that they may be signs whereby Christians may be externally recognized,[36] but much more (*sed magis*) that they may be a sign and a testimony of God's will toward us . . ." (AC XIII 1), then enough has been said, and it is precisely this that we assert. For again we have to ask, what sort of Lutheran would not consider the reception of the divine gift of the Sacrament as the primary goal of the Sacrament? Yet Pastor Rietschel blames me, of course, for twisting the statement and thinks that I remind him of the "presumptuous scholars" that are dealt with in the Apology (Ap XXIV 68). By way of an answer, we only need remind him of Matthew 7:12 ["Whatever you wish that others would do to you, do also to them"]. We hope that in the future Pastor Rietschel will work more carefully at portraying historical facts and judging ecclesiastical questions.

In brief, with this thesis the Confessions explicitly acknowledge that it is a purpose of the Sacrament *ut sint notae professionis inter homines* ["that they are

35 FC SD VII 115 (*BSLK* 1012). Ep VII 27 (*BSLK* 801).

36 In Latin: "*ut sint notae professionis inter homines.*"

signs of confession among men"]. It cannot even be asserted with the same certainty that this *non modo* ["not only"] here in the Augustana is directed against the one-sided emphasis of this factor on the part of the Zwinglians, just as in the negative thesis of the Formula of Concord. At least, the expression (*nota*) ["marks"] chosen here alludes at the same time to other contexts. And, in any case, there are other sources of proof than this "*non modo*." The confessional basis that Rietschel marshals, to our great surprise, is to be found in one of the great chief and cardinal statements of the Augsburg Confession and her Apology, in the very concept of the Church. The *ecclesia* is to be sought there, so the Augustana teaches, where, next to the proclamation of the Word, "*recte administrantur sacramenta*" ["the Sacraments are rightly administered"] (AC VII). However, precisely for this reason the Apology teaches explicitly concerning the correct use of the Sacrament that it is a *nota ecclesiae* ["a mark of the Church"]; explicitly: "*pura evangelii doctrina et* ***adminstatio sacramentorum consentanea evangelio***" are "*externae notae, ut agnosci possit ecclessia*" ["the pure teaching of the Gospel and administration of the Sacraments according to the Gospel are **external marks** by which one may recognize the Church"] (Ap VII–VIII 5ff.). This is not said of the Body of Christ or of the invisible Church, but rather of the Church as a confessional church (cf. Ap VII–VIII 20). If, then, the administration of the Sacraments serves to the end that one is able to recognize where the *pura doctrina* ["pure doctrine"] and a living Church that confesses in accordance with the Gospel is to be found, then, on the one hand, a confession of the Church is present in the administration of the Sacraments, and, on the other hand, a demand is made of the individuals to decide whether they share this confession. Where these individuals seek the Sacrament should determine where they hope to find the Church that rightly teaches and confesses. This corollary is so self-evident and incontestable that in the article concerning the "*usus sacramentorum*" ["use of the Sacraments"] the confession can simply assume it as a conceded presupposition: "*non modo ut sint notae professionis inter homines*" ["they are not only marks of profession among men"]. It is simply unnecessary to look for an array of individual statements in the Confessions. This understanding can only be characterized as a fundamental presupposition of the entire Lutheran understanding of the Church. Additionally, we know of a public expression, which is already much older, applied by Luther to the matter in the Latin Mass. Concerning the application of the *usus sacramenti* ["use of the Sacrament"] in practice, Luther wrote: "*nam hujus communio coenae est pars confessionis*" ["for communion in this Supper is a part of confession"].[37]

One could say concerning this last expression—which is echoed in the addition of "the Christians" in the German version of the Augsburg Confession—that

37 ["*Nam huius communio caenae est pars confessionis, qua coram Deo angelis et hominibus sese confitentur esse Christianos*" (WA 12:216.25; cf. AE 53:34). MH]

it is more reminiscent of the manner in which the *professio* in the Supper is emphasized by Zwingli and the other Reformed. For what we have above deduced from the concept of the "*nota ecclesia*" ["marks"] is not the general profession of Christians, but rather the specific confession, inasmuch as it serves to express taking a position within the visible Church. Thus with each reception of the Supper within one's own fellowship, the relationship of the individual to the Church as member is renewed in the same sense in which [one's] first Communion meant the acceptance of that same individual into conscious Church membership. Conversely, however, the expression in the Latin Mass turns out to be qualified in another way by the immediate context. For here there is no talk of admission, but only that the communicant should line up at a particular location in the church so that he is visible to all. It deals with external ceremonial conduct, the inner significance of which is demonstrated by Luther.[38] This passage is only valuable inasmuch as it is one of the earliest explanations to show how erroneous it is to characterize this line of thought as originally and exclusively Reformed or Zwinglian. However, we will discuss this below in more depth.

Conversely, Luther's explanations read much differently where the concern is the confession that distinguishes between pure doctrine and false doctrine in the fellowship of the Supper. All of Luther's statements that were cited above in the account of his practice fall into this catagory. There is no brotherhood in the sense of church fellowship without unity in doctrine, faith, and confession. Indeed, the act of confession comes into consideration for our particular question in just this way.

But Luther also discussed the question exhaustively and deduced (just as we have asserted it as a corollary of the Lutheran concept of Church) the second proposition that altar fellowship is confessional fellowship [*Bekenntnisgemeinschaft*] directly from the definition of the *notae ecclesiea* ["marks of the Church"]. In his writing *On the Councils and the Church,* an entire section deals with the issue: "By which signs the Christian Church is to be recognized." In the first place, he names the Word of God, and specifically where it is publicly confessed before the world (W[1] 16:2785ff. [*Von den Konziliis und Kirchen*, 1539; WA 50:509–653; StL 16:2144ff.; AE 41:3ff.; Aland 382]), then Baptism, and, finally, in third place the Supper (W[1] [16:]2788ff.). "Third, one recognizes God's people, or a Christian, holy people, in the holy Sacrament of the Altar, **where it is properly distributed according to Christ's institution, believed and received**. For it is also a public sign and treasured relic [*Heiligtum*] left behind by Christ, whereby His people are sanctified, where they practice **and publicly confess** that they are Christians, as they do with the Word and Baptism. . . . So, **when you see such a Sacrament**

38 The passages where Luther emphasizes in opposition to house Communion that "the Sacrament" is "a public confession" or should be "a public and common confession" belong here as well. W[1] 10:2738ff. [*3-7-35 an Barbara Lisskirchen*; WA Br 6:86; Aland Br 2184].

distributed in its proper use, then you may know for sure there is God's people. And though quite a few false and unbelieving Christians are secretly among them, they do not, however, desecrate the people of God, especially because they are unknown. For the Church or God's people does not suffer those who are openly false, but rather punishes and sanctifies them also, or when they will refuse, it expels them."

These passages are no less conclusive because they, in a way similar to the expression of the Symbols, betray a certain vagueness regarding the visible and invisible Church. As is known, the relationship of the predicate to the subject in "*communio sanctorum*" ["communion of the saints"] in Article VII [of the Augustana] is subject to the same misunderstanding. It would be a great injustice to the reformers were someone to attribute to them the position that they had viewed the Lutheran Church as *ecclesia proprie sic dicta* ["the Church strictly speaking"]. The Apology already distinguishes the *notae* ["marks"] somewhat more clearly as a consequential factor for the *agnosci*, that is, for the tangible appearance of the true Church.

Historical context makes the expression understandable. At the beginning of the Reformation, there were not fully developed, coexistent confessional churches as we now have. Rather, within the one large fellowship which had, however, fallen into false public teaching and patronage [*Spendung*], the evangelical believers existed as "*sparsi*" [i.e., those strewn among the multitude]. They were still not bound by any sort of external unity, whereas on the Roman side one could point to the one head and the episcopal organization. Only from pure teaching and the correct administration of the Sacraments could one recognize where the Gospel had dominance. The recognition of orthodox teaching and administration of the Sacraments served, at first, as a division over against the old church fellowship. That is why Luther mostly addresses this in connection with the reception of the Sacrament *sub una* ["under one kind"]. However, as soon as divisive doctrine and use of the Sacrament emerged among the Protestants themselves, we see Luther applying the exact same principles against the Reformed, and thus the concept of *nota* ["mark"] and of a confessional decision in the choice of the Supper among the individual confessional churches. It is within this context that the decision was put before the Frankfurters as to "whether they should go with the crowd to the Sacrament" where the preachers "neither teach nor believe that the body and blood are truly in bread and wine" (W^{1} 17:2436 [*Ein Brief an die zu Frankfurt am Main. D.M. Luther*, 1533;[39] WA 30/3:558–71; StL 17:2007ff.; Aland 225])—or as Luther expresses it in another place: "If we accept them as brothers, then we must be complicit in their doctrine" (W^{1} 3:2617 [*5. Mose* 9, 12–19–29; WA 28:737–63; Aland Pr 1106).

39 See also Jon Vieker's translation in chapter 1 of this book: above, pp. 1–19.

Subsequently, if we observe that the entire practice and all of the expressions of faculty opinions are founded upon this principle, then it is not an overextension of the original principle, but rather the very expression of the long-recognized consequence of the Lutheran principle. Thus the opinion of the Wittenberg faculty from 1568, quoted above, reads:[40] "**Thus the use of the Supper is, as are all Sacraments, a public testimony and confession as to which Church an individual belongs and which doctrine, faith, and religion each individual maintains, believes, confesses, and holds to be doubtless as the eternal and unchanging divine truth**. When, therefore, it becomes apparent through a rejection of our doctrine and confession that someone is not a member of this Church and that he condemns the same Church as errant in his conscience, then such a one may not be accepted among us into fellowship in God's Church through the enjoyment and use of this Supper. For such an acceptance begs to be seen as silent praise and approval of inappropriate and false condemnation of the Church's faith or (and this is even more heinous and despicable) as contemptuously casting to the winds that which one believes and maintains concerning this Supper."

An opinion of the Leipzig faculty from 1648 makes the appeal that this understanding of the use of the Sacrament has always been characteristic for the Church. "It is certain and the apostle Paul clearly teaches (1 Corinthians 10:17) ["Because there is one bread, we who are many are one body, for we all partake of the one bread"] that among the ends of the Holy Supper, besides strengthening faith, this is by no means the least, namely, that the communicants thereby signify the **unity of faith** that they share with one another in the measure in which this Communion has been treasured since the beginning of Christianity and in all places as a sign of the unity in faith. For through the admission of persons of a Calvinist inclination, those who do not have the true faith concerning the Holy Supper are inappropriately brought into this unity."[41]

All of the casuists judge similarly: "*Cum quibus de eadem coena participamus, cum his communionem habemus et doctrinam eorum tacite approbamus*" ["If we participate in the same meal with such persons, we have communion with them and tacitly approve their doctrine"], says [Friedrich] Balduin [1575–1627].[42] He refuses, therefore, the admission of all who are not *eccleсsiis nostris fide conformes*[43] ["in agreement with the faith of our churches"]. G[eorg] König [1590–1664] explains the Supper as *nota et tessera religionis, quam quisque profetur* ["signs and

40 Dedekenn 1:634ff.

41 Dedekenn (Appendix) 4:433. This is also a proof that Rietschel unjustly seeks to explain the more lax opinion of the same faculty from 1626 as the result of a "more mild viewpoint" that was previously present.

42 *Tractatus de casibus conscientiae*. Wittenberg 1628 II, 12. p. 326

43 *Tractatus de casibus conscientiae*, 814.

tokens of the religion that one professes"] and demands the explicit confession of the consumption of the body and blood while cognizant of the various types and numbers of those who are to be examined.[44] See also [Ludwig] Dunte [1597–1639], *Decisiones casuum* 1664. p 507. [Friedeman] Bechmann [1628–1703], *Theol. conscientiaria* 1692. p. 199 et al. Even still in [Salomon] Deyling [1677–1755] we find the unperturbed clarity of the old doctrinal expression: "***Sacramenta sunt notae confessionis****. Qui coeunt et iisdem utuntur sacramentis, eandem profitentur fidem, et sunt ejusdem ecclesiae membra, spirituali unione inter se conjuncta*" ["The Sacraments are marks of confession. Those who make use of the same sacraments profess the same faith and are members of the same Church joined together in a spiritual union"]. Upon this he establishes the necessity of a reciprocal exclusion from altars.[45]

Such mediating characters as [Johann Conrad] Dannhauer [1603–66] and [Philipp Jakob] Spener refused to mediate here. The former, in his "Reformed salvo,"[46] calls it the "sacramental watchword" or "the flag." Spener, however, invokes that "this Sacrament is regarded by every part of Christianity as the bond of their unity." Even in view of the peaceful compromise of the Reformed Synod at Charenton (see below), he holds fast to the opposite position: "Because Communion with a congregation entails approving of that congregation's doctrine, especially in the article on the Sacrament . . . I do not see how we can make use of Communion among those churches whose very doctrine of Communion we do not believe or confess to be correct and therefore make one confession with the **mouth** and another by our **deed**." "Thus this Sacrament has always been regarded in the churches as a *publicum symbolum* ['public expression'] and *tessera* ['token'] of religion and confession of faith." Much offense has been taken at my expression that the Supper is a "**watershed**" in this sense (Rietschel, p. 29). But Spener says: "Therefore, this point is the most obvious partition between both religions. . . . How, then, can they have a common Supper with one another?"[47]

In terms of ecclesiastical jurisprudence, this was called *effectus externus* or *judicus*. According to [Justus Henning] Böhmer [1674–1749] it is "*principalis effectus externus, qui etiam juridicus est, quod communionis et fraternitatis jus indicat, ut qui ad S. coenam admittitur, pro membro ecclesiae habeatur*"[48] ["the principle external effect, which is also judicial, which indicates a right of Communion and fraternity that whoever is admitted to the Holy Supper is considered a member of the Church"]. . . . Hence the formula of the ancient Church:

44 *Casus consientiae*. Altdorf, 1654. pp. 596ff.

45 *Institutiones prudentiae pastoralis*, ed. Küstner (Leipzig, 1768).

46 Cf. Delitzsch, *Die bayrische Abendmahlsgemeinschaftsfrage*, 29.

47 *Letzte theologische Bedenken* 2:4ff. and 3:81, 83ff.

48 *Jus ecclesiasticum*. Tom III, lib. 3, tit. 41, § 42.

Ne quis ex catechumenis, ne quis ex audientibus, ne quis ex infidelibus; ne quis ex haereticis!" ["No one who is a catechumen, no one who is a hearer, no one who is a pagan, no one who is a heretic, (shall commune)!"]

We conclude this proof with Johann Gerhard's main propositions concerning the relevant doctrine. Hopefully, Pastor Rietschel will admit him as an unsuspicious witness of the Lutheran doctrinal perspective. He treats the *notae ecclesiae* ["marks of the Church"] exhaustively in vol. XI pp. 187ff., and the *finis* and *usus* ["purpose and use"] of the Holy Supper in vol. X, 363ff., ed Cotta.[49]

---

49 Vol. XI, p. 192: "The Word and Sacraments are, simply speaking, marks of the church. For, wherever the word is spoken and the holy Sacraments are administered, there is the church to some extent. However, because there are not the same level of purity and sincerity in the churches, we say: the pure preaching of the Word and the legitimate administration of the Sacraments are marks of the church from which the pure church may be distinguished from the corrupt and impure."

p. 194: "As pertains to the meetings of the heretics, if a legitimate and complete Baptism is administered among them and if they have preserved uncorrupted the principle parts of the doctrine of Baptism, then it cannot be denied that to some extent the church is gathered among them before God." Therefore, even in the seventeenth century, it was not taught that the Lutheran Church is **the** Church. (Cf. Rietschel, p. 39.) Cf. 212: The Lutheran church is true and sincere as the orthodox church.

p. 195: "Just as the church may be distinguished from profane meetings outside of the church through the preaching of the Word and the administration of the Sacraments, so through the pure preaching of the Word and the legitimate administration of the holy Sacraments the church is distinguished from those meetings of the heretics who are in the church."

p. 198: "What sort of church it is, is judged by what sort of doctrine is spoken in the public ministry of that church."

p. 206: "Although the reprobate are mixed in with the elect and the bad with the good in that assembly in which the Gospel is purely preached and the holy Sacraments are legitimately administered, that is, in the particular churches . . . nevertheless because of this pure preaching of the Word and legitimate use of the Sacraments we know that there are some of the elect there and, consequently, the church which we can safely join.

p. 207: "'Lutherans confess that their churches do not lack freckles' (Bellarmine). By freckles which stick to the church we do not mean heretical doctrines, but rather opinions which do not fight against the basis of faith."

p. 212: "The legitimate use of the Sacraments should be judged from their essentials."

Vol. X, p. 371: It belongs to the "lesser goals of the Holy Supper": "that we give testimony that we approve the doctrine which is preached in that church in which we consume the same bread together with others and drink from one chalice (1 Cor. 10:17)."

p. 184: "We do not doubt that there are, indeed, a great number of hearers in the churches of the Calvinists who have purer ears than the lips of their teachers; however, if we want to judge the writings and arguments of the adversaries, we must confess that the question is not concerning the mode of presence but rather concerning the very presence of the body and blood of Christ" (cf. above XI, 212, the "essentials").

p. 381: "But not all Christians should be admitted indiscriminately to the Holy Supper (1 Cor. 11:28, cf. vv. 26, 31). Therefore all who are imbued with heresy are excluded, that is, those who obstinately and stubbornly persevere in an error against the basis of faith, having

After all of this, it will be impossible for Rietschel to turn a blind eye to the fact that his second thesis, "that it is un-Lutheran to characterize altar fellowship as an act of confession," also contains a gross distortion of historical facts. Whoever is not more certain of his case should have misgivings about writing off men, as they are listed on p. 25, with the question: "Where is the proof?" In a matter in which proof can be found among any one of the Lutheran dogmaticians, it might perhaps be permitted to assume some knowledge of this. In any case, the desired proof has been delivered.

Rietschel errs no less by characterizing our understanding of the act of confession as a distinctive of the Zwinglian—that is, Reformed—doctrinal view.

Admittedly, Reformed dogmatics, as is known, teaches something closely related: for example, Calvin says (*Inst.* IV 1,8): "*Ecclesiae visibilis signa sunt sincera verbi praedicatio et sacramentorum legitimus usus; ita, ut pro ecclesiae membris agnoscamus, qui et fidei confessione et vitae exemplo et sacramentorum participatione eundem nobiscum Deum ac Christum profitentur*"[50] ["The signs of the visible Church are the sincere preaching of the Word and the legitimate use of the sacraments; in this way we may recognize the members of the Church who by confession of faith, example of life, and participation in the sacraments profess with us the same God and Christ"]. This fundamental perspective also explains why for the most part during the time of strict observance the same practice is to be observed on the Reformed side as among most Lutherans (see above, pp. 16ff.). However, this would not therefore characterize it as an original distinction, nor do the Reformed derive from this principle that confessional character which they specifically attribute to the consumption of the Supper which Pastor Rietschel also has in mind. Considering that this aspect tends to be treated by them in an entirely different place, he could have been more careful in his application. That confessing which has been emphasized by all of the Reformed since [Huldrich] Zwingli and [Johannes] Oecolampadius [1482–1531] is essentially thanksgiving. This completely explains the use that the Reformed make of this concept in the catechism especially in connection with the Supper.[51] Paired with this thanksgiving is the confession of the benefits bestowed to Christians in the death of Christ, and this confession of the death of Christians becomes a confession of the Christians as Christians at the Supper. Calvin gives the clearest expression to precisely this thought (IV, 17, 37): "*Coena Domini nos admonet, ne tam . . . effusae beneficientiae*

disregarded the steps of admonition; since, therefore, they have separated themselves from fellowship in the true church, they should by no means be admitted to the Sacrament, which is the church's own goods, who obstinately deny the true and substantial presence of Christ's body and blood in the Holy Supper."

50 Cf. the other witnesses in Schweizer, *Die Glaubenslehre der evangelisch reformierten Kirche* (Zürich, 1847), 2:670ff.

51 Cf. my *System der Katechetik* II, 1. S. 302f.

ingrati simus, quin potius landibus [sic] praedicemus eam. Celebratur in memoriam Christi mortui, that is, publice palam fateri, totam salutis ac vitae fiduciam in moret domini nobis positam esse, ut nostra illum confessione glorificemus et alios nostro exemplo exhortemur. Secundus usus ad confessionem externam attinet, tertius est exhortatio ad sanctimoniam vitae.—Ergo" (he says, listing the *usus* altogether)—"*ergo (1) confirmatio fidei, (2) confessio externa, (3) excitatio ad officium.*" ["The Lord's Supper admonishes us, lest we be unthankful for such abundant benefits, that we should rather proclaim it with praise. It is celebrated in the memory of Christ's death, that is, it is openly and publicly confessed that the entirety of salvation and faith is given to us in the death of Christ, that we might glorify Him by our confession and exhort others by our example. The second use pertains to external confession; the third is an exhortation to a holy life.—Therefore, it is (1) a confirmation of faith, (2) an external confession, (3) a call to service in one's office or vocation.] That there is, however, no essential difference between the later Reformed and Zwingli can be shown from the latter's words (*Opp.* III, 240): "*Christus hac coena voluit jucundam sui commemorationem fieri, gratias publicas haberi pro beneficio, quod in nos liberaliter expendit; est enim eucharistia gratiarum actio. Qui . . . huic interest, toti se ecclesiea probat, ex eorum esse numero qui Christo fident, unde et communio vocatur*" ["Christ wanted this meal to be a pleasing remembrance of Himself, a public thanksgiving held for the benefit, which He liberally gives among us. It is His concern to prove that of the whole Church, there is a number who trust in Christ, whence it is also called a communion"]. Here it is a matter of a confession toward **God** of a general Christian sort, as Luther calls it in a somewhat related way in other passages cited above (pp. 44ff.) Conversely, we speak of an act of confession, which gives testimony before men, namely, the Church, as to which confessional fellowship one adheres. And we have established this to be the Lutheran perspective from the Symbols' concept of the *notae ecclesiae* ["marks of the Church"]. Now what does the one have in common with the other, and what should we call it when someone undertakes on account of this concept to accuse a Lutheran of a Zwinglian view?

When Pastor Rietschel uses the fact that I cite sources such as Schleiermacher and Nitzsch to raise suspicion, I regret to have to characterize this again as a conspicuous misunderstanding. Of course, these two absolutely could not serve as witnesses for such a confessional exclusivity. Rather, we have simply taken the opportunity to point out what place Schleiermacher himself and his successor, as systematicians of practical theology, grant to the Supper in worship and for the concept of education in the Church [*Kirchenbildung*]. Whoever considers, as they do, the Holy Supper to be the actual goal of the catechuminate must consequently also recognize it as the thing which makes the particular church [i.e., a church of a particular confession] exclusive in its worship. I have expressed myself on this exhaustively enough elsewhere, so I consider myself safe from such misjudgments.[52]

Finally, the not insignificant circumstance rightly emphasized by Pastor Rietschel—that the older Lutheran Church did not put such an emphasis upon the distribution formula as would be expected by their view of the Sacrament as an act of confession—requires a word of correction. It is entirely correct that a great diversity of practice in the use of the distribution formula can be observed in the Lutheran agendas of the sixteenth century. It is not uncommon that the use of such a formula is not even mentioned.[53] It can be ignored even less that later on a greater emphasis was placed upon the distribution, and in the course of the struggles against the Union it achieved the significance of a completely indispensable act of confession. In this, too, we can only agree with Pastor Rietschel that the distribution formula, considered in and of itself, is nothing more than the expression of individual application as it has been carefully expained by the older Lutheran authorities.

But precisely this last viewpoint serves well as an explanation why the older Lutheran teachers believed they could do without this aspect of confession. We have already seen that the Formula of Concord itself characterizes the auditory confession of the Words of Institution over the elements to be an indispensable part of a correct celebration of the Supper [*Abendmahlshandlung*]. Among its negative theses is the statement that whereas "the Words of Institution are omitted by some in the celebration of the Supper," this may "by no means" occur.[54] In the affirmative, on the other hand, it is emphasized as a particular purpose [of the Words of Institution] that "the faith of the one who hears . . . would be strengthened . . . concerning the presence of the body and blood of Christ." Thus the act of confession is to be sought in the word of consecration, an assertion collaborated by comparison with the above quotes from Chemnitz. The application could not in any way say anything new or different. However, the focus of the confessional struggle of that time was the Words of Institution. Luther, therefore, always only referred to these for matters of practice. This also helps to understand why at Luther's suggestion the act of consecration itself was in many cases divided such that the chalice was consecrated and distributed only after the same was done with the host, so that the distribution of each part was connected much more directly to the consecration and to prevent the distribution from being made into an independent, isolated act. Additionally, as can be abundantly attested, the hymns sung

52 Cf. *System der Katechetik* I, 439, 723, and 443.

53 Mostly following Bugenhagen's example: "How a common Mass should be held," Wittenberg 1542. It corresponds to the fact that Bugenhagen exclusively valued the consecration. Cf. for the latter the evidence in Dedekenn 1:576 and König, Dedekenn 1:515.

54 FC SD VII 121. Cf. the affirmative thesis, FC SD VII 79ff.

during Communion were conceived as a confession of the congregation, for which Luther's Communion hymns "Christus unser Heiland" ["Jesus Christ, Our Blessed Savior"] and "Gott sei gelobet und gebenedeiet" ["O Lord, We Praise Thee"] were particularly suited.[55] The confessional position which the fellowship took toward the Words of Institution was, so to speak, the general confession about the form in which the Words of Institution are applied, namely, the sense with which it presented the Sacrament to its members [i.e., a clear confession of the body and blood of Christ in the Sacrament].

This is why Lutherans called the words of consecration not only *verba invocationis et sanctificationis*, but even "*sermo* ***testificationis***," which the Leipzig faculty explained on January 12, 1620, as "a certain testimony, that here the servants of the Church act as stewards of God and want to bestow this mystery, that by virtue of the order and institution of Christ the blessed bread is a participation in the body and the wine is a participation in the blood of Christ, and that not only bread and wine but at the same time the body and blood of Christ are received and enjoyed by the communicants."[56] This is why here, too, the necessity of the words of consecration is asserted as absolute. In this sense, Chemnitz calls them nothing less than "the proper, only, actual word of this Sacrament."[57]

Conversely, regarding **distribution**, the Wittenberg faculty explained in various opinions of 1616 and 1619 that the formula of distribution is "not [to be considered] as an essential piece belonging to the substance nor as an integral piece belonging to the proper completeness of the Supper." This is expressly because the Words of Institution already do the corresponding work. However, the distribution formula is recommended so that the *actio* [i.e., action of distribution] would not be *muta* ["silent"] and to increase edification. With this the opinion from 1616 suggests that those territorial churches in which the formula "Take [eat], this is the body, etc." had not been in use should use the formula in the future for the sake of uniformity. Likewise, an opinion of the Leipzig faculty gives preference to this formula among various forms in question.[58] It is a mistake when Rietschel says that the formula "the true body" was approved (p. 32). A reference to the Saxon Church Order of 1580 could set him straight (cf. Richter 2:439).

The matter had to gradually take on another form after union formulae had been consciously suggested or introduced. The Heidelberg dispute between [Tilemann] Hesshusius [1527–88] and Wilhelm Klebitz [1533–68] is the

55 This corresponds to the use of the Greek Church, where in the place of any other words the choir sings the following during the distribution: "Take the body of Christ, drink from the immortal spring. Hallelujah, Hallelujah, Hallelujah!"

56 Dedekenn 1:575.

57 Dedekenn 1:576.

58 Dedekenn 1:577ff. The Lutheran casuists of the seventeenthth century take the exact same position. Cf. Dunte, 509. Bechman, 222. Especially König.

first example of this sort. Requested by the count of the Palatinate to mediate, Melanchthon proposed the distribution formula: "The bread which we break is the fellowship of the body"[59] as a union formula ("*remotis contentiosis prodest reliuos de una forma verborum convenire*" ["benefits the contentious, distant parties to agree on one formula words for the future"]). On the other hand, the crypto-Calvinists in Saxony used the fomula: "Take and eat, may your faith in the sacrificed body of Christ sustain you unto eternal life" (cf. Richter 2:439).

Under such circumstances the earlier relatively inconsequential nature[60] of this issue had to end, as the Saxon Church Order of 1580 demonstrates. Indeed, under such circumstances the words of distribution were no longer made to serve merely the application but rather the explanation of the meaning by partisan tendencies within the Church. Already from this point on a *status confessionis* ensued, although the old tradition continued to have an effect for some time. As is known, the form "the true [*wahre*] body" stems from the crypto-Calvinist disputes, a form which **Hunnius** was particularly active in spreading in northern Germany.

The same thing applies today to the distribution formula of the Union: "[Take eat.] Christ says [this is My body], etc." (Prussian Agenda).[61] The intention is unmistakable. Although even for this formula one could point to an instance from a more harmless time. It was used early on in Ulm, whose first ecclesiastical institutions admittedly stem from Bucer. However, the case of Seiler has been decisive for the spread of this formula in our century. In his time, he recommended it with the characteristic words that "he had already used it among certain enlightened persons, and it had been received quite well."[62]

---

59 *Corpus Reformatorum* 9:962. Opinion from November 1, 1559. Melanchthon's misuse of these words is suggested in FC SD VII 59ff.

60 It is not absolutely certain whether the Erbacher Agenda from 1560 (Richter *Kirchenordnungen* 2:223) can be judged as a strictly Lutheran agenda purely according to the criterion of harmlessness given its form: "Recall that the body of Christ is given for you in death."

61 My honored friend Kahnis perhaps no longer maintains all of the statement of his polemic against Nitzsch on "The Matter of the Lutheran Church over against the Union" (1854). However, he has very recently given a clear and straightforward testimony to the significance of altar fellowship as an act of confession. (Reformation program v. 1868. cf. d. Referat in Luthard, *Allgem ev. luther. Kirchenzeitung* 1868. pp. 81ff.)—Concerning the use of the united distribution formula on the part of a Lutheran it reads: "As often as you stand at the altar and administer the Sacrament according to the agenda you are committing a denial of your own confession" (p. 80). The general correctness of the Lutheran position in the struggle over the Sacrament in the Church is characterized by the testimony of the Reformation program (op. cit. p. 86): "If Luther and his sort were of the firm conviction that their doctrine was the only evangelical one—which no one can dispute—then it lay within their position to surrender unity rather than give up the truth."

62 *Allgem. Sammlung liturgischer Formeln* 1804. vol. 3, p. 16.

We have come to the end of our historical evidence for the theory and practice of the Lutheran Church in its normative epoch. A few things about the subsequent development can serve as a transition to the current status of the issue. The result of that epoch is, however, doubtless: the administration of and admittance to the Supper were generally conceived of as an act of confession and duty of the confessor, and the Reformed were as a matter of principle viewed as excluded from the Lutheran Supper. The main question for the present consists in how far the conduct of those who belong to the Union churches is to be subordinated to the same norms that applied to the Reformed in the normative epoch.

III. THE PRESENT STATUS OF THE ISSUE

The seventeenth century brought with it a certain mitigation of the old antagonisms. The Peace of Westphalia [1648] brought an end to the ignoble condition of intolerance according to which those to whom ecclesial fellowship was denied on account of confessional opposition were not even tolerated as citizens. Of course, afterward a second stage of development followed in which—without any changes having occurred in the confessional conflict—even the exercise of the Church's position on altar fellowhsip was decried as intolerance. All the same, the victory of the political worldview, won in the throes of the Thirty Years' War, over the theological worldview took longer than would have been expected. The ecclesiastical conscience was too deeply rooted no less among the Reformed as a whole as among the Lutherans.

Pastor Rietschel mentions a case in which a theological faculty of such stature as Leipzig (which we have observed to give strong opinions expressing a different view [from standard orthodox positions] around this time period and even later) encouraged a Lutheran pastor to administer the Office of the Ministry [*Amt*] to a Reformed congregation and alongside Reformed clergy and to make all sorts of concessions in ceremonies. These are not completely isolated instances (the case in question occurred in the year 1626).[63] But the Wittenberg faculty rendered judgments in these very instances in a completely opposite manner.[64] Instead, it appears to us that they cannot be explained apart from the false view, which had gained ground in the Lutheran Church, concerning the ecclestical authority of territorial patronage [i.e., the prince was forcing his will contrary to Lutheran teaching]. It is worth noting that already Balduin had asserted the right of the congregation against such a misuse of the authority of patronage. Balduin judged in the context of cases such as the one mentioned above: "*Fit hoc interdum in amplissimis rebus*

63 Dedekenn, *Appendix*, 474ff. The case in which the Leipzig faculty also had to provide advice (1651) was somewhat different. Dedekenn, *Appendix*, 600ff.

64 Cf. *Consil. theol. Witeberg*. 2:127ff.

publicis, ubi multi sunt errores, sicut in magnis fluminibus multae sordes"[65] ["Now and again it happens that there are many errors in very public matters, just as there is much filth in large rivers"]. The theological faculty at Jena decided much differently and strictly in cases where the conflict appeared much smaller, even where only private circumstances were affected.[66]

Tholuck has painstakingly (and with a list of records rarely available) sought out examples of more lax practice in the seventeenth century and has only found those few that were published in the *Deutschen Zeitschrift* 1852, no. 16.[67]

Even irenic-minded theologians have come to conclusions contrary to Rietschel. We have already mentioned Spener's understanding of the Sacrament (p. 45). A few testimonies will demonstrate the consequence it had. Although he also pastored the Reformed in Frankfurt as those assigned to his congregation,[68] he warned against them as false prophets in public sermons in Frankfurt.[69] He disapproved of a mild form of the admission of the Reformed that was popular in Württemberg.[70] And he confessed that in danger of death he would rather take the Sacrament from a layman of his Church than from a Calvinist clergyman.[71] Here should be mentioned especially those passages in which he goes as far as to deny to the Reformed the name of brother. "Since," he writes in one place,[72] "Christianity has been divided into numerous parties on account of false doctrine which has crept in, I can call no one brothers except those who confess themselves members of the Lutheran Church." The other most explicit witness is found in the last *Theologische Bedenken* (1:605): "As concerns external brotherhood which is founded upon the fellowship of the faith or religion that one believes, all Lutherans are my brothers since they confess and adhere to one faith. But not one of the Reformed, as long as he remains such, is my brother, because he professes adherence to another religion—in fact, such a religion which I believe has recognized dangerous errors." Spener's return to Luther's position is even more significant considering that already at the Religious Dialogue of Cassel [July 1–9, 1661] the theologians of the University of Ritteln (among whom was [Johann] Musäus [1613–81]) had pledged the name brother to the Reformed—admittedly under

65 Balduin, *Tractatus de casibus conscientiae*, 345.

66 Dedekenn, *Appendix*, 709ff.

67 Cf. Tholuck, *Das kirchliche Leben des 17. Jahrhunderts* I, 50.

68 *Theologische Bedenken* 1:285.

69 *Letzte theol. Bed.* 3:272; cf. Canstein's *Vorrede*, 61, and Hossbach, *Spener*, 152.

70 *Consil. lat.* 1:391.

71 *Consil. lat.* 1:448.

72 "*Uebereinstimmung mit der Augsburger Confession*" (Spener's decisive writing against those at Wittenberg from 1695), 226.

protest from various Lutheran provinces.[73] Accordingly, Pastor Rietschel is admittedly right to use an exclamation point to underscore his misgivings [to the fact] that I talk about Reformed "brothers." I hope to be able to justify myself.

The theologically mediating [Johann Franz] Buddeus [1667–1729] renews and even intensifies all the old principles against mixing confessions when in 1712 he was called upon to give an opinion regarding the proposal for the unification of both Protestant churches. "The fraternal fellowship in all spiritual goods, especially in the Holy Supper, is impossible where there is no fellowship of faith. This, however, cannot humanly [*menschlicher Weise*] be presumed where all points of doctrine are not correct which are necessary for faith, so that such a fellowship would be produced and maintained among us."[74] A comparison of the 1721 *editio novissima* of [Johann Benedict] Carpzov's [1565–1624] famous *Jurisprudentia consistorialis* according to its main section with the *Additiones* from Beyer (which in a separate section adds all of the retractions) provides an insight into just how long legal policies which the Peace of Westphalia had already revoked remained in effect, particularly in Saxony. When finally at the end of the eighteenth century the ecclesiastical legal constitution, repugnant to the spirit of age, had been entirely forgotten, a sort of social sense of propriety had survived. This was used as a principle to at least excuse that which in practice no one dared advocate any longer. An instructive example of this is a work that had faded into obscurity even in Saxony: *Praktische Anweisung zu richtiger Anwendung der Kinchenrechte in den chursächs. Landen*, Wilhelm Friedrich Kunze [1735–1805] (pastor at Dippoldiswalde), Dresden, 1789—not without worth as a source for historical facts. Here in part III. c. 8. paragraph 5 (p. 221) the case is explicitly addressed as to whether "one [may] administer the Supper to Christians of another confession in an emergency." "The objection," so it reads, "made by a few is that the communal use of the Holy Supper belongs to the close association of the members of a Church who are at one in their opinions and doctrinal views. Anyone else, therefore, who differs from our doctrinal views and does not view himself as a member of our Church cannot be drawn into that close association. He is in error, and because he will not give up his error, we cannot accept him into the closer unity of the Church. The withholding of the Supper cannot be viewed as an injustice and atrocity. It is not an injustice, because it is not unjust to withhold something from someone that he did not otherwise want and would also not desire in the future under different circumstances. It is not an atrocity, because the external act of the Supper saves no one, but only the faith which does not depend upon the external act." So far the arguments of the others.

---

73 Calov, *Hist. syncret.* 629; cf. 613.

74 Cf. Sal. Cyprian, *Abgedrungener Untericht von kirchlicher Vereinigung der Protestanten* (Leipzig, 1726), 404. (Cf. 411.)

"I [Kunze] answered: The common use of the Holy Supper through the office and administration of a preacher of the Church admittedly belongs to the closer association of the members of this Church. In this respect, a Christian of another confession belongs to this closer association just as little as a stranger belongs to an exclusive society. However, just as it can occur that someone may out of Christian love allow a stranger access to the goods reserved for an exclusive society, so also one may serve a Christian of another confession, who in this respect is not a closer member of our Church, with the most excellent acts of the divine office." Of course, the unionistic theology of our day has learned to defend its positions with other means.

The Reformed, too, held firmly to the old strict observance. [Ernst] Salamon Cyprian [1673–1745], in the foreword to the book from which we quoted that objection by Buddeus, brings to mind the explanation "of a most renowned Reformed teacher" (he means [Francis] Turretinus [1623–87]), almost contemporaneous with Buddeus): "Ecclesial fellowship cannot take place among those who are divided regarding the basis of faith," etc. (p. 7). Only the French Reformed Church officially altered the practice. "The Decree in Favor of Our Brothers, the Lutherans," released by the Synod of Charenton in 1631,[75] is so beautiful that only with a full sense of the pain of having to learn to live with brothers who have been separated in a Church in conflict can one read such a statement without feeling entitled to the corresponding counterstatement. Whoever judges appropriately will, along with Spener, recognize that it is their belief concerning the Supper which draws tighter borders around Lutherans.

In Germany, in particular, the confrontation was much harsher. Wherever the Reformed were locally dominant, there was no lack of oppression that was just as hateful as that which was elsewhere experienced by the Reformed at hands of the Lutherans. If reading about the oppression and harassment of the Reformed by the Hamburg *ministerium*[76] can only arouse sadness and disgust, then it must be said the treatment of the Lutheran Church and clergy under Duke Moritz of Hesse [1672–1732] is an example of intolerance without parallel on the other side.[77] Moreover, take a look at conditions in East Friesland[78] or pay attention to the testimony of reliable witnesses in this matter, such as that of Max Göbel in his account of Christian life in the Rheinland and Westphalia. "The relationship of the

75 It was the 26th French National Synod, which is to be regarded as the prototype of a free church governance. The 29th Synod, 1659/60, held at Loudün, confirmed the decision of Charenton, however not without certain provisos. The latter may be found in the *Evangelisch-Reform. Kirchenzeitung from Stähelin*. 1857. No. 39. 40.

76 Dedekenn, *Appendix*, 112ff.

77 Cf. Rommel, *Neuere Geschichte von Hessen* II, pp. 518ff.

78 Cf. Schlegel, *Kirchen- und Reformationsgeschichte von Norddeutschland und den Hanoverischen Staaten* II, pp. 430ff.

Reformed religion to the Lutheran was as a whole just as hostile and harsh as to the Catholic religion. Here the Reformed were clearly far more the oppressors than the oppressed, not so much in teaching and polemical preaching as in hindering worship and the establishment of congregations. Just as they had suffered grave injustice at the hands of Catholic rulers and their counsels and theologians, so they with the help of their Reformed territorial government committed grave injustices and through such measures of force embittered the Lutherans, who strove all the more acrimoniously against them in speech and print."[79]

Accordingly, it would be a one-sided and a completely ahistorical judgment to accuse only the Lutherans of harshness in their ecclesial exclusion of the Reformed. As long as both sides fought with means of state-sanctioned measures of force, the relationship was bound to bear a hateful character on both sides. How was it, once again, anything other than raw force with which the Prussian Union sought to oppress the renitent Lutherans in Silesia? What else has been the means with which this struggle has been renewed besides the intolerance of those states in which the union has been introduced, the intolerance with which congregations that wanted to live in the freedom of their old Lutheran congregational status are now at most granted the privileges of sects [*Sectenrecht*]?

However, the firstfruits of all of this for the Lutheran Church has been what blessed [Klaus] Harms [1778–1855] prophesied: "Luther's bones were given new life."[80] An ecclesial consciousness has recently been awakened which no one had considered possible in the the 1820s or even in the 1830s, an ecclesial consciousness which—praise God!—generally rejects anything other than weapons of the spirit and churchly, pastoral means for defense. If there are isolated occurrences of hatefulness, we stand in judgment of these. We could, however, at the same time cite scores of attempts of the most unworthy methods of warfare employed top-down by the principal organ of the Union.

We prefer, however, to return to the chief question. What is our present position toward the older principles of the Lutheran Church? First of all, we have to say that our agenda is littered with all sorts of questions and cases that did not exist back then. Besides the Reformed, we now have the United who demand rights as guests at altars of the Lutheran Church. Nevertheless, it would be easy to find parallels to these were the union to appear everywhere—as, for example, in the Palatinate—as a confessional union whereby the one confessional church unites with the other as such. But besides the confessional union there are also the unions of ecclesiastical government, whereby expressly the Reformed confessions are to retain their validity for congregations as well as for teachers and individuals. Thus

79 Göbel a.a.O. II, pp. 62ff. 65. Cf. 55.

80 [Harms produced 95 *Theses* against the Union and warned that if it were consummated above Luther's grave he would rise again in protest, and then woe to you! MH]

the United fall into three categories of those who demand rights as guests: those who are united in conscience and principle, those who want to remain Reformed within the union, and lastly those who are Lutheran within the Union. An awful mess! Old Spener was a prophet when in the face of the union proposals of his day he expressed the concern: "Two parties will turn into four!" Those who are conscientious among the Reformed have turned away in disgust just as conscientious Lutherans have. We had long since matured into a clear and simple situation of separate, peaceful lives and a relationship as neighbors. Why sacrifice this to a phantom of peace? In truth, admittedly, there are very real political interests at stake. Spener had already clearly perceived this when he declared suspect the proposals for union made in his own day on account of implicit political interests.[81]

The simple consequence of this would, of course, be that the altars of both confessional churches would be all the more indiscriminately open to all who desire admission in the name of the evangelical faith. Whether one talks about a right as guest or "a right and duty of administration" makes no substantive difference. In any case, it must be said that this all leads to the result of contributing to the general dominance of the principle of the Union. Among all that he has to say about an artificially achieved union, I cannot discern any conclusive testimony against the principle of a union in Pastor Rietschel's writing. No one even needs to ask him what his practical position on the most practical case is, namely, that men who have commanded influential offices in the Lutheran Church have no misgivings about accepting positions within the United Church which at the outset grant them the right of being regarded only as Lutherans within the union. Whoever has no objection to this betrays without a doubt that his supposed statement of principle lacks the seriousness of factual consistency.

Whenever the old Lutheran principles are invoked as the basis of church fellowship, the consequences are undeniable. According to that which we have above observed to be the result of history, it follows as a matter of course that there are no new factors [*Instanzen*] upon which the decision over against the Reformed and members of the confessional union is contingent. Lutherans who speak of a justified altar fellowship with such will, if they are upright and well-instructed, simply admit that they favor a more lax practice than was customary within our Church or allowed by her principles. The laws of church fellowship remain even when the opposition has been theologically formulated in manifold different ways and when living conditions among one another have changed. I, for my part, returning to that to which I earlier alluded, can do nothing else than recognize faithful members of those churches as brothers. In this matter we are only drawing other conclusions from old Lutheran premises. It was, in fact, consistent when men like Spener asserted that they could not call the Reformed as such brothers as long as

81 *Consil. lat.* 1:103.

one had to say of the Reformed confession that it denied essential, sacred things [*Heiligtümer*] of our Christian faith. Only those who show themselves to be children of God have the right to be called brothers, as far as human judgment has a right to [make such a judgment]. Those children of God are hardly all members of the Lutheran confessional Church, and yet, on the other hand, this Church itself has at all times acknowledged that there are children of God everywhere where there is but Word and Sacrament. Thus we say now as a consequence of the last statement: we call all believing Christians from every confession brothers.[82]

Whoever shares this position will gladly offer his hand in any form of free exchange regarding Christian concerns as far as no act of church fellowship is thereby included. I, in my own day, have had to suffer suspicions from Lutherans because I held apologetic lectures upon request in Reformed Basel. What would have been said were it generally known that in memory of the love of my dear friends there I have a "Basel room" in my study house, which would be open anytime to a pious Reformed Christian from Basel. A study house is, to be sure, not a church.

Nevertheless, I did not promise this to those at Basel until I had their statement that they were not unaware of my confessional stance and that a Lutheran of such a stance would be welcome to a brotherly helping hand. Also, my friends there could, unprovoked by me, provide a testimony to many conversations on altar fellowship. As little as they agree with me in principle, all the more they recognize, for example, that if Lutherans in general shared these principles, Lutheran congregations would have existed in every major city in Switzerland for some time now, just as much as there are Reformed congregations everywhere among us, and this to no disadvantage of the mutual growth of the Church.

It is easy to understand, then, that we are not asserting the difference in altar fellowship as a Christian duty, but rather as matter of ecclesiastical faithfulness, namely, as a faithfulness to the confessional Church. It is a witness to Rietschel's sense for justice that he wants to see the administration of the Means of Grace extended even to Catholics in emergencies (pp. 44ff.). But would he not have to admit that what would be considered an emergency would be completely different in the case of a Catholic as it would among the Reformed? The right and duty of a Christian is not alone decisive, but rather the Church's confession in its repercussions for the Supper. Therefore, we adopt this statement from Luther entirely: "**The Supper is not the Christian's, but rather the Lord's**." According to our interpretation, this means: The Lord's institution and the belief in this institution determines the position of each Church's conscience, and not the thoughts of men on the extent of fellowship boundaries. In matters of Christian brotherly love, a brother

82 Even Spener recognized this distinction; cf. *Letzte theologische Bedenken* 1:604ff. Cf. 3:408ff. [See the Preface to the Book of Concord. MH]

has claim to me and my service, even a brother of another confession. In matters of Church and ecclesiastical grace, however, that [Church] in which I serve is not mine, nor is it at my disposal. The institution of the Lord is binding in the understanding and confession of the Church which I serve.

If Pastor Rietschel draws his conclusions from the general right of Christians to the forgiveness of sins, then there is a preliminary question that needs to be answered first, which is presently of the greatest practical significance. The forgiveness of sins is not only obtained in the Holy Supper. The question is whether the private, yet official [*amtlich*, that is, delivered by the pastor] assurance of the forgiveness of sins does not have a wider legitimate use than the bestowal of a sacrament to which belongs the Church's celebration within the fellowship. Admittedly, in times past, narrower boundaries were drawn around this, but more so in casuistic circles without universally valid ecclesiastical norms. I am not asserting that I do not recognize these boundaries and would take it upon myself to derive from the generally recognized right to baptize children of another confession the right to grant the consolation of private Absolution to members of another confession in emergencies. But then, one could rightly demand of such that they let this suffice and not desire what belongs to the congregation as such according to the institution of the Lord, and which is an official act of the congregation and is at the same time always kept within the bounds of a confessional fellowship.

The difficult situation in which Lutheran pastors of the Baltic provinces presently find themselves is well-known. The nationals who let themselves be misled by false promises to convert *en masse* to the Greek Church now, overcome with remorse, desire the Sacrament in the Lutheran Church. However, because in this land of complete caeseropapism no one is allowed to convert from the Greek Church to another confession, they have to seek it out in secret. So in the face of an official affiliation with the Greek Church, they seek the false comfort of a secret affiliation with the Lutheran Church. For this reason they are not satisfied with desiring consolations of another sort; rather, they long especially for the enjoyment of the Supper. It would be difficult for such a person to persuade himself that he has any claim to membership in the Lutheran Church, if in the affliction of his conscience he were to be granted the forgiveness of his sins only in private. And yet he would have something far more substantial if he truly sought this than if he wanted to be able surreptitiously to consider himself a member of the Lutheran Church by means of some kind of seizure of the Holy Supper. It would be easy to determine whether he were motivated by the sincere need of his soul or by the desire for a false reassurance. However, it might obviously be feared that, by accommodating the desire of secret admittance to the Sacrament, the Lutheran Church of the Baltic provinces would put itself in danger of quieting her conscience with regard to another of her sacred duties. That is, I do not see how the Lutheran Church of the Baltic provinces can evade her duty of officially and as one man protesting against the unprecedented tyranny, which offends the justified sense for tolerance in every Christian nation, that is government policy against conversion to other confessions. What is now given the force of a law originally had only the bearing of an individual measure ordered in a handful of cases. (Cf. Harless, *Geschichtsbilder aus der lutherischen Kirche Livlands*, 28, and *Zeitschift für Prot. und Kirche*, June 1868, 369ff.)

In connection with the last mentioned confrontations, the question has been contemplated afresh by Lutheran theologians in particular as to whether or not all duties which confessional faithfulness otherwise dictates take a backseat in *articulo mortis* ["at the point of death"]. There is evidence at hand that our Church formerly held firmly to the consequence of being a confessional church even in this case. Yet here, too, another consequence may be juxtaposed. At the passage into eternity all of the rights of the Church militant are ceded. To this I add another open confession. I recognize the possibility of genuine, fervent cases of distress and conscience wherein the duty of confession can take a backseat to the pastoral [*seelsorgerlich*] faithfulness of the common office of Christian, ecclesiastical comfort. If, even in such cases, a Lutheran pastor would not dare administer the Sacrament, but instead out of duty limited himself to all other means of brotherly comfort, I would have to agree that he had acted legitimately. Consequently, I would urge anyone who thinks he should deal differently, that he should not do so without likewise admitting himself guilty of violating his duty in regard to his confessional church. However, I do recognize such emergencies in which I would submit myself to the duty of admitting my guilt and nevertheless, in the fear of violating a higher divine duty, would come to the aid of a truly distressed conscience with my church's service of the Sacrament. However, it seems to me that for such cases, which belong in the sphere of special care, private Communion is in order as a form of administration.

Of course, such emergency cases would require more justification than that a few of the Reformed or United had to travel a good distance to the next Reformed or United congregation and had difficulty doing so because of mundane circumstances. In such cases, I consider it the duty of every faithful servant of a confessional church not only to observe the boundaries of his church's confessional stance but also to strengthen the others in like duty to their own church. Oddly enough, Pastor Rietschel assigns this last duty only to Catholics. True Christian love and ecclesial patience is demonstrated in helping make it possible, even were it by one's own means and efforts, that those who as foreign church members desire to receive the Sacrament locally are able to do so by means of a traveling preacher or that they be provided with travel to the nearest parish of their confession. I would at any time offer assistance in establishing a Reformed parish for isolated members in a city where they were in sufficient number. I will not deny the difficulties of a practical implementation in larger cities (cf. Rietschel, pp. 52ff.); however, social situations provide still greater difficulties for the faithful administration of the office within one's own church. To simply point a gun at them means nothing other than abandoning the Church, whereas consistent faithfulness in individual circumstances has been blessed at all times, so that by means of such faithfulness new ways of structuring the Church have been opened up and recognized that are appropriate to the changed situation of the world and preserve the old faithfulness. It serves as a proof of just what is possible with determined faithfulness despite all the obstacles presented by social conditions that the Lutheran ministerium of a Bavarian city with a population of 20,000, of whom 17,000 are Protestant, a city in full industrial bloom, maintains the practice of permitting no one to receive the Holy Supper without an announcement, and directing to the closest Reformed congregation all those who are Reformed and United and do not want to convert to the Lutheran Church.

With this we have already approached the other question as to how to behave toward church members under a Union government with concern for the basic principles of the Lutheran Church. Wherever a confessional union does not determine the confessional stance of the individual members of a united territorial church, one has to decide on the basis of the confessional stance of the individual members or (under the assumption that such lack the seriousness of maintaining church fellowship in their own home church in the form of a certain and unanimous confessional stance) take the stance against them as a whole by denying all the right of being a guest at the Sacrament.

This brings to mind another excess of supposed ecclesial faithfulness that can be observed in a number of instances. Lutheran communicants go as far as to believe that they have to abandon the altars of clergy faithful to their confession even when these have expanded the borders of altar fellowship only in individual cases and for pastoral reasons. This goes beyond everything that was imposed by the old teachers as a confessional duty in regard to admission to the Supper and has already been characterized by my honored friend [Franz] Delitzsch as an incorrect consequence.[83] When a parson admits the heterodox not only in individual cases, for pastoral reasons, and with care taken against any sort of altar fellowship that does not regard confession, then it is justified to bear witness against this. Were a Lutheran clergyman to go even further and basically confess himself part of a mixed altar fellowship, then the right would have to be attributed to the congregation members to request a dismissal and seek altar fellowship where faithfulness to the Confessions prevails. In general, that faithfulness to the Confessions prevails must suffice for reassurance of every communicant. Besides that which each individual seeks for himself and his soul in the Holy Supper, that faithfulness to the Confessions demanded is limited to the fellowship with the Church of the same

83 Delitzsch, *Die bayrische Abendmahlsgemeinschaftsfrage*, 42.

confession. If, however, congregation members believe that they must be vigilant with regard to the Holy Supper to make sure, for instance, that a member of the Union Church does not go next to them to God's table, then it may be feared they are less concerned than they should be with the needs of their own souls and the distress of their own sins. And if, finally, they do presume the right to criticize the practice of a pastor in individual cases whose stance with respect to the confession is otherwise sufficiently certain, then they are liable to the judgment of having encroached upon the office of another (1 Peter 4:15) ["But let none of you suffer as a murderer or a thief or an evildoer or as a meddler"].

Such cases have occurred earlier and again recently, especially in university congregations. This is doubly deplorable, especially because the enforcement of old ecclesial requirements is subject to particular difficulties especially in regard to students of theology. Temporarily, members of the university of a Lutheran territory are entrusted to the spiritual care of the one who oversees the parsonage of the university congregation during their stay. Although it may be demanded that they be conscious members of the Church to which they belong, on the other hand they are clearly on their way, for the first time, to becoming certain of their ecclesial doctrine in the form of theological cognizance. Can anyone demand any more from such than that upon desiring the Sacrament they bear witness that they wish to receive it as Christians with a Lutheran belief in the Sacraments and to preserve the faithfulness to the Sacrament for the future of the Church from which they now desire it? If freedom in pastoral discretion and treatment is to be granted anywhere, then [it is certainly appropriate] here in individual cases. Only one thing may be demanded with certainty: personal announcement before the Sacrament. It is easier here than in a hundred other cases to determine how a conscientious conduct of the pastoral office is at all possible.

Our position on the question of how to deal with Lutherans within the union has already been generally indicated with the requirements in this particular case. First of all, it is impossible to view United churches in another way than according to their historical development and factual existence. If, then, the Lutheran Church has to, as a matter of principle, reject a United church governance which always simultaneously assumes the right to syncretistic altar fellowship no less than a confessional union does, then her conduct toward the individuals can nevertheless not be determined by confessional oppositions. It should, rather, be recognized as a fact that in Prussia there are entire fellowships of pastors and congregations within the union who assert all of the rights of the Lutheran Confessions and more or less resolutely attempt to maintain altar fellowship according to the position of the Lutheran Confessions. To simply refuse them the Sacrament at altars of Lutheran territorial churches would be in conflict with old ecclesial principles. If Lutherans are within the union and do that which they profess, then I do not know how anyone could deny them the rights of members with a good conscience. Reasons for excluding these Lutherans would have to be sought somewhere else than in the old traditions of the Lutheran Church and her Confessions. One among these reasons that many may see as valid is that this is owed to those who lead the fight for faithfulness to the point of separating from the union. And, in fact, as far as I am aware, those Lutherans who have been separated by the union are being recognized within all the Lutheran territorial churches to the effect that members of their congregations are recognized as members of the Lutheran territorial churches without being questioned. The question would be whether more testimony is required. To try to prove that those Lutherans who are still fighting for the rights of full independence as Lutherans generally lack complete faithfulness would be both difficult and not without sin in making a judgment against closely bound brothers. No other obligation can be derived from principles of Lutheran fellowship practice than to demand of those Lutherans from the union during the examination before the Supper to seek the Sacrament when they are home only in those congregations in which doctrinal discipline is practiced for altar fellowship according to Lutheran principles.

The situation is different, however, when the confessional stance and independence of the Lutheran Church is in danger in one's own homeland. Then regard for the right that individuals within the union apply to their confessional stance takes a backseat to the overall character of the union and the threat posed by the union's disregard for confession. Even here judgment is flexible. Faithful Lutheran clergy have always recognized a struggle against an anti-churchly principle of time within the struggle against the union and have already for a long time, before anyone had a notion of the ecclesiastical consequences of the year 1866, had misgivings about granting admittance to the Supper to just any adherent of a United church. For the thought and urgings of the union to gain ground, it was necessary to offer resistance to any possible faithfulness. In any case, it has to be admitted that the increased danger of a general victory of the union over the confessional stance of the Lutheran territorial churches by means of an opposing altar practice has not been altered since 1866.[84]

However, what should be said about the new Prussian provinces whose ecclesial situation has recently been of particular interest for the Lutheran conference paper? Indeed, they have the king's word that their traditional confessional status

---

84 Cf. Delitzsch, *Die bayrische Abendmahlsgemeinschaftsfrage*, 41. Already in 1854, Kahnis said of Saxony: "There is already enough union stuff floating around in the air. Until now, it has only fallen down as water." Cf. *Die Sache der lutherischen Kirche gegenüber die Union*. p. 3. [In 1866, Prussia annexed the Kingdom of Hanover (then converted into the Province of Hanover), the Free City of Frankfurt am Main, the Electorate of Hesse, and the Duchy of Nassau (combined as the Province of Hesse-Nassau), as well as the Duchies of Schleswig and Holstein (becoming the Province of Schleswig-Holstein), all prevailingly Lutheran territories where Lutherans and the minority Calvinists had not united. Wikipedia, "Prussian Union Churches." MH]

will be left untouched. Of course, at the same time the hope has been repeatedly expressed that they would not resist the traditions of their new crown in the long run. And the actual situation speaks more clearly than anything else. There can be no more doubt that the Lutheran churches of these provinces simply by being placed under the summepiscopate [i.e., the head of state is the head of the church] have already been viewed as having been assimilated into the entire Prussian territorial church. A start has already been made with decreeing a new church constitution for them in the name of the Prussian territorial church.

Admittedly, they still have not been incorporated into the organism of the United church government in a strict sense. All the more so, the concern for them is that the parish union should not become a reality. The other thing would happen automatically. Treating a parish as united begins in that moment when indiscriminate participation in the Supper at the altars of the new Prussian provinces is demanded as a right for all evangelical members of the old Prussian territorial church. **And this is happening.**[85] As soon as this principle succeeds in being implemented generally and without resistance, then the situation of the Lutherans in these provinces will be essentially the same as that of the Lutherans within the Prussian Union. A union which is implemented at the level of church governance has less of an immediate effect on the confessional status of a church than an altar practice that is robbed of any doctrinal discipline.

Anyone who can turn a blind eye to the fact that the independence of the Lutheran Church is in the greatest danger in these new Prussian provinces and that the point at which this danger hits closest to home is altar practice cannot possibly be serious in his opposition to the union and his love for his ancestral church. "*Tunc tua res agitur paries quum proximus ardet*" ["It is your matter when your neighbor's wall is on fire"].

Unless all insight has abandoned me, there can be no other advice for these provinces than to stand relentlessly by the demand that members of the Prussian Territorial Church be served by the establishment of independent united congregations within the territory, because the Lutheran congregations of the provinces cannot otherwise ensure the independent existence they have heretofore enjoyed than by simply excluding all members of the United Church. If this seems harsh, they should simply appeal to the fact that they are not the cause of this painful struggle and that they would behave differently in less dangerous times. Those who denounce this emergency measure as a misuse of the Supper for "political ends"

85 It is a completely unproven assertion that this right is demanded only as a "guest's right," because there is no place for subordination under the United Church's superior council [*Oberkirchenrat*], as Rietschel thinks. Rietschel will not even admit what Kahnis says of the united territorial church: "Wherever there is altar fellowship **according to the church order**, there is church fellowship according to the church order" ("Reformationsprogramm bei Luthardt," *Kirchenzeitung* 7 [1868]: 113).

should be ashamed when not a word has been said against how the other side is treating political borders as ecclesiastical ones without thinking twice. It also should not be forgotten that it was actually the union theology that first treated the Supper and altar fellowship as a first step toward securing the union.[86] Admittedly, the establishment of independent united congregations as a concession seems to be the necessary flipside of a consistent exclusion from the altars of the Lutheran congregations and also the best proof that such practice is not exercised as a result of unfairness and bitterness. Furthermore, it is also the best test of whether the Prussian church governance is serious about recognizing the independence of these Lutheran church provinces **alongside** the united Prussian territorial church.

In the lecture that was attacked by Rietschel, I did not say a word concerning church practice in Saxony as far as it did not have something to do with proceedings that have a related significance for the states of the North German Federation [*Nordeutsche Bund*], such as those requirements in reference to altar fellowship in the new Prussian provinces. The pastoring of Prussian military congregations as such without concern for the churchly stance of their members cannot be viewed any other way. These are the beginnings of that which in other places has become a dominant and a nearly complete condition. When I had to refute a similar attack by Prof. Fricke, I had already then brought to mind that every freedom of the Lutheran confession, with the single exception of the separate Old Lutherans, has been suppressed within the ecclesiastical arm of the Prussian Army. Anyone from the Lutheran provinces who has to become a soldier is treated thereby *eo ispo* as a member of the United Church and may not lay claim to any other pastoral care. An edict issued to Hesse even explicitly refused any access to liturgical care by the separated Lutherans. How is it that Pastor Rietschel does not have a word to say against such a coercion of consciences? Demanding friendship toward Prussian garrisons in the Lutheran territorial churches without testifying to the gross violation of our fellow believers in the Prussian Army—such demands require a double standard to say the least.

In any case, the situation is such that there is cause to conscientiously resist any initiatives. Can anyone really think that had the Lutheran Church ceased to exist as an independent church in Hannover, in Schleswig-Holstein, or in Hesse that the ecclesiastical legal status quo in Saxony would counter with an effective: "so far and no further"?

At the moment, anyone who does not want to establish the norm for the task ahead in this conflict from those situations in which Lutheran independence is most threatened—I repeat—that person is not serious about maintaining independence. "What is the point of continuing to live exclusively as Lutherans within the union, that is, within the large German national church? The uniqueness of

86 Cf. Kahnis, "Reformationsprogramm by Luthardt," *Kirchenzeitung* 6, p. 91.

the Lutheran confession or, said more correctly, the uniqueness of the Lutheran theological perspective can be preserved here nevertheless." If one were to be completely honest, this is the hidden crux behind this irenicism.

The other side continues to suspect our church struggle to be the product of political opposition against Prussia. I want to make it clear once again as a sincere man that I condemn—indeed, I hate—mixing political particularism with church struggles. Today, any genuine man of the Church should be fine were the Main River no longer to divide Germany politically so that the king of Prussia were the only ruler in Germany, if Prussia would understand that it should do—if I may say so—that which alone is worthy of its greatness and its Protestant mission, if it understood and were capable of proclaiming the great noble principle of **ecclesiastical freedom**. I have been regarded as a man of intolerance while my friends and students know that I am a fierce advocate of the freedom of the Church within the state. Only when this morning dawns upon our people and we Lutherans above all will have learned to stand on our own two feet, only then will the churches reciprocally accept the worthy character of respecting each other's independence and uniqueness as long as the struggle remains relentless for the Church militant. At least then there would no longer be the illusion that church and political parties as such have identical interests.

How can someone turn a blind eye to the fact that the secret of the union from the first *Henotikon*[87] in the Christian Church up to the fantasies of a Prussian-German national church is pure caeseropapism! If there was a prince who in his efforts to effect a union had originally intended it as an act of the inner conviction of his subjects, it was Friedrich Wilhelm III of Prussia [1770–1840]. However, as his hope for unification in this way proved to be illusory, he then unashamedly seized power as a territorial lord. His explanation reads:[88] "Now, since the honorable clergy do not so desire, nor are able, and it is impossible to make it just for everyone, and since this divergence **may no longer take place** in one and the same (!) church, **I, like my ancestors, will make use of the liturgical right conceded to me**." As is well-known, it was [Friedrich] Schleiermacher who energetically raised his voice against this "liturgical right of the evangelical territorial prince."[89] The Reformed saw clearly much earlier, and we have to accept the accusation that it was originally the Lutheran territorial churches in which the thought of a union was implemented, thanks to the dubious principle of the Lutheran summepiscopate.[90] In that article from the Reformed periodical [*reformierte Kirchenzeitung*]

87 ['Ενωτικόν, "act of union." In 482, the Byzantine emperor Zeno forced a union between the supporters and opponents of the Council of Chalcedon. MH]

88 Cf. Eylert, *Charakterzüge*, 3:1, 351.

89 *Sämmtl. Werk.*, I. Section. vol. 5.

90 [I.e., the idea that the head of the state was also the head of the church. MH]

from which I took the quote from the Synod of Charenton, it reads: "The modern union is a plant which has generally grown on essentially Lutheran soil and which is homogeneous with the efforts of the Lutheran consistorial constitution which aims at territorial unity, which efforts are more or less tainted with caeseropapism."[91]

Where has the principle of the sovereign ecclesiastical authority of the territorial ruler ever been given such a blatant expression than has just now been done by Rödenbeck against the faithful fighters for the independence of the church in Hesse? And in what German territorial church other than in the Prussian Church are such declarations by the church governance possible like those which very recently appeared in the church papers: ". . . to submit that the sustained and conscious abstinence from sacramental fellowship in the territorial church is tantamount to a renunciation of church authority."[92] The most remarkable thing about this is that men who otherwise pay homage to principles of Protestant unification in their suggestions for the new formulation of the church constitution unabashedly make the principle of the ecclesiastical sovereignty of the territorial ruler, that is, the absolute right of the state over the church, the starting point for their entire church policy in Prussia. Wolter's recently published writing "On the History and Constitution of the Ev. Church in Prussia" [*Zur Geschichte und Verfassung der evang. Kirche in Preußen*][93] provides some of the most instructive evidence of this. While he wants to see every "specifically ecclesiastical qualification" excluded for active and passive electability to the synod (p. 102), he puts the following sentence at the apex of his entire explanation: "that, with the exception of the state power, Prussian state jurisprudence has acknowledged the *jus reformandi* ['right to reform'] since time immemorial, and still acknowledges it." It is as if in Prussia the Altenstein Ministerium[94] is to live on immortally with the Hegelian theory that the church has to be dissolved into the state.

All sorts of well-meaning illusions can be connected with a German national church. Any blind man can see that to produce such a church would mean nothing other than to consummate the caesaropapistic thought of a church fellowship that is still ultimately defined by political borders and to degrade the Lutheran Church to a theological direction or a sect. And there is no need for any Prussian court preacher to blurt out the secret for someone to be able to recognize that they are headed straight at this goal.

---

91 *Sämmtl. Werk.*, I. Section. vol. 5, 305.

92 From the Supreme Church Council dated September 25 of this year, on the occasion of the refusal of church marriage to Irvingites.

93 Berlin, 1869, by Franz Lobeck.

94 [Karl vom Stein zum Altenstein (1770–1840, same dates at Friedrich Wilhelm III!) was the first minister of culture in Prussia. From 1817 his department was tasked with reforming the church into the newly forced Union. MH]

Such a danger cannot be met with pseudo-irenic theories about Lutheran principles without any historical basis of truth. What we need now are men who demonstrate a courage to witness and an unyielding steadfastness against unjustified concessions, in the manner of Luther. We will gladly bear the accusation of intolerance until God in His grace inaugurates for our people those days when all friends of the freedom of religious conviction recognize that the struggle for the independence of the Church upon the basis of her own principles is the way to the peace of the churches among one another and with the state.

CHAPTER FIVE

LOEHE CORRESPONDENCE ON UNIONISTIC COMMUNION PRACTICE IN THE BAVARIAN CHURCH

TRANSLATED BY ROLAND ZIEGLER WITH MATTHEW C. HARRISON

WILHELM LOEHE (1808–72) AND HIS FOLLOWERS IN the Bavarian Lutheran Church protested the union nature of that church in a formal document on October 9, 1851. C. F. W. Walther and F. D. C. Wyneken of the LCMS were present at that meeting and supported the protest. In doing so, they lost access to funding for the LCMS seminaries from the Bavarian queen. See Matthew C. Harrison, *At Home in the House of My Fathers* (St. Louis: Concordia, 2010), 57ff. As the following correspondence indicates, Loehe and his compatriots are on the verge of being ejected from the Bavarian Church. They were fighting for their ecclesiastical lives and, more important, for the fundamental New Testament and confessional truth that unity in true doctrine is a prerequisite for Communion. Harless then replaced his unionistic predecessor, and tensions eased. These letters are translated from Deinzer, *Wilhelm Loehe's Leben*, Nuremberg (1873), vol. 2, pp. 391ff. MH

Schwabach, October 9, 1851
Royal High Consistory!

Concern:
With the most humble and obedient thanksgiving, and petition of the undersigned, concerning the ceasing of Communion fellowship between members of different confessions.

The most humble, obedient undersigned hereby acknowledge, with complete and sincere thankfulness, the paternal gentleness with which the Royal High

Consistory had deigned to answer their petition of July 2, last year. And they neither can nor want to fail to express their unfeigned thanksgiving to their superiors.

However, they neither can nor are able to conceal the fact that they cannot agree with the opinion regarding the Bavarian ecclesiastical conditions, which the Royal High Consistory has communicated to them, since they have a different conviction. They express this with reverence and moderation because they believe that, above all else, they should bring an open heart to their superiors. But they take the gracious statement of the assurance of an undiminished existence of a Lutheran Church in Bavaria as a guarantee for the churchly, Lutheran decisiveness of their superiors. And they greet the promise of unceasing efforts to establish a purely confessional separate church with the joyous conviction of its success and most beautiful victory. Trusting in this statement and this promise they declare hereby that they want to remain, also in the future, within the body of the territorial church, waiting for improvement. They desire to serve the church and her congregations with the old proven faithfulness and the old obedience of which they are conscious. There is only one point which would violate our consciences deeply, if we are forced to bare it in the old way. It is Communion fellowship with the United and Reformed. We do not recognize this as a mere emergency or exceptional state [*Not- oder Ausnahmszustand*]. It burdens our consciences as a sin. No peace can be made with this situation. It is to be renounced as soon as possible and in every way. As convinced as we are to wait for the further development of a truly Lutheran Church of Bavaria, trusting the Royal High Consistory, we are just as convinced we have to confess to our fatherly superiors:

> that we cannot recognize any Communion fellowship with Reformed and United [Christians];
>
> that we cannot recognize as Lutheran any pastor or other Christian who consciously remains in such a Communion fellowship;
>
> that in all our official, practical circumstances we must follow this conviction, as difficult and sorrowful as this could be for ourselves here and there.

The Word of God, which forbids any fellowship with false doctrine and its persistent followers, thus especially forbids Communion fellowship. The Lutheran Confessions and their "we reject" [*reprobamus*], the old practice of the Church, the spiritual well-being of the congregations which is clouded and endangered through mixed Communion fellowship, the salvation of our own souls [all] urge us to implore our gracious superiors to abrogate this blackest spot in our ecclesiastical circumstances, in accordance with the position given them by God. It cannot be excused with us by any [alleged] need or emergency against which the need of our own [consciences] raises its voice loudly. If we are not mistaken, then also some voices from the congregations will unite with us when they become aware of this matter via the sad situation of their shepherds. How much thanksgiving would not only come to our superiors but also rise toward God if the sad union of the divisions [of differing confessions of faith] at altars would go away.

Remaining in supreme devotion,
The Royal Protestant High Consistory's most humble, most obedient
W. Loehe, Pastor in Neuendettelsau
E. Stirner, Pastor in Fürth
F. Wucherer, Pastor in Nördlingen
Fischer, Pastor in Aufsess
Volk, Pastor in Rügland
Roedel, Pastor in Mengersdorf
Fischer, Pastor in Artelshofen
Bauer, Catechist in Nuremberg
Semm, Vicar in Memmingen

November 5, 1851

In the Name of His Majesty the King,

Concerning the petition directed immediately to the Consistory from the 9th of October regarding the abolition of Communion fellowship of members of different confessions, by Pastors Loehe in Neuendettelsau, Stirner in Fürth, Wucherer in Nördlingen, Fischer in Artelshofen, Volk in Rügland, Fischer in Aufsess, and Roedel in Mengersdorf, and Candidates Friedrich Bauer in Nuremberg and Wilhelm Semm in Memmingen, the response is:

At the release of the decision of September 19 of this year [1851], concerning the abolition of Communion fellowship with the Reformed and the United, the Royal High Consistory had hoped through the explanation given in this decision the wrong opinions of the petitioners of the legal position of the Lutheran Church in Bavaria would be corrected and that their conscientious concerns would be calmed concerning the exceptional circumstances regarding Communion practice.

According to the content of the said petition of October 9 of this year, this hope has not been fulfilled. The participants declare [their intent] "to continue to remain within the organization of the territorial church" and have therefore given up their decision to leave it. But at the same time it had to be deduced from that petition, with great regret, that the signers not only persist in their erroneous concept of the situation of the territorial church but also assert the consequence of their opinion that they cannot regard any pastor or other Christian for a Lutheran who consciously participates in the so called Communion fellowship of Lutherans, Reformed, and United. They regard this as a sin and as the blackest spot on our churchly situation. And they declare that they have to act on this conviction in all their official practical relations.

The Royal High Consistory desires in no way not to give appropriate consideration to the conscience of individuals, if in certain cases in the exercise of their immediate vocation they have come to misgivings that cannot be avoided. But the supreme church government cannot allow individuals to express this as a right and to claim this right for themselves. In doing so they make their subjective judgment in their official practical relations a measure of their actions, even severing church fellowship. Thereby they make claim to a special position in the territorial church. This cannot be allowed by the supreme church government. Such action endangers all churchly order. It renders church governmental leadership impossible, and it introduces a process, which if allowed in the Church, would create a growing measure of confusion and disorder hard to estimate. Thus the supreme church government is forced to demand seriously that the signers of the petition of October 9 again take counsel with their consciences. The supreme church government demands that they either faithfully and obediently rejoin the territorial church, without the conditions [presented], which harm churchly order and fellowship, or resign an office which they can no longer hold by insisting on these conditions . . . [Etc. Etc.]

Munich, November 5, 1851
Royal Protestant High Consistory
Friedrich v. Arnold[1]

[Neuendettelsau][2]
November 20, 1851

. . . Although it may be uncommon in our time to urge sacramental unification of the Church [i.e., unified practice], and though we may be unable to demand that the importance of an issue, which has been forgotten by most for a long time, be quickly recognized and reintroduced, we have trusted in the patience of government. We have demanded for ourselves from the beginning that we be able to act in a godly, Lutheran manner, and only at the confessional booth and at the altar. We only wanted to ward off sin. If only our protest, necessary for the sake of our consciences, could be tolerated, we would have liked to wait for our brothers who are as yet undecided in confessional matters. In that way, truth and love, justice and mercy seemed to be retained and balanced. Having rendered this

1 Arnold, whom Loehe called a "rationalistic jurist" (Deinzer 2:412), retired and was replaced as president of the High Consistory by Harless on September 20, 1852. Harless brought immediate Lutheran improvement in the Bavarian church leadership and calmed the tensions with Loehe and his followers. Deinzer 2:413. MH

2 The translation is from the excerpted version of the letter in Deinzer 2:400–403.

decision for ourselves, and praying for the entire Lutheran people, thus and in no other way we approached the Royal High Consistory on October 9.

We foresaw, nevertheless, that in the practical execution of our principles, some brother might be harmed and that we might be injured ourselves. Although nobody knowing the subject matter could have accused us of exercising the ban (how could that have happened since the ban is the end of a process which we cannot even start, and the Lutheran Church does not know of an excommunication of unknown persons or groups). Furthermore, though we are completely certain that we in no way want to create disorder, we cannot avoid pointing out old disorder in order to attack it. Thus the feelings created cannot rise from order. It is not our fault that we found so much confessional and sacramental confusion. We were unaware of so much misery, which is now evident to us. For example, we had never thought that in the organizational edict for the pastoral offices of the city of Nuremberg of April 10, 1810, (published again in the *Nuremberger Intellegenzblatt* of 1833, no. 104, September 4; paragraphs 6 and 7 of the Royal General Commission Council of the Pegnitz area, as the general deanery) sacramental union of the Lutherans and Reformed of Nuremburg is outrightly intended and decreed. But thus it is! A few weeks ago we would not have believed that we would have to deal with so many sacramental abuses. Unfortunately, in this unsuspected find there is only renewed confirmation that our consciences are not erring consciences.

After all this, may the Royal High Consistory allow the most humble, most obedient signer to give his explanation to the very significant letter of the 5th of this month in the following way.

The principles thus explained and formulated in the document of the 9th of October cannot destroy churchly order and the true fellowship of the Church, because these principles themselves are rather pillars of churchly order. I cannot give up these principles. They are not subjective. They are demonstrably the property of the Lutheran Church from the beginning. Neither can I resign my office in this local congregation with the conviction that I am being faithful. The entire church council, together with the better and larger part of the congregation, has signed the church council's petition of October 12 recognizing my position as the correct one. For a long time I have been burdened heavily by my office. My flesh would be pleased if I no longer had it. But I feel connected to this congregation since the petition of October 12, and by those signatures I have been connected to it more than ever. How should I view that which pleases my flesh? On the contrary, I will once again express as clearly and as distinctly as possible how I envision the exceptional sacramental-confessional position of Lutheran pastors and congregations in Bavaria, with the heartfelt petition that this relationship remain undisturbed.

1. I will never serve Communion to a Reformed or United [person].

2. I will never serve Communion to a person who has stood in Communion fellowship with the Reformed or United, without his having been previously taught, admonished, and brought to the confession of his errors and his sins.
3. I cannot regard Communion fellowship with other believers, whether and however it may exist, as an emergency. I have to regard it as sin, to testify against it, and to warn against it.
4. I cannot recognize, therefore, any Christian or pastor as Lutheran who practices such Communion fellowship or defends it. I have to warn against it or dissuade [others from such practice] as much as I am able.
5. I have to receive at my altar any Lutheran Christian who has severed his confessional relationship [*Beichtverhältnis*] [with his pastor and congregation] because of mixed fellowship in the Lord's Supper, and who has given me proof of it, and who has followed the procedure in the handbook. I must strengthen him in his determination when he comes to me, wants to be received, and has an otherwise good witness.
6. Finally, I have to confess the truth in and toward all circles of which I am a member. I will also make the requests of, and beseech conventions and churchly authorities, until I am heard, namely, that the sinful, deplorable state of affairs end soon.
7. In the same way I acknowledge it as my indispensable duty to bear witness against all other confessional abuses and defects. I shall pray and plead until the Lord hears and improvement comes.

From these sentences the Royal High Consistory certainly will recognize the most humble [undersigned's] faithful will not to give up his convictions and to serve his congregation. But one cannot fail to recognize that with the current mobility [of people], individual congregations come into a thousand contacts with the greater whole and its parts. So there is no question that a movement may also proceed from an individual congregation effecting wider circles. This causes harmful contacts with dissimilar elements [i.e., practices] and defies all resolution to work only inside the [individual] congregation . . . .

With this I place everything into the hands of the gracious superiors in Christ. I pray to the Lord and ask these superiors to abolish the sinful abuses in the Sacrament. And I hope that, along with other pastors of the same opinion, I might be retained in the exercise of such a churchly faithfulness, which we can justify before God and man.

With the high respect and devotion owed the Royal High Consistory, I remain your most humble, most obedient,

Pastor Wilhelm Loehe

CHAPTER SIX

Fellowship in the Lord's Supper and Church Fellowship in the Ancient Church[1]

Werner Elert
Translated by Wolf Dietrich Knappe

I.

By limiting our subject to the Ancient Church, I not only want to fill in a gap in the literature (though only in sketches) but also to counter a narrowness in the way the whole question is being asked. Fellowship in the Lord's Supper [*Abendmahlsgemeinschaft*] has become the object of church orders and of theological consideration ever since the split of Christianity. Since when? Hans Asmussen [1898–1968] puts the responsibility on the "confessional churches" which originated since the Reformation. "The separation at the Lord's Table, as we have it today," he opines, "happened in a history which extends for four hundred years" (*Abendmahlsgemeinschaft* [1937], 5). The following explanations show that this means that this was the case for only the past four hundred years. But this is an obvious error. The split between the Roman Catholic Church and the Orthodox Church in the East [AD 1054], still in force today, happened half a millennium before the Reformation, the separation of the Monophysite Church and that of the Nestorians a whole millennium before that. These splits are just as decisive for the outward image of Christianity today as the consequences of the Reformation.

1 "Abendmahl und Kirchengemeinschaft in der alten Kirche," in *Koinonia: Arbeiten des Oekumenischen Ausschusses der Vereinigten Evangelisch-Lutherischen Kirche Deutschlands zur Frage der Kirchen- und Abendmahlsgemeinschaft*, ed. Lutherischen Kirchenamt der Vereinigten Evangelisch-Lutherischen Kirche Deutschlands (Berlin: Lutherisches Verlagshaus, 1957), 57–78. MH

There is no Communion fellowship between these churches (with the exception of a minority of Eastern churches that are united with Rome) ever since they excommunicated each other. The claim, assiduously spread by a certain side, that the Reformation is to blame for all "confessional divisions" is therefore false. True, the above-mentioned churches do not call themselves confessional churches, that is, churches with a confession. But whoever considers this epithet not as an insult but as an honorary title cannot deny it to them.

But the "separation at the Lord's Table," rightfully deplored by Asmussen, is still much older. If today, within the ecumenical movement, the confession [of faith in] "Jesus Christ, our Lord and Savior" is considered a sufficient criterion of a Christian Church, one cannot deny this to the church of Marcion either, which split from the majority Church during the middle of the second century and existed for centuries. The same goes for the Novatians, Valentinians, Arians, semi-Arians, and Donatists. Nevertheless, all these were excommunicated by the majority Church [*Grosskirche*]. Therefore, they did not have any fellowship in the Lord's Supper with the latter. Neither did they have it with one another. And the expression "majority Church" did not always indicate the greater number, as if the others were only marginal phenomena. Around the middle of the fourth century the whole world was wondering, according to St. Jerome, "how the whole world had become Arian."[2] And, finally, even in the New Testament there is enough talk of splits and false teachers, and by no means only in the Pastoral Letters. Try as I may, I cannot imagine that Paul would have wanted to celebrate the Lord's Supper together with those who were "peddlers of God's word" (2 Corinthians 2:17; 4:2); or with one who "proclaims another Jesus than the one we proclaimed, or if you receive a different spirit from the one you received, or if you accept a different gospel from the one you accepted" (11:4); with "false apostles, deceitful workmen, disguising themselves as apostles of Christ" (11:13); with "[Satan's] servants, [who] disguise themselves as servants of righteousness" (11:15). No, the division in the Church did not just start during the Reformation. The divisions are from the beginning a part of its historical image, and therefore it had to face, from the days of the apostles on, the question of how these divisions affected fellowship in the Lord's Supper.

Therefore, even today, we cannot speak about this whole question as if it were just a private matter of our age, or of our own confession, or as if it applied only to our relationship to this or another confession. The answers we are looking for have to be able to be defended before the entire Christian Church. Therefore, the voice of the Ancient Church cannot be a matter of indifference for us. Here we often have to see the difference between East and West. In any case we are closely related to the ancient Greek Church, because the dogma it formed has

2 NPNF^2 6:319. MH

remained the unquestioned presupposition for the Lutheran Reformation and for Lutheran theology.

There is yet another very instructive reason for studying its relationship to our special subject. The reasons, which today make the question of fellowship in the Lord's Supper so timely and also so difficult to answer, exist exactly in the same way in the Ancient Church of the East. The often astonishing parallels can be explained by the relationship, one could almost say the identity, of the confessional situation. The different Christian confessional churches live in close proximity. Before Constantine [ca. 272–337], the Church, which we are used to calling *a posteriori* the majority Church, had no means to prevent mutual contacts by using forceful means. In Alexandria, there was no way to control the back and forth from one assembly to another, as one can see from a description of the local bishop Dionysius (Euseb. VII, 7,4). Later, forceful measures by the state have only given the wrong impression of temporary successes, just like the post-Reformation territorial church government. Only a few decades after the strict laws concerning heretics by Theodosius [347–395], all outlawed heretics and schismatics have their own houses of worship in the capital again. Socrates [of Constantinople, ca. 380] tells of a Jew who let himself be baptized several times in Constantinople and "made a lot of money through this technique" (VII, 17). First he was with the Arians, then with the Macedonians, and finally he tries it with the Novatians. However, there he is unmasked by Bishop Chrysanthos. Around the year 500, when Emperor Anastasius I [430–518] extends the right of asylum to the churches of the heretics (Theodor Lector, II, 24), the picture of the confessions in the capital could hardly have been less colorful than in a German or English metropolis of today.

Of course, the divisions are painful for every serious Christian, then as today. Zacharias Rhetor [ca. 465–536] opens his church history with moving complaints that because of Chalcedon the seamless robe of Christ had been torn apart. Times of bitter polemic alternate with attempts at union, just as today.

II.

In order to understand how the Lord's Supper was practiced [*Abendmahlspraxis*] under these circumstances, we also have to consider the doctrine of Communion of the Ancient Church. I can assume that in our circle it is known and also acknowledged that early on this was permeated with unevangelical views and theories. This means especially the interpretation of the Lord's Supper as a priestly sacrifice and the teaching of transubstantiation, which can be found already with Chrysostom [345–407]. In our context, the teaching of transubstantiation is of no importance. It is still in its early stages and not in any firm theological connection.

On the other hand, the theory of sacrifice immediately leads us to the central question of our subject: "fellowship in the Lord's Supper and church fellowship."

This theory in its medieval and modern Catholic form concentrated the entire weight of the eucharistic process upon the priest and his action. In the strictest sense, the congregation is only spectator. The so-called Mass sacrifice is valid even if no congregation is present. With this, the "fellowship character" of the Lord's Supper has been completely lost.

The beginnings of this development lie, as mentioned, where the imagining of a priestly sacrifice in the Eucharist starts, and this certainly is the case in the third century already. But only the beginnings. The Roman description, which tries to put the present status of things already into the first centuries, is historically false. In the *Apostolic Constitutions* there is the lapidary sentence for the beginning of the eucharistic celebration: "The bishop assembles his congregation." The Eucharist in all Ancient Church orders and liturgies is a congregational celebration. In the theological interpretation as well as in the views of laypeople, for which there are plenty of testimonies, the fellowship character is never forgotten. At least in the East, with Eutychius of Constantinople in the sixth century and with Anastasius Sinaita in the seventh—that is, in both of the first monographs about the Lord's Supper—the fellowship character outweighs the view of the priestly action.

The significance of this fact for our subject is clear. Both subjects, that of the Lord's Supper and of church fellowship [*Kirchengemeinschaft*], immediately move toward a close connection, even though the Lord's Supper is "fellowship" [*Abendmahl "Gemeinschaft" ist*]. Church and Lord's Supper, then, are somehow put together through the concept of fellowship. If one interprets the Lord's Supper as a Mass sacrifice, this is by no means the case. Of course, what does "fellowship" [*Gemeinschaft*] mean here? Lest we misinterpret Ancient Church sources with the help of this German word, we first have to clarify its various German meanings.

In Luther's day, the word *fellowship* [*Gemeinschaft*] was still new. It was uncomfortable. In the Large Catechism, where he understands the formula *sanctorum communio* as an apposition to *sancta ecclesia*, he wants to render *communio* with "*Gemeine*" ["congregation/community"] in German. He rejects the term *fellowship* [*Gemeinschaft*] as a name for the Church. On the other hand, in his Bible translation, he rendered the word *koinonia* (1 Corinthians 10:16), where it is used for the Lord's Supper, with "fellowship" [*Gemeinschaft*]; and in the *Great Confession on the Lord's Supper* (1528), he gave more detailed explanations. Here also he is not very happy about the German word. The lack of understanding of the doctrine of the Lord's Supper by his antagonists he derives in part from this, and he gives this reason for it: "It is not as clearly German as I would have it. For to have fellowship [*gemeinschaft*] is commonly understood as to have something to do with a person. But here (1 Corinthians 10:15) it is supposed to mean, as I have explained above, that many use a common thing together, enjoy it, or take part in it. This I have to translate with *gemeinschafft*. I was unable to find a better word for it" (WA 26:493.2).

Thus Luther does not want to apply the attribute *fellowship* to the Church, and to the Lord's Supper only if it is not used in the meaning of the common language of his day. That meaning is "to have something to do with a person." Certainly one cannot use it in this way if it is to correspond to the word *koinonia* in 1 Corinthians 10:16, for that means that many use, enjoy, or take part in one common thing. This contrast shows what Luther is concerned with. What unites the communicants in the Lord's Supper is not that the one has something to do with the other—that is, not their human relationships and ties with one another—but the common good in which they all partake.

Let us now compare corresponding remarks from more recent theology. [Friedrich] Schleiermacher [1768–1834], about the Church (*The Christian Faith*, par. 2): "The common concept of the Church, if there is something like that, has to be taken chiefly from ethics (he means philosophical ethics), since in any case the Church is a fellowship [*Gemeinschaft*], which originates only through free human acts and can only continue through such." Here one can see how the essence of the Church is directly derived from the essence of fellowship. What grave consequences this deduction must have one sees by the fact that Schleiermacher gives the concept of fellowship exactly the meaning which Luther rejects resolutely when it is applied to the Church and to the Lord's Supper: fellowship originates from actions of free people in relationship to one another.

The application of the concept of *fellowship* to the Lord's Supper has become a firm convention through Luther's translation of *koinonia* in 1 Corinthians 10:16. There is hardly a German commentary of it which would not contain that word. Ed. v. Dobschuetz, for example, comments on *koinonia* here thus: "Fellowship of communicants, first among each other."[3] Here also there is an exact contrast to Luther's understanding. Luther says: *koinonia* does not mean here that people have something to do with each other, not "first of all with one another," but the relationship of the many to the common good of which they are partaking. Dobschuetz, on the other hand, says it is especially "first of all with each other." Of course, Dobschuetz does not overlook the relationship to the common good (body and blood of Christ) in the text. Therefore, he believes that in the end he can define the whole as "an association of the body and blood of Christ" [*Genossenschaft*]. The concept of association once more underlies the previous understanding of fellowship. Fellowship is a coming together of people to an assemblage, an association, a corporation. Fellowship understood as association is just about synonymous with the concept of congregation [*Gemeinde*].

We return to the Ancient Church. Of course, everybody has the right to use the word *fellowship* as he pleases, in order to express his own opinion. However,

3 Dobschuetz, "Sakrament u. Symbol im Urchristentum," in *Theologische Studien und Kritiken* (1905): 12, 28ff.

we do not have this freedom when the word is to render concepts of an ancient language. In our case that means the concepts of *communio* and *koinonia*. In all the places where the word *communion* appears in the language of the ancient world and of the Ancient Church, according to the *Thesaurus Linguae Latinae*, it never means an association, never a corporation, never an organization. Roman law, when referring to corporation matters, used instead the concepts of *corpus, universitas, collegium, sodalitas, societas*. But we have to limit ourselves here to the Greek use of the language. *Koinonia* also never means a corporation, never an organization, never an "association," neither in profane nor theological or church use. Whoever translates *koinonia* in 1 Corinthians 10:16 with "fellowship" [*Gemeinschaft*], and interprets fellowship as association, commits a falsification, whether consciously or unconsciously.

This statement is of basic significance for our subject, because the concept of *koinonia* is used for the Lord's Supper and also for church fellowship in the Ancient Church. Church fellowship is called κοινωνια εκκλησιαστικη or κοινωνια της καθολικης εκκλησιας or something like it. Whoever is part of the fellowship is called κοινωνικος; whoever is excluded is ακοινωνητος. As already mentioned, this brings the concepts of Lord's Supper and Church closely together, since *koinonia* is used for both of them. However, one must not be too quick in drawing conclusions from this. The concept *koinonia* does not mean the same thing here.

We cannot deal here with the great number of other possibilities for the use of the concept *koinonia*. As far as they occur in the New Testament also, they have been analyzed and distinguished in the most complete and precise way in the exegetical homilies of Chrysostom. The difference in applying it to the Lord's Supper or to church fellowship becomes clear immediately once one derives the noun from the corresponding verb. If it means church fellowship, one must derive it from κοινονειν τινι. In this case, τινι means the dative of the person. In this connection, κοινωνειν of course can also mean: to communicate something to someone, let him partake. The result, then, is the *koinonia* which Paul gathers for the congregation in Jerusalem and which Luther translates with "*Steuer*" ["tax"]. But if Justin [ca. 100–165] says of the Gnostics: ων ουδενι κοινωνουμεν, or if it says in Athanasius, Arsenios wishes κοινωνειν ημιν, or if heretics or an illegitimate bishop are excluded and this also applies to παντες οι κοινωνουντες αυτω, without any doubt the meaning is: to have fellowship with someone. In this case κοινωνειν is also connected with the dative τη εκκλησια, and accordingly also with τη αιρεσει. *Koinonia* here does not mean the Church as corporation nor the totality of the members or parts of the Church, but a relationship of members that exists within the Church or is mediated by it, or a relationship of members, or a part of them, with the Church as a whole. The unity of the Church (Ephesians 4:3ff.) is not just established through this *koinonia*. It is rather objectively given beforehand.

But if in contrast the term *koinonia* is applied to the Lord's Supper, it has been taken over from 1 Corinthians 10:16. Then one must derive it from κοινωνειν τινος, τινος meaning the common good, that is, here σωμα and αιμα ["body and blood"] of Christ. In any case, the entire theology of the Ancient Church has understood this passage, and one cannot deny that they had a feeling for the Greek language. Κοινωνια του σωματος means participation, *metalepsis*, *participatio* of the body of Christ. Instead of many quotations [here is] only the definition of Isidore of Pelusium [died ca. 450]: "*Koinonia* means the receiving of the divine mysteries, because thereby is given to us the union with Christ and because it makes us partakers of His kingdom" (Ep. 1.228, PG 78:325: κοινωνια κεκληθαι η των θειων μυστηριων μεταληψις δια το την προς Χριστον ημιν χαριζεσθαι ενωσιν και κοινωνους ημας της αυτου ποιειν βασιλειας). *Metalepsis* or μετοχη is used a hundredfold, even in the church orders and the liturgies, without any addition, as a synonym for *koinonia* and always means the sacrament of the Lord's Supper. The equation comes from 1 Corinthians 10:17: οι γαρ παντες εκ του ενος αρτου μετεχομεν. Των θειων μυστηριων is dual and indicates the consecrated elements.

Here the Lord's Supper is defined as *koinonia*, but there is no mention whatsoever of a relationship of the participants with one another. Since the fourth century the corresponding verb κοινωνειν is also used in an absolute way, without addition, corresponding to the later expression "communing." Communing is also said about the individual, without necessarily implying a connection with others. This apparently completely individualistic expression corresponds to the Johannine understanding of the Lord's Supper, for in John 6 there is also talk exclusively of the relationship of the receivers to Christ, but not a word about their relationship to one another. However, that does not mean that the relationship of the partakers to one another was overlooked, or even denied, in the theology of the Ancient Church.

We already saw that the Eucharist in the Ancient Church is always understood as a congregational celebration. Melanchthon, in rejecting the sacrifice theory, appealed to the term *Synaxis* (Ap XXIV 79). This is completely correct; only this expression was used for a long time for any kind of congregational assembly. It has become a popular term for the Lord's Supper only since the fourth century, but gradually, and never exclusively. If we wanted to derive the fellowship character from this term, we would grossly falsify the understanding of the Lord's Supper in the Ancient Church. The corresponding verb συναγεσθαι or συνερχεσθαι means the action of the assembly participants. They come together, συνερχονται επι το αυτο; the *Synaxis* is, to say with Schleiermacher, the result of free human actions. The fellowship character of the Lord's Supper would then happen because people of goodwill are united in the decision to celebrate it.

This is just about the direct opposite of the understanding of the Ancient Church. Already in the eucharistic prayer of the *Didache* the word group συναγεσθαι receives a different turn. Here it is God who is being asked: "Συναξον ['Gather together'] (namely, the congregation) the holy one from the four winds!" (10, 4). The participants here are not subjects but the object of the union.—The *koinonia* concepts finally point in the opposite direction. It means *metalepsis* ["participation"] of the body of Christ, and only for this reason it also means a relationship of the participants to one another. Cyril of Jerusalem [ca. 313–86]: Through the κοινωνειν, the partaking of the body and blood of Christ, the receiver becomes συσσωμος και συναιμος of Christ (*Concorporalis et consanguineus* ["bodied and blooded with Christ"], *Cat. Myst.* IV, 3). Everybody thus becomes *Christophoros* ["a Christ-bearer"], he adds. Here the *koinonia* is said only about the individual. Cyril of Alexandria [ca. 376–444] picks up this thought, but gives it a new twist: "We all are συσσωμοι ['bodied together'] in Christ" (74, 560d). "We, who have been divided into individual persons, so to speak, one being Peter or John, Thomas or Matthew, have become συσσωμοι in Christ, nourished by one flesh, and sealed into unity through the Holy Spirit, if Christ is truly indivisible, for He cannot be divided under any circumstances. We are all one in Him" (*Dial. de trin.* 75, 697b).

For this, Cyril of Alexandria refers to 1 Corinthians 10:17: "If we all partake of the one bread, we all have completely become one body. For it is impossible for Christ to be divided up. Therefore, the Church is also called 'body of Christ,' but we, according to our measure of partaking (κατα μερος, cf. εκ μερους, 1 Corinthians 12:27), are members, according to the understanding of Paul" (72, 560b). One can hardly understand that in any other way but that Cyril saw in the Pauline formula of 1 Corinthians 10:17 the origin of the term "body of Christ" for the Church. What he further mentions concerning the oneness and union [*Einigkeit*] is based on Ephesians, but here also he once more finds the συσσωμα (Ephesians 3:6) and the formula "one body and one Spirit" (4:4). "The many are one in Christ and in the Holy Spirit, bodily and spiritually" (75, 697c). The bodily union happens in the Eucharist. It unites all with Christ, but therefore also with one another.

Of course those who take part in the Eucharist also have to come together. But neither their decision, nor the common way to the Church, makes them into εν σωμα ["one body"], but the eating of one and the same bread. The fact that they then together are the Body of Christ is in no way the result of "free human actions," but exclusively based on the fact that "the bread which we break is the κοινωνια του σωματος του Χριστου" ["participation in the body of Christ"] (1 Corinthians 10:16). The body of Christ, which has been given before all human decisions and actions, is what also unites the participants with one another. As they are united spiritually through the Holy Spirit, they are also united bodily through the *metalepsis* ["participation"] of the body of Christ.

III.

We now turn to the practice of the Lord's Supper of the Ancient Church, as far as it applies to our subject, first in the view of the local congregation, later in the relationship from church to church. I will give reasons for this distinction later. In deference to today's linguistic use, I say local congregation, or also just congregation, even though the Ancient Church made no distinction in terminology here. The local congregation also is called *ecclesia*: the *ecclesia*, the church of Rome, of Corinth, of Antioch. We start with the local congregation because naturally church fellowship, the κοινωνια εκκλησιαστικη, is experienced in the most immediate way in the local boundaries of the assemblies, the agape [meals] and other events and institutions, and because even many important synodical decisions, for example, concerning the exclusion from the Sacrament, are based on local conditions. How does the κοινωνια εκκλησιαστικη ["church fellowship"] of the local congregation manifest itself? If one compares the congregational phenomena of the primitive church with the local congregation of the time of Constantine, or even later, it is difficult to give a general answer. The greatest change happens very early in the constitution: from the charismatic dynamic to a professional clerical hierarchy. Ignatius [died ca. 112] already would give a short answer to the question of what holds a congregation together, namely, the bishop. The structure of the society also has changed. Paul was still able to give a letter of recommendation to an escaped slave. This nonsense is forbidden once for all by the Council of Chalcedon: επιστολαι συστατικαι ["letters of recommendation"] are to be issued only to persons who can claim a special task. This means, first of all, members of the clergy. The others have to be satisfied with ecclesiastical "letters of peace," which we will be interested in later.

But in a fourfold way the local congregation has basically remained the same. (1) It is brotherhood (with charitable care); (2) it is subject to a strict discipline, even in the private sphere; (3) it is confessional fellowship; and (4) it is exclusive in its Divine Services [*geschlossen*; "closed"]. The character of confessional fellowship is shown in the fact that every applicant, before being received as full member in Baptism, offers the baptismal confession. In the problem of church fellowship during the second half of the second and the first half of the third century (from Dionysius of Corinth to Novatian), the *regula fidei* ["rule of faith," i.e., creed] plays a decisive role. Its formal relationship to the baptismal symbol is being questioned in historical research. This much is certain, that even materially it forms an early step to the later synodical confessions which we usually call "dogma."

The closed character [*Geschlossenheit*] of the congregational services is seen in the fact that their worship assemblies are not public. Origen [185–254] emphasizes this as being different from the pagan philosophical school (*Contra Celsum* III, 51). Nonmembers are admitted only as listeners to the Service of the Word, after having received private instruction and after promising to lead an orderly life. Before the beginning of the Eucharist not only the listeners but also the catechumens have to leave the assembly. During the Eucharist, the doors are guarded by the deacons and subdeacons (*Apostolic Constitutions* VIII, 11, 11). Tertullian [ca. 160–225] criticizes severely the opposite actions of the heretics (*De praescr.* 41, 1f.; [ANF 3:263]).

The worship assembly of the Ancient Church is a closed one [*geschlossene*], not a public one. Especially the participation in the celebration of the Lord's Supper is absolutely restricted to the saints. Why? An attempt was made to find the reason for this in the "arcane discipline," that is, the duty for the "initiated" to keep the worship events, especially Baptism and Lord's Supper, secret from the "uninitiated." In this case, the pagan mystery religions would have served as an example, for whom this obligation was a firm rule.

This reasoning is untenable. The concept of arcane discipline, the specific mystery terminology, and the secrecy based on it can be authenticated only since the fourth century. The fact that Tertullian [ca. 160–225] already at times (*Apol.* 7 [ANF 3:23]) compares the Christian Sacrament with the pagan mystery does not mean any more than Paul's comparing the pagan sacrifice with it (1 Corinthians 10:19). Keeping strangers away from the Eucharist does not mean keeping a secret. Whoever wants to learn about the Christian mysteries only has to read the *Apology* of Justin Martyr, which is no secret writing but was directed half a century before Tertullian "to Emperor Antonius Pius . . . the holy senate and the whole Roman people" [ANF 1:163ff.]. In it the rites of Baptism and Lord's Supper are reported with all liturgical details so openly and extensively that this description even today is the best source for us. Thus there is no such thing as arcane discipline in the second century. Therefore, it cannot have been the reason for the closed Communion [*geschlossene Kommunion*] of the Ancient Church.

The strict limiting of those entitled to take part [*Teilnahme*] goes back to the most ancient time. But what is important for it is not the secrecy, but the keeping away of the unholy from the holy, according to the Old Testament concept of holiness. "No one should eat or drink of your Eucharist except those who have been baptized in the name of the Lord, for here also the word of the Lord applies: Do not give the holy to the dogs!" (*Didache* 9:5; cf. 10:6). This word of the *Didache* also resounds in the formula "Holy things for holy people!" which precedes the distribution in the old church liturgies. Only the baptized are admitted. They are the holy ones. That corresponds to the ancient understanding of Baptism: Christ has sanctified His *ecclesia* by cleansing it through the water bath in the Word (Ephesians 5:26). Paul had called attention to the danger of "unworthy" eating and drinking (1 Corinthians 11:27ff.). Therefore, he had pledged every participant to a strict self-examination, and for this reason alone one could not admit indiscriminately any curious person. But of course the whole congregation was also responsible so that no one would run blindly into destruction, so to speak. Therefore, the most basic condition was to be baptized, because Baptism was preceded by an examination of the conduct of life and of honesty, as well as instruction and confession. But Baptism itself was a precondition, inasmuch as holy things should be received only by holy people. According to the understanding of the Ancient Church, that meant the baptized.

Cyril of Jerusalem uses the term *koinonia* for Baptism also. He says that the baptized have *koinonia* with the suffering and dying of Christ (II, 7; *Euch. Ser.* 20, 2). This is in essence completely Pauline, and through this *koinonia*, just as in the Lord's Supper, the *koinonia* of the baptized with one another is also established. Baptismal *koinonia* and *koinonia* in the Supper are both exclusive by their very nature. But both are not the same. Baptism for every Christian is a one-time event while partaking [*Teilnahme*] of the Lord's Supper is a repeated event. What Paul says about the *metalepsis* in 1 Corinthians 10:16 and what Jesus says about it in the Lord's Supper address in John 6 is not yet received in Baptism. Here basically is the reason for the practical distinctions, which were made by the Ancient Church between baptismal fellowship and fellowship in the Lord's Supper. The baptismal fellowship became a problem when the Church had to decide whether Baptism performed by heretics should be considered valid once [the baptized] converted to the catholic Church. After difficult inner debates, [the Church] affirmed this, at least in principle—under the condition that it was a trinitarian Baptism. The question why it dealt differently with the fellowship in the Lord's Supper we have to delay, because it applies already to the relationship of one church to another and therefore goes beyond the realm of the local congregation.

IV.

Within the local congregation, the problem of fellowship in the Lord's Supper is conditioned through those three categories of brotherhood, discipline, and confession. First of all, fellowship in the Lord's Supper and brotherhood. We remember the statements of Cyril of Jerusalem, that through the *metalepsis* in the Lord's Supper we become συσσωμοι ["bodied together"] with Christ, and those of Cyril of Alexandria, that in Christ we also become συσσωμοι ["bodied together"] with one another. The participants become "one body and one Spirit." Therefore, nothing that separates must stand between them, otherwise what separates them would also wound the Body of Christ.

For this reason, the ancient church orders establish the duty for all participants to remove all arguments that exist between them beforehand. Since the *Didache*, one is always reminded of the word from the Sermon on the Mount which demands reconciliation before bringing an offering [Matthew 5:23]. The *Didascalia* [*Apostolorum*; ca. AD 230] orders that before the congregational prayer the deacon asks in a loud voice whether anyone has something against a brother. In this case, the bishop should create peace between the squabbling parties (54, 1). Cyril of Jerusalem quotes this in order to give a reason for the kiss of peace. The kiss of peace, which the participants exchanged with one another, has its fixed place in the liturgy, either at the beginning of the eucharistic part or later, but always after the dismissal of the catechumens and before the Communion proper.

The kiss of peace and the duty to be reconciled were supposed to prevent human dissensions from destroying the unity of the Body of Christ. If it is impossible to reach a reconciliation, there is not supposed to be any Communion. It is obvious that this is in the final end an appeal to the conscience of each participant, because hatred and enmity are beyond the observation of others. If one acts against conscience, what the apostle said about unworthy eating and drinking will be fulfilled. For this reason alone one should not belittle the fact that the ancient liturgies call for the fulfilling of the brotherly duty at every celebration of the Supper. The fact that the kiss of peace happens precisely during celebration of the Supper reminds us that the brotherly side of church fellowship finds its purest expression in the fellowship in the Lord's Supper.

As for the second point, the discipline: the practice of the Lord's Supper is closely connected to the practice of repentance. This development drags on through the entire history of the Ancient Church. It is so complicated, there are so many questions being researched, it is interpreted in a totally different way in Catholic research than in Protestant research, so that we are unable to exhaust this subject at this point. We have to limit ourselves to a few basic trends. First, it is certain that the Ancient Church since the days of Paul practiced excommunication; second, that it already knows the difference between *excommunicatio major* (exclusion from the Church altogether) and *minor*, not under these terms, but in essence; third, that in both cases the exclusion from the Eucharist is the first and most natural thing. There was agreement from the beginning that obvious sinners, as they are characterized by Paul in 1 Corinthians 5:11ff., with whom, according to his instruction, one should not "eat together," even if they "are called brother," are at least to be excluded from the Sacrament. All the controversies over repentance always dealt with receiving [the sinner] again. Major sins are called more precisely "mortal sins" (during the Middle Ages, "capital sins"). Which ones were counted as such we can leave aside here. The exclusion from the Sacrament is by no means limited to mortal sins. The synod at Elvira [ca. 305–306] (canon 34), for example, decrees that people who light candles in the cemeteries during daytime *arceantur ab ecclesiae communione* ["are to be excluded from the Communion of the Church"]; the one at Arles (314, canons 4 and 5), that charioteers (during a race) and actors, as long as they practice their trade, are to be excluded *a communione* (*separari*).

The oldest existing canons of repentance stem from a time when in the Ancient Church it was clear that all Christians succumb to the daily temptations even after Baptism and are always in need of forgiveness. Proof for this is the *exhomologese* ["confession"] in the liturgy, which is expected from all. Even the Montanist Tertullian does not want to be excluded from it. A man like Basilius, who himself created a large collection of repentance canons, expresses very clearly that before God every sin is a mortal sin. Sins that are subject to the discipline of repentance are those that have become publicly known and have stirred up a scandal in the congregation. Where one has sinned publicly, there is also need for public repentance. As long as this does not happen, the sinner is considered to be unrepentant. But how alive the feeling was that the condition of unrepentance is incompatible with receiving the Lord's Supper, even if it was known only to the sinner, can be seen as an example in the "Testament of Our Lord Jesus Christ" (probably Monophysite, fifth century). According to this, the deacon calls out at the beginning of the Eucharist: "Lift your hearts to heaven! If someone hates his neighbor, let him be reconciled; if someone knows about his unbelief, let him confess it; if his mind is far from the Commandments, let him leave; if someone is in a fallen estate, he should not keep it a secret; it is godless to hide; if someone suffers from a sickness of the soul, let him not approach; if someone is dirty, not steadfast—the same; if someone is far from the commandments of Jesus, let him go away; if someone despises the prophets, let him be separated; let him watch out for the wrath of the only (Son)—so that we do not despise the cross!" (p. 250, Quasten). Those are early Christian sounds. Every participant is being warned once more. If he has not repented, he should forgo the Lord's Supper of his own free will, even if he has not been reached by the discipline of the congregation.

The process of repentance had a different development in the East and the West. In the West there is a judicial action early on. The bishop becomes the judge, who assigns punishments *usu forensi*. This is one of the consequences of the theory of sacrifice which led to a mistaken perception of the fellowship character of the Lord's Supper. In the East the thought of punishment is not lacking either. But here it is outweighed by the thought of healing, through the pedagogical purpose of the entire process. Between the repentance process and the exclusion from the Lord's Supper one sees an essential connection. The congregation cannot let the unrepenting sinner, who has been designated as such publicly, take part in the Lord's Supper [*Teilnahmen lassen*], for his own sake. But it cannot do it for its own sake either. The fact that it seeks to protect itself from defilement and infection by excluding [the sinner] should not be understood as a narrow-minded police action (*Didascalia* VI, 14.10). Behind the seriousness with which the participation is guarded, there stands the Pauline understanding of the Lord's Supper. The *koinonia* of Christians among themselves is, according to its essence, *koinonia* in the body of Christ. Therefore, it cannot "eat together" with the unrepenting sinner, to use Paul's expression. Otherwise one would simulate a *koinonia* in the Body of Christ which does not exist.

The Ancient Church made an exception only *in articulo mortis* ["in the case of imminent death"]. The Nicene Council of 325 determined in general that "in every case" the bishop should grant the Eucharist to a dying person desiring it, "under examination" (μετα δοκιμασιας) (can. 13). If the sick remains alive contrary to expectation, he has to be placed again among those who are allowed to partake only in prayer. For this the council refers to the "old canonical law," which "is to be kept even now." Thus the exception must be based on a long tradition. In fact, it was required already by Dionysius of Alexandria (247/248–264). His only difference from the Nicene order is that he does not mention the bishop, and that in the case of recovery, as long as the sinner is not again backsliding, the reconciliation should stand (Pitra I, 546, manuscript).

Third: It has never been doubted in the Ancient Church, either in the Church at large nor in any other, that the fellowship in the Lord's Supper of the local congregation is conditioned and limited by the criterion of confessional fellowship. And they all dealt accordingly. "This food," says Justin already concerning the Supper, "is called by us the Eucharist. No one is permitted to take part of it except one who believes in the truth of our teaching, who has been washed in the bath for the forgiveness of sins and the new birth, and who lives according to the tradition of Christ" (*Apology I*, 66, 1 [ANF 1:185]). The heretic contradicts the confession of the Church and therefore is *ipso facto* excluded from its fellowship. Since the bishop of Antioch Paul of Samosata [200–275] has "gone over from the Canon (the *regula*) to false and illegitimate doctrines," thus is the judgment of the third synod held against him, therefore he "is outside" (εξω; Eusebius VII, 30, 6). The *Didascalia* demands that the deacon question every stranger to find out whether he belongs to the Church or to a sect (*haeresis*) (II, 58, 1). *Haeresis* can also mean schismatics. In the constitutions, this has been enlarged to the demand to ask for a church membership certificate from every one. In the so-called Clementine liturgy, the deacon calls out before the Eucharist: "None of the listeners, none of the unbelievers, none of the heterodox should partake!" (*Apostolic Constitutions* VIII, 12, 2). Heretics are not allowed to enter the church, as long as they remain in heresy, that is, as long as they have not asked to be received or to be received anew. On the other hand, believers are not to enter the buildings of worship of Jews or heretics in order to pray or to worship. Clerics who transgress here are dismissed; laypeople excluded (Laodicea can. 6, can ap. 64 [63]).

Anyone transferring from the Catholic Church to a heresy, but then returning, has to do penance for ten years before the Lord's Supper is granted to him again (Elvira, can. 22). The penance has to be performed for the previous apostasy. It is not demanded from heretics or schismatics who did not belong to the Catholic Church before. There are different conditions for reception. The ones (e.g., Arians, Macedonians, Novatians) are being received by anointing after furnishing a written declaration that they have anathemized all heresies that diverge from the Catholic Church. Others (e.g., Montanists, Sabellians) are received first as catechumens, who have to be baptized again. All of them have to be instructed first and have to memorize the orthodox Creeds. In every case, the participation in the Lord's Supper is the final step in the reception into church fellowship. Without it, it is denied under all circumstances. Exceptions here also are made only *in articulo mortis* ["in the face of imminent death"].

John of Damascus: "We have to hold on with all our strength to this: neither to receive the Lord's Supper from heretics nor to give it to them" (*De fide orth.* IV, 13; PG 94:1153b [NPNF² 9:84]: παση δυναμει τοινυν φυλαξωμεθα μη λαμβανειν μεταληψιν αιρετικων μητε διδοναι).

V.

So far we have looked at excommunication in the view of the local congregation. But by its nature it is also a process of the Church at large. Every excommunication is an exclusion from the Church at large. The expressions which Paul uses for the exclusion of immoral sinners in 1 Corinthians 5:4ff. leave no doubt here. Later excommunications, even if they have been performed only by a single bishop, never have another meaning (against Hatch, *Gesellschaftsverfassung*).[4] The Ancient Church at first made sure of this by communicating to other congregations via a circular letter the excommunication performed in one place. Since the third century, numerous examples for this have been preserved.

However, this method could be used against famous heretics, but not against the more or less numerous adherents and followers who were spread out over entire provinces. There are many reports about attempts by excommunicated [members] to sneak again into the orthodox church fellowship in a different place. In order to safeguard itself against cheaters, the Ancient Church early on developed a process which reminds us of modern methods. Anyone moving in from the outside had to present a written certificate from his former bishop before *koinonia* was granted to him. Marcion [ca. 85–160] already had difficulties being received in Rome because he could not present a certificate from his bishop, his own father (Epiphanius). In the fourth century, this kind of proof of identity, the form, the authorization, etc., is precisely regulated through numerous synodical decrees. The certificates have different names and are of different character. The main difference is between επιστολαι συστατικαι ["letters of commendation"] and *litterae communicatoriae* or also (later) επιστολαι ειρηνικαι ["letters of peace"]. The first Synod at Carthage 345/348 announced a practical purpose for them: No cleric or layperson should be permitted to take the Lord's Supper in another church (canon 7) without a "letter

4 [Edwin Hatch and Adolf von Harnack, *Die Gesellschaftsverfassung der christlichen Kirchen im Alterthum: Acht Vorlesungen gehalten an der Universität Oxford im Jahre 1880* (Giessen: Ricker, 1880). MH]

of his bishop." The traveler, or one moving, is also referred to the new bishop in this way.

The letters of fellowship or of peace are an expression of Church liberality. It is unlimited in space, but limited in the "realm of the Church." The referral to the bishop of the new place of residence indicates that no one can belong to "the Church" without belonging to a certain parish. This guarantees that there is no transgression of the orthodox confession. For, of course, the certificates are recognized only by a bishop who is in church fellowship with the one who issues them. The Synod at Nimes in 394 dealt with a group of clerics coming from the East who do present *epistolia* ["letters"], but with an "unknown signature." This is considered proof of a "simulated religion." But within those established borders there is the assurance that through the church fellowship of the local congregation a Christian also has a part in the universal church fellowship of the Church at large. The concrete expression of the fact that the small circle is a member of the large one is seen in this, that the Christian who transfers from one congregation to another is permitted to take the Lord's Supper in the new one also. The *koinonia* of the Lord's Supper of the local congregation is surrounded and carried by the fellowship of the Lord's Supper of the Church at large.

Special attention is given to the certificates of clerics. Even bishops have to present their credentials in this way. The special attention is justified by the fact that bishops and clerics should enjoy the privileges of their position in a strange place also (Chalcedon, canon 5). They can affirm the church fellowship also through practicing their liturgical function wherever they go. The bishop as well as the priest can everywhere "say Mass," as one would say today. Because this is a matter of privilege, he has to prove his legitimacy when received by a strange congregation.

A cleric who cannot produce a certificate can "receive Communion only as a layperson (ως λαικος κοινωνειτω)." This formula is also used in a different context, which shows that the so-called lay Communion for clerics can also be assigned as punishment. The admission to the *communio laica* can also mean a reconciliation for the cleric, just as it is given to the repenting layperson. Cornelius of Rome (251–253) writes about a bishop who had taken part in the schismatic election of Novatian, but afterward repented this step: "Upon the request of the entire congregation we communed (*kommunizierten*) with him as with a layperson" (Euseb. VI, 43, 10). One can understand this only in such a way that this bishop was not allowed to administer the eucharistic Sacrament, or even to con-celebrate, but that he could receive it together with the laypeople. Since before, by taking part in the schism, he had *ipso facto* excluded himself, the admission to lay Communion meant the readmission into church fellowship, even though not a restitution to the office of bishop. But the fact that he is not permitted to celebrate or con-celebrate (the Mass) is under all circumstances a punishment.

What does this mean for the fellowship in the Lord's Supper that is practiced between local congregations? First of all, it is clear that here also is an expression for the difference between clergy and laypeople. The layperson, provided that he is legitimate, may receive the Lord's Supper in other congregations also. But bishops and presbyters [clergy] may also "celebrate" in other congregations, provided that they have been proven to be legitimate. But under some circumstances the cleric is denied [the right to] celebrate, he is only allowed to "commune as a layperson."

This fact, which existed beyond any denial in the Ancient Church, apparently seems to justify those who in today's interconfessional relationships want to make a difference between a half or a whole church fellowship, or one under certain conditions. Full church fellowship should be demonstrated by the fact that strange clergy should be granted the right to celebrate, that is, to administer the Sacrament; the restricted fellowship would be expressed by admission to the reception of the Sacrament or, in the language of the Ancient Church, to the *communio laica.* We are not going to take a position in regard to this Solomonic judgment, but only state the fact that it absolutely has nothing to do with the practice of the Ancient Church, except that there is a difference between communing and celebrating.

In the Ancient Church, church fellowship is not first established by receiving foreign communicants or those who celebrate. Rather, it is in each case the indispensible condition. Either there exists church fellowship between two congregations or their bishops—both conditions have equal significance—in which case laypeople can commune in both places and bishops and priests can celebrate in both places; or there exists no fellowship, in which case neither the one nor the other is permitted. If a layperson is forbidden to take the Lord's Supper in one congregation, because he is excommunicated or is in a state of repentance, he is also forbidden in the other. If a cleric has been refused to celebrate in one congregation, he is not permitted to do it in another either. If he can commune only *inter laicos* ["among the laity"] in one congregation, he cannot celebrate in another either. The withholding of the right to celebrate happens in connection with deposition, degradation, suspension, and of course with the [great] excommunication. That is a punishment for personal unworthiness. But it never happens in the relationship between two congregations and their bishops that laypeople are permitted to commune while clerics are refused to celebrate because somehow church fellowship is incomplete, or because the congregations and their bishops have a different confession, or agree only in part in their confession. The objection that the Ancient Church could not have made use of this possibility because the coexistence of different confessions is a phenomenon of modern times is misleading. On the contrary, in this regard it was in the same situation as is the case today. This fact, which we already touched on, we now have to take a closer look at.

VI.

We are now going to trace the way the Ancient Church used the word, and also call the local congregation, "Church." Therefore, we can also speak of churches in the plural. Ever since the institution of an individual episcopate, *ecclesia* as a rule means a church assigned to one bishop. We do not have to pay attention to the exceptions (Egypt) at this point. If we were to follow Cyprian [d. 258], church fellowship would not be a problem where there are bishops. In his opinion, the unity of the Church is represented by the bishops. How could fellowship between churches under bishops present any kind of problem? But reality by no means corresponds to this dogmatic statement. The bishops of the Ancient Church represent disunity as much as unity.

In the second century, the individual churches under bishops in a legal way are still completely independent of one another. Whether they can have fellowship with one another is a question. What criteria are determining for this? The constitution for bishops, which they all have in common, is in no way sufficient for this. Just a few examples! Hegesippus [ca. 110–180], who under Anicetus (ca. 154/166) came from the East to Rome via Corinth, states with satisfaction that in all the churches under a bishop which he visited he found the same doctrine. That means that it has to be decided in each case whether there exists worthiness for fellowship [*Gemeinschaftswürdigkeit*], and its criterion is the doctrine. Bishop Victor of Rome [bishop 189–199] excludes Bishop Polykrates of Ephesus [ca. 130–196] from church fellowship, together with all [churches of] Asia Minor, because they have a different date for Easter. He is criticized for this by Irenaeus, because this was not a sufficient reason. According to Irenaeus [130–202] also the decisive criterion is the doctrine. Through the rise of synods and the metropolitan constitution, there comes the possibility that bishops can also be deposed by bishops. The Ancient Church made frequent use of this. Dionysius of Alexandria [bishop 248–265] corresponds with the congregation in Antioch behind the back of its bishop. Even the apostolic succession, despite all the claims of its advocates to the contrary of then and now, does not guarantee in the least that the churches under bishops who possess it can keep church fellowship with one another.

The episcopal constitution is no criterion whatsoever which would belong only to the majority Church. Even Marcion is called "bishop" by his adherents. The Theodotians in Rome attempt to claim their own bishop after having been excluded. Even bishops of the majority Church join the Montanists. The constitution of the Novatians for bishops is the same as that of the majority Church. After Nicaea [325] one does not even have to ask about it anymore. The great anti-Nicene parties are led by bishops who can claim apostolic succession. The same is true with schisms on the grounds of Nicene orthodoxy (Apollinarians, Donatists). The great heretics of the following century—Nestorius [archbishop of Constantinople, 428–431], Dioscurius, Severus [born ca. 465]—are legitimate patriarchs of Constantinople, Alexandria, and Antioch. Because of Chalcedon [451], the unity of the Church of the East is irreparably lost to this day, despite the unity in its constitution. The Church of Armenia, the Nestorians, Monophysites—they all have an episcopal constitution and all are eager to keep apostolic succession. That is how the unity of the episcopate looks in reality, which was to guarantee the unity of the Church, according to Cyprian. The great synods by no means overcome an existing dissent by winning the majority of those dissenting for the consensus. The minority is outvoted, or they leave the assembly before the decision. The majority decides dismissals and excommunications. This causes or favors the formation of particular churches.

Therefore, there is no point in time in the Ancient Church when the question of fellowship from church to church would not have been most urgent. At first the problem seems to be simplified step-by-step by the uniting of individual episcopal churches into metropolitan districts, provincial churches, and patriarchates. However, in the very moment when in Nicaea apparently a maximal unity has been achieved, the problem returns in an intensified form. Now it becomes a special confessional problem. The boundary lines of the confessions are no longer geographic, as was the case before with conflicts between provincial churches. Nicene churches, semi-Arians, Eunomians, Macedonians, Apollinarians all meet in the same space. The pre-Nicene special groups—for example, the Novatians—for a long time and at the same time have covered several parts of the same area with a net of congregations. In addition, after Chalcedon there are the Monophysites, who themselves split up and finally push the orthodox imperial Church in large areas into the minority. All these groups have their church buildings next to each other, especially in the large cities.

The reasons for the splits and the following formation of particular churches are varied, just as is the case today. In part they lie in the area of discipline (Novatians, Donatists), but there can hardly be a modern denomination which would not have its prototype in the Ancient Church, beginning with the Valentinians which correspond to today's Christian fellowship (*Christengemeinschaft*), to Islam, which has an exact copy in today's Mormons. Here like there [there is] a new book, which pushes Jesus in relation to the founder of the sect into a subordinate role.

However, it was the dogma that proved to have the greatest power in splitting [the churches]. This lies in the nature of the matter. The dogma wants to proclaim the pure teaching, and therefore always contains a polemic element. Whoever demands orthodoxy within or from the Church has to be prepared for divisions, for the very concept of orthodoxy presupposes the possibility of heterodoxy. The moment when, for example, the formula "Creator of heaven and earth" was incorporated into the baptismal confession, the contrast to all Gnostic direction and also to Marcion became apparent. It also had become unbridgeable. This contrast still exists today.

But this is only one side of the matter. The dogmas of the Ancient Church do not want to be mere *theologoumena*, not just opinions of theological schools, but binding pronouncements of the Church at large. As doctrine they are the binding norm for the teaching office [*Lehramt*] of the Church, but as confession [binding] for all who include themselves in the "we confess" or "we believe," which stands at the beginning of all teaching decrees of the synods. For this reason they not only provoke divisions, but they also bring about unity. To orthodoxy belongs, according to Basil [of Caesarea, 330–379], homodoxy [i.e., unified confession and praise]. The truly healthy faith leads "to fellowship and unity of those of equal faith" (ομοδοξοι) [Ep. 28, 3]. Until the opposite is proven, all parties assume that a person means what he is saying. Therefore, in the excommunication of anything heretical, those are always included who think "their own" [views] or "the same." What the constitution of the bishops alone does not yet accomplish for the unity of the Church, only the dogma does. It is *homodoxy* in the orthodoxy. Behind the homodoxy stands the harmony in the φρονημα της πιστεως ["convictions regarding the faith"]. Of course, this must not be misunderstood in a subjective way. The confession is a pronouncement of faith as a confession in that which is believed. Not the subjective act of faith, but the objective content of the faith works the unity.

For this reason, the unity of the Church is wounded most deeply through heresy, much more deeply than through differences in discipline. Because homodoxy in dogma is the basic condition for church fellowship, the Ancient Church is unbending in excluding heterodoxy. The question of what is orthodox and what is heterodox is the subject of its formation of the dogma. The question of who is orthodox and who is heterodox leads to the problem of church fellowship. It is clear that the answer for the first question is the indispensable condition for the answer of the second.

VII.

Our historians of dogma tell us what caused the schisms. They also [tell] of successful and unsuccessful attempts at union, but even in modern church-historical and legal histories one learns very little about the methods of confirming the fellowship between homodox churches. We cannot go into this now, but have to limit ourselves to the effects upon the practice of the Lord's Supper. For this also a few practical examples have to suffice.

First: Where there is fellowship from one church to another, fellowship in the Lord's Supper is also granted from one church to another. Irenaeus reminds Victor of Rome that Victor's predecessor "sent the Eucharist" even to those who were "from parishes" that had a different date for Easter than the Roman one

(Eus. V, 24, 15). Sending the Eucharist, which can only mean the consecrated elements, should apparently make possible the "eating of the one bread" in which the *metalepsis* ["participation"] in the body of Christ is accomplished. This reminds us of the notice of Justin, that parts of the blessed elements were also brought by the deacons to absent widows, orphans, sick, and imprisoned (*Apology I*, 67, 5ff.). But the remark of Irenaeus indicates that the Eucharist was also sent abroad. Rightfully he sees in this a proof for the fact that the Roman bishops in this way gave a witness for the fellowship from church to church. Later the Synod at Laodicea [363–364] forbade this practice, probably because of the possibility of misuse. But that does not lesson the strength of the proof of the practice of the Roman bishops in the sense of Irenaeus.

As a further proof, Irenaeus mentions that Anicetus of Rome [bishop, ca. 158] granted the Eucharist to Bishop Polycarp of Smyrna [69–155] when the latter visited Rome (Eus. V, 24, 17). Since Polycarp is in Rome not incognito—that is, not as a private person but as a bishop of his Church—it must be understood that Anicetus permitted him to celebrate. In any case it is without doubt what is important to Irenaeus in this context, namely, that in this way the fellowship of the Church of Rome with the Church of Smyrna is affirmed. Irenaeus therefore presents the proof that there is fellowship between the churches of Rome and Asia Minor by showing that their fellowship in the Lord's Supper is affirmed. That means that, on the other hand, he could not imagine fellowship in the Lord's Supper without church fellowship, and he could not have worked with these proofs if he had assumed that Victor of Rome was of a different opinion. The fact that Victor withdrew the fellowship with the [churches of] Asia Minor, and thereby also cut off fellowship in the Lord's Supper, is for Irenaeus himself and for the other bishops who protest the exclusion of the [churches of] Asia Minor without doubt the reason for the entire presentation of the proof.

With the accomplished split, fellowship in the Lord's Supper ends automatically. Novatian [antipope 251–258] demands from every participant in the Lord's Supper the renunciation of the bishop of the catholic majority, Cornelius [bishop of Rome 251–253]. Cornelius is upset about this, but acts exactly the same way, for he readmits a person who up till now was a follower of Novatian only after that person confessed his fault and denied Novatian again (Eus. VI, 43, 10. 18ff.). The fact that a Christian indeed could not commune in both Roman bishops' churches, the catholic and the Novatian, but had to make a decision for the one or the other was an unavoidable consequence of the schism, according to the conviction of all involved. According to the description of Epiphanias, exactly the same happened during the schism between Bishop Meletius of Lycopolis [died ca. 325] and Peter of Alexandria [bishop 300–311]. The latter was successfully removed through the efforts of the Council of Nicaea. The schism starts with the lifting of sacramental fellowship and is removed when it is put in force again.

In Ephesus (431), there is no common meeting of the general synod, called there by the emperor. Majority and minority are meeting separately and deny legitimacy to each other. The majority excludes the Antioch minority from church fellowship. In order to make this exclusion effective, it [the majority] attempts to prevent the Antioch people from holding their own services. The imperial commissar Candidian, called by the Antioch people, decides: "It is my will that neither party should celebrate, lest there be a schism of the holy and orthodox Church" (Schwartz, *Acta* I, 4, p. 44, 3).[5] The dogmatic difference separating both parties, according to his opinion, still hangs in the balance. He himself only has the order to prevent it from growing into a schism. Therefore, he has to prevent under all circumstances that the parties celebrate separately; for as soon as that happens, the split is perfected. To deny *koinonia* in the Lord's Supper means the completion of splitting the Church.

Fifty years later the fight about Chalcedon broke out between East and West. Pope Felix III [483–492] in 483 sends the Bishops Vitalis and Misenus to Constantinople in order to call the emperor and the local patriarch Acacius [471–489] to order on account of the *Henoticon*. However, the legates are found to be willing to have the Lord's Supper with Acacius. With this, they witness publicly that there is church fellowship between Rome and Constantinople. But this not only contradicts their mission, it does not reflect the facts either. According to Rome's perception, church fellowship can only be granted if the *Henoticon* is withdrawn. Therefore, Vitalis and Misenus are relieved of their office as bishops by a Roman synod and excluded from the "unsullied *koinonia*." They themselves are not accused of any heresy. Despite this, their exclusion is according to canonical orders. Bishops and clerics who commune with heretics or schismatics are themselves excommunicated.

Neither side questions the fact that church fellowship is as indivisible as the Church itself. Its integrity demands integrity of all partners. Whoever communes with an outsider who is a heretic or schismatic, or for any other reason has not been received into total fellowship, himself becomes unworthy of fellowship, because he hurts the integrity of the whole. Archbishop Theophilus of Alexandria [patriarch 385–412] excommunicates his archpresbyter Petrus—and another presbyter, Isidore, who stuck with him—because Petrus admitted a Manichaean woman to the Lord's Supper who had not renounced her heresy. This is perfectly legitimate, only Petrus claims that the archbishop had previously declared his agreement. Isidore and the four "tall brothers," Egyptian monks, attempt to receive in Constantinople an intervention in favor of those who, according to their opinion, had been excluded unjustly. They are received with honors by the local patriarch John

5 [Wissenschaftliche Gesellschaft in Strassburg and Eduard Schwartz, *Acta Conciliorum Oecumenicorum* (Berlin: de Gruyter, 1927). MH]

Chrysostom and are not prevented from attending the services (των ευχων). But he is unwilling to grant them *koinonia* in the Lord's Supper until the matter is investigated. Theophilus, who is instructed about this, claims wrongly that Chrysostom also granted them the Sacrament. He uses this occasion to put Chrysostom in the wrong, and thus works into the hands of the enemies of the patriarch at the court, who finally achieves his dismissal (Socrates VI, 9; Sozomen VII, 12ff.).

One can see how a single case, the perceived or real incorrectness in admitting the Manichaean woman to the Lord's Supper, creates ever wider circles. The archpresbyter is excluded because of it. If this exclusion is justified, the "tall brothers" also have to be excluded, because before and after they remained in fellowship with him. Chrysostom acts correctly, inasmuch as he refuses the Sacrament to them. He only gets into trouble because he only suspends the *koinonia* in the Lord's Supper with them, because in doing so he acknowledges that the original case is in need of a revision. Then again, Theophilus of Alexandria takes the behavior of Chrysostom as a reason to suspend fellowship with him. The entire process has symptomatic significance for the Communion practice of the Ancient Church, even if Theophilus uses it only as an excuse.

The principle that impermissible *koinonia* in the Lord's Supper hurts the integrity of church fellowship is the same in the non-catholic churches also. The schism within the Novatian Church begins with the fact that Sabbatios separates himself from the Novatian congregation in Constantinople, because supposedly unworthy people had been admitted to the Lord's Supper. The fact that Paul the Black [patriarch 550–575], Monophysite patriarch of Antioch, was willing, once or twice, to commune with the Synodites, the adherents of the Synod of Chalcedon, makes him unworthy of fellowship with his own fellow believers. It is one of the accusations which cause the refusal of church fellowship with him by the Egyptian Monophysites, and finally his dismissal (John of Ephesus KG II, 3; IV, 15ff.).

VIII.

The dogmatic fights often are protracted over a long time before they lead to a complete split between churches. This is quite natural. Each party at first attempts to refute the other theologically and, if possible, to win it for its own side. A retarding element, especially during the time of the Arian controversies, is also the pressure of the state, which is interested in unity. All parties seek to keep up, as long as possible, the fiction of the unity of the imperial Church. How this affects the practice of the Lord's Supper the following example will show.

Philostorgius [ca. 368–439] reports that the Arians, despite their teaching, which is opposite to that of the orthodox Nicaeans, nevertheless take part [*teilnahmen*] in their "prayers, songs, councils, and almost all other things, except the mystical sacrifice"; that is, they did not partake in the celebration of the

Supper. This relatively peaceful condition only the radical Aetius [Flavius Aetius, 396–454?] put an end to by causing the homodox to found a separate congregation (III, 14). Sozomen also reports that under Constantine, the Arians did not yet form a separate congregation, but rather that all except the Novatians, Phrygians (Montanists), Valentinians, Marcionites, and Paulinianists—that means all except the pre-Nicene heretics and schismatics—assembled together and maintained fellowship. Sozomen blames a general imperial prohibition of small group meetings for this, which obligated all Christians to visit the same houses of worship. Both reports let us see how the dogmatic conflict that broke out after Nicaea was reflected even in individual local congregations. However, both reports can be correct only within their limits of space and time. In Egypt especially things were different, but that does not detract from the importance of the report of Philostorgius.

As mentioned before, Philostorgius lets the complete separation of the congregations begin only with the appearance of Aetius (middle of the fifties). But it is important for him [to state] that his Arian fellow believers did not have complete church fellowship with the Nicenians even before then. They visit their services but do not take part in [*nehmen ... nicht ... teil*] their Lord's Supper. One could think that in the places that are covered by this report they were prevented from doing so by the orthodox majority or its clergy. But Philostorgius presents the matter as a voluntary resignation of fellow believers, and since there is also talk of common consultations, it seems most likely that the abnormal rule happened with agreement from both sides.

Of course, this rule could be thought of only as a moratorium. No party wants to take up the odium of a complete split between churches. Up to the Synod of Sardica in 343, as mentioned before, the fiction of the unity of the imperial Church is kept up from all sides. Only in Sardica a formal secession of the anti-Nicene Eusebians happens, and another one and a half decades pass until Aetius and Eunomius [died ca. 393] from Constantinople organize a special Church by ordaining bishops for Asia Minor. Thus the moratorium happens at a time when a clear decision concerning the exclusion of the one or the other party from the majority Church has not yet happened. But exactly because of this, it has a symptomatic significance which goes beyond the momentary situation. We do not learn whether the equal behavior of the Arians in different districts is directed by a central agency or whether the local groups act spontaneously. In any case, a central direction would be thinkable. However, since at that time there is no central jurisdiction of Arian bishops outside of their own dioceses, it would have been ineffective if the disparate groups would not have agreed because of their own conviction. In any case, the rule that was established presupposes the view of the congregational members themselves. The doctrinal controversy is understood in the congregations, namely, as a confessional controversy, which demands a personal decision from every church member. Some make a decision for the *homoousia* of the Son with the Father; the others, against it. These, the Arians, draw the conclusion that because of the disunity in the confession one cannot commune together. According to everything we know about the Homoousians, it is a matter of course that they do not think differently.

This process has exemplary significance for the entire Ancient Church. Today's opinion is often that the churches may differ in many things—in confession, organization, the liturgy—but that despite everything should celebrate the Lord's Supper together as a witness to their unity. The Arians do the exact opposite. They take part in the meetings of the Nicaeans, in their prayer service, their debates, and in "almost everything else," but not in their Lord's Supper. Here and there the Lord's Supper has a special significance for the unity of the Church. In the first case, according to that modern understanding, the partners know that they are not united in important areas. Despite that, they want to celebrate the Lord's Supper together, because they wish to be united and because they consider the Lord's Supper the proper means to witness to this desire. One can only come to this conclusion if one sees the "fellowship character" of the Lord's Supper in the uniting of the participants for a common meal, and if one is of the opinion that one is at liberty to use this means to achieve the purpose of unification.

In the other case, with the Arians, the partners also know that in fact they are not united, in this case not in the confession. They also wish to re-create the full unity of the imperial Church, else they would not take part [*teilnehmen*] in the local consultations of the Nicene congregations. But they cannot commune with them, because for them the unity of the Church is not the purpose of the celebration of the Lord's Supper, but its indispensible precondition. In this regard they share the understanding of the Lord's Supper with the entire Ancient Church. The *koinonia* of the Lord's Supper is a *metalepsis* ["participation"] in the body of Christ, which humans are free to carry out as they please, a fact which is to be respected by all people, which they should follow. Therefore, the participants are obligated to eliminate the existing dissensions. As long as there is still something separating them, they cannot commune together, for every disunity which is taken into the Lord's Supper will wound the Body of Christ.

In this way, participation [*Teilnahme*] in the Lord's Supper itself, as well as its refusal, becomes an inner-church act of confession. There are many examples for this from the Ancient Church. They are not always pleasant. The imperial bishop Makedonius of Constantinople (342/348 and 350/360) seeks to win the Novatians in the capital for a union. When the Novatians definitely refuse, βια των μυστηριων μετεχειν τους ανδρας ηναγκαξον (Socrates II, 38). Thus this prince of the Church seeks to create a church legal fact through a forced Communion. For this purpose, the mouths of the obstreperous men are forced open with a piece of wood, and then the Communion elements are stuffed in. This method is no longer used today. But that Christians are put under pressure in order to make them partake [*Teilnahme*] in a celebration of the Lord's Supper, which lacks the condition that agrees with their faith, happened in the nineteenth century and is still happening today.

But it would be wrong to conclude from this and similar events that in the Ancient Church the renunciation of fellowship in the Lord's Supper between the churches would necessarily have meant constant fighting and arguing. We only have to think once more of the Arian moratorium. When Bishop Paulus of the Novatian congregation in Constantinople died (439), he made, as Socrates reports, "at his funeral all different confessions [αιρεσεις] so to speak into one Church, for they all accompanied his body to the grave, singing psalms" (VII, 46).

One last example from the student congregations of the Ancient Church. Zacharias Rhetor tells how he studied jurisprudence, first in Alexandria, then in Berytos, together with Severus, the later Monophysite patriarch, and how gradually he tried to win him for the teaching of the Church. Severus had not yet been baptized. In Berytos they joined together with other like-minded students, visiting together the services in the city churches, and also praying together. But when Severus declares that he is ready to receive Baptism, and asks the friend to become his sponsor, Zacharias turns down the request because he does not commune with the bishops of Phoenicia who adhere to Chalcedon, since he is a Monophysite (*Vie de Severe*. PO II, 1 p. 78, 6). Thus he behaves like the Arians during the time of the moratorium. Despite the fact that the student circle by no means consists only of Monophysites, they visit together services in Berytos, dispute theological questions, and also pray together. But the Baptism of Severus would have to be followed by the Eucharist, and this last completion of fellowship the young law student must deny himself, because between him and the bishop of the city there is this difference in the confession.

According to the understanding of the Ancient Church, the confession qualifies the entire person as orthodox or heterodox, but the one like the other can be only "in fellowship." What kind of fellowship one belongs to, that is, what church one belongs to, is seen by where one communes. The fact that the Princess Sophia, before the enthronement of her husband (Justin II [ca. 520–578]), received the Eucharist from a Monophysite priest was for everybody proof that she did not want to have fellowship with the members of the (Chalcedonian) Synod. On the other hand, "she fell," as John of Ephesus called it, "into the fellowship of the Synod members" the moment she started "to commune together with the Synod" (KG II, 10). By partaking in the Lord's Supper of a church, the Christian bears witness that the confession of this church is also his confession. Because one cannot agree with two different confessions at the same time, one cannot commune in two churches of different confessions either. Whoever does it anyway either denies his own confession, or he does not have any. This is how one thought and acted in the Ancient Church.

CHAPTER SEVEN

Opinion Concerning Communion Fellowship

Read before Some Friends by Pastor Loehe in Neuendettelsau 1863[1]

Translated by Wolf Dietrich Knappe

You know, my brothers, what efforts some pastors in the Bavarian *Landeskirche*, some of us included, have made during the last decades in order to get rid of the evil of mixed Communion which has spread among us, as it has in all the German *Landeskirchen*. They tried to restore the faithfulness in regard to Communion fellowship which is fitting for the Lutheran Church. These pastors not only kept the faith on their part, giving public witness in periodicals and tracts, but also did not neglect to make requests and presentations before the governing authorities of the Church and the general synods. During the last general synod, they no longer wanted to tackle this matter; the debate of our presentations was denied, as if there could be the danger that the outward peace of the *Landeskirche*, which it had taken so much trouble to establish, could be disturbed. You will all agree with me that now our means are exhausted and that we have come to the end with all our efforts to bring about better conditions in general.

It is impossible to make this confession without deep sadness. It is no small part of our life which we have dedicated to this sacred matter. For its sake we have suffered to be in a state of protestation for such a long time. We suffered bad reports, tolerated the misery of being hated, and much other grief and hardship which is known to you and to God. And after all this we are burned out and in general are unable to do any more. We got older, and almost all of us turned gray over this, and instead of being able to congratulate ourselves, we can do nothing

1 Wilhelm Loehe, *Gutachten in Sachen der Abendmahlsgemeinschaft* (Nördling: C. H. Beck'sche, 1863).

but put down our weapons and mourn that the holiest and best cause for which we stood in our life, in general, did not find the response it deserved.

We would be very ungrateful toward God if we were going to say that we did not accomplish anything. Our voice in this sacred matter has been heard in many places, both on this side and on the other side of the ocean. There are quite a few individual pastors here and there whose conscience has been stirred so much that they found better ways in their practice of the Lord's Supper than before. It is also clear that in our own immediate homeland our numbers have been growing. Even younger pastors have joined us in this cause, and in their attitude they give us a certain kind of guarantee that the witnesses and the witness will not die out after we are gone. But we do not want to measure or count our successes, not present them in a lengthy way, so that we do not appear as praising ourselves more than thanking God, and that we do not provoke our enemies to an unjust contradiction and zeal and thereby raise new obstructions to the truth. But no matter what we could say to the praise of God about the success of our witnessing, though conscious of our own mistakes and sins, the fact still is that in general nothing has become better.

When at first we raised our voices in this matter, everywhere consciences were stirred: To almost everybody the mixed Communion appeared if not as sin, at least as an evil which one had to get away from, even though one could not overcome it with one strike. During these many years, we had enough time and means to get rid of the evil, but in general only a few weak attempts have been made. The old evil is still a burden everywhere, as one could easily prove, and, what is worse, one has learned to look at the matter with totally different eyes. What was an evil at the beginning, one to get rid of with all power, has now become an evil which you cannot get rid of, which one must bear, and one that can be borne since in the final instance it does not endanger the existence of the Lutheran Church. Thus one gradually falls asleep, and after a while one will have found not just excuses but also will have discovered reasons to defend the present condition. Perhaps one will call this progress within the Church, a throwing away of the harshness of the Reformation when one offers Communion across the confessional fences. One will find a few isolated examples for mixed Communion during earlier times of the Lutheran Church and use them as proof, the longer the more convincing, that even in former times there was no agreement in this matter. Finally, one will praise the nineteenth century because this, like other questions of earlier days, has finally found a happy solution.

And yet nothing is more simple than the conclusion:

St. Paul says in Titus 3:10: "A man that is an heretick after the first and second admonition reject" [KJV].

The Reformed and the Union Christians are heretics. Therefore, we are to reject them.

If one should reply to this: Of course this conclusion is simple, but first one has to prove that the Reformed and Union people are heretics, only then the conclusion is valid—it is very easy to bring the proof in regard to the Reformed. True, it has become customary in our century not to bring critical questions to a final solution, we let arguments and counterarguments stand at the same time. But in this point we would quickly be victorious, even in our time, not only through clear and unanimous witnesses from the Lutheran tradition but also through simple exegesis, a simple description of what God's Word is saying. The idle talk about sister churches would easily be exposed as nothingness. One could bring the sweeping proof that even if there was some meaning to the word "sister church," this would not remove the limits and differences between the churches, or make permissible the most intimate union, that of the Sacrament, and overthrow all the confessional fences. It is unnecessary to persecute a heretic with fire and sword, nor with hatred, ridicule, derision, or insult. I can recognize a person as a heretic without throwing aside fairness and love that excuses things. Even according to the judgment of our severe fathers, I can still recognize him in a certain sense as a member of the Church, and yet avoid him—avoid him personally, but especially in the Sacrament. After three centuries, after such a long separation and living next to each other, we should have learned to keep the name heretic, in calm determination, even mutually, and to bear it without dipping it into the fire of bitter hatred. One could possibly have learned to call a church a sister church, because of such close relationship, and yet avoid it because of the heretical teachings it keeps as different, separated from the true Church. The name heretic means nothing else but the judgment that a person, despite the clear divine Word in a certain article of faith, dares to keep and defend his own human opinion, even though he has received sufficient admonition. Whenever I have to make this judgment, I have to avoid my opponent in church matters, not only out of love to myself, lest I become lukewarm toward the truth, but also out of love for him, so that he will not become completely at home in the lie. I have to bother him, bother him with my opposition, through my opposition in word and in life, so that he will not become completely hardened in the lie. It is clear that I do not give up loving a person by calling him a heretic and as such avoid him.

As far as the word *avoid* goes, no reasonable person will arrive at the thought that the apostle only wanted to forbid the personal relationship in daily life. In 1 Corinthians 7:12–16, he does not permit a Christian to break off a marriage with a Jew or pagan. Much less would he permit the personal relationship between spouses to be interrupted because of heresy. This is a powerful example which throws light on any relationship, especially one of less intimacy. And if avoiding does not forbid every kind of personal relationship, what else could be forbidden except the churchly relationship? Or: If the personal relationship would really be forbidden, would the churchly relationship not have to be forbidden much more, since it is a spiritual relationship and therefore a most intimate one? And if the avoiding refers to churchly relationship, does it not have to mean especially sacramental fellowship, which includes the fellowship of spirits at their greatest depth? And if I have to avoid every heretic in church and in the Sacrament, would I not have to avoid the Reformed heretic especially? His heresy refers to the Sacrament itself. He wants to take away from Holy Communion its highest value and therefore also the power of its sacred effect. At least he acts that way, perhaps without understanding that he becomes guilty because of such an attempt. How you can extricate yourself from all this and despite the apostolic commandment keep Communion fellowship with heretics, I do not understand, and with all my desire for love and fellowship I cannot excuse it, except by first assuming that the Lutheran who acts in this way, himself does not know and has not experienced what the Sacrament is and what it gives to a person.

One will rather be inclined to admit all this in regard to the Reformed than to the Unionists [members of the Union Church]. The fact that the Unionist, as stated above, is simply put next to the Reformed and should be a heretic just as this one, many will not want to admit. I myself admit that there is a difference between Unionists and Unionists. I find it possible that somewhere in the complex of a United *Landeskirche* there could be a congregation which, though completely following Lutheran teaching and Lutheran life, is only called United because it is under a United church government. In my opinion such a congregation is not United at all. The church governments of the *Landeskirchen* are unavoidable superstructures. From the fact that they are tolerated one cannot always conclude what the condition of the individual congregation is. If there was such a congregation which kept its special Lutheran position in doctrine and Sacrament, despite a United government, I would no more consider it United than myself. In my eyes it would be as good a Lutheran as I am myself, even though for half a century I have lived and still live under a Roman Catholic supreme bishop. But I also admit that in reality so far I always found myself mistaken whenever I tried to ascribe the necessary separation in doctrine and sacramental fellowship to a congregation living in a United complex.

However, if I think of truly United Christians, I really do not know how they could avoid being called heretics by true Lutherans. Either a member of the Union Church will find the words of the Lord and His apostles and evangelists concerning the sacred Supper unclear, and therefore does not have the courage to subscribe to the teaching of the ancient churches concerning the presence and the distribution of the body and blood of Jesus. Or he will find these words clear, so that he personally shares the teaching of the ancient churches, but without attributing to his own knowledge and that of the ancient churches the importance which is given to it by the ancient churches, especially the Lutheran, so that he would not break off Communion fellowship with those who think otherwise. In both cases he stands before the Lutheran Church as one who has to be avoided in church matters, especially if he has been admonished more than once. In the first case, he resists completely the divine Word, which could not speak more simply and clearly than in the sacramental words, and through them takes captive any soul of goodwill under the obedience of faith. In this case there cannot be a lack of knowledge, only of the will. The human will refuses not only the commonly accepted understanding of all the ancient churches but also the clearest words of God Himself. Here is a heresy of the will. Basically, and in its consequences, it is no less to be rejected than any other heresy. But in the second case, where one does not want to consider the clearly known Word as authoritative for others, and the clear trumpet call of the divine Word is stamped as a private opinion, I cannot see anything else as in the first case: a heresy of the will, which in the end makes me shudder even more than the Reformed heresy, which in the end admits at least some subjective honesty and uprightness. Or should one excuse the latter United opinion with blindness? Is it possible to acknowledge the essence of Holy Communion without recognizing its greatness and its glory, its effects and blessings? Can a person know what he has in Holy Communion without attributing to it the greatest significance for the life of the individual and of the congregation? Can a person really be so nearsighted that he let himself be admonished without coming to any clarity? I confess that I have great doubts about the inner moral condition of the so-called principally United. But even if this was not so, how can I translate the churchly behavior of the United into a simple word? Do I not have to say either: "The United does not want to recognize the essence of the Sacrament, its importance, and its effect"; or "He knows its essence, but he does not want to admit its importance and its effect"? Do I not have to say in both cases: "He does not want to see the truth, does not want to recognize the greatness, the importance, the effect of the truth"? Does he push the sun into the fog in order not to be forced by its light to act according to apostolic principles? And do such sentences not deserve to be heresies of the will? And is the seat of heresy not generally in the will, not in reason? I find a difference between the heresy of the United and the Reformed, but to the disadvantage of the United who wants to extinguish the light of the centuries in order to walk in darkness. I confess that when it comes to the Sacrament, I do not want to have anything to do with the Reformed, but indeed even much less with those who are United in principle.

In our time, there rises from the Protestant Church a superficial, broad new direction, the Protestant direction of the nineteenth century. With a certain grandiosity and nobleness, it rises over all confessions, namely, over the Protestant ones, and according to its opinion completes the Reformation by stamping the different doctrines of the individual confessions as mere opinions which everybody should tolerate, and the Sacrament should be a point of uniting everybody. Spurgeon in a sermon on verse 19 of the Epistle of Jude:

> Under God's wide sky there is no Christian from whom I am separated. I always invited all Christians to take part of the Lord's meal with us. If someone would tell me that I am separated from the Episcopalians, the Presbyterians or Methodists, from the Lutherans or Calvinists, I would tell him that he doesn't know me; for I love them with honest and burning heart, and I am not separated from them. This is a rather hard talk for all exclusive church fellowships. I do not want to offend anyone through harsh pronouncements, but these Christian brothers separate themselves from the great universal Church. They say they do not want to have Communion with others, and if someone comes to their table of the Lord who does not have the same forms of the faith, they turn him away. The lifeblood of the Body of Christ is Communion—the sacred Supper—and woe to the church that tries to heal the evils which the Body of Christ may be suffering from by stopping its pulse. I consider it a sin to refuse having Communion with someone who is a member of the Church of our Lord Jesus Christ. I would accuse myself of a giant mistake, if I would meet at the steps of the altar a truly repentant child of God who does not have the name of my own church fellowship and I would say to him: "No, you do not agree with us in certain points—I believe you are a child of God—but I don't want to have anything to do with you." I would remember that this very text would bear witness against me: "These be they who separate themselves, sensual, having not the Spirit." . . .

It does not matter what the Lord meant with His sacramental words, but everybody, no matter what opinion he has of the Sacrament and other doctrine, should come to His meal upon His command, and let the same work whatever He decided, but one ought only to strive for unity and love. All come, enjoy bread and wine, proclaim His death, let go of all disagreements, and on this way of nonchalance they become one Church. This is the meaning of Protestantism, which, if I see correctly, has first appeared in the forests of America and from there started out to conquer the old world. It will also succeed. Everything Protestant belongs to it in the whole world with the exception of a few Lutherans. It is the grandiose United Church—destroying meaning of the new Church—and the head from which it is born, like Minerva, is none but the Reformed Church. With all its unbelief in the words of Christ about the Last Supper, it wanted from the beginning Communion fellowship, that is, the most intimate union among all Protestant parties. Its greatest heresy does not show itself in the different confessions concerning the Lord's Supper, but in the sentence that any confession concerning it should not be church dividing and that the teaching about Holy Communion should not be listed among the church dividing articles, as Luther had done. With this the Lord's institution has lost its meaning, the Church has been deprived of the God-given power of renewal, and the altar, which more than anything else gathers the Church and keeps it and should keep it, has been pushed into the fog of opinions. Not only that person has become Reformed who accepts the Reformed confession of Communion, but also the one who in any way does homage to the Union and strikes the doctrine of the Holy Supper from the register of church dividing teachings. The power of the Reformed Church lies in the Union. But the grandiose heresy of the United will has the consequence to lead to any Reformed confession, even the most negative one. It will take away the ark and the *Shechinah* and leave behind an empty temple, which waits for a different coming of the Lord Jesus Christ. With these thoughts one can understand why I detest the nebulous heresy of the United will more than the Reformed confession. I shy away from it, flee and avoid the United more than the heretic of the Reformed confession.

I know that in all the above my sole foundation is the apostolic word: "a heretical person you shall avoid." In its clear simplicity it is all sufficient. But the entire Scripture is full of the same spirit.

If the mixing of the Sacrament has been thus demonstrated as something infamous, its infamy can also be shown quite simply by other invincible reasons. Take the question: Who confers the office to a pastor? Quite plainly the Church to which he himself belongs. And for whom does it confer the office to him? Without any doubt for the members, and only for its own. In the first place he is there only for the congregation to which he has been called. Beyond its borders he may be capable to administer the office, but he does not have the authority. Thus a pastor may not even extend his activity across his parochial borders without sinning against the word of the apostle which forbids one to interfere in a foreign office (1 Peter 4:15). Other congregations of the same confession may be served by him only according to a certain rule and order. The parochial borders limit his activity, and yet the confessional separation, which is of much greater significance, is so easily ignored! Who indeed has called you to the service of the Reformed or United? With the Romans, whose doctrine of the Sacrament could satisfy a Lutheran much more than that of the Reformed, you understand your limits. And with the Reformed and United you do not comprehend them? Even if, because of other differences in doctrine, you consider yourself more separated from the Romans than from the Reformed, and rightly so, and if the agreement with the Reformed in other doctrines spreads sand into your eyes so that you do not recognize the tremendous difference in regard to the Sacrament, you should at least respect the parochial borders of the Reformed according to your Lutheran viewpoint. Even the Reformed belongs to his own congregation, or has to seek it for the sake of God and because it is right, if he does not have it. But you consider him a sheep without a master, and without giving it a thought you act as if it was your right. Even if Reformed pastors, in the spirit of their church and in order to carry out the principle that Holy Communion should not be church separating, would grant us the right not to observe the parochial borders, we should not do it, even for the sake of the Lutheran principle that Holy Communion is church dividing.

If someone answers to this that all this is well-known, even admits everything, but that at times one is compelled by mercy to grant the Reformed their wish, one should remember that mercy in this case could not be very deep, hearty, and painful, because here is no mention of mercy, only about what is right. One changes the evil into mercy, so that one can do it, instead of awakening the conscience for what is right or not. A Lutheran abroad is categorically forbidden to let himself be served with the Sacrament, he has to be content with the *crede et manducasti,* and yet he misses out on so much. But the Reformed—who does not even seek what we give him in Communion, does not take it, and does not miss it; who, looking at it from the Lutheran standpoint, does not miss much of anything—would challenge so many Lutheran pastors to have mercy! Should it not be easy to send him away? Every year he travels long distances for pleasure, and should he be in such trouble that calls for mercy if he has to walk a few hours, ride or take a train in order to find a congregation that he belongs to or should be assigned to? Should one have pity on him if he does not want to do that, and would it be so hard for a merciful heart to tell a person of this kind: "Go where you belong!"? If one has true mercy, one would teach the poor Reformed first the fact that his Reformed Communion also should be worth some trouble; second, that in the Lutheran Church the Sacrament is considered so great, high, and bringing a blessing that before receiving it one must first recognize the immeasurable gift and appreciate it. In short: True mercy must teach a pastor and compel him to lead the Reformed to the Lutheran Church, so that he will not remain a stranger, but a native and a citizen at the altar. But if a Reformed does not want to be taught, wants to go to Communion in Bavaria with the Lutherans and in his Reformed home again with the Reformed, in his private view of the Sacrament always remaining Reformed, one should not talk about mercy toward the Reformed. One should rather examine oneself whether one is not a weak slave of miserable churchly conditions, of peaceful comfort, or even being a belling-serving pastor who does not want to miss the donation of the often wealthy Reformed. This donation might be sufficient to make it possible for the Reformed to travel to his own fellow believers and his own Communion. Of course, what is said here about the Reformed also applies to the United.

After such a long struggle and manifold discussion of the matter, it is clear that all this is said not in order to teach, but as a witness. It may and must be repeated because it is necessary. One loves to talk in such a way as if the sacramental mixing among us was only an exception. However, it is not hard at all to bring proof and evidence that in many congregations—in fact, almost everywhere where there is a Reformed and United *diaspora*—the exception has become the rule. Looking at the perceptions of the matter which have been formed in the course of time, there is not much hope that conditions could change, if here and there one would have an isolated case and one could say that truthfully one could either drop the protestation or raise it only against this single case. But that is not how it is, and we avoid it mainly to bring the proof, which in Bavaria is known by everyone anyway, so that no one can reproach us for making a public display of the shame of our Lutheran *Landeskirche*. As things are, one can indeed say that the Communion fellowship of the Bavarian Lutheran Church (and as far as we know also of all other *Landeskirchen*, as it hardly can be any other way) could be taken by people of ill will as a witness that our fathers, with Luther at the head, acted very unjustly not only to establish the necessary separation from the Roman Church but also from the Reformed Church, and thereby tear and split apart the poor people even more. Our fathers apparently are shamed by our actions. If we are not the people who would have made such a separation, we should at least keep up the existing separation. By being a little serious this would be easy. We do not do it, and certainly not out of faithfulness! Apparently we do not live by Lutheran but by Reformed principles: thousands and thousands of examples of mixed Communion prove that we no longer consider the doctrine of the Sacrament as church dividing. We make the faith of all churches, with the exception of the Reformed, in the real presence and the true distribution of the body and blood of Christ a matter of private opinion, just like the Reformed. For even though we share this faith with the Ancient Church, we tolerate it that from the northern border of Bavaria all the way to Lindau hundreds and thousands approach our altars who do not think of joining the Lutheran Communion confession. They remain faithful to their unbelief or the nebulous home of their churches. From whatever standpoint you can say what you want, but looking at it simply and in a churchly way, the Reformed principle is triumphing, and so much more the longer it lasts, and the more through the long duration sense and understanding of pastors and congregations become hardened.

Or what kind of effect should such conditions have? One could solve this question, as we Germans like to do, without taking a look at reality. In theory we could determine the extent of our proceeding, and then we could imagine that things were so. But what good is that for us who are standing in the middle of the life of the Church? If we want to know what kind of pastoral effect our mixing of Communion has, we only have to go into the congregations where it rules. There we can see the results. If in such a congregation the right person, under the right circumstances—not touching finances of churches and pastorates, etc.—will move to become a Union church, the entire congregation will agree, especially if the Reformed are smart enough to leave artwork and altars in place and not to insist that one celebrate Communion in the most naked Swiss form, perhaps serving it on the cover of the baptismal font or on the organ. In such congregations there rules indifference toward confessional borders, not only ignorance of the different doctrines but also aversion toward them. There is no feeling for the Sacrament, its power, its effect. One remembers the death of the Lord in the most superficial way, with many different explanations, and also makes the Sacrament a gathering place for the most diverse, mixed-up members of the congregation. There can be no talk of Lutherans influencing the Reformed, unless here and there a Reformed person would notice that the Reformed service—for example, those in Switzerland—are much too bare! The Sacrament for a Lutheran must be the one and all not only of churchly life but also of all Christian life. The Sacrament forms, the Sacrament sustains, the Sacrament advances and perfects the congregation if it is comprehended, explained, administered, and used as it should be. In it the center is given for the leading of the congregation and the individual soul; in it are concentrated in an understandable and present way all the doctrines of the Church, most of all those concerning justification and sanctification. Whoever knows this and has experienced it knows also what is taken away from the congregations that practice a mixing of the Sacrament, and what has been made impossible for them. He will also know what has been taken away and has been made impossible for the Reformed *diaspora* in such congregations. The mixing of the Sacrament and the Union do not permit a pastoral use of the Sacrament, remove the Lord's Supper from the center into the periphery, and in the altar and its rich divine blessing they take away from the poor congregations the power to resist the world and its tendencies, the devil, his works, and his being. Pastors and congregations who have agreed to the sacramental Lutheran direction have, I firmly believe, a promise that the gates of hell will not overcome them, if indeed they have agreed not only on a human but also on a spiritual level.

This kind of unity we have wanted to make possible, this was our goal, and our distress is the fact that in the end we had to say that we have not achieved what we considered possible and achievable. Under certain circumstances we still dare to hold to it. Now we—I mean you, my dear brothers, and myself, since in this matter we are one heart and one soul—could just accept this sad necessity. We pastors who agree with one another have no problem in our places. So far no one has forced us, or was able to force us, to lead our office according to other principals than those which we have. And none will force us. Our congregations and our penitent confessors either are in complete agreement with us or at least do not resist us. We could be content with our immediate conditions, pasture our flocks to the best of our ability and understanding, and leave the further care to God the Lord who knows all things. We could also, as mentioned above, be comforted with the fact that we have many followers in this conviction and in the conducting of their office. There are more of us now than there were during that assembly in Schwabach, where we had to discuss the mysteries of the kingdom of heaven and how to lead the congregations in the Sacrament right under the eyes and ears of a police officer.

However, the sacramental direction that is faithful to our Lutheran Church also has a *diaspora*. All over the country there are isolated families and people who have the same convictions as we do, who waited together with us for help, prayed and struggled for it. Their pastors and congregations paid as little attention to their protest and their presentations as the entire *Landeskirche* did to our combined efforts. Just as we became irksome to the *Landeskirche* because of our efforts, they also became irksome to their pastors and congregations. And since as a result of the last general synod human help has disappeared, they stand there perplexed, embarrassed, and isolated. Here and there the faithful pastors had to leave, or the previous pastor died. There is a lack of leadership, or those left behind have not yet joined the successors of their shepherds, etc. What is going to happen to those poor people, some of whom cling frantically to the witness of their leaders? Here and there they no longer went to Communion in their home churches, because in their confusion they did not know anything better, and during the time of the protest and the struggle they would rather take one step too many than to do too little. Here and there they were completely right, and it was their duty to abstain: With their convictions, what were they to do before altars where openly the un-Lutheran practice was not only tolerated but also practiced and made the rule? The hope that things would improve made abstinence tolerable for them, or they bore the reproach to be considered desperate people, and with a letter of dispensation from their pastor would go to other altars where there was no danger of Communion mixing. But what now? Should those people, whose center and star of their earthly life was the Sacrament, now that their hope for improvement is gone, be content for the rest of their lives with a *crede et manducasti*? Should they forever, even to old age, be on a pilgrimage for the high enjoyment of the sacramental celebration? Or should they do, as here and there some have done—should they let go of their conviction, their faithfulness to their conviction, because they are weary of fighting, weary of waiting, and thus, without blaming their former behavior, or able to blame it, join those pastors and congregations they had avoided and thus in the future go to God's Table without any further regard of all Communion discipline? Perhaps it may happen with a grim resignation, with the feeling of apostasy, having left the first direction and having gone to another for which they have no respect. Perhaps then, in the misery and despair, they become people of the world who loudly scorn the first and the second direction and give their hungry souls the husks of this world to eat, because they could not receive the food and drink of eternal life the way they wanted it. There are already examples for this. By reaching in despair for the Communion fellowship that is forbidden by the Lord, they were driven on by the spirit of despair to the communion with the world and the devil. Should we tolerate this, dear brothers, and not give advice to our own *diaspora*? May the Lord forgive those who would rather have Communion with the Reformed or United than to do their duty and help the poor lambs of Jesus. Despite all their weaknesses and transgressions, He nevertheless looks at them with more mercy, since He has bought and won them, than those sheep who had no shepherd and whom He delivered from physical starvation on the green grass of the mountains of Galilee. This we may not do, and my main intention in the following words is to advise them and keep the necessary faithfulness for them. Listen and examine what I now want to say.

It is and remains a difficult task to give meaningful advice. A number of years ago many of those for whom it took too long to wait for help in their churchly trouble emigrated to America. There, in the Franconian colonies in Michigan, or by joining other congregations that were founded by our students and emissaries, they were safe from mixed communions, and are safe still. The same way even now our brothers in the *diaspora* could set out and go across the ocean. They could also join our colonies in the Saginaw valley, or the colony of St. Sebald by the Spring, or other congregations of the Lutheran Iowa Synod, and they would be removed from all trouble. However, our colonies in the Saginaw valley are in the hands of Missouri pastors and thus Missourians, and we have become heretics in their eyes because of our doctrine of the ministry and because of our eschatological direction. Our colonies and former disciples in America can tolerate this, because they are of the opinion that they have remained more faithful to the divine Word than we, and they had to give up their connection with us by necessity for the sake of Christ. But our friends in Germany see, watching the way our North Americans went, into what danger of fanaticism of churchly opinions and of ingratitude they could come, and they do not want to go that same way. The American colonization has come to a complete halt since the defection of our colonies and disciples, and as much as emigration to America for a while was popular because of the trouble in the church of our homeland, all excitement has been killed because of the Missouri movement. No one wants to go to America anymore in order to escape the church troubles. Nor does anyone want to go to Iowa anymore. Despite the intimate connection of the Iowa Synod with us, one does not trust the American air any longer. The congregations of the Missouri Synod formerly were also intimately connected with us, and yet there was the disastrous split. Of course, it would be better if our like-minded brothers in the *diaspora* would go to Iowa than to remain in their congregations at home, where they wait in vain for improvement, have a hard time to keep up, and are hovering in constant danger to fall away from their dearest convictions and suffer damage of their souls. But this seems to be a thing of the past, especially with the present war troubles of the North American states.

So what can one advise? As the next thing following the previous counsel one should say: If you do not want to go to America, join a German congregation where you are safe from mixed Communion. There are more such congregations; you do not have to go to Neuendettelsau. Sell out and settle in a safe place. But upon this there comes the answer: Which congregation is safe? Under the order of advancement in Bavaria, there can be no consideration to place pastors in such a way that the successor would work in the same spirit as his predecessor. Even the better pastors accept calls elsewhere, or they die. Thus one of our brothers could change his town with great loss and sacrifice, and tomorrow he might be in the same misery. After all, what is a regular congregation to do if the new pastor goes a perverted way, especially if it is not completely unanimous? No one pays attention to the embarrassment of the souls of those who follow a correct Communion practice. There is no consideration for this, nor can there be. The Neuendettelsau congregation years ago witnessed to the church government its unanimous consent with its pastor in his Communion principles. Perhaps even now the greatest majority would declare the same thing if there were a change of pastors, especially since they would have leaders, since the institutions here are built on exactly the same principles. Certainly they would not join a pastor who would promote mixed Communion. As miserable as Dettelsau is, who knows whether there is another congregation in our fatherland in which a mixing pastor would have as little chance for being effective and successful. If anywhere, there seems to be a certain measure of effectiveness and security here. And yet, if there is any change, here also a disaster is possible, especially if the continually growing institutions would come to the point to which they have to come eventually: they will achieve a more independent and special sacramental license through their own pastor. Thus when it comes to the calling of a pastor [for the village church], one no longer would have to give any consideration for the institutions. If like-minded friends would move to Neuendettelsau with the intention to keep their sacramental faithfulness, victory would easily be possible, since God the Lord gives success to the upright. A like-minded, or almost like-minded, congregation could be born, where sacramental faithfulness would become tradition and unbreakable rule. But safety is here as little as in other places. There is no place in the world that would have the promise that the divine Word would always be there. Anyone who demands security should forget to make any move, especially since at the end it could also be that through a change of pastor in the near future he might get a shepherd according to his own heart. This has always been what our friends thought. How often have we said during the time of the emigration to America: "You do not have to move to America. Come to us. There are farms for sale where you could make a living." But who paid attention to this? Conditions here were not as trustworthy as in America. People rather turned their back to the entire fatherland than to make a change at home, where with all their confessional faithfulness sooner or later there could be a change again. Even though in America, just as here in Germany, there is a lot of moving around and a man sometimes moves four and five times in his life, this happens for other, earthly reasons in America as a common habit. But in church matters, at least here, no one believes he can be certain of success.

One could imagine people who would have the courage to move to a place like Dettelsau. That would have to be people who made the decision to move after the Gospel and the Sacraments, as often as the divine gifts themselves are moving and change places; people who never become permanent residents, inside are never at home. Instead of a comfortable home and earthly rest, they put the joy to stand by Christ and walk with Him, never to remain where He is not, where His Word, His Sacrament, its right administration and fellowship do not remain. But who will give our dispersed people such a pilgrim and wandering sense? Where are the people who have enough courage and steadfastness to say: "I follow my Lord. I will never stay longer than He does with His pure Word and Sacrament. I may now with my whole will and all joy move to Dettelsau, and if things change here, I will move on. I will risk everything that is temporal, I will have no regret for the good. Whether my spiritual and churchly wandering life will bring me temporal harm or gain, I will leave it up to God who knows my intent and my faithfulness." And even if somewhere a man or a woman would want to live by this principal, would the spouse want the same thing? The parents, children, cousins, and friends? Hardly any person, let alone several, will lift himself to such simplicity and height of thinking. In the end our like-minded friends and their Communion-mixing pastors will feel what Margrave George pronounced: "God's Word would not be difficult if only there was no self-interest." In short: Whoever can comprehend and do it, let him start out and move to a place where Christ happens to live and rule, and if He moves away, let him go with Him and follow Him. One must give up the dream, especially in our days, as if the kingdom of God would permanently remain in one place. Whoever seeks the kingdom of God and His righteousness first has to consider his earthly home lightly, the longer the more, and has to plan a spiritual nomadic life. However, such advice is not good for most of our friends. They are so tired and so depressed that they are incapable of such mobility. They say, "Where should I wander? I live here." The reason why they cannot run after Christ, His Sacrament, and its proper administration and fellowship lies in their fields, their meadows, and houses—in short, in their residency.

But since they would like to be freed from their church misery, how can one counsel them? "If there would be a church, a Lutheran Church more Lutheran and Christian than the state and *Landeskirche* in the country or in the neighborhood, I would leave the *Landeskirche* and join that church, and thus I would not go fro, but to the Lutheran Church." Many a person says so, and who knows whether he would not do it, if this were the case. But it is not, and even if it were, it would still be a question whether you would act that way. It is easier to leave fatherland and home altogether and to join a remote church or congregation, where things are going the right way, than to remain at home and to leave the inherited *Landeskirche*, to which belong the entire family, relatives, friends with whom one is connected by a thousand strings, and they all want to remain there, undisturbed. This you have never tried, and you cannot talk about it. You, who cannot do the easier thing, would hardly be able to do what is harder. And such a church does not exist, so there is no need to even talk about it. So how should one counsel now? We come ever closer to the advice, and perhaps once it is finally given, it will not be without danger either, only given in a dilemma, full of difficulties, so one could despair of a blessed success, unless there is with those who want to follow it above all things one condition. This condition is not only standing but growing in faithfulness in the sacramental-confessional conviction. Anyone who started wavering is incapable of acting; he first has to confirm his conviction. There is not only a great multitude of pastors on the opposite side, but also among them there are many who are excellent in their office and their position in life. They are also men whose knowledge and wisdom, piety and virtue cannot be denied. It is no small matter for a modest person to contradict all of them and to tell them they are wrong in matters of sacramental unity. For this one needs great simplicity and a firm conviction. No reasonable person can be happy to declare himself right, especially in such a principal matter and against such excellent people. Anyone who knows himself will be afraid of a position in which he would have to ascribe to himself a prominent wisdom. Every simple person will say with inner truthfulness: "Things would be bad in this world if my poor insight would be the mountaintop of the light given to humans." It is much sweeter and more satisfying to share the wisdom with a great multitude. But what help is there? In the end one cannot become unfaithful to the truth one has received because of the fellowship of many and better people. There has to be a way in which one can keep the truth over against many and excellent defenders of the opposite, without hurting humility and modesty. One must not leave the truth. One has to cling to it, get to know it ever more accurately and completely, and live in its service the longer, the better. This also applies to the truth of Communion fellowship. If someone would want to remain faithful to the way of sacramental Lutherans only because he did it until now, out of stubbornness, it would serve him right if he would find much trouble and aggravation on this way. Whoever is tired of the matter and it has lost significance for him, and yet he wants to go with the horde of its defenders, is a miserable hypocrite to whom God will give his reward together with all hypocrites. Above all, everybody should examine himself, how he stands in this matter, whether he still thinks the same way as before, whether right and truth of those representing it is still firmly established, and whether he could still do everything for it out of love for it. If this is the case, if the truth and his conscience constrain him, only then one can talk about counseling him. Then he will also accept the counsel with his reason and not follow it like a fool, just to do something and somehow help himself out of the embarrassment, but afterward find himself worse off than before and perhaps fall into the temptation to abandon the truth.

Taken for granted that a brother is so minded as we wish, we advise him that he would in no way, not even in the way we want to suggest ourselves, go to the altar of a Sacrament-mixing congregation, as long as he can help himself in some other way. If a pastor gives him a notice of dismissal [*Dimissorium*], whether willing or unwilling, let him go to the next congregation where things are done right. Let him go as often as possible to the Sacrament, so that through a richer experience of its power and grace he will bear the trouble of having to walk so much more joyfully. Experience shows that people who can have the Sacrament with little trouble in the closest distance often lose the zeal they had before, when it took a sacrifice to go after the heavenly goods. One will also be more receptive for the gift of faithfulness in the truth when one is farther away from the enemies than when one is closer to them. During a certain separation, one can even keep and practice love and honoring those of a different mind more carefully than when one lives in daily aggravation.

However, if there are unconquerable obstructions against walking, so that one could not walk because of sickness, age, or weakness or because the distance is too great, one may no longer be satisfied with the *crede et manducasti*, as long as at the hometown altar, even with the mixing, the confession of Communion, consecration, and distribution are formally in order.

This word remains a comfort when it is impossible to receive the body and the blood. But the people to whom the great grace is given, as to us, to know the great importance and the effect of the Sacrament which are rich in blessings, can the least condemn themselves to miss it, if it is at all possible to receive the Sacrament. If, therefore, all hope is gone to make the pastor change the sacramental mixing through a self-denying witness, then it is all-important not to become a partaker in the mixing. If that is somehow possible, I at least do not consider it sinful if someone, driven by the misery and the desire of the soul for the Sacrament, would receive the body and blood of the Lord from the hands of a Lutheran—I do not say a Union or even a Reformed—but a mixing pastor. I say that only under the condition that one is unable to walk and that one does not become partaker of the guilt of mixing. Under no circumstances may we do injustice with others. Therefore, in this given case, it is all-important that the following advice truly avoids a common guilt. Even in this given emergency one would have to reject the counsel and be satisfied with the *crede et manducasti* if a common guilt cannot be avoided.

There is no talk about an inner sharing of the guilt by partaking of the wrong opinion of the adversaries: we only try to give advice to those people who are of our conviction. We only speak of a common guilt through outward participation. When the apostle says that one should avoid the heretics, he forbids the church fellowship with heretics which nevertheless is practiced by our adversaries. But we want to keep church fellowship with our opponents, because we do not know how we can satisfy our high need and our hunger for the body and blood of Christ, and yet we do not want to have fellowship with the heretics with whom they practice fellowship. This basically means only this: we do not avoid the heretics, and yet want to have avoided them. One can see how miserable the situation of those is who happen to be counseled by us. What I myself would do in this case, whether I would break through and find some other way to still my need for the Sacrament, whether I myself would follow my counsel, is a question. Nevertheless, I will no longer be distracted from pronouncing my advice. It is the following: "Go with one or two witnesses to your pastor, declare to him your hunger for the Sacrament, your inner objection to his mixing, which makes him disobedient to the apostolic prohibition, and the great trouble of conscience into which he puts you and other like-minded through his unfaithful behavior. Protest as before God against his practice and call before his ears to the Lord as witness, that you will have no part in it, and that the responsibility is all his and those who tolerate his practice and approve of it against the teaching and practice of the Lutheran Church. Tell him also that you will voice your objection in the same way against anyone who either has to know it, or with whom you may talk about this matter occasionally, and that you cannot do otherwise than to keep away from those who become an offense to the Church and those who believe otherwise through their perverted Communion fellowship. Since you are unable to stem the evil, you will raise your objection even louder and become more intimately united with those who remain in the state of protest and contradiction. However, in your trouble you will no longer refrain to receive the Sacrament from him, your pastor, and that you will try to bear it to go with such a contradiction with him to God's Table." That is the miserable counsel I have to give. This advice will be so much harder to follow because our opponents will hardly be able to put themselves in the place of those who should follow it and want to do it. They will demand from them an irreproachable conduct, even in formal matters and in expression. It does not help a person to be in the right. He has to defend and keep his right in such a way that one cannot attack him. A wrong defense destroys any victory of the right, especially before unreasonable and unjust people. Since we and our brothers not only know this, but also have often experienced it, we cannot avoid the request to proceed without blemish in the above-mentioned conduct of protest. The difficult task has to be solved with all modesty and consideration, with holy discretion and keeping the right measure in word and behavior. It is well justified to add this serious remark to our counsel.

But one should not be unaware of the fact that even the correct execution of this counsel can be dangerous for the soul. A smart pastor of the opposition party may well listen to you and let you talk, counts it already a gain if only the separation would somehow end, and is confident that such a protest will have no consequence, no effect, if indeed there is participation of his Communion. Nobody will care about it. In the end he is smart enough to calm you through love and friendliness, somehow considers your viewpoint as valid, and will touch it with a tender hand, just like a wound. On a butchering day one can let the sun go down with some glory, as long as it goes down. If the pastor is very smart, he treats you as one recuperating, with a lot of attention, tries to lift up related sides between his and your conviction, shows in this and that part that is important to your solicitude, strictness, care, etc., and in this and other ways he tries to make his relationship with you as good as possible, to avoid the fact that you would regret joining him, to embed you with good mortar into his Communion fellowship. Those of like mind with him will praise him as having great pastoral wisdom, that you will give in at the end, become lukewarm in your knowledge, in your protest, and at the end you will be reconciled with the opinion of the enemy, which you should never share. Here is danger, without any doubt.

Indeed, the opposite party will interpret the observing of this method as victory; there will be no lack of derision and triumph. Whoever permits himself to be made tired and worn-out will always be in danger inwardly to step over to the opposite side. In that case it would have been better to save oneself, even with extreme effort, into a congregation where one can go in peace to God's Table. Whoever gives up his standpoint of resistance and somehow joins his enemies, without inwardly wanting to join them, starts out on a way that is so steep that it takes a high and holy soul not to perish on it. Since I have given the above counsel a number of times, I already have a little experience when it comes to it. Those to whom I gave this advice either told me that they felt like apostates as often as they tried to implement it, or those who followed it carried the new condition as a heavy burden. In either case one could tell how anyone following this advice had to jump over a deep chasm. Therefore, I do not want to give it any higher value than is possible. It is an emergency solution, given in a great emergency. But the smaller it shows itself, the more important is the obligation to take up all courage and power in order to be able to walk on the other helpful ways mentioned above. Here also the Word applies: "Whoever would save his life will lose it, but whoever loses his life for My sake will find it" [Matthew 16:25]. Therefore, I would not have attempted to give this advice if I would not fear the great weakness of our brothers and that terrible shying away from what is good, which can attack and perhaps even destroy our poor people. They may be talked into walking on an even more difficult way, or follow authority without having the necessary confidence and the necessary force of conviction. Whoever acts beyond his capability [will find that] even the best action can become sin and a burden. "Whatever does not come from faith is sin."—In the end my counsel says no more than this: I will not criticize or insult the one who follows it the right way and in such a way that he gives no offense, but a bright and clear witness.

In the case that this counsel should nevertheless come into life, it would also cause a change in the behavior of our opponents. At least this would be possible. If examples would become known, telling that some of those of the same mind with us had gone with protest to Communion served on mixed altars, it could also happen that pastors and congregational members would come from their mixed altars to us, wanting to receive the Sacrament from us. This would be less objectionable as the opposite, when those like-minded with us would want to receive the Sacrament from mixed altars. Nevertheless, one would have to witness to such brothers that even before them a protest would have to be raised that would liberate them from their error. If we act faithfully in such cases, our enemies will avoid us, and there will not be many such happenings. But if it happens, there will be less danger for us as in the opposite case. As much as both cases before pure reason seem to be the same, nevertheless in life and in practice the second case is a completely different matter and makes a completely different impression. There have been some incidents of Reformed or United seeking Communion fellowship with me, for their conviction gives them courage. But the opposite happened very seldom, that people who consciously practice mixing would want to go to God's Table with me. To be exact, I have to say that it never happened. If people who were unaware and without knowledge, confident to be faithful members of the Lutheran Church, and wanting to be that, would come from mixed altars, I always treated them gently and with patience. Also, my duty to witness never forced me to take on the role of a great inquisitor, given the general confusion in the land. I always considered all to be of the same mind, if I did not know the opposite, and while in general I have a severe position in this matter, my mildness in individual cases was blessed, so that people who were unclear, without any polemic from my side, through my mild behavior were put in the mood to recognize the truth and from now on to live according to it. Whoever wants to put a principle into practice must not be critical in all minutiae, else he will cause the pillar which he wants to erect to shake, sometimes to fall before even having sunk it in the ground.

So far we have talked only of cases which can happen within the Lutheran *Landeskirche* of Bavaria. But our like-minded people also come into lands that are outside of Bavaria, just as we receive people from there. Just as we ourselves could easily find the right procedure with Reformed and United people, our like-minded brothers can easily see that they cannot go to Communion with openly Reformed or United. But how are things with the *Landeskirchen* and with congregations that have been incorporated in the Union, who claim to be faithful to the Lutheran Church? Let us sort out the cases and ask, first of all, how we are to treat the members of Lutheran *Landeskirchen* and United Lutherans when they come to us. In the first case we will without doubt act with mildness. If we treat members of Bavarian Lutheran congregations as like-minded, unless we know something to the contrary about them and their congregations, we will be no less good-hearted toward members of other *Landeskirchen*. Ignorance excuses and justifies us in the latter case more than in the first. What good would a sharp inquisition do us if we cannot obtain a true witness? If we were to bring the fellowship into beds that are too narrow, we would come eventually to the point where we have no fellowship at all. In order to give a witness or to offer a protest, one must first of all be able to prove that there is a cause for giving a witness or offering a protest. In general we know very well that in other *Landeskirchen* things are not better, rather worse than here with us in Bavaria. But who can judge the individual congregation according to the judgment which one can have about those terribly mixed up *Landeskirchen*? It is possible that things are well in a congregation, and because it is possible, I take it for granted in all cases where I do not know anything to the contrary. This is how love and the Eighth Commandment teach me to act. I act in a similar way with Lutherans from the Union who assure me that all things were the same with them as with me. I may suspect the opposite, perhaps I find it very likely. I may not even trust that the one who gives me that assurance has the right knowledge. But since I do not know the local conditions and cannot get the information in a hurry, and since my suspicion may be wrong and it might be as I have been told, I let the testimony of the person who seeks my fellowship stand, until I know better, as long as he promises confessional faithfulness for the future and all possible cases and renounces solemnly the mixed Communion before witnesses in *optima forma*. I act this way despite the fact that my experience tells me that usually the Communion fellowship in United-Lutheran congregations is not in order and was not even in order in places where I was assured that it was. With all my experience, I cannot deny the possibility that here and there circumstances, insight, wisdom, strength, and steadfastness of the pastor could be thus that what I was assured of could be true. The pure church-governmental Union I do not accept, especially with the progress of United Lutherans. Whoever shows Lutheran faithfulness at the altar, I take him for Lutheran. Whether this faithfulness is being practiced I can only know in rare cases. But I accept the witness of unsuspected people, and I do not know how to act otherwise. Many an erring brother has been brought to the right way through such mildness.—Whatever else concerns our like-minded brothers and sisters abroad, this will show what they have to do. It is easier for them to come to clarity in the places where they want to go to Communion since they are right there. They can research; no one holds that against a stranger. They have a greater responsibility than the pastor who is supposed to accept strangers. If a Christian staying abroad, after researching the circumstances, does not find a reason to doubt, he may go to the Sacrament. He is not an inquisitor either. It is self-understood that the stranger cannot get to the bottom of things the way a native can, if he wants to. In general those like-minded with us would do well before traveling to inquire about church conditions in the congregations where they are going. They should also ask their pastor for a certificate that witnesses to their own church faithfulness and their character, and abroad they should be ready to give an answer to everyone who asks for a reason for the hope and the faith that is theirs. Such a certificate is more useful and necessary than a government passport, which any reasonable traveler would have.

From what has been said so far, one can tell that how a pastor or his parishioners act under our miserable circumstances is not an easy matter. Everybody should act according to the best of his fidelity. Even so, he will not get to the point where mistrust or ill will would always be content with his behavior. It can happen that people accuse one to make exceptions at times, while one has no intention to do anything except to live faithfully to the holy rule. In the life of a pastor and *Seelsorger*, casuistic knowledge and wisdom is a virtue of all virtues. For the uninitiated and unreasonable the life of a pastor can appear full of contradiction, inconsequence, and exceptions, while perhaps in every case only that happened which the holy rule demanded. One has to learn to bear unreasonable judgments. One would have a lot to do if one would always want to justify oneself. I, for instance, often have to question whether I can admit an insane person, a mentally or emotionally sick one, a demonic, or one burning up with a fever to God's Table or not. I know what it means to do the right thing and how few people I can please. I have to carry my burden alone and count on the mercy of the archshepherd [*Erzhirten*] and bishop of the congregation. Therefore, I also would not dream to pull before my judgment other pastors with experienced principles. If I can trust them in general, I do not consider myself authorized to attack their faithfulness in the details upon the gossip of pious people. Even if they fail, perhaps fail openly, I am not inclined to judge severely, because all fail, and especially in the area of Communion practice it is easiest to fail. For faithful and honest disciples of the right churchly doctrine, one must request what is requested from them: strong principle, mild execution.

After all this, it should be said for the benefit of our like-minded brothers and sisters that the Communion discipline and fellowship is different from the discipline of life. I mean that one ought to be more strict in avoiding those who live in heresy, because it is possible to be more strict. Many of our brothers have demanded the same thing from today's pastors in regard to the discipline of life, ordered by our Lord and His apostles, as in regard to heresies. But even with the best intentions and burning zeal of a pastor in matters of life and behavior of his parishioners, one cannot deny the fact that our miserable conditions in the congregations present extraordinary difficulties for a faithful steward of the mysteries of God. No one any longer practices the discipline of love in the way it has been commanded. There are no degrees of admonition, no process of discipline, no public ban. It is impossible to have all this, in part because the church governing authorities claim the right of the ban. To exercise this, they lacked the capability, not only in our time but always, in part because of personal insufficiencies of knowledge and experience and lack of divine power; in part because the individual congregations, to whom without doubt the Lord and His apostles gave this right and this duty, cannot or do not want to exercise this right, the way most of them are, unless they took it in the devil's name and applied it to the saints of God. The stewards of the mysteries of God stand alone with their sanctuary and their pearls, and in the whole world there is not a single one, not even the most gifted, who could deal with his parishioners in matters of life according to the meaning of Christ and His apostles. In the best case we are pillar saints [stylites] [*Säulenheilige*], standing above the congregations, not on the same level with them, separated from them and deserted in matters which cannot happen without fellowship. We are able to avoid heretics, though even here it is difficult to gain the appreciation of even a single congregation. But in matters of discipline of life, we should do whatever is possible. In principle, our congregations and their members shy away here, not wanting to step into our light, not wanting to have their works known or to have them punished. Our eyes lack the capability to see all the details of the life of our parishioners from our high lookout. I contradict myself here, and yet am understood: There is an open and yet intangible hypocrisy of the public and unrepenting sinner, and there is fearful and evil silence of the better parishioners. There are so many other hindrances which any pastor reading this can insert here. How little one can do here; how much goes unmentioned or with just a slight reproach! What a screaming contradiction is found here between the inner knowing, the personal recognition and the conviction of a pastor, and the treatment which he can give to the sinners! In addition, the gift of pastoral counseling is very rare, and most pastors are standing on the field of their most important work not only without this gift but also without weapons and the art of warfare. Where can one learn something for these kinds of struggle? Therefore, the behavior of even a faithful pastor often looks worse in the eyes of pious and faithful parishioners than it actually is. They see the open evil conditions, which have grown higher than all the trees of the world because of the neglect of Jesus' commands of discipline, and without thinking they demand from the pastor to come to the aid through an official procedure of discipline. If that does not happen, the parishioners sometimes do not ask for the reason, nor do they ask what the pastor in these matters really did or wanted to do, but they immediately want to have order restored, while there is no understanding, no wisdom, no power, no security, no steadfastness, not with the isolated pastors and even less with the good people who make unreasonable demands from them. True, if a pastor in principle rejects discipline, does not acknowledge the commands of the Lord, one should flee from him and avoid him. But if he cannot and is unable to do what he acknowledges to be necessary and divine, what he has neglected to do according to his own conviction to the ruin of the congregation, one has to suffer with him and strengthen him. But one should not flee from him or his office, but go with him as long as it is possible. Of course, the lack of discipline of a congregation can reach such a height that the pastor ought to be permitted to shake off the dust from his feet and walk away, and that the parishioners should be without blame if they leave the tired and weak pastor and the whole congregation without discipline, especially if they know where they should go. But under normal circumstances we did not advise even our strictest teachers, those who practiced the greatest severity in regard to heresies, to separate themselves, but to remain in the miserable conditions for a never-ending witness and protest, for fervent prayer.

Into all this trouble we are led by the sin of the Church of God on earth, in our case mainly the sin of our Church. There are untold sins against us, against ours, against the dispersed fellow believers, against the poor brothers and sisters of Jesus, against Jesus Christ Himself. There are also plenty of sins against the Reformed and United, who, because of mixing, cannot be led to the knowledge and the truth. But the greatest evil is this, that such few recognize the sin. Most of them have lost any feeling for the evil; some praise the condition of the *Landeskirche*, not just in comparing it with other *Landeskirchen* but in and by itself. It cannot be otherwise, dear brothers: We, with our continued pushing and our constantly repeated complaining, under the widespread way of thinking have to become more and more something to be avoided and an abomination, and our admonition an object of loathing. All it would take to make the misery complete would be if we also would become lukewarm and lazy, tired of our miserable position, and remove the last thorn from the conscience of our enemies by going over to their camp and acknowledging that the whole misery of our position is our own fault and learn to look at it as deserved suffering for our stubborn error. Thus this matter also, as so many others, would go off into the sand [*im Sand verlaufen*], and after a while one would quietly go to sleep on the mountains of sin. But may the Lord preserve us from this in His great mercy! Even if we could not help our brothers to come to the knowledge of their sins, nevertheless our whole future behavior should give the proof that we remain faithful to the truth we have come to know. Nothing is farther from us than to approve of their behavior, which certainly is not justified by anything, least of all through experience. One can see the disastrous consequences everywhere: the spiritual life that is dying everywhere. Even our better parishioners are on an extremely low level of the most intimate connection with the sacramental leadership. Even if our brothers do not see, we at least in this case have been given the eye. May that not be darkened through any dust of circumstances as long as we live. But even if by us someone would be befogged and fall asleep, the eye of the Lord is awake nevertheless, does neither slumber nor sleep, and His hand without any doubt will bring to the light the evil which stems from the lack of discipline in doctrine and life. Perhaps then many a person will wake up from his sleep and turn to that truth and wisdom which is not comfortable for our condition, does not spare it, but in the end will be the only saving anchor when the ship of the Church is being tossed around and the Lord will execute the judgment of His own. A confessional life without sacramental leading of the congregation will end in a miserable orthodoxism and confessionalism which fractures and splits up the Church, kills true life, and in its place puts the arguing of the school opinions, which cannot satisfy any soul. Against this the concentration of all spiritual and churchly life in the Sacrament is not only the best way to keep the divine truths but also the best way to introduce them into the life of the soul and of the congregation. The Sacrament is not only the high point of the divine acts for the salvation of mankind but also the highpoint of all the revelations of God in time and of all doctrines of the Church. And all of this becomes easy to comprehend, so that a rich sacramental life is a living book. By reading it under skilled leading, even the dullest can become wiser and more pious, just as with the brightest and most simple symbolical book. Whoever puts the Sacrament in its place and opens the floodgates for it helps the Church, and in it all humanity. But whoever places it in the dark does not let it rule or be king, hinders the life and the blessedness of the congregation. This is exactly the curse of sacramental mixing, which spreads a rotten graveyard peace [*Kirchhoffrieden*] over the Church, and fosters a fleshly love, but kills the love which has the Spirit and life.

Whoever has these convictions will become very worried looking at our *Landeskirche*. He will shiver thinking of the responsibility of those who practice mixing. They think they are building the Church and render God a service while the opposite is happening: the Church is cheated of its life well [*Lebensbrunn*], at least of its richest stream of blessing, and the Lord of the Church is offended. Therefore, we, dear brothers, must recognize our sacred duty and pray that God's judgments will be turned away from our *Landeskirche* and that our opponents may be converted. But above all may the Lord convert us in everything where we need it and listen also to our prayer for the conversion of our brothers in regard to the Sacrament. Let us pray for this without ceasing, without pharisaism, even the fear of being accused of pharisaism, with great seriousness to God the Father for the sake of Christ in the Holy Spirit.

CHAPTER EIGHT

REGARDING THE QUESTION OF FELLOWSHIP IN THE LORD'S SUPPER

FRIEDRICH WILHELM HOPF
TRANSLATED BY WOLF DIETRICH KNAPPE[1]

1.

The question of fellowship in the Lord's Supper [*Abendmahlsgemeinschaft*] between members of the Evangelical Lutheran Church and members of churches of other confessions has become intensified since the Prussian Union entered the scene with a common celebration of the Supper in 1817.[2] The custom of breaking the Communion host, until then practiced only by the Reformed churches, was the outward sign of a united celebration of the Supper, which was celebrated on the anniversary of the Augsburg Confession on June 25, 1830. On April 4, 1830, King Friedrich Wilhelm III [1770–1840], in his decree concerning the upcoming celebration of the 300-year anniversary, had said: "It seems proper to me to add further steps to this happy event, which will enable us to bring the wholesome work of union even closer to completion, in the spirit of my decree of September 27, 1817."[3] In order to accomplish these "further steps," almost all the Breslau clergy addressed to their congregations "A Word of Brotherly Instruction concerning the Union of the Reformed and Lutheran Confessions into an Evangelical United

1 *Zur Frage nach der Abendmahlsgemeinschaft*. Von Friedrich Wilhelm Hopf in *Vom Sakrament des Altars: Lutherische Beiträge zur Frage des heiligen Abendmahls*, Hermann Sasse (Leipzig, 1941, Verlage von Dörffling & Franke), pp. 234–56.

2 Cf. the descriptions by Bishop [Rulemann] Eylert [1770–1852] in Hermann Sasse, *Union und Bekenntnis* (Munich: Chr. Kaiser Verlag, 1936), 13ff. [English translation in *The Lonely Way*, vol. 1: *1927–1939*, ed. Matthew C. Harrison (St. Louis: Concordia, 2001), 273–74. MH]

3 J. G. Scheibel, *Aktenmässige Geschichte der neuesten Unternehmung einer Union* II (Leipzig: Fleischer, 1834), 35.

Church." In this document they informed [their people that]: "Both Confessions, the Reformed and the Lutheran, have accepted the new hymnal, designed for Silesia, including the order of service. And the solemn words and prayers that are spoken during official acts of the Church are, from now on, the same for both confessions." It was believed that through "a hint of divine providence" now "everything has been brought to the point from which the work of union can easily and without difficulty be accomplished."

"In serious consideration of the above remarks, a number of good men of a Christian mind have met and come together in the decision to celebrate the coming completion of three centuries since the delivery of the Augsburg Confession with a common observance of the Holy Supper with the rite of breaking the bread. This is the way our Lord Himself originally performed this sacred act. They gave the well thought-through, free, and firm declaration that from now on the party names *Reformed* and *Lutheran* should cease and that both confessions should be considered as *one united Evangelical Church*." After the assurance that everybody should continue to belong to his church "organization" and that by no means "even a single person would be persuaded, or his conscience hurt or forced in such a highly important and holy matter," the certain expectation is expressed: "We hope that many members of our congregations will take part in the service of the Holy Supper that has been planned for the celebration of the three centuries as a symbol of unification. We believe that most of them have advanced so far in their Christian insight that they can see that doing this they will advance a good work, pleasing to God."[4]

This declaration of the Breslau clergy, which the two Reformed pastors signed with special approval, is one of those characteristic documents that helps us to understand the special emphasis which Lutherans, faithful to their Confessions, adopted since the introduction of the Union regarding the question of fellowship in the Lord's Supper. Inter-confessional fellowship in the Lord's Supper and confessional separation for Communion always stood and stand opposite to each other as sensible and consequent expressions concerning the way of the Church. Even today the basic Lutheran attitude cannot be witnessed differently from the way it was done in the petition of the *Breslau Lutheran* [*Breslauer Lutheraner*] on June 27, 1830: "We cannot be pacified by the fact that everything that is contrary to the teaching in which we seek our salvation has been carefully avoided. This (teaching) itself, in its unique independence, in its glory and power, must decisively be brought forward and permeate and enliven the entire service. It was no secret regarding the hope that a service, thus splintered, after the most essential elements of the proper life have been destroyed, would cease completely and would disappear in the common Union, so desired. This has been pronounced

4 Scheibel, *Aktenmässige Geschichte*, 79ff.

publicly, and certainly this is no empty hope."[5] [J. G.] Scheibel [1783–1843] correctly recognized that even biblical words and customs, as well as old Lutheran orders of service, can be misused in order to circumvent the question of truth and to pretend a unity which does not exist. He points out that a mere quoting of the words of Christ leaves the congregation the "ignorance in the faith."[6] "The preacher ought to give an account, not only of his own faith but also of the faith of the congregation entrusted to him (in order that he may lead them to faith)." Besides that, he asks the question: "If it is such a laudable thing to celebrate the Lord's Supper with the Reformed, why not also with the Catholics? Is it less loveless to exclude them? Or is what the Reformed Church teaches closer to us than what Catholics are teaching?"[7]

In order to calm down emotions, it has always been emphasized that there is "no change of confession" connected with a Union Communion. But behind it there was the thought that precisely the confessional difference was lifted. On the one hand, one should see to it that "the individuals who do not favor the Union should receive the Supper according to the existing rite." On the other hand, one acted against such "stubborn and selfish attempts" with the principle: "Partaking of the Lord's Supper in an evangelical congregation of the other confession no longer is a sign of converting . . . since through the Union the act of the Lord's Supper can no longer be considered as different for the two evangelical confessions. Besides, there is no act of the Church that carries the character of difference."[8]

The struggle against the Union Lord's Supper is also expressly directed against a Union Lord's Supper that is being celebrated with as many Lutheran forms as possible. "Thousands are shouting: Why in the world are you fighting so stubbornly? For this very reason, because the semblance of Lutheranism is being imitated. For its essence is gone. The same liturgy is fitting for the Reformed Church and has been introduced there. This is contrary to the essence of Lutheranism. . . . Yes, one says, both celebrations and confessions should be allowed next to each other. One consistory counsel, one superintendent appoints preachers to a Lutheran or a Reformed altar, whether they are Lutheran or Reformed. Thus the Church is being destroyed.[9] Outwardly few words have been changed; but with

5 Scheibel, *Aktenmässige Geschichte*, 85.

6 [A reference to the Union Agenda's distribution formula: "Take eat. Christ says, 'This is My body.'" Just what exactly that means, well . . . YOU decide! MH]

7 Letter to Senior Hagan, August 29, 1830; Scheibel, *Aktenmässige Geschichte*, 114ff.

8 *Hirtenbrief* of General Superintendent Bobertag to the Clergy of Silesia, May 31, 1830; Scheibel, *Aktenmässige Geschichte*, 233.

9 [In time, the people no longer knew what the confession of their congregation had been or whether they themselves were Lutheran or Reformed. Sasse, a pastor in the Church of the Old Prussian Union from 1920 to 1933, complained precisely about this in his Berlin congregations. MH]

them the faith, the Church [are being changed]. Therefore, we fight. . . . Yes! Even though Lutheran words may still be permitted in the prayers for the Lord's Supper, our Lord's Supper must not be celebrated together with the Reformed. Jesus' institution is no game" (Scheibel).[10]

2.

Within the Lutheran territorial churches, no Lutheran, faithful to the Confessions, could ignore the decisions and separations to which the Silesians had been led. In this regard there is a connection between the struggle of the Lutheran Church in Prussia and the discussions concerning fellowship in the Lord's Supper which have been conducted in the territorial churches between 1840 and 1870. But despite this, the conditions were different here. For the legal validity of the Lutheran Confessions in these territorial churches stood firm from the beginning, as well as the exclusive right of a celebration of the Supper which agreed exactly with the Lutheran Confession. True, the practice often suffered from the results of the rationalist past and the unionizing tendencies of the time. The Union Supper as such was not subject of the intra-Lutheran discussion, but rather the question whether Reformed and Union people should be admitted to the Sacrament at unquestionably Lutheran altars. This question has not been uniformly answered by Lutherans faithful to the Confessions. But they were all agreed in their common rejection of the Union Supper, and in the basic judgment concerning the threatening danger of the Union.

In the most decisive way, Wilhelm Loehe [1808–72] made the question of admission [to the Lord's Supper] a *status confessionis.*[11] The "mixing of the Supper" [*Abendmahlsmengerei*] within the Bavarian *Landeskirche* forced him more than once not only to consider leaving the *Landeskirche* but also to prepare to leave and to give detailed explanations for doing so. Only the urgent advice of his friends in the free Lutheran Church in Prussia prevented him from carrying out his decision. They pointed out to him the legal status of the Lutheran Confession which had been acknowledged again and again and the corresponding order in Bavaria. They advised him to keep fighting and acting, without giving up by separating prematurely. When [Adolf von] Harless [1806–76] was called as leader of the *Oberkonsistorium* ["supreme consistory"] in Munich and made vigorous efforts for a new constitution for the *Landeskirche,* based on the Confession, Loehe believed that it was all right to stay, especially since he could depend on his like-minded congregation and by claiming a special position for himself and his

10 Scheibel, *Aktenmässige Geschichte*, 249ff.

11 Cf. J. Deinzer, *Wilhelm Löhes Leben*, vol. II (Neuendettelsau: Buchhandlung der Diakonissenanstalt, 1935), 273ff.; Siegfried Hebart, *Wilhelm Löhes Lehre von der Kirche, ihrem Amt und Regiment* (Neuendettelsau: Freimund Verlag, 1939), 199ff.

friends. However, his hope for a completely new constitution, especially in regard to sacramental practice, was not fulfilled.[12] For the rest of his life he suffered with this intense problem.

Loehe's position was formulated in the sharpest way in the so-called *Schwabach Declaration* of October 9, 1851. The decisive sentences are: "We have stated that there is *no emergency* which would necessitate a mixed celebration of the Lord's Supper, and we claim that there cannot be one. Necessity knows no commandment, but it knows God's commandment, and God's Word is above all necessity. And God's Word forbids fellowship in the Supper with those who have strange doctrines and will not let go of them, for it forbids any close relationship with them. This latter [statement] is clear for anyone who reads verses such as Romans 16:17; 1 Timothy 6:3ff., especially v. 5; 2 John 10ff. simply and without prejudice. This also makes clear the simple and powerful conclusion in regard to the Holy Supper. . . . But if our conclusion is valid, all the emergencies become sins, the exceptional conditions become sinful conditions that deserve no forbearance. If other differences do not prevent one from having fellowship in the Lord's Supper, should not the difference regarding the Lord's Supper itself prevent one? There cannot be anything more undignified than a 'yes and no' at the altar, a splitting up over the Sacrament during the Sacrament!—It is undignified—and it is **sin**! Sin against the word of Christ. Sin against the Holy Supper. Sin against the Church, which in its uniqueness was formed only through the struggle about the Supper, and which loses everything it owns once it loses its precious jewel. Sin against the Confession of the Church, which is sacred in its antitheses, which prohibit fellowship, as also in its thesis. Sin against the better practice of our fathers, who were steadfast in their struggle against fellowship with the Reformed—with the Reformed and the neutral who wanted to stay that way. Sin against the congregations, which cannot come to an appreciation of the Holy Meal because they cannot tell the difference. Sin against those of a strange faith, who are lacking the true witness concerning the Holy Supper. Sin against our own poor souls, because we cannot remain in so much sin without hurting our souls, especially if we know what we are doing. . . . *Union at the altar is union above all unions*! . . . Above all, it is necessary that fellowship in the Supper with all United and Reformed, who are unwilling to publicly renounce their fellowship and convert to the Lutheran

12 Cf. the weighty judgment of such a competent reporter like Stählin: "In regard to fellowship in the Lord's Supper, much has been put in order, but for the diaspora congregations, especially the evangelical congregations in Munich, Harless never strove for or applied a change" (D. v. Stählin, *Realencyklopädie für protestantische Theologie und Kirche*, 3rd ed. [Leipzig: J. C. Hinrichs'sche, 1899], v. 7, 429, 22ff., s.v. "Harless").

Church, be discontinued. Then—but only then—a mortal blow is given to every essence of the Union."[13]

Not a few influential leaders of Lutheran theology and the Church agreed only in a limited way with this clear position of Loehe.[14] One of their best speakers was Franz Delitzsch [1813–90], at that time in Erlangen. In principle, he shared Loehe's refusal of the Lord's Supper and church fellowship with the Reformed and United, which was a consequence of the Lutheran Confession concerning the Lord's Supper. "*The basic position of the Lutheran Church, according to the Confession, toward the Reformed and United is the norm for the practice of the Office of the Ministry of the Lutheran Church office. It (the office) must not admit Reformed and United Christians, who want to remain so, to fellowship in the Supper with our Church; it must not put the members of the Lutheran congregation into fellowship in the Lord's Supper with them. Mixed fellowship in the Lord's Supper cannot be justified with any kind of emergency. For nothing can become a duty of love which is against the duty of faith. In mixed congregations with a Lutheran name and of the Lutheran Confession, one should declare openly that it is expected and demanded from all who want to participate in the Lord's Supper that they are willing to belong to the Lutheran Church with heart, mouth, word, and deed.*" While agreeing basically with Loehe, Delitzsch now turns against "the false consequences" which he sees with Loehe: "That one might believe one would have to leave a church in which the Lutheran Confession rightfully exists, because there is an un-Lutheran practice here and there, as long as the free Word is not bound which punishes them, and as long as one acts according to one's conscience which keeps itself unsullied and is not ridiculed." Delitzsch also considers it a false consequence "if one thinks that a lax practice in the admission to the Lord's Supper would deprive the Sacrament of its meaning"; or "if one would consider a pastor, who has not yet become convinced of his duty to have a stricter practice of the Lord's Supper, as un-Lutheran, despite his otherwise proven Lutheran conviction" and for making it "an objective confessional duty" not to partake if a Lutheran administered the Lord's Supper under this condition.[15]

---

13 *Declaration of Several Pastors concerning Their Relationship to the Bavarian-Protestant Landeskirche* (Nuremberg: 1851), 13ff. [C. F. W. Walther and Friedrich Wyneken of the Missouri Synod were present at Schwabach with Loehe in 1851 and voiced their explicit approval. See "The Trip Report," in *At Home in the House of My Fathers* (St. Louis: Concordia, 2010). MH]

14 [Walther and Wyneken were in fact with Loehe in Schwabach and raised their hands in affirmation of this document! See "The Trip Report" and the full Schwabach Letter of Loehe and his compatriots (p. 109) in *At Home in the House of My Fathers*, 24ff. and 10 ff. MH]

15 Franz Delitzsch, *Die bayerische Abendmahlsgemeinschaftsfrage. Ein Anfang eingehenderer Erörterung* (Erlangen: Theodor Bläsing, 1852), 21, 41ff.

Delitzsch's criticism is indicative for other Lutherans also, some of whom went even farther in their critique of Loehe. They all demanded a confessional administration of the Sacrament, even in regard to admission. But at the same time they were willing to bear with the practical needs, for instance, in the *diaspora* or in the case of members of a different faith moving into an all-Lutheran area. The necessity to break with a Lutheran *Landeskirche* because of the "mixing of the Lord's Supper" existing in it was not acknowledged outside of the circle around Loehe.

Special difficulties for the confessional practice of an order of admission in the Lutheran *Landeskirchen* arose when members of the Union wanted to come to the Sacrament. They would confess their personal agreement with the Lutheran teaching about the Lord's Supper, and besides that they could claim that in their home congregation, despite the Union, there still existed a Lutheran administration of the Sacrament. [Gottlieb Christoph Adolf von] Harless, already in 1843, had pointed out the fact that, because of the Union, "innumerable people who do not belong to the Lutheran Church completely agree with its teaching, especially concerning the Lord's Supper. According to their opinion, they do not even think that they ever became unfaithful to the Lutheran Confession." He then judged that admitting such members to the altars of the Lutheran Church should by no means be considered a sign that the pastor who receives them belongs to the Union. On the contrary, "the communicant by coming to the Lord's Supper confesses publicly and solemnly that he accepts the Confession of the Lutheran Church."[16] Even Loehe—at least in later years—admitted Lutherans from the Union to the Sacrament, if they could assure him [that] "with us everything is just as with you." He considered this witness valid, even if it seemed dubious to him, as long as he was not convinced of the opposite. However, he made this a condition, that the communicant "for the future and for all possible incidents promises confessional faithfulness and solemnly renounces before witnesses the mixing of the Supper [*Abendmahlsmengerei*] *in optima forma*" [i.e., "absolutely"].[17]

16 G. Ch. Adolph Harless, *Die evangelisch=lutherische Kirche in Bayern und die Insinuationen des Herrn Professor Döllinger* (Erlangen, 1843), 35ff. Compare also the letter of Harless to the Erlangen *Philadelphia* ["fraternity"], December 14, 1855; *Korrespondenzblatt für die ev.=luth. Geistl. in Bay.*, 322ff. (no. 35; August 31, 1937).

17 Wilhelm Loehe, *Gutachten in Sachen der Abendmahlsgemeinschaft* (Nördlingen: C. H. Beck'schen, 1863), 40ff.: "I do not accept the Union that is purely ordered by a church government, especially since the Lutherans in the Union have made such progress. Whoever shows Lutheran loyalty before the altar, I consider Lutheran. Whether this loyalty is being practiced, I can know only in the most isolated case. But I accept the witness of people not under suspicion, and I do not know how to act otherwise. Through such mildness many an erring brother has been brought back to the right way." Besides that, Loehe knew very well that the practice of the Supper of the Lutheran *Landeskirchen* toward individual Lutherans from the Union must never put in question the solidarity with the free Lutheran Church in Prussia. As an example, in the *Schwabach Declaration* he chastises the fact that "north of the Bavarian borders" Prussian enclaves of Union congregations are being served by Bavarian

3.

Toward the end of the great debates concerning fellowship in the Lord's Supper between 1830 and 1870, there is an article by Gerhard von Zezschwitz [1825–86]. The history of its origin leads to a new phase of the struggles for the preservation of the Lutheran Church. After the Prussian annexations of 1866,[18] and finally after the founding of the empire in 1870/71, plans for a German *Reich* and national church emerged. The Lutheran *Landeskirchen*, bound by their Confessions, were to be absorbed by it. In a presentation about "the tasks which the duty of independence of the Lutheran Church poses, based on the events of the last years" (June 4, 1868),[19] Zezschwitz had kept to the principle that fellowship in the Supper is only possible among those who, as "confessing congregation," are in agreement, especially also in the confession concerning the Sacrament of the Altar. Thereupon Georg Rietschel [1842–1914] claimed that, according to the Lutheran Confession, admission to the Sacrament could not be refused even to the Reformed and United. This attack caused Zezschwitz to write a comprehensive rebuttal, which he based on comprehensive examples from the teaching and practice of the old Lutheran Church.[20]

In the first part, he poses "the conditions for the admission to the Holy Supper according to Lutheran principle" (pp. 3–41). Rietschel had based his thesis mainly on the fact that, according to Lutheran teaching, the worthiness consisted only in the faith in the words "given and shed for you for the forgiveness of sins," but not in a faith in the presence of the body and blood of Christ under the bread and wine. Therefore, the admission of faithful Reformed and United Christians would, "consequently, be completely Lutheran." Zezschwitz was able to prove, already from the confessional writings and also from contemporaneous sermons and

---

pastors. While they do this, they are "Pussian Union pastors," who are "in the same relationship with the Lutheran Church of Prussia as all Lutherans in the Union. And yet they are able to return to the service in the Bavarian Church without recognizing and confessing their sin. Having been under the government of the Prussian Union, in fellowship in the Supper with the Union, in contrast to our brothers in Prussia, they can without any problem come back to us, into our fellowship in the Supper, our dioceses, our parishes" (*Declaration of Several Pastors* . . . 1851).

18 [The Austro-Prussian War resulted in the consolidation of northern German states into Prussia. MH]

19 [Gerhard Zezschwitz, *Über die Aufgaben Welche Die Selbstständigkeitspflicht der Lutherischen Kirche auf Grund der Ereignisse der Letzten Jahre Stellt: Vortrag auf Ddr Lutherischen Conferenz zu Leipsig Den 4. Juni 1868* (Leipzig: J. C. Hinrichs, 1868). MH]

20 Recently Hans Asmussen has made extensive use of the proof-texts gathered by v. Zezschwitz without admitting that he by no means can claim all of his historical material as his own research. Much of it is exclusively the work of v. Zezschwitz, whom he ridicules condescendingly. Cf. the collection *Abendmahlsgmeinschaft?* (Munich: Chr. Kaiser, 1937), 5–37. [The rebuttal by Zezschwitz is included above, pp. 85–143. MH]

church orders, that "faith" in Christ's forgiving word includes the right faith in the meaning of the teaching concerning the Sacrament according to the Scriptures. In the second part, the "partaking of the Lord's Supper according to the Lutheran concept" is described as an act of confession (pp. 42–57). In the 300-year history of the Lutheran Church, Zezschwitz found so many examples that in summing up he could write: "The indubitable result is that the giving of the Lord's Supper, and the admission to it, was in general understood as an act of confession, as a duty of the confessor [*Bekennerpflicht*], and that the Reformed in principle were considered excluded from the Lutheran Supper. The main question for the present time is to what extent the behavior of United Christians is to be subjected to the same norms which applied to the Reformed in the normative period" (p. 57).[21] Therefore, the "status of the question in the present time" is discussed in the third part (pp. 58–80). Zezschwitz holds on to the refusal of fellowship in the Lord's Supper with the Reformed and those united by consensus,[22] for the sake of the faithfulness which he owes to the confessional Lutheran Church, based on its sacramental administration which is according to its institution. He acknowledges "the possibility of individual, burning cases of troubled consciences"—not only in mortal danger—"when the confessional duty can take second place to the pastoral faithfulness of the general office of Christian comfort of the Church. . . . In such cases I would come to the help of a truly troubled conscience with the sacramental service of my Church." "For such cases which belong to the sphere of special pastoral care" Zezschwitz sees the proper form of service in private Communion. Over against a Union that is only based on church government, where one can think even of Lutheran pastors and congregations, Zezschwitz offers a double possibility for consideration: either an equal refusal of the right of guests at the altars of the Lutheran Church for every Lutheran living under the church government of the Union, or a separate decision for each individual case, which would require the consideration of the status of confession of the individual. As long as the old Prussian Lutherans within the Union "insist on all the rights of the Lutheran status of confession and seek to achieve a corresponding fellowship in the Lord's Supper," Zezwitsch opines—much like Loehe in his "*Gutachten*" of 1863—that one could

21 The quoting of examples from the sixteenth and seventeenth centuries takes up a lot of space in the debate of the nineteenth century. Cf., among others, Loehe in *Deinzer* II, 558, no. 4 et al.; Delitzsch, *Die bayerische Abendmahlsgemeinschaftsfrage*, 28–41: "All the voices of our Church, even that of Georg Calixt [1586–1656], agree that fellowship in the Lord's Supper between Lutherans and Reformed is not permissible." "There is not only total agreement that a Lutheran could not take part in a Reformed celebration of the Supper (including the most extreme consequences), but also that those who steadfastly confess Calvinism cannot be admitted to the Lord's Supper in our Church" (p. 28). S. Fritschel also quotes much ancient material: *Allg. Ev.=Luth. Kirchenzeitung*, 1869, col. 769ff., 817ff.

22 [There are various types of union churches. "Consensus union" is the blurring of confessional distinctions in virtually every way at the parish level. MH]

not simply refuse them "the Sacrament at the altars of Lutheran *Landeskirchen*." But in these cases he demands that the Lutherans within the Union "at home seek the Sacrament only in congregations that practice doctrinal discipline according to Lutheran principles for fellowship in the Lord's Supper" (p. 73). But in view of the actual conditions within the Prussian Union, one would have to ask whether these conditions could exist at all.

But it is very important that Zezschwitz reckons with conditions that make fellowship in the Lord's Supper with Union Lutherans impossible in every case. "The situation and the danger of church independence in view of the infiltrating Union can at times necessitate intensity" (p. 71). Since the Prussian annexations of 1866, the Lutheran *Landeskirchen* in the new Prussian provinces were threatened by the Union (e.g., in Hannover). "Of course, they have not yet been incorporated in the organism of the church government in a more narrow sense. That makes it so much more important for them not to let the local congregation become a Union church. The rest would then follow by itself. But the treatment of the local congregation as a United one starts the moment when participation in the Holy Supper is demanded as a right for all evangelical members of the old Prussian *Landeskirche* without exception" (p. 74ff.). Because of this danger of Union, Zezschwitz advises the threatened *Landeskirchen* to secure their status quo by "simply excluding all members of the Union Church" and to demand for the Evangelicals that move into the territory "the founding of independent United congregations" (p. 75).

Here one can see that the question of fellowship in the Lord's Supper entered a new phase around 1870. The refusal to admit United [members] to a Lutheran celebration of the Lord's Supper becomes a shibboleth in the defensive struggle of the Lutheran Church in Germany over against the plans for a German national church, emanating from Prussia. "One can connect all kinds of well-meaning illusions with a German national church. But any blind person can see that its creation would certainly result in caesaropapism, establishing a church fellowship that is only based on political borders. But the Lutheran Church would be degraded to a sect" (p. 79). "That kind of danger [caesaropapism of a national church], which would mean the end of the Lutheran Church, cannot be met with false irenic theories of Lutheran principles that are not based on historical truth. What we need now are men who demonstrate the courage to be witnesses, and with unbending firmness against unlawful concessions, according to Luther's uncompromising way.—We will gladly bear the accusation of intolerance, until God in His grace will bring about for our people the days when all the friends of the freedom of religious conviction will acknowledge the fact that the struggle for the independence of the Church, based on its principles, is the way to peace for the churches and for the state" (p. 80).

What Zezschwitz outlined did not remain without contradiction. The further dispute cannot be described here.[23] The struggles of the Lutheran Church of the nineteenth century concerning fellowship in the Lord's Supper have been characterized sufficiently by the witnesses quoted. For the Silesian Lutherans, the position concerning fellowship in the Lord's Supper had to result in a decision for or against the Union, for or against the Lutheran confessional Church. Loehe's struggle, on the other hand, is an internal church struggle for a confessional order, against the toleration of a fellowship with false teachers which is forbidden by the Word of God. Zezschwitz's train of thought finally presents proofs, in connection with historical and dogmatic arguments and in view of dangers that were then acute, that the indiscriminate admission of all "Evangelicals" to the Sacrament at Lutheran altars would hollow out the Lutheran *Landeskirchen* from the inside, so that in the end they would no longer have any strength to resist the ceasaropapism of a national church. Of course, this presents the danger that the practice of admission will no longer be used exclusively for the sake of the Sacrament and its use. The nonadmission of United [members] becomes a means of fighting for the Lutheran Church, which has to defend its borders because its freedom is threatened. It must not be overlooked that our Church in its many struggles has succumbed more than once to the danger of emphasizing the confessional principles of fellowship in the Lord's Supper one-sidedly for the sake of its ecclesiological-political significance. In doing so, it de-emphasized the connection with the actual use of the Sacrament. Of course, this development is understandable as a reaction against the ever greater dissolution of any confessional practice of the Lord's Supper. An exaggerated order can be misused as an inflexible principle, and then it no longer serves the building up of the living congregation. But even then it is to be regarded more important than fundamentally giving up any confessional order.

The lasting result of the debates of the Lutheran Church concerning fellowship in the Lord's Supper in the nineteenth century lies in the fact that here dogmatic insights were connected with the witness of what the Church actually did [in practice]. In this way a binding heritage could be passed on to the following generations of our Church. The content of this heritage, which the Lutheran fathers of the nineteenth century have left, can finally be summed up in three thoughts,

23 Cf. here Hermann T. Wangemann, *Die Neulutherische Begriffsverwirrung in den Kirchenideen Hervorragender Stimmführer in Deutschen Lutherischen Landeskirchen als ein Vornehmliches Hinderniß für die Ausgestaltung der Una Sancta* (Berlin: Selbstverl. des Verf, 1883), *Una Sancta*, book 4; vol. II, 2. For an evaluation of Wangemann's treatment of the history: Johannes Nagel, *Zur Geschichte der ev.=luth. Kirche in Preussen, Ein Zeugnis gegen Dr. Wangemann* (Leipzig, 1884); also Reuter, "Die lutherische Bekenntniskirche, ein Tatzeugnis gegen die Union," *Theologisches Zeitblatt* 1 (1909): 117ff. (especially pp. 124ff.); and the work that is just coming out about Scheibel by Martin Kiunke. [Martin Kiunke, *Johann Gottfried Scheibel und Sein Ringen um die Kirche derlutherischen Reformation* (Göttingen: Vandenhoeck & Ruprecht, 1985). MH]

which without question agree with the teaching and the practice of the Lutheran Church of the sixteenth and seventeenth centuries: (1) A part of the "*worthiness*" (according to 1 Corinthians 11:27–29) has to be the faith in the words of Christ, in which the Lord witnesses to the forgiveness of sins as certainly as to the presence of His body and blood under the bread and wine. (2) Partaking [*Teilnahme*] of the sacramental celebration includes the common confession of the communicants. Because of this they have to agree in faith and doctrine. (3) Based on this unity in the confession, fellowship in the Lord's Supper becomes a witness to the existing church fellowship.[24]

4.

At the present time, the question of fellowship in the Lord's Supper has to be answered on the basis of renewed dogmatic deliberation. It is absolutely necessary to remember the historical experiences of our Church with this question. Only in this way will the decisions of the twentieth century attain their proper background, which unites them with the life of the Church in the past and at present. Nevertheless, a noncritical transfer of church decisions from the past to the present, jumping to conclusions, must be avoided. The point of origin for answering the question that has been posed for us is the responsibility of the Church for the administration of the Sacrament in accordance with its institution. The Lutheran teaching concerning the Holy Supper has been given in our confessional writings, and since then has been defended again and again, so that the Sacrament of the Altar can indeed be administered and used according to Christ's institution. No theories or consequences, least of all church-political goals, were determinitive for bearing witness to the teaching of the Lord's Supper according to the Scripture, but only the obedience of Christ's command, and with it the gathering of the congregation for the receiving of the body and blood of Christ. Therefore, every sentence of our confessional writings concerning the use of the Holy Supper leads first to the determination of the celebration of the Supper, and then to the pastoral preparation of the communing congregation.

The indissoluble connection between the doctrine of the Holy Supper and its celebration is based in the essence of the Sacrament according to Christ's institution. There is no receiving of the sacramental gifts from the hand of the Lord without His living and strong Word, with which He accompanies, interprets, and

24 An exact description of all the debates about fellowship in the Supper in the nineteenth century can only be done in the framework of a monograph devoted to that purpose. From the material that was collected for this purpose, only a few typical examples have been quoted in this paper. But the fact should also be mentioned that the insights and experiences that were gained in Germany at that time have also been applied in very significant ways in the young Lutheran churches of North America, Brazil, South Africa, and Australia, as well as on the Lutheran mission fields.

imparts His gifts. Therefore, the explanation and proclamation of the sacramental words is an indispensible part of any celebration of the Supper that is in accord with its institution. Christ's gift in the Sacrament must not be darkened or misinterpreted through the practice of the Church, be it through unclear talking about the celebration of the Supper itself or through levity while preparing and admitting the communing congregation. The teaching of the Lord's Supper of our Church has to be given expression at every use of the Sacrament. But the witnessing of the correct doctrine can never be separated from the rejection of false doctrine. For all false doctrines are not merely historically conditioned opposites, restricted to an only temporary effect. Behind the changing forms and formulations the same powers remain in effect as constant temptations for the congregation, again and again leading it toward unbelief and the doubting of the Word of the Lord. If the Sacrament of the Altar is to be administered in the Lutheran Church according to its institution, the false teaching regarding the Supper must always be rejected, directly or indirectly, and conquered through the Word of God. The liturgical form of the Divine Service of the Lord's Supper and the content of the sermon at the Supper must fulfill the duty to reject always the Reformed teachings regarding the Supper, and in the same way also defend against the Roman teaching of the Sacrament. This does not require dogmatic-historical explanations or confessional polemics in the sacramental service, but an unequivocal and truthful witness to that which is given us in the Sacrament—in contrast to all falsifications.

With this delineation against the false doctrines of the Supper of other churches, there is no judgment pronounced on whether the celebration of the Sacrament of other churches, based on wrong doctrine, is a Supper of the Lord at all, whether body and blood of Christ are received at all. We cannot be judges of that. For we cannot limit the grace of God nor the efficacy of His Means of Grace. As long as there is still a remnant of the act according to the institution—as, for instance, in the Mass of the Roman Church (despite the Mass sacrifice and all other errors)—we can believe and hope with Luther that even there the Sacrament is also received. But from this faith in the *one* Church among the confessional churches we can by no means conclude that we may acknowledge the sacramental celebration of another church besides the Lutheran as being according to the institution and of equal validity. As long as the teaching about the Supper from the altar and the pulpit of a church does not completely agree with the words of Christ and the teaching of the apostles, and as long as a unity of teaching with the Lutheran Church cannot be established, a common celebration of the Lord's Supper is impossible. That means: members of the Lutheran Church, because they are bound to the Word of Christ, are not allowed to celebrate the Sacrament at altars of a different confessional church or to receive it from the hands of a pastor who does not teach Lutheran [doctrine]. It is just as impossible that those who teach differently should preach from Lutheran pulpits about the Holy Supper and distribute [*austeilen*] the Sacrament from Lutheran altars according to a faith and a doctrine which we have to reject as false faith and doctrine. Any attempt to bring about an inter-confessional fellowship in the Supper through a common celebration of the Supper has to lead to the point where celebration of the Supper and the doctrine of the Supper are torn apart. The celebration of the Supper will be robbed of the certainty that is built on Christ's Word and is turned into a celebration of religious communion [*Gemeinschaftsfeier*] performed by pious people.[25] The doctrine of the Supper that is separated from the celebration at the altar becomes an object of discussion for schools of theology, perhaps also a shibboleth of church-political parties. However, as long as the indissoluble connection between doctrine and the receiving of the Sacrament in the meaning of the Lutheran Confession is adhered to, an inter-confessional fellowship in the Lord's Supper must be rejected.

The connection between *the doctrine of the Supper and the congregation receiving the Supper* is also important for our question. For even if at every celebration of the Supper there is a strict tying together of proclamation and liturgy in the unique Lutheran way, the communing congregation could possibly consist of members of different confessions. In almost all German Lutheran *Landeskirchen*, the indiscriminate admission of all "Evangelicals" is being practiced.[26] Can one justify these conditions from the Confessions and from Scripture? The final applicable measure here is the biblical demand of a "worthy" eating and drinking at the Lord's Table (1 Corinthians 11:27–29). But first we must consider in what way humans can even ask the question of "worthiness" or answer it. From St. Paul's teaching about the Supper, it follows that the misuses at the Supper in Corinth and the despising of the Sacrament, which they expressed, could be deducted from a culpable ignorance and lack of understanding of the gifts which the Lord Christ offers to His congregation under the bread and wine. The apostle fights against this lack of true knowledge by first speaking about the receiving of the body and blood of Christ in light of the Words of Institution, and then calls for a self-examination. In this way he wants to help the congregation to "distinguish" the Sacrament from other eating and drinking. Whoever lets himself be led to such "distinguishing" through the words of the Lord and through self-examination will eat and drink "worthily." Luther finally unlocked this word of Scripture with the article of justification when he explains: "That person is truly worthy and well prepared who has faith in these words: 'Given and shed for you for the forgiveness of sins.' But whoever does not believe these words or doubts is unworthy and unprepared. For the word 'for you' requires all hearts to believe."[27] The Lutheran Church can apply the measuring stick

---

25 [I.e., Schleiermacher! MH]

26 See the opinion of Albert Hauk, *Realencyklopädie für protestantische Theologie und Kirche*, 3rd ed. (Leipzig: J. C. Hinrichs'sche, 1908), v. 20, 260, 38ff., s.v. "Union."

27 SC V.

of "worthiness" only by taking care of the prerequisites on which the "differentiation" which the apostle Paul requests depends. But this "differentiation" is nothing but the obedient and thankful faith in Christ's Words of Institution. Therefore, the proclamation and explanation of these words remain the only means to assist the congregation toward a worthy enjoyment of the Sacrament.

The admission to the Supper depends basically on the fact that the communicants have been instructed according to God's Word about the gift of the Lord Christ, and therefore know that they receive Christ's body and blood under the bread and wine. Open and stubborn refusal to repent will necessitate exclusion from the fellowship of the Supper only because this shows that in this case forgiveness is not desired. In contrast, a general nonadmission to the Supper at Lutheran altars for members of other confessional churches can be justified only in this way: that they lack the basic condition of the right "differentiation," since they have been instructed about the Sacrament according to a false doctrine. But by drawing this line, the present task is by no means fulfilled. In an individual case one can instruct those coming from non-Lutheran churches and wanting to come to our Lutheran altars for the Sacrament. Whoever denies openly and expressly the true presence of the body and blood of Christ under the bread and wine must not be admitted to the Sacrament by the Lutheran Church. This principle must be applied, first of all, even toward such members of the Lutheran Church who break from the scriptural confession of our Church, despite serious instruction and repeated pastoral efforts. In that case the "differentiation" demanded by the apostle is lacking, because the Word of Christ is not truly believed. On the other hand, there are other communicants who have not received Lutheran instruction, yet they are perfectly willing and thankful to follow the scriptural proclamation. Basically there is no reason to deny them admission. But it must not be overlooked that by having been admitted to a Lord's Supper of the Lutheran Church they can no longer belong to another church.

Thus inter-confessional fellowship in the Supper for the Lutheran Church is just as impossible in view of the composition of the communing congregation as in regard to the celebration of the Supper. The fact that the Holy Supper is administered "according to the Gospel" (*recte*) is connected with everything else that belongs to the existence of the Church of Christ on earth. The administration of the Sacrament in its confessional significance is one of the two signs of the Church (*notae ecclesiae*). For the receiving of the Holy Supper is of significance not only for each individual Communion guest but also for the congregation as such (1 Corinthians 10:16ff.). The Church as the Body of Christ is being built and sustained through the physical connection with the Lord in the Sacrament (Ephesians 5:29–31). Therefore, the common reception of the body and blood of Christ corresponds with the common confession of the return of Christ (1 Corinthians 11:26). From this viewpoint also, fellowship in the Lord's

Supper becomes impossible if the communicants do not agree in faith and confession toward the gifts of Christ, which they receive in the Holy Supper.

The application of the Lutheran principles concerning fellowship in the Lord's Supper always belongs to the area of church orders, which are created by humans. They cannot be taken directly from the Holy Scriptures and can never be imposed upon the congregation as a divine Law. They can be changed according to place, time, and other circumstances of a certain congregation. But all these church orders have to serve exclusively [the purpose] that the ecclesiastical office [*kirchliche Amt*] can serve the whole congregation with Word and Sacrament, according to its divine commission. All the church orders concerning fellowship in the Supper and the practice of admission are also subject to this demand. Its sole purpose—even if it means to erect barriers around the Lutheran altar—consists in this: that through it the actual use of the Sacrament, the blessed receiving of the body and blood of Christ, is not hindered but furthered.

5.

The practice [*praktische Handhabung*], which corresponds to the dogmatic reflections of the question of fellowship in the Supper, presupposes that the Lutheran teaching about the Supper agrees with the witness of the Holy Scripture. Regarding this point, our Church does not know of any "open question." As long as the Lutheran interpretation of the New Testament texts about the Supper cannot be refuted through the clear witness of the Scripture, the claim of our confessional writings must be maintained, that this doctrine of the Supper alone demands validity in all of Christendom. A further condition for today's practice of admission is the judgment concerning the Reformed Church which today stands opposite to us. In this matter the understanding regarding certain "concerns" of the Lutheran doctrine, found already in Calvin, cannot be decisive, but only the question whether by any chance Reformed theologians would be willing, in the name of their Church, to reject the old false teachings and to agree with the confession of the presence of the body and blood of Christ under the bread and wine. If there are Lutherans who are already on the way to fellowship in the Supper with the Reformed,[28] they must not be satisfied with just expressing their opinion concerning the difference in the understanding of the Supper. Their decision must be affirmed publicly before the Lutheran Church through a clear confession [about] whether we do receive the body and blood of Christ with our mouth or not.

As long as we hold fast to the teaching of the Lutheran Confessions on the Supper for the sake of the Word of God and its eternal truth, the confessional significance of fellowship in the Supper cannot be in doubt. The Lutheran Church cannot admit anyone to the Sacrament whose confession does not accord with

28 Cf. Hans Lauerer, "Der Weg zur Abendmahlsgemeinschaft," *Das Luthertum* (1938): 65ff.

the words of Christ. The Lutheran Church cannot acknowledge fellowship in the Supper between itself and other churches which cling to a false doctrine about the Lord's Supper. The Lutheran Church must seriously warn its own members not to receive the Sacrament at strange altars. The Lutheran Church must especially reject the inter-confessional fellowship in the Supper with responsible representatives of different confessional churches, since this would give a false impression of a unity of faith which does not exist. There must be nothing dubious in the practice of the Supper over against Reformed and United Christians, who are standing in known and declared opposition to the confession of our Church. As long as they are not permitted to come to a Lutheran Lord's Supper but still desire it, one must give to the individual a witness of the pure teaching according to the Word of the Lord. This pastoral [*seelsorgerliche*] effort must not cease to give a friendly but also firm admonition toward confessing the orthodox faith of the Lutheran Church for the sake of the truth.

However, the application of these confessional principles is usually frustrated by the complete ignorance of the "evangelical population" in confessional matters. In fact, we in the Lutheran *Landeskirchen* have to count on the fact that at the altars of larger city churches we have a communing congregation whose confessional knowledge is very unclear. The number of Lutherans who have been well instructed in the Fifth Chief Part of Luther's Catechism must not be overestimated. Very seldom do we meet Reformed [members] who are aware of which confession they belong to because of faith and doctrine. And we will hardly meet members of the Union Church who know anything about the confessional separation or about their own position. Besides that, one cannot overlook the fact that rationalism as the "basic religion" of the natural man has flooded the congregations of all confessions. One can assume that the concept of Communion of the "enlightened" citizen, as long as he still wants to be a Christian, is straight Zwinglianism. We use this term without any confessional accent. Of course, there are still congregations that have a distinct confessional consciousness. In cities and in the country there are many traces of the blessings of faithful Lutheran witnesses clearly recognizable, as well as the good fruits of firm church orders. But the total picture in evangelical Germany is not marked by a churchly confessional order but by total Protestant-unionist disorder and devastation.

What kind of a task do these conditions present for an administration of the Sacrament in accordance with the Confessions? What the Lutheran *Landeskirchen* for decades have been guilty of and have neglected can today no longer be repaired by judging individuals according to confessional assumptions which they have lost a long time ago. It should be taken for granted that we do keep the strict confessional practice with all those who witness of their opposition to Lutheran doctrine. But toward the large majority a different standard has to be applied which we find expressed very clearly in our confessional writings. We are up against ignorant people who are in need of instruction just as much as the congregations four hundred years ago, about which Luther wrote: "Help, dear God! What misery have I seen! The common man knows so little about Christian teaching, especially in the villages (today often the opposite is true!), and unfortunately many pastors have no skill or ability to teach. And these want to be called Christians, be baptized, and enjoy the sacred Sacraments, yet they know neither the Lord's Prayer nor the Creed nor the Ten Commandments. They live like dumb animals and ignorant swine" (Preface to the Small Catechism). "Yes, it still happens daily that one finds uncouth, old people that have known nothing of this, nor know it now. And yet they go to Baptism and the Sacrament and use everything that Christians have, even though those going to the Sacrament ought to know more and have a more complete understanding of all Christian doctrine than boys and new scholars" (LC Shorter Preface). The forms of ignorance and the extent of not knowing may be different today than in those days. The problem itself exists again to a large extent, and according to human judgment it will further increase. Therefore, the Lutheran Church faces the task of finding new forms of administering the Sacrament in view of the ignorance and indifference of the congregations. The ways that are shown in the Confession for this are these: a thorough instruction in the doctrine of the Supper, regular preaching about the receiving of the body and blood of Christ and its significance for salvation, and in connection with this inclusive proclamation of the Sacrament the conscientious practice of a truly pastoral [*seelsorgerlichen*] order for the admission to the Lord's Table.

Based on the order of admission it will be decided whether we are really willing to apply our confessional principles of fellowship in the Supper for the sake of the Sacrament, or whether we apply them only for other reasons. As an example, it is perfectly possible today to communicate to all members of our Church, orally or in written form, the meaning of going to the Lord's Supper in the Lutheran Church and why a personal announcement by all communicants (individually or by families) must be required. The instruction can and must often be repeated, especially for newly arriving members. Of course, in that case the announcement has to be received by the pastors themselves—at predetermined times, not just on the day the Supper is celebrated, but even a week in advance. Mass Communions must be divided up in smaller sacramental celebrations. Here one educates for the long term. Besides the pastoral office, especially the church government should be responsible for this. Even a Lutheran mission among the people [*Volksmission*] can be used for regular cooperation in this area. Only within the framework of a newly established pastoral order of admission will it be possible to establish church discipline according to God's Word for the public and unrepentant sinners. Only with this prerequisite is it again possible to talk with individual Christians from Reformed and United churches concerning their relationship to the Confession of the Lutheran Church. Here also a clear word can be addressed to all members of the congregation, as long as our Church has the courage to establish a true church order for the sake of the Sacrament. The purpose of this should not be some legalistic determinations, but to invite, and at the same time admonish, pointing to the biblical message concerning the reception of the Sacrament.

The question concerning fellowship in the Lord's Supper must and will be answered by the concrete action of the Lutheran Church. We fight for this, that our Church will act according to its Confession in its governance and in the spiritual guidance of individual congregations. But any individual decision is in agreement with the Lutheran Confession only if three things are witnessed to emphatically:

Fellowship in the Lord's Supper is possible only where the celebration of the Supper in its form, and the communing congregation in its Confession, agree with the Lutheran doctrine concerning the Sacrament of the Altar.

Fellowship in the Supper is always church fellowship; therefore, it is impossible between the Lutheran Church and other confessions, which are separated from the orthodox Church by false doctrine.

Fellowship in the Supper requires *an order for admission to the Sacrament* according to the principle of the Augsburg Confession: "This custom is practiced by us: the Sacrament will not be given to those who have not first been examined and absolved" (AC XXV 1).

CHAPTER NINE

Luther's Teaching on the Lord's Supper

Ernst Sommerlath[1]

Translated by Albert B. Collver

Luther's doctrine of the Lord's Supper and Luther's consequent understanding of the Lord's Supper in the high Mass of the Lutheran Church cannot be based on, as it is sometimes claimed, Luther's capacity for stubbornness or on a biased exegesis of the Words of Institution,[2] which Luther insisted upon. Indeed, it is in fact true with respect to questions concerning the Lord's Supper that Luther emphatically depended upon Scripture. He felt constrained by the Words of Institution,[3] which for him were the final foundation of his certainty. Also, today in the Lutheran Church, this is not a matter of mere adherence to a dogma confessed from ages past. It is a testing of the truth, which she sees confessed in the New Testament. Also, the official discussion between the Lutheran and Reformed churches in recent times was nothing else than a contemporary and serious examination of the teaching about the Lord's Supper[4] from the Scriptures. But Luther "stood" not only on the wording. He understood the words very much in the context in which they stand, with the *entirety* of the saving reality of God. His understanding of the Lord's Supper is connected most closely with belief in the God of the New Testament and with the New Testament understanding of the Holy Spirit. But Luther especially has the relationship of the doctrine of the Lord's Supper to Christology very clearly before his eyes. Luther views the union of the bread and wine and the body and blood of Christ in a way that corresponds to the

1 "Abendmahl III. Dogmatisch, Lutherische Lehre," in *Die Religion in Geschichte und Gegenwart* (Tübingen: J. C. B. Mohr [Paul Siebeck], 1957), vol. 1, pp. 34–38.

2 *Abendmahlsworte* [literally: Lord's Supper words].

3 *Einsetzungsworte*

4 *Abendmahlslehre*

way the divine and human natures are joined together in Christ. Therefore, for him, the Lord's Supper is a foundational part of New Testament revelation.

It is the incarnation of Christ, the infleshing of the divine in the earthly, which produces the foundational fact. It is, first of all, the way of God with man. Thus Luther sees the Lord's Supper in the framework of the entire reality of salvation as it presents itself in the New Testament. Therefore, for him, Christ Himself is the proper, the original, Sacrament.[5] All that matters to him is that as in Christ God truly is on earth, so also in the Sacrament Christ is entirely and bodily with us. The real passion in Luther's teaching on the Lord's Supper, and that of the Lutheran Church, is the bodily presence of Christ in our earthly manner of existence. It is the opposite for all fanaticism,[6] that the embodiment of salvation is at the heart of the Lord's Supper. While one must "swarm" [*schwärmen*] over the entire earth in order to have Christ and yet not find Him, He permits Himself to be grasped and to be caught here. While with Calvin the presence is thought of only as an "as if" ("*non secus ac si corpore adeset*" ["just as if the body were here"], *Institutio* VI, 123). With Calvin there is always an "upward movement" in which the soul sweeps upward, in order to unite itself with Christ in the heavenly and spiritual sphere. In the Lutheran Church, faith's fervor is over the presence of Christ's body here. That is the meaning and the serious belief in the teaching of the *manducatio oralis* [i.e., the body and blood of Christ are received by the mouth]. As the incarnate Christ was bodily on earth, thus He will be received also in the Lord's Supper, bodily and with the mouth. Article X of the Augsburg Confession emphatically says of the body and blood of Christ that they are *vere adsint et distribuantur* ["truly present and distributed"].

This indeed presupposes that the Sacrament not only points to the salvation gift, but it is contained in itself and it *brings it about*. This was not simply self-evident, even for Luther. In his confrontation with [Roman] Catholic sacramental teaching in *The Babylonian Captivity* of 1520, he interprets the Sacrament (his earliest teaching regarding the Lord's Supper) that it is a sign (*signum*) of God's graciousness, and thus it can be compared with a seal on a deed. In the Lord's Supper, that which is certainly offered and spoken to us in the Word is made certain with a visible sign. The Sacrament and thus also the Lord's Supper is in such a manner a visible Word set forth. This assurance function of the Lord's Supper, namely, the psychological meaning it has for the weak in faith, is to be highly valued. Individuals are each given a sign for the strengthening of faith and certainty, to which they can hold on to in the trials [*Anfechtungen*] of life. But the function of the Lord's Supper is not thereby exhausted. Even then Luther firmly maintained that the Lord's Supper itself is the body and blood of Christ, and more

---

5 *Ursakrament*

6 *Schwärmertum*

and more this certainty came into the foreground of the interest of faith for him, [namely,] that the Lord's Supper bears in itself what it indicates. It is a vehicle or a bridge, by which the gift itself comes. It is the conduit, through which the water flows, which gives drink to the thirsty. "Meaning" and "work" of the Sacrament coincide. The Sacrament as visible Word does not at all exhaust the content of the Lutheran teaching of the Lord's Supper. It is better to see the Sacrament and thus also the Lord's Supper more closely connected with the Word. The power of the Lord's Supper consists in Christ's Words of Institution.[7] First of all, the Word interprets the gift for us, and the Word imparts to us the gift intended for us. The Word with its "for you" makes personal faith possible, without which no right reception of the gift of grace would be possible. But the Sacrament is not simply subordinate to the Word. The Lord's Supper also stands next to the Word as a particular gift, as has again been acknowledged in recent dogmatic studies. If one asks about the *proprium* of the Lord's Supper, then one will have to locate it in the spiritual-bodily communion with Christ. It is impossible here to examine how this *proprium* relates to Baptism. Over against the Word, in any case, the connection with the corporality of Christ is the very sort of fellowship that is given nowhere else. Luther can speak eloquently of the special nature of this communion. It is so close that we become "one cake, one bread, one body, one drink" with Him. No other union is for him as close as the union of the food[8] with the one fed. For the food is changed as to its nature and becomes one essence with the one fed.

It is understandable that, for Luther, as for the Lutheran Church, faith is directed toward the elements and that the question of the *real presence*[9] plays a decisive role. Everything in the Lutheran teaching depends upon it. The bread and wine are Christ's body and blood. Luther had no interest in *how* it happens. Neither did he fight against [*bekämpft*] the [Roman] Catholic teaching of transubstantiation, that is, that the substances of the bread and wine were transformed into the substances of the body and blood of Christ, even though he did not believe it was correct. If indeed one would insist on a theory as to a how it happens, then he would note how in the person of Christ divine and human natures are bound together. They are not changed into the other nature, but very closely united into a personal union [*unio personalis*]. Thus Luther conceived of a very close unification of bread and body and of wine and blood of Christ in a sacramental union [*unio sacramentalis*], without transubstantiation. This union could not be considered to be too close or tight a unity. Even the doctrine, so often noted as a distinct mark of the Lutheran understanding, that the body of Christ is "in, with, and under" the bread did not satisfy Luther as a precise theological manner of speaking.

---

7 *Einsetzungsworten Christ*

8 *Speise*

9 *Realpräsenz*

Theologically, he adhered to an identification [of the bread and body]. The bread is the body. Thus as in the case of a hot glowing piece of iron, fire and iron become entirely one, so also the bread and the body of Christ. But this is only one way to think of the union. Also his teaching of ubiquity (that is the teaching that Christ's body has the capacity to be everywhere) is only a theory, which he was forced to set forth as the result of Zwingli's assertions. His teaching was not based upon ubiquity, rather only upon the fact that bread and body, wine and blood of Christ are one.

This unity [of bread and body] is for the Lutheran understanding of the Lord's Supper not merely a mode of the presence of Christ, but it is the thing itself. If today now and then it is asserted that Reformed and Lutheran views of the Lord's Supper are in agreement on the assertion of the presence of Christ and only conceive of the mode of the presence in different ways, then the proper concern of the Lutheran teaching is not understood at all.

To presume that in this valuing of the elements [there is] a retreat from faith and from the personal significance of the Sacrament would be a total misunderstanding. The Lutheran teaching on the Lord's Supper, from Luther on, insists here with all earnestness that the body and blood of Christ be received in repentance and faith and be appropriated personally. Without faith, no one receives the blessing of the Sacrament. But with equal seriousness it is maintained that the Sacrament originates [*Zustandekommen des Sakramentes*] completely and entirely independent of our faith. It depends only upon the institution of Christ. The Sacrament is undisturbed by the vicissitudes and half-heartedness of our faith. This comes to expression in the doctrine of the *manducatio impiorum*. Unbelievers also receive the body and blood, though not to their salvation but to their condemnation.

By this unified view of the objective action of Christ and subjective personal approbation of faith, the accusation [that the Lutheran view is somehow] a magical understanding can only be described as absurd

If the Lord's Supper is the true/actual[10] body and blood of the Lord, then it demonstrates itself at the same time [to be] the Sacrament of fellowship.[11] Those who eat the body of Christ become one body, which is the Body of Christ, the Church. The Lord's Supper as the "Sacrament of love" unites [the Church] with Christ the Head and the members with one another. The Lord's Supper is fundamental to the Church.[12]

This particular presence[13] of Christ—viewed temporally—unites past and future in the present. The past, that is Christ, as He was bodily on earth, becomes

10 *wirklich*

11 *Gemeinschaft*

12 *kirchen-konstitutiv*

13 *Gegenwärtigkeit*

present; the future, that is Christ who will come again, is anticipated and present. The presence of Christ in the Lord's Supper is, in a special sense, the breaking of eternity into time. The table of the Lord's Supper is the "entrance to heaven" [*Pforte des Himmels*] on earth [Genesis 28:16–17].

CHAPTER TEN

The Lord's Supper
Our Life Together in Doctrine and Practice

John T. Pless[1]

Introduction

Writing in the early 1940s, J. Michel Reu (1869–1943) posed the question: "Can We Still Hold to the Lutheran Doctrine of the Lord's Supper?"[2] Reu, of course, will answer in the affirmative after surveying and critiquing a variety of theologians from Schleiermacher to the middle part of the twentieth century who question not only the meaning of the Lord's Supper but also its origin. I take my assignment for this conference to look at the dogmatic foundations inherent in the confession and practice of the Lord's Supper and their implications for our life together in the Church. Given the spirit of the age that can be very dogmatic in asserting its rejection of dogma, an atmosphere in the Church that insists on a dogma-free Christianity, to paraphrase Hermann Sasse, I realize the difficulty of this undertaking especially in making the claim as I intend to do that the doctrine of the Lord's Supper is critical not only for liturgical forms but also for the proper pastoral care of those who are admitted to the Sacrament and those who are not. Nevertheless, this is a task that we may not shy away from if we are to be faithful to the Holy Scriptures and the Lutheran Confessions. Given all that has been written in scholarly and popular domains on the Lord's Supper and the way in which assumptions and assertions have subtly or not so subtly influenced teaching about the Sacrament and sacramental practices in our midst, we need to examine fundamental doctrinal categories as they are exhibited in connection with the Lord's Supper. Luther's exposition of the Sacrament of the Altar in the Small Catechism is a demonstration of his "catechetical-systematics," to borrow a term from Oswald

1 Presented at Missouri District Pastoral Conference, October 2013, in Osage Beach, MO.

2 J. Michel Reu, "Can We Still Hold to the Lutheran Doctrine of the Lord's Supper?" in *Two Treatises on the Means of Grace* (Minneapolis: Augsburg, 1952), 1–38.

Bayer. Luther starts not with a general theory of the "sacraments" or with a liturgical event but with the words of the Lord. That is where we shall start as well.

EXEGETICAL TRENDS

It is instructive to note how so much of contemporary scholarship refuses to begin with the *verba testamenti.* Joachim Jeremias, whose *Eucharistic Words of Jesus* would have a profound effect on twentieth-century New Testament scholarship, exemplifies this trend: "The wrong way to develop an understanding of the last supper is to be begin from the words of interpretation, because in this way the so-called 'founding meal' is isolated. Indeed, it ought really to be said that this isolation of the last supper through the centuries has made it very difficult to recognize its . . . significance. In reality, the 'founding meal' is only one link in a long chain of meals which Jesus shared with his followers and which they continued after Easter. These gatherings at table, which provoked such scandal because Jesus excluded no one from them, even open sinners, and thus expressed the heart of his message, were types of the feast to come in the time of salvation. . . . The last supper has its historical roots in this chain of gatherings."[3]

Jeremias makes the move from Jesus' meals with those deemed outcasts and unrighteous to the Lord's Supper. He sees a continuum between these meals and the Sacrament. The contrast between the meals where Jesus sits at table with sinners and the Last Supper is overlooked by Jeremias. In the Last Supper, Jesus gathers only the twelve. It is not an open meal, but a supper with those called to the life of discipleship; they had followed Jesus throughout His public ministry. It is no ordinary meal that Jesus partakes of with His followers, but the Last Supper where He institutes the Sacrament of the New Testament—the meal of His body and blood.

The particularity of this supper sets it apart from all previous meals. On the eve of His crucifixion, Jesus says of the bread "this is My body" and of the cup "this is My blood." No mere cipher for the gift of Himself or His acceptance of the unrighteous, these words speak of His impending sacrifice. They declare the fruits of His sacrifice—body and blood given and shed for those who betray Him.

The words of Christ's new testament like the cross itself are an offense. They may not be reduced to vague assertions of presence, encounter, or mystery, as does Eduard Schweitzer who writes: ". . . the real presence of Christ in the Lord's Supper is exactly the same as his presence in the world—nothing more, nothing less. It is an event, not an object; an encounter, not a phenomenon of nature; it is Christ's

---

3 Joachim Jeremias, *New Testament Theology*, vol. 1: *The Proclamation of Jesus*, trans. John Bowen (London: SCM Press, 1971), 289–90. For a refutation of Jeremias, see Reu, "Can We Still Hold to the Lutheran Doctrine of the Lord's Supper?" 1–38.

encounter with his church, not the distribution of a substance."[4] Rather the words of Christ, says Werner Elert, are "extraordinary . . . without analogy of any kind."[5]

Historical-critical approaches to Holy Scripture created skepticism as to the reliability of the Synoptic and Pauline accounts of the Sacrament's institution.[6] If uncertainty exists as to the accuracy of the institution narratives, the practice of the Lord's Supper is linked either to the meals of the historical Jesus or the meals of the Early Church thought of as experiences with the risen Christ.[7] Both of these approaches shift away from body and blood to events and acts. This shift is demonstrated in the *Manual on the Liturgy—Lutheran Book of Worship*, as the authors seek to make the case for the omission of the post-Communion blessing, arguing: "This blessing which is provided is optional for a number of reasons. It is a reflection of the medieval mentality which saw the Communion in terms of things—bread and wine; body and blood—rather than in terms of a personal

---

4 Eduard Schweitzer, *The Lord's Supper according to the New Testament*, trans. James M. Davis (Philadelphia: Fortress, 1967), 37–38.

5 Werner Elert, *The Structure of Lutheranism*, trans. Walter A. Hansen (St. Louis: Concordia, 1962), 303.

6 For example, Willi Marxsen writes: "It is extremely difficult to refer the contents of the Pauline formula back to Jesus; and in the face of all that we can ascertain about the preaching and activity of Jesus, it is still less likely to assume the institution of a cult by Jesus. Thus the supposition that Jesus instituted the Lord's Supper on the eve of his death poses so many difficulties that the careful historian must put more than just a question mark here" ("The Lord's Supper as a Christological Problem," in *The Beginning of Christology*, trans. Lorenz Nieting [Philadelphia: Fortress, 1971], 112). By way of contrast, the apostle Paul understands the Lord's Supper as proceeding from its institution by Christ and its administration in the Church. See 1 Corinthians 10:14–17 and 11:20–30 (12). What Paul has received from the Lord becomes the basis for how he assesses the Corinthian congregation's administration of the Holy Supper. Note Werner Elert's defense of the veracity of the Pauline account: ". . . the report of the institution of the Lord's Supper transmitted by Paul is of the greatest importance. It reveals from where the Pauline congregations actually derived their celebration of the Sacrament. Paul cannot have transmitted it to the congregations of Asia Minor in a manner other than he did to the Corinthian church. Thus the institution is older than the oldest Pauline congregations. It has, as it were, prehistoric significance. . . . The possibility that Paul invented the Sacrament—aside from all other impossibilities here—is ruled out by the very fact that Holy Communion, as already stated, cannot be derived from any other of the Gospel's themes. If Paul had invented it, in what way might this have helped him clarify or explain the great themes of the Letters to the Romans and to the Galatians? Might not the introduction of a ritual act, which he himself considers to be in dangerous proximity to the pagan sacrificial meals, obscure rather than clarify the connection between promise and faith, faith and works, Law and Gospel?" (*The Lord's Supper Today*, trans. Martin Bertram and Rudolph Norden [St. Louis: Concordia, 1974], 13–14).

7 See Oscar Cullmann, *Early Christian Worship*, trans. A. Steward Todd and James B. Torrance (Philadelphia: Westminster Press, 1978), and *Essays on the Lord's Supper*, trans. J. G. Davies (Atlanta: John Knox Press, 1958).

encounter with the risen Christ."[8] The language of "personal encounter" reflective of the existentialism of much of middle to late twentieth-century theology is not sufficient to convey the truth that the body and blood of the crucified and risen Lord are present and bestowed under bread and wine in the Sacrament.

LITURGICAL STUDIES

Closely linked to the language of encounter is the piety of human activity. Behind the Second Vatican Council's notion of "liturgy as the work of the people" is an understanding of liturgy that is rooted in ritual performance, reenactment, or cultic activity. The key figure here is Gregory Dom Dix, whose book *The Shape of the Liturgy* would exert wide influence in the liturgical reforms that swept across Christendom in the wake of Vatican II. Dix asserts that early eucharistic liturgies exhibit a fourfold pattern: (1) taking of bread and wine; (2) giving of thanks over bread and wine; (3) breaking of bread; (4) eating and drinking.[9]

For Dix and his disciples, the celebration of the Sacrament is seen as adhering to the pattern of Jesus in the Upper Room. It is a sort of liturgical application of WWJD—what would Jesus do? Jesus took bread, gave thanks, broke it, and gave it to His disciples to eat and drink. Thus the Sacrament is primarily a cultic *mimesis* of Jesus' Last Supper. Here the accent is not on the promise and gift of Christ's body and blood but on ritual action. The liturgy becomes dramatic reenactment. The similarities with Zwingli are apparent. Performance of the Sacrament memorializes Jesus and spurs faith to the knowledge of His atonement. But where are the fruits of the atonement located? Not in body and blood given under bread and wine but in communal, eucharistic memory.

Faithful teaching of the catechism, and liturgical practice coherent with it, will maintain that this Supper is the Lord's Supper, not the Christian's supper, to echo Luther. Potent trends within the last century have challenged Luther's assertion as one-sided or narrow. I have already noted the influence of Gregory Dom Dix. Significant also was the work of the Swedish archbishop Yngve Brilioth In 1925–26, Brilioth wrote *Eucharistic Faith and Practice*, dedicating it to the ecumenical pioneer Nathan Söderblom. In this book, Brilioth attempts to forge a path

---

8 Philip H. Pfatteicher and Carlos R. Messerli, *Manual on the Liturgy—Lutheran Book of Worship* (Minneapolis: Augsburg, 1979), 246–47.

9 Gregory Dix, *The Shape of the Liturgy* (New York: Seabury Press, 1982), 48. Dix's influence in the LCMS can be seen in the 1969 *Worship Supplement* in "The Holy Eucharist II" with its four actions of taking, blessing, breaking, and sharing. See Commission on Worship-LCMS, *Worship Supplement* (St. Louis: Concordia, 1969), 60–62. See Oliver Olson's examination of the *fractio panis* uncritically adopted by Lutheran liturgies of this period. Oliver Olson, "The Liturgy and the Concomitant Aspects of the Lord's Supper," in *Lord Jesus Christ, Will You Not Stay: Essays in Honor of Ronald Feuerhahn on the Occasion of His Sixty-Fifth Birthday*, ed. J. Bart Day et al. (St. Louis: Concordia, 2002), 121–29.

through the doctrinal divisions hardened into closed altars throughout modern Christendom. Through a selective examination of liturgical texts, Brilioth sought to isolate distinctive themes or dimensions of the Sacrament accented by various traditions. While arguing that the central motif of the Sacrament is the mystery or holy presence, Brilioth sees other dimensions to the Holy Meal as thanksgiving (eucharist), communion, commemoration, and sacrifice. He concludes his treatment by asserting that no one tradition in Christendom has captured the Sacrament in its wholeness. Instead, he says that the Sacrament is like a precious jewel which "shows endless changes of light and colour as it is regarded from different angles. But the light which it refracts is one and the same: the holy Presence, the Mystery. It is true to say that the other aspects of the eucharist are only different sides of the Mystery, or, from the human point of view, different ways of approaching it; and the various forms of liturgy and systems of doctrine which we have surveyed have helped to show the richness of its variety in constantly changing forms. But it is also true that since the early centuries no part of Christendom has succeeded in expressing all aspects together, in their harmony and completeness."[10]

For Brilioth, the catechism's confession of Christ's body and blood given under bread and wine for the forgiveness of sins could be no more than one aspect of the Lord's Supper.[11] So in Brilioth's estimation, Luther corrected some aspects of a distorted medieval piety but was finally unable to recapture the fullness of the Sacrament itself, and whatever territory Luther reclaimed was finally lost in Lutheran Orthodoxy, Rationalism, and Pietism.

Along with Dix's liturgical proposal and emerging historical-critical renderings of the place of the Lord's Supper in the New Testament, Brilioth's work would be influential for Lutherans in revising both the doctrine and the practice of the Lord's Supper. In the 1960s and '70s, when air was heavy with ecumenical optimism prompted by the achievements of the Second Vatican Council and the prospect of uniting segmented Lutheran churches, the map charted by Brilioth would be eagerly followed by both, ecumenically and liturgically. On a popular level, this can be seen in a small book written by LCMS pastor Herbert Lindemann in 1971 entitled *New Mood in Lutheran Worship*. Lindemann praises the achievements of the Liturgical Movement and gives practical advice as to how they might be implemented in Lutheran congregations to create a new atmosphere for worship marked by celebration and joy. As the title indicates, a different mood is sought. Worship ought to be celebratory, welcoming, and participatory.

---

10 Yngve Brilioth, *Eucharistic Faith and Practice: Evangelical and Catholic*, trans. A. G. Hebert (London: SPCK, 1965), 288.

11 Brilioth writes: "This one-sided emphasis was only intensified by the fact that Luther himself used the term 'forgiveness of sins' in a broad sense to cover the whole fact of God's gracious coming to man; and the common use of the term in the narrower sense resulted in serious impoverishment of the idea in the Lutheran churches" (142).

Systematic and Ecumenical Theology

Six years later, in a lecture series at Yale Divinity School, the German ecumenical theologian Wolfhart Pannenberg delivered two lectures that would be published in a book entitled *Christian Spirituality*. Like Brilioth before him, Pannenberg thought that Luther preserved the medieval preoccupation with guilt. This prevented the reformer from moving beyond the categories of repentance and the forgiveness of sins. In fact, Pannenberg suggests that the Reformation may have made matters worse, for it accented an individualistic notion of faith in a forensic declaration of justification which did not lead to transformation.

Steven Paulson provides a summary of Pannenberg's proposal: "To get rid of Protestant guilt and isolation he proposed a search for a better piety, and he believed he had just the one that would help. He called it 'eucharistic' piety, which required a new liturgy. Instead of centering everything on preaching law and gospel, and so the forgiveness of sins, he proposed a new liturgy that would produce joy instead of guilt, and sponsor communal, rather than individual, faith. This new piety would center on feelings of joy and the work of giving thanks, and it would be composed of signs indicating that worshipers are visibly united while making Eucharist together. In short, he laid out the rationale for what has become known in Lutheran churches as the new 'eucharistic celebration.' Communion is joy, not guilt; communal, not individual, and so is not the act of forgiveness of sinners but the public symbol of the united, joyful kingdom of the resurrected Christ as it makes its pilgrim journey to the promised land. Instead of death, celebrate life; instead of the cross, resurrection; instead of guilt, joy. It was quite glorious to contemplate, as glory always is."[12]

The action in Holy Communion is anthropological, that is, it is the human action of ritual celebration. Michael Welker writes: "The recognition that in holy communion a gathered community celebrates a symbolic community meal is indispensable—and, as we will see, has major consequences."[13] This meal has symbolic function. Here Welker is consistent with the *Arnoldshain Theses* as this document defines the Sacrament: "The Supper is an act of worship of the community gathered in Jesus' name."[14] This act is constituted as "with prayer, praise, and thanksgiving, bread and wine are taken, the Lord's words of institution are spoken, and bread and wine are given to the congregation to eat and to drink."[15]

---

12 Steven D. Paulson, "What Is Essential in Lutheran Worship?" *Word & World* (Spring 2006): 55. Here also Oliver K. Olson, *Reclaiming the Lutheran Liturgical Heritage* (Minneapolis: Reclaim Resources, 2007).

13 Michael Welker, *What Happens in Holy Communion?* trans. John F. Hoffmeyer (Grand Rapids: Eerdmans, 2000), 29.

14 Welker, *What Happens in Holy Communion?* 36.

15 Welker, *What Happens in Holy Communion?* 36.

Welker observes that the term *Eucharist* has found wide acceptance among both Roman Catholics and Protestants as it takes the focus away from the elements to the communal action of the assembly.[16] It is an ecumenically-friendly term that is attractive both to Rome and the Reformed. Alasdair I. C. Heron comments:

> Very early in the ancient church, "Eucharist" became the established name for the sacrament, as recorded around the middle of the second century by Justin Martyr and perhaps even earlier. It has remained in use ever since in both the Eastern, Greek Church and the Latin, Western Church; and appropriately so, for this is the great **act of thanksgiving** at the very heart of Christian worship. Calvin himself spoke of "the kind of sacrifice which we have called eucharistic" (i.e., the sacrifice of thanksgiving), and insisted "this kind of sacrifice is indispensable in the Lord's Supper." It is no very great jump from Calvin to restore the word itself as an alternative to "Supper"; and by doing so we make available to ourselves the most universally used and understood name for the sacrament, one which is free from narrower denominational or confessional associations, and which has for that reason been increasingly employed in modern ecumenical dialogue.[17]

---

16 Welker, *What Happens in Holy Communion?* 57–58.

17 Alasdair I. C. Heron, *Table and Tradition: Toward an Ecumenical Understanding of the Eucharist* (Philadelphia: Westminster Press, 1983), xiii. Lowell Green observes that the term *Eucharist* is used only twice in the Lutheran Confessions. See L. Green "The Holy Supper," in *A Contemporary Look at the Formula of Concord*, ed. Robert Preus and Wilbert Rosin (St. Louis: Concordia, 1977), 207. On the other hand, the Tetrapolitan Confession of 1530 uses *Eucharist* to identify the chapter on the Lord's Supper. See *Reformed Confessions of the 16th Century*, ed. Arthur C. Cochrane (Philadelphia: Westminster Press, 1966), 75. Zwingli's preference for "Eucharist" is noted by Geoffrey Bromiley: see G. Bromiley, "Lord's Supper," in *The Westminster Handbook to Reformed Theology*, ed. Donald K. McKim (Louisville: Westminster/John Knox, 2001), 142. My colleague Professor Naomichi Masaki pointed me to this line by Theodor Kliefoth: "The Lord's Supper is held to in terms of what the congregation does in it, namely, remembering and showing forth the death of Jesus, thanksgiving, etc. Therefore they (the Reformed) prefer to call the Lord's Supper by the name Eucharist" (*Die ursprüngliche Gottesdienstordnung in den deutschen Kirchen lutherischen Bekenntnisses, ihre Destruktion und Reformation* [Rostock: Stiller'sche Hofbuchhandlung, 1847]), 27. For a Lutheran analysis of the use of the term *Eucharist* for the Sacrament, see Gerhard Forde, "What's in a Name? Eucharist or the Lord's Supper?" *Logia* (Eastertide 1993): 48. Forde comments: "An age which has already reduced God pretty much to a meaningless cipher, a sentimentality characterized as 'love in general,' cannot afford to lose sight of the fact that this sacrament is the Lord's Supper not ours. He gives it. He is the gift. We are indeed to give thanks for this unspeakable gift. But the thanksgiving must be quite distinct; it must not displace the gift itself. When the Lord's Supper becomes the Eucharist everything is run together and confused and the sheer gift of the gospel is obscured, if not lost" (48). For Sasse's critique of the terminology of "Eucharist," see Hermann Sasse, "Consecration and Real Presence," in *Scripture and the Church: Selected Essays of Hermann Sasse*, ed. Ronald Feuerhahn and Jeffry Kloha (St. Louis: Concordia Seminary Press, 1995), 300–303. The liturgy contains a "eucharistic prayer." It is Luther's post-Communion collect of 1526 that gives thanks for the salutary gift of Jesus' body and blood and implores God

Alongside of the activity of thanksgiving, the Supper functions as a sign of mutual acceptance. Welker writes: "Yet along with thanksgiving, there is a second center: the communal taking, breaking, and distributing of the bread, and the corresponding symbolic action with the cup and the wine. The action in connection with the bread and wine expresses human beings' welcome and acceptance of each other."[18] This theme then translates into a completely open altar. The apostle's words in 1 Corinthians 11 are taken to mean: "The community, the church of Christ, must attend to the right celebration of the Supper. Each person must judge him—or herself. But no one has the power and the authorization to exclude a particular person or a particular group of persons from participation in the Supper! On the contrary, Paul's reproach to the Corinthians applies precisely to a celebration of the Supper which is misused to exercise moral control and for some persons to dominate others."[19]

A LUTHERAN CRITIQUE

Hailed by many as an ecumenical breakthrough, the new liturgical theology did not deal with the question of what is received in the Sacrament as consensus was seen instead in a common ritual pattern. Hermann Sasse saw this consensus as a compromise that spelled death to the Lutheran doctrine of the Lord's Supper. His

---

that this gift would strengthen the communicants in faith toward Him and fervent love toward one another. Eucharist happens in the world as those who have received Christ's body and blood now give themselves to the neighbor in love. For more on this point, see Paul Rorem, "Augustine and Luther For and Against Contemporary Spirituality," *Currents in Theology and Mission* (April 2003): 102–3. Also see John T. Pless, "Taking the Divine Service into the Week," in *Christ's Gifts in Liturgy: The Theology and Music of the Divine Service*, ed. Daniel Zager (Fort Wayne: CTS Press, 2002), 71–82. Welker notes that the term *Eucharist* is more friendly to feminist theologians who find the language of the "Lord's" Supper offensive (Welker, *What Happens in Holy Communion?* 3). See the critique provided by Oswald Bayer, "The Ethics of Gift," *Lutheran Quarterly* (Winter 2010): 447–68, where he states: "Whoever calls the Lord's Supper as a whole 'the Eucharist,' and understands it as such—as an act of thanksgiving—subsumes the 'downward' gift and promise within the 'upward' offering of praise in such a manner that the thanksgiving nullifies the gift. The pure gift is thereby practically overshadowed and, indeed, distorted by the response and the gift in return—even when these are understood pneumatologically in a Trinitarian context and thus relieved of the suspicion of works righteousness" (454).

18 Welker, *What Happens in Holy Communion?* 67.

19 Welker, *What Happens in Holy Communion?* 71. Compare *A Declaration of Eucharistic Understanding and Practice* from the Florida-Georgia District of The Lutheran Church—Missouri Synod. Contrast with Werner Elert, *Eucharist and Church Fellowship in the First Four Centuries*, trans. Norman E. Nagel (St. Louis: Concordia, 1966). Elert sees this understanding as "man-centered" and representing the trajectory of Schleiermacher. Elert writes: "The concept of fellowship which is here said to characterize the church does not derive from the nature of the church, but the nature of the church is derived from the concept of fellowship" (2).

writings on the Sacrament beginning in the 1930s and continuing until near the end of his life in 1976 sought to defend the Lutheran doctrine and deepen in congregations an appreciation for a practice consistent with this confession. His writings on the Sacrament of the Altar are in so many ways prophetic of our current circumstances. Sasse saw a genuine Lutheran confession of the Sacrament jeopardized by both a nonsacramental, unionizing Protestantism and a Romanizing liturgical movement. Both are unacceptable alternatives as each surrenders the evangelical character of the Lord's Supper. This happens as Lutherans, in order to accommodate the Reformed, set aside the confession that the Word of Christ Himself gives us His very body and blood to eat and drink. Reformed tendencies are not to be countered by becoming more Roman. Sasse was critical of the Liturgical Movement for adopting Roman liturgical practices without giving consideration to how these practices embody an alien doctrine that would transform the testament of Christ into a sacrifice. For Sasse, the answer to those Lutherans who sought their identity with the Reformed as well as those who saw themselves as drawing their theological identity from Rome was to be found in Article VII of the Formula of Concord.

It was from the Formula that Sasse would argue that the difference between the Lutherans and the Reformed on the doctrine of the Lord's Supper is as lively today as it was in the sixteenth century. It is not merely a debate over the *how* of Christ's presence but rather *what* is present. No Christian believes in a *real absence*. That was not the issue at the time of the Reformation nor is it the issue now. Thus Communion announcements that ask that those who come to the altar "believe in the real presence of Christ in the Sacrament" are meaningless. As Dr. Albert Collver has demonstrated, the language of the real presence is not yet a confession of Christ's body and blood.[20]

The themes that we have isolated in contemporary ecumenical theologies of the Lord's Supper provide a frame of reference for understanding the assumption and insistence that access to the altar is a matter of entitlement not to be denied to anyone. After all, if the Supper is a communal recognition of the presence of Jesus as the one who welcomes sinners and an activity of thanksgiving, why ought not all people be urged to participate? Hence the preference of the terminology of "eucharistic hospitality" over against the older language of altar and pulpit fellowship. However, this category does not do justice to the gift of the Lord's Supper, a meal which is both inclusive and exclusive. "Open Communion is not Communion at

20 See Albert B. Collver III, "'Real Presence': A Confession of the Lord's Supper" (Phd thesis, Concordia Seminary, St. Louis, 2001).

all; it may be a fascinating rite, a religious experience, but it is not the Sacrament of the New Testament,"[21] observed Sasse in a 1957 essay on "Selective Fellowship."

In His Supper, the words of Christ stand. He gives us His body to eat. He gives us the blood of His new testament to drink for the forgiveness of our sins. "Around the Lord's Table is gathered the church. At the Table of the Lord, the church knows what it most profoundly is: the body of Christ. There has been no doubt of this since the days of the apostles. Where the Lord's Supper is no longer known or celebrated, there the church dies, irretrievably lost,"[22] wrote Hermann Sasse in 1941.

One of Sasse's "letters to Lutheran pastors" is entitled "Word and Sacrament: Preaching and the Lord's Supper."[23] This letter points to the crucial connection between sermon and Sacrament, preaching and the Lord's Supper. Preaching is essential to the Sacrament. In a sermon on 1 Corinthians 15 from 1532–33, Luther asserted: "For the pulpit can and must alone preserve Baptism, Sacrament, doctrine, articles of faith, and all estates in their purity."[24] Sermon and Sacrament stand or fall together. One is not to be played off against the other.

Preaching does more than provide commentary on the Church Year or parts of the Divine Service. It is not merely "setting the table" for the Lord's Supper. Here preaching is not seen as the delivery of the words of Jesus, words that are spirit and life, but preaching stands only to interpret the liturgy or point to that which is to come, the Sacrament. Preaching is liturgical not only because it occurs in the context of the Divine Service but because it is of one piece with the liturgy where the Lord Christ Himself is giving out His gifts. The sermon itself is a speaking of Absolution. Through the words of preaching, God is forgiving sins. Preaching that conforms to the prophetic and apostolic Scriptures is God's Word. The Sacrament evokes liturgical preaching, that is, preaching that lays open the new testament of Christ's blood for troubled consciences. It is not talk about the Gospel or the Sacraments but a proclamation of the Gospel that also encompasses the externality

---

21 Hermann Sasse, "Selective Fellowship," in *The Lonely Way: Selected Essays and Letters*, vol. 2: *1940–1976*, ed. Matthew C. Harrison (St. Louis: Concordia, 2002), 262.

22 Hermann Sasse, "Preface to *Vom Sakrament Des Altars*," in *The Lonely Way: Selected Essays and Letters*, vol. 2: *1940–1976*, ed. Matthew C. Harrison (St. Louis: Concordia, 2002), 12. Sasse was a man who called the church to repentance. It is a salutary thing that Matthew Harrison, Ronald Feuerhahn, and others are making Sasse available to us today. We have much to learn from him when it comes to the place of the Lord's Supper in the life of the congregation. He lived and suffered through the decay of Lutheranism in Germany. He has much to say to our situation as well. For an overview of his contributions, see John T. Pless, "Hermann Sasse (1895–1976)," in *Twentieth-Century Lutheran Theologians*, ed. Mark C. Mattes (Göttingen: Vandenhoeck & Ruprecht, 2013), 155–77; and John Stephenson and Thomas Winger, eds., *Hermann Sasse: A Man for Our Times* (St. Louis: Concordia, 1998).

23 Hermann Sasse, "Word and Sacrament: Preaching and the Lord's Supper," in *We Confess the Sacraments*, trans. Norman E. Nagel (St. Louis: Concordia, 1985), 11–35.

24 AE 28:62.

of the body and blood we are given in the Supper. In this way the reminder of Gerhard Forde is helpful that the Sacrament will not allow the Word "from disappearing into the inner life."[25]

Preaching the Lord's Supper is not done by way of analogy but by proclaiming the Lord's words, their "for you" character. These words Luther understood as the words of Jesus' testament. Incarnation and atonement are comprehended in the word *testament*,[26] for the God who makes this testament takes on flesh and blood in order to die. "What is the whole gospel" Luther asks "but an explanation of this testament?"[27]

Along with preaching, there is catechesis. Luther's treatment of the Sacrament of the Altar in the catechisms has the aim of preparing people for a salutary reception of the Lord's body and blood. His pastoral goal was that the Christian would know what the Sacrament is, the blessings given in this gift, and how it is to be used in faith. The conclusion of the Apostles' Creed confesses "the forgiveness of sins, the resurrection of the body, and the life everlasting." These gifts are delivered to the communicant in the Lord's Supper, as Luther notes that the words "given and shed for you for the remission of sins" show "that in the Sacrament forgiveness of sins, life, and salvation are given us through these words. For where there is forgiveness of sins there is also life and salvation." Forgiveness of sins is not merely an entry way into life with Christ and preliminary to life and salvation. The forgiveness of sins constitutes the Christian's existence.[28]

---

25 Gerhard Forde, *Theology Is for Proclamation* (Minneapolis: Fortress, 1990), 160. Forde observes: "Sundered from the sacraments, that is, the spoken word can go awry and fail to reach its goal. 'Help' must come from the outside, from a more irreducibly external word. . . . They will not let the Word be swallowed up in our internality. They remain always external, from without. They guarantee the character of the Word as what Luther could call an 'alien' Word, a Word from without, from out there in the world of things and bodies" (169).

26 See AE 36:38 and 35:84.

27 AE 35:106. Also see Gerhard Forde, "The Lord's Supper as the Testament of Jesus," *Word & World* (Winter 1997): 5–9. Forde writes: "The conceptuality of testament sets forth and insists upon the gospel character of what occurred" (6). Also see Reinhard Schwarz, "The Last Supper: The Testament of Jesus," *Lutheran Quarterly* (Winter 1995): 391–403.

28 Here note Kenneth Korby: "The forgiveness of sin is both the beginning and the goal. We do not start with forgiveness and then move on to something higher, greater, or better. The East saw the gift of immortal life as the gift of the Eucharist. The West saw the immaculate offering of the church to her Lord—but in communion only an appendix with the forgiveness of sins (but not of mortal sins so as not to degenerate the sacrament of penance). The mystics saw in the Lord's Supper the mystery laden-liquification of the individual in the awe. But Luther concentrates on the center, the forgiveness of sins" ("The Use of John 6 in Lutheran Sacramental Piety," in *Shepherd the Church: Essays in Pastoral Theology Honoring Bishop Roger D. Pittelko*, ed. Frederic W. Baue et al. [Fort Wayne, IN: Concordia Theological Seminary Press, 2002], 131–32).

The Small Catechism, without engaging in explicit polemics against either Rome or the Sacramentarians, addresses both of these errors.[29] Question 1, "What is the Sacrament of the Altar?" and question 3, "How can bodily eating and drinking do such a great thing?" confess the gift of Christ's body and blood under the bread and wine and connects the physical eating and drinking with faith in Christ's words. These questions seem to be addressed particularly to those followers of Zwingli who would deny the presence of Christ's body and blood and see in the Sacrament nothing more than a spiritual eating and drinking. Question 2, "What is the benefit of such eating and drinking?" and question 4, "Who, then, receives this sacrament worthily?' address Roman abuses of the Sacrament as Luther confesses the forgiveness of sins at the heart of the Sacrament and faith in Christ's words as necessary for worthy reception. Bayer helpfully observes: "Luther does not concentrate on the threefold repetition of the two phrases 'given for you' and 'shed for the forgiveness of sins' just by chance. God's turning toward the sinner, the promise that creates faith, empowered by the death and resurrection of Christ, cannot be summarized any more succinctly and specifically than by using these words. This must be stated clearly as a critique of the depersonalizing speech about the 'bread of life' or the diminution of the Lord's Supper to become a generic lovefest. The Lord's Supper is not some diffuse celebration of life but defined in a precise way in its essence by means of the connection between the Word of Christ that has the effective power and the faith."[30]

The Large Catechism addresses these same themes but in a more explicit fashion. Luther notes that the Lord's Supper is established by the Word of Christ and is to be used according to His Word: "All this is established from the words Christ used to institute it. So everyone who wishes to be Christian and go to the sacrament should know them. For we do not intend to admit to the sacrament and administer it to those who do not know what they seek or why they come."[31] For Luther, the right administration of the Lord's Supper assumes that those who are admitted know what the Sacrament is and why they need it.

Eating and drinking the Lord's body and blood *worthily* requires instruction. Admitting the uninstructed and therefore unexamined, whether they are adults or infants, was out of the question for Luther.

Already in 1522, Luther provides a descriptive template for the structure of the catechism: "Thus the commandments teach man to recognize his sickness, enabling him to perceive what he must do or refrain from doing, consent to or

---

29 See Charles Arand, *That I May Be His Own: An Overview of Luther's Catechisms* (St. Louis: Concordia, 2000), 170–72. Also see Timothy Wengert, "Luther's Catechisms and the Lord's Supper," *Word & World* (Winter 1997).

30 Oswald Bayer, *Martin Luther's Theology: A Contemporary Interpretation*, trans. Thomas Trapp (Grand Rapids: Eerdmans, 2008), 272.

31 LC V 1–2 (Kolb-Wengert, 467).

refuse, and so he will recognize himself to be a sinful and wicked person. The Creed will teach and show him where to find the medicine—grace—which will help him to become devout and keep the commandments. The Creed points him to God and his mercy, given and made plain to him in Christ. Finally, the Lord's Prayer teaches all this, namely, through the fulfillment of God's commandments everything will be given him. In these three are the essentials of the entire Bible."[32] Instruction in and confession of these essentials of the Christian faith are a prerequisite for admission to the Lord's Supper. Four years after writing the catechisms, in 1533, in his "An Open Letter to Those in Frankfurt on the Main," Luther writes: "It is quite true that wherever the preacher administers only bread and wine for the Sacrament, he is not very concerned about to whom he gives it, what they know or believe, or what they receive. . . . However, because we are concerned about nurturing Christians who will still be here after we are gone, and because it is Christ's body and blood that are given out in the Sacrament, we will not and cannot give such a Sacrament to anyone unless he is first examined regarding what he has learned from the Catechism and whether he intends to forsake the sins which he has again committed. For we do not want to make Christ's church into a pigpen [Matthew 7:6], letting each one come unexamined to the Sacrament as a pig to its trough. Such a church we leave to the Enthusiasts!"[33]

In the Large Catechism, as in the Small Catechism, Luther catechizes for an evangelical use of the Sacrament. That is, he wants the Sacrament to be recognized for the gift that it is and received accordingly. The Lord's Supper refreshes and strengthens the Christian in the ongoing fight for survival against the wily devil, the treacherous world, and the deceptive flesh: "Therefore, it is appropriately called food for the soul, for it nourishes and strengthens the new creature. . . . Therefore the Lord's Supper is given as a daily food and sustenance so that our faith may be refreshed and strengthened and that it may not succumb in the struggle but become stronger and stronger."[34]

Luther exalts the Sacrament on account of Christ. The forgiveness of sins won on the cross is delivered and distributed in the Supper. "Therefore it is absurd for them to say that Christ's body and blood are not given and poured out for us in the Lord's Supper and hence that we cannot have forgiveness of sins in the Sacrament. Although the work took place on the cross and forgiveness of sins has been acquired, yet it cannot come to us in any other way than through the Word."[35] Thus Luther urges that the Sacrament be received frequently not as a work or expression

32 Luther, *Personal Prayer Book*, AE 43:14.

33 Luther, "An Open Letter to Those in Frankfurt on the Main," trans. Jon D. Vieker, *Concordia Journal* (October 1990): 343. See also chapter 1 in this book.

34 LC V 23–24 (Kolb-Wengert, 469).

35 LC V 31 (Kolb-Wengert, 469).

of human piety but on account of our deep need. "What I mean is that those who want to be Christians should prepare themselves to receive this blessed sacrament frequently. For we see that people are becoming lax and lazy about its observance."[36] Christ's command and promise coupled with our own condition ought to draw us to the Sacrament: "We must never regard the sacrament as a harmful thing from which we should flee, but as a pure, wholesome, soothing medicine that aids you in both soul and body. For where the soul is healed the body is helped as well."[37]

Pastors, as stewards of the Lord's Sacrament and shepherds of those entrusted to their care, will attend to this need. Just as a pharmacist does not distribute medication without a physician's prescription and directions for proper dosage, so it is pastorally irresponsible to administer the Lord's body and blood without regard to His Word. Hence the Augsburg Confession approvingly notes that "Chrysostom says that the priest stands daily at the altar, inviting some to Communion and keeping others away."[38] Pastors may not neglect this responsibility. Our confessional practice is not intended to drive people away from the Lord's Table but to shepherd them by Christ's words to a salutary eating and drinking of Christ's body and blood with us in the unity of faith and confession. It is to make clear that the fellowship we share is actually the *koinonia* in Christ's body and blood given and shed for the forgiveness of sins and not reduced to a religious exercise or an extension of familial or personal intimacy.[39]

APPENDIX I: CRAFTING A CONFESSIONAL COMMUNION STATEMENT

1. Assumption: The practice of not inviting all worshipers to commune goes against the cultural grain of North American Christianity largely influenced by American Evangelicalism. In his book *The Democratization of American Christianity* (Yale University Press, 1989), Nathan Hatch points out emphasis on personal decision and the Church as a spiritual democracy. Evangelicalism's stress on the autonomy of the believer and the immediacy of spiritual experience downplays the place of Church (i.e., unity in doctrine) and the Sacrament. Sacraments become metaphors open to individual interpretation and usage.

36 LC V 39–40 (Kolb-Wengert, 470–71).

37 LC V 68 (Kolb-Wengert, 474).

38 AC XXIV 36 (Kolb-Wengert, 71).

39 Also note Elert: "The unity of faith is not merely some shared sentiment. Paul had already made it clear not only that there is no faith without *kerygma*, but also that believing with heart is coupled with the confessing with the mouth (Rom. 10:8ff.). . . . Fellowship is possible only on the basis of the confessed faith" (*Eucharist and Church Fellowship*, 71).

2. Communion practice is a confession of the truth of Jesus' words that give us His body to eat and His blood to drink for the forgiveness of our sins (see Matthew 26:26–28; Mark 14:22–24; Luke 22:19–20; 1 Corinthians 11:23–25).
3. Our practice seeks to guard both the unity of the Church (i.e., integrity of confession; here see Elert and Sasse) and protect the potential communicant from spiritual danger by eating and drinking in the Sacrament without discerning the body and blood of the Lord (1 Corinthians 11:27–32).
4. Eating and drinking the Lord's body and blood together presupposes unity in the Lord's teaching (see Acts 2:42). The Sacrament presupposes oneness in the faith rather than creating it.
5. Communion statements sometimes say too little or too much. A well-crafted statement will be clear to the visitor. Wordy statements tend to assume that the guest has at his or her disposal a developed doctrinal vocabulary. On the other hand, a short statement might come across as negative and harsh. The best statements will clearly articulate our practice in an evangelical way with a winsome invitation for guests to set up an appointment to visit with the pastor regarding instruction and admission to the Lord's Supper.
6. The statement should, in some way, reflect the fact that admission to the Lord's Supper is made not on the basis of a personal confession of faith but is tied to the confession of the altar where one communes. Note Elert: "Since a man cannot at the same time hold two differing confessions, he cannot communicate in two churches of differing confessions. If anyone does this nevertheless, he denies his own confession or has none at all" (*Eucharist and Church Fellowship in the First Four Centuries*, 182).
7. Pastors may wish to develop a longer tract that will go into more detail explaining the biblical and pastoral rationale for closed Communion. Here see the 1999 CTCR report *Admission to the Lord's Supper: Basics of Biblical and Confessional Teaching*. For a sample of such a tract, see *What Your Eating and Drinking at This Altar Confesses* by John T. Pless (available on my webpage at www.ctsfw.edu/pless/documents).

APPENDIX II: THESES ON INFANT/TODDLER COMMUNION[40]

1. The question of admission to the Lord's Supper is addressed from the instituting words of the Lord which also disclose the purpose and beneficial use of the Sacrament.

40 See also chapter 20 in this book, which is an explanation of these theses.

2. The apostolic teaching that a man is to examine himself (1 Corinthians 11:28) cannot reasonably be interpreted as to exclude the noetic dimension of which infants/toddlers are incapable.
3. Baptism is an absolute prerequisite for admission to the Lord's Supper, but it does not follow that all the baptized are categorically to be admitted to the altar.
4. Arguments for infant/toddler Communion bypass the truth that in Baptism we receive "victory over death and the devil, forgiveness of sin, God's grace, the entire Christ, and the Holy Spirit with his gifts" (LC IV 41–22 [Kolb-Wengert, 461]), as though the promise of Baptism remained unfulfilled without the Lord's Supper. By waiting until children have been instructed, examined, and absolved before admitting them to the Lord's Supper, they are not being deprived of Christ.
5. Faith does not make the Sacrament, but it is only by faith that the benefits of the Sacrament are received. Faith is precisely trust in these words "given and shed for you for the forgiveness of sins" (SC). In the Small Catechism, eating and drinking are joined together with trust in the spoken word "given and shed for you." The Lord's Supper is given precisely to strengthen the faith of those who through the accusation of the Law recognize their sin and whose terrorized consciences acknowledge their need and desire for the forgiveness of their sins. "For people are admitted only if they have first had an opportunity to be examined (*explorati*) and heard. The people are also reminded about the dignity and use of the Sacrament—how it offers **great consolation to anxious** consciences—so that they may learn to believe in God and expect all that is good from God" (AC XXIV 6–7 [Latin, Kolb-Wengert, 68]).
6. The Lutheran Confessions assert that none are to be admitted to the Sacrament who have not been instructed, examined, and absolved. See LC V 1–3 [Kolb-Wengert, 467]; AC XXV 1–3 [Kolb-Wengert, 73]).
7. Lutheran theology does not begin with a generic category of sacraments but works instead from the Lord's mandates for Baptism and the Supper. Each has its own distinctive features. They are not interchangeable. It does not follow that arguments for the Baptism of infants are to be applied for the Communion of infants/toddlers.
8. The Lord's Supper is the new testament of the Lord, not the new Passover. Hence it does not follow that because infants/toddlers were included in the Passover meal that they are to be communed.
9. Evidence for the Communion of infants/toddlers in the Early and Medieval Church is there in some places, but it is not clear that the practice was

universal or when it was first practiced. Lutheran liturgical practice is not based on historical precedent but on the Lord's mandates. Not all practices of the Early Church are to be emulated. Infant/toddler Communion is one of those practices.

10. Arguments for infant/toddler Communion reveal a problematic hermeneutic of the Lutheran Confessions which undercut a *quia* understanding of confessional subscription.
11. Luther may not be cited in support of infant/toddler Communion. He knew of the practice among the Hussites, and while he would not condemn them as heretics (those who deny the fundamental Christological and trinitarian dogma), he did not accept their practice as correct.
12. Infant/toddler Communion is a novel practice in the Lutheran Church. In American Lutheranism, it gained traction only in the 1970s, fueled by particular aspects of the liturgical and ecumenical movements.
13. The fact that children who have been instructed, examined, and absolved may be admitted to the Sacrament at a younger age than has been the general custom in The Lutheran Church—Missouri Synod is not to be confused with the admitting of infants/toddlers to the Altar. Churchly and pastoral concerns for unity in practice are important considerations. But the Communion of infants/toddlers is not an adiaphoron to be left up to individual parents, pastors, or congregations.

BIBLIOGRAPHY

Bayer, Oswald. "The Lord's Supper." Pages 270–73 in *Martin Luther's Theology: A Contemporary Interpretation.* Translated by Thomas Trapp. Grand Rapids: Eerdmans, 2008.

CTCR. *Admission to the Lord's Supper: Basics of Biblical and Confessional Teaching.* St. Louis: LCMS, 1999.

Elert, Werner. *Eucharist and Church Fellowship in the First Four Centuries.* Translated by Norman Nagel. St. Louis: Concordia, 1966.

Elert, Werner. *The Lord's Supper Today.* Translated by Martin Bertram and Rudolph Norden. St. Louis: Concordia, 1973.

Gibbs, Jeffrey A. "An Exegetical Case for Close(d) Communion: 1 Corinthians 10:14–22; 11:17–34." *Concordia Journal* (April 1995): 148–63.

Klän, Werner. "Eucharist and Ecclesiology: Marginal Comments concerning the Inherent Coherence of the Theology of Hermann Sasse." Pages 153-65 in *Lord Jesus Christ, Will You Not Stay: Essays in Honor of Ronald Feuerhahn on the Occasion of His Sixty-Fifth Birthday.* Edited by Bart Day et al. Houston, TX: Feuerhahn Festschrift Committee, 2002.

———. "The 'Third Sacrament': Confession and Repentance in the Confessions of the Lutheran Church." *Logia* 20 (Holy Trinity 2011): 5–12.

Koester, Craig. "Infant Communion in Light of the New Testament." *Lutheran Quarterly* (Autumn 1996): 233–39.

Kolden, Marc. "Infant Communion in Light of Theological and Pastoral Perspectives." *Lutheran Quarterly* (Autumn 1996): 249–57.

Korby, Kenneth F. "The Use of John 6 in Lutheran Sacramental Piety." Pages 129–44 in *Shepherd the Church: Essays in Pastoral Theology Honoring Bishop Roger D. Pittelko.* Edited by Frederic W. Baue et al. Fort Wayne, IN: CTS Press, 2002.

Lassman, Ernie V. "'Discerning the Body' and Its Implications for Closed Communion." Pages 112–15 in *A Reader in Pastoral Theology.* Edited by John T. Pless. Fort Wayne, IN: CTS Press, 2002.

Lockwood, Gregory J. "Unworthy Reception of the Sacrament." Pages 369–410 in *Concordia Commentary: 1 Corinthians.* St. Louis: Concordia, 2000.

Luther, Martin. "An Open Letter to Those in Frankfurt on the Main, 1533." Translated by Jon D. Vieker. *Concordia Journal* (October 1990): 333–51.

McCain, Paul T. *Communion Fellowship*. Waverly, IA: International Foundation for Lutheran Confessional Research, 1992.

Nichol, Todd. "Infant Communion in Light of the Lutheran Confessions." *Lutheran Quarterly* (Autumn 1996): 241–47.

Nagel, Norman. "Closed Communion: In the Way of the Gospel; In the Way of the Law." *Concordia Journal* (January 1991): 20–29.

Olson, Oliver K. "*Adiaphora, Mandata, Damnabilia.*" *Lutheran Forum* (Spring 2010): 22–25.

———. *Reclaiming the Lutheran Liturgical Heritage* (Reclaim Resources, 2007).

———. "The Liturgy and Concomitant Aspects of the Lord's Supper." Pages 121–29 in *Lord Jesus Christ, Will You Not Stay: Essays in Honor of Ronald Feuerhahn of the Occasion of His Sixty-fifth Birthday.* Edited by Bart Day et al. Houston, TX: Feuerhahn Festschrift Committee, 2002.

Peters, Albrecht. *Commentary on Luther's Catechism: Baptism and Lord's Supper.* Translated by Thomas Trapp. St. Louis: Concordia, 2012.

Pless, John T. "Can We Participate Liturgically in the Atonement?" *Logia* (Eastertide 2010): 39–48.

———. "Hermann Sasse and the Liturgical Movement." *Logia* (Eastertide 1998): 47–51.

———. "The Lord's Supper in the Life of the Congregation." Pages 133–48 in *Divine Multi-Media: The Manifold Means of Grace in the Life of the Church.* Edited by John A. Maxfield. St. Louis: Luther Academy, 2005.

Reu, J. Michel. "Can We Still Hold to the Lutheran Doctrine of the Lord's Supper?" In *Two Treatises on the Means of Grace.* Minneapolis: Augsburg, 1952.

Sasse, Hermann. "Consecration and the Real Presence." Pages 271–317 in *Scripture and the Church: Selected Essays of Hermann Sasse.* Edited by Jeffrey J. Kloha and Ronald Feuerhahn. St. Louis: Concordia Seminary Press, 1995.

———. "The Lord's Supper in the Life of the Church." In *Witness: Sermons Preached in Erlangen and Congregational Lectures.* Translated by Bror Erickson. Saginaw, MI: Magdeburg Press, 2013.

———. "The Lord's Supper in the Lutheran Church." Pages 87–99 in *Letters to Lutheran Pastors.* Volume 1: *1948–1951.* Edited by Matthew C. Harrison. St. Louis: Concordia, 2013.

———. "The Lord's Supper in the New Testament." Pages 49–97 in *We Confess the Sacraments.* Translated by Norman E. Nagel. St. Louis: Concordia, 1985.

———. "Theses on the Question of Church and Altar Fellowship." Pages 331–38 in *The Lonely Way.* Volume 1: *1927–1939.* Edited by Matthew C. Harrison. St. Louis: Concordia, 2001.

———. *This Is My Body: Luther's Contention for the Real Presence in the Sacrament of the Altar.* Minneapolis: Augsburg, 1959.

———. "Word and Sacrament: Preaching and the Lord's Supper." Pages 11–35 in *We Confess the Sacraments.* Translated by Norman Nagel. St. Louis: Concordia, 1985.

Schöne, Jobst. "Pastoral Letter regarding the Divine Service and the Sacrament of the Altar." *Logia* (Reformation 1998): 31–39.

Schulz, Charles. "The Worthy Communicant in SD VII." *Logia* (Eastertide 1991): 31–38.

Throntveit, Mark. "The Lord's Supper as New Testament, Not New Passover." *Lutheran Quarterly* (Autumn 1997): 271–89.

Tranvik, Mark D. "Should Infants Be Communed? A Lutheran Perspective." *Word & World* (Winter 1995): 83–90.

Volk, Ernst. "Evangelical Accents in Understanding the Lord's Supper." *Lutheran Quarterly* (Summer 1987), 185–204.

Wendebourg, Dorethea. "Traveled the Full Extent of Rome's Erroneous Path?" *Lutheran Forum* (Winter 2010): 18–33.

Wisløff, Carl F. *The Gift of Communion.* Translated by Joseph Shaw. Minneapolis: Augsburg, 1964.

Wittenberg, Martin. "Church Fellowship and Altar Fellowship in Light of Church History." *Logia* (Reformation 1992): 25–59.

Ziegler, Roland. "Should Lutherans Reserve the Consecrated Elements for the Communion of the Sick?" *Concordia Theological Quarterly* (April 2003): 131–48.

———. "The Eucharistic Prayer and Justification." *Concordia Theological Quarterly* (January/April 2013): 79–99.

CHAPTER ELEVEN

CHURCH FELLOWSHIP AND TELLING THE GOOD NEWS ABOUT JESUS

AN ESSAY PRESENTED TO THE CONVENTION OF THE LUTHERAN CHURCH—MISSOURI SYNOD

CARL C. FICKENSCHER II

JULY 17, 2001

As kids growing up in California, we learned very early that you could do *almost* anything with anybody. Some of our best friends in school and in the neighborhood were Asian and Hispanic. Our family dentist was African American. Tante and Onkel Goldberg were like another set of grandparents. You got together with all kinds of folks for all kinds of things. For those few things you *didn't* do with everybody, you knew there was a reason far more important than age or color or accent.

As a young professional in Washington DC, I attended an ecumenical Reformation service one year at the National Cathedral. We got together with a whole lot of folks, and it was a magnificent event—huge organ, a thousand voices, vestments I'd never seen before. But somehow, it wasn't Reformation—and not just because we sang "A Mighty Fortress" using the "wrong" translation.

As a green, new pastor in Michigan, I was speaking with a visitor before the service. He was from the ALC congregation in town, but he was a former Missouri Synod member, and he was beginning to recognize the differences between the synods. This sounded to me like one of those "extraordinary circumstances" requiring "responsible pastoral care," "by their nature, relatively rare."[1] Unfortunately,

1 "The Synod affirmed in 1986 Res. 3-08, and reaffirmed in 1995 Res. 3-08, 'that the pastors and congregations of The Lutheran Church—Missouri Synod continue to abide by the

after his communing and my calling on him, he told me his friendships on the softball team were pretty strong, and he'd decided to stay where he was.

Later, as a pastor in Texas, I had a little better visit one evening when a lapsed and unchurched Baptist told me, no, he wasn't offended that he couldn't come to Communion; he really appreciated finding a church where "everything you people believe is laid right out." After adult instruction, he and his wife, their grown son and daughter, and their families became some of our strongest members, and he and his wife were out with me making evangelism calls.

For our time this evening, I'd like to continue Dr. Gibbs' and Dr. MacKenzie's discussion of church fellowship, but for this session, let's talk specifically about how our Synod's fellowship practices impact our doing evangelism, "Telling the Good News about Jesus." Could it be that our understanding of fellowship is a straitjacket, that you simply can't do evangelism within our church's guidelines of closed Communion and against unionism? Let me answer that question by asking and at least beginning to answer quite the opposite question: "Why is our practice of fellowship *vital* to fulfilling the Great Commission?"

I.

"Go therefore and make disciples of all nations, baptizing them in the name of the Father and the Son and the Holy Spirit" (Matthew 28:19). We all know very well what Jesus has commissioned us to do, don't we? In fact, you know it well enough to quote the part of the Great Commission I left off: "teaching them to observe all things I have commanded you" (28:20a). "Make disciples of all nations . . . baptizing them" and "*teaching them to observe all things.*" That's an essential part of the Great Commission, isn't it?—not just an afterthought.

I remember, back when I was a brand-new Sem I student, first year at the seminary, really naive, talking to another first-year student, an equally reliable theologian, about various evangelism methods. Kennedy was big back then.[2] My friend's words of wisdom were: "You just give it to 'em down and dirty at first, then you clean up the theology later." I nodded in agreement.

Boy, was I dumb! "Teaching them to observe all things" is not an afterthought; it's the Great Commission; it's cutting-edge evangelism. In the Greek text, "baptizing" and "teaching" are parallel participles, just as they are in English. Both—equally—describe means by which we make disciples. Baptizing and the preaching

---

practice of close Communion, which includes the necessity of exercising responsible pastoral care in extraordinary situations and circumstances,' and beseeched the Synod in love to remember that 'situations of emergency, and special cases of pastoral care, or extraordinary circumstances' are, by their nature, relatively rare." 1998 Resolution 3-05 "To Reaffirm Our Practice of Admission to the Lord's Supper," *Convention Proceedings*, 115.

2 That is, the evangelism method offered in D. James Kennedy, *Evangelism Explosion*, foreword by Billy Graham (Wheaton, IL: Tyndale House, 1977).

and teaching of the Word create and sustain disciples. It's not as if you do evangelism to make a disciple then teach doctrine to fix a disciple. Baptizing and teaching, together and as a lifelong process, are evangelism, and, obviously, both are to be done right the first time.

I've always been bothered a bit by the distinction between mission and maintenance ministry. The suggestion seems to be that some of the work we do in teaching and preaching isn't mission, it isn't evangelism. It made me wonder what I was doing as a pastor. I was making nonmember visits every Monday night and training others to do them; I was continually leading adult instruction classes; I was baptizing and confirming new members. And I was making shut-in visits—some of which were adult instruction classes; I was preaching to my regulars every Sunday; I was baptizing babies and confirming eighth-graders. So what was I doing? Mission or maintenance? This was evangelism—that is, proclaiming the "evangel," the Gospel; all of it was. It was all evangelism, making disciples by baptizing *and* teaching them to observe all things whatsoever Christ commanded. To appreciate why our Synod's fellowship practices are so vital to fulfilling the Great Commission, it's first crucial to appreciate that teaching all things is an essential part of the Great Commission.

Why does Christ give teaching all things such priority? If everybody who believes in Jesus goes to heaven, why doesn't Jesus just say "give it to 'em down and dirty at first, and, if you've got time, clean up the theology later"? Because, quite simply, Jesus knew that clean theology is what gets people to heaven. "Teaching them to observe all things" is essential to the salvation of souls. Let's say that again: "Teaching them to observe all things" is essential to the salvation of souls. "Down and dirty" results in souls spending eternity in hell.

Now don't get me wrong. It's not a person's orthodoxy on every point that earns him salvation. Certainly countless people who hold theological errors will be in heaven, because there are countless such people who still hold simple faith in Jesus' death and resurrection for the forgiveness of their sins, and everyone who believes that *will* be in heaven.

But it is also only Baptism and orthodox teaching that gets them there. No one ever comes to faith in Christ by anything false he's been taught. Only the truth creates and sustains faith. Now a person may have heard the truth in a heterodox church; she may have heard the Gospel mixed with lots of error and still become a believer. But it was not the error that brought her to faith. Jesus says, "You shall know the truth, and *the truth* shall set you free" (John 8:32). Paul writes, "You were included in Christ when you heard the word of truth, the gospel of your salvation" (Ephesians 1:13a). James agrees: "Of His own will He brought us forth by the word of truth" (James 1:18).

It was not when a revival preacher falsely invited the audience to come forward and accept Christ that people became believers; it was when, earlier in his sermon, he proclaimed the cross that the Holy Spirit created faith in their hearts.

It was not by the faith of the parents that a baby baptized in a Presbyterian church was saved; it was by the washing of regeneration in the child's heart, even though the congregation denies it. We sincerely rejoice with the angels in heaven when a sinner comes to repentance at the preaching of an ELCA pastor, but that new faith was in no way enhanced by the fact that the pastor was a woman. It's the truth, not errors intermingled with the truth, that fulfills the Great Commission.

We probably all agree with that. It's obvious enough. But what about the flip side? Only truth fulfills the Great Commission, but is error really so bad? Does a little false teaching really hurt? Can't you do evangelism well enough, as long as most of what you're saying is true? Are *all things* that Christ commanded really necessary to doing evangelism? Aren't some teachings pretty peripheral? Two ways we might get at the answers.

First, let's ask ourselves why God gave the truth as He did. Why sixty-six books? Why a doctrine of Baptism? Why Christ's real presence in the Lord's Supper? For that matter, why would God forbid a little thing like coveting, and, for the Old Testament people, why not boil a kid in its mother's milk (Exodus 23:19a)? Well, if we believe that "all Scripture is breathed out by God and profitable" (2 Timothy 3:16a), then, as Paul says in Romans, "whatever was written in former days was written for our instruction, that through endurance and through the encouragement of the Scriptures we might have hope" (Romans 15:4). And that hope which does not disappoint us is this: "Since we have been justified by faith, we have peace with God through our Lord Jesus Christ" (5:1). That is to say, as John does about his Gospel, "These things"—all these things—"are written so that you may believe that Jesus is the Christ, the Son of God, and that by believing you may have life in His name" (John 20:31). That's evangelism. That's "Telling the Good News about Jesus." Every word, every doctrine, of Scripture God gave for one purpose: the salvation of souls. Let's say *that* again: Every word, every doctrine, of Scripture God gave for one purpose: the salvation of souls. We don't always understand fully, but nothing is expendable. God didn't give a single word, a single doctrine, for *His* good. Somehow every teaching leads us to Christ. In other words, replacing *any* truth with any error takes away some of what God intended us to use in doing evangelism. Regardless of what our reason, our observation, may suggest, you cannot do evangelism as well without all of God's truth. "Teaching them to observe all things" is essential to the salvation of souls.

A second answer to the question about error: How much harm to evangelism can a little bit of false teaching really do? We each have dear Christian brothers and sisters in erring churches who are "on fire for the Lord," who are out there doing evangelism like we wish we were. And we give thanks that God is using them to bring people to saving faith. They're doing evangelism. Why should we be concerned about their errors?

For starters, can there be any doubt that souls are spending eternity in hell because our dear, sincere Baptist friends didn't baptize thousands and thousands of babies? Haven't some been lost? Or have you ever counseled with one of your college students who was now questioning his salvation because of what friends at school said? His friends believed that revival preacher and told your young man he wasn't really saved unless he made a decision for Christ. Can there be any doubt that a false teaching of conversion has caused someone along the line to lose the security of his salvation, to despair, and to spend eternity in hell? And what about the woman pastor? She defends her claim to the office by alleging that clear passages of Scripture on the order of creation and the role of the sexes were time-bound and no longer relevant. Do we doubt for a minute that that has caused someone else, somewhere, to disregard other passages of Scripture, perhaps on sexual morality, and fall into impenitent sin . . . and spend an eternity in hell? When truth is compromised for error, ultimately other truth will be lost. As Paul says in Galatians, "A little leaven leavens the whole lump of dough" (Galatians 5:9).

That's a hard reality, isn't it? Maybe this is why all of us at times struggle with our practice of fellowship. Because we each have dear friends in other churches, because by everything we see we're confident of their sincere personal faith, maybe sometimes in our heart of hearts we just don't believe anymore that false teaching can really be so dangerous.

But when truth is lost, souls are lost.[3] Any error, even among our sincere brothers and sisters in Christ, works against fulfilling the Great Commission. The Great Commission, "Telling the Good News about Jesus," requires "teaching them to observe all things."

II.

That is precisely what our Synod's fellowship practice is designed to do. Our fellowship practice is vital to fulfilling the Great Commission because it serves—and in fact is necessary—to "teach all things." Let's talk first about how that's true for the unbeliever we hope to evangelize. Then we'll see how it's also true for our own members doing the evangelizing.

At first blush, this may not seem true at all. We all want to be out there, sharing Christ, seizing every opportunity to proclaim the Gospel to as wide an audience as possible. You get an invitation to preach at a high school baccalaureate; you want

3 FC Ep XII 30: "All these and similar articles, together with their erroneous implications and conclusions, we reject and condemn as wrong, false, heretical, and contrary to the Word of God, the three Creeds, the Augsburg Confession, the Apology, the Smalcald Articles, and the Catechisms of Luther. *All pious Christians, of high degree and low, must guard against these if they dearly love their soul's eternal welfare and salvation*" (Theodore G. Tappert, trans., *The Book of Concord: The Confessions of the Evangelical Lutheran Church* [Philadelphia: Fortress, 1959], 500, emphasis added).

to do it. The community has a Thanksgiving service; you want to participate. A son of your congregation is getting married in his fiancée's church; you want to get the young couple off on the right foot with God's Word and, even more, preach Christ crucified to their friends who may not be in church another day in their lives. Your own church is packed on Friendship Sunday or Confirmation Day, and you don't really want to burst the bubble by having to say no about the Communion table. These are all opportunities, it would seem, to do precisely what we need to do: "teach them." But there's that troublesome fellowship practice of ours getting in the way.

The truth is, it doesn't always get in the way as much as we think. Our understanding of unionism is caricatured when people suggest we can't do *any* of the things I just mentioned. Not only should we always be eager to cooperate with others in externals, activities in which the sacred—God's Word and Sacraments—are not involved,[4] but what's more, there are many sacred activities outside our church walls in which, for example, an LCMS pastor as the sole functionary can freely proclaim the Gospel without compromise.

A couple of months ago, we had a terrible tragedy in our seminary family. The teenage son of one of our students was killed in an automobile accident while picking up his sister—right out in front of her middle school, as dozens of her friends watched. I welcomed the invitation to preach for the memorial service in chapel at the sem, but I was tremendously surprised and even more pleased to be invited by the young man's public high school to preach for a memorial service there the same afternoon. I asked some questions, was assured there would be no clergy of other denominations involved, and went for it. A fabulous opportunity to declare to a thousand-plus young people the faith in which this young saint had died! Afterward, the principal said to me, "You never thought you'd be able to do *that* in a public school, did you." Then he whispered in my ear, "It'll just be our little secret." Oops. I guess it's out.

Not only, though, is our fellowship practice not the hindrance we may think. More important, our understanding of fellowship, properly practiced, actually enhances our teaching all things. Yes, it's even necessary.

Perhaps you'd agree: for me as a pastor, evangelism was not primarily Friendship Sundays and flashy ads and hot programs that got people in the door. For the most part, it wasn't even those special settings for proclamation. An awful lot of evangelism was sitting down in the homes, talking, asking and answering questions. Teaching—adult instruction class two hours a week for nearly four months, teaching about the Trinity and creation, the Ten Commandments, the redeeming work of

4 Examples of ways in which our Synod has historically cooperated with other church bodies in externals are given in: Commission on Theology and Church Relations, *Inter-Christian Relationships: An Instrument for Study* (St. Louis: The Lutheran Church—Missouri Synod, February 1991), 29. See also CTCR, *Theology of Fellowship* (n.d.), 28, and CTCR, *A Lutheran Stance toward Ecumenism* (November 1974), 14, 16.

the Son, the Holy Spirit, the Sacraments, prayer, liturgy. Then there was Baptism or confirmation. That was evangelism. Teaching them to observe all things.

As many times as I did that, like thirty-two classes in fifteen years, I would often have loved to shorten the process. But I wanted my adult converts to take very seriously the Third Commandment and justification and their prayer life. I was trying to convey that this mattered. It wasn't optional. Remember, I believed all of this was important to the salvation of their souls. You didn't teach the Third Commandment and then say, "But, of course, worship isn't really that big a deal. You can still get to heaven without it."

Now, then, a new visitor comes to worship and presents himself for Communion. He's Baptist or Methodist or ELCA. If, knowingly, I let him commune, how will I answer my adult class members this week when they ask, "What do Baptists or Methodists or ELCA Lutherans believe? Does infant Baptism really matter? How about the real presence? Is homosexuality still wrong? Oh, and how about the Third Commandment and justification and prayer?"

This is just one example. But in your church, like mine, it's an example that comes up week after week after week. The same could be said if I stand with pastors of those other denominations for a joint wedding or funeral or Reformation festival. In order to teach all things to the unbelievers we hope to evangelize, it's necessary that we continue and follow our Synod's practice of fellowship.

By the way, you notice that I said "unbelievers." The waters become very muddled if we forget we're trying to win *unbelievers* for Christ. See, we're often afraid that our fellowship practices will offend people. But whom would we offend? And with whom might we commune and lead worship? Very few among us would consider communing or leading worship with open unbelievers. The issue is whether we admit *other Christians* to our altars and pulpits. They're the ones some might bend the policy to avoid offending. But what we've just said is that they're already Christians. They're not the souls we're hoping to win for Christ. We don't want to confuse LCMS evangelism with simply increasing our numbers at the expense of another Christian church's. Of course, we always welcome Christians who come to us from other denominations, but for only one reason. Not for numbers, but that they may now share in the *pure* preaching of the Gospel and administration of the Sacraments, "all things Christ commanded." That is, if we believe we have the pure preaching and Sacraments, and if we believe false teaching matters. And if we do, then we surely cannot give those inquirers from other Christian churches less by any fellowship practices which compromise that doctrine.

I said before that, for me as a pastor, an awful lot of evangelism was all that visiting and teaching I did with prospects. The other thing that "doing evangelism" meant for me as a pastor was this: educating and motivating my own members to "Tell the Good News about Jesus" every day at work, at school, wherever God put them. Here, too, for our own members, our fellowship practices not only enhance but are necessary to "teach all things."

A few years ago, in one of the more famous case studies in marketing research, an ad agency for Curtis Mathis Televisions made an interesting discovery. Curtis Mathis was at that time offering a full line of TVs, from small black-and-white portables to huge color consoles. Their researchers found that their market share and profitability were very strong with the big, jazzy models while all their other products were mediocre or worse. So even though it would cost them total sales, they recommended dropping everything else and pushing one kind of TV. Their advertising slogan became (maybe you remember) "Curtis Mathis: the most expensive name in television and darn well worth it." Their profits soared.

Now, we in the Missouri Synod are not going for snob appeal, and we're certainly not expensive. But we do have something on which we are very strong, and we should be aware of it and feature it. It's our doctrine. In order to do evangelism with full commitment and enthusiasm, our own members need to know that they, we, have something very unique to share with the world, something that saves souls for eternity: pure doctrine. Not everything else we've got is so good—at least not uniquely so. Even if we did admit everybody to our altars, we might or might not be the friendliest church in town. Even if our pastor is visible at every community worship event, he might not out-hustle the nondenominational minister down the street. But we have what we believe, teach, and confess only the true Evangelical Lutheran Church has: "all things Christ commanded." If our folks think their job is to market "friendly," "great programs," "inspiring worship," then their motivation is purely human. If they realize that they are sharing the pure Word of God, a Word which alone can save souls, a Word the friendly church around the corner doesn't have quite purely, then their motivation is from God Himself.

I'm not sure our own members know what a unique treasure from God we have in our doctrine. But I am sure they will never know if we do anything that suggests differences in doctrine don't matter.[5] Our Synod's fellowship practices, properly carried out, help to make this clear.

I happen to believe that our own failure to appreciate our unique treasure of doctrine is the greatest hindrance to evangelism that we are struggling to

---

5 Ironically, some LCMS members may actually be *embarrassed* about our doctrine on this very matter, fellowship, believing that it is unfriendly or unloving and thus a detriment to evangelism. They might be surprised to read the following from the catechism of another denomination often admired for its evangelistic activity: "8. *Why ought not Baptists to commune with believers of other denominations?* Not because we think we are better Christians than they, but because we believe that they have not been baptized or that they are not walking orderly in their relation to the church" (W. E. Davidson, *A Catechism of Bible Doctrine* [Nashville, TN: Broadman Press, n.d.], 24). It is especially noteworthy that "the Catechism came to America out of the mission field" (Davidson, *Catechism of Bible Doctrine*, 2). The reality is that the great majority of the world's Christians practice close(d) Communion.

overcome today. Conversely, really appreciating our doctrine again may be the key to becoming powerful tools for God. Years ago, at a time of phenomenal growth in our Synod, an official publication of another Lutheran body, one not in fellowship with us, wrote this about our church:

> It may be out of place to enter minutely upon the history of the Missouri Synod, the greatest and most important of the Lutheran synods of our country; but there is one fact that I do not like to pass over in silence. . . . I see before me no more striking instance of the blessing which God bestows on men's faithfulness than this very Missouri Synod. If it had not with such iron tenacity held to its confession of pure doctrine; if it . . . had not fought against each and every deviation from . . . the only true way; if it had adapted itself in ever so small a measure to the views of our rather impressionable age, it would not have achieved the results it may now claim. . . . [T]hat attitude of hers the Lord has rewarded. In the view of the earliest and the present members of the Missouri Synod, the glory of God and the unalloyed truth of His Word . . . is to be esteemed more highly than the favor of men. . . . If the Lord God had not taken pity upon the Lutheran Church in America by placing the Missouri Synod in its midst, we would today be an insignificant band.[6]

Today, in a totally new era, we still desire to be a blessing to those around us by "Telling the Good News about Jesus." We want everyone to hear of the Savior so that someday we can do everything with everybody. In the meantime, for those few things we can't do together, let's understand that it's for a vitally important reason. It's because God has called us to continue that confession of pure doctrine, "teaching them to observe all things," those things that alone can save their souls.

OUTLINE

WHY IS OUR PRACTICE OF FELLOWSHIP VITAL TO FULFILLING THE GREAT COMMISSION?

I. Because the Great Commission requires "teaching them to observe all things" that Christ has commanded.

   A. Christ's command to "teach all things" is an essential part of the Great Commission—not just an afterthought.

   B. "Teaching all things" is essential to the salvation of souls.

II. Because our fellowship practice is necessary to "teach all things."

   A. For the unbeliever to be evangelized

   B. For our own members to do evangelism

---

6 *Pilger durch Welt und Kirche* (a publication of the General Council), 5:370; quoted in W. H. T. Dau, "At the Milestone," in *Ebenezer 1847–1922: Reviews of the Work of the Missouri Synod during Three Quarters of a Century*, ed. W. H. T. Dau (St. Louis: Concordia, 1922), 530–31.

CHAPTER TWELVE

STUDIES IN HOLY COMMUNION

H. P. HAMANN

STUDY 1
THE LORD'S SUPPER AND THE AUTHORITY OF SCRIPTURE

HISTORICAL SETTING AND BACKGROUND OF THE LORD'S SUPPER

Jesus instituted the Lord's Supper on the night in which He was betrayed. On this night He and His disciples were gathered together in an Upper Room in Jerusalem for the festival of the Passover meal. This festival dated back to the deliverance of Israel from bondage in Egypt. To break the stubborn resistance of Pharaoh, who refused permission to Israel to return to the Land of Promise, God had given warning that all the firstborn in Egypt were to be slain. There was only one way, God said, by which the firstborn among the Israelites could escape from this death: the people were to kill a lamb for each household and put the blood on the two sideposts and on the top crossbeam of the doors leading into their houses. The flesh of the lamb was to be roasted and eaten with unleavened bread and bitter herbs. Upon sight of the blood, the angel of the Lord on his mission of death throughout Egypt would "pass over" their homes, and their firstborn would not be slain.

The Israelites acted on the instruction of the Lord. Death did not strike their firstborn. Saved by the blood of the lamb, they moved out from the bondage of Egypt into the freedom God had promised them.

In remembrance of this great deliverance, the people of Israel thereafter each year by divine command celebrated the Passover festival. The lamb slain and eaten at each annual Passover celebration, however, was not only to remind them of their past deliverance from Egypt, but above all, of the still greater deliverance from the bondage of sin and death and hell that was to be effected for them and all men by the Lamb of God that was to be slain for the sin of the world. Jesus Christ is the true Passover Lamb, and at the Passover festival for which He was gathered with His disciples in the Upper Room, He was to be sacrificed to save lost and condemned mankind. "For Christ, our Passover lamb, has been sacrificed" (1 Corinthians 5:7).

The Old Testament Passover had served its purpose. The Lamb of God to which it had pointed had come. In His great love, Jesus now gave His people a "new" Passover meal—a Passover meal to remind them of His great sacrifice for them. He instituted the Lord's Supper.

The Real Presence of Christ in the Supper

The Lutheran Church teaches concerning the Lord's Supper that it is:

> the true body and blood of our Lord Jesus Christ, under the bread and wine, for us Christians to eat and to drink, instituted by Christ Himself. (SC)

Or

> Concerning the Lord's Supper it is taught that the body and blood of Christ are truly present and are distributed to those who eat at the supper of the Lord. They condemn those who teach otherwise. (AC X)

Christ, according to Lutheran teachings, is not present in the Lord's Supper merely in the sense that He is everywhere present. Nor is His presence a mere spiritual presence, as He is present, for example, when His people gather for worship. The presence of Christ in the Lord's Supper as taught in the Lutheran Church is a *real* presence. In a manner that is beyond human understanding, the body and blood of Christ are truly given with the bread and wine and are orally (with the mouth) received by the communicant whether he believes or does not believe.

> No matter whether you are worthy or unworthy, you here have Christ's body and blood by virtue of these words which are coupled with the bread and the wine. (LC)

In teaching the real presence of Christ's body and blood in the Lord's Supper, the Lutheran Church is completely in agreement with the whole catholic tradition, Roman and Greek. The latter, of course, go beyond Scripture when they teach that the bread and wine are changed into Christ's body and blood (they err also in some other aspects of teaching in regard to the Supper), but they do accept the teaching of Scripture that the body and blood of our Lord are truly present in the bread and wine.

The United Testimony of Matthew, Mark, Luke, and Paul

A careful comparison of the four places (see the appendix to this study) where the Words of Institution of the Lord's Supper are found (Matthew 26:26–29; Mark 14:22–25; Luke 22:19–20; 1 Corinthians 11:23–28) will bring to light both the differences and likenesses in the various accounts.

When comparing the four accounts, you will find, above all:

1. All four have the same, identical words: "This is My body";
2. The different ways of expressing what the cup is (Matthew and Mark: "This is My blood of the covenant"; Luke and Paul: "This cup is the new covenant in My blood") evidently say the same thing and must be understood exactly like the words concerning the bread;
3. The various additions or omissions found by your comparison do not affect the meaning of the central words.

The Words of Institution Are Clear

The Lutheran doctrine of the real presence (that is, of the body and blood of Christ *in the bread and the wine*, not of His personal presence somehow in the Supper) is in accordance with the simple understanding of the New Testament witnesses. The words of Jesus, no matter which of the four reports is taken up, are clear and straightforward. The Lutheran teaching is a fitting, adequate, faithful statement of what Jesus said in the situation in which He said them. The real presence could not have been expressed in words more clear than the ones He used. To put it differently: if Jesus at the Last Supper with His disciples had said, "Take, eat; this is fish" or "this is very good bread," then there would be no problem at all in regard to the meaning of the words. As it is, the words Jesus did use in the Lord's Supper are just as clear as the words we have supposed.

Why Some Reject the Real Presence

When some Christian individuals, groups, or churches refuse to accept the teaching of the real presence of Jesus' body and blood in the Lord's Supper, it is not because the Words of Institution are unclear or uncertain or even ambiguous (capable of being understood in more than one way). The problem is that these people cannot understand with their reason how Jesus can give His body and blood with the bread and the wine. Their reason stands in the way of their accepting with the faith of a child the teaching of the real presence so clearly expressed in Jesus' words.

More Support from the New Testament

The meaning of the four accounts of the institution of the Lord's Supper is in no way questioned or placed under any doubt but is rather supported and confirmed by other statements of the New Testament in relation to the Lord's Supper. If, for example, you study St. Paul in 1 Corinthians 10:16 (*not* the *New English Bible* or even the *Good News Bible*, which translate wrongly and probably deliberately wrongly) you will see that he speaks of a *fellowship*, a union or communion, a participation of the body in the bread and the blood in the wine (cup). Receiving the bread of the Supper, you receive the body of Christ. Likewise, receiving the wine in the Supper, you receive the blood of Christ. First Corinthians 11:27 in a different way also supports the realistic view of the Supper.

Words cannot more clearly set forth the doctrine of the real presence.

"Scripture Alone" or Reason?

If the last sentence ("words cannot more clearly set forth the doctrine of the real presence") is true, then it is clear that the Lutheran Church cannot give up its teaching on the Lord's Supper. If it did, it would be acting against one of its fundamental principles: that the prophetic and apostolic writings of the Old and New Testaments are the sole (only) and infallible (unerring) rule according to which we ought to judge all doctrines as well as all teachers. There is no authority in the Lutheran Church that can be set on a level with Holy Writ: not Luther, not the Confessions themselves, not reason, not philosophy, not science, nothing. Now, if the Lutheran Church were to abandon its realistic understanding of words so clear and direct and unmistakable in their natural meaning because of problems derived from human reason and not from Scripture, it would be directly attacking and contradicting the scriptural testimony *at a central point.* Scripture alone would no longer be the source of its teaching, but rather Scripture plus reason (or Scripture as interpreted and accepted by human reason). No principle of "Scripture alone" could exist after such a capitulation (surrender) to human reason. Having once given human reason a voice in determining teaching, especially in such a vital matter as the Lord's Supper, the Lutheran Church could no longer insist on "Scripture alone" as a source of doctrine. The Lutheran teaching of the real presence is a test whether the principle of "Scripture alone" is taken seriously or not.

Some Points for Discussion

1. Try to express the doctrine of the real presence more clearly than the words of Jesus say it.
2. What would you say of Luther's "in, with, and under the bread and wine"?
3. Discuss in-depth the last sentence of the presentation. Is there a flaw in the argument?

Appendix to Study 1

A Comparative Presentation of the Words of Institution

Matt. 26:26	Now as they were eating,
Mark 14:22	And as they were eating,
Luke 22:19	And
1 Cor. 11:23	For I received from the Lord what I also delivered to you, that the

Matt. 26:26	Jesus took bread, and
Mark 14:22	He took bread, and
Luke 22:19	He took bread, and when He
1 Cor.11:24	Lord Jesus on the night when He was betrayed took bread, and when He
Matt. 26:26	blessed, and broke it, and gave it to the disciples and said,
Mark 14:22	blessed, and broke it, and gave it to them and said,
Luke 22:19	had given thanks, He broke it and gave it to them saying
1 Cor. 11:24	had given thanks, He broke it, and said,
Matt. 26:26	"Take eat; this is My body."
Mark 14:22	"Take; this is My body."
Luke 22:19	"This is My body which is given for you. Do this in
1 Cor. 11:24	"This is My body which is for you. Do this in
Matt. 26:27	And He took a cup, and when He had given
Mark 14:23	And He took a cup, and when He had given
Luke 22:17	And He took a cup, and when He had given
Luke 22:20a	remembrance of Me." And likewise the cup after supper
1 Cor. 11:25	remembrance of Me." In the same way also the cup, after supper,
Matt. 26:27	thanks He gave it to them, saying, "Drink of it, all of you;
Mark 14:24	thanks He gave it to them, and they all drank of it. And He said to
Luke 22:17	thanks He said, "Take this, and divide it among
Luke 22:20a	saying,
1 Cor. 11:25	saying,
Matt. 26:28	for this is My blood of the covenant, which
Mark 14:24	them, "This is My blood of the covenant, which
Luke 22:20c,b	"This cup/is the new covenant in My blood./which
1 Cor. 11:25	"This cup is the new covenant in My blood. Do this,
Matt. 26:28	is poured out for many for the forgiveness of sins.
Mark 14:24	is poured out for many.
Luke 22:15	is poured out for you/And He said to them, "I have earnestly desired
1 Cor. 11:25	as often as you drink it, in remembrance of Me."
Matt. 26:29	I tell you I shall not drink again of this
Mark 14:25	Truly, I say to you, I shall not drink again of the
Luke 22:18	for I tell you that from now on I shall not drink of the
1 Cor. 11:26	For as often as you eat this bread and drink the cup, you proclaim

Matt. 26:29	fruit of the vine until that day when I drink it new with you in My
Mark 14:25	fruit of the vine until that day when I drink it new in the
Luke 22:18	fruit of the vine until
1 Cor. 11:27	the Lord's death until He comes. Whoever, therefore, eats the bread
Matt. 26:29	Father's kingdom."
Mark 14:25	kingdom of God"
Luke 22:18	kingdom of God comes."
1 Cor. 11:27	or drinks the cup of the Lord in an unworthy manner will be guilty of

STUDY 2
THE LORD'S SUPPER AND THE GOSPEL

THE HEART OF THIS STUDY

The heart of this second study concerning the Lord's Supper is this: the Lord's Supper as an institution of Jesus Christ is the source of the apostles' proclamation of the Gospel. It is our Lord's instruction to His apostles and the Church concerning His person and work.

THE LORD'S SUPPER AND THE CONTINUITY OF THE GOSPEL

Many theologians today teach that there is no real continuity, no direct link or connection, between the teaching of Jesus and the teaching of the earliest Church. The idea at the back of this is that the Early Church did not receive its teaching from Jesus but that it thought up its own theology or doctrine. This idea is shattered by the fact of the Lord's Supper. The first letter of Paul to the Corinthians was written shortly after AD 50, that is, only about twenty years after Jesus instituted the Lord's Supper. Now, in the section of the letter dealing with the Lord's Supper, 1 Corinthians 11:23ff., Paul quotes the Words of Institution not as though they were something new and previously unheard of in the Church, but as words that were already firmly established and used by the Church in its teaching. In other words, he quotes them as a fixed tradition ("for I received from the Lord what I also delivered to you"). Just because of the shortness of the chain of tradition: Jesus-tradition-Paul—a chain hardly more than twenty years along—the chance of early Christian interpretation or reinterpretation or misrepresentation is extremely slight, to say the least. Here, in the Lord's Supper, we have continuity of teaching; that is, there is no break between what Jesus taught His disciples and what they in turn taught others. The Words of Institution contain truths concerning Jesus and

His work which, with their implications, are the source of the whole of Christian teaching. The importance of the Lord's Supper for the doctrine of the Church will now be pointed out in a number of specific instances.

THE LORD'S SUPPER AND THE INCARNATION

(Incarnation = the action by which Jesus, the eternal Son of God, became a true man.)

"And the Word became flesh and dwelt among us . . . full of grace and truth" (John 1:14). Jesus, the eternal Son of God, became a true man. The words of Jesus in the Lord's Supper, when understood to say that His body and blood are truly present in the bread and wine in this Sacrament, teach us to think rightly of the incarnation. Whenever and wherever the Supper is celebrated to the end of time, Christ is present, His body and blood are distributed, received, eaten and drunk. In other words, Jesus, the Word made flesh, remains the incarnate one forever. He was God in the flesh not only while He was here on earth, but He is so still today and will remain so to all eternity. It is so easy to think of Jesus as a mere man of the past, as one who exists in the present only by the influence He exerts, like some great figure in history, for example, Socrates of ancient Greece and the Buddha. But the words of Jesus in the Lord's Supper, telling us that He gives us His true body and blood with the bread and the wine, makes it impossible for us to think of Him in this way. How can Jesus be a man of the past when His body and blood are given whenever the Lord's Supper is celebrated? He is God in the flesh to this very day and will always remain so.

It should also be pointed out that, in the Words of Institution, Jesus gives a hint of the resurrection and of the new life which lies before Him. His death is clearly implied, but His resurrection is taught almost as clearly by His statement that whenever His Supper would be celebrated it would be a proclamation of His death "*until He comes*" (1 Corinthians 11:26). This statement implies life for Jesus after His death and burial, life of a new kind which was to begin a few days after His institution of the Supper.

THE LORD'S SUPPER AND THE ATONEMENT

The atonement is the great work of Jesus Christ by which He, through the voluntary sacrifice of Himself on the cross, once and for all paid the ransom price for the sins of the world to God and so brought reconciliation (peace) between God and humanity.

In the Lord's Supper Jesus presents this wonderful truth to us in a nutshell.

Note the following points in the Words of Institution:

1. Jesus clearly speaks of His body being given and His blood being shed. The separation in the words of body and blood would suggest that Jesus saw His death as a *sacrifice*.

2. Jesus states plainly for whom His body was given and His blood was shed (see Luke and Paul). Paul's words concerning the bread ("This is My body for you") contain the idea that Jesus died to expiate, that is, pay the penalty for men's sins (see Romans 5:6–8; 14–15; 1 Corinthians 15:3), and that His death was a victorious one, a death for sinful people (Galatians 3:13; 2 Corinthians 5:21). Likewise, Paul's word concerning the *cup* (wine) is a direct reference to Jesus' death and includes the thought of a violent death to pay the penalty for men's sins in order thus to shame them.
3. Jesus points to the great purpose for which His body was given and His blood was shed: "for the forgiveness of sins," for the establishment of a "new covenant" (testament) of reconciliation and peace between God and mankind.

Put all this together and we have the Gospel of the atonement in a nutshell. It is not too much to say that Paul's teaching of the atonement is merely an unfolding of Jesus' Words of Institution.

The Lord's Supper and the Second Coming of Christ

The actual Words of Institution do not directly teach the second coming of Christ, but it is a truth that Jesus clearly taught in connection with His Supper. Mark and Matthew report the statement: "Truly, I say to you, I will not drink again of the fruit of the vine until that day when I drink it new in the kingdom of God." Luke has a similar sentence, and Paul writes to the Corinthians in 1 Corinthians 11: "as often as you eat this bread and drink the cup, you proclaim the Lord's death until He comes." The death of the Lord and His second advent belong together.

The Lord's Supper Unites Past and Future in the Present

The death of Christ is an event that lies a long way back in history. A period of more than 1,900 years lies between that event and us. The cross seems so far away. All sorts of ideas have been devised to bridge the distance, to bring it nearer and closer to us. One favorite way by which people have tried to do this is by the idea of re-presentation. But it is difficult to see how a once-for-all act in the past, removed from us by more than 1,900 years, can be re-presented now. We can recall it, we can vividly picture it to ourselves in our imagination, we can reenact it in some fitting kind of dramatic action, but all this is not to make it happen again in any real way at all. The idea of re-presentation is artificial. It lacks enough substance to be of any real value to most Christians. We who have the true Sacrament in our confession of the real presence have no need at all for devices to bring the death of Christ nearer to us. The Lord's Supper does this to perfection. The Supper bridges the nineteen centuries lying between Calvary and us and makes the sacrifice of Christ *ever present*, because the body given into death *then*, and the blood shed, is the same as that which we receive *now* at this time and place.

The Lord's Supper and Justification by Faith

(Justification by faith = God declares those righteous who trust in Jesus as their Savior.)

There is a close connection between the heart of the Reformation, justification by faith, and the Lord's Supper.

Gift and reception—giving and receiving—this is the heart of justification. God is the giver. The forgiveness of sins He gives, the verdict by which He declares the guilty righteous and by which humanity is reconciled to and put right with Him—all that is already there, perfectly whole and complete in the death and resurrection of Christ. It is not something to be won, achieved, worked, earned, and gained by human beings and their work. It is there as a *gift*—a gift to be received—to be received by faith, simply by believing that God for the sake of Jesus forgives our sins and declares us righteous.

Gift and reception—giving and receiving—this is also the heart of the Lord's Supper. Jesus is the giver. He gives His body and blood, and, with His body and blood, the forgiveness of sins, *life, and salvation* He has won for us by means of them. All communicants do is to receive. As worthy communicants they receive in faith. They receive the body and blood of Christ and His gift of forgiveness, life, and salvation. If they are unworthy (unbelieving) communicants, they still receive the body and blood of Christ, but not the forgiveness of sin, life, and salvation He offers in His Supper. Such communicants receive the Supper to their condemnation and not to their blessing (1 Corinthians 11:29). The gifts of God are never without their proper result.

Gift and reception—giving and receiving—is the heart of both justification and the Lord's Supper. We have a perfect parallel between the Word of the Gospel and the Sacrament.

Some Points for Discussion

1. Can a symbolical, figurative view of the Lord's Supper give the same teaching concerning the Christian faith as the realistic view has been shown to do?
2. Why is it undesirable to speak of the congregation as sacrificing when they celebrate the Lord's Supper?
3. Discuss this sentence: If you want to keep the Gospel, you must keep the true Lord's Supper.

STUDY 3
PRESERVING THE TREASURE OF THE LORD'S SUPPER

THE LORD'S SUPPER: A TREASURE TO BE PRESERVED

Our previous two studies on the Lord's Supper have shown how great a treasure the Church possesses in this Sacrament. It is the source of the apostles' proclamation of the Gospel; it is the heart of the Gospel.

A treasure needs to be preserved. For this to happen in the case of the Lord's Supper, we need, first and foremost, to gain an ever deeper and better understanding of it. We need regularly and frequently to partake of it. We need to treat it with reverence, celebrating it with the most suitable and dignified forms we can devise. Indeed, the history of the Church shows that some of the noblest praises of the Church in liturgy, worship, and music are connected with the celebration of the Lord's Supper.

CONFESSION AND DEFENSE ESSENTIAL FOR PRESERVATION

Confession and defense are essential for the preservation of the Lord's Supper. We need to *confess* the *true* Lord's Supper, the Supper in which Jesus in, with, and under the bread and wine gives us His true body and blood, and we need to *defend* this true Supper against all who by false teaching would deprive or rob us of this treasure. To put the point quite sharply, it means saying quite clearly and unmistakably, but also quite lovingly, that those who deny the real presence (the true presence of the body and blood of Christ in the bread and the wine for us Christians to eat and to drink) are destroying the Sacrament; that they are putting a man-made ceremony in the place of the institution of Christ. It means saying that a supper in which the bread and wine are seen merely to represent the body and blood of Christ is no supper at all or, at least, that there is very great doubt whether it is the true Supper even when the Words of Institution are actually used.

Confession and defense of the Lord's Supper means taking seriously this sentence of Luther:

> Therefore it is my honest advice which before God I owe you who are at Frankfurt and whoever else may be in need of it. If anyone knows that his pastor teaches the Zwinglian way publicly, he ought to avoid him. He should rather abstain from the Sacrament all his life than receive it from him, and even die and suffer all things. (For Luther, Zwinglians were people who spoke of a real presence in an ambiguous way.)

Confession and defense of the Lord's Supper means taking seriously also these words of the sainted Dr. Sasse:

> The Lutheran Church . . . has never recognized the Sacrament of the Altar in those communities which deny the Real Presence, and consequently

does not allow even in a case of emergency or in the moment of death to receive Holy Communion in such churches.[1]

So Lutherans will not receive the Lord's Supper in a church where the real presence is denied. They will not take part in celebrations where a church (or churches) that teaches the real presence communes together with a church (or churches) that denies the real presence. They will not permit those who deny the real presence to commune at their altars.

THE PRINCIPLES INVOLVED IN CLOSE COMMUNION

The practice of refusing certain Christians Communion at a Lutheran altar (this practice is true generally of the Catholic churches) is called *close Communion*. Two important principles are involved in this practice:

1. It should be quite clear that those who teach the real presence cannot celebrate the Lord's Supper together in one act with those who deny it. It is impossible for a thing to *be* and *not to be* at the same time. A thing either *is* or *is not*. Jesus' body and blood are either present in the Lord's Supper or they are not. You cannot therefore with one breath say that they are present and then with the same breath say that they are not present. But this is the very thing that a person who believes in the real presence does when he communes with those who deny this presence. He is saying, "Yes, Jesus' body and blood are present," but they at the same time are saying, "No, they are not present." By communing with other people, a person declares: "I hold the same confession and belief in regard to the Lord's Supper as they do." But this is simply not true if he believes in the real presence and those with whom he communes do not. Words and actions must be truthful. No one who truly accepts the real presence as the very Word of God can grant a person the right to deny it and to commune with him at the same table. Just so, no Presbyterian, for example, who declares that there can be no real eating and drinking of the body and blood of Christ, could really want to receive the Supper at an altar where just this thing impossible to him is confessed and taught.
2. The second principle takes us into the wider area of church fellowship. Lutherans who practice close Communion cannot exclude Catholics (that is, Roman Catholics, Eastern Orthodox, some Anglicans) from their altars on the ground that they do not believe in the real presence, for Lutherans and Catholics agree on what the Lord's Supper is. Why, then, do Lutherans and Catholics not commune at the same altar? One reason for this is that they are not agreed on all points of teaching in regard to the Lord's Supper. But it is not only the teaching in regard to the Lord's Supper that is

1 Hermann Sasse, *This Is My Body* (Adelaide: Lutheran Publishing House, 1977), 372.

involved. This Supper cannot be divorced from the rest of Scripture. It does not stand by itself, in isolation, apart and separate from the whole body of Christian truth. There is a close, intimate, inseparable tie-up between it and the other doctrines of Holy Scripture. The Lord's Supper is an integral part of the whole witness of Scripture to the Gospel of Jesus Christ. In the Lord's Supper, therefore, the whole of Christian truth is involved. This means that only those who are truly agreed on all points of Christian teaching can commune together. The Lord's Supper, according to the will of God, is a sign, a token, a testimony of the unity of faith. When communing with other people we are saying in effect, "We believe the same as they do." If, therefore, those who are not in unity of faith commune together as though there *were unity of faith*, we have an untruthful situation. A false impression is being created, an impression of a unity, a oneness, that does not exist; truth is not being confessed and served. The proper thing for churches separated by division as to what the Gospel is, is to reach agreement, oneness in the Gospel. Then communing together is a truthful witness or testimony of a oneness that does in very fact exist.

Close Communion Not Contrary to Love

Many people outside our Lutheran Church of Australia, and quite a few within it, would not agree with what has been stated, not because it is wrong, but for other reasons. They, for instance, claim that by excluding members of other denominations from our altars we are saying that they are not Christians. But nothing of the kind is being said. What is being said is that we are not united in confession and faith and that therefore we cannot commune together.

Another objection frequently raised against the practice of close Communion is that it displays a lack of love. But it is difficult to see how this objection can be upheld. The very opposite is the case. It is love to tell other people that they are wrong if they are wrong. It is love to take other people's teachings and positions seriously even if they are wrong, and then to take the action required of us by God in His Word. But when people say that they are right and others wrong, and then say, "Well, it doesn't really make much difference; we can commune together just the same," then obviously they are not taking the other people's point of view seriously at all. They are treating their opinion as though it were not really important. And what is more, they are treating their own teaching as though it did not really matter either.

Confession Calls for Action

Confession is not only claiming to teach so and so, but it is acting in accordance with the claim to teach so and so. Confession, in other words, is not merely a matter of *saying* but also of *doing*. What we confess, we must also practice. We need very carefully to note what James says in his epistle, chapter 2:14–16. He hits very hard those who say they have faith when their whole conduct and way of life show that they really have no faith at all. To prove that we sincerely and seriously believe in the real presence and the true Supper of our Lord, we need to do two things:

1. Commune only where others who have the same faith as we commune;
2. Gently but firmly exclude from our altars those who deny the real presence and those who in other ways oppose the Gospel of Jesus Christ and depart from the truths of the Word of God.

Some Points for Discussion

1. The general rule behind close Communion is given in the exposition above. Can you think of situations where the rule may be broken though? And for what reason(s)?
2. Discuss more fully what love really means in this sentence: "Thou shalt love thy neighbor as thyself."

Study 4
Preserving the Treasure in the Christian Life

The Lord's Supper—Source of Spiritual Nourishment

The Lord's Supper is pure Gospel. It is the Gospel in its purest and most concentrated form. As such, it is a constant source of nourishment for the Christian life. What food and drink are for the body, the Lord's Supper is for the spiritual life of the Christian. This is probably why an ancient understanding of the petition "Give us this day our daily bread" saw in it a prayer for the nourishment given in the Eucharist (a name for the Lord's Supper derived from the Greek word for "giving thanks"). The Lord's Supper and the other two Means of Grace, Baptism and the Word of the Gospel, are the instruments the Holy Spirit uses to bring people to faith or to recall them to the faith, and then to nurture and to preserve them in the faith.

The faith and spiritual life of Christians are constantly in need of nourishment. As little as their physical lives can survive without food, so little can their spiritual lives. For this reason Christians need to feed on the Word of God regularly and to partake of the Lord's Supper frequently.

The Lord's Supper—A Reminder of the Need of Repentance

Since the Lord's Supper is for sinners and gives them the body and blood of Christ for the forgiveness of sins, it is, in particular, a continual reminder of the need to repent (to see and to confess one's sins) and a call to such repentance. The Lord's Supper is for *sinners* and *sinners only*—no one is *worthy* in himself of being given such a gift, but "he is truly worthy and well prepared who has faith in these words 'given and shed for you for the remission of sins.'" The Lord's Supper can be received with blessing and profit only by those who know that they are sinners and in contrition acknowledge themselves as such before God.

Because of this, Christians are exhorted to examine themselves before partaking of the Lord's Supper. This self-examination must be carried out in the light of the divine Word. It is only as Christians thus examine themselves that they can learn to know their sins and to bow in humble contrition before God.

The Lord's Supper—A Reminder of God's Bounty

The Lord's Supper is a reminder of the need to repent. At the same time, however, it is a reminder to Christians that they live by the bounty of God. The Supper is all gift, the gift of the body and blood and of the forgiveness of sins, and with it, life and salvation. In the celebration of the Supper the Christian does nothing but receive what Christ offers: "Take, eat; this is My body! Drink of it, all of you; this is My blood!" Christians remain beggars all their lives—as Luther said of himself on his deathbed—and the very heart of this life is a taking, receiving, appropriating of all the blessing, goodness, and salvation that God promises.

The Lord's Supper—The Center of Christian Worship

Finally, the Lord's Supper is the center of Christian *worship*. It is this in two ways:

1. There are many activities which make up Christian services: Confession and Absolution; prayer and praise and thanksgiving; proclamation and preaching and teaching of God's Word. None of these activities identify you as a Christian in the way that attendance at the Lord's Table does. You may sing hymns because you like singing, listen to the sermon because you like good speaking, and no one knows whether you are taking part in the Confession of sins or not, or taking the Absolution to heart or not. But when you attend the Lord's Supper, you are making a distinct confession of your faith in the Gospel. "Take, eat, etc.," and when you receive it, you are saying to all present, "This I believe." The altar is the layman's pulpit where he proclaims the Gospel, which these studies have shown to be concentrated in the Supper. Only on the very rare occasion of an adult Baptism and in confirmation services is there a similar clear individual confession of faith in the Christian service.
2. The Lord's Supper is also the clearest demonstration of Christian fellowship. All Christians are one Body in Christ because they all eat of the one body in the Sacrament (1 Corinthians 10:16–17). Let us think again of what goes on

in the Christian worship service. There is proclamation of the Word in one way or another: in readings from Scripture, in the sermon, in most hymns, in the Absolution. But does it mean that when the Word is preached, the people hearing it together are necessarily in fellowship with one another? Hearing the Word together with other people is not a demonstration or expression of Christian fellowship. People may be in church who are merely curious, seekers after truth, casual visitors, non-Christian friends, etc. It is somewhat different with those parts of the worship service devoted to prayer, praise, and thanksgiving. Here there is indeed some display of fellowship, certainly far more than in hearing the Word together. But the greatest demonstration and expression of fellowship is given in the celebration of the Lord's Supper when Christians together receive what the Lord gives them in His Supper: His body given for them and His blood shed for the forgiveness of their sins. There is no closer fellowship than the fellowship of the altar.

Questions for Discussion

1. Baptism is also at the heart of the Christian life. See Romans 6:4–11 and Luther's Small Catechism, namely, his explanation of Baptism in the Fourth Chief Part. Compare Baptism and the Lord's Supper as nourishers of the Christian life.
2. Study the Christian worship service from the point of view of reception of God's gift. Are we doing something for God in our worship or receiving from Him?
3. Compare our services with the aspects of Christian services as described to us in the New Testament. The following texts have been grouped to make this comparison easier:

   Acts 2:46–47; 20:7–12; 1 Corinthians 10:16–17; 11:20–30; Ephesians 5:19–20; Colossians 3:15–17; 1 Timothy 3:16; Revelation 5:9, 12, 13; Romans 8:15–17; 10:9–10; 1 Corinthians 8:5–6; Philippians 2:22; 1 Timothy 2:8–14; Hebrews 13:7–16; 1 Corinthians 16:19–22 (more general ideas).
4. How frequently should our congregations celebrate the Lord's Supper?
5. How often should we receive the Lord's Supper?
6. What things should Christians seek to find out about themselves in their self-examination before partaking of the Lord's Supper?

CHAPTER THIRTEEN

THE CONFESSIONAL PRINCIPLE

CHURCH FELLOWSHIP IN THE ANCIENT AND IN THE LUTHERAN CHURCH[1]

TOM G. A. HARDT

I. THE ANCIENT CHURCH

1. THE FALSE CONCEPT OF THE ONE, COMPREHENSIVE ANCIENT CHURCH

When dealing with this topic, we face a mass of serious misunderstandings and distortions of how the Christian Church throughout the ages has handled the question of church fellowship both theoretically and practically. This is due to the fact that we stand today under the pressure of the ecumenical movement which by all means propagates the idea that the Church has at least originally been one, that originally all Christians exercised church fellowship with one another, and that a divided Christendom is a comparatively new fact. Our duty would then be to return to the originally existing oneness.

This idea is already to be found with a man like the Swiss reformer Zwingli and with his spiritual father Erasmus. In his debate with Luther at the castle of Marburg in 1529, Zwingli appealed to this ideal Church, the one primitive Church, where you could hold different opinions but yet, of course, as an absolute necessity practice church fellowship with those deviating from you doctrinally. We find the same view among different ecumenists in the seventeenth century. The idea of the one primitive Church in the course of time gained the strongest foothold in England and the Anglican Church, whence it has been acquired by the present-day high-church schools of thought within the various confessions and also by the ecumenical movement of the day.

We find a most touching and very beautiful picture of this dream of the one Church in the words in the will of the Anglican Bishop Thomas Ken (1637–1711),

1 This essay was a lecture delivered by the late Tom G. A. Hardt (+June 1998) in Riga, Latvia, in May 1996. Tom Hardt was pastor of St. Martin's Lutheran Church, Stockholm.

where he confessed: "I die in the Holy Catholic and Apostolic Faith, professed by the whole Church, before the disunion of East and West." We hear a nostalgic leaning toward the past, a longing for a peace no more at hand, yet consoled by the additional final sentence: "more particularly I die in the communion of the Church of England, as it stands distinguished from all papal and puritan innovations." An even more fascinating expression of the longing for the one, undivided Church we find with Bishop Bo Giertz of Gothenburg, the well-known and much-admired Swedish conservative theologian. In his very popular and widely spread *Kristi kyrka*, chapter "Una sancta," he says about the primitive Church: "From Spain one could travel along the whole Mediterranean and deep into Arabia and up among the mountains of Armenia, and wherever one came or whenever one went ashore, one could go into the churches, partake of the Lord's Supper, and experience as a wondrous truth what some unknown hymn writer from these centuries wrote in the Ambrosian hymn of praise, our *Te Deum*: *Te per orbem terrarum Sancta confitetur ecclesia:* (The Holy Church in every place throughout the world exalts Thy praise)."[2] The Council of Nicaea, where our Nicaean Creed was accepted in 325, is, for Giertz, "the great day of triumph for the one world-encompassing Church." The Church was "united and strong under the leadership of her bishops."[3]

To Giertz, as to so many others who follow this fascinating, glowing picture that has spellbound many souls, the one Church is one because she is "catholic" in the sense of "broad-minded," "dogmatically comprehensive." This is of utmost importance for the treatment of our topic. Giertz writes: "The distance between a Jew in Jerusalem, a believer in the ancient faith converted to Christianity, and a recently converted Greek slave was certainly greater than the natural distance, as it manifests itself, between a Pentecostal and a Roman Catholic. But despite these violent tensions unity was preserved. It rested upon a holy obligation."[4] According to Giertz, the unity of the Church does not rest upon the unity in doctrine. The Church is to Giertz a kind of organism, an entity that grew out of the apostolic congregations, constituted by this historical connection, despite the ever-changing forms. This organism Giertz calls the "body of Christ," which thus describes the outward, visible corporation, exactly as the Romantic Movement of the nineteenth century saw the ancient nations and political institutions of Europe as such "bodies." This kind of terminology permits, of course, the idea that by "splitting" the body, the body gets "wounds" through separations, etc. Accordingly, Giertz writes: "If the apostles appeared today, and if they were confronted with the splintering in a single, average, Swedish community, they would be horrified and would

---

2 Bo Giertz, "Una sancta," in *Kritsti Kyrka* (Stockholm: 1946), 65.

3 Giertz, "Una sancta," 63.

4 Giertz, "Una sancta," 61.

reproach us with having cut to pieces and lacerated the holy body of Christ."[5] The fact that a Roman Catholic and a Pentecostal do not celebrate the Sacrament together is thus to this admittedly conservative theologian a sin that has split the Body of God. Not to have church fellowship is thus a sin.

Giertz is, however, not fully unaware of events running contrary to the harmonious picture given above. "From time to time there arose divisions," writes Giertz, but "some of them healed themselves. Others survived as locally limited or insignificant minorities. The more tenacious ones led to the coming into being of independent national churches, often in distant countries far beyond the bounds of the Roman Empire. Yet all the time the great mother church was there in constant growth. For more than eight centuries she possessed existence."[6] As Bishop Ken, Bishop Giertz aims at the separation between East and West, and accordingly the years 867 and 1054, when the bonds between Rome and Constantinople broke off, are the years of limits of the "great mother church." Its destruction is not caused by false doctrines but by cases when practice is set against practice, in this case when papal centralism is set against the autonomy of the local churches. Faced by this tragedy, Giertz calls out with a German theologian: "Back to the One, back to the whole! Beyond the confessions to the undivided Christ!"[7] Rightly—according to the foundations of the theology now developed—the confessions, also the Confessions of the Lutheran Church, are put under condemnation, as they have indeed most certainly caused splits within Christendom.

What we have now heard out of the mouth of a most influential, conservative leader within Lutheranism can equally well be heard from what can be termed a pronouncedly ecumenical work such as Stephen Charles Neill's *A History of the Ecumenical Movement 1517–1948*. Like Giertz, the dogmatic tensions are regarded as having the "nature of family quarrels,"[8] and excluded are only those who are no Christians at all, like the Gnostics. The criterion of the true Church is that she was worldwide, "the Council of Nicaea represented the Church from Spain to the slopes of Hindu Kush." The restrictions in admission to the divine services, which the author actually does know about, are thought to be directed against pagans and spies. The author assures us that the doctrine that "anyone who . . . communicated . . . with a tainted sheep thereby became tainted himself" has been developed by "puritans such as Lucifer of Cagliari," a name that through its demonic associations aptly describes the origin of the idea that church fellowship should

5 Giertz, "Una sancta," 65.

6 Giertz, "Una sancta," 66.

7 Giertz, "Una sancta," 74.

8 Stephen Charles Neill, "Introduction: Division and the Search for Unity Prior to the Reformation," in *A History of the Ecumenical Movement 1517–1948* (London: SPCK, 1954), vi.

not be liberally exercised. Neill knows a little more than Giertz about the presence of heretics, but they do not play any prominent role in the history of the Church.

2. The Real Ancient Church Is the Church of Closed Communion, Excluding Heretics

This long presentation of a view that certainly is not mine and that certainly is not true has its place in this essay simply to make clear what the presuppositions of any treatment of our subject really are. All that has been said up to now is regarded as self-evident, standing to reason, raised above all discussion. Yet that very discussion must be raised, and it has been raised and more than that. The utterly scholarly and trustworthy work by the late Werner Elert, professor of Erlangen, *Abendmahl und Kirchengemeinschaft in der alten Kirche, hauptsächlich des Ostens* (*The Eucharist and Church Fellowship in the Ancient Church, Mainly in the East*) has, as a matter of fact, completely destroyed the false presentation to which you have had to listen for a while. Its English translation by the Missouri Synod's Concordia Publishing House in St. Louis may be a sign that it has not been welcome outside the camp of conservative Lutheranism. It runs so entirely against what is acceptable within the established, ecumenical, theological world. Probably the real argument against it is simply that it does not serve any reasonable purpose, does not promote some good cause, has no actuality, as learned men say when they want to silence some scandalous academic work. There is only one other similar work, that one by Martin Wittenberg, formerly professor at Neuendettelsau, Bavaria, entitled *Kirchengemeinschaft und Abendmahlsgemeinschaft*. It has recently been reedited in German and published in English (*Logia* 1, no. 1, Reformation 1992) and in Latvian. This presentation, as far as the Ancient Church is concerned, builds mainly on Elert.

We now turn to the Ancient Church and ask some questions: What were the regulations concerning church fellowship? Could one, "wherever one went ashore," communicate? Are the limitations aimed only at the "grave" heretics, who by definition were not Christians at all? Where were the heretics to be found? Were there only a few of them? Was the Ancient Church dogmatically comprehensive?

Undoubtedly there were in the Ancient Church at least some people of the modern attitude, to which we have listened. Tertullian does speak of heretics, who "come together, listen together, pray together" with those of different faith, yea, without even differentiating between baptized and unbaptized. Tertullian's remark implies, however, that he speaks about something quite extraordinary and unusual, hardly believable. Those heretics also prove their falseness through other openly offensive forms of behavior such as lay preaching, including preaching women. If this all must be understood as exceptional, one has to admit that, on the other hand, it is possible to deduce from the many safety measures against heretical infiltrations that there were Christians who more regularly tried to get access to altars where they were not welcome. There are complaints by St. Basil the Great (ca. 330–379) that lukewarm Catholics grow accustomed to participation in the heretical worship of the very much dominating anti-Nicene party. St. Basil asks for letters from others to stop this violation of the rule forbidding church fellowship with heretics.

These rules were not man-made disciplinary regulations but, of course, were founded on the clear doctrine of the New Testament, where Christ says: "Beware of false prophets" (Matthew 7:15), and St. Paul asks us to "avoid" those of different teaching, as in Romans 16:17. Even the exchange of the liturgical, Christian greeting with the heretic is forbidden, "for whoever greets him takes part in his wicked works" (2 John 11). The Pastoral Letters of St. Paul, the canonical nature of which were never questioned before the time people wanted to live in a pluralistic church, are quite clear concerning the question of church fellowship: "As for a person who stirs up division, after warning him once and then twice, have nothing more to do with him" (Titus 3:10). We should in this connection consider the fact that the inability to recognize such words as genuinely apostolic builds on the strange idea of a necessary evolution, which presupposes that such words cannot have been written before a long process of thought has taken place, bringing us from the simplicity of the first Christians to the well-regulated, well-disciplined but also less spirit-minded Early catholic Church. This is, however, an entirely unfounded assumption with no proofs to sustain it, except the equally unfounded dogma of evolution. Today's discovery of the very well-regulated life of the Qumran sect teaches us besides that the New Testament was written in a world where all the marks of a firm ecclesiastical order were present. To summarize: everything was there from the very beginning.

The Church Fathers often present the doctrine of church fellowship in connection with the treatment of the Sacraments. Both St. Ignatius of Antioch (ca. 35–107) and St. Justin Martyr (ca. 100–165) affirm the prohibition to have fellowship with the heretics at the same time as they stress belief in the incarnation and in the real presence. St. Ignatius makes it quite explicit that only those who assent to the apostolic teaching are admitted to the Sacrament, which the Christians teach to be the body and blood of Christ. It is not to be imagined that St. Ignatius would have admitted anyone teaching that the same body and blood "are not here." The *Didaskalia* (early third century) thus makes it necessary for the deacon to demand from any visitor information as to whether he belongs to the Church or to a sect. The *Apostolic Constitutions* (late fourth century) in that case demand a document of legitimation, as do the Synods of Elvira (306) and Arles (314). The Synods of Antioch (341) and Carthage (345–348) repeat the prohibition against admitting unknown persons to the liturgy. The Synod of Laodicea (360) even prohibits the outward presence of any heretic in the church building and forbids the Catholics to be present in heretical church buildings. In all these cases fellowship is not merely thought of as fellowship in the Sacrament but as fellowship in prayer as well. (When Elert thinks that in two cases some fellowship in praying the Psalms with heretics has been exercised, he is in my opinion mistaken. The singing of Psalms was the task of one man, where the others listened, hymnals still waiting for their existence.) The closed doors that forced visitors to leave the church after the sermon were closed before the prayers started. It should also be remembered that this strictness was also exercised in the hour of death. It is an often-heard opinion that *in articulo mortis* fellowship had to be granted the heretics, but it is due to a misunderstanding of canon 13 in the decisions of the Council of Nicaea, which clearly speaks of penitents whose time of penitence is shortened if they are expected to die.

That the rules concerning *communicatio in sacris* were actually applied in all their severity is shown by the unfortunate lot of the Church Father St. John Chrysostom (ca. 347–407). In Alexandria an archpresbyter had given the Eucharist to a heretic Manichaean woman and was accordingly excommunicated for this. Since another presbyter and four monks, known as "the tall brothers," continued to have sacramental fellowship with the archpresbyter, they also were excommunicated. They turn to St. John Chrysostom in Constantinople, who grants them fellowship in prayer, which can be regarded as the level attainable for penitents before their final admission to the Eucharist. The end of the story is that St. John Chrysostom as a result of this veritable chain reaction is deposed and thrown into exile.

Also on the other side of the fence the same conditions rule. When a Monophysite patriarch of Antioch once or twice has communicated with the Catholics, he is as a consequence refused Communion by his own brethren and is finally deposed. The rule of no fellowship with heretics or schismatics (*nulla comunicatio in sacris cum haereticis aut schismaticis*) is universally recognized and can claim to be an ecumenical belief, the only one really existing. All agree that you must agree before taking Communion together.

That common Communion meant a common Church was thus universally recognized. When the state, as so often, wished to have the stability of a unified state church, the state's only wish was to have a common Communion, not to meddle in any way into theological matters. Everyone was permitted by the state to have his own belief, as long as he took the Sacrament in the prescribed way. Thus in AD 369 a Catholic bishop is admonished by an Arian emperor to communicate with the Arians in order that peace shall be established. The bishop refuses, celebrates his own catholic Mass, and is sent into exile by the emperor. The bishop has thereby shown that to confess the Nicene Creed is not an academic matter, not to repeat a formula, but to put the Nicene Creed into practice, to let the final condemnations that actually are fixed to the end of the Creed work out at the altar rail, as always the dogmatic "We condemn" that follows the "We teach" has meant that the heretics are refused admission to the Sacrament.

Against this background we can understand the great ninth-century dogmatician St. John of Damascus when he says: "We must with all strength hold fast to the principle neither to receive the Eucharist from heretics nor to give it to them."[9] This is a voice not from an undisturbed, unafflicted, homogenous, closed world but from a suffering Church under the yoke of Muhammadanism. This conflict with a heathen state did not make the fight against heresies less important and did not open the closed altar.

We have already heard some people are inclined to regard what we have now described as directed against such grave heretics who had as a matter of fact already left the Christian faith. This is, however, not in agreement with the existing facts as we know them. The Council of Nicaea demands, for example, rebaptism only of the followers of Paul of Samosata, who denied the Trinity. Other groups are regarded as having a valid Baptism. Later on Montanists, Sabellians, and Eunomians were also included among those who did not have valid Baptism. Far more important, however, is that Arians, Macedonians, Novatians, Apollinarians, and others were regarded as lawfully baptized. With few exceptions the authority of the biblical canon is recognized, and to its wordings references are made in the dogmatic conflicts.

Werner Elert has collected cases which are to prove that the exclusion of heretics from the liturgy did not correspond to a general aversion against their persons. A certain theological cooperation against a third party could be developed, mutual discussions take place in a friendly way, and even a certain humor shown. The subjective honesty of the opponent could be taken for granted. Generally speaking there is not much place for the "speculative temperament of the Levant," a concept that Bishop Neill introduces in his learned attempts to explain the history of the Ancient Church. This concept corresponds in a most regrettable way too well to another similar notion, that of "prelogical man," an invention of modern and not very logical scholars. The people of the Ancient Church were all like us, as wise and as stupid as we. They knew their fellow men as well as we do. They certainly, however, differed from us in the doctrine of church fellowship.

3. The "Everywhere" and the "by All" of Heresy

We will not treat here the original meaning of the expression "*semper, ubique et ab omnibus*," the always, everywhere, and by all, which is to be found with St. Vincent of Lérin (died before 450), and which is thought to be a way to discover the Christian truth. Let it suffice to say that it has been very misunderstood, and

9 Werner Elert, *Abendmahl und Kirchengemeinschaft in der alten Kirche, hauptsächlich des Ostens* (Berlin: Lutherisches Verlagshaus, 1954), 102.

whatever it meant, it did not help poor St. Vincent very much, as he finally fell into heresy. Today we use it to mean that contrary to what is often said, heresy is most definitely not something insignificant, not something silenced simply by looking at the Great Church, the Church above discussion. Heresy has been predicted by Christ's words that "*many* will come in My name, saying, 'I am the Christ,' and they will lead *many* astray" (Matthew 24:5). Heresies are accordingly large, impressive movements, whereas the Catholics find consolation in being the little flock predicted by Christ.

First of all, we can let Elert point to a few interesting facts that show us the Catholic Church as one of many churches. Before Constantine, the Catholic Church had no privileged position over the heretical bodies. At this time the various churches could not even control the changes of confession by their members, for example, in Alexandria. Even after the directives of Emperor Theodosius in 380 against the heretics, they could, despite everything, have churches in the capital city itself. An Ancient Church historian tells us about a Jew who for the sake of gain let himself be baptized in Constantinople by the Arians and the Macedonians only finally to be exposed during his visit to the Novatians. Elert maintains that about the year 500 "the capital city presented a motley of denominations quite comparable to that of a German or English metropolis today." Another vivid description by Elert runs: "Nicaeans, Semi-Arians, Eunomians, Macedonians, Apollinarians live side by side in the same locality. The pre-Nicaean Novatians had at the same time spread and continued for a long time to spread a net of congregations over many parts of the same area. To this there came after Chalcedon the Monophysites, who in their turn split again."[10]

Even apart from Elert and before him, minor points have been advanced to prove that the heresy in the Ancient Church extended far more widely than has been customarily supposed. Eusebius's silence concerning the church life in middle and eastern Asia Minor might be due to the fact that Christianity in these areas was heretical. St. Ignatius of Antioch, too, in his letters omits naming certain churches of Asia Minor which appear in the Book of Revelation, despite including the rest of these churches. It is tempting to assume that St. Ignatius looked upon the omitted churches as now having become entirely heretical. The heresy mentioned in the Book of Revelation could then have choked the orthodox Christendom in the time before the letters of Ignatius. One may, moreover, point out that the letters in Revelation 2, as a matter of fact, are occupied with the *communicatio in sacris cum haereticis*, for which sin otherwise praiseworthy orthodox congregations are accused (Revelation 2:14, 15, 19). The mere presence of heretics in a congregation—the Balamites, the Nicolaitans, a female teacher—is a sin to be repented of.

10 Elert, *Abendmahl und Kirchengemeinschaft*, 113.

Just as heresy thus can ascribe to itself the *ubique*, the "everywhere," it is also embraced *ab omnibus*, "by all." When I wrote the first version of this lecture about forty years ago (!), I carefully made an exception for St. Augustine, with whom I found the thought that the legitimacy of the Church could be proved from her numbers and geographic catholicity. I no longer believe in this wisdom of the textbook. When St. Augustine, for example, says that the authority of the Catholic Church has led him to the Gospel, he certainly does not mean that nonsense that we hear from Roman Catholics. He spoke about the first, Early Church, which could testify to the authenticity of the Gospel, not about any kind of later Church, pretentiously claiming for itself an authority above the Gospel. Likewise, when he speaks about the true Church being spread everywhere and the heretics being local, he thinks of his own Church in unbroken succession of the first, primitive Church, where the apostolic churches founded everywhere retained a true doctrine while the heretic innovators could not trace their dogmatic pedigree in that way but were local appearances without the bonds to the apostolic past, to the apostolic "*ubique*." St. Augustine would thus not have become a Donatist, even if they had succeeded in spreading everywhere, while St. Augustine's followers would have been limited to his see, Hippo Regius in Northern Africa. To that extent, I think it quite correct to see him in full unity with his fellows, the other Church Fathers whose testimony we now are to quote.

Before I do so, I will note the source of these quotations, which will show that what I present to you is part and parcel of the Lutheran heritage, that the orthodox Lutheran Church has always been conscious of its full agreement with the Church Fathers on these points. The following references are all taken from the great Lutheran seventeenth-century dogmatician Johann Gerhard (1582–1637), who brings them in his famous *Loci*. It should not be forgotten that the word "patrology" originally is taken from his great collections of patristic material, and that the Lutherans, especially the so called Gnesio-Lutherans in the sixteenth century, were the first to open this field for scholarly theological investigation. Gerhard's quotations were revived in the nineteenth century by the great Lutheran confessionalist and liturgist Wilhelm Loehe of Neuendettelsau (1808–72), who reprinted them in his *Drei Bücher von der Kirche* (*Three Books on the Church*). It should not astonish you to hear that Loehe's most well-known follower today is Professor Martin Wittenberg, to whose work on fellowship I have already referred you.

The Lutheran fathers of all times have thus reverently listened to the testimony of St. Basil the Great, who, himself plagued by a heretical majority in his diocese, as we know, speaks of the three men in the fire and writes: "They teach us what should be done when no one is of our opinion. In the middle of the flames they praised God; they looked not upon the multitude which spoke against them, but were satisfied to be in agreement though they were only three."

Theodoret the Lector (early sixth century) mentions in his church history an exchange of words between Pope Liberius (352–366) and the Arian emperor, who asked the pope: "How large a part of the earth have you behind you, who contradict in this way?" Liberius answered: "Through my loneliness the Word of Truth loses nothing. There were also once only three who put themselves against the edict of the king."

Also against the Arians, St. Gregory of Nazianzus (329–389) writes the following words: "Where are they who judge the church by number and despise the little flock, who measure the divinity with measure and place the people so high, who place sand high and despise the light of the world, who collect mussels and despise pearls? They have the houses, we the inhabitants—they have the churches, we God; yea, we are the temple of the living God, a living sacrifice, a spiritual burnt offering. They have the people, we have the angels; they audacity and daring, we the faith; they threats, we prayers; they gold and silver, we the pure doctrine of the faith."

St. John Chrysostom speaks the same language: "What is most useful, to have much straw rather than precious stones? Not in the number of the multitude but in the sincerity of the strength consists the true majority. Elia was only one, but the whole world did suffice not to outweigh him."

To sum up, we quote St. Jerome (ca. 342–420), who says against a Pelagian: "That you have many like you will not at all make you a Catholic; on the contrary it proves that you are a heretic."

II. The Lutheran Church

1. Martin Luther on Church Fellowship

In his famous letter to the Christians of Frankfurt on the Main[11] of 1533, we find Luther's doctrine on church fellowship very well illustrated. That is probably the reason why it has not been translated in the new American edition of Luther's Works, and as the knowledge of German is quickly vanishing in Scandinavia and the USA, its content is likely to be forgotten. We should therefore the more carefully penetrate into it.

The Christians of Frankfurt on the Main, who are exposed to Luther's violent attacks, are no ordinary fanatics or even Zwinglians. They are rather a church of what later on would be called the Melanchthonian type. Luther's epistle especially arouses a great deal of discontent with the mediating theologian Martin Bucer (1491–1551), the man who is today hailed by Stephen Charles Neill as "the most constant promoter of church unity among all the sixteenth-century church leaders."[12] He finished his life as an Anglican professor in Cambridge, having been the adviser of Archbishop Thomas Cranmer in his creation of the constitutive

11 [See above, pp. 1–19.]

12 Neill, *History of the Ecumenical Movement*, 44.

documents of the Anglican Church. The editors of the German edition of Luther's works rightly say about Bucer that: "In this letter he saw his own mediating position to the Lord's Supper attacked, a position which veiled the contradictions and variations in it."[13]

Luther in his letter does not only attack false doctrine but also and even more the unwillingness to stand up for what the opponents believe to be true. They do not wish to fight for their own doctrine. Luther aptly formulates the nature of the conflict: "Thereto belongs a twofold hell: one that they contradict the Word of God, the other that they deny and do not freely confess their own teaching which they praise as the Word of God."[14] The conflict between Luther and his ecumenical opponents is thus not primarily a disagreement about the Sacrament, but it is a conflict about the nature of the conflict, where Luther sees the conflict as decisive for the unity of the Church while the others do not. The Christians of Frankfurt want to keep the interpretation of the dogma open, in this case the doctrine of the real presence, and have found that it is enough to believe that which Christ meant, to believe that we receive what Christ meant. This ecumenical attitude is to Luther a purely satanic dishonesty: "Who would not gladly be a pupil here? When we get tired of the labor of teaching and preaching and can refer the burden of both to Christ and say: I believe what Christ says?"[15]

As a consequence of this looseness and defective concept of faith, the pastors in Frankfurt no longer hold any confessional altar but exercise Communion in sacred things without dogmatic restrictions. Luther's reaction to this kind of Communion is vehement. He does not see it as the triumph of Christian love but of pure evil. Luther makes clear that a Lutheran who out of ignorance takes part in that kind of Eucharist is miserably deceived and receives only bread and wine, as the Reformed Lord's Supper is no sacrament. Furthermore, Luther writes: "It is terrible for me to hear that in the same church and the same altar both parts should take and receive the same sacrament, and one part should believe it receives mere bread and wine but the other part believe it receives the true body and blood of Christ. I often doubt that it really is possible that a preacher or pastor could be so hardened and wicked and keep silent about it and let both parts go according to its own faith. If there is such a man, he must have a heart which is harder than any stone, steel, or diamond. He must truly be an apostle of wrath. . . . These fellows must be the right high archdevils who give me only bread and wine and let me regard it as the body and blood of Christ and thus be so miserably deceived."[16]

---

13 WA 30/3:555.

14 WA 30/3:560.

15 WA 30/3:562.

16 WA 30/3:565.

As a defense of the altar, the use of the confessional is stressed. Luther speaks in this context not about the confessional as the place where the Sacrament of Holy Absolution is given, but as a place where the father confessor can scrutinize the Christian faith of the penitent and examine him or her about the catechism. He says, "But it is true that if the preachers give mere bread and wine as a sacrament, it is not important to whom they give it, or what those who receive it know and believe. There one pig eats with the other. . . . We will not and cannot give the Sacrament to anyone unless he has first been examined as to what he has learned from the catechism and if he wants to leave his sins which he has committed. For we do not want to make out of the Church of God a pigsty, and let everyone go unexamined to the Sacrament, as the pigs run to the trough. Such churches we leave to the enthusiasts. And such we have received from the beginning of Christendom."[17] So Luther well knows that the closed, fenced altar, protected by the pastor in his confessional, is a heritage from the Ancient Church, never to be given up.

After this penetration into Luther's defense of the closed, confessional altar, we can turn to a number of statements where Luther deals with the difficulties that arise when an orthodox Christian lives in an area with only heretical administration of the Sacrament. In a letter to Queen Mary of Hungary in August 1530 [WA Br 5:527; StL 10:2228; Aland Br 1674] it is made clear that all Communion with the Romans under one form is impossible. So is also any kind of lay celebration. Thus one has to keep away from the Sacrament forever, which in such a case is no sin. In Augsburg in 1533 Luther points to the possibility of creating a congregation of one's own in order to get the Sacrament, if one no longer wishes to travel to an orthodox congregation for one's Communion [WA Br 6:492; 6:507]. In Luther's famous *Table Talk*, we find that Luther regards it as impossible to commune with the Bohemians, the followers of John Hus, as they have fellowship with the pope, which would make the Lutherans partakers of popery. Luther apparently has in mind the fact that the Bohemians made use of occasionally visiting Roman bishops to get their new priests ordained.

2. The Lutheran Church on Church Fellowship

As strongly as Luther, the Lutheran Confessions defend the closed altar and the examination of the communicants. In the Lutheran churches that subscribed to these documents, the doctrine of fellowship was followed as strongly as in the Ancient Church. *These churches formed a conscious, confessionally-minded fellowship, knowing about its borders from the very beginning.* It is wrong to assume that this consciousness grew only gradually, as time passed and the souls hardened in their attitude of defense. We can see this in the formulations by Luther' closest

17 WA 30/3:567.

friend, the bishop of Naumburg, Nicholas von Amsdorf (1483–1565), when he excommunicates a priest who has committed the blasphemous and heretical act of distributing an unconsecrated host at the celebration of the Sacrament. This man is not to be tolerated "in our Christian church," that is, "in the fellowship of all Wittenbergian Christian churches." The word "Wittenbergian" here apparently serves as the name of denomination, pointing to churches that receive one another's communicants but also accept the excommunication issued by one particular church or bishop. In principle this fellowship reaches also outside the churches that have passed through the reformation of the Latin Church at the beginning of the sixteenth century. In one case Luther is known to have issued a letter of recommendation for an Ethiopian deacon, Michael. The intention is apparently to make it possible for Michael to receive the Sacrament; the similarity between the outward forms of the Lutheran and Ethiopian eucharistic liturgy being stressed. Michael was said to have accepted all our articles of faith, "*omnibus nostris articulis*." This unexpected declaration of fellowship between the Wittenbergian churches and the Church of Ethiopia may have been based upon a misunderstanding, but it yet speaks about the openness of Luther's mind and his consciousness of belonging to the Church of the holy Fathers.

When negotiations about Church unity took place, as in Wittenberg in 1536, no joint Communion could take place until full agreement had been reached. In Marburg in 1529 no joint eucharistic celebration occurred, as Zwingli was refused the hand of brotherhood. In this connection I wish to make clear that it is a mistake when it is said that Luther would in some way have admitted prayer fellowship with the Reformed at that occasion. When grace is being mentioned once in the sources, common meals apparently not existing as a rule, it is said or sung by Luther, assisted in the responsories and hymns by summoned schoolboys. At this occasion only one non-Lutheran is present, which does not mean more than he observed the passive presence acceptable to anyone.

This abstinence from joint prayer was as a rule respected by both parts. In 1645, at the so-called charitable colloquy at Thorn in Poland between Roman Catholics, Reformed, and Lutherans, the Roman Catholic president demands, however, that the Lutherans, the "domini Augustani," the men of the Augsburg Confession, must pray with the Roman Catholics and the Reformed. The Lutherans reject this proposal, referring to a custom established already at the colloquy at Ratisbon in 1541 but also to the belief of the Romans: "The Roman Catholic part prohibits prayer with heretics," a fact well-known to every English schoolboy from the words of the Roman Catholic Mary, Queen of Scots, to the ambitiously assisting but entirely undesired Anglican clergyman on the scaffold of Fotheringay: "I shall not say Amen to your prayers nor you to mine." This common, ecumenical ground should be observed. The men of the Augsburg Confession demand that when the Romans have finished their prayers, they should be permitted to say theirs. This is, however, not granted, and instead it is decided that the men of the Augsburg Confession may be absent from the common prayers, say their prayers in another room, and then join the others. The Lutherans have carefully developed their many arguments on this point; no less than seventeen carefully worded reasons were presented. First among them is the simple, biblical: "The apostle forbids fellowship with darkness and the spiritual Babylon, 2 Corinthians 6 and Revelation 18." The church orders of the Lutheran Church fully correspond to this persuasion. It is made clear, for example, in the Swedish Church Order of 1571 that exclusion from the fellowship of the Church does not only include the Sacrament but also all the liturgy as well, though presence during the sermon is permitted.

In the church oders of the seventeenth century it is presupposed that the altar is literally fenced, that is, by a rood screen with one or two doors, through which the communicants had to pass under the scrutinizing eye of the pastor and verger. This rood screen has often been thought to have been a medieval introduction to separate priests and laity, destroyed by the Reformation in the name of the priesthood of all believers. This is all wrong. It was built by orthodox Lutherans, who believed in the closed altar. The attitude that we have now described was observed in its full strictness also at the deathbed of a heretic. The drafts for different Swedish church orders in the seventeenth century, as well as their final version, the Church Order of 1686, make clear that not even this situation can change the fundamental laws of church fellowship. Yet the prescriptions for the conduct of a clergyman, summoned to a dying heretic, show the greatest pastoral concern for the dying and his eternal welfare. All doctrinal disputes must be kept away from the deathbed; only the atonement and its universality must be proclaimed. No "controversial and deep questions and disputes" are permitted, but the Lutheran pastor is only to draw the dying person "through the word of truth to believe and confess that God wants all men to be saved, and that Christ died for all and therefore calls all sinners to Him." The stress on the universality may point to the fact that the dying person is probably Reformed and that the soul-destroying heresy of limited atonement must be refuted. In the case that the dying person would request to be received into the bosom of the Evangelical Lutheran Church, rejecting his former heresies, he is, of course, immediately granted access to the Sacraments. If this conversion does not take place, he is to hear "the general promises of grace."

The draft to the Danish-Norwegian Church Order of 1685 repeats the same prescriptions, stressing that "a good servant and priest of God ought to conform himself to the old rule that has always been kept in the Church of Christ: "*Infideles non prius ad societatem communionis admittantur, nisi haeresi legitime abnegata*," which means: "No unbeliever should be admitted to the fellowship of Communion, until he has properly rejected his heresy." An interesting example of how such a case could be treated with pastoral tact and Christian care is the deathbed of the non-Lutheran, Reformed philosopher, historian, and politician Hugo

Grotius (1583–1645), who, shipwrecked and dying after a storm in the Baltic, was cared for by a prominent Lutheran professor of theology at the faculty of Rostock, Johann Quistorp Sr., summoned to the deathbed. Quistorp afterward wrote to the leading man of Lutheran Orthodoxy, Abraham Calovius, that Grotius died as a pious, penitent sinner, trusting in the merits of Christ. So acted, wrote, and felt the men of Lutheran Orthodoxy, all of whom observed so very carefully the limits of church fellowship.

In order to avoid all misunderstanding we should stress that, though not only the Sacrament but also the entire liturgy was regarded as not belonging to those not of the household of faith, there was always the possibility for visitors to observe a passive presence to their own edification. We have, for example, descriptions of the Lutheran High Mass in the Great Church of Stockholm by members of the French embassy to the Swedish court, which convey the greatest admiration of what was seen and heard. Other similar reports also exist.

3. The Abolition of the Lutheran Doctrine of Church Fellowship

We have now seen the theory and praxis on fellowship as observed in the Lutheran Church. We know already, however, that these conditions did not last, and that they would eventually not only be changed but even entirely forgotten. What we have brought forth in this essay is thus likely to cause surprise and even doubt as to its veracity. How did the change come about?

We already know that there were Reformed influences behind the development to come, but it may be a bit one-sided to merely blame the Reformed. A deviation from the Christian revelation lies after all within the capacity of all flesh, even non-Reformed. No one has to learn to sin, as we know how to do that by ourselves. Powers were at work within Lutheranism itself that would eventually bring forth the change. We now look more closely at these events.

Some of the occurrences that look like a breakdown of the ancient principle of church fellowship are really at closer inspection in accordance with it. Such are the cases of the so called *simultaneum*, when one and the same church was used by two different confessions, mostly Lutherans and Roman Catholics. This did not imply any real breakdown of the walls of fellowship but was a kind of arrangement by the civil authorities, whereby the recurring question about the right to a certain church was solved in this Solomonic way. Other cases were far more serious. It could, for example, happen, as in Halberstadt in Germany, that the canonical hours were sung together by Lutheran and Roman Catholic canons. The solemn Mass was celebrated by a Lutheran priest under the assistance of a Roman Catholic deacon, which deeply upset visiting prelates from Rome, who reported these things to the pope. Yet such things, in themselves undoubtedly contrary to all sound principles of fellowship, were never based on dogmatic convictions. They were only practical arrangements for some much too practical reason, exactly as when, under Chemnitz's vehement protests, his duke, Julius of Brunswick, ordained two of his sons Roman Catholic priests simply to get a sufficient princely income for them. Detestable as such a thing sounds and soul destroying to those involved, it hardly constituted a habit to be continued.

In my opinion, the first signs of a breakdown of the principle of fellowship can be detected in connection with infant Baptism. Both the church orders of the seventeenth century as well as dogmaticians of that time such as Johann Gerhard and David Hollazius admit Lutheran Baptism of infants whose parents are heretics, rejecting Lutheranism, and also the possibility of Lutheran parents calling for a heretical Baptism of their child. What makes this far more serious than the other cases is the kind of defense that is offered in favor of such a practice. Gerhard sees the case of Lutheran parents using a heretic pastor to baptize as defensible, because (1) such a Baptism is apparently valid, (2) because in the Old Testament the evil high priest always was in possession of his ministry, (3) because the parent could always at the time of the Baptism protest against the pastor's heresy, (4) because there are always a few real believers even in a heretical church. These theological grounds could later on be taken over by the pietistic movement, which repeated all these four arguments for completely breaking down all respect for the fellowship principle, staying in a heretical church body despite its shortcomings. The four reasons can defend anything and have defended anything.

If we now turn to the Reformed who once were to take advantage of concessions of the type mentioned, we must first make a kind of reservation to our former description of them. When the ecumenically minded Bucer of Strassburg succeeded in establishing church fellowship with Wittenberg—we must add: through pure deception and false double talk—his more serious-minded brethren in Zürich prohibited Swiss students studying in Strassburg from taking Communion there anymore in order not be tainted by the Lutheran heresy. Similar examples of a Reformed strict observance of the fellowship principle exist.

Yet it remains true that at bottom the broad-minded attitude of the Reformed as to what was regarded "not essential" made them open to Communion with the Lutherans. The Calvinist synod of Charentone, the Calvinist chief church in Paris, in 1631 formally through a decision opened the holy tables for any Lutheran. We must consider that the same Calvinists were in full fellowship with the Church of England, as the famous Bible commentator Archbishop Ussher of Armagh (1581–1656) points out: "I profess that with like affection I should receive the blessed Sacrament at the hands of Dutch ministers if I were in Holland, as I should at the hands of the French ministers if I were in Charentone."[18] Archbishop Wake

18 Samuel Miller, *The Primitive and Apostolic Order of the Church of Christ Vindicated* (Philadelphia: Presbyterian Board of Education, 1840), 324.

of Canterbury (1657–1737) erected in 1717 a formally recognized church fellowship between the Church of England and the Reformed Church of Zürich. When in 1718 an invitation for closer cooperation was issued from some English bishop to the Lutheran Church of Sweden, it was thus self-evidently strongly rejected by the responsible Swedish bishops. To have Communion with a church which was in fellowship with the chief churches of the Reformed faith was naturally impossible.

The way to break down the Lutheran stiffness on fellowship went, however, through a more general approach to the matter, that is, through the introduction of open Communion without any confessional demands. In 1857, the bishop of London A. C. Tait (1811–32), later archbishop of Canterbury, celebrated the first open Communion at a YMCA conference. Although the future archbishop thus seems to have been a liberal-minded person, it did not mean that he lacked firm persuasions. In church history he is remembered as a firm persecutor of those conservatives believing in the real presence and practicing private Confession. In some cases his victims among the Anglo-Catholic clergy had to spend a considerable time in prison. Besides, he insisted, though in vain, that the Athanasian Creed should be abolished from the Anglican Divine Service. These features give you a certain insight into the kind of ecumenism at work. The liberal attitude knows its limits. This development within the established church circles had its full counterpart in the so-called evangelical circles. C. H Spurgeon (1834–92), the famous revivalist and denier of baptismal regeneration, could preach against those not practicing open Communion using Jude 19: "It is these who cause divisions, worldly people, devoid of the Spirit." Confessionalism is thus to Spurgeon the only thing that separates from the Church universal.

The final attack on the Lutheran Church was to take place in Germany, where for many centuries the Calvinist House of Hohenzollern waited for the moment when it could fulfill the will of the so-called Great Elector Frederick Wilhelm (1640–86) to "exterminate the ungodly ceremonies of the Lutherans." By virtue of being what he called "der oberste Bischof," "the supreme bishop," the Prussian king Frederick Wilhelm III (1797–1840) commanded in 1830 all his subjects, Lutherans and Reformed alike, to commune together. Everyone was permitted to keep his own former beliefs, but through common Communion one had to concede that these beliefs were not church divisive. In most places the ecumenical celebration of the Sacrament took place with the obedient subjects marching toward the altar to military regiment music. In a special decree of "The State Department for Church, School, and Medicine" a warning was issued against those who used the apostolic warnings against fellowship with heretics as referring to his majesty's newly created church and its officers. The warning was necessary. The faithful Lutherans refused to celebrate with the Calvinists and were in some cases thrown into prison. The Lutheran Church was persecuted. Its priests could only administer the means of grace during nighttime. Only after a long time of hard suffering were the Lutherans conceded freedom of religion, at which time many Lutherans had already emigrated to foreign countries. The so-called Union was then gradually introduced all over Germany. It can now be said to have been established everywhere with the exception of the small independent Lutheran churches.

The Scandinavian Lutheran churches were naturally not involved in the German development. They were approached by the Reformed spirit in other ways. Before we treat this, however, it is necessary to make clear that the entire foundation of the established churches both in Germany and in Scandinavia had been thoroughly undermined by skepticism and denial among the educated classes. It is interesting to study how the undoubtedly Reformed initiatives of the pious Prussian king were welcomed by his officials on a plainly secular basis. The Reformed faith, open Communion, and ecumenism appeared to these people to be more according to the times, more civilized, more enlightened, while Lutheranism stood for the Middle Ages, for belief in satanic powers, for mysterious, superstitious Sacraments, for dogmas. The choice was not difficult. The Reformed attack had been well-prepared, yea, actually anticipated, and when it came, it would after some time be absorbed by the secular powers that had helped it to open the Lutheran Church doors.

In 1908 the first contacts between the Church of England and the Church of Sweden started which later led to full intercommunion. In 1929 in Uppsala and in 1927 in Canterbury the first joint episcopal consecrations took place. They did not continue during the time 1959–76 because of the introduction of priestesses in Sweden, but since the Church of England came to share the official Swedish view, the joint episcopal consecrations started anew. It is, of course, apparent that the existence of the apostolic succession in the Church of Sweden has been the main cause for the Anglican approach. If we turn the question and ask why the Swedes accepted this approach, we have to face two important forces. First of all, the Swedes were not immune to the general development and the general dissolution of dogmatic Christianity that had dominated the theological world for such a long time. Second, they had in their midst a person who was about to create the worldwide ecumenical movement, the future Archbishop Nathan Söderblom (1866–1931). He was an extreme theological modernist, who, according to one of his admiring biographers, Bishop Tor Andrae of Linköping, introduced a total reformation of the Christian religion, "*to the exclusion of everything supernatural*." Söderblom could himself state that the Christian religion as we know it in the history of the Church and in its creeds was "doomed." No single letter of Holy Writ was left. Söderblom wanted to replace this former Christian religion by two substitutes. The first was mysticism, Christian and non-Christian, hence his great interest in St. Bridget of Sweden and her mystical revelations. The second one was the ecumenical movement, which should use the impressive structure of the established churches, their cathedrals, liturgies, and offices to acquire a role in political life, the new task of the new religion after the disappearance of "everything supernatural." Here unlimited church fellowship becomes absolutely necessary. Here we find the reason why we are not permitted to hear one single word about the testimony about church fellowship from the lips of the Church Fathers and reformers. Any indication about the presence of such a belief is to open a door which must remain closed to the ecumenists of today.

The claim for intercommunion today never stops but must go on, until limitless intercommunion is practiced. After the Lutherans in Germany had accepted the Reformed at their altars, they soon had to accept also Methodists, Baptists, and Mennonites. This is natural because the presumption of all modern negotiations about church fellowship is that there is no certain truth, that we live in a darkness where any claim to possess the truth is immoral. So the emissaries of the archbishop of Canterbury who knock at the church doors of the Cathedral of Riga have not come to make the Latvians Anglicans nor to make them believe as the *Common Prayer Book*. They are there to tell the Latvians what Luther already saw as the real motive behind Martin Bucer, the grandfather of Anglicanism, that everyone is saved by his own faith. Against this we must cling to Luther's admonition to the Christians in Frankfurt on the Main to keep to the fenced, confessional altar, not to let "everyone unexamined go to the Sacrament, as the pigs run to the trough. Such a church we leave to the enthusiasts. And this we have received from the beginning of Christendom."[19]

19 WA 30/3:567.

CHAPTER FOURTEEN

C. F. W. WALTHER ON ADMISSION TO THE LORD'S SUPPER

TRANSLATED BY CHRISTIAN TIEWS[1]

ARTICLE 15
ANNOUNCEMENT FOR THE LORD'S SUPPER

Because a preacher should be not only a teacher but also a shepherd, bishop, and watchman (Ephesians 4:11; 1 Timothy 3:1; Hebrews 13:17; Ezekiel 3:17–21); not only a distributor of the holy Sacraments but also a steward over them (1 Corinthians 4:1); and [because he] has the earnest command not to give what is holy to dogs or to throw his pearls before pigs (Matthew 7:6); he therefore has the holy obligation to require that those who wish to receive the Holy Supper *announce* personally beforehand and to use [the announcement] faithfully and wisely for an *examination*. (Cf. above, Article 6, comment 7.)

COMMENT 1

First, as far as the *necessity* of the so-called announcement for Communion is concerned, let us include here an essay in volume 4, number 21 of *Der Lutheraner*. It is entitled "Something on the Custom of Also Inviting People to Participate in the Celebration of the Holy Supper Who Have Not Gone to Confession." The following saying of Chrysostom precedes the essay as an epigram: "I would sooner lose *my* body and life than to allow the body of the *Lord* to be given to someone unworthily, and I would sooner have *my* blood shed than sanction giving *His* most

1 The following is from chapters 15, 16, and 18 of Walther's *Americanish=Lutherische Pastoraltheologie*, (St. Louis: Concordia, 1906). This text has been amended from the translation of Christian C. Tiews published in Walther's Works: *Pastoral Theology*, ed. David W. Loy (St. Louis: Concordia, 2017).

holy blood to an unworthy person" (*Hom. 83 in Matthew*). The essay itself is the following.

> Not a few preachers of this country are in the habit, whenever they carry out the celebration of the Holy Supper, of first addressing all those gathered and inviting them all—not even excluding the members of other confessions who are present—to participate. In particular the German Methodist preachers here ["in America," *hiesigen*] use this means to make inroads with scattered German Protestants living here. The latter have often had to go for years without public preaching and receiving the Lord's Supper; if a Methodist preacher now comes one time into their loneliness, and if he not only preaches to them but also does not even put the smallest obstacle in the way of celebrating the Lord's Supper among them and readily accepting each one,[2] then with that he has usually already won the people for himself. He uses the Holy Supper as bait, that is, as a cheap means of coaxing souls into the net of his enthusiasm and sectarianism.
>
> But wouldn't even many so-called "*Lutheran*" preachers like to follow a similar practice (manner of acting)! Yet we have—unfortunately!—experienced that not a few of even those preachers who call themselves Lutheran (in the belief that this is properly evangelical [or "Gospel-centered," *evangelisch*]), when they have prepared the holy table for the administration of the Sacrament, now call everyone who wants to come to this offering of grace and admit [them] without an examination of their faith and life. In fact, it is to be feared that many act in this way out of the impure motive of being seen among the members of all parties as truly "dear, open-minded" men and being praised as such; it is to be feared that many surrender the Holy Sacrament to everyone and even serve it to the manifestly godless because they also want to be in good standing with the godless, do not want to bring the anger and hatred of the world upon themselves, and do not want to lose their somewhat lucrative pastorate. For it is certainly true: there is hardly anything in all of pastoral care [*Seelsorge*] that causes more trouble for a faithful minister of the Church than wanting to deal conscientiously with admission to the Holy Supper. If an orthodox Lutheran preacher takes responsibility for a new congregation, and if he now does not want to admit any of its members to the table of the Lord until he has spoken with and heard from the mouth of every single one that he believes in God's Word from the heart, that he sincerely longs for grace and the forgiveness of sins in Christ's blood, that he also has the earnest intent to follow Christ in a holy life unstained by the world, and the like—what harsh resistance he then usually runs into immediately! How many enemies he then usually makes for himself immediately by doing so! How seldom it then continues without divisions ensuing! How often does he see himself immediately

2 [Literally, "does not cause the least amount of trouble regarding inviting each one of them." CCT].

forced to take up his walking staff again and still to have it said of him that he wanted to lord it over the congregation! —

What? Is a preacher doing the right thing in this if he would rather endure everything—in fact, even give up his ministry—than admit someone to the Holy Supper without examination? Is the generosity of many preachers in this country in this regard really so reprehensible? We reply yes! But in order to judge properly in this matter, it is necessary first to consider what kind of matter the Holy Supper is.

This is a very different matter than preaching the divine Word; the Word is given not only to keep a believer in the faith but also to awaken a person out of the sleep of sin, to bring him to knowledge of his sins, to repentance, and to faith, and to convert [him]. In fact, without the Word, all of this is impossible. For this reason, of course, no one can and should be turned away from the preaching of the Word, for this would be locking the only door of grace on him.

It is not the same with the Holy Supper. Through it a person is not to be *brought* to repentance and grace in the first place, but *strengthened* in them; through it a person is not to *obtain* grace and *become* a Christian in the first place, but the grace obtained through the Word is to be sealed in him and he is to be *kept, preserved*, and *nurtured* in Christianity; through this Meal a person is not *awakened* to life through [*aus*] God in the first place, but is to be *nourished* and *refreshed* when he is already spiritually alive. Therefore, whoever wants to receive the Holy Supper in a worthy manner and for his salvation must already have come to repentance and faith beforehand; he must already have received grace and become a true Christian beforehand, must already beforehand have been awakened to life through God and been born again [*wiedergeboren*].[3] Therefore, only someone who has already become a child of God through the washing of rebirth—that is, through Holy Baptism—should receive the Holy Supper, just as in the Old Testament only he was allowed to partake of the paschal lamb who had already been received into the divine covenant of grace through the sacrament of circumcision.

To partake of the Holy Supper is not a good thing per se. Instead, it depends on *how* one partakes of it. It does not work by virtue of simply being done

3 *Luther* writes concerning this in his *Church Postil*: "Christ also did the same: He preached to the crowds, to everyone, as the apostles also [did] later, so everyone heard it, believers and unbelievers. Anyone could take hold of it. We must also do the same. But we should not cast the *Sacrament* to the people in the crowd in this way as the pope did. When I preach the Gospel, I do not know whom it touches. But here *I should believe* that it *has* touched the one who comes to the Sacrament. I must not doubt this, but be certain that the person to whom I give the Sacrament has grasped the Gospel and believes rightly—just as if I were to baptize someone. In the same way, he who takes it or gets baptized should not doubt" (*Kirchenpostille, Am Ostertag, vom Empfang des heiligen Sacraments*. See StL 11:608ff.).

[*ex opere operato*]![4] It is not like a medicine that one need only ingest for it to work; it is rather a treasure trove whose riches can be taken, gathered, and retained only by the hand of faith. Whoever does not have faith certainly also receives the real and whole Sacrament—that is, he receives not just bread and wine but actually and truly [receives] in, with, and under these elements the body and blood of Jesus Christ in his mouth as a precious pledge of grace and forgiveness. However, he goes away devoid of the blessing for the salvation of his soul which lies in it. For how can a pledge, however precious and valuable it may be, help a person, and how can it serve to assure him of a matter, if he does not believe that it is such a precious and valuable pledge? — Yet whoever partakes of the Holy Supper without the correct faith and thus unworthily will not only not receive the grace which lies in it but will also find in it instead of grace, wrath; instead of life, death; instead of blessing, curse. He becomes, as St. Paul writes, "guilty of the body and blood of the Lord. [. . .] He eats and drinks judgment on himself by not discerning the body of the Lord" [1 Corinthians 11:27, 29]. Terrifying is the sin one commits, and dreadful the ruin he brings down on himself, if he partakes unworthily of the Lord's Supper; and those who say, "But we should be glad that people are still coming to the Holy Supper," thereby reveal the sad condition of their knowledge of this Holy Sacrament.

Another unique characteristic of the Holy Supper—and of the holy Sacraments in general—is that it belongs to the hallmarks [*Charakteren*], to the banners of the church, and to the seals of doctrine and faith (Romans 4:11; see also 1 Corinthians 10:21; Exodus 12:48). The church in which one participates in the Holy Supper is the church and doctrine that one confesses. There can be no deeper brotherly fellowship than that in which one meets those in whose fellowship one receives the Holy Supper. "For," the holy apostle says, "as often as you eat this bread and drink the cup, you *proclaim* the Lord's death until He comes" (1 Corinthians 11:26), and "because there is one bread, we who are *many* are *one body*, for we all partake of the one bread" (1 Corinthians 10:17). So there is a great difference between listening along to a sermon in a different church fellowship one time and participating in the celebration of the Holy Supper there. One can certainly listen along to the preaching there on occasion—perhaps to get to know the doctrine of that group—without thereby participating in a heterodox worship service. By contrast, Holy Communion is an act of confession; if one communes in a different church [*in einer fremden Kirche*], one actually joins it, acts as a witness for its teaching, and declares its members to be one's brothers and sisters in the faith.

This being the case, what should we make of the custom of inviting everyone present to participate without distinction during the celebration of the

4 [Literally, "by carrying out the work," that is, performing it without faith in Christ, as if it were a magic trick. CCT]

Holy Supper and of admitting [communicants] without examination? — Preachers who do not themselves believe that the body and blood of the Son of God are present in the Holy Supper and are received by all participants, preachers who believe the Holy Supper is a mere memorial meal, a mere ceremony, such as the Reformed, Methodist, and most United-Evangelical [*Unirtevangelischen*]—it is entirely natural for them to do this. But when those who want to be *Lutheran* preachers and are persuaded of the truth of the Lutheran doctrine of the Holy Supper act in this way, it is inexcusable.

First, such preachers are acting against the command of God: "Do not . . . take part in the sins of others" (1 Timothy 5:22). For whoever can prevent a sin, yet not only fails to prevent it but actually promotes it, makes himself a participant in it. Now those preachers could certainly quite often prevent the terrible sin of participating in the Lord's Supper unworthily, but they not only fail to do so—partly out of fear of people, partly out of a desire to please people—but they even promote this sin with their careless invitations. Oh, how terrible their responsibility will therefore be some day! How terrified they will one day be, when God reckons to them as their own all the guilt against the body and blood of Christ which the unrepentant, unbelieving, and false believing people admitted by the [preachers] *without any examination* brought upon themselves! Certainly, if unworthy communicants will be damned one day, then those who tempted them to it will have to suffer a tenfold damnation. *Luther* writes in the *Unterricht für die Visitatoren*, "One should also not permit anyone to go to the Holy Sacrament unless he has been *individually examined* by his pastor as to whether he is fit to go to the Holy Sacrament. For St. Paul says in 1 Corinthians 11:27 that those who receive it unworthily are guilty of the body and blood of Christ. *Now not only is the Sacrament dishonored by those who receive it unworthily but also by those who distribute it negligently to the unworthy.*"

On top of this, in doing so a preacher commits a particularly grave sin by being an unfaithful, careless, and unscrupulous caretaker of souls [or "pastor," *Seelsorger*]. The Word of the Lord in the prophet Ezekiel, ch. 3:17–18, applies to every preacher: "Son of man, I have made you a *watchman* for the house of Israel. Whenever you hear a word from My mouth, you shall give them *warning* from Me. If I say to the wicked, 'You shall surely die,' and you give him no warning, nor speak to warn the wicked from his wicked way, in order to save his life, that wicked person shall die for his iniquity, but *his blood I will require at your hand*." The Word of the Lord spoken to Peter also applies to every preacher: "I will give you the keys of the kingdom of heaven, and whatever *you bind on earth* shall be bound in heaven, and whatever you loose on earth shall be loosed in heaven" (Matthew 16:19). The apostolic word applies to every preacher: "Make an effort to present yourself to God as an upright and blameless worker *who rightly divides the word of truth* [. . .] and *correct[s]* the rebellious. God may perhaps grant them repentance leading to a knowledge of the truth, and they may come to their senses and escape from the snare of the devil, after being captured by him to do his will" (2 Timothy 2:15, 25–26). It says about all righteous preachers: "They *are keeping watch over your souls, as those who will have to give an account*" (Hebrews 13:17).

A preacher does the opposite of all that [these passages] expect of him as a caretaker of souls if he admits everyone to the Holy Supper without examination. He should proclaim to the godless, "You must die," but by admitting him to the table of grace he says to him, "You shall live." He should bind the unrepentant, yet he looses them. He should correct the rebellious so that they come to repentance, yet he proclaims them righteous, so that they become even more recalcitrant. He should guard their souls, yet he turns out to be a "silent dog" who, as Isaiah 56:10 states, "cannot rebuke, [who is] lazy, lies down, and loves to sleep." He should help souls out of sin and damnation, yet he bolsters them in their impenitence and only plunges them ever deeper into sin, God's wrath, death, hell, and damnation. Alas, it is certain that, no matter how fervent a preacher might be otherwise, if he does not *to the best of his ability* protect souls from unworthily receiving the most Holy Sacrament, even this one thing will make him blameworthy and will bring down on him a severe judgment as a hireling, as an unfaithful caretaker of souls, even as one who corrupts souls. This is why *Luther* writes in his incomparable *Vermahnung an die Pfarrherrn, wider den Wucher zu predigen* ["Warning to pastors to preach against usury"] in 1540: "If such usurers want to rage because you do not absolve them or administer the Sacrament to them or bury them . . . then say first that you are forbidden by God from regarding any usurer as a Christian. . . . 'And why should I put my soul on the line for you and stand by you and condemn myself with your sin because you are such a money grubber. . . . Nor would it help you—and it would condemn me—if I simply absolved you. For God and the emperor do not accept this in their law. Therefore, repent and do the right thing. If not, then you can just as well go to the devil singly without me and my Absolution as if you went to the devil as a duo with my Absolution and took me along, too, because of your guilt, although I was not guilty. No, fellow. What is appropriate is: "You go ahead; I will stay here." I am not a pastor so I can accompany everyone to the devil, but rather so I can bring everyone to God with me.' "

It is true, however, that a preacher must also consider that he is called by God to be a "*steward* of the mysteries of God" (1 Corinthians 4:1). Yet a steward cannot use and abuse what has been entrusted to him as he pleases without serious liability. Instead, he must abide by the instruction that he has been given for administering the office. But in the Holy Scripture we preachers have such instruction—and, in fact, the most fitting [instruction]—for properly administering the Holy Sacrament. It prescribes for us in clear words who may be admitted [and] who may not. Christ says, among other things: "Do not give dogs what is holy, and do not throw your pearls before pigs, lest they trample them underfoot and turn to attack you" (Matthew 7:6). Christ says furthermore: "If he refuses to listen even to the church, let him be to you as a Gentile and a tax collector" (Matthew 18:17). St. Paul writes further: "If there is someone who lets himself be called a brother and he is guilty of sexual immorality or greed, or is an idolater, reviler, drunkard, or swindler, *with him you shall also not eat.* [. . .] Remove from yourselves whoever is evil" (1 Corinthians 5:11, 13). The same apostle writes furthermore: "If anyone does not obey our word, mark him with a letter and *have nothing to do with him*, that he may be ashamed" (2 Thesalonians. 3:14). Finally, John writes in his Second Epistle: "If anyone comes to you and does not bring this teaching, do not receive him into your house or give him any greeting, for whoever greets him takes part in his wicked works" (2 John 10–11; cf. 2 Thessalonians 3:6; Romans 16:17; 1 Timothy 6:3–5; 2 Timothy 3:1–5; Titus 3:10–11; 2 Corinthians 6:14–18). Accordingly, Christians should not associate with anyone who is a manifest sinner, with anyone who despises the Christian congregation, with anyone who does not want to be disciplined, and with an unbeliever or heterodox person as if they have a brotherly fellowship of faith with him. For in [these passages] every preacher has the fitting instruction that God's Word gives him regarding the administration of the Sacrament. For it is obvious that all those with whom Christians do not have the brotherly fellowship of faith and whom they should exclude from themselves should also not be admitted to the Sacrament, through which the deepest brotherly fellowship of faith is expressed and brought about.

What, then, are preachers doing who admit everyone without distinction? They prove themselves to be unfaithful, careless stewards of the mysteries of God. They usurp God's office and make themselves *lords* over His Holy Sacrament when they are only His *ministers*. Woe to them forever and ever if they do not reflect on this at some point! There will come a day when they will have to atone terribly for having ruined the Lord's goods and for having misused them for their dishonest purposes. The Lord will summon them to Himself and will cry out to them: "What is this that I hear about you? Turn in an account of your management, for you can no longer be manager" (Luke 16:1–2).

However, some will perhaps say, "What should a preacher do to rescue his conscience?" In closing, I only want to have our Luther speak about this. He writes, namely, in his *The Christian Way to Go to the Lord's Table* [*Formula Missae et Communionis*] of 1523: "On this matter we should have the same procedure and order that we maintain in Baptism, namely, that the bishop or pastor is first *informed* which [people] wish to receive the Sacrament, and they should personally request that he give them the Holy Sacrament so that he may know their names and what kind of lives they lead. Then, even if they request it, he should still not admit them until they have given an answer regarding their *faith*, and especially given a response to the question whether they understand *what the Sacrament* ***is****, what it is useful for and* ***gives****, and to what end they want to* ***use*** *it*—that is, whether they can recite the words about the Sacrament with the explanation from memory and show that they go to the Table of the Lord because they, with a troubled conscience or a fear of death on account of sins, or plagued by some other tribulation of the flesh, the world, or the devil, hunger and thirst to receive the Word of grace and salvation from the Lord Himself through the ministry of the minister, so that they are comforted and strengthened, just as Christ has given and instituted this in this Lord's Supper out of inexpressible love with these words: 'Take and eat . . . .'

"But I believe that it is good enough for someone who desires the Sacrament to be questioned and examined in this way *once* a year. Indeed, he might have such a good understanding that he may be questioned once in his whole life—or not at all. For with this regulation we want to guard against the worthy and the unworthy running to the Table of the Lord together, as we have seen up until now under the papacy, where all that people sought was to *receive* the Sacrament. But the papists ignored the faith and gave it no second thought. But there was neither talk nor thoughts about faith, consolation, and the correct usage and benefit of the Sacrament—indeed, they took pains to hide the words of the Sacrament, which is the Bread of Life. Indeed, they treated it with the greatest senselessness, [claiming] that whoever received the Sacrament did a good work, which was good on account of its own worthiness, not that they received and strengthened faith through Christ's goods. However, we wish to exclude and separate from the fellowship of this Sacrament those who do not know how to respond to the points mentioned above as those who lack the wedding garment [cf. Matthew 22:12].

"Then, if the pastor or bishop sees that they understand all this, he should also pay attention to whether they *prove* their faith and knowledge by their *lives* and *habits*—for even Satan understands all these things and can also speak of them. That is, if [the pastor] sees a whoremonger, adulterer, drunkard, gambler, usurer, gossip, or [someone who] otherwise has a reputation for another manifest sin, he must certainly exclude him from the Lord's Supper, *unless he can prove with manifest signs that he has changed and improved his life.* However, not only should one *not deny* the Sacrament to the others who occasionally fall and return, and who are sorry that they have fallen, but they should also know that it is *instituted* precisely for their sake to refresh and strengthen them. 'For we all stumble in many ways' (James 3:2), and it is right that the one bears the other's burden, because the one is onerous for the other (Galatians 6:2). For here I am talking about the despisers, who sin unashamedly without fear and yet nonetheless boast greatly in the Gospel.

> "Regarding private confession before Communion, I still believe as I have taught up until now, namely, that it is unnecessary and should not be required, but is useful and is by no means to be despised" (see *Luther's Werke*, Halle [Walch] 10:2764–67).
>
> Our public confessional writings, incidentally, claim the same things that Luther says privately here. For example, Article XXV of the Augsburg Confession says, "The custom is preserved among us of not offering the Sacrament to those who have not been *examined* and absolved *beforehand*" [AC XXV; *Triglotta*, p. 69]. Furthermore, the fifteenth article of the Apology reads: "With us the people use the Lord's Supper willingly, without constraint, every Sunday, but *after having been first examined* as to whether they are instructed in Christian doctrine, whether they know and understand anything of the Lord's Prayer, the Creed, and the Ten Commandments" [Ap XV 40; *Triglotta*, p. 325].

Thus far the essay mentioned above.[5]

Incidentally, *announcement for Communion* is especially needful where *private confession* is not exercised. [The latter] was retained in our church in part precisely for the sake of what announcement for Communion should aim at. For example, the *faculty of theology at Wittenberg* writes as follows on June 15, 1619:

> We do not deny that *private confession* is not being used in all orthodox Lutheran churches, since the forgiveness of sins and worthy use of the Holy Supper is [there] in any case; therefore, the confessional is not prescribed to achieve these goals for anyone. But there are chiefly *three reasons for this institution*, namely:
>
> (1) So that the preacher and caretaker of souls has the opportunity to speak privately with each one who intends to go to the Lord's Table, to hear from him how he is prepared for it—whether he examines himself properly and sufficiently, whether he is sufficiently instructed in the doctrine, reconciles himself to his neighbor, seriously intends to set aside any coarse sins he might have [*behaftet*]—and thus whether [the pastor] can safely admit him. If a defect [*ein Defectus*] should also occur in the one and the other, it may be amended [or "restored," *erstattet*] with instruction and admonition.
>
> (2) If the hearer should have a *special concern* or should discover other vice in himself, and if he should wish to talk to his caretaker of souls on account of it and to receive instruction from him [*Bericht bei ihm zu holen begehrte*], he could have the best occasion [for doing so] in confession, since he should above all test and examine his conscience.

5 [C. F. W. Walther, "Etwas über die Sitte, bei der Feier des heiligen Abendmahls auch solche Leute, die nicht gebeichtet hatten, zur Teilnahme einzuladen," *Der Lutheraner* 4, no. 21(1848): 161–63. This translation is based on an unpublished translation by Joel Baseley. CCT]

(3) Thus also the grace of God and the forgiveness of sins that occur through Christ, which otherwise come to all believers corporately in the Word, are *personally applied* to a repentant sinner in confession. (*Consil. Witebergens.* 2:139)

Comment 2: Faithfulness in Using the Institution of Announcement for Communion

Faithful and wise use of the institution of announcement for Communion means that the preacher will focus solely on the salvation and blessing of the person wishing to commune and will above all explore the following:

1. Whether the person in question believes the Word of God to be the Word of God
2. Whether he knows what is necessary for salvation
3. Whether he realizes that he is a poor sinner, finds consolation in Christ's merit alone, and does not have evil intent in his heart (Psalm 66:18) or is still unreconciled with someone (Matthew 5:23–24)
4. Whether he believes in the mystery of the Holy Supper and seeks in it forgiveness as well as strengthening of faith and salvation
5. Whether in general he confesses the Lutheran Church and doctrine, as the latter is set down in Luther's Small Catechism, to be the true Christian Church and doctrine

In doing so, the preacher should make every effort not to scare off the simple or aggravate the reluctant with solemn, official airs and emotional affectation, nor to turn a friendly conversation into a rigorous examination or torture. The preacher must try to learn what is necessary according to the circumstances without the person who is being examined getting the impression that he is being examined. The greater the prejudices are in a new congregation against the institution of announcing for Communion if it has become unfamiliar to them, the more the preacher must avoid everything through which the members of the congregation could become suspicious and resistant to this institution. In order to win over those who oppose it out of ignorance, etc., the preacher must not let it irritate him to visit them personally, if they will not at all come to him, and to conduct the necessary examination in a thoughtful manner there. *Luther* writes to Pastor Balthasar Thuringen in Coburg: "I have written the pastor *that he should not torture unknowledgeable people with long examinations when they want to go to the Lord's Supper, yet should not admit them without examination and questioning.* For wanting to admit them without examination is not useful for anything. We rebuke the adversaries for serving their bellies, but our people are stubborn and hold grudges. I therefore ask you for God's sake to work very hard to teach the Gospel in a modest way" (Walch Edition 21:1348). It is despicable if a preacher uses announcement for Communion to pry into secret sins or family matters and to encourage boasting.

COMMENT 3: ANNOUNCEMENT FOR COMMUNION SHOULD NOT BE DEALT WITH LEGALISTICALLY

Not only is it *unnecessary* to examine each person *before every Communion* (it is sufficient to do this from time to time, roughly once per year), since examination is based not on a Law but only on the need of souls, but the actual exploration can even be *omitted altogether* for certain proven Christians [who are] known to be knowledgeable and upright. Thus Luther writes, for example:

> In addition to this freedom, we retain the practice that the penitent should relate several sins that oppress him most. And we do this not for the sake of those who understand, *for our pastor,*[6] *the chaplain,* M. *Philipp,*[7] *and such people who know very well what sin is—we do not demand this of them,* but because the dear *youth* are growing up every day and the common man understands little, for their sake we retain this practice, so that they will be trained in Christian discipline and understanding. For the point of this (private) confession is not that they list all their sins, but that they are *examined* as to whether they know the Lord's Prayer, the Creed, the Ten Commandments, and the other things in the Small Catechism. For we have certainly experienced that the common people and the youth learn little from preaching if they are not individually questioned and examined [*gefragt und verhöret wird*]. But where can one do this better and where is it more necessary than when they are preparing to go to the Sacrament? Certainly, when preachers distribute nothing but simple bread and wine in the Sacrament,[8] it does not matter to whom they give it or what those who receive it know and believe. . . . But since we intend to raise up and leave behind Christians, and [since we] distribute the body and blood of Christ in the Sacrament, we should not and do not want to give this Sacrament to anyone unless he has first been examined regarding what he has learned from the catechism and whether he wants to desist from the sins that he has committed contrary to it. . . . And because a pastor is supposed to be a faithful servant of Christ, he must, as much as he is able, not cast the Sacrament before swine and dogs, but instead hear who the people are. If they deceive him and do not tell the truth, then he is excused, and they have deceived themselves. (*Sendschreiben an die zu Frankfurt*, 1530; Walch Edition 17:2449)[9]

---

6 [Johannes Bugenhagen? CCT]

7 [*M. Philipp*. That is, Melanchthon. CCT]

8 [That is, in Zwinglian churches. CCT]

9 [See also above, pp. 1–19. MH]

Luther's declaration has already been quoted above: "that it is good enough for someone who desires the Sacrament to be questioned and examined in this way *once a year*. Indeed, he might have such a good understanding that he may be questioned *once in his whole life—or not at all*."

Comment 4: Procedure When There Is a Bad Rumor about the One Announcing

If a *bad rumor* is circulating regarding those who are announcing or if they are explicitly *accused of a crime*, they should be confronted with this. However, according to the maxim "the Church does not judge what is concealed" [*De occultis non judicat ecclesia*], if they deny the accusation against them and their guilt is not otherwise proven, such as by several witnesses, then they should not be suspended from the Lord's Supper but should be treated as innocent. Even those who are pursuing a presumptively legitimate lawsuit—that is, against nonbrothers[10]—should certainly be warned earnestly against vengefulness and implacability, but should not be turned away from the Holy Supper because of it. The *faculty of theology at Wittenberg* writes as follows about a case in which two people who desired Communion were testifying against each other but the true circumstances could not be determined:

> From the letter you addressed to us we learn what a complex case [*intricatus casus*] has arisen for you, in which a man among you is accused of having fornicated with a person who not only accuses him before the authorities and the ministerium but also presents herself as a suffering sinner and requests forgiveness with a penitent heart, desires the Holy Supper, and has obediently submitted herself to church discipline. But when turned away, she appealed to Christ, the supreme Bishop. The accused man, however, has consistently denied [guilt] before the authorities when admonished on various occasions. And because he cannot be rightfully convicted because of lack of witnesses, he likewise requests that [you] regard him as a Christian and admit him to the Sacrament. The gentlemen desire our opinion as to how they should deal with the two parties.
>
> Even though it cannot actually be learned from the gentlemen's report whether the matter has proceeded to regular legal proceedings before a legitimate judge—in which case it is no secret for the gentlemen that such persons should not be denied the desired confession and Absolution as

10 [Yet suing fellow Christians is even worse: 1 Corinthians 6:1–8. CCT

Walther here distinguishes between lawsuits against fellow Christians, on the one hand, and lawsuits against non-Christians, on the other. However, we need to remember Ap XVI 7: "Public redress, which is made through the office of the magistracy, is not advised against, but is commanded, and is a work of God according to Paul, Romans 13:1" (*Triglotta*, p. 331). So the sin is the motive of revenge and/or the refusal to reconcile—and—restore where that is possible. The use of civil courts is not a sin in and of itself (comment by Martin Noland).]

> long as the legal proceedings have not been concluded [*pendente lite*]—nevertheless, we believe that, even without regard to that, both persons could certainly be admitted to the Sacrament [*ad sacra*] if sufficiently warned beforehand and if they continue their insistence [on their respective stories], as long as there are not *strong* suspicions that the accused man is being treated unjustly.[11] Where there is no such suspicion, the woman is to be regarded as a poor, penitent sinner from whom, especially because she appeals to Christ when denied, Absolution and the Holy Supper cannot be withheld, especially because she also obediently submits to church discipline. The man, however, could be that much more sharply warned in the presence of the authorities not to use the Holy Sacrament as a ruse, as so many people do, but to know that while the Sacrament is going to be administered to him, he will nevertheless have to answer for it gravely on that day if it should turn out that he is guilty in his heart. Otherwise, since a ruling has not yet come down, the mere accusation and the malicious gossip that arises from it cannot exclude him from the Sacrament [*Sacris*]. Should he receive the Sacrament unworthily, the preacher who has duly warned him and cannot see into his heart does not bear any guilt for it. The ministerium is unable to judge concealed sins; mere suspicion cannot bar anyone from the Sacrament. God knows hypocrites the best; in His time He will know where to find them. Wittenberg, April 21, 1624. (*Consil.*, 2:125)

Regarding situations in which there is a bad rumor about someone announcing for Communion, *J. L. Hartmann* writes:

> We say that no suspicion is sufficient to turn a person away from the Holy Supper entirely; but we are speaking about a person under suspicion whom one has diligently examined but who persistently denies the deed. For a person is not always guilty of the crime of which he has been accused. Then it is an erroneous supposition that a clear and explicit confession of every individual sin, in particular those of which one is accused through a rumor or a strong suspicion,[12] is necessary; in Scripture there is no command about this. The former supposition is also no less erroneous—that someone who does not explicitly confess before the father confessor the sins he has committed is not truly sorry for them. Besides, there are other means available to lead a person suspected of wrongdoing to recognize it. In particular, one must conduct an inquiry into whether he recognizes that he is guilty of, for example, adultery (or whatever) and admonish him to take good care not to heap sin upon sin.[13] This is why sainted *Dr. Höpfner* notes in his *Isagog. coen.*, pt. 1, p. 358: "Where there are only reasons for

---

11 [In which case the woman would have invented the affair and should not receive the Sacrament. CCT]

12 [See AC XI. CCT]

13 [In this case, to add to the sin of the sin of adultery (Sixth Commandment) the sin of lying (Eighth Commandment). CCT]

suspicion and the people suspected of a fundamental error or an evil deed will not confess this specifically, but acknowledge in general that they are miserable sinners, they should not be suspended from receiving the Holy Supper. For if they will not confess such a sin either voluntarily or even after being admonished by the father confessor and yet persist in asking for Absolution, then they should be judged according to their words and left to their conscience." *Luther's* judgment is therefore valid here: If someone comes to confess and is suspected of a wrongdoing, then I (if I am acting as father confessor) must look into the matter according to the circumstances. But if he denies [wrongdoing], then I should give his no more weight than my suspicion; and if he insists on being admitted to the Holy Supper, I am required to give it to him.[14] (*Pastorale evangelicum*, p. 791)

ARTICLE 16
CONCERNING CONFESSION

The Augsburg Confession clearly testifies "that *confession is not commanded by Scripture* but instituted by the Church" (Article XXV [*Triglotta*, p. 71]). However, it also confesses: "Concerning confession it is taught that one should *retain* private Absolution in the Church *and not permit it to fall into disuse*" (Article XI [*Triglotta*, p. 47]); and its Apology says, "We also retain confession *on account of the Absolution*, which is the Word of God through which the power of the Keys absolves us from sins. Therefore, *it would be against God*" [*impium esset* = *es ware gottlos*, "it would be ungodly"] "*to remove Absolution from the Church.* Those who despise Absolution do not understand what the remission of sins or the power of the Keys is" (Article concerning Confession and Satisfaction [*Triglotta*, p. 281]). Therefore, a preacher cannot demand the introduction of *private confession* as an indispensable element [*conditio sine qua non*] of a Lutheran congregation or prefer for [the congregation] to be robbed of the pure preaching of the Gospel and to perish rather than for private confession not to be introduced; moreover, he must beware of the inclination to introduce it with impetuosity where it has already fallen into disuse or, where there is a desire to abolish its exclusive use, to hold fast to maintaining it exclusively at any price. On the contrary, using instruction and admonition as well as praise of [private confession], he should work in an evangelical manner [*evangelischer Weise*] toward its being used regularly *alongside general confession* at first, and, finally, where it is possible and advisable, [he should

14 Incidentally, confession before people is *necessary* only if one's neighbor would be harmed by one's not confessing—if, for instance, an innocent person would have to suffer because the guilty party did not confess. Apart from this case or apart from confession, a preacher should also therefore never himself *ask* someone accused or suspected of a sin whether he actually committed this or that sin. For in so doing he would compel the guilty person either to reveal to him a sin which is still concealed or to lie.

> work] toward its reintroduction as the exclusive custom—and, where it already exists, toward its being upheld. In any case, he may not under any condition give in to a congregation that does not even want to allow the use of private confession and Absolution by individual members, because "to *remove* Absolution from the Church" would certainly be "against God."[15]

Comment 1: The Great Value of Private Confession

We can see from *Luther's Sendschreiben an die zu Frankfurt, sich vor Zwinglischer Lehre zu hüten* ["Warning to the congregation in Frankfurt to stay away from Zwinglian teaching"] (1533) how highly he regarded *private confession.* He writes the following (among other things): "*Even if I owned thousands upon thousands of worlds, I would rather lose it all than to allow even the slightest bit of this confession to slip from the Church.* . . . For it is Christians' first, most necessary, and most useful school, where they learn to understand and exercise God's Word and their faith, which they do not do as powerfully in public readings and sermons" (see Luther's *Volksbibliothek* 4:61; cf. pp. 54–66).

In 1522, while Luther was being hidden at the Wartburg, Karlstadt began his iconoclastic reform[16] in Wittenberg and also abolished private confession, among other things. Luther hurried from his place of shelter despite the elector's prohibition in order to resist as a faithful shepherd the wolf that had broken into his flock. Arriving in Wittenberg on March 6, he held a sermon daily from Invocavit Sunday until Reminiscere[17] and, with God's help, quickly restored order to everything that the disgraceful enthusiast Karlstadt had confused and destroyed with a rough hand. In the last of his eight sermons, Luther comes to private confession. We cannot help but quote the following from it:

> Third, there is also a confession when one confesses to another and takes him aside and tells him what his trouble and need is, so that he may hear from him a comforting word so he may assuage his conscience. The pope sternly commanded this confession and turned it into a wretched affliction. I have condemned this *compelling and forcing* and attacked it severely when I have preached and written concerning confession. And I will not go to confession just because the pope has commanded it and wishes it. For he should leave confession *free* for me and not make of it a compulsion or command, which he has no power or authority to do. Yet I will nevertheless let no one take private confession away from me and *would not give it up for all the treasures in the world,* since I know what comfort and strength it has given me. No one knows what private confession can do except one who must often fight and struggle with the devil. I would long ago have

15 [Both quotations from Ap citation above. CCT]

16 [Smashing stained-glass windows, statues of saints, etc.—anything that smacked of the Medieval Church. CCT]

17 [That is, for a whole week, from the First to the Second Sunday in Lent. CCT]

> been defeated and killed by the devil, if this confession had not sustained me. For there are many doubtful and confusing matters which a person can neither resolve by himself nor comprehend. Now, when he is in such doubt and does not know a way out, then he takes his brother aside and tells him his trouble; laments to him of his weakness, his lack of faith, his sins; and asks him for comfort and advice. For what does it harm him, if he humbles himself a little before his neighbor and puts himself to shame? So if you receive a word of comfort from your brother, accept him and trust him, as if God Himself had said it to you. . . . *But whoever has a firm, strong faith in God and is certain that his sins are forgiven him may certainly ignore this confession and confess to God alone. But how many of you have such a firm, strong faith and confidence in God? Let each person take heed of himself here so that he does not lead himself into temptation.* (Erlangen Edition 28:249 [cf. AE 51:98–99])

On Luther's advice, the exclusive use of private confession and Absolution was therefore stipulated as a matter of church order in almost every church order of the churches in fellowship with the Wittenberg [Church] in the sixteenth century, whereas general confession was not permitted. For instance, the church order [of Wittenberg] of 1542, signed by Luther, reads: "For a pastor to gather in a group those who decide in the morning to commune and to grant them a *common* Absolution:[18] *that should not be in any way*" ["Ordenung vom eusserlichen gotsdienst und artikel der ceremonien"].

[Private Confession Is Not Absolutely Necessary]

Admittedly, whoever does not believe that Christ has already completely redeemed the entire world and that the good news of the Gospel is therefore nothing but an Absolution based on this redemption which has already occurred and which should be brought to the whole world (which [Absolution] demands nothing but faith in it or, in a word, acceptance for [the world] to obtain its blessed fruit); or whoever has never yet come to the experience of the weight of his sins—he will certainly also never be able to persuade himself of the precious nature of private confession and Absolution. And if a preacher does not use this wonderful means of consolation himself—as unfortunately! often happens—[and] thus cannot speak of how wonderful it is from experience, then it should certainly not be surprising if his teaching with regard to this institution [or "rite," *Institut*] remains unsuccessful in his congregation.

We permit ourselves to mention an article in *Der Lutheraner* (volume 6, no. 15) which appeared under the title "Wie groβ und verderblich der Irrthum

18 [Or "corporate Absolution." Corporate and individual confession and absolution existed side by side in early Lutheranism. The reference here is from *Constitution und artikel des geistlichen consistorii zu Wittemberg . . . 1542*, in *Die Evangelischen Kirchenordnungen Des XVI. Jahrhunderts*, ed. Emil Sehling (Leipzig: O.R. Reisland, 1902), first half, p. 202. MH]

derjenigen sei, welche den Predigern des Evangeliums die Macht absprechen, auf Erden Sünden zu vergeben" ["How great and pernicious the error is of those who deny preachers of the Gospel the authority to forgive sins on earth"].

Comment 2: Private Confession Not Absolutely Necessary

Regardless of how esteemed private confession and Absolution has been in our Lutheran Church up until now, it has nevertheless not been practiced in all Lutheran churches. Nor did our orthodox fathers deny a church the attribute [*Prädicat*] of being a true Lutheran church if that institution had not been introduced in it. Thus the faculty of theology at Wittenberg writes in a theological opinion from 1619: "Because we do not deny that private confession is *not being used in all orthodox Lutheran churches*, since the forgiveness of sins and worthy use of the Holy Supper is [there] in any case, therefore the confessional is not prescribed to achieve these goals for anyone" (*Consil. Witebergens.*, 2:139; Dedekenn, *Thesaur. consil.*, 2:749).

Furthermore, theologian *F. Balduin* of Wittenberg writes: "If private confession can be omitted by someone under certain circumstances in those churches where it is *in use*, then in places where it is *not in use*, yet the doctrine of the Lord's Supper is maintained purely (as in some towns in *Upper Germany*),[19] they can omit it even more and still receive the Holy Supper for salvation. For customs, which are indifferent matters, cannot detract from the essence of the Sacrament" (*Tract. de cas. consc.*, p. 467).

Theologian *Hieronymus Kromayer* of Leipzig writes as follows: "Although this" (private confession) "has *no divine command* and has been abolished as an indifferent matter *by many orthodox churches*—for example, by the [churches in] *Strassburg, Sweden*, and elsewhere—it still has *examples* in Scripture and its benefits, which should not be despised. . . . The fact that no one is admitted to the Holy Supper in our churches unless he has confessed his sins comes from *ecclesiastical* arrangements. Meanwhile, they do not condemn other churches which do not have that private confession" (*Theol. positivo polem.*, pp. 584f.).

Theologian *Conrad Dannhauer* of Strassburg writes as follows: "*Private Absolution is established in the articles of the Augsburg Confession, and yet Christian freedom is also permitted.* Thus private Absolution was retained in St. Nikolai Church in Strassburg on account of Marbach, who was a student of Luther, and it is still retained" (*Theol. casual.*, p. 99).

Finally, theologian *F. Bechmann* of Jena writes as follows: "One objects: many churches of the Augsburg Confession retain only *public*" (general [or "corporate"]) "confession in practice. Answer: This is admitted, but just as we do this out of

---

19 [South of the Main River and in parts of Saxony and Thuringia. CCT]

Christian freedom, other churches of the Augsburg Confession retain private confession out of the same Christian freedom" (*Theol. polem.*, 1702, p. 865).

Theologian *Balthasar Meisner* of Wittenberg writes regarding so-called *general* confession:

> None of our teachers condemned or rebuked as godless the kind of general Absolution which is in use not only in Reformed churches but also in some Lutheran churches. For we know by God's grace that the Word of Absolution which the minister of the Church proclaims *corporately* [*insgemein*] in the name of and by the command of Christ to all those confessing is the same word that is applied in our churches not to everyone in general but to each person *individually*. And that is why we say that *the former* Absolution is a true and efficacious one, but *the latter* is not only true and efficacious but also more appropriate in light of the reasons stated. (*Colleg. adiaphorist.*, disputation 7, 1616, E.2.b)

Nonetheless, no preacher may allow the congregation to *forbid* private confession, even if it does not have exclusive validity there [*wenn (die Privatbeichte) auch . . . nicht ausschließliche Geltung hat*]. This is why *Luther* (along with Melanchthon and Jonas) advises concerning the negotiations in Smalcald: "Although we do not wish to have someone forced or urged to" (private) "confession in the case of a mortal sin, nor to obligate recounting all sins, nor to torture consciences as under the pope—yet intending to *forbid* confession and therefore driving Absolution out of the church should be tolerated just as little. . . . What else is Absolution than the Gospel spoken to an individual person who receives from it comfort for the sins of his which he knows?" (*Luther's Werke*, Walch Edition 16:2177).

It is known, incidentally, that *Nectarius*, bishop of Constantinople [d. 397], when a wrongdoing was committed by his deacon in private confession and a great offense was caused and the entire congregation was filled with aversion toward private confession, immediately eliminated it in the year 391. In doing so, he clearly revealed that Christians in that era recognized Christian freedom even on this point.

Comment 3: Where Private Confession Is to Be Held

Private confession is best held in an unlocked and accessible place, ideally in a confessional booth [*Gittergestühle*], where the father confessor and the person making confession can be *seen*, but where they are at such a distance from others who are present that the latter cannot *hear* what is being said. In the Saxon General Articles we read:

> At the same time, for numerous important reasons, confession and examination of those wishing to go to Communion should not take place in the home of the pastor and deacon, nor in the sacristy, but publicly in the

> church in the choir [*im Chor*],[20] so that everything can be done with great modesty and solemnity, in the presence of and with the prayers of the people. . . . Since . . . when the people are in church for confession . . . [they] are surrounding the father confessor such that no one can present his need to the pastor confidentially and the minister of the Church cannot speak with them appropriately, ministers of the Church should observe such a regulation in each place that in the cities the ministers of the Church sit in the choir in places far away from one another, and the people remain outside the lattice or choir, [and] they go to the father confessor one after another, [so] he can speak with them without others in the church hearing. In the villages, however,[21] the pastors should require their penitents to remain seated until the one who has just confessed has left the choir. (*Des Durchlauchtigsten etc. Herrn Augusten [etc.] Ordnung*, Leipzig, 1580, fol. 298f.)

Comment 4: Procedure If There Is a Bad Rumor about the One Confessing

While the preacher has the obligation, if he has heard a *bad rumor* about a person making confession, to ask him about it, [he should] not refuse to give the person Absolution if he claims that the report is baseless and nothing can be proven against him. Probing into secret sins is contrary to [the preacher's] ministry [*wider sein Amt*]. For this reason, the Saxon General Articles read: "The ministers of the Church should not *ask* their penitents out of idle curiosity about what is not confessed. For this confession is not instituted for inquiring into secret and concealed sins, but above all and only for instructing the ignorant and for comforting sorrowful and burdened consciences" ([*Des Durchlauchtigsten etc. Herrn Augusten*], fol. 297).

But to the question "Whether a pastor in the confessional may also confront a person when there is a public outcry," the following answer is given in Dedekenn:

> Certainly, for Luke 16 says that the unfaithful manager was *accused* before his master of having wasted his goods, from which the master finds cause to speak to him and says, "*What is this that I hear about you?*" [Luke 16:2]. He does not say, "*I know for a fact* that you are not managing my household properly." Thus a pastor, because he is a watchman over the people and will someday have to give an account, therefore, if he hears something bad—that one of his parishioners is not managing [things] properly—it would certainly be inappropriate for him to remain silent. We read in 1 Corinthians 1[:11]: "It has been reported to me by Chloe's people"; and

20 [The "choir" is the area at the front of the church where the monks and all priests used to sit, separate from the congregation in the nave. It is usually enclosed by an altar rail in our sanctuaries (comment by Martin Noland).]

21 [Where the churches are not as large as in the cities. CCT]

in 1 Corinthians 11[:18]: "I hear that there are divisions among you. And I believe it in part"; [and in] 1 Corinthians 5[:1]: "There is a public outcry that there is sexual immorality among you." Here Paul finds cause from a public outcry to write to the Corinthians.

Luther writes:[22] "If someone comes to confession and I have an idea and suspicion, then I should diligently ask about all the circumstances. If he simply denies it, then I should give his no more weight than my suspicion. If he continues to ask for the Sacrament, I should give it to him." Chemnitz, in the *Examination of the Council of Trent* (p. 365), where he discusses the benefit and correct use of private confession, establishes these words (among others): "One also asks if one believes they are stuck in certain sins. — What if a pastor also had causes that compelled him to confront his penitent with the evil clamor? Then Paul says, 'Do not be hasty in the laying on of hands' (1 Timothy 5[:22]). Likewise, Dr. Luther: 'Not only do those people desecrate the Sacrament who *take* it unworthily, but also those who *give* it unworthily. However, if I am to learn whether someone is worthy, I must certainly ask him about what it is I am hearing about him and then hear from his response whether he is worthy and is sorry for his sins and wants to improve.[23] For if he still defends the sin and is, in short, an impenitent sinner, the pastor may not absolve him.' — What if the blessed moment were to come now in confession in which God would work recognition [of the sin]? For people cannot recognize their sins on their own, and even if they know they have done something, [and even if] they also know that what they did was wrong [and] also that many people are aware [*daß es auch Vielen unverborgen sei*] of it, still they do not pay attention to it, but go to the Sacrament anyway—in fact, as Dr. Luther writes, many cover up their sins, disgraceful actions, and vices by receiving the Sacrament, because the people do not recognize their sins themselves or have no sorrow about them, but God must work contrition and sorrow in them. But He works contrition and sorrow not without means, but through means. That is why it is necessary for a pastor to talk with his penitent about that bad rumor concerning him, if God would give repentance through his ministry so that the penitent begins to repent and gain contrition and sorrow about the sin committed up until now." (S. *Thesaurus Consilior.* by Dedekenn, 2:752)

Balduin writes as follows on this same topic:

If someone's sin is known by way of rumor but has not yet been admitted, but the one who stands under suspicion nonetheless desires Absolution from sins, then he should be politely heard, even if he himself does not make any mention of that offense in confession, but the father confessor must bring the rumor to his awareness and *dispassionately* inquire what

---

22 [For source, see next Luther quotation. CCT]

23 See above, Article 15, note on comment 4.

> is happening, whether he is conscious of it in his conscience [*im Gewissen bewußt sei*], and ask him not to withhold anything about it.[24] If he confesses the offense and is sorry for it and promises to discontinue it from now on, then he should be welcomed with open arms as a penitent sinner, absolved of the sin, and admonished in a brotherly way to beware of the sin in the future. However, if he not only denies the deed but even defends himself extensively, then he should not be forced to admit the deed, either by denial of Absolution or by any other means, because a minister of the Church is not a torturer of consciences. Nevertheless, the circumstances of the deed should be explained to him, and he should be warned that here, before the face of God, he is unable to fool the one who knows hearts, and he should therefore be asked to free himself from his burdened conscience by a sincere confession, with a reminder of what a great sin it is to intend to deceive God, who examines heart and mind[25] and who threatened His people with all His wrath when they denied and whitewashed their transgressions (2 Kings 17:9). [He should also be warned] that people who whitewash their transgressions will not succeed (Proverbs 28:13) and that they cannot partake of the Sacrament worthily, but become guilty of Christ's body and blood (1 Corinthians 11:27). However, if nothing is accomplished with such admonitions, but the person stubbornly denies the deed about which there is an outcry, then the matter should be commended to God, and Absolution should not be denied to the one who is requesting it. In His time, if God wills it, the truth can surely become more clear through other means. *The power of the Keys is given not to examine secret sins but to heal manifest ones.* (*Tractatus de casibus conscientiae*, pp. 1123–24)

Already *Augustine* writes: "We can turn no one away from Communion unless he has voluntarily confessed or has been either indicted or convicted in a secular or ecclesiastical court. For who can presume to be both prosecutor and judge of someone?" (Serm. 351, § 10).

Comment 5: Suspension of the One Coming to Confession

While no preacher has the authority to exclude a member of his congregation *absolutely*, completely from the Holy Supper and thus to place him under the ban,[26]

---

24 Cf. [previous note].

25 [Literally, "heart and kidneys" ("*Herz und Nieren*"); this is based on the Luther Bible translation of Psalm 26:2 (כִּלְיוֹתַי וְלִבִּי, literally, "kidneys and heart"), which the ESV renders as "heart and mind." CCT]

26 *Completely* denying the Holy Supper to a congregational member and fully excluding him from it is, namely, certainly to be regarded as the same as excommunication. In the Large Catechism, in the chief part on the Sacrament of the Altar, *Luther* quotes the following words from *Hilary*: "If a sin was not committed such that someone could not rightly be *removed from the congregation* and regarded as a non-Christian, one should not *stay away*

cases can nevertheless occur in which a preacher would himself grievously sin, would profane the Holy Supper, would participate in the sin of receiving the Holy Sacrament unworthily by a communicant, and would cause a great scandal if he were simply to admit to Communion someone who had announced for confession and the Lord's Supper. This would be the case, for example, under the following circumstances: if the person announcing [for the Lord's Supper] had fallen into a public, mortal sin, or was living in it, and had shown himself to be impenitent; if he had committed theft and yet did not want to return the stolen goods; if he had insulted and grieved someone, whether an individual or a whole congregation, or had been insulted by someone and did not want to reconcile with the party who had insulted him or whom he had insulted (Matthew 5:23–25; 18:28ff.; Luke 17:3); etc. Then the preacher, though without authority to excommunicate a congregational member, is in the position of being able not to distribute the Holy Supper to him. Such situations invoke the need for so-called *suspension* from the Holy Supper, by virtue of which a member of the congregation is denied the Holy Supper—not absolutely, as someone already excommunicated [*Gebannten*], but *temporarily* until the issue has been resolved—or [by virtue of which] a deferral in reception [of the Sacrament] is demanded—until, that is, the one who desires Absolution and the Lord's Supper shows signs of repentance or reconciles with his neighbor as far as he is able, and the like.

As certain as it is that a preacher may not and cannot take part in the sins of others (1 Timothy 5:22), it is equally certain that he must have the right to *suspend* people from the Holy Supper in every such case in which he would knowingly assist in committing a serious sin by admitting [someone] to the Lord's Table, thus participating in the sins of others. Thus just as decisively as our older orthodox theologians therefore deny preachers the right to excommunicate without the congregation, they equally decisively ascribe to preachers the right to *suspend* from the Holy Supper. *Amsdorf,* Luther's close friend,[27] for example, writes in an opinion from the year 1561: "If the consistory wants to remove the binding key [*clavem ligantem (Bindeschlüssel)*] from ministers and not leave them free, or to prevent or forbid private *suspension* from the Sacrament, then one cannot and should not consent to it. However, if it reserves public excommunication for itself, so that a pastor does not *excommunicate* anyone without the knowledge and consent of the consistory, then it is acting rightly and properly" (Löscher's *Unschuld. Nachrr.*,

---

from the Sacrament, so that one does not rob himself of life" [LC V 59–60; *Triglotta*, p. 767]. Accordingly, it is clear that, because a person who does not belong under *excommunication* should not *stay* away from the Holy Supper, the pastor should likewise *drive* him away from it to an even lesser degree. If he does this, then the preacher, for his part, is putting the one driven away under excommunication, which, however, he has no authority to do.

27 Luther regards Amsdorf as one of the "most worthy and excellent theologians" of his day, alongside Brenz and Rhegius (Erlangen Ed. 62:292).

1722, pp. 29f.). Furthermore, *Saubert* (died 1646) writes: "Although every called minister of the Church has the authority by virtue of the binding key to *refuse reception of the Holy Supper* to someone who is knowingly impenitent—because in this case he should pay attention to both himself and his flock (Acts 20:28) and should not throw what is holy before the dogs (Matthew 7:6)—he is nevertheless not authorized to appropriate the *greater excommunication* for himself alone without the previous knowledge of a Christian consistory" (*Zuchtbüchlein*, ch. 5, p. 49). Finally, the old theologian from Rostock, *Paulus Tarnov* (died 1633), writes: "Every pastor can *suspend* from the Sacrament, since he has the command to admonish every one of his hearers who sins (Ezekiel 3:17–18, 20); to pay attention to himself and the whole flock in which the Holy Spirit has made him a bishop; to pasture the congregation of God (Acts 20:28); and to take care not to give dogs what is holy (Matthew 7:6). However, only the presbytery or consistory, which represents the whole Church,[28] has the authority to *excommunicate* (Matthew 18:17; 1 Corinthians 5:4; 2 Corinthians 2:6)" (see Dedekenn's *Thesaurus*, 2:699).

[Suspending People from Confession]

However, there are also certain statements in the writings of our faithful fathers which seem to deny preachers the authority to suspend as well as the authority to excommunicate. Thus *Gerhard* writes:

> With regard to degrees, a twofold excommunication is established: a lesser and a greater one. The former is exclusion or suspension from the use of the Lord's Supper; the latter is removal from the communion of the church. . . . *Neither greater nor lesser excommunication should be employed by the minister of the church apart from a judgment of an ecclesiastical senate or consistory*, because the power to excommunicate is not the possession of any one bishop, but rather is the possession of the presbytery, which represents the entire church. ([Commonplace [XXVI], *On the Ecclesiastical Ministry*], §§ 194, 286)

Furthermore, *J. Conrad Dietrich* writes: "It is the *general* opinion of Lutheran theologians that no preacher should or can excommunicate, *suspend*, or deny [the Lord's Supper] with the greater excommunication [*excommunicatione majori*]—with the ban or with the lesser [*minori*]—with exclusion from the Holy Supper" (*Consilia und Bedenken*, p. 304). Even the Saxon General Articles note: "No one may be excluded from the Holy Supper based solely on the pastors' own judgment [*Erkenntnis*]" (art. 7).

However, the contradiction between these last statements and the ones cited above is only an apparent one. The following passage in the church order

28 Thus the *ministerium* should not be confused with the presbytery [*presbyterium*] or consistory [*consistorium*], because the former represents not the entire Church but only a part of it, namely, the teaching estate [e.g., pastors].

of Württemberg, known as the *Cynosura*, is among those that resolve this apparent contradiction: "Ministers may *advise against Communion, forbid it, or suspend [from it] by way of request*, but no minister should exercise *public excommunication* by his own authority [*propria autoritate*]" (see M. S. Eckard, *Pastor conscientiosus genuinus*, p. 177). Thus it is well within the authority of a preacher to "advise against" Communion for someone, even to "forbid" in the name of the Lord or to "suspend by way of request" someone who is clearly impenitent or unreconciled. However, if such a person is unwilling to obey it, and if he protests against the judgment of the pastor, then the [pastor] should not regard himself as the highest judge in this. Instead, he should immediately report the case to the presbytery, consistory, or congregational assembly [*Presbyterium oder Consistorium oder der Gemeindeversammlung*]—depending on the existing constitutional form—so that the final verdict about it is rendered by this body.

Comment 6: Absolution Should Always Be Unconditional

If the preacher has strong doubts as to whether the penitent is truly repentant and honest, yet without being able to convict and deny [him Communion], then he may not try to ease his conscience by adding all kinds of *conditions* or even *warnings* and *threats* to the formula of Absolution. *Deyling* writes: "It is the almost unanimous opinion of our theologians that the *formula of Absolution* should be understood *categorically* and should be free of any added condition. For each person confessing is presumed to be penitent and believing, unless the opposite is known with the greatest certainty and without any doubt whatsoever (which can only rarely be the case). For whoever was previously the most evil knave can now have come contritely to true repentance and an entirely different outlook" (*Inst. prud. pastor.*, p. 3, ch. 4, § 38, p. 447). — Nevertheless, this is naturally not meant to deny that in principle every Absolution, even an absolute one, is in a certain sense conditional. *Luther* writes in his letter to the city council at Nürnberg in 1539: "Even mental Absolution is conditional, in the way that a public sermon and every Absolution is also. Both public and private have the condition of faith. For without faith, it does not loose [sins][29] and is therefore not a false key. For faith is not based on our worthiness, but only means that one accepts the Absolution and says yes to it" (Walch Edition 21:424).

Comment 7: Preserving the Confessional Seal

A preacher must not reveal what is confessed or [made] known to him in confession, or even [just] as a preacher. Instead, he must keep it secret because of the *seal of confession*. It says in *Luther's Table Talk*:

29 [In the sense of Matthew 16:19 or 18:18. CCT]

> Someone asked Dr. M. Luther and said, "If a pastor and father confessor absolved a woman who had strangled her child, and [the deed] later became public and known through other people, would the pastor, too, if he were asked about it, have to testify before the judge?" He answered: "Most certainly not! For one must distinguish between the ecclesiastical and secular government;[30] since she did not confess anything to *me* but to the Lord *Christ,* and since Christ keeps it secret, I should also keep it secret and immediately say, 'I have heard nothing; if Christ has heard something, let Him say it.'" (Walch Edition 22:879 [cf. AE 54:395])

When *Luther* was told that the city council in Venice had condemned to the fire a monk who had absolved a murder confessed to him by someone but had then let himself be persuaded to disclose it through bribery, Luther replied, "This is a proper, good, and reasonable ruling and a wise opinion on the part of the council, and it was fitting to burn the monk as a traitor" ([Walch] 22:880). At any rate, a preacher who gossips [about things revealed] in confession has ruined his ministry and deserves to be removed. (Cf. Deyling, [*Inst. prud. past.*], § 41; Saxon General Articles, 7, final §.)

Fecht writes: "That obligation" (not to break the seal of confession)

> is based on a silent agreement between the one hearing confession and the one confessing. For if the minister of the Church were not obligated to the most rigorous silence, then the hearer would be acting foolishly if he entrusted to the former at his own risk something he could, according to Lutheran principles,[31] keep secret. Moreover, in this act the minister of the Church is not regarded as a prosecutor or examiner or judge. Finally, not only the Roman but also our whole Lutheran Church commands that this confidentiality be kept holy. However, with regard to the seal of confession, we should note that it extends not only to whatever is discussed with the prior promise of secrecy in the confessional between the one hearing confession and the one confessing but *also to all other, even private, interactions that occur pastorally between the father confessor and the one confessing*, unless he explicitly stated that he was speaking with him in a different capacity. (*Instruc. pastoral,* ch. 13, § 33, p. 151)

Therefore, the preacher should make every effort to guard his tongue, and even if he should present a particular case confessed to him without names for instructional purposes, he should be careful not to present the situation in such a way that people could guess the person about whom he is talking. He should

30 [The doctrine of the two kingdoms. CCT]

31 [As opposed to the Roman Catholic position, according to which all committed sins must be told. "If anyone says that the confession of all sins, such as the Church observes, is impossible and is a human tradition to be abolished by the godly . . . let him be anathema" (the Council of Trent, quoted in Chemnitz, *Examination of the Council of Trent* [St. Louis: Concordia, 1978], 2:591. MH]

destroy letters containing confessions as soon as they have fulfilled their purpose. Incidentally, in discussing this topic, *Avianus* notes quite correctly regarding this point: "A *penitent*, too, should be discreet and not gossip afterward about what was said to him during confession" (see Dedekenn's *Thesaur.*, 2:758).[32]

The teaching about preserving the seal of confession [*Sigillum Confessionis*] has nevertheless also been overdone by some. For instance, Cardinal Petronius approved the horrible statement of a French Jesuit: "If the Lord Jesus were still walking on earth and someone confessed to him [the Jesuit] that he intended to kill [Jesus], [the Jesuit] would rather allow the Lord Jesus to be killed than betray the one who had entrusted it to Him" (see [J. S. Adami], *Der gewissenhafte Beichtvater*, Leipzig, 1692, p. 49). Against this we should first note that if someone confesses *a sin still to be committed*, this does not at all fall into the category of confession. While such admissions should also in no way be revealed except in the most extreme emergencies, if what is revealed concerns a sin that would harm another person, perhaps an entire community—a planned murder, maybe the assassination of a king, the poisoning of a well, arson, treason, and the like—then [the pastor] must above all appeal with all means to the conscience of the one blinded not to carry out his plan. However, if this is unsuccessful, the matter must be reported to the proper authorities (without names, if *this* is enough to avert the danger; however, where this is not the case, then also by naming names). *Fecht* explains: "Those sins which, if they remain concealed, involve the destruction of either an entire community or several [people] should not be kept secret, since a community should be the object of greater concern than an individual. In this all theologians agree unanimously. However, one should proceed as considerately in such a disclosure as the holiness of the seal of confession demands. The persons must be protected as long and as far as possible" ([*Instruct. past.*], p. 152).

Deyling writes:

> We distinguish between sins that have already *occurred* and those that *have yet to be committed.* The former are rightfully kept secret and covered with complete silence, provided the general well-being and the command of the highest authorities do not command something else, as was the case with the notorious Lips Tullian.[33] With regard to future sins and sins *still to be*

---

32 *Deyling* notes: "Hippocrates obligated doctors under oath not to reveal the hidden weaknesses of the sick. How much more confidentiality is necessary for a spiritual and soul doctor! . . . Nepomuk, who was father confessor to the spouse of King Wenceslaus of the Bohemians, could not be moved by flattery or by imprisonment and torture to betray the secrets of the queen that had been entrusted to him under the seal of the confessional. He was therefore thrown into the river from the Prague Bridge, and he drowned" ([*Inst. prud. past.*], pp. 452, 454).

33 [The pseudonym of a leader of bandits in Saxony in the early eighteenth century, whose real name was Elias Erasmus Schönknecht. "Lips" has nothing to do with the English word "lips." CCT]

> *committed*, there is less concern. For if an offense revealed under the seal of confession and keeping that same [sin] secret would lead to the destruction of the highest authorities or the state or the neighbor—for instance, if a conspiracy, treason, the poisoning of a well, and arson were confessed—and the person confessing persisted in his evil plan after being warned by the preacher, in this case he, as an impenitent, may not be absolved nor may his horrific crime be kept secret, if the one hearing confession does not wish to act contrary to the law of nature, which commands us to prevent every destruction of the neighbor, [and if he does not want] to make himself a participant in the same sin and guilty of shedding innocent blood. Thus that Jesuit could have prevented the murder of King Henry IV of France if he had not kept secret the plan of Ravaillac which had been revealed to him. And even if someone who confessed the intention to commit a crime *promised not to commit the crime* after stern reproach by the father confessor, it would still be in accordance with love and prudence, while keeping the one who confessed anonymous, *quickly to inform* the people whose well-being is at stake, so that they may exercise care and ward off the danger. In fact, if the well-being of the highest authority or of the republic requires it, he may not conceal even the *name*. In light of all of this, it is not difficult to answer the question whether a confession should be revealed if, by concealing the confession of the guilty person, an *innocent person would lose his life*, even if he had not revealed his innocence himself. Our theologians correctly answer the question in the affirmative, but with a distinction between revealing the criminal and [revealing] the crime; only the latter is permissible here. ([*Inst. prud. past.*], § 43, p. 456)

Dannhauer writes:

> It is true that what is confided in confession is to be kept secret, in accordance with natural obligation (Proverbs 11:13), in accordance with the ancient practice of the church, and because the preacher acts in the stead of Christ—because the latter covers up the sins of the repentant, the one absolving must not disclose them, especially secret and nonoffensive sins. But if silence would harm the state or love of one's neighbor (if, for example, a conspiracy, treason, poisoning of wells, or the danger of arson were confessed), then the one who confessed this is to be urged either to disclose the matter himself or explicitly to allow it to be revealed. Otherwise he will not receive the blessing of the loosing key. If he does not want this, then more concern should be had for society than for an individual person, and there is no seal in the divine Law that could be held over the mouth in this case.[34] (*Hodomor. Spirit. Papaei*, p. 1456)

L. Hartmann shares a response by the faculty of theology and law at Jena from 1624 about a poor woman who had been accused of practicing magic but was

34 [Literally, "in divine Law there is no seal that could be pressed on that mouth." CCT]

innocent. During the torture used against her, on account of the pain, which she could not bear, she confessed that she was guilty, because she preferred to suffer death rather than [to suffer] the agony of torture further. However, after her conviction she confided to her father confessor that she was innocent, but with the request to tell to the judges nothing for God's sake. In this case, the father confessor was, of course, instructed to break the seal of confession—not only so that the innocent woman would not leave this world with a lie but also so that the authorities would not stain themselves with innocent blood (*Pastoral. Ev.*, 3, 36, pp. 741ff.). Finally, *Hartmann* recommends that before an inexperienced preacher breaks the seal of confession, he should always first seek input about the case from his superiors or other experienced theologians using the fictional names of Cajus and Sejus[35] ([*Pastoral. Ev.*], pp. 747f.).

Comment 8: The Preacher Should Also Go to Confession before the Holy Supper

In a case of necessity [*selbst im Nothfall*] a preacher may go to the Holy Supper *without confession*,[36] although this should not be done by him except in the case of necessity. Even every *preacher* should rather select his own specific father confessor, confess regularly to him, and receive Absolution from him. Even the preacher needs this important means [of grace], and how can he expect and demand that his hearers hold the holy pastoral office in high esteem if he himself gives the smallest appearance of disdaining it? We will return to this topic again in the discussion of self-Communion by the preacher.

Article 18
Who Should Be Admitted to the Lord's Supper

As far as *communicants* are concerned, only those should be admitted to the Holy Supper

1. who are already baptized;

---

35 [Ficticious names used commonly by ancient Roman lawyers in discussing case law. See Plutarch's *Morals*, question 30. MH]

36 In the *Unterricht für die Visitatoren* [*Instructions for the Visitors*] of 1538, *Luther* writes: "If the pastor or preacher himself, who deals with it daily, wishes to go to the Sacrament *without confession* or examination, nothing should be forbidden him in this regard. The same should also be said about other wise people who know well how to confess themselves. So that such confession does not become a new papal compulsion or necessary custom again, we should and must have it freely. And I, Dr. Martin, have gone many times without confession, so that I do not make it into a necessary custom in the conscience for myself, yet on the other hand [I] use confession and do not wish to go without, most of all on account of the Absolution (that is, God's Word)" ([Walch] 10:1937ff. [WA 26:216; AE 40:263ff.]).

2. are able to examine themselves;
3. cannot be proven to be non-Christians or heterodox believers, who would therefore be taking the Sacrament unworthily; and, finally, of whom
4. there is no reason to believe that they need to reconcile with someone or to provide restitution beforehand.

Comment 1

Since Holy Baptism is the Sacrament of rebirth into[37] the kingdom of God and of initiation [while] the Holy Supper is the Sacrament of refreshment, only those who are already *baptized* should be admitted to the latter. This is analogous to the Passover meal, to which, according to Exodus 12:48, only those who had already been received into the covenant of grace by circumcision were to be admitted.

Comment 2[: On Confessing Persons Who Cannot Commune]

Since, according to God's Word, everyone desiring to go to the Lord's Table should first examine himself and discern the body of the Lord (1 Corinthians 11:28–29), the Holy Supper should not be administered to *children* who are not yet capable of this. It was an obvious abuse when this was done quite commonly in the third through fifth centuries—as the examples of Cyprian and Augustine themselves show—with the endorsement of even Innocent I. [It was] based on a misunderstanding of John 6:53, which was understood to refer to sacramental reception. This abuse was also practiced among the Bohemian Hussites, and it is still the law today in the Greek Church. *Luther* writes: "I cannot agree with the Bohemians, who give it" (the Holy Supper) "to children, even though I do not call them heretics for doing so" (letter of 1523 to Hausmann; Walch Edition 21:841).

[People Who Are Not to Be Admitted to Holy Communion]

Those who cannot examine themselves and should therefore not be admitted to the Lord's Table also include people who are *sleeping, unconscious, in the throes of death and unaware of what is happening, insane,* and the like. In 1623, the Wittenberg theological faculty answered the question "Whether one should give the Holy Supper to someone who is dying and no longer hears and understands what is about to be done for him" as follows:

> One should not give the Lord's Supper to such a dying person [*seelzogenden*]. For salutary use of it requires a proper faith, which rightly distinguishes the body of Christ from other common food, accepts the merit of Christ, and proclaims the death of Christ; it requires a certain examination, by

37 [Alternatively, also means being "born from above" as the Greek word ἄνωθεν in John 3:7 indicates. CCT]

> which the communicant should examine for himself how he stands before God, so he does not use it unworthily; it requires a sincere desire [*herzliches Verlangen*] for this salutary food for the soul. None of this is true of a person who is in the throes of death and is so close to death that not even the short time required for the consecration is available. For these reasons one should prefer not to administer the Lord's Supper to the dying, so that one does not perhaps administer it to someone who is unworthy and give others reason for offense and security, as if the mere act of using the Lord's Supper is sufficient, even if it is taken without faith, without self-examination, without sincere desire, and as if its use may therefore be delayed even until the hour of death. (*Consil. Witebergens.*, 2:115)

However, even if it were already improper—since the Holy Supper does not work physically, like a bodily medication which has its effect if it is simply ingested—to administer the Holy Sacrament at the insistence of relatives to someone who is already lying unconscious in the process of dying [and] who bore the signs of true faith during his life, it would be even more reprehensible to administer it under these circumstances to a person who had despised the Word of God and the most holy Sacraments until the hour of death. *Luther* writes to Lauterbach concerning this in the year 1544:

> What else will you do with people who delay taking the Sacrament until the last moment of their lives besides remind them publicly that they should guard against and fear such danger? Afterward warn them that, if anyone delays taking the Sacrament until his reason and senses are gone, the Sacrament cannot be administered to him any more than to a pig or a dog. For with people such as this one cannot talk about repentance or ask them what they believe or do. Therefore, they cannot become more fit to receive the Sacrament [*Darum sie des Sacraments nicht empfänglicher sein können*]; it is administered to them in vain. Let their blood be on their own heads if they despise Word and Sacrament their whole lives while they are still healthy. By doing so they become less fit for it from one day to the next, so that they would rightly be robbed of the Sacraments at the end of their lives by their own fault. May they therefore consider growing accustomed to using the Word and the Sacraments while they are still alive and healthy, since they can still hear, respond, explicitly confess their sins and faith. If they do not, may they also finally, when reason and senses fail, do entirely without the office of preaching, the Sacraments, and the communion of the Church, just as they desired and earned in their lives. We are commanded not to throw what is holy before dogs and not to throw pearls before pigs [Matthew 7:6]. This is how we admonish our people, and this is what we do. ([Walch[1]] 21:1527)

[People Who Are to Be Admitted to Holy Communion]

As far as *insane, raving mad,* and *possessed people* are concerned—about whom there will be occasion to write in more detail later—*Gerhard* writes: "If they have lucid moments in between, they should not be excluded from using the Holy Supper, provided they clearly demonstrate that they can examine themselves" (*Loc. Th. de s. coena,* § 225).

Also *deaf-mute* people, if they show signs of faith and of understanding the holy act, should not be turned away from the Table of the Lord. Luther writes:

> Many people have asked whether one should offer the Sacrament to deaf-mute people. Many people want to deceive them in a friendly way and believe one should give them unconsecrated hosts. This insult is not good. It will not please God, who made them Christians just as [He did] *us,* and they deserve precisely what we do. Because they have reason, and one can note certain signs that they desire it out of true Christian devotion, as I have often seen, one should leave the Holy Spirit to His work and not deny him what he demands. It may be that they have in them greater understanding and faith than we do; no one should impudently oppose it. (*Sermon von dem Neuen Testament*; Walch Edition 19:1302; cf. Deyling, *Instit. prud. past.*, 3, 4, § 45)

In one case, the person who desired the Holy Supper had become *so weak in his understanding and memory* that he was able to examine himself only with the help of the preacher and could only repeat what had been said to him, although he had shown himself to be a righteous Christian when his mental powers had been better. The theological faculty at Jena recommended that he be admitted [to the Lord's Supper]. See Dedekenn, *Thesaur. Consil.*, vol. 1. pt. 2, f. 357.

Comment 3

It is well worth noting that a preacher does not have to be certain that the people he should and wants to admit to the Holy Supper are *Christians* with a living faith[38]—after all, who could discern this?—but only that their lack of Christian faith [*Unchristentum*; that is, their *absence* of faith] may not be demonstrable or obvious. To act according to his moral conviction when admitting to or turning away from the Table of the Lord is to rule over consciences in an inexcusable way. Even the Lord, who in His omniscience certainly knew that Judas would consume the Holy Supper to his judgment, still admitted him, because he was not yet manifest before man. On this point, *Gerhard* writes:

---

38 [Walther is not implying that people of other religions (that is, Judaism, Islam, etc.) should be accepted to the Lord's Table. After all, in the nineteenth century neither the United States nor Germany were pluralistic, with a diversity of religions, as these countries are today. The vast majority of the population was at least Christian—whether with a "living faith" or not. MH]

> Christ certainly allowed Judas to partake of the Holy Supper along with the others, as we deduce from Luke 22:20–23. For even though Judas already intended in his heart to betray Christ at that time—in fact, had already received the reward of injustice at that time—this most grave sin was nevertheless still known only to Christ at that time, but not in any way to any of the apostles, for they were asking each other "which of them it could be who was going to do this" (Luke 22:23). This is why Christ, after first warning Judas to abandon that sin, admits him to the Holy Supper along with the others. Thus, in accordance with Christ's example, a minister of the Church should not exclude from receiving the Holy Supper those whose sins are still concealed. Instead, he should vigorously warn against harmful consumption by the unworthy and urge true repentance. (*Loc. Th., de S. Coena,* § 223; cf. regarding Judas's participation at the reception of the Lord's Supper, § 235)

Regarding the necessity and proper use of prior announcement for Communion, see above, [Article] 15, comments 1–2; regarding turning away and suspending from the Holy Supper, see above, [Article] 16, comment 5.

Comment 4[: People Who Are Not to Be Admitted to Holy Communion]

Anyone who cannot confess faith that the true body of Jesus Christ is actually and truly present in the Holy Supper and is therefore consumed by all communicants—both the worthy and unworthy—is incapable of discerning the body of the Lord (1 Corinthians 11:29). For this reason, he should not be admitted to the Holy Supper under any circumstances. Cf. *Gerhard*, [*De S. Coena*], § 222. But even someone who confesses this cannot be admitted in accord with good order[39] if he is not a member of our orthodox Church but instead is either a separatist, Roman Catholic, Reformed, so-called Protestant [*Evangelischer*] or United Protestant,[40] Methodist, Baptist—in short, is a member of a heterodox fellowship and wishes to remain so. For the Sacrament, just as it is a seal of faith, is also a banner of the fellowship in which it is administered. *Michael Müling* writes: "The holy Sacraments are symbols, mottos, banners of the Christian confession of heavenly truth, of living faith, and of the true fellowship of the churches of Christ. Those who consent to false, erroneous doctrine cannot use the holy Sacraments without a bad conscience and name—yes, not without offending the weak faith" (Dedekenn, *Thesaur.*, vol. 1, pt. 2., f. 364).[41]

---

39 Except in the case of mortal danger, which we will address later.

40 [Pertains to the forced union of Lutheran and Reformed churches in nineteenth century German lands (beginning with the Prussian Union in 1817) and not really to the American scene of the nineteenth century. CCT]

41 See the "Thesen über Abendmahlsgemeinschaft mit Andersgläubigen" contained—along with an excerpt of the proceedings conducted about them—in the fifteenth Synodical

COMMENT 5: THE UNRECONCILED CANNOT BE ADMITTED TO THE LORD'S TABLE

Those who have insulted or given offense to others (whether an individual or an entire congregation) and have *not yet reconciled* with them, or who have been insulted or offended and have *not yet sought reconciliation*, should be *suspended* from the Holy Supper on the basis of Matthew 5:23–25 until they have recognized their guilt and done what is in their power to bring about reconciliation. What the old theological faculty at Wittenberg wrote in a response is undoubtedly correct:

> There is a clear difference between *inner, actual unworthiness* [*indignitate intreseca*], which flows from unrecognized mortal sins, and *exterior unworthiness based on accidental* [*(indignitate) accidentali*] *circumstances* (which is what offending one's neighbor is), of which the penitent is often unaware and which might be called an accidental *obstacle* [*obstaculum accidentarium*] rather than actual *unworthiness*. However, if the father confessor is aware of it and it is well-known [*notorium*] or is such that the offense cannot be separated from the external fact, he is obligated to mention it and to admonish the penitent to avoid such a scandal, which would make his repentance suspect. (*Consil. Witeberg.*, 2:128)

If *personal* reconciliation is impossible, it can also be done *in writing or through others.* If this also is impossible, then a discernible, *honest desire* for it is sufficient, because God alone sees the heart. This is why *Balduin* writes: "If the offended party is present, then the offending party is obliged to go to him and ask for forgiveness according to Christ's words in Matthew 5. No one will be absolved until he has provided satisfaction to the other whom he has insulted. But if the [offended party] is absent and no meeting can be arranged with him, then inner reconciliation of the heart is sufficient, as is testifying before others that he is prepared to ask for forgiveness" (*Tractat. de cas. consc.*, 4, 17, 5, p. 1256). *Chemnitz* also notes the following regarding Matthew 5:23: "Because time and place often do not permit going to the offended brother, and this often does not help the brother, the point is to form and have the sincere, good intention in the heart to appease the offended brother and, as far as it is up to us, to do everything to make the offended brother a friend again" (*Harmon. ev.*, on the passage cited). Finally, *Augustine* writes: "If something of that sort comes to mind regarding someone who is absent and possibly living on the other side of the sea, it is absurd to believe that the gift should be left at the altar so that one can sacrifice it to God after traversing nations and seas. This is why we are compelled to take our refuge inwardly in spiritual adherence to the command so that we can understand what has been said without absurdity" (*De sermon. dom. in monte*, bk. 1, ch. 10).

Report of the Western District of the Synod of Missouri, etc., from 1870. [A translation of these theses can be found above, pp. 21–74. MH]

Regarding the fact that bad rumors, suspicions, indictments, or carrying on just legal proceedings are insufficient reasons for denying someone the Holy Supper, compare above, [pp. 181–83], § 15, comment 4, and [pp. 189–91], § 16, comment 4. *Luther* writes to a person involved in *legal proceedings*:

> But if the matter is being settled in court, then let it be done and wait for the ruling. This does not at all hinder going to the Sacrament. Otherwise we and our princes would be unable to go to the Sacrament either, because the matter between us and the Papists is being settled [legally]. Commend the matter to the courts [*Rechten*], but in the meantime liberate your conscience and say, "Whoever wins the judgment was in the right [*Wem das Recht gefällt (zufällt)*]; meanwhile, I will forgive the one who has done wrong and will go the Sacrament." This way you will not go unworthily, because you desire justice and are prepared to suffer injustice, whether the judge declares the matter to be just or unjust. (Walch Edition 10:2736)

What to Do When Only the Preacher Knows about the Sin of the One Announcing

Concerning a case *in which the sin of a person coming to Communion is known only to the father confessor and the sinner, Polyk. Leyser* writes:

> In this case, a preacher can neither simply admit nor publicly refuse a person who confesses it. That is, he should earnestly encourage the sinner and warn him, on account of the harm to his soul, to refrain from the Holy Supper until he shows sincere fruits of repentance, so that he does not grow accustomed to sins contrary to conscience, which would make him guilty of the body and blood of the Lord Christ [1 Corinthians 11:27]; and [the preacher] should point out means and ways by which [the sinner] can truly repent and get free of this sin—and if he promises to follow this faithful advice, he will be fittingly absolved and admitted. *However, if he does not follow through with this promise and ignores the admonition and appears with the other communicants, the preacher cannot publicly refuse him, because it is a secret offense.* And even though it was revealed to the preacher, *the preacher should not be a revealer of confessions*, which is what would happen if he were not to admit him to Communion and thus hurt his reputation among his fellow brothers. As, for example, if a young, single woman had sinned against the Sixth Commandment, but because she was not pregnant and no one knew of the deed, she kept wearing the virgin's wreath [*Kranz*],[42] but revealed her case to the pastor. He should certainly admonish her to take off the wreath. Since she wishes to come to the Table of Christ, who knows her deed and cannot be deceived but would certainly punish her, it would therefore be better to suffer temporal dishonor than to expect eternal [dishonor]. However, if she nevertheless appears with the wreath, the preacher cannot publicly refuse her. Doing so would reveal to

42 [The customary head ornament for virgins. CCT]

> everyone that she is guilty of a misdeed, but a preacher cannot and should not be a traitor to his penitents.[43] (Dedekenn's *Thesaur. Consil.*, vol. 1. pt. 2., fol. 353)

Absolution, of course, is a totally different matter. Since it can be withheld without having to reveal publicly what was confessed, it should also be withheld in the case described,[44] just as the theological faculty at Wittenberg also declared it to be the proper procedure according to God's Word in a similar case in 1612 ([Dedekenn, *Thesaur. Consil.*], fol. 758). Compare what was said about keeping the seal of confession, above, [pp. 194–97], § 16, comment 7.

Those Living in an Ungodly Occupation[45] Should Not Be Admitted to the Lord's Supper

Those living in an ungodly occupation should also be suspended from the Holy Supper until they leave this occupation [*sie diesen Stand verlassen*] and dedicate themselves to a God-pleasing vocation [*Beruf*].[46] *Leonhard Hutter* answers the question "Should *actors* be admitted to the Holy Supper?" as follows: "In his Epistles 1 and 60, St. Cyprian answers in the negative, because it is consistent with neither the divine majesty nor church discipline for the honor and purity [*pudor*] of the Church to experience such a shameful and dishonorable contact and to be sullied by it" (*LL. Th.*, art. 19, ch. 4, q. 7, n. 3, p. 728). *Friedlieb* writes: "Excluded from this Sacrament are . . . magicians, necromancers (fortune-tellers, especially those who consult the dead), pimps, and murderous duelists. All of these are to be excluded if they do not desist from these arts and forbidden acts and show true repentance [*wahre Buße tun*]" (*Opus novum*, f. 376). *Balduin*:

> Acrobats and tricksters, who seek to make a living by a certain flexibility of their bodies or by deceiving the eyes, ply foolish trades, and I seriously doubt whether the lifestyle [*Lebensart*] of such people pleases God. For they cannot be reckoned to one of the divine estates, nor are their skills useful to anyone. Instead, they lead others away from honest work to idleness and are themselves more inclined toward idleness than to work. Because their arts consist of no work, or at least useless [work], therefore they are not easily received into a well-arranged state, but instead drift back and forth like shiftless do-nothings [*geschäftige Nichtsthuer*] as a warning to young people to learn something better and more useful. (*Tractat. de cas. consc.*, pp. 1007f.)

---

43 [Literally: "cannot or should not be the betrayer of his confessing children." CCT]

44 [That is, the matter of the prostitute with the virgin's wreath. CCT]

45 [*Stand* can be translated as "status" or "circumstance," but it also has the meaning of "vocation" or "rank." CCT]

46 [This whole passage addresses not only ungodly lifestyles, but also vocations. MH]

However, a profession should not be considered ungodly just because what it produces is for the most part misused.

The *excommunicated* [*Gebannten*], above all, are included among those who should be turned away from the Lord's Supper until they are reconciled with the Church again, unless they suddenly come into *mortal need*. Concerning this case the church order of Lower Saxony says:

> If the excommunicated person should perhaps also be afflicted by a serious, burdensome, deadly illness before reform can be seen in him,[47] friends should join the pastor in admonishing, calling to mind, and pointing out to him with all possible diligence the divine wrath about such sins, so that he takes his sins to heart and confesses them and desires, along with reconciliation to the church which he offended, forgiveness of his sins by God through Christ. In such a case and instance, the pastor should administer Absolution to him along with the Holy Supper in the presence of a number of witnesses, with the condition that, if God helps him back out of his situation, he will not neglect public repentance and Absolution before the congregation of God. (Dedekenn, *Thesaur.*, vol. 1, pt. 2, fol. 687)

Comment 6: Return of Stolen Goods Must Occur Prior to Communion

The well-known proverb "There is no remission of sin without restoration of what was stolen" [*Non remittitur peccatum, nisi restitituitur ablatum*] is undoubtedly correct. A person is a thief as long as he unlawfully keeps someone else's property. During that period, he therefore cannot receive the Holy Supper worthily. *Dannhauer* writes concerning this: "One must make restitution for *all of it*; one must return *the same thing*, either in kind or by a corresponding means with *the same worth*, as measured by the damage that was inflicted, [and] should be compensated. (Such a [means], if one has to restore someone's good name, is a retraction.) One must, if he can, make restitution to the one *from whom the article was stolen*; if one cannot do this, then to his *heirs*; if this also is impossible, then to the poor" (anonymously, of course). "If the one obligated to make restitution [*Wiedererstattung*] is unable to do so, then he must make restitution by *wishing* and by *promising* to do so when his circumstances improve (Luke 19:2)" (*Lib. consc.*, 1, p. 314). Under certain circumstances, restitution can occur secretly through others without the victim finding out who returned the stolen goods to him.

Comment 7

If two preachers are serving the Holy Supper at the same time, and the first one has already given the consecrated bread to someone without the other being aware of it, the latter, to keep from mutilating [*verstümmeln*] the Sacrament,

47 [Literally: "before any (spiritual) improvement in (this person) can be felt." CCT]

should not deny the communicant the consecrated chalice, even if he might otherwise have a legitimate reason to do so. Cf. *G. König*, *Casus catech.*, p. 1, ch. 6, cas. 5, pp. 467–76; and *Hanneken*, in *Opus novum*, fol. 578.

Comment 8: In a Case of Necessity the Preacher Can Commune Himself

Regarding the question "*May a preacher serve the Holy Supper to himself under certain circumstances?*" we repeat what we have already shared elsewhere about this:

First, as far as our dear father *Luther* is concerned, it is true that he writes as follows in his work *The Christian Way to Go to the Lord's Table* [*Formula Missae*] from 1523: "Then let him distribute the Sacrament both *to himself* and to the people while the *Agnus Dei* is sung" ([Walch[1]]10:2760). However, it seems to contradict this when Luther writes in the Smalcald Articles:

> But if anyone should advance the pretext that as an act of devotion he wishes to administer confession or Communion *to himself*, he is not in earnest. For if he wishes to commune in sincerity, the surest and best way for him is in the Sacrament administered according to Christ's institution. But for one to administer Communion to himself is a human notion, uncertain, unnecessary—yes, even prohibited. And he does not know what he is doing, because without the Word of God he obeys a false human opinion and invention. So, too, it is not right (even though the matter were otherwise correct) for one to use the common Sacrament of the Church according to his own private devotion and to trifle with it without God's Word and apart from the communion of the Church. (SA II II [8–9; *Triglotta*, p. 464])

However, these latter words only *seem* to contradict the former ones. There the topic is self-Communion of the preacher *with the congregation*; here an alleged self-Communion that *excludes* the congregation in a so-called silent or sacrificial Mass. Luther justly rejects the latter—in part, because it is only pretended where one is ashamed to admit that he wants to sacrifice Christ; in part, because Holy Communion is a Sacrament given to the fellowship of saints and thus presupposes several participants. None of these reasons and reproaches are relevant to the *former* self-Communion. It is therefore in no way declared to be inadmissible in itself here by Luther, and thus in our symbols, as some let themselves believe.

[In Cases of Necessity the Preacher May Commune Himself]

While the later Lutheran theologians are far from declaring self-Communion by the preacher to be the normal manner of distribution, only in the case of necessity mentioned above do they declare it to be unquestionably admissible.[48]

48 Namely, when, as happens not seldom here, preachers are so isolated and far removed from brothers in ministry that, if they were unwilling to administer the Holy Supper to themselves, they might have to go without it for years on end. Needless to say, the congregation

Thus *Johann Gerhard* writes in his *Locis Theologicis*:

Here it is asked whether a minister of the Church may administer the Holy Supper to himself. Dr. Pelargus denies this in his *School of Faith* on Article X of the Augsburg Confession, citing the following reasons: (1) Because two persons are required for the Holy Supper, one who gives and one who receives, it would seem to be more correct and more in accord with Christ's institution if he took the Sacrament from someone else rather than from himself. (2) If there is an analogy between the Sacraments of Baptism and the Lord's Supper, and if Christ did not baptize Himself but employed the ministry of the Baptist, by whom Christ's disciples were also baptized, as is believed, then what is to prevent us from asking others to administer the salutary bread and salutary drink to us in the Holy Supper? (3) Since no one is able to absolve himself, and since it also does not say, "When you forgive yourself your sins," but "if you forgive the sins of any" (Matthew 16:19; John 20:23), then why should one not also, just as he must ask for Absolution from a faithful minister according to the custom of the whole Church, do the same with respect to the Holy Supper? (4) In order to declare unanimity in religion and true faith, the presence of another pastor or minister of the Church seems necessary; and so that the recipient may confess that he is a member of a certain church by means of this symbol of reciprocal brotherly love which is administered to him by the other, he should also adopt a neighboring co-worker in the church as a witness to his true faith. (5) On account of the reverence due to the ministry, so that, because Christ instituted this sacred order, whoever takes the Sacrament from a minister of the Church may willingly bear witness that he, too, reveres and holds in esteem other ministers of the Church. (6) For the sake of a fuller strengthening of faith, for it can happen that one wavers and is full of doubts and must be lifted up and strengthened by the voice of another; sometimes [one must] also be admonished with respect to life and morals, especially when one has promised improvement and a new life. For that reason Paul is commanded to come to Ananias (Acts 9:6), and Cornelius is commanded to send for Peter (Acts 10:5). (7) We also do not read that it was customary in the ancient apostolic church for someone to offer himself the bread and wine in the celebration of the Sacrament. — Yet Pelargus is correct to add in this passage that *the case of necessity is an exception*. If, therefore, some village pastor cannot summon or come to his neighbor because of his isolation, let him test and examine himself first, ask God for the forgiveness of his sins, and then take the body and blood of the Son of God, not as if from his own hand but as from the hand of Christ, which offers both to him. As far as the passage from Luther

(in the Smalcald Articles)

---

should first be instructed about the validity of self-Communion so that [his practicing] it does not cause offense.

> is concerned, it is actually opposed to papal private Masses, of which it is believed that the people watching receive some kind of benefit from it. (*Loc. de Sacra. Coen.*, § 18)

Johann Benedict Carpzov writes the following about the passage from the Smalcald Articles which has been mentioned several times:

> This must be understood correctly about the custom of communing oneself. For even though (1) our church does not approve the fifth canon of the Council of Toledo, in which it is established as absolutely necessary that the presbyter administering Holy Communion to others must also serve the Eucharist to himself and always commune at the same time; (2) even if what the Council of Trent declares in session 13, c. 8, is not true—namely, that it has always been a tradition in the church of God for priests administering the Eucharist also to commune themselves and that this tradition, as one which derives from apostolic tradition, must be retained as a matter of law—yet (3) in our churches this tradition is not absolutely disapproved, as if it would contradict the essence of the institution of the Meal of the Lord. Concerning this, what Chemnitz called to mind in the second part of his *Examination of the Council of Trent*, folio 296, can be looked up. And for this reason, (4) these words of Luther in the Smalcald Articles must be understood only in [light of] the specific concern that they have, namely, about a Communion or a Holy Supper in which the one holding the Mass carries out a private Lord's Supper that he does not have in common with anyone, so that he—the one consecrating it—is the only recipient. It is therefore one thing to serve the Holy Supper *to yourself as well* when it is also served and distributed to others; it is something different to take and serve the Holy Supper to *oneself alone* to the exclusion of others. Here Luther is not rejecting the former but the latter—which we presently reject as well. (*Isagog. in Libb symb.*, p. 794)

Speaking even more decisively in favor of the right of a preacher to commune himself are *Caspar Erasmus Brochmand*, the famous Danish theologian—see *System. th., loc. de coena*, f. 485, as well as *Quenstedt* in his *Theologia didactico-polem.*, p. 4, ch. 3, fol. 1033, and all of our casuists.

CHAPTER FIFTEEN

1 CORINTHIANS 11:29—"DISCERNING THE BODY"

AND ITS IMPLICATIONS FOR CLOSED COMMUNION

ERNIE V. LASSMAN

"For anyone who eats and drinks
without discerning the body
eats and drinks judgment on himself."

INTRODUCTION

Beginning with Martin Luther, the Lutheran Church has consistently understood 1 Corinthians 11:29 as referring to the real presence of the body of Jesus Christ in His Supper. Luther makes this abundantly clear in such writings as *Against the Heavenly Prophets*[1] and *Confession Concerning Christ's Supper.*[2] The "second Martin," Martin Chemnitz, also made this clear in his writings.[3] And this understanding of 1 Corinthians 11:29 is the teaching of the Book of Concord.[4]

Such an understanding of 1 Corinthians 11:29 has implications for the teaching of close(d) Communion. A communicant who partakes of the Lord's body without "discerning" or "recognizing" its presence with the bread eats judgment

1 AE 40:185, 186.

2 AE 37:347, 348.

3 Chemnitz writes in *Ministry, Word, and Sacraments—An Enchiridion* (trans. Luther Poellot [St. Louis: Concordia, 1981], 130): "But the following are they that eat unworthily, as one can very clearly gather from Paul, 1 Cor 11:1. They that do not discern the body of the Lord, that is [they] that do not hold that the very sacred food of this Supper is the body and blood of Christ, but handle and use it with no greater reverence and devotion than other common foods."

4 The Book of Concord has two references to 1 Corinthians 11:29: Ap XI (Tappert 18, p. 5) and FC Ep VII (Tappert 484, p. 18).

to himself. Thus, one of the reasons for closed Communion is pastoral concern to prevent such unworthy eating (1 Corinthians 11:27). The Lutheran Church has consistently associated unworthy eating with "not discerning the body."

However, some have understood "not discerning the body" as referring to the Church and not to the real presence: "In the center stand not the elements or substance of bread and wine but the action of the fellowship as the body of Christ in the knowledge that it is dependent upon his blessing and subject to his Lordship. To be guilty of the body and blood of the Lord (v. 27) signifies an act of one brother against another."[5] Such an interpretation of "discerning the body" weakens the rationale for closed Communion and takes less seriously the possibility of Christians communing at Lutheran altars not for blessing but for judgment.

During the course of my fifteen-year ministry I have come into contact with Lutheran pastors who have understood "discerning the body" as a reference not to the real presence but to the Church. Regrettably, this understanding was associated with an indifferent attitude toward the historic difference between the Lutheran and Reformed understandings of the Lord's Supper and resulted in the practice of open Communion, defined as all Christians being welcome at the Sacrament. Little or no concern for the necessity to believe in the real presence as taught in the Book of Concord was evident in these cases.

I believe that my personal experiences are simply a microcosm of a larger problem in the Church involving the teachings of the real presence, open versus closed Communion, fellowship and its practices, and even Lutheran identity itself. This problem is becoming more evident as the Evangelical Lutheran Church in America moves toward altar fellowship with Reformed churches as articulated in the document "A Common Calling." *Forum Letter* observes, "The document treats the dogmatic differences between the two traditions in the critical areas of christology and sacramentology as nuances of theology and differing emphases. . . . It is our opinion that Lutheranism has traditionally regarded its differences with the Reformed tradition as rather more fundamental. . . ."[6] In *Lutherans in Ecumenical Dialogue—A Reappraisal* the observation is made, "After having carefully examined the materials produced by three series of dialogues with the Reformed, questions arise concerning the absence of in-depth theological treatment of all the issues which have traditionally separated Lutheran and Reformed churches."[7] There is, then, a perception among many Lutherans that the Lutheran Church in North America is experiencing a crisis of identity not unlike the one experienced

5 Colin Brown, ed., *The New International Dictionary of New Testament Theology*, vol. 1 (Grand Rapids: Zondervan, 1976), 237.

6 Paul Hinlicky, ed., *Forum Letter* 21, no. 5 (May 28, 1992): 6.

7 Joseph A. Burgess, ed., *Lutherans in Ecumenical Dialogue—A Reappraisal* (Minneapolis: Augsburg, 1990), 44.

in the nineteenth century.[8] Dr. Samuel S. Schmucker advocated what was known in his day as "American Lutheranism" which threatened the distinctive characteristics of Lutheranism with the result that Lutheranism was hardly distinguishable from other Christians of the Reformed tradition.[9]

I introduce our study of 1 Corinthians 11:29 in this manner in order to illustrate some of the basic issues at stake. Let us now turn our attention to the text itself.

THE CONTEXT

Clearly Paul is talking about two closely related problems in 1 Corinthians 11:17–34. There were divisions in the congregation: "For, in the first place, when you come together as a church, I hear that there are *divisions* among you, and I believe it in part" (v. 18); "Do you not have houses to eat and drink in? Or do you *despise* the church of God and *humiliate* those who have nothing? What shall I say to you? Shall I commend you for this? No, I will not" (v. 22); "So then, my brothers, when you come together to eat, wait for one another" (v. 33).

On the other hand, there were at least some who did not understand the Lord's Supper and its purpose or, while knowing the purpose, *abused the Supper.* This is brought out by several verses: "for there must be *factions* [*heresies*] among you in order that those who are genuine among you may be recognized. When you come together, *it is not the Lord's Supper that you eat.* For in your eating, each one goes ahead with his own meal. One goes hungry, another gets drunk" (1 Corinthians 11:19–21).

Because they were coming together to simply satisfy their hunger and thirst, Paul repeats the Words of Institution and the purpose of the Supper. He reminds them that the Supper is a Means of Grace giving the benefits of Christ's suffering and death on the cross, forgiveness. This is communicated in verses 24–26: "And when he had given thanks, he broke it and said, 'This is My body, *which is for you. Do this in remembrance of Me.*' In the same way also He took the cup after supper, saying, 'This cup is *the new covenant in My blood.* Do this, as often as you drink it, *in remembrance of Me.*' For as often as you eat this bread and drink this cup, *you proclaim the Lord's death until He comes.*"

The Corinthians' bad treatment of their poorer members was the result of a misuse of the Supper itself. In other words, had the Corinthians recognized the

8 This crisis has been noted by a number of individuals. vol. 22, no. 8, p. 6 of "Forum Letter" calls the readers' attention to a monograph by Luther A. Gotwald, Jr., "The Trial of Luther A. Gotwald—A Lutheran Identity Crisis," delivered in April of 1993 to the annual meeting of the Lutheran Historical Society. In addition, reference is made to David A. Gustafson's *Lutherans in Crisis: The Question of Identity in the American Republic.*

9 See Vergilius Ferm, *The Crisis in American Lutheran Theology* (St. Louis: Concordia, 1987), 117–235; and E. Clifford Nelson, ed., *The Lutherans in North America* (Philadelphia: Fortress Press, 1975), 120–24, 127, 217–27, 233.

Supper as a Means of Grace, and taken seriously the real presence of the body and blood of Jesus Christ, they would never have treated their fellow members in such a shameful manner. They could satisfy their hunger and thirst at home (v. 33). Such activities have no place in the Lord's Supper; it has other purposes. Were the Corinthians to start using the Supper for its intended purpose and receive it with reverence by remembering and believing in the real presence of Christ's body and blood, they would, as a result, stop shaming those who were less fortunate. Such disunity and favoritism would never have shown itself had the Corinthians had the right understanding of the Supper and treated the Supper accordingly.

THE MEANING OF Σῶμα

According to the lexicons σῶμα has four basic meanings:[10] (1) The body of a man or animal. (2) The bodies of plants and heavenly bodies. (3) The Christian community. (4) The body of Jesus Christ in the Lord's Supper.

When we examine the use of σῶμα in 1 Corinthians we find the following uses: (1) The human body: 5:3; 6:13, 15, 16, 18–20; 7:4; 9:27; 13:3. (2) Plants, heavenly bodies, spiritual bodies: 15:35, 37, 38, 40, 44. (3) The Church: 10:17; 12:13–20, 22–25, 27. (4) The Lord's Supper: 10:16; 11:24, 27.

The frequent use of σῶμα as "Church" in chapter 12 should not determine the use of σώμα in chapter 11 because the immediate context (vv. 23–28) has more influence on the meaning of σῶμα than the more remote context. Chapter 12 is dealing with a new subject as indicated by περὶ in verse 1 (the ESV translation "now"). Paul uses this format frequently in 1 Corinthians to introduce new subjects: 7:1, 25; 8:1; 12:1; 16:1, 12. In addition, the subject matter of chapter 12 is not the Church *per se*, but spiritual gifts. The subject of Church as the Body of Christ and the illustration of the human body is a sub-theme made necessary to discuss the subject of spiritual gifts. In chapter 12, the Lord's Supper is not referred to as the basis of unity in the Church, but the unity comes from having the same Spirit (12:4), the same Lord (12:5), and the same God (12:6).

In contrast, chapter 10 has more bearing on the use of σῶμα in chapter 11 than does chapter 12 because of the subject matter. Chapters 10 and 11 are clearly related to each other in the discussion of the Lord's Supper. As chapter 10 speaks about the Lord's Supper in relation to idol worship and the meals associated with

10 Grimm and Wilke. *A Greek-English Lexicon of the New Testament*, translated and revised by Joseph H. Thayer (Wheaton, IL: Evangel Publishing Co., 1974), 611; W. Bauer, *A Greek-English Lexicon of the New Testament*, translated and edited by W. Arndt, F. Gingrich (Chicago: The University of Chicago Press, 1953), 806, 807; G. Kittle and G. Friedrich, eds., *Theological Dictionary of The New Testamen*t, trans. by G. Bromiley (Grand Rapids: Eerdmans, 1964), 1024–94. Bauer, Arndt, Gingrich and Kittle understand σῶμα in 1 Cor 11:29 as a reference to the body of the Lord in the Supper. Thayer makes no reference to 1 Cor 11:29.

the worship of idols, chapter 11 speaks about the relation of the Lord's Supper to the worshiping congregation.

The word σῶμα is used five times (including the disputed time in v. 29) in chapters 10 and 11. If we do not count verse 29, three of the four references refer not to the Church, but to the Lord's Supper (10:17—Church; 10:16; 11:24, 27—the Lord's Supper). This means that in the immediate context of verse 29 the only body that is referred to is the body of Christ in the Lord's Supper (vv. 24, 27). The immediate context then favors σῶμα as referring to the Lord's Supper, not the Church.

Had Paul written "not discerning the body *and the blood*" exegetes would not have thought his words strange at all, because the context of the verses immediately preceding verse 29 speaks of the Words of Institution, and about being guilty of the body and blood of Jesus, and so the need for self-examination (v. 28). Had Paul written "not discerning the body *and the blood*," no one would say, "Isn't it strange that Paul would talk about the real presence at this point in his letter?" Such a reference clearly fits the immediate context. What has been perplexing and has caused confusion for some is why Paul only mentions the body and not the blood of Christ. Here are some considerations:

1. Paul is using synecdoche, a figure of speech where a part is put for the whole, for example, "The ranch is run by fifty hands," or as in Acts 27:37 where "soul" is used for the whole person. In *The Expositor's Greek Testament*, G. G. Findlay calls it an aposiopesis—the leaving of a thought incomplete.[11]
2. In chapter 11 Paul uses "to eat" to include *drinking* as well as eating: "When you come together, it is not the Lord's Supper that you *eat*. For in *eating*, each goes ahead with his own meal. One goes *hungry*, another gets *drunk*. . . . So then, my brothers, when you come together to *eat*, wait for one other" (vv. 20, 21, 33).
3. This usage of "to eat," including the drinking, is seen in Matthew 26:17: "Now on the first day of Unleavened Bread the disciples came to Jesus saying, 'Where will you have us prepare for you *to eat* the Passover?' "

In chapter 11, Paul never uses σώμα in reference to the Church (not counting the disputed use in v. 29). But ἐκκλησία occurs three times: "If anyone is inclined to be contentious about this, we have no such practice, nor do the *churches* of God" (v. 16); "For in the first place, when you come together as a *church*, I hear that there are divisions among you. And I believe it in part" (v. 18); and "What! Do you not have houses to eat and drink in? Or do you despise the *church* of God and humiliate those who have nothing? What shall I say to you? Shall I commend

11 W. R. Nicoll, ed., *The Expositor's Greek Testament*, vol. 2. (New York: George H. Doran Company), 833.

you in this? No, I will not!" (v. 22). In these and the preceding verses Paul deals with the sectarianism and uncaring behavior of some of the Corinthians. It is not necessary for him to repeat it in verse 29. Beginning with verse 23 Paul is concerned with the Lord's Supper itself and how it is being misused and abused and the consequences of judgment. In verses 23–26 he repeats the Words of Institution about the essence and purpose of the Lord's Supper. In verses 27–29 he talks about the consequences and implications of the Lord's Supper in the Corinthian congregation. Being reminded of the purpose and blessings of the Lord's Supper, Paul expected the problem of disunity at the Lord's Table to be corrected.

THE MEANING OF Διακρινεῖν—DISCERNING

The basic meanings of this word include "to part," "to sift," "to make a distinction," "to differentiate," "to judge," "to doubt," "to separate," "to discriminate a person/thing from the rest."[12] As we study the use of this word in the New Testament we learn what we *are* to discern and what we are *not* to discern.

It is proper to διακρινεῖν (discern) ourselves: "But if we *judged* ourselves truly, we would not be judged" (1 Corinthians 11:31). It is also permitted to discern legal disputes (controversies): "I say this to shame you. Can it be that there is no one among you wise enough to settle [*judge*] a dispute between the brothers?" (1 Corinthians 6:5). It is also proper to do this with the devil: "But when the archangel Michael, contending with the devil, was *disputing* about the body of Moses, he did not presume to pronounce a blasphemous judgment, but said, 'The Lord rebuke you'" (Jude 9). People also discern the sign of the sky: "He answered them, 'When it is evening, you say, "It will be fair weather, for the sky is red," and in the morning, "It will be stormy today, for the sky is red and threatening." You know how to *interpret* the appearance of the sky, but you cannot interpret the signs of the times'" (Matthew 16:2–3). This last reference is a good parallel to 1 Corinthians 11:29 as διακρινεῖν is used in a sense to see something that is not obvious to the uninformed person. To the uninformed person it is only a red sky, but the informed see more, what kind of day it will be. Likewise in the Supper there is more than meets the eye. There is more than simply bread and wine; the body and blood of Christ are present as we have been told by the Words of Institution.

This understanding is reinforced in 1 Corinthians 10:15–16 where Paul uses the verb κρινεῖν in connection with the real presence of the body and blood of Jesus Christ in the Lord's Supper. Paul says, "I speak as to sensible people; *judge* for yourselves what I say. The cup of blessing that we bless, is it not a participation in the blood of Christ? The bread that we break, is it not a participation in the body of Christ?" Paul is asking people to judge, to discern, that there is more than bread

12 BDAG, 184; Kittle, 3:922; Thayer, 138.

and wine in the Lord's Supper. Though this is not evident to the eyes, it is evident by the Words of Institution which are accepted in faith.

Furthermore, διακρινεῖν does not appear to be the appropriate verb to use if σῶμα refers to the Church. If by "Church," "people" are meant, a word study on διακρινεῖν shows that this is something that we are *not* to do in the Church, that is, to fellow believers. Some examples: "He made no *distinction* between us and them, having cleansed their hearts by faith." (Acts 15:9); "For who sees anything *different* in you? What do you have that you did not receive? If, then, you received it, why do you boast as if you did not receive it?" (1 Corinthians 4:7); "Have you not *made distinctions* [*discriminated*] among yourselves and become judges with evil thoughts?" (James 2:4). The point is that we are *not* to discern the Body of Christ, that is, the Church. We are *not to* make distinctions and show discrimination among fellow believers. But this is precisely what Paul speaks against in verses 17–22 as he mentions the sin of despising and humiliating the Church. However, in verse 29 Paul says the *opposite* of this: "For anyone who eats and drinks without discerning the body [of the Lord] eats and drinks judgment on himself." He criticizes the Corinthians because they *should* be discerning the body, and they are not. This leads us to conclude, then, that Paul is not using the word σῶμα to refer to the Church, fellow believers.

CONCLUSION

In summary, the phrase "not discerning the body" refers to the real presence of the body of Jesus Christ in the Lord's Supper and not to the Church. We have based this conclusion on: (1) The immediate context of the verse (vv. 17–34, especially the verses containing the Words of Institution, and chapter 10, especially vv. 16–17); (2) The meaning of σῶμα in the immediate context; (3) The meaning of the word διακρινεῖν and its appropriate use in reference to the real presence, and its inappropriate use in reference to the Church; (4) That the frequent use of σῶμα in chapter 12 should not influence the interpretation of "discerning the body"; (5) If Paul had the Church in mind he had precedent in chapter 11 to use ἐκκλησία (vv. 16, 18, 22) again in verse 29 but did not.

There were two closely related problems addressed by Paul in 1 Corinthians 11. The presenting problem was the division and discrimination manifested when the Corinthians came together. However, the root problem was a false view of the Lord's Supper with reference to the real presence of Christ's body and blood. In verse 29, Paul is addressing this root problem. He warns all who come to the Supper of the Lord that belief in the real presence is required of all to partake in a worthy manner and not receive a judgment. As such, Paul's words still apply today and have implications for the issue of open versus closed Communion.

CHAPTER SIXTEEN

STEP UP TO THE ALTAR
THINKING ABOUT THE THEOLOGY AND PRACTICE OF THE LORD'S SUPPER

JOEL D. BIERMANN

ONE OF THE SINGULAR DELIGHTS OF STUDYING theology is the depth and breadth of the subject. Name a subject, that is, a *locus*—any will do—and the possibilities of exploration and discussion are endless. This is the case because theology is not (as we well know, but seem sometimes to forget) a series of discrete articles strung together by convention or long tradition. Augustine did not write theology, neither did Melanchthon nor Pieper; each merely explicated and articulated what was already there. Theology is in fact nothing more than God's reality, His truth. It is a simple unity, and one pulls it loose into component parts only at the risk of sacrificing the whole truth. So it matters little which door one chooses to enter into the exploration; sooner or later every topic comes into focus and every *locus* is relevant. All this serves, I suppose, both as warning and justification for what follows. While it might seem that I have lost my way, or wandered into avenues irrelevant for the present discussion, hopefully the connections will eventually be evident and convincing to all. The avenue by which we are to embark on this theological contemplation is the Lord's Supper, specifically the "theology and practice" of the same. The topic is a welcome one, and the invitation has satisfied my growing desire to lend some thoughts to the lively debate that continues to thrive in our midst.[1]

I. WHO SHOULD BE COMMUNING AT OUR ALTAR?

It would seem that there is little to debate about our theology and practice. Everything is laid out beautifully in the Small Catechism:

1 This article was originally a paper given at the Minnesota South District Theological Conference on September 29, 2007. My thanks to Charles Arand for his helpful criticism of an earlier draft of this essay.

> What is the Sacrament of the Altar? Answer: It is the true body and blood of our Lord Jesus Christ under the bread and wine, instituted by Christ Himself for us Christians to eat and drink.
>
> How can bodily eating and drinking do such a great thing? Answer: Eating and drinking certainly do not do it, but rather the words that are recorded: "given for you" and "shed for you for the forgiveness of sins." These words, when accompanied by the physical eating and drinking, are the essential thing in the Sacrament, and whoever believes these very words has what they declare and state, namely, "forgiveness of sins."
>
> Who, then, receives this Sacrament worthily? Answer: Fasting and bodily preparation are in fact a fine external discipline, but a person who has faith in these words, "given for you" and "shed for you for the forgiveness of sins," is really worthy and well prepared. However, a person who does not believe these words or doubts them is unworthy and unprepared, because the words "for you" require truly believing hearts.

That is it. Everything we need is right there. Luther gives us what we need to know about the Sacrament. *Satis est.* It is enough. Or is it? Well, that depends. Did Luther provide the sufficient and complete answer for the Christian contemplating her right reception of Holy Communion? Absolutely. It is an issue of faith; simple trust in the promise of Christ and thirst for forgiveness makes one a worthy recipient. Period. Luther accomplished his purpose: he provided instruction for the simple believer. But, do Luther's beautifully wrought words provide the sufficient and complete answer for the congregation or the pastor seeking understanding about who should commune at the altar entrusted to them? Certainly not. That is another question altogether. In the first instance the question being addressed is, "Am I worthy to be at the altar receiving the Sacrament?" The second situation, however, asks a different question entirely: "Who should be communing at our altar?" Luther's explanation in the Small Catechism provides part—but not all—of the answer to that question.

To reach a faithful and responsible answer to the second question requires a careful consideration of a few more areas of theology. It is not merely a matter of prompting people honestly to ascertain their state of repentance and their understanding of the miracle of Christ's presence in the Sacrament. Actually, it would be cause for some hope if all of our Lutheran Church—Missouri Synod (LCMS) congregations consistently made a serious effort to do this much. Still, if that is as far as we go in our practice of the Lord's Supper, then we are guilty of misrepresenting the full significance of the Sacrament's communion, guilty of misleading people into an incorrect understanding of unity in confession, and guilty of failing to exercise the role of "steward of the mysteries of God"(1 Corinthians 4:1). No, to be a faithful steward of the profound mystery that is the Sacrament of the Altar, one must take into account more than the sacramental understanding of those at the rail. The "real presence" litmus test is inadequate. To put it bluntly: Not every communicant worthy by the standards of the Small Catechism is necessarily a Christian brother who should be communing at your altar.

This way of framing the question, it should be evident, is in full agreement with the position developed in the 1999 document from the Commission on Theology and Church Relations (CTCR), *Admission to the Lord's Supper: Basics of Biblical and Confessional Teaching*.[2] Recognizing the ready availability of this important document, and heartily commending its study and the avid appropriation of its argument and conclusions, the present study will endeavor to avoid redundancy by considering at least two attendant areas of theological interest not exhaustively treated in this CTCR document: first, a failure to appreciate the responsibility of oversight, and, second, a misapplication of "Law and Gospel." These topics, which will comprise the bulk of this study, are not chosen randomly or arbitrarily, but grow out of a need to address questions that continue to swarm around the Communion practices of individual congregations in the LCMS.

These areas of further exploration both grow directly out of a common concern: The fact that, despite the oft-repeated LCMS position embracing and encouraging the practice of closed Communion, surveys as well as anecdotal evidence indicate that a substantial number of LCMS congregations disagree. While it may be that there are only a handful of pastors and congregations that are willing openly and vocally to question the LCMS position on closed Communion, the number of congregations and pastors that are actually practicing what may be best described as "functionally open Communion" is quite significant. Clearly, a definition of functionally open Communion is in order. A church's Communion practice is functionally open when the determination of who is an appropriate recipient (and not merely a "worthy" recipient) is left exclusively in the hands of the individual contemplating eating and drinking, and when the Church's concern is limited to an individual's worthiness without further consideration of that person's confession.[3] In other words, professed agreement with the idea of closed Communion is irrelevant if actual practice leaves it up to individuals to determine whether they should commune.

II. THE PASTOR AS STEWARD OF THE MYSTERIES OF GOD

The simple solution to the problem of functionally open Communion is to reassert and reaffirm the role of the congregation and especially its pastor in overseeing

2 A Report of The Lutheran Church—Missouri Synod Commission on Theology and Church Relations, *Admission to the Lord's Supper: Basics of Biblical and Confessional Teaching* (St. Louis: The Lutheran Church—Missouri Synod, 2000), www.lcms.org/graphics/assets/media/CTCR/admisup.pdf.

3 This distinction is helpfully explained and applied in *Admission to the Lord's Supper*, 41–48.

the celebration of the Sacrament. This means that one of the primary contributing forces behind many congregations' practice of functionally open Communion is in reality a denigration of the Office of the Pastoral Ministry—often perpetrated by the pastors themselves. The pertinent *sedes doctrinae* are 1 Corinthians 4:1: "This is how one should regard us, as servants of Christ and stewards of the mysteries of God," and Acts 20:28: "Pay careful attention to yourselves and to all the flock, in which the Holy Spirit has made you overseers, to care for the church of God, which He obtained with His own blood." As one would expect, the Lutheran Confessions reinforce the role of pastor as God's chosen means of administering the Sacraments. Article V of the Augsburg Confession actually binds the article of justification to the Office of Preaching: "To obtain such faith God instituted the office of preaching, giving the gospel and the sacraments" (AC V 1). Furthermore, Article XVIII makes it clear that, while there is much bishops should not do (running a government or leading an army, for instance), it is their responsibility to administer God's grace: "Our people teach as follows. According to the gospel the power of the keys or of the bishops is a power and command of God to preach the gospel, to forgive or retain sin, and to administer and distribute the sacraments" (AC XXVIII 5–6).

As bishop or overseer of the Church in a given place, it is the responsibility of the pastor to provide for his flock and ensure that the Gospel and Sacraments are being delivered rightly. As with the faithful prophets of Israel, the pastor does not operate on his own initiative or even according to his own preferences or ideas. He is God's spokesman and must take the task of administration and oversight seriously. When he delivers the host to a communicant, he should be quite confident that the one receiving this gift of the Gospel is receiving it rightly: in faith and in the confession of the truth. He cannot freely pass out the goods without a thought to those who are receiving, as if their actual presence proves the legitimacy of their reception. Contrary to much popular thought, the Sacrament is not just between Jesus and the individual. The pastor is not an insensible spiritual vending machine without responsibility for those who are receiving. The Sacrament is Christ's presence, His gift to the Church; and the Church celebrates this gift in the unity of their confession. It is the celebration of that gathering of people. The pastor oversees this celebration and takes care that it is being shared by those who belong to that unity. This is his task. This is what it means to be pastor. To do less is to shirk the responsibility of the Office. To push onto the visitor the decision about whether to commune is to abdicate his pastoral responsibility.

To refine a point in this argument, I am saying that reliance on an announcement in the bulletin that the Sacrament is for those who are baptized, repentant, and "believe in the real presence" is completely inadequate. Such a practice clearly amounts to nothing but functionally open Communion. The practice of relying on bulletin announcements places the decision entirely in the hands of the individual. This practice makes it obvious to the church visitor that it is his choice whether to commune—which, of course, is precisely the way that just about everybody wants it to be. In a society that celebrates the individual, dismisses the role of community, and operates with an entitlement mentality, giving the decision to the individual is reasonable and easy. It is a common thought: "Let each person decide. It is between the visitor and God, I'm just delivering the Gospel, just passing out hosts." Wrong. The pastor is the steward. It is his responsibility to invite people to the rail, to exclude those who should not commune, and, yes, even to refuse to commune those who may present themselves at the altar inappropriately. This is neither easy nor fun. Practicing oversight and administering the Sacrament can be altogether uncomfortable and demanding. The pastor would do well, then, to recall those prophets of old who frequently found themselves carrying out distasteful and unpopular tasks not by their choosing or according to their preferences, but at the behest of the Lord whose call they had been compelled to answer. So it is with the Lord's servants in the twenty-first century, or so it should be.

To accomplish such a shift in the practice of the Lord's Supper will require a corresponding shift in the way that pastors and people view the Office. Yes, pastors are there to proclaim the Gospel, to dispense the forgiveness of sins, and to comfort souls. But it is patently obvious in Scripture and the Confessions that they are also "there" to use the Keys: to convict sinners, exclude the unrepentant, and oversee the right practice of the Sacraments. Functionally open Communion amounts to pastoral neglect. The corrective is not pastors as dictators, but pastors as responsible stewards diligently administering God's Means of Grace so that the broken are healed and the unrepentant are admonished. As stewards, they will also see that the Lord's Supper, the meal that feeds and binds the Church to Christ and to one another in the unity of their confession, is celebrated by those for whom it is intended: the members of the Church in that place. Those who are not part of that particular community of faith but who are present at the celebration of the Sacrament should learn to see their participation as privilege and not as right or entitlement. They should assume that this celebration does not include them unless they are specifically invited to join—hence the time-honored, but now typically disregarded, practice of conversing with the pastor before the celebration. To make the point sharper yet, assuming such a conversation occurs, it is imperative that the pastor does not perpetuate the erroneous notion that if the visitor "believes in Jesus and the real presence," then she is welcome. There is much more to it than that, and the pastor needs to communicate this fact by his conversation and his decision . . . and it is *his* decision. He has been entrusted with this responsibility by his Lord and the priesthood in that place. He is accountable for his practice in administering the Sacrament.

While such sacristy conversations are rarely fit settings for detailed discussions about the doctrine of the Church, Sacraments, and fellowship, it is a place to establish a relationship with visitors who are inquiring about their participation in the

Sacrament. The those who are not in fellowship with the congregation should be told that the congregation eagerly desires their participation and would be delighted to welcome them when it is clear that there is unity in confession. Clearly, such a response will demand additional conversation, but if the proper tone is set, this need not be automatically negative and offensive. Admittedly, individuals steeped in American, democratic culture will frequently struggle with such an "exclusionary" position. The best pastoral practice is certainly demanded in such situations. It bears remembering that the Church is, by Christ's own definition, exclusionary. While all are indeed welcome and urged to come to worship, only those in Christ are part of the community.

III. Denying the Sacrament to Christian Visitors

Before embarking on the next major area of discussion, the misuse of the Law and Gospel paradigm, a quick word needs to be said about the Church's squeamishness about actually telling a real person that he is not at present welcome at the Communion rail. It seems that the driving force for most twenty-first-century American Christians—including those in LCMS pews—is the need to be nice. So most LCMS people who take 1 Corinthians 11 seriously recognize the need to keep people who do not "discern Christ's body" away from the rail. These nice Lutherans see the need to reserve the Sacrament for those who are worthy in the Small Catechism sense of worthiness. It is done for the sake of the uninformed or unbelieving visitor. Letting an unbeliever commune to his own condemnation is definitely not being nice.

These same people for the same reason, however, may chafe at the thought of denying the Sacrament to a Christian visitor who believes in the "real presence" but just happens to be a Methodist or a member of the ELCA. Telling such nice people "no" to the Sacrament is not nice and therefore deemed unnecessary or even unchristian. The steward of God's mysteries needs to educate his people about the importance of the Sacrament on many planes and particularly needs to emphasize the corporate and confessional aspects of the Sacrament that are present along with the individual's communion with Christ. Ultimately, the goal is to adjust the Church's culture so that nice people are able to recognize that a person should not expect to commune at any and every altar at which he happens to be present. Guests do not impose on their hosts or simply anticipate being treated like those who are part of the community where they are present. Oddly, people seem quite capable of accepting this fact in many areas. Guests at country clubs, business events, and military ceremonies recognize and accept that some aspects of these occasions are only for those who are part of that community. This distinction is understood even within the life of the Church. For instance, a visitor present at a baptismal service certainly would not think it appropriate to bring his own child immediately to the font so that he could also participate in the activities of the community, nor would the pastor or those sitting near the guest encourage him to do so. By necessity, such a process of reeducation will progress slowly and sensitively, but where faithful stewards are heeding their Lord's call, it should begin.

A pastor acting as a steward of the mysteries of God is a *sine qua non* for an acceptable practice of the Sacrament. Both pastors and people, however, too often diminish and trivialize such stewardship to counting cups or hosts to ensure that there will be no embarrassing shortages during the distribution. On the other hand, stewardship may be equated with finding creative ways to "speed up" the sacramental liturgy and distribution so that it can be done more efficiently and within the confines of the sacred 60-minute rule; this is deemed necessary to satisfy the needs of the hypothetical visitor who is, it sometimes seems, the unwitting and unappreciative center of the entire worship event. Stewardship that is marked by a serious effort to elevate the Sacrament's significance and to guard its distribution only to those who are part of the community of the faith in that place is difficult. But the difficulty is not merely the hard reality of strained relationships or the threat of being thought a bully or close-minded and intolerant. No, what makes such faithful stewardship extremely difficult, if not altogether rare, is that in addition to personal preferences, relationship demands, and social pressure, theology is involved. The reasoning and arguing of many who resist or completely reject the practice of closed Communion is based on more than feelings or fear; it is an issue of theology. In fact, some would insist that good Lutheran theology actually demands the practice of open Communion. The argument is that Christ's Gospel is available to all and the steward's job is to deliver it to all. Certainly, such reasoning should apply to the Lord's Supper. Thus we arrive at what I believe to be the very heart of the issue that provokes such passionate and acrimonious debate about appropriate Communion practices in our churches. The central problem plaguing unity in understanding and practice of the Lord's Supper is a misunderstanding and misuse of the Law and Gospel paradigm.

IV. THE MISUSE OF THE LAW AND GOSPEL PARADIGM

Lutherans who have been steeped in a heavy atmosphere of "grace alone" and "the Gospel must predominate" have been conditioned to be wary of anything that smells or even remotely feels like Law. If it is Law, it has to be bad. Obviously, establishing and adhering to criteria about who may and who may not attend the Lord's Supper has more than a little whiff of the Law about it. The aversion to such legalistic ideas is compounded in the case of the Lord's Supper by the fact that the Sacrament is a God-given Means of Grace. It is pure Gospel: the delivery of Christ's blood-bought forgiveness for unworthy, undeserving, and unassuming sinners who come to the rail with empty hands and broken hearts. To befoul the sacred Gospel with the filthy Law is unconscionable. So it is that those who advocate a more open practice of the Lord's Supper are often perceived as those who take the high road and who more fully understand and value the reality of the Gospel. Of course, by implication, those who insist on a closed Communion practice are therefore either still benighted or more horribly simply arrogant Pharisees who love tradition and "doctrine" more than people and the Gospel. Consequently, if one is going to make a case for closed Communion as the right practice of faithful stewards who love their Lord, their flock, and the lost, then one must address this apparent conflict between Law and Gospel.

Clearly, we have now broached an area of theology more critical, more sweeping, and more fundamental than even the doctrine of the Office of the Ministry. A thorough treatment of the problem of the polarization of Law and Gospel and the often-devastating consequences of such a polarization for God's people lies well beyond the confines of this study. Still, since this topic is essential to a right understanding of our practice of the Lord's Supper, a brief introduction is in order. The crucial contribution to this discussion came in 1993 when David Yeago, an ELCA theologian, published his seminal article "Gnosticism, Antinomianism, and Reformation Theology."[4] In this essay, Yeago argued convincingly that today's Protestant Church is perilously infected with insidious forms of the "isms" identified in his title. Their pervasive yet often unrecognized presence within Protestantism he traces to a misconstrual of the polarity between Law and Gospel. Yeago argues that when Law and Gospel are set against each other, the Gospel inevitably gains its definition in antithesis to the Law itself. The Gospel becomes our liberator not from our failure to keep the Law and the consequent just wrath of God; rather, it becomes our liberator from the Law *per se*. Hence any word that comes to a Christian as command, direction, or guidance is ruled out by the liberating Gospel. "If the law/gospel distinction is a final antithesis," Yeago argues, "then *any* call for one ordering of life rather than another, will by definition be the law from which the gospel frees us."[5]

In this theological climate, antinomianism thrives. "Indeed," Yeago charges, "much twentieth century Protestant theology has been antinomian all along; the practical antinomianism now regnant in many churches is simply a long-standing

4 David S. Yeago, "Gnosticism, Antinomianism, and Reformation Theology: Reflections on the Costs of a Construal," *Pro Ecclesia* 2, no. 1 (1993): 37–49.

5 Yeago, "Gnosticism, Antinomianism, and Reformation Theology," 42 (emphasis in original). Once freed from the Law, it should be noted, people are at liberty to choose whatever pleases them and to take their cues about acceptable behavior from the culture or from whatever other source is convenient or comfortable.

theoretical antinomianism achieving the courage of its convictions."[6] Yeago's accusation of Gnosticism derives from the same thesis of a misconstrual of the Law and Gospel dichotomy, but that discussion must be deferred. Yeago has no patience for the practices in ordinary church life which derive from the antinomian and Gnostic theology rampant among Lutherans. He laments the "contemporary tender-minded rhetoric about all those 'hurting people' who need more than anything else to be liberated from all order and absolved of all expectations by the redemptive 'inclusivity' of the antinomian church."[7] Yeago also denounces the effects on worship, education, and ethics as congregations increasingly jettison extensive catechesis and ritual/liturgical observances in favor of formats deemed less "demanding," more contemporary, and presumably more "meaningful." Yeago's incisive analysis has been reaffirmed by a number of other theologians including Robert Benne,[8] Reinhard Hütter,[9] and Gilbert Meilaender.[10] The lesson is clear and disconcerting: Law and Gospel cannot be made the final paradigm on which to hang all theological reflection and practice.

Scholars have offered various solutions to the problem of the misuse of the distinction of Law and Gospel and its misconstrual as a polarity. I will present what is, I am fully persuaded, the best way to solve the dilemma, the way followed by the reformers: the understanding of the two kinds of righteousness. Essentially, the two kinds of righteousness is the recognition that individuals live in two distinct realms: one before God and the other before the world. Before God, human beings are always totally dependent and passive, simply receiving the grace that God delivers in Christ through the means. Before God, the Christian is unconcerned about his own works, recognizing that only Christ's work matters. In the realm of this world, however, Christian people live as responsible creatures obligated to fulfill certain tasks for the sake of the neighbor who depends on that faithful service. In this realm, the Christian is active and is quite concerned about the quality and quantity of his works.[11] The significance of shifting from a paradigm of Law and Gospel to one based on the two kinds of righteousness is profound,

6 Yeago, "Gnosticism, Antinomianism, and Reformation Theology," 42.

7 Yeago, "Gnosticism, Antinomianism, and Reformation Theology," 42.

8 Robert Benne, "Lutheran Ethics," in *The Promise of Lutheran Ethics*, ed. Karen L. Bloomquist and John R. Stumme (Minneapolis: Fortress Press, 1998), 11–30, esp. 27–28.

9 Reinhard Hütter, "The Twofold Center of Lutheran Ethics," in *The Promise of Lutheran Ethics*, ed. Karen L. Bloomquist and John R. Stumme (Minneapolis: Fortress Press, 1998), 31–69, esp. 42–43.

10 Gilbert Meilander, "Reclaiming the Quest for Holiness," *Lutheran Quarterly* 13 (1999): 483–92, esp. 488.

11 For more on the two kinds of righteousness, one may begin by consulting Charles P. Arand and Joel Biermann, "Why the Two Kinds of Righteousness?" *Concordia Journal* 33 (2007): 116–35.

especially for the way that one thinks about the Christian's life of obedience and the place and necessity of good works.

It is essential to recognize that a congregation's practice of the Lord's Supper is shaped by both kinds of righteousness. Certainly, the reception of the Sacrament is God's delivery of the Gospel *par excellence*. This is passive righteousness before God in all of its glorious, inexplicable grace. However, the Christian's righteousness before the world, that is, before other men, also comes into play. Here it is important to remember that the congregation and its pastor are held responsible for the right practice of the Lord's Supper; for the sake of their fellow creatures, they must take care that the Sacrament is being properly celebrated and received. Thus the congregation that correctly understands the Lord's Supper as God's gift and as its celebration of unity with God and with one another will establish guidelines and directions for the right celebration that will uphold and teach the truth about the Sacrament. In other words, a conscientious and serious practice of closed Communion is not antithetical to the Gospel, but actually necessary and supportive of the Gospel and its gracious delivery.

A pastor acting as steward of God's mysteries is acting for the sake of the Gospel, his flock, and the worship visitor when he practices closed Communion. All will benefit when God's will for the Sacrament is followed. Of course, this truth is more than a little counterintuitive. While not everyone may cheerfully recognize or appreciate the value of such a faithful and careful Communion practice, God's revealed will is always to be followed, even when the immediate results appear less than encouraging or satisfactory. The situation is not so different than that of pastoral ministry to a cohabitating couple. One could argue that the Gospel must predominate, and that any attempt to apply the corrective of the Law will only result in alienation and estrangement of the couple. Thus the "Gospel-oriented" pastor would overlook the breach of God's Law (i.e., God's will!) and proceed with some more "loving" plan of action. Such behavior, of course, would amount to nothing but bare-faced antinomianism, with all of its sometimes distant—but always disastrous—consequences. When God's will is thwarted, God's creation always suffers. Gospel motives do not redeem a sinful choice. Moreover, one cannot help wondering whether fear is not as great a motivator in such situations as one's professed love for the Gospel. The same question applies with equal force to the present discussion about right Communion practice. It is perhaps more than a little convenient that acting in the name of the Gospel also happens to be the easy route of least resistance and least offense. Claiming the Gospel as a cloak for cowardice and laziness is still, in the end, just run-of-the-mill antinomianism and disobedience.

V. The Abuse of Pastoral Discretion

Finally, a few brief words must be addressed to the problems of autonomy and the abuse of pastoral discretion. While congregational autonomy may be ensconced in the documents and the hearts of the LCMS, it has deleterious effects in the life of Christ's Church when claimed as a right. Both pastors and congregations need to recognize and cherish the interdependence and unity that exits between them and all other pastors and congregations. A congregation is never acting on its own. Whatever it does or fails to do has an impact on every other gathering of Christ's Church—even if that impact is not directly or immediately experienced by any of those involved. No man and no congregation has the right to "do his own thing" regardless of other pastors and congregations. We are bound to one another and must not ignore one another in our desire to walk faithfully in the ways of our Lord. If nothing else, circuits and districts serve as stubborn reminders of our mutuality and responsibility for one another. There is no place for the Lone Ranger, and there is no place for shunning or disdaining the brother or brothers who appear to be out of step in our walking together as a synod.

Pastoral discretion, then, is to be upheld and guarded as in the best practice of pastoral care. It is not, however, to be abused as an excuse for inaction or reluctance to deal forthrightly with a potentially difficult situation. Neither is a claim of "pastoral discretion" an acceptable justification for blatant and persistent disregard for the express position of the LCMS and its agreed practice. A congregation with functionally open Communion is not exercising pastoral discretion. That congregation is being inconsiderate of her sister congregations, disloyal to the will of the Synod, and—above all—disobedient to the will of God. Cases of pastoral discretion should be rare and the cause of much careful thought and conversation among brother pastors. Recourse to pastoral discretion should never become the norm for a congregation's Communion practice. On the other hand, it is also vital to reiterate that cases of pastoral discretion do exist. When a pastor makes a decision which is clearly an exception to the normal practice of closed Communion, he should expect and welcome the questions and concern of his brother pastors, but he should also expect their trust and willingness to cast his actions in the best possible light. We must be willing to allow one another freely to practice the stewardship of our shared Office of the Holy Ministry without fear of needless criticism or reprisal. Obviously, such mutual trust is cultivated when all involved act with a spirit of cooperation and an awareness of our mutual interdependence and shared life in Christ.

VI. Conclusion

The nature of this topic is that much needs to be considered and said, and much is at stake. The theology and practice of Holy Communion is a topic laden with serious doctrinal questions and concerns, but that does not make it impractical or irrelevant to the life of the Church; that much is hopefully clear by now. Indeed, if this study has succeeded in some small way in persuading even one reader of the serious importance of right doctrine for right practice, then its purpose has been accomplished. The Church's doctrine has everything to do with the Church's vitality and the Church's faithfulness. We dare not forget this truth in our consideration of the theology and practice of the Lord's Supper.

CHAPTER SEVENTEEN

THE LORD'S SUPPER TODAY

WERNER ELERT
TRANSLATED BY MARTIN BERTRAM

THE PLACE OF THE DOCTRINE OF THE SACRAMENTS

Christ's position between God and man as mediator is affirmed in the Church's proclamation in which we hear the voice of His Paraclete. It follows that our belief in Christ is of necessity trinitarian; and if dogmatics wishes to follow the inner logic of the Gospel it must join the doctrine of the work of the Spirit to the doctrine of the work of Christ. All the while dogmatics must also speak of the Church, because the Spirit's exhortation (*paraclesis*) reaches us only through the Church's proclamation (*kerygma*). The proclamation of the Gospel is necessary for the existence of the Church in more respects than one. It determines the Church's unique essence, which distinguishes it from all other human societies that are outwardly similar.

But Gospel proclamation is not the only distinguishing mark of the Church. The Church has also been charged with the administration of the cultic acts of Holy Baptism and of Holy Communion, which activity can by no means be regarded as a mere adjunct to the proclamation of the Word. Since these two sacramental acts are not subordinated to but coordinated with the proclamation of the Word, they confront dogmatics with special questions of methodology, the answers to which are indispensable for the correct understanding of the acts.

Both Sacraments demand separate places in the total domain of dogmatics. In Holy Communion Christians come into immediate contact with the exalted Christ. Therefore it must be treated in conjunction with the doctrine of the person and work of the Redeemer. It is directly connected with the work of the Spirit only insofar as faith is involved—faith which is linked to the *paraclesis* of the Paraclete. To be sure, Baptism is also joined to the work of Christ, but in a reverse sort of a way. It is immediately related to Christ also insofar as the baptized person's incorporation into the Church as "the Body of Christ" is carried out in it. On the other hand, since the Church belongs to the work of the Spirit and there demands a special place, Baptism must be discussed also within the doctrine of the Church as an incorporative act. Since Baptism and Holy Communion, in distinction to the proclamation of the Word, partake of the nature of acts, it is advisable to examine this common feature before we enlarge on the doctrine of Holy Communion.

The dogma taught by the Church is the subject of dogmatics, the content of its dogma coinciding with its kerygma. In dogmatic theology the Church, as it were, checks and double-checks its dogma and thus also its kerygma. The Church is to fulfill its Christ-given commission with regard to the kerygma. By checking on it the Church renders an account as to whether and how it fulfills this commission. However, the commission does not declare, relative to Baptism and to Holy Communion, that there is to be only *teaching* about these, but that they should be *administered*. To be sure, the commission to baptize appears in close association with the commission to teach. Holy Communion likewise appears in close association with the commission "to proclaim the death of the Lord." And in the Lutheran Confessions "Word and Sacrament" are always closely joined together. But precisely this side-by-side position lends the Sacraments an independence of Gospel proclamation.

Self-evidently, there has always been a doctrine on the Sacraments. But just as there is a material difference, for example, between military science and the actual conduct of war, so there is a difference between the Sacraments themselves and the doctrine concerning them. In both instances the action enjoys the real and essential priority over the teaching. Just as wars were waged before the birth of military science, so Baptism and Holy Communion were administered before a doctrine pertaining to them was formulated. Baptism and Holy Communion must be administered by the Church because this was commanded by Christ. This commission is executed by action, not by teaching about it. The performance of this action is independent of its theological conception, for right dogmatic understanding has nothing to do with creating a sacrament.

Thus the doctrine of Baptism and of Communion owes its special place to the fact that it takes its departure not from the kerygma of the Church but from its cultic action. It must proceed from these two facts: (1) the ordination of a sacrament by Christ and (2) its performance by the Church. In relationship to the remaining contents of dogmatics, these two facts must be regarded as characteristic of the Sacraments. Thus it is doubtful whether the doctrine of the Sacraments can for that reason be brought into a systematic association with the whole of dogmatics. A number of deviations from the doctrine of the Sacraments can be traced to the fact that, despite the contingence of the above two points, a systematic connection with the remaining dogma was simply postulated and the validity of the Church's Sacraments thus made dependent on such a systematics. Such a devious course resulted because the deductive process was applied. We proceed deductively when we try to deduce the inner necessity of Baptism and of Holy Communion from some part of the kerygma. That is impossible. Neither can they be deduced from the doctrine of divine creation and preservation; nor from Christology or Pneumatology; nor from the doctrines of reconciliation, justification, and redemption; nor from the doctrine of conversion. Nor can they be viewed as the outgrowth of something preceding them, as good works, for example, result from faith. The New Testament offers no support whatsoever for that.

The New Testament does not even contain a common expression for the actions of Baptism and Communion. Already for this reason every doctrine about them is suspect in advance—suspect of beginning with the nonbiblical term "sacrament" and then investigating whether and how this general term fits both actions. A second wrong procedure in methodology is connected with this. We follow it, for example, when the Augustinian definition of a sacrament as the visible Word (*verbum visible*) determines the structure of the doctrine of the Sacraments, in the sense that the validity of the Sacraments is made dependent on their relationship to the proclaimed Word. The Apology of Melanchthon, too, employed this formula (Ap XIII 5). But here it is quoted as an afterthought, that is, after the author has first stated the necessary facts about each Sacrament. And further, it is here only designed to emphasize the externals. On the other hand, in Neo-Protestant theology it serves to support the thesis of "the Church of the Word only." The Church is, so the argument runs, purely a church of the Word; consequently a sacrament can be but another form of the Word or the confirmation of the Word.

This *quid pro quo*—this something-for-something-else approach—is transparent. Such a doctrine of the Sacraments can be viewed only as an attempted flight from the Sacraments themselves. Therefore a theology which championed or still champions this kind of an argument is chiefly responsible for the actual abandonment of the Sacraments during recent generations. Under no circumstances may its advocates appeal to Luther. For it is precisely he from whom we learn that the formula of the "Church of the Word only" is refuted by the Sacraments. During his entire life Luther comforted himself and others with the fact that he and they were baptized, not with the fact that there is a *doctrine* of Baptism.

The only systematic viewpoint that must be presupposed for the doctrine of the Sacraments is this: Whatever is taught about Baptism and Communion dare not contradict the kerygma of the Church and thus also not its dogma in general. If contradictions should arise between the two facts previously asserted for Baptism and Holy Communion and the dogma of the Church, it is well to assume *a priori* that the Church's dogma needs to be revised. For the facts stated before—the institution of the Sacraments by Christ and their administration by the Church—are not subject to revision. Naturally this rule must be kept in mind especially when the Church's doctrine regarding itself is being considered.

If we avoid the error of thinking that something theological might be learned about Holy Baptism and Holy Communion from the term *sacrament*, no objection can be raised to its use in the sense current in the Church. The concern of Schleiermacher and of others is particularly unfounded, namely, that the use of "sacrament" might move us dangerously close to the Roman doctrine of the Sacraments. On this basis one might also take exception to the expression "Baptism," and finally to our entire dogmatic terminology. Quite to the contrary, we must say that only the use of commonly understood terms enables us to express differences in concepts.

Schleiermacher is correct in stating that a dispute with the Roman Church on the sacramental concept as such is quite superfluous. When we come right down to it, the dispute has to do with the difference in the number of the sacraments. Roman theology operates under the authority of conciliar decree, which even for formal reasons has no binding force for us. Furthermore, when the *Catechismus Romanus* declares in its definition of the word "sacrament" that the idea of sacrament in many scriptural passages denotes "nothing other than a holy, hidden, and mysterious thing" (II, 1, quest. 2), this seems, to be sure, a somewhat unrevealing paraphrase of the biblical "mystery" (μυστήριον). But there is no deeper reason for attacking the use of the term.

However, when Roman theology makes the designation "sacrament" dependent on the fact that the sacramental action is instituted by *God*, we can counter this only with our linguistic usage, which makes this term dependent on the fact that the action was instituted by *Christ*. And that immediately brings a deeper factual difference to the fore. The Roman concept of a sacrament is wide enough to encompass marriage. Substantively speaking, this puts marriage into the same category with Holy Baptism and Holy Communion, and this will never do. Roman theology sees a point of contact in the dispensation of "grace" in marriage as well as in Baptism and in the Lord's Supper. We cannot agree to this, because marriage is a function of the order of creation. As such it dare not be understood at all—or at least not in the same sense as Baptism and Holy Communion—as a New Testament Means of Grace. In order to avoid such inadmissible mix-ups we restrict the term "sacrament" to the cultic acts ordained by Christ.

The oldest Lutheran Confessions apply the term "sacrament" not only to Baptism and Holy Communion but also to Absolution; the Apology, also to "the Ministry of the Word" (*ministerium verbi*, Ap XIII 7ff.). This is based on the conception, as Article VII expresses it, that the Sacraments are rites "which have God's command and promise of grace" (*qui habent mandatum Dei et promissionem gratiae*). The context shows that by the "mandate of God" the commission of Christ is meant. The later restriction of the term "sacrament" to Baptism and Holy Communion is not rooted in an internal change of the concept, it only takes account of the insight that Baptism, Holy Communion, Absolution, and the Office of the Ministry are all based on the institution by Christ and on His promise, but that only the first two combine the promise with an external rite, that is, with a cultic act. It says that after all Baptism and Holy Communion occupy a special position in the things that Christ instituted.

When in addition to Christ's commission the Confessions stress also the promises connected with these acts, the initial step toward a proper theological conception is taken. This step is not derived from the concept of a "sacrament" nor from any other part of the Church's doctrine. As will be shown later, it is drawn from Christ's commission. It is evident immediately that an understanding of the Sacraments derived from the promise attached to them is, at least in the initial step, in accord with the basic content of all evangelical proclamation, for the Gospel is promise. But for that very reason the question now arises as to how cultic acts can fulfill promises, in view of the fact that the promises of the Gospel are proffered in the spoken Word and are perceived with the ear and in the heart.

This inevitable question explains why the attempt has been made again and again in the Church—from the earliest times to the present day—to conceive of Baptism and Holy Communion as analogies to non-Christian rites. Undoubtedly such analogies exist in great abundance. And it makes little difference whether we have mainly Old Testament rites in mind, as in the Ancient Church, or the cults of mystery religions whose parallels to Christian mysteries gratified their discoverers, especially since the eighteenth century. In either case the resemblance consists in the sacral character of human acts, and both are thought of as associated with some transcendent holy thing. The disclosure of these analogies, particularly by religio-historical research at the turn of the last century, rendered theology a great service. It freed it from the obsession that the Christian mysteries might be understood only symbolically, proving that early Christianity at least understood them differently. Heitmüller's exegetical conception did justice to the New Testament statements on Baptism and Holy Communion far better than the entire "pneumatic" exegesis of the following years. It is sad that these studies in comparative religion were not carried out under theological auspices. But it is still sadder that the circuitous route via non-Christian parallels was necessary to take the apostolic conception of the Sacraments seriously again.

This detour is not merely superfluous; in another respect it also fairly obstructs the path to a theological understanding. Similar to the proclamation of the Word, the study of the Sacraments cannot be gained from the *form*, but only from the factual *content*. For that matter, also the evangelical kerygma and its acceptance by the hearer as the Word of God has, as far as form is concerned, non-Christian parallels. Its factual content, however, finds no analogy among pagan religions. Its content is disclosed only to him whose heart is open to it. The same is true of the Christian Sacraments. Their understanding hinges on acknowledging the authority of Him who instituted them, and it is conditioned on belief in His promises. The understanding of a sacrament depends on the right attitude of the recipient.

This leads us to a second viewpoint for proper understanding. The Sacraments can be understood only in the attitude of the recipient because they, infar as they are administered by man, involve reception; they are acts for receiving the promises. What is received in them is the content. This must be examined separately in Baptism and in Holy Communion. But now already it must be stated that their fulfillment can by no means be considered as resulting from man's cultic acts. That marks the difference between sacramental action and sorcery. The sorcerer purposes to effect, to generate, or even to compel something. Whenever associated with a deity, sorcery attempts to pressure the deity. To conceive of the Christ-ordained Sacraments in that light would be blasphemy. What is man's part in sacramental acts? In them man plays the same receptive role as in the proclamation of the Word. It follows from this that when the Sacraments are understood as acts whereby man confesses his faith, this has to be considered incidental; it cannot have constitutive meaning for the Sacraments.

The third viewpoint, having to do with the understanding of both Baptism and the Lord's Supper, pertains to the character which is peculiar to all of Christ's promises. He who hears them must apply them to himself. They call him out of the enclosed circle in which he has isolated himself and enroll him in the domain and dominion of Christ. And that is the kingdom of the exalted Christ. What is promised in Baptism and in Holy Communion is received from the risen Christ, just as the promise of the kerygma is. Therefore we can conceive of the Sacraments as only a recollection of the historical Christ as little as they may be conceived of as mere acts of human profession. We can neither baptize nor celebrate Holy Communion as though Christ had not risen. By the same token, we can also understand the promises attached to the Sacraments only if the death to which they are linked is the death of Him who overcame death.

A final mark shared by Baptism and Holy Communion is found in the fact that they were correctly designated as Means of Grace (*media salutis*) by our old theologians. The application of this term to both Word and Sacraments points out the essential feature here. It is directed against all forms of "enthusiasm," that is, against the delusion of an "inner light" which is supposed to "illuminate" without any external means. In the Augsburg Confession (AC V 2) the inclusion of the Sacraments and the external Word (*verbum externum*) as instruments of the communication of the Spirit is opposed to this view. Luther declares in the Smalcald Articles (III VIII 10): "Whatever is attributed to the Spirit apart from such Word and Sacrament is of the devil." The proclaimed Word and the sacramental acts have in common that they, in relationship to faith, are external. If there is no working of the Spirit and consequently also no faith without them, they are, in the words of ancient dogmatics, the instrumental cause (*causa instrumentalis*) of faith and also of the certainty of salvation. They protect faith from doubt, just as though it were its own producer. The mark of externality is particularly prominent in the Sacraments. And that lends a new urgency to the question: How can external acts be means for the fulfillment of promises? This, too, demands a separate answer for Baptism and for Holy Communion.

THE INSTITUTION OF HOLY COMMUNION

The doctrine of Holy Communion, as was said previously, must take its departure from two facts: its institution by Christ and its administration among Christians. This order is also followed by Paul, to whom we are indebted for the oldest report by far on Holy Communion, and who is at the same time its first interpreter. In 1 Corinthians 10:14ff., he presupposes its administration in the Church as a fact, and he seeks to make it intelligible *a posteriori*. He proceeds in the same manner in 1 Corinthians 11:20ff., where he first of all affirms the fact of the Sacrament's institution and then draws deductions from this.

The report of institution, which he reproduces here, is of special significance in several respects. First, Paul here refers to a historical event in Christ's life as immediately and exactly as to no other. This report is Christendom's oldest document of the words of Christ in direct speech. Second, it attests that the celebration of Holy Communion antedates the oldest documents that have been transmitted to us. And third, it occupies a special position inasmuch as it is not immediately connected with the other themes of Paul's proclamation. The theme of the Church as the "Body of Christ," which at first blush seems to be an exception to the above statement, is in reality a deduction from the fact of Holy Communion. In no other instance, outside of Baptism, did Paul so unreservedly restrict the independence of his apostolic proclamation in favor of what was transmitted to him as at this point.

Paul's claim to have "received it from the Lord" can but refer to his apostolic authority in general. Whatever he did to and in the Corinthian congregation was done by virtue of his apostolic authority. Vested with this authority, he had founded the congregation through the proclamation of the Gospel and through Baptism, the latter having been administered sometimes by others, sometimes also by himself (Acts 18:8; 1 Corinthians 1:14ff.). When he in the First Letter to the Corinthians presupposes that Holy Communion is celebrated in the congregation, it has to be assumed that he himself introduced it during the year and a half of the congregation's existence (Acts 18:11). The remark in 1 Corinthians 11:23 reflects that he was also authorized to do this as an apostle of Christ. But it says nothing about the manner in which the report of the Sacrament's institution was made known to him. Just as he found the command to baptize and the practice of Baptism in the Church at the time when he himself was baptized, thus he also found the administration of Holy Communion—and consequently also information regarding its institution—when he arrived on the scene.

Therefore the report of the institution of the Lord's Supper transmitted by Paul is of the greatest importance. It reveals from where the Pauline congregations actually derived their celebration of the Sacrament. Paul cannot have transmitted it to the congregations of Asia Minor in a manner other than he did to the Corinthian church. Thus the institution is older than the oldest Pauline congregations. It has, as it were, prehistoric significance.

With regard to age, the Synoptic writers' reports on the institution are far later than Paul's. Nevertheless they, too, demand particular attention—first, because of their divergences. The fact that Paul's report was known in the Pauline congregations implies that the evangelists' reports are an independent tradition. The Synoptic reports are important, second, because they prove that the Early Church saw no contradictions in these divergences. The latter consist partly in supplements, partly in shortenings, partly in slight shifts in the wording. But none betrays the slightest polemics against Paul. Third, the reports merit attention because of their agreement with Paul. They demonstrate the extent to which there was complete unanimity throughout the Early Church with regard to the institution of this Sacrament.

A comparison of the reports is rendered difficult at one point by an uncertainty in the transmission of Luke's text. In manuscript D and in several Old Latin manuscripts the sentences contained in Luke 22:19b–20 are missing. Accordingly the report on the institution breaks off here with the words "This is My body." The words about the traitor in verse 21 are missing from two other Old Latin and from Syrian manuscripts. Instead, they first quote the words regarding the cup at this point, which is reported by most of the manuscripts in verses 17–18—consequently prior to the breaking of the bread. Thus their Luke text at this point, excepting slight deviations, corresponds to the report of Matthew (26:26–29) and to that of Mark (14:22–25). Furthermore, they add: "which is for you. Do this in remembrance of Me" to the words "This is My body." Consequently we have in this reading the very words that are found in the corresponding passage of Paul's version. Finally, all the Greek manuscripts except D contain the accepted text of Luke 22:19b–20. (This agrees essentially with 1 Corinthians 11:24–25a.) In addition they report in verses 17–18 the words regarding the cup—thus before the reference to the breaking of bread.

E. Lohmeyer explains the variations of the Luke texts by attributing them to liturgical differences which prevailed in different sections of the Church; he therefore regards it as possible that the accepted text is a condemnation of a special kind of congregational celebration, such as the Corinthian celebration (*Theol. Rundschau*, 1937, pp. 177ff.). Most scholars today incline to the view that the original text actually stopped short with the words "This is My body." But then what prompted the author to break off there? Various conjectures might be considered here. At all events, it is safe to say that the breaking off at this critical point cannot intimate any opposition to Paul on the part of Luke. And furthermore, it is not sure that this really marks a breaking off; for it is inconceivable that the report might have ended with the words "This is My body."

The most important deviation of Paul's report from those of the Synoptic writers consists in this: Paul's version adds to the distribution of bread and wine the command of repetition: "This do . . . in remembrance of Me." This is missing in Matthew and in Mark. In Luke this command is found only in conjunction with the distribution of the bread. But as was said, this may possibly have been entered by a later hand and copied from Paul's report. But if Paul is the only proof for the command to repeat the Sacrament, the question arises whether its absence from the report of the first two Synoptic writers permits the conclusion that Christ never gave this command. The Heidelberg rationalist Paulus was the first to espouse this view; and it was disseminated particularly by Strauss and later by Jülicher. In the end it makes little difference whether one joins Wellhausen and makes Paul the inventor of the institution of Holy Communion, or whether one agrees with later scholars who have the "cult-legend" evolve from the community meals of the early congregations. In either event, Holy Communion ceases to be an institution of Christ.

The possibility that Paul invented the Sacrament—aside from all the other impossibilities here—is ruled out by the very fact that Holy Communion, as already stated, cannot be derived from any other of the Gospel's themes. If Paul had invented it, in what way might this have helped him clarify or explain the great themes of the letters to the Romans and to the Galatians? Might not the introduction of a ritual act, which he himself considers to be in the dangerous proximity of the pagan sacrificial meals, obscure rather than clarify the connection between promise and faith, faith and works, Law and Gospel? Might a cultic act not appear as thwarting his Pneumatology? What connection is there between it and the burning Corinthian problem of charismatic busyness? But if it was undertaken in the situation of the letters to the Thessalonians, the absence of drastic eschatological features in the Words of Institution, such as marks the reports of the Synoptic writers (they make no mention of Christ's returning), would really be incomprehensible. Viewing the entire body of Paul's theology, it might be more reasonable to assume that Holy Communion forms an alien part in it than to conclude that Paul could be its author in any sense or to any degree. There is absolutely no reason to believe that Paul subsequently invented Christ's authorization for a rite which he already found in use when he came on the scene. Paul cannot be the inventor of the Words of Institution and thus also not of the command: "Do this in remembrance of Me."

That brings us to the primitive Church. Did the Church have its own version of the Words of Institution? To refer to the silence of the Synoptic writers regarding

Christ's command to repeat the Sacrament till He returns is insufficient evidence for such a claim. Paul, the earliest witness, had the Words of Institution transmitted to him ready-made, as it were. Accordingly, what Paul received must be presupposed not only for the congregation of Antioch but also for the congregation of Damascus (Acts 9). In view of the personal, geographic, and chronological relationship, it can be traced back into the immediate environs of the primitive Church in Jerusalem. Mark's report cannot be more recent. If the author of Mark's Gospel—it matters not whether we speak of the canonical Mark or of an earlier form—is identical with John Mark mentioned in the New Testament (there is no reason to doubt this), he was intimately acquainted with the sacramental life of the first congregation which met in his mother's home (Acts 12:12). And Mark would know about Holy Communion before reading about the Feast of Unleavened Bread mentioned in Acts 12:3. There are therefore no external reasons whatsoever for ascribing any knowledge of the institution of Holy Communion to the early congregation other than is contained in these reports; at least not in the features in which Paul agrees with Mark and Matthew.

The oldest preserved Christian documents are the two letters to the Thessalonians, the letter to the Galatians, and the first letter to the Corinthians. From these we learn four facts pertaining to Christ Himself: (1) He died on the cross, (2) He arose from the dead and appeared to the disciples, (3) He promised to return (*parousia*), and (4) He instituted Holy Communion. In other words, the kerygma of the crucified and risen Lord, who instituted Holy Communion on the night in which He was betrayed, is the oldest that was transmitted to us from authentic sources. If the total image which we believe to have gained of Christ from the Synoptic writers does not include that He "instituted a sacrament," then this image has to be false. Christ's death on the cross, His resurrection, the promise of His return (*parousia*), and the institution of Holy Communion are the four bonds that join the Pauline kerygma to the Christ pictured in the Synoptic writings, though as a matter of documentation the latter are much later.

We have no means for setting aside the Church's knowledge regarding its own origin and for trying to correct such knowledge later on. This knowledge leaves absolutely no room for a cultic legend to evolve from the administration of a Holy Communion based on any customs which may have been observed at some time. Therefore if it is not assumed that the apostles contrived and devised the Sacrament between Easter and Pentecost—an assumption on par with that of the ancient rationalist who declared that someone had stolen the body of Christ—nothing remains but to believe that they attributed its repeated celebration to the will of Christ Himself. And that dismisses every reason for trying to brand Paul's report of institution wrong at this point by referring to the Synoptic writers.

A further deviation of the first two Synoptic writers from Paul has to do with Christ's words of distribution accompanying the presentation of the cup.

According to Matthew and Mark they read, "This is My blood of the covenant." To this Mark adds "poured out for many," and Matthew "poured out for many for the forgiveness of sin." Paul evidently follows a tradition different from that of the Synoptic writers. Had he known about these additions, there would have been no manifest reason for him to omit them. He in particular stresses the atoning power of the blood of Christ, especially also its significance for the remission of sin (see Romans 3:25; Ephesians 1:7; 2:13; Colossians 1:20). And he adds "for you" after the words "This is My body"; these two words are not contained in Matthew and Mark. In the Synoptic writers, on the other hand, the additions are important, since they do not in other connections refer to the saving significance of Christ's blood (cf. only Mark 10:45; Matthew 20:28). Therefore one might almost say that the additions found in the Synoptic writers ("poured out for many," "poured out for many for the forgiveness of sins") bear a Pauline stamp, although he himself omits these words. At all events, the divergence in the additions reflects no theological difference in the Words of Institution.

The variation in the words of distribution implies, as Jeremias has pointed out, no factual difference whatsoever. When the words read in Synoptic writings, "This is My blood of the covenant," the reference of course is to the wine in the cup. And when Paul says, "This cup is the new covenant in My blood," the meaning there too is not the cup itself but its content, that is, the wine. The Synoptic formula designates the wine as "My blood of the covenant." From this we must infer that the blood does not belong to the covenant incidentally but necessarily: the blood guarantees the covenant. The Pauline formula designates the wine as "the new covenant in My blood." The covenant is in the blood; the blood guarantees the covenant. Both formulas designate the wine as the blood of the Donor, belonging to the covenant and guaranteeing it. The material connection between wine, blood, and covenant is the same each time. We shall note later that also the Pauline addition "new" contains no change in the meaning.

The third, greater deviation from St. Paul's version of the Words of Institution seems to be different. Following the words of distribution for the cup, Matthew (26:19) and Mark (14:25) add Jesus' announcement, "I shall not drink again of this fruit of the vine until that day when I drink it new [with you] in the kingdom of God [in My Father's kingdom]." The words in brackets are found only in Matthew. They imply no change in meaning. Christ's announcement at this celebration conveys His awareness that this was His last earthly meal. The words of distribution again simply show His awareness of His imminent death. Furthermore, they repeat His earlier promises concerning the kingdom and His *parousia*. To be sure, this announcement is not found in the Pauline version, but the matter is fully covered there when Paul adds, "For as often as you eat this bread and drink the cup, you proclaim the Lord's death until He comes" (1 Corinthians 11:26). Here, too, the reference to His death and the reference to His promise of the future are joined together. Paul appropriately links this sentence to the preceding word *remembrance*, which for Paul concludes Christ's words of distribution for the cup. His omission of the eschatological announcement found in the two Synoptic writers, namely, that our Lord would not drink of the wine again until He had entered the Father's kingdom, proves that he was either unacquainted with this or that he did not regard it a component part of the institution of Holy Communion. However, this does not denote a theological difference.

On this point Luke, too, must be compared with the other two Synoptic writers. Luke cites the eschatological announcement in a somewhat abridged form preceding the breaking of the bread (22:18). There it exactly parallels the words accompanying the eating of the Passover, "I shall not eat it until it is fulfilled in the kingdom of God" (verse 16). Since it is improbable that the eschatological announcement was spoken over the cup twice in succession, we might ask whether it is found in the correct place in Matthew and Mark, or in Luke. Undoubtedly the Luke account notes the right place, for otherwise it would be separated so far from the parallel sentence on the Passover—separated by the breaking of bread, the presentation of the Communion cup, and the accompanying words of distribution—that the parallelism would be lost entirely. It is thus eliminated from the actual institution of Holy Communion, which according to Paul, Mark, and Matthew begins with the breaking of the bread. The first two Synoptic writers attached the eschatological statement at the end, because it was transmitted in association with the Words of Institution. But only Luke shows us its full meaning as he combines it with the eating of the Passover (22:15–18). It clarifies the relationship between the latter and the institution of Holy Communion.

Also the other two Synoptic writers leave no room for doubt that the Sacrament instituted by Christ was directly associated, at least temporally, with the last Passover celebrated by Him (Matthew 26:17ff., 26ff.; Mark 14:12ff., 22ff.). The objection raised against this again and again has its origin in the Gospel of John, which seemingly presupposes that Christ's trial occurred before the Jewish Passover (18:28). This seeming or real difference understandably led to disputes over the chronology of the Passover story as early as the second century, particularly over the month of Christ's crucifixion and resurrection, because of its importance for the computation of the Christian Easter. However, the chronology of John's Gospel cannot contribute to an understanding of the Christian Holy Communion, if for no other reason than that it does not even report on its institution. The harmonious Synoptic presentation of the relationship of the Lord's Supper to the Passover can by no means be invalidated by anything that John's Gospel seems to say or does not say.

The connection between Holy Communion and the Passover, as was said, is clearly seen in Luke's report, at least in one respect. The eschatological prospect (Luke 22:16, 18) accompanies Christ's eating of the Passover. It stresses that this is the last meal eaten in common with the disciples before the advent of the kingdom. However, the uniqueness of this meal does not derive from the fact that it is Christ's last meal with the disciples, as some exegetes maintain. For how could Christ then have said that He had "earnestly desired" it (v. 15)? Some meal had naturally and necessarily to be the last meal with them. Rather, those words of Christ can only be understood as His desire that none other than the Passover meal should be their last meal. And as the dawn of the kingdom is here placed over against the last Passover, this action acquires the character of a solemn closing act of salvation history, for which act the Passover possesses essential significance.

In the same night "in which He was betrayed" the appointed guardians of Passover religion took the final steps to destroy Christ in the name of that religion. The moment when that goal was reached Passover religion in its appointed exponents was turned from a fulfillment of the will of God to enmity against God. Henceforth no one can eat the old Passover without entering into communion with those who killed the Son of God. The last Passover which Jesus ate with His disciples does more than signify the end of the old covenant; its completion actually marks its end, for it was the last Passover which was celebrated in conformity with God's will.

Two factors now enter the vacuum that resulted for the disciples: the reference to a reunion with Christ for a common meal and the institution of the new Sacrament by Christ. Theoretically it was possible that the disciples, following the testimony that the risen Christ bore of Himself, equated the two. The resurrection of Christ is the dawn of "the last things," consequently also an important moment in the dawn of the kingdom. It was not far-fetched to conceive of Holy Communion as a meal with the exalted Christ who had promised His presence—thus a fulfillment of the prospect of a common meal in the kingdom. However, the entire New Testament does not lend support to such a conception. On several occasions the possibility of a common meal with the resurrected Christ lies close at hand. But there He either gave the disciples the bread (Luke 24:30; John 21:13), or He "ate before them" (ἐνώπιον αὐτῶν, Luke 24:43); but He never ate *with* them. These accounts show convincingly that the fulfillment of the eschatological time (Luke 22:16, 18) has not yet come. Therefore also the celebration of Holy Communion cannot be interpreted in that light. It cannot have had the meaning of a restoration (or continuation) of Table fellowship with the exalted Christ.

The very independence that the institution of Holy Communion had from the beginning from eschatological prospects lends it a character other than that of Table fellowship. Naturally it is Table fellowship, just as the Passover is. But the factual meaning of this meal embraces more than that. What Holy Communion is results from something on which all of the writers agree. Christ hands the disciples the blessed bread with the words "This is My body." Thus Holy Communion, just like the Passover, attains its character from the bread dispensed there. Matthew,

Mark, and Paul are unanimous also in their reports on the presentation of the cup with the words of distribution that go with it.

The connection of the eschatological time with Holy Communion is moved into a new light by Paul. Christ's death and resurrection are events of the past. The *parousia* lies in the future. Holy Communion joins both together: "As often as you eat this bread and drink the cup, you proclaim (καταγγέλλετε) the Lord's death until He comes" (1 Corinthians 11:26). The καταγγέλλειν in this sentence does not, of course, express the platitude that Christ is dead. Rather, it is the καταγγέλλειν of the testimony of God to which Paul himself witnesses in the same letter (2:1), that is, the witness of the crucified Christ (v. 2). He speaks of the crucified Christ as "in a mystery" (1 Corinthians 2:7 KJV) because it was, contrary to appearances, "the Lord of glory" who was crucified (v. 8). This mystery is also proclaimed through the eating and drinking in Holy Communion. This proclamation is not a lament for the dead. Nor is it, as today's exponents of a one-sided eschatological conception of Holy Communion would have it, a mere profession of the *parousia*-expectation and of the advent of the kingdom, for why then are we told to "proclaim the Lord's death"? Rather, it attests the death of Him whose resurrection proved Him to be the Lord of glory. And in that way it is simultaneously a profession of the dawn of the new kingdom.

What about the new kingdom? According to Paul's words concerning the cup, Christ's blood is the blood of the new testament, or covenant (διαθήκη). Even if the word "new" is missing in Matthew and Mark, it can appropriately be supplied here. In the New Testament the expression διαθήκη designates, on the one hand, the provisions for salvation once made by God and the old order of salvation decreed thereby (Luke 1:72; Acts 3:25; 7:8; Romans 9:4; 11:27; 2 Corinthians 3:14). But on the other hand it means also the new order ushered in by Christ and founded on Him (2 Corinthians 3:6; Hebrews 7:22; 8:8ff.; 9:15; 10:29; 13:20; cf. J. Behm's article on διαθήκη in TDNT, 106–34). Evidently only the new order can be meant with the word διαθήκη, also in Matthew and Mark. According to the words of distribution, this new order is guaranteed by the blood of Christ. Therewith the sacrifice of Christ enters into analogy with the sacrifices which guaranteed the old order. Just which Old Testament sacrifices might be named here is hard to say; but this is also quite inconsequential for the analogy. It is surely most natural for a Christian to be reminded here of the reflections of the letter to the Hebrews.

In Holy Communion, the disciples receive the blood of the new covenant. It becomes evident here that Holy Communion really enters the vacuum which occurs with the solemn termination of the old order through Jesus' last Passover meal. And that applies not only to the first celebration of the Sacrament, which bore an anticipatory character since Christ's sacrifice was first carried out on the following day. No, it applies to every celebration of Holy Communion. Theodor Zahn says correctly, "The Church's celebration of Holy Communion is not a celebration commemorating its institution, but a celebration of the entire Christ-wrought redemption of His Church as typified in the Jewish Passover."[1]

PAUL'S CONTRIBUTION TO THE UNDERSTANDING OF HOLY COMMUNION

As an act of reception Holy Communion requires a readiness on the part of the communicants to receive something from the Donor. The Donor must be known to the recipients. It was for good reason that the ancient Church withheld the Sacrament from the view of all outsiders. After all, of what concern is it to outsiders what only Christ's disciples may receive? The proper attitude for receiving also demands that we are open to the Donor's invitation. He becomes known to us through the declaration: "Behold, the Lamb of God, who takes away the sin of the world!" The invitation adds to this: "Be reconciled!"

This Christ to whom John the Baptist points and who summons us to Himself is the Donor of the food which is dispensed in the Sacrament and by which this meal is distinguished from every other. He Himself dispenses the bread and wine. And when He accompanies this gift with the words "This is My Body" and "This is My Blood," it is in fact His body and blood. How can anyone who in faith hears His invitation, knowing that only as a believer he can and will receive the benefits of Christ's gifts—how can he conceive the idea that this is not Christ's body and blood? How can there be "a distress" about Holy Communion, as some people say today, if it is received with this attitude of faith? Of the Early Church we read that Christians "broke bread." In view of the following liturgical note, this is undoubtedly a reference to Holy Communion. And they broke bread "with gladness and singleness of heart" (Acts 2:46 KJV). How can this gladness, which our Holy Communion liturgy also aims to express, become "distress"? And above all, how can anyone hold Luther's doctrine of Holy Communion responsible for that, considering that his whole struggle was directed against no other opponent than doubt regarding Christ's own words? And how can there be doubt about words which, among all those transmitted of Christ, have the very oldest testimony in their favor and without which Holy Communion would be an empty ceremony?

If there is "a distress" of Holy Communion, and if it is founded on anything outside the general secularism which had weaned all of us away from the gladness of the Early Church, it can consist only in the fact that the Christians who complain about this distress have lost that "singleness of heart" with which the Early Church celebrated the Sacrament. The opposite of singleness (*Einfachheit*) is doubleness (*Zwiefalt*), from which "doubt" (*Zweifel*) derives its name. Zwingli taught that Jesus meant something different from what He said. His was the crassest presentation of doubleness. What is more, in trying to exonerate himself, he imputed

1 Theodor Zahn, *Einleitung in das Neue Testament* (Leipzig: A. Deichert'sche, 1900), 513.

this duplicity to Christ. One of today's "experts" in the area of Holy Communion declares that whoever claims that the situation of Marburg still exists at present and feels impelled to turn against Zwingli was shutting open doors. A grave error! To the present day this Zwingli dominates by far the largest area of the entire literature on Holy Communion. All that is added by contemporary writers is the variation in expressing doubleness.

Among today's Calvinists, especially among those who emphatically call themselves "Lutheran"—and people for whom the designation "Crypto-Calvinists" would be ridiculous euphemism—this doubleness is reflected in the assertion that Calvin expressed what Luther meant. Naturally none but the authors of such a preposterous idea can have any interest in it. This sham has the same meaning for them as Zwingli's theory had for him. In their own heart they feel the objective difference between Luther and Zwingli, but they suppose that they can dissolve it by dialectics, that is, by saying both yes and no. The Luther of Marburg is just as irreconcilably opposed to these "Lutheran" Calvinists, to their Calvin, and to the "Luther" fashioned by them as he was to Zwingli. For singleness and doubleness can never, never be reconciled. Here it is of no great consequence—at least not for us—whether Wittenberg or Geneva is right in the end, as little as it matters whether Rome is right in the end. For us Luther is not a formal doctrinal authority; he is our exemplar, particularly in this matter of retaining singleness of heart over against Christ's words in Holy Communion. Singleness is not simplicity. Consequently it is not the opposite of smartness or mature judgment but of doubleness. It is the opposite of saying both yes and no.

To cite formal "scriptural proof" does not yet guarantee a true, single conception of Holy Communion. Its only reliable basis is found in Christ's own words. But these words are not a doctrine about Holy Communion. The recipient of Holy Communion can sense what they mean only as he applies them directly to himself. And they presuppose, as was stated, that the recipient is aware of the One by whom they are spoken and from whom something is received. Here the entire problem of Christology arises behind the doctrine of Holy Communion; and Christology is, of course, only a part of the total conception of the Gospel. So long as the Gospel as a whole is understood differently, it is utopian to assume that one can arrive at an agreement "in obedience to Scripture" by the exegesis of individual New Testament words. How can one arrive at an agreement with a theology whose Christ-image does not concede that Christ "instituted a sacrament"? Our concern must be to ascertain the meaning of Holy Communion as the apostles and the Early Church understood it, and this always in relationship to their overall testimony of Christ.

As an initial step in this direction, we consider the addition to the words "This is My body," "This is My blood." The additions show how the disciples themselves understood Christ. To the first of these two statements Paul's version adds "which is for you." To the second the Synoptic writers add "which is shed for you." These additions are explanatory insofar as they point to the bloody sacrifice and death of Him who adds them. That imparts an anticipatory character to the act of institution, for the sacrifice was first carried out on the following day. The term *testament*, which is sealed by the blood, also contributes to this explanation.

Herewith the Words of Institution touch the core of the entire Gospel, and they do this in complete agreement with it. For the Gospel is the "Word of the cross," the "Word of reconciliation." This, because Christ is "the sacrifice for our sin," because His death effects atonement, or because the incarnate Word is the Lamb of God that bears the sin of the world, as John put it. It will suffice to call attention here to the parallels in the first letter of Peter, in the letter to the Hebrews, in the Book of Revelation. In this connection the words are of great importance, for at this central point they form the bridge between the Synoptic Christ-image and the remaining testimonies to Christ in the New Testament. To be sure, the idea of a sacrificial death is indicated also in the Synoptic writers by the declaration that the Son of Man will have to suffer and die and that this will be done "for many" (Matthew 16:21; 17:22; 20:18; Mark 10:45; Luke 13:33). The writers are familiar also with the application of Isaiah 53 to Christ (Matthew 8:17; 27:60; Mark 9:12; Acts 8:32). Moreover, the detail with which they portray His great Passion (*passio magna*) can be explained only by the fact that they ascribe to it the same central significance as do the remaining witnesses of the New Testament. As for Christ's Words of Institution as recorded by the Synoptic writers, they as no other words teach us the meaning of His sacrificial death as He Himself purposed it.

Thus when the question is put, as theology must put it: Is the Gospel as the Word of reconciliation perhaps only a subsequent interpretation of Christ's death and one that was foreign to the earthly Christ Himself? The only ultimately decisive answer comes from the Words of Institution. In them is found the origin, not of reconciliation itself, of course, but of "the Word of reconciliation." Assuming that there is a contradiction between the Early Church's conception of the Sacrament and its other testimonies of Christ, this may be tersely dismissed thus: *The entire Gospel of reconciliation proceeded from the Christ who instituted Holy Communion.* Quite obviously, the Words of Institution cannot be divorced from the act. By reason of His death Holy Communion as a whole is Christ's legacy to His disciples. To be sure, they did not formally derive from this the commission to proclaim the Gospel, but surely the basic content of their message has its source in Christ's words. Holy Communion is not a marginal note, not some symbolic arabesque on the Church's ceiling. It is part of the foundation on which the Church is constructed.

But the Early Church did not consider Holy Communion only in the light of its institution. It celebrated the Sacrament regularly because it believed the promise contained in it for its life. Holy Communion is an act of reception. It is not the dead but the exalted Christ who is present in His Church and who is the Donor here. His food is received here and now. With "the table of the Lord" (1 Corinthians 10:21) and "the Lord's supper" (1 Corinthians 11:20) Paul means, as the context clearly shows, "the cup of blessing which we bless" and "the bread which we break" (1 Corinthians 10:16). What is meant is not the meal of long ago, the meal of institution, but the meal of today, the meal we keep repeating.

Paul says of this cup that it is "participation in the blood of Christ," and of this bread that it is "participation in the body of Christ." Note well that he also says the first—the statement about Christ's blood. Not a few exegetes of today simply ignore that and then compromise with the rest of the sentence in such a way that, in keeping with other Pauline statements, they equate "participation in the body of Christ" with membership in the Church. These are the same exegetes who envisage Holy Communion merely as Table fellowship. However, that interpretation is inadequate also in this context. Paul compares Holy Communion both with the Jewish and with the pagan sacrificial meals. But with regard to the Christian, Jewish, and pagan meals the point of comparison does not lie in the trivial event of eating together but in the fact that in all three instances the eating affords participation in the sacrifice. And this is precisely true with regard to the physical eating. That is convincingly proved by the following verses, which speak of eating the food offered to idols in the homes of pagan hosts. The possibility of a Christian's participation in a pagan sacrificial act is entirely out of the question.

Also the exegesis which sees the "participation" in Christ's body and blood as participation in the liturgical benediction (εὐλογοῦμεν, v. 16) founders on this comparison. Neither Table fellowship as such nor the benediction can afford participation in Christ's body and blood; only the eating and drinking do that. The fact that the blood is mentioned in addition to the body forbids the symbolic interpretation that "body" stands for the Church. If the words "We who are many are one body" (v. 17) refer to the Church as the Body of Christ, then the context here compels a very realistic conception! "Because there is one bread, we who are many are one body, for we all partake of the one bread." Logically this sentence can have no other meaning than that a physical oneness of the communicants is effected through the eaten bread, that is, through each communicant's reception of a part of the broken bread. But since it is the liturgically broken bread and the liturgically blessed cup which are received here, thus also this physical oneness is a common physical sharing in the body and blood of Christ.

This writing of Paul shows the simplicity of heart (ἀφελότης) of the Early Church very clearly, that is, a truly single—not double—conception of the Words of Institution which he himself cites later on. Because Christ Himself dispensed the bread and the wine with the words "This is My body," "This is My blood," the eating of the bread and the drinking of the cup can be nothing other than oral eating and drinking (*manducatio oralis*) of His body and blood. The question whether Christ meant, or possibly could have meant, anything other than what

He said is not raised at all. For that would be nothing other than the old question of the tempter, "Did God say?" Further, Paul does not inquire here whether the "participation" in Christ's body and blood promised and fulfilled here conforms to the picture of Christ he projects elsewhere. This question is superfluous from the beginning, because he grounds the promise on the order established by Christ Himself. What he "received from the Lord" (1 Corinthians 11:23) became an integral part of his own testimony to Christ, and it is accordingly just as determinative for his conception of Christ as is all that he received otherwise from Him or about Him. And finally, there is not the slightest intimation of a gap of any kind between the physical eating and drinking and the "participation" in body and blood. Both coincide completely in one and the same act.

Any doubt that may still arise on this score is removed by the practical conclusions drawn by Paul (in 1 Corinthians 11:27ff.) from the tradition he had received concerning the institution of the Lord's Supper. Prompted by the abuses which appeared in Corinth, he ponders the possibility of an "unworthy" eating and drinking. To be sure, the unworthiness manifests itself in the outward conduct of the Corinthians (1 Corinthians 11:17–22); but in Paul's opinion, this simultaneously reveals an inner unworthiness. This may be inferred from the admonition that each should examine himself, that is, examine his inner attitude, before eating and drinking (v. 28). The danger of becoming guilty is explained by the fact that the unworthy communicant fails to "discern the body," that is, that he eats the bread as though he were thereby not receiving the body of Christ. The point is that he becomes guilty by eating and drinking (v. 29). Therefore, apart from his inward unworthiness, he encumbers himself with guilt by partaking of food and drink. Of course, this guilt does not spring from eating and drinking bread and wine in general, but from eating and drinking *this* bread and *this* wine, because the bread and wine used in the Sacrament effect our participation in Christ's body and blood. If the apostle meant that only the inner unworthiness made man guilty, then he should have stated in verse 27 that the unworthy person incurred guilt over against Christ. But this verse reads: He "will be guilty of profaning the *body* and *blood* of the Lord." Therefore, the unworthy communicant is guilty over against the received gift because this is not—also in an unworthy reception—only bread and wine but in every instance the body and blood of Christ. The "eating of the unworthy" (*manducatio indignorum*) is an unworthy reception of the body and blood of the Lord.

All the objections raised against this conception of the *manducatio indignorum* proceed from the thesis that the gift of Holy Communion, like all of Christ's gifts of salvation, can be received only by faith. While this thesis cannot be disputed, it does not apply here. These objections tacitly presuppose that Christ's body and blood are gifts for our good under all circumstances, also to those who commune unworthily. But this superficial assumption is revealed as illusion by these very reflections of Paul. That becomes fully clear when he numbers also sickness and premature death among the punitive consequences of an unworthy reception (1 Corinthians 11:30). The context forbids to construe this as a general chastisement for any kind of unworthiness. Rather, the punitive physical consequences correspond exactly to the physical eating and drinking and therefore also to the physical reception of the Lord's body and blood. (Cf. 1 Corinthians 10:16.)

The treatise in the letter to the Hebrews reflects that the Early Church was acquainted with a becoming guilty of Christ's blood also otherwise (Hebrews 10:29; cf. 6:6 and Matthew 27:25). The disputants of the doctrine of the *manducatio indignorum* are as a rule also proponents of the doctrine that Holy Communion is only *verbum visible*. But even if it were only this, they should ask themselves whether the unbelieving hearing of the Word, which would be comparable to the unworthy reception in Holy Communion, deprives the Word itself of its objective validity. They must surely concede that the Word of God, when it is heard by an unbeliever and thus finds its way into his inner self, still remains the Word of God when spurned, assailed, rejected. But as little as an unbeliever can prevent the Word of God, which he hears with his ears, from penetrating into his inner self and there fulfilling its task (κειτικός, Hebrews 4:11), so little can an unworthy communicant prevent his receiving of Christ's body and blood in Holy Communion. In the former instance, he hears the Word to his own condemnation; and in the latter, he eats and drinks Christ's body and blood to his own condemnation. There is no neutral vacuum in either instance.

JOHN'S CONTRIBUTION TO THE UNDERSTANDING OF HOLY COMMUNION

If the rest of the New Testament contained testimonies regarding Holy Communion at variance with Paul's testimony, we might be confronted by difficult decisions. However, under no circumstances would that warrant a reinterpretation of the Pauline testimony. An occasion for doing this has been offered time and again by Christ's words recorded in John 6:26–59. To be sure, these words have in turn been interpreted most variously. The analysis of the sources, outwardly supported by an uncertainty as to the transmission of the text of verse 51, has frequently contributed to this. Only if we can prove that in John 6 Christ refers to the Sacrament will this yield anything for dogmatic understanding.

Luther, as we know, disputed this relationship. In the sentence "The flesh is of no avail," he found—and surely rightly so—a repudiation of the "Capernaitic" understanding of Christ's words. If Christ's entire discourse tends toward this thought, then the *manducatio spiritualis*, the reception of Christ by faith, appears as the antithesis to the Capernaitic eating. In view of verses 40 and 47ff., this antithesis is very correctly discerned. Luther himself had to stress this because involved was a defense of his own conception of Holy Communion against the accusation of Capernaitism. For that reason his weekday sermons emphasized that he, too, was aware of a spiritual reception of Christ in Word and Sacrament. However, apart from this reception of the bread from heaven by faith, the second part of Christ's words (v. 51ff.) speaks so realistically of the eating of Christ's body and the drinking of Christ's blood that the reader of the Gospel of John is inevitably reminded of Paul.

The statement that it is "the Spirit that gives life, the flesh is of no avail" (v. 63) has often been construed as an epigrammatic summation of the entire discourse, or at least of a part of it. However, that is impossible, for the discourse itself, at least in its last part, moves in the opposite direction. When Jesus stresses here in ever new terms that the bread which He gives is His own flesh (vv. 51–56), the greatest importance is assigned precisely to His flesh. But the words of verse 63 appear to say just the opposite.

If the section comprising verses 51–59, which we may call the third part, were an interpolation by a later redactor (Bultmann), the contrast between flesh and Spirit would have to correspond to the antitheses governing the first (vv. 26–29) and the second part (vv. 32–50) of Christ's words. In the first part He places the procuration of imperishable food (v. 27), which according to verse 29 is faith, over against the desire for the dispenser of earthly food (v. 26). The words of verse 63 might possibly be fitted in here, that is, if the two were immediately joined. However, the conversation takes a new turn due to the question of the Jews (vv. 30–31). The second part of Christ's words contrasts the bread which God Himself dispenses from heaven (vv. 32–33), the bread which is Christ Himself (v. 35), with the miraculous food of the wilderness. This bread enjoys a double distinction over the manna of the wilderness. First, it really "comes down from heaven" (v. 33); second, it appeases hunger forever (v. 35).

As this double theme is carried out, each of the two distinguishing marks provokes the Jews to contradiction, and each receives greater sharpness as the charges are being refuted. The first objection of the opponents is directed against Jesus' claim that He came down from heaven (v. 42), the second that He calls His own flesh the bread of life, which when eaten fully satisfies one's hunger, for it conveys eternal life (v. 52). The second objection and its repudiation belong to the execution of the double theme exactly as the first one does. Thus verses 51–59, which contain it, cannot be the interpolation of a later redactor. And the antithesis of flesh and Spirit in verse 63 possesses the proper continuity only if it is part of the theme, for it is only with verse 51 that the discussion about the flesh begins. Without this third section there would be no reason for contrasting flesh with Spirit. The first two parts speak only of bread. Verse 63 is intelligible only because this bread is designated as Christ's flesh in the third part and only because the Jews disputed (v. 52) this claim of Christ.

Admittedly the words pertaining to Spirit and flesh were no longer addressed to the great mass of Christ's hearers but only to the narrow circle of His disciples. Christ's discourse induced a crisis. Its "partly very defiant and blunt formulations signify an intentional endurance test for the relationship of Jesus' adherents to their Master."[2] Many forsook Him because they could not bear the "hard saying" (vv. 60, 66). The fact that also the disciples "murmured at it" reveals that they heard Jesus' words with the same unbelief as the Jews did. Therefore the words with which Jesus countered their "murmuring" can only have the purpose of strengthening their faith. And Peter's later profession demonstrates that the words fulfilled their purpose. As always so, here, too, the strengthening of their faith resulted from a promise—from the promise of the exaltation of the Son of Man and from the promise of "the Spirit that gives life" (v. 63).

But now, what is the meaning in this context of the words "The flesh is of no avail"? If this addition is only an epilogue for the disciples, it may have a double meaning for that part of the discourse to which the word "flesh" is joined. It may either intensify or weaken the offense (*skandalon*). It would weaken it if with its help the expression "flesh" were to be made intelligible subsequently in the third part of the discourse, that is, if, in a sense, apology were to be made for it. And thus it is actually understood by many exegetes. But, to be exact, it would then not be a weakening but a refutation. For if the general statement "The flesh is of no avail" is to be a subsequent interpretation of Christ's words, then His flesh cannot be the "food indeed" (v. 55) and cannot impart eternal life (v. 54). Then these sentences would be stripped of the *skandalon* only because they are subsequently carried *ad absurdum*. Consequently, that general statement of the epilogue can only intensify the *skandalon*, as if to say: "Although the flesh is of no avail, the words which I have spoken are Spirit and life." The expression "which I have spoken" (λελάληκα, not λαλῶ, as Luther read), of course, refers back to the discourse itself. The disciples, too, cannot and shall not be spared the *skandalon*. But as always so, here, too, their faith shall be strengthened by the words of their Lord (cf. John 16:1) in defiance of the *skandalon*.

The answer to the question "Do these words of Christ relate to Holy Communion?" is dependent on the other question: "What constituted the *skandalon* for the disciples here?" Christ's claim to be the bread of life cannot by itself have been an offense to them. To be sure, the Jews were offended by such and similar claims (John 5:18; 7:20; 8:12, 52; 10:20, 31), but not so the disciples. However, here they, too, recoil. From what? Because Christ was vulgarizing the beautiful figurative speech of the bread of life, which may be appropriated by faith, by speaking of His flesh and blood? Did He perhaps offend them when He attached

2 Gustav Stählin, *Skandalon: Untersuchungen zur Geschichte eines biblischen Begriffs* (Gütersloh: Bertelsmann, 1930), 244.

so much importance to the "flesh"? The evangelist John can surely not have thought of the offense in that way, because according to his doctrine the entire mystery of Christ's mission consists in the fact that the Word became "flesh" (John 1:14; cf. 1 John 4:2; 2 John 7). Also the generalizing interpretation of the words "The flesh is of no avail" founders on this Johannine doctrine. No, the offense stemmed from the fact that Jesus had spoken of the eating of His flesh (τρώγειν, vv. 54, 56ff.) and the drinking of His blood, which excluded any figurative understanding. And the epilogue retracted nothing of this. It might be inferred precisely from this that the third part of the discourse, in the Johannine presentation, indeed has Holy Communion in mind. The Jews are entirely unable to comprehend this eating and drinking. In the case of the disciples, their human offense as such is joined by the terrifying thought that these words, if they should materialize, would make their Lord a corpse.

The epilogue first gains its full meaning from this perspective. The flesh which was mentioned is not the flesh of a corpse, as the disciples assumed and from which idea they recoiled. They would behold the Lord "ascending" (v. 62). This cannot refer, as John 12:32–33 does, to the ascending on the cross. In view of the allusion to the place whence He came (ὅπου ἦν τὸ πρότερον), it can refer only to His ascending after His death. If verses 62 and 63 are not completely unrelated, the words regarding Spirit and flesh must refer to the exaltation. And this reference is perfectly clear. Without the exaltation, the flesh (of the corpse) is of no avail. But it is "the Spirit that gives life." Aside from this verse, the expression "to give life" (ζωοποιεῖν) occurs in only one other passage in this Gospel, namely, in John 5:21. And here it is used as a parallel to "raising the dead." In John 6:63, the Spirit is said to give life because He again breathes life into the flesh of the corpse, which flesh without Him is of no avail. Thus the Spirit leads the dead to ascend to life. Accordingly the words pertaining to flesh and Spirit do not refer to a manner of eating but to the promised food itself.

Thus the entire discourse contributes to the understanding of the Sacrament. Very probably the Fourth Gospel encounters here the same adversaries as are to be presupposed in John 1:14 and in 1 John 1:1 and as are clearly identified in 1 John 4:3 and 2 John 7. In its realism, the strong expression used for eating (τρώγειν) corresponds exactly with Thomas's meeting with the risen Christ (John 20:27) and with the seeing with eyes and the touching with hands that is mentioned in 1 John 1:1. This same realism that is affirmed for the real presence of Christ's body and blood in the Sacrament is expressed by Paul in the *manducatio oralis* and the *manducatio indignorum*. Perhaps even the words pertaining to the traitor, in which the term τρώγειν occurs (John 13:18), may be construed as a reference to the *manducatio indignorum*. At all events, any thought of a mere commemoration of the dead Christ or any thought of a mere table fellowship with the exalted Christ is entirely out of the question in John.

We are further reminded of Paul and the Synoptic writers when in John 6:51 we find "for the life of the world" added to the "giving of the flesh." In the "for" (ὑπέρ) there lies, as in Mark 14:24 and in 1 Corinthians 11:24, a reference to the sacrificial death. At the same time, John's closer designation of purpose implicit in the word *life* leads beyond that. This may perhaps also be inferred—to be sure, as contrast to any thought of punishment—from Paul's remark about those fallen asleep prematurely (1 Corinthians 11:29–30). And throughout his proclamation the emphasis on "life" or "eternal life" is a variously modified theme. But in the Johannine treatise on Holy Communion, the reception of Christ's body and blood is directly placed into the purpose of life. In fact, one might almost say that it is subordinated to it. To eat Christ's flesh and to drink His blood is necessary for the attainment of life, eternal life (6:53 ff.). Eating and drinking are the means, "life" is the goal. The "life" that Holy Communion purposes to give is indispensable. The "living Father" sent the Son, who lives "because of the Father;" therefore he who eats Him will "live because of the Son" (v. 57). With this conception of Holy Communion, one of the chief themes of the Gospel of John reaches its conclusion.

The double aspect in which life appears elsewhere in John is found here too. It is in the present and at the same time in the future. "He who eats My flesh and drinks My blood *has* eternal life" (v. 54)—that is the present. "He *abides* in Me and I in him" (v. 56)—that is the present outlook. "He who eats this bread *will live* forever" (v. 58)—that is the future consummation. The present "having" of life through the reception of Christ's body and blood assures the resurrection, for He says, "I will raise him up at the last day" (v. 54). Ignatius's oft quoted formula regarding Holy Communion, "The medicine of immortality and the antidote which prevents us from dying" (Ephesians 20:2), is only a linguistic modification of the Johannine conception. For today's differentiation between immortality and eternal life, which was necessitated by the reinterpretation of the Enlightenment, is appropriate neither to John nor to Ignatius. Ignatius, too, is aware that there is no resurrection without dying, both for Christ and for us (Trallians 9:2). Thus immortality is not an uninterrupted extension of physical life into the infinite. As his whole letter to the Romans shows, death is a necessary passage to eternal life. Ignatius writes, "To be close to the sword is to be close to God" (Smyrnaeans 4:2).

Immortality is also an integral component of Johannine eschatology (11:25ff.). Also in John's words on Holy Communion not only eternal life (v. 58) but also the nondying of him who has eaten Christ's bread (v. 50) appears as contrast to the necessary dying of the fathers. Thus that formula of Ignatius is sound Johannine doctrine. The reception of Christ's body and blood is death's antidote because it guarantees the resurrection.

On the basis of the Pauline and Johannine conception, perhaps many a further statement of the New Testament might be construed as a reference to Holy Communion. With regard to 1 Corinthians 5:6ff. and 1 Peter 2:3 this is quite generally acknowledged. Luther's translation of δεῖπνον with "Abendmahl" (literally, "evening meal," also used to designate the Last Supper, or Holy Communion) has long directed attention to other passages (John 13:4; Revelation 3:20; 19:9; cf. also Luke 14:16). In Revelation 22:17–21, Lohmeyer beholds "the barely disguised final celebration of the Eucharist." According to him, D. Plooj believes that Hebrews 8–10 also contains a Holy Communion homily.[3] Perhaps new light would be shed on many an additional New Testament statement if it were understood from the viewpoint of Holy Communion—for example, on the "mystery, which is Christ in you" (Colossians 1:27) or on the "partakers of a divine nature" (2 Peter 1:4). However, the meaning of the Sacrament itself, as derived from the reports of its institution and their further elaborations by Paul and the Gospel of John, can neither be enriched nor impaired by all of these uncertain allusions.

THE DOGMATIC CONCEPTION OF HOLY COMMUNION

The New Testament conception of Holy Communion as presented is binding for dogmatics because such understanding is drawn from the original institution of the Sacrament as well as from its repeated celebration together with the "word of reconciliation." However, also at this point the history of dogma may not be ignored. The return to the "singleness of heart" with which the Early Church celebrated the Sacrament cannot take place if dogmatics tries, as it were, to secure a place for itself outside the history of dogma. The investigations of the last century prove that the conception of Holy Communion, when kept aloof from the questions and problems of the Church's confessional writings, became enmeshed in ideologies which were alien to early Christianity. To be sure, dogmatics cannot trace the entire history of the doctrine of Holy Communion. However, we dare not close our eyes to the fact that within the Church and within theology "singleness" was again and again jeopardized and destroyed by "doubleness" (cf. above "Paul's Contribution to the Understanding of Holy Communion"). A critical line of demarcation must always be drawn against this.

If the Gospel is correctly understood as the word of reconciliation, then the doctrine of Holy Communion must reflect this understanding. Consequently, when the Roman doctrine proceeds from the insight that atonement is effected by sacrifice, and when it accordingly associates the Eucharist with the sacrifice of Christ, we can but concur. But it errs when, proceeding from this basis, it conceives of the Eucharist as a sacrifice which must be repeated by the priest. It is true that at present this idea often recedes into the background. However, it is recorded in the decrees of the Council of Trent. Try as we will, and despite the anathema pronounced at Trent, we can discover no intimation in 1 Corinthians 11:24 and

3 Ernst Lohmeyer, *Vom Urchristlichen Abendmahl* (Tübingen: Mohr, 1938), 196, 312.

Luke 22:19 that Christ ordained His apostles as priests to sacrifice His body and blood. Christ's sacrifice was carried out and completed in that one historical act of His death on the cross, which is neither capable of nor in need of repetition. In Holy Communion, we partake of Christ's body and blood (κοινωνοί, 1 Corinthians 10:18) and partake of His sacrifice. But this participation cannot consist in the act of sacrificing Him.

That does indeed not imply that Holy Communion is only a reference to the one-time event of the crucifixion or even to the historical event of the institution. We can never act—and that goes for Holy Communion too—as though the living Christ were not really present. In the same letter Paul calls the Christ who instituted His Supper in the night of His betrayal the "Lord of glory" who rose again and who initiates the resurrection from the dead. According to apostolic testimony, the Christ whom Christians encounter in Holy Communion is not a dead Christ but the risen, living, glorified, exalted Lord. Whoever infers from the word *remembrance* that the Lord's Supper was celebrated in commemoration of the dead reads his own "doubleness" into the apostles' words, regarding it possible that they believed in two different Christs: a dead one and an exalted one. The remembrance of His death is not a sentimental reminder of the late Jesus but a reference to the sacrifice He offered by His death; and this sacrifice has the force of Christ's real presence for the forgiveness of sin. Christ is present only by reason of His resurrection; for "if Christ has not been raised, your faith is futile and you are still in your sins."

Therefore, when Christ promised to give His body and His blood in His Supper, it is not the flesh of a corpse which we receive, as the Capernaites misunderstood, but the flesh and blood of the exalted Lord of glory. The monk Ratramnus, one of the participants in the controversy revolving about this Sacrament in the ninth century, raised the question whether the body received in Holy Communion was "the same body that was born of Mary and suffered, died, and was buried, and that rising and ascending to heaven sits at the Father's right hand" (*ipsum corpus, quod de Maria natum est et passum, mortuum et sepultum, quodque resurgens et coelos ascendens ad dexteram Patris consideat*). This question is understandable, especially in view of the conception expressed by the opposition. And yet it contains the germ of serious error. The more recent dogmatic historians are wont to reproduce the question in this abridged form: "Is the historical body of Christ involved here?" But that is only half of the question. Characteristically, Ratramnus does not differentiate between the "historical" body of Christ—that is, the born, dead, and buried body—and the risen body which is seated at the right hand of the Father. Since he fails to distinguish between these two, he treats it as a foregone conclusion that this body can be only in heaven, and consequently not in Holy Communion.

The point of truth in this thought is obvious. In keeping with apostolic testimony we cannot doubt the identity of the body of the risen Christ with that of the earthly Christ. And yet it does make a difference whether we are speaking of the body that is still destined to die or whether of the one that has already overcome death. With death the laws of this cosmos in general are set aside. What is promised beyond death is not a duplication of cosmic existence but in every respect its very opposite. That is clearly stated in 1 Corinthians 15:42–53. Therefore from the outset it is inadmissible to apply the cosmic categories of physical being to the body of the exalted Lord. It seems almost too trivial to emphasize that this, of course, applies also to the categories of mass and of space.

Yet, the above must be said, since that monk of the ninth century was not the only one who failed to note this. Ratramnus is here directly influenced by Augustine, just as Calvin was at a later date. To the present day Augustine is the author of all the types of "doubleness" with regard to the doctrine of Holy Communion in the West. Within the framework of the doctrine of Holy Communion he went ahead with the impossible thesis that Christ's body is localized in heaven and is thus spatially restricted. And from this he logically deduced that this body could not be present in the Sacrament. Thereby he simultaneously became the author of all attempts to assign to Christ's words on Holy Communion a meaning which is different from what they really express. The elements, bread and wine, must necessarily come to the fore of his entire doctrine of Holy Communion. As signs and figures they are said to represent what one imagines was Christ's meaning. In this respect, Zwingli is Augustine's most faithful disciple. But also the Roman Church's doctrine followed him in his thesis of the localization of Christ's body and its spatial restriction in heaven, even though this is but cautiously intimated in the canons and decrees of Trent.

Augustine's view bore fruit above all others in Calvin. Here is where all of Calvin's labored endeavors originate: to wrest a meaning from Christ's words on Holy Communion which does not directly contradict them. Whether he thinks from the top down and says that the Spirit, as it were, gives presence to the spatially removed body of Christ, or whether he thinks from below to above and has faith surmount the barrier of space by its soaring to heaven, it is always the localization myth that keeps him from professing the here-and-now fulfillment of Christ's promise. It is because of this that all the strenuous attempts to reduce the difference between Calvin and Luther to the question of the "how" of the real presence of Christ's body are refuted and must fail. Viewed from Luther's position, Calvin never taught more than a quasi presence: ". . . not otherwise than as if He were present in the body" (*non secus ac si corpore adesset*). This "as if" in the first edition of his *Institutio* (W 1:123) remained the label for his doctrine of the Sacrament down to the last edition (IV:17, 18).[4]

4 Johannes Calvin—Otto Weber (Übers. u. bearb.), *Unterricht in der christlichen Religion—Institutio religionis christianae* (Vier Bücher in 3 Bden., compl.).

The localization myth founders on the New Testament conception of heaven, which is not a space but the "abode" of God. Therefore, it also founders on the conception of Christ's ascension and His sitting at the right hand (*sessio ad dexteram*). If heaven is not space but lies beyond the cosmos and beyond all temporal-spatial existence, then the body of Christ, exalted in heaven, cannot be understood as localized in it. And it is this body which is promised us in the Sacrament. If there were any room for doubt regarding the real presence of the whole exalted Christ, it would be removed for all believers not only by His words in Holy Communion but also by the promise of His presence contained in His commissioning command (Matthew 28:20). All the while, the statement of the real presence is only an auxiliary thought for the doctrine of Holy Communion. It is indeed incontrovertible, but it does not yet touch its profoundest content of the Sacrament. For Christ's promise does not declare that His body will be present in the Sacrament but that it will be received there by us. This is self-evident for every theology that still acknowledges these words of Christ: "This is My body." The fact that the real presence was nevertheless questioned in the very context of the Lord's Supper suggests motives which are not rooted in apostolic testimony on this point but in other considerations.

These motives are found, first of all, in Christology. They are found in the Nestorian-Calvinist doctrine of the real presence of Christ in which the incarnation of God is delimited by the capacity of the human nature. This doctrine asserts of the earthly Christ that the Son of God left part of His deity behind in heaven to enable Him to become man. It says of the exalted Christ that He leaves His human nature in heaven to enable Him to be present on earth.

This is the doctrine with which Zwingli and Oecolampadius in Marburg attempted to refute Luther's doctrine of the real presence. They declared that Christ was present only according to His divinity (*secundum divinitatem*). Here the human nature is the *finitum* which cannot share in His presence. For Calvin, the human nature is only the flesh (*caro*) of Christ. However, that is dealing only with a restricting word, not with the substance. God's incarnation consists in His becoming *caro*. If in any degree He were again to detach Himself from this *caro*—for example, if He left it in the heavenly sphere to enable Him to be present on earth—then He would again divest Himself of the entire human nature in the same degree. Therefore the Heidelberg Catechism (quest. 47) is consistent when it excludes the human nature of the exalted Christ from His presence here on earth in general.

Consequently, it is not only misleading but also unjust to Calvin when his present-day interpreters treat the Augustinian localization theory as of only minor importance to him, or when they even ignore it entirely. It is a necessary part of his Christology; and whoever does violence to it destroys both his Christology and the core of his entire theology. For, generally speaking, this involves the relationship of God and man. Together with Luther we view this relationship from the perspective of Christ's person, and that, we believe, is in harmony with the New Testament testimony. Calvin and the theologians patterning after him, on the other hand, place their doctrine of the relationship between God and man ahead of Christology. This doctrine, in a manner of speaking, forms a system of coordinates into which Christology is subsequently sketched in. This fact cannot be covered up, not even when Karl Barth abruptly introduces Christological statements on the first page of his dogmatics. At all events—and Niesel's assertion to the contrary notwithstanding—there can be no doubt regarding the secondary position which Christology occupies for Calvin.

Calvin's doctrine of predestination, which deprives Christ's person and work of their central position, offers cogent proof for this. He assumes that he must leave room for a conception of God that is not altogether centered in Christ. Therefore the belief that we in our relationship to God, also in our relationship as His creatures, should always deal with the one who became *caro* is insufferable to him. Luther, on the other hand, professed at Marburg: "I know of no other God than the one who became man; nor do I want any other" (WA 30/3:157.33). It is folly to say that the disagreement in the doctrine of Holy Communion, which came into the open then and endures to the present day, involves nothing more than insignificant theses. Two theologies—two types of belief in God—confronted each other at Marburg. There can be no compromise between the two. This situation was not altered by Calvin, nor can it be made obsolete by any "new exegetical situation."

The conception of the Gospel as a whole is at stake here. If "God was in Christ" only incompletely, He was not in Christ at all, for there is no incomplete God. If the Son of God became *caro*, He also remained *caro*. If it were otherwise, then the end of the incarnation would mark also the end of reconciliation and redemption. Then there would be no justification either. Then there would also be no Holy Communion, merely a sentimental commemoration. The fulfillment of the Holy Communion promise implies that the incarnation is still in effect, that is, that Christ remained *caro*.

As always, faith goes hand in hand with the here-and-now promise. If the promise comes to us *hic et nunc*, the fulfillment also comes to us *hic et nunc*. If the promise is fulfilled now, it is also fulfilled here. If the exalted Christ is present now, He is also present here. Whoever interprets this differently cannot in truth speak about His presence. If Christ is here now, He is here entirely, not fractionally. If He comes to us, He does not expect us "to soar to heaven." If in the Sacrament at hand He gives us His body, we must not seek Him in distant places. That is our conception of the real presence. The gulf which separates Christologies also separates the doctrines of Holy Communion. The doctrine of Holy Communion is the test for the genuineness of our belief in the incarnation.

But perhaps we are doing many a doubter an injustice or accord him too much honor when we deduce his rejection of the real presence in Holy Communion from his Christology. Perhaps his deeper reason for this rejection inheres in a certain worldview. As already said, not only the real presence is involved here but so is also the eating (*manducare*). In the end, the doubter's question will always be that of the Capernaites: "How can this man give us His flesh to eat?" (John 6:52). This question does not stem from any Christology, for the Capernaites had none. With them it sprang from very natural considerations, and these we need not analyze. Very likely the same considerations elicit this same question from present-day doubters. These only lack the pathos of a natural revulsion to eating Christ's body, which marks the Capernaites and excuses them for their gross misunderstanding. To point to a lack of faith in miracles here, whether by way of reproof or excuse, is not to offer anything helpful. For here the miraculous nature of a happening is not at all in question; it is its actuality. Just as little may this be characterized as a doubt regarding God's omnipotence. For what doubter does not speak of the "Almighty"? And who would maintain that he is not sincere about that?

No, the worldview or feeling at the root of the rejection of the real presence looks different. It is the feeling of living in a world bereft of deities. The cosmos has become subservient to us, since we suppose that we have penetrated the mystery of its laws. We paid a high price for that. We sold ourselves to the insight that we ourselves are with body and soul consigned to the cosmos and its laws. There is no longer any room for mysteries in the world. It has become secular in every respect. The feeling of modern man for the uniform, unvarying secularity of all cosmic happenings might be the ultimate reason for the strangeness he feels over against Christ's Supper. As the experience of recent decades teaches, he stands ready to have theology inform him that the cosmos finds itself in a "crisis" by reason of its earthly relativity. He construes that as an entirely natural matter. But the fact that his secular, everyday knowledge is confirmed by "revelation," or is seen from the perspective of "origin" or "end," merely imparts to it, so he thinks, the sacral tone of a funeral dirge that accompanies the coffin into the crypt of the crematory.

Eating and drinking is the most secular matter in the world. With respect to it there is perhaps no essential difference between today and the time of the apostles. If the apostles' acquaintance with the pagan sacrificial meals gave them a different private opinion regarding eating and drinking, this could not be important to us today. However, they had another, far different reason for not feeling bound solely to the cosmos or thinking naturalistically when eating and drinking. The Fourth Petition of the Lord's Prayer had taught them to receive their daily bread from the hand of God. The giving of thanks, with which their Lord was wont to break His bread, corresponded to their manner of receiving food. To be sure, that does not impart a sacral character to natural eating and drinking, but it does reflect the belief that even the most profane matter of the cosmos may be blessed by

God Himself. And it is indeed blessed by God when received from His hand. That applies not only to eating and drinking but also to all else which Luther's explanation of the Fourth Petition adds to this. It applies to everything that links us with the cosmos.

There is admittedly no direct transition from here to Holy Communion. But it is impossible to discuss the doctrine of Holy Communion with anyone who lacks an understanding of everyday eating and drinking. For this type of eating and drinking must first be learned before one can understand what the Lord's Meal (κυριακόν δεῖπνον, 1 Corinthians 11:20) is. We do not eat bread symbolically, but really. And it is not a sign that we receive from God's hand, but the substance. This kind of reception of earthly things marks the end of the meaningless secularity which characterizes that "cosmic" feeling of which we spoke. The Creator Himself extends His hand over it, and He leads us to believe that this earthly cosmos is still His creation. If He blesses what is creaturely, then His blessing is the justification of creatureliness. It is not a theological opinion to deduce the body's appointment for death from its creatureliness. Death is the wages of *sin*, not the penalty of our creatureliness. That we are and remain God's creatures despite sin is one of the presuppositions of our belief in the resurrection.

Bodily food is promised also in Holy Communion. To be sure, it is of a kind different from our earthly bodies that receive it. But that does not justify our attempt to reduce this food to a mere *thought* or *symbol* of Christ's body. The body of the exalted Lord, which He promised in Holy Communion, is indeed no earthly body; it is the body which overcame death. When He vanquished death, His "lowly body" became His "glorious body" (Philippians 3:21). His glory cannot be forced into earthly categories. Calvin disputed Luther's doctrine by saying that the "glorified" body of Christ was not given to locality nor form (*nullo loco, nulla forma*). His adherents nowadays try to outdo him in his polemics and at the same time try to defend their position as they protest that they are unable to "picture" Christ's body in Holy Communion to themselves. Nor can we! None of us can "picture" to himself anything that lies beyond the grave, because that lies beyond our sphere of observation. For the same reason we cannot "picture" the risen Lord to ourselves. Nor can we "picture" His coming in glory or the final judgment or eternal life to ourselves.

The question is whether God's promises, which transcend earthly life, depend on what we think is possible or impossible of fulfillment. A mere reference to the difference between the "invisible" and the "visible" gains nothing here. If that is to mark the boundary line between the earthly and the nonearthly, we would first have to define "invisible" and "visible" from the perspective of the bearers of these attributes. Sin is also invisible, and yet it is earthly. And conversely, the kingdom of God is nonearthly and yet it will become visible (John 3:3). If we try to solve the problem by construing the contents of the promises rationally or "mentally" (*geistig*)—not only ancient Alexandria but also the present day furnishes many such instances—the whole concept of divine promises is destroyed. For all that is present "mentally" (*in mente*) is already there and need not first be promised.

All these attempts to "intellectualize" the eschatological promises, or to make them tractable to us through the category of invisibility, deprive them of the supernatural quality they in fact possess, a quality that is opposite to our earthly existence. The imperceptibility of their contents is not a mere detail to be deplored; it is part of their essence. Since God's promises have to do with truths that lie beyond earthly things, they define the way as to how we are to perceive them. They do address themselves to our perceptive capacity. To designate that which lies beyond the realm of perceptibility, they use words which are intelligible to us: power, body, life, crown, inheritance, priesthood. They speak of God's kingdom—of His riches. His abode. His ways. However, all of these words are marked by or are accompanied by attributes which begin (or end) with syllables of negation: immortal, endless, indestructible, unfading, unfathomable, inscrutable, invisible, unchangeable, inexpressible, immovable, imperishable, not made by hand. (In Greek, note the *alpha privativum*: ἀθανασία, ἀΐδιος, ἀκατάλυτος, ἀμαράντινος, ἀνεξερεύνητος, ἀνεξιχνίατος, ἀόρατος, ἀπαράβατος, ἀπρόσιτος, ἄρρητος, ἀσάλευτος, ἄφθαρτος, ἀχειροποίητος.)

To be sure, the attribute of invisibility too is found among such words, but it is only one among many. Whatever the conception that is appealed to, they at once want to set limits on it or, what is worse, to neutralize it entirely. At the same time these attributes keep us from construing this mode of speech symbolically or figuratively, that is, to see it only as a comparison. It is possible to do that with Jesus' parables or, in a quite different way, with the imagery of the Apocalypse. But there we find no limitations set by such attributes. Where these are added, there the subject which they modify is meant to be really what it is designated to be—life, power, body, inheritance—but this only in contrast to all that is otherwise designated in such a way and of which we have a conception.

The fact that we, as one might say, cannot "picture" anything of Christ's body in Holy Communion to ourselves expresses no more and also no less than our inability to picture to ourselves anything pertaining to the contents of our Lord's eschatological promises. Since the exalted Lord forms the content of the Holy Communion promise, the latter, too, belongs to the promises of "the last things." All that lies beyond death falls into this category. But this "beyond" is not limited chronologically. It dawned with the resurrection of Christ, and the Holy Communion promise tells us that it has dawned also for us. Yes, Holy Communion is the dawn for us. For as the resurrected Lord presents us with His body and blood, He does away with the boundary line between the realm of the physical, which is appointed to death, and the realm of the other, which has overcome death. As always, we can be only the recipients, because not we but only the resurrected Lord removed the line. But we actually receive what He promised: "He who eats My flesh and drinks My blood has eternal life, and I will raise him up on the last day" (John 6:54). That may seem presumptuous to a theology which seeks to understand the relationship between God and us only dialectically, that is, from the contrast between God and us. We understand it from the fact of the atonement.

In Holy Communion, promise and reception correspond to each other exactly as promise and faith do in the kerygma. This by no means involves only an analogy. Christ's body is truly given for us and His blood truly shed for us for the remission of sin. This implies, as Paul tells us, that there is also an "unworthy" reception of His body and blood, just as there is in some a hardening of the heart over against the kerygma. As for Holy Communion, it is received worthily only by faith, a faith which is indeed not devoid of penitence, a faith which receives forgiveness. Thus it may seem that Holy Communion is but a duplication of what faith receives by and through the proclamation of the Gospel. However, what is presented us is not only the Word, nor is our reception of it only by faith. The gift distributed to us is Christ's body and blood, and our reception takes place by means of eating and drinking. These cannot be dissociated from each other.

As we saw in a previous chapter, there may be an unworthy eating and drinking and thus also an unworthy receiving. That is a reception without faith. This fact points to a real conflict between the recipient's outward act and his inward state of heart, as even they who reject a *manducatio indignorum* must concede. For by participating in the act of receiving, such a recipient surely puts himself at variance with his inner attitude. Conversely, through his eating and drinking in faith a conflict is resolved—a conflict that is not yet removed only by hearing the proclaimed Word in faith. In fact, it is through the proclaimed Word that a hearer may become especially aware of the discord between body and soul. The *manducatio oralis* of the believer is the only earthly act in which this discord is completely overcome. Therefore this act, together with the real presence of the exalted Christ, is the dawn of the last things.

The opponents of the *manducatio oralis* need not worry that by such a belief we lapse into a "magic" conception of Holy Communion. Magic is sorcery. Sorcery purposes to exercise supermundane powers through using human action and human means to achieve self-chosen aims. Such a feature could be found in Holy Communion only if the human action, that is, the distribution and the eating and drinking of bread and wine, were motivated by human aims. But that is not the case. This human action does not spring from our will; it is our obedience, our compliance with the commission given us. We do not pursue any aim of our own in this; we merely receive what is promised us. In this respect, our attitude is the same as when the Gospel is proclaimed to us.

Along with the eating and drinking, bread and wine, too, do not have the function of magical means here. They obtain their place in Holy Communion by the act of institution and by Christ's words of distribution associated with this act. The recitation of these words as the celebration of the Sacrament is repeated does not have the significance of a magic formula, as though it had a magical effect on the bread and wine. The words merely repeat the promise of Christ, just as other promises are repeated in a sermon.

The Lutheran Confessions correctly reject the opinion that bread and wine, by virtue of the benediction spoken over them, retain sacramental value or effect also outside the administration of Holy Communion (*extra usum*, FC SD VII 83ff.). It is by the act itself that bread and wine have the significance which Christ assigned them by His words and action. There is neither reason nor justification for any speculation regarding a material relationship between Christ's body and blood and the elements. Nowhere do the Lutheran Confessions blur the distinction between Christ's body and blood and the earthly means. They contend against the doctrine of transubstantiation, and they forego the scholastic problems of impanation, coexistence, concomitance, and the like. It is evident from the language used elsewhere in the Confessions that the "in, with, and under" phrase (*in, sub, et cum*) is not intended as a speculative substitute for any scholastic formula.

The Augustana declares that Christ's body and blood "are present, distributed, and received under the form of bread and wine" (AC X, only in the German text); in place of this, the Apology states: "*cum his rebus*" (Ap IV 57, only in the Latin text); Luther, in the Small Catechism: "under the bread and wine"; in the Large Catechism: "in and under" (LC V 8); the Formula of Concord: "with bread and wine" (FC Ep VII 6). The change in the choice of prepositions demonstrates that their task is not that of precise definition. They paraphrase the simple fact that bread and wine remain bread and wine, but that in the administration of the Sacrament they are bearers of the presence, of the presentation, and of the reception of Christ's body and blood.

Finally, there is also no magical effect connected with the reception. With regard to physical effects of an unworthy reception, of which Paul speaks in 1 Corinthians 11:27–32, the judgment is evoked by the act of eating and drinking. Its cause is an inner impenitence. But also that elimination of the conflict between body and soul through the *manducatio oralis* is not the effect of magic. It produces no enduring condition, neither a spiritual nor a physical state. Nor does it produce an immortality (ἀθανασία) or incorruptibility (ἀφθαρσία) of the human body. It has reality only in the act of reception, just as the reception of the Spirit has reality only in the act of faith. However, in the act of reception the *manducatio oralis* is the dawn of the last things. For this act leads us to the boundary line that separates our body, appointed to death, from the body of Christ, which overcame death. It is simultaneously the actual obliteration of that line of the separation. The dawn is here related to the consummation as this present "life," which according to John is promised by Christ, is related to the resurrection on the Last Day.

To be sure, here the limitations fixed for dogmatics become perceptible as nowhere else. The doctrine of Holy Communion cannot replace Holy Communion itself. When theology speaks of the Word of God, it is itself under the authority of the Word, even as it itself carries out the act of faith of which it speaks. However, what is carried out in Holy Communion can at best be paraphrased (or circumscribed) but never described. The immortal (ἀθάνατον) and the indestructible (ἀκατάλυτον) is not only the eternal (ἀΐδιον). It is most profoundly also the inexpressible (ἄρρητον).

HOLY COMMUNION AS SYNAXIS

The Lord's Supper is not the private experience of individuals. Rather, it belongs to the Christian community. It unites the many recipients into "one body" (1 Corinthians 10:17). It is fellowship, or communion.

The term *communion* (*communio*), which is used also in dogmatics and which has been adopted into common church usage as well, is ambiguous. It is intended to reproduce the term κοινωνία. It is true that elsewhere in the New Testament, even with Paul, this term designates also the communion (or fellowship) of Christians with one another. In connection with the Lord's Supper, however, Paul uses it to mean "participation" in the body and blood of Christ (1 Corinthians 10:16). These two meanings are not the same. On the contrary, in the Pauline sense communion among Christians is related to participation in the Lord's Supper as effect is related to cause. Therefore, whenever we employ the term *communio*, we must always inquire which of the two meanings is intended.

In order to forestall any confusion it would be advisable to use the expression of the Early Church for the Lord's Supper as the communion of Christians, namely, the term σύναξις. In the Book of Acts (20:7; cf. Revelation 19:17) the verb form of this word is used to describe Christians coming together for the breaking of bread. Paul uses it to speak of Christians "meeting together" and "coming together," though not necessarily for Holy Communion (1 Corinthians 11:20, 33). The expression recalls John's statement that the purpose of Christ's death was "to gather into one the children of God who are scattered abroad" (συναγάγῃ εἰς ἕν, John 11:52).

As synaxis, the observance of the Lord's Supper is not the Christians' own doing, as little as is their coming together to hear an evangelical sermon. In both instances, God has called them together. The only other thing that makes their outward coming together an act of true oneness is that together they hear and receive the one Lord. In this respect, the Lord's Supper has the same constitutive significance for the Church as have the proclamation of the Gospel and Baptism. No one of these three functions can be reduced to either of the other two. They are coordinate with one another. In this coordination, however, each in its own way actualizes not only the Church's existence but also its unity.

Precisely because they constitute the Church's unity, they also form the marks by which that unity is identified. Alas, they are also the marks whereby its disunity, that is, its splintering into individual denominations, is recognized. Organizational or liturgical differences need not disrupt the true unity of the Church. On the contrary, such differences may provide an excellent object lesson on what is truly essential and what is unessential for the Church's unity. However, the major splits within the Christian Church reveal a disunity precisely in the essentials. To be sure, there is already disunity with respect to how far the essentials extend. Among the essentials the Eastern churches include also their polity, and so do the Roman, the Anglican, and most of the Reformed churches. All of them, of course, regard as essential also the Church's doctrine. Disunity in the proclamation is a sad sign. It cannot be remedied by viewing it as unimportant. To set up, in the face of this disunity, a merely external unity or union is not only to use a poor substitute but also to deny that which makes an assembly of people the Church in the first place. The question may be asked whether the split in the Church, which in the case of its proclamation reaches down to its very foundation, may not be overcome by uniting in—or using as aids—the other two functions: Baptism and Holy Communion.

This question underlies the current insistence upon altar fellowship, which aims to bridge the gulf between denominations. It is difficult to see, really, why a beginning should not rather be made with baptismal fellowship. For in many respects the situation there is far more favorable. In the major denominations which practice infant Baptism there is far-reaching agreement on the baptismal rite, though of course it is more than a rite when Baptism is really administered in the name of the triune God. Moreover, such Baptism in one denomination is accepted as valid by the others, even by the otherwise very exclusive Roman Church. So we could say that baptismal fellowship is already a reality.

However, the mutual recognition of Baptism is reduced to practice only in the event of membership transfers from one church body to another, and that, as far as total church bodies are concerned, deals with an exception rather than the rule. Still, if one were to apply to Baptism the demands currently made for altar fellowship, one would have to insist that the exception become the rule. That could and would happen if parents of one church body had their child baptized in another. That would be a profession of the cross-denominational unity of Christ's church. The proponents of altar fellowship should ask themselves whether they stand ready to do this. And since they recognize as valid the Baptism of the Roman Church, they should not, of course, exclude this either.

For this they would not be ready, and rightly so. They will assert that the administration of the Sacraments and the Church's proclamation are inseparable, since these are constitutive of the Church only when they are kept together. To recognize another church body's Baptism does not imply that doctrinal differences and other distinctions are of no importance. But if baptismal fellowship were to be carried to the extremes indicated, then of necessity the other differences and distinctions would have to be regarded as unimportant. The same reasons stand in the way of altar fellowship.

We are not questioning whether other denominations intend, with their celebration of the Lord's Supper or the Eucharist or the Mass, to conform to the will of the Founder as they understand it. But even if we were in agreement with their understanding of the Lord's Supper, a joint celebration would be in place only if there were unanimity also on all the other factors which sustain the Church. Such unanimity would not be necessary if the other factors were adiaphora, or matters of indifference. Of course, then there would no longer be a line of division. Then the Lord's Supper would no longer need to bridge a gulf, because no gulf existed. But where this is not the case, altar fellowship signifies *ipso facto* a sense of indifference to everything else as well. Then it signifies the denial of the fact that the Sacraments establish and sustain the Church only in association with the kerygma. Accordingly it is only in this association that the Sacraments realize their unity.

When even those who are fully aware of the constitutive significance of the other functions of the Church explicitly urge this altar fellowship, we may assume that they are motivated by the thought of the synaxis. The Lord's Supper appears to them as the appointed way on which the separated ones may again "come together." They frequently complain that the Church's restriction of altar fellowship reduces the Lord's Supper, which was designed to be a supper of love, into a supper of strife. But this charge simply does not square with the facts. For even if the Roman doctrine of the sacrifice of the Mass and the doctrinal disputes on the Lord's Supper between the Reformed and the Lutherans did contribute materially to denominational divisions, we must nonetheless ask: Did the Lord's Supper in any one of these communions thereby forfeit its character as synaxis? Surely no one will maintain or concede that it did. We for our part concede that it retained this character also with Zwingli, and that not only in his theory but also in the practical administration of the Lord's Supper in his Zürich church. It is utterly inconceivable how a congregation, in regular service assembled and united by faith and confession, could celebrate the Lord's Supper as a supper of strife.

It is precisely in the situation of a local congregation that the Lord's Supper fulfills its function as synaxis most meaningfully. This is the situation from which Paul's statements about synaxis in 1 Corinthians proceed. It was the local situation which occasioned his reproofs against lovelessness. Likewise in such a situation, and only in such a situation, is there opportunity for a concrete *agape*, which is still something different from a general love for mankind. We cannot concede that the love which we owe also to those outside the boundaries of our churches is impaired when in our liturgical fellowship we unite locally for the celebration of the Lord's Supper.

Synaxis is experienced within each celebrating congregation. The substantive content of this synaxis is of course not confined to such a congregation. Since synaxis depends upon the Lord's own call—and since it achieves its reality through the food received in this meal—this synaxis is practiced to the extent that His call is obeyed and this food is received. That is why the oft-quoted prayer of benediction from the *Didache* could already compare the synaxis (συναχθέν) of the bread, which as grain had been scattered across the fields, with the synaxis (συναχθήτω) of the Church "from the ends of the earth to Thy kingdom" (9:4). Here, as in the eucharistic prayer of thanksgiving, God is being asked to grant the synaxis of His Church (σύναξον, 10:4).

What this says, first of all, is that the synaxis in the Lord's Supper is not achieved by the mere assembling of Christians. Rather, it is the work of Him who calls them together and makes of the many one body. At the same time, these prayers point to an expanding of the synaxis beyond the here and now, referring to the final fulfillment that exceeds all earthly bounds. Whether in a single celebration of the Lord's Supper there are ten or a hundred Christians who participate, this makes no difference as far as the eschatological character of this synaxis is concerned. Also as synaxis is the Lord's Supper the dawn of the last things. While we must designate it as only the dawn, it is nevertheless truly the dawn; for this dawn all the denominational lines that have been drawn have been removed. But that is a removal pertaining to the last things and is thus beyond our comprehension.

CHAPTER EIGHTEEN

Altar Fellowship, Church Fellowship, and Ecclesiastical Federation

Hermann Sasse
Translated by Matthew C. Harrison

Christmas 1952[1]

Dear Brothers in the Office!

The events of this year now passing in the Church, particularly the great ecclesiastical sessions of Willingen (World Mission Council), Hanover (Lutheran World Federation), Stuttgart (German Evangelical Kirchentag) and Lund (Third World Conference for Faith and Order), have with great urgency directed anew to us Lutherans the question of what the theological conditions are for altar fellowship, church fellowship, and ecclesiastical federation. The question is certainly not new. It had already been thoroughly dealt with in the nineteenth century—so thoroughly, in fact, that one is amazed at the thoughtlessness with which the theology of our time dismisses the answers given then, though these answers still today have significance at least for canonical law. But perhaps it is asking too much of our generation, whose experience of church history began with Barth's *Römerbrief* of 1919,[2] or even only first with the German church struggle of 1933, yet to understand the struggle and work of the fathers of the previous century, upon whose shoulders we stand. Still less can this be expected of the American Lutherans who since 1917 together with their nation have undergone a transformation the depth of which can only be compared to the transformation which the Russian nation

1 *Briefe an lutherische Pastoren* 28: *Abendmahlsgemeinschaft, Kirchengemeinschaft und kirchliche Federation* (North Adelaide, December 1952). The original was published in *Lutherische Blätter* 5, no. 30 (1953). Huss number 297. MH

2 *The Epistle to the Romans*, trans. Edwyn Clement Hoskyns (London: Oxford University Press, 1933). MH

has undergone since 1917. The American of 1952, even if he should belong to the Lutheran Church, is an entirely different man than the American before the outbreak of the First World War. If Lutherans at the beginning of the century could read their church and synodical newspapers of today, they simply would not recognize their church in them. Thus it appears senseless to appeal to the faith and decisions regarding matters of the faith of the fathers when the great question of the relationships of the churches is the matter under discussion. We must go back to the Confessions of the Lutheran Reformation and to the teaching of the New Testament.

1

The decision regarding the relationship between the Lutheran and the Reformed Church, as is well-known, was rendered at the Marburg Colloquy [1529] and dogmatized in the Confessions. All attempts to reinterpret the meaning of *Augsburg Confession* Article X have ended in failure and have only led to the forsaking of the Lutheran Church. The *improbant secus docentes* ["they reject those who teach," AC X 2] of this article is only a mild form of the *anathema* which precludes church fellowship with the deniers of the real presence as it is taught in the catechism. *The Wittenberg Concord* of 1536, too, by which the South Germans and the Lutherans were united, can be understood in no other way than as it was interpreted and taken up by the *Formula of Concord*. The decisive question is whether Luther was justified when at the conclusion of the Marburg discussions he refused to the Reformed altar fellowship and the recognition as brothers which they had sought. It was not that he was not basically inclined to oblige Christians who thought otherwise. This is shown by the *Marburg Articles* themselves, in particular by the formalization of the article on the Supper, and also by the last offer for union which he made and which the trustworthy [witness] [Johannes] Oecolampadius has preserved for us:

> We confess that, by virtue of these words "This is My body" "This is My blood," the body and the blood of Christ truly, that is, substantially and essentially, not, however, quantitatively or qualitatively nor locally, are present and offered in the Supper. [Cited according to W. Köhler, *Das Marburger Religionsgespräch 1529, Versuch einer Rekonstruktion*, 1929, pp. 131ff.]

Luther was satisfied with the mildest form of the doctrine of the real presence in the sense of a substantial and essential [presence], though not a local and quantitative presence of the body and blood of Christ under the elements. But where this was not acknowledged there could be no altar and church fellowship for him. The denier of the real presence was for him no Christian brother, and he well knew what he did when in Article XV he maintained that each side ought to show Christian love to the other, then added the words: "so far as every conscience can allow" (WA 30/3:170.30ff.).[3] While the Zwinglians and the later Reformed have always declared that the Lutheran doctrine of the Supper is indeed false but not Church dividing, Luther and the Lutheran Church, as long as they took their Confessions seriously, have always viewed the difference on the Supper as Church dividing and the Reformed doctrine on this point as a heresy precluding church fellowship. For more than four hundred years the right hand of fellowship of the Reformed has remained outstretched. For more than four hundred years we Lutherans with our reformer have had to hear the accusation of unbrotherliness and lovelessness, because we have refused this hand.

This fact must give us serious cause ever and again to examine whether or not Luther's conscience was perhaps on this point an erring conscience. Woe to us if we would base the denial of altar fellowship on the tradition of our Church or the example of Luther. If we did this, we would no longer be Lutherans. Perhaps our opponents have not been totally incorrect if they have often felt our standpoint were essentially only traditionalism. With many Lutherans this is actually the case. This renders their position dubious and explains the defection of so many Lutheran churches from the position of old Lutheranism. In Sweden today it is declared without concern (as it happened only a short time ago with the World Conference on Faith and Order) that the old rules of church order are a holdover [from the past]. Those who come to the altar are not questioned concerning their confession; rather, one is prepared to give the Sacrament to anyone because the Lord does the same thing at our altar that He does at the Reformed and Anglican altar, namely, He gives Himself in the real presence. Thus open Communion is advocated. In fact, if we have to do here only with a human tradition, then the Swedes and their Nordic and German neighbors are entirely correct when they defect to the practice of open Communion which has been advocated by the Reformed since Marburg. But before we follow their example, the Swedish Luther scholars must explain to us then why Luther so firmly held to the literal meaning of the Words of Institution and what these words meant for his faith. Why, for instance, did he demand from the Bohemians, whom he so kindly addressed in *On the Adoration of the Sacrament* of 1523,[4] the acceptance of the doctrine of the real presence as a condition for church fellowship? Indeed, he did so for exactly this reason: the Words of Institution are the Gospel, which one must simply accept and may not change:

---

3 *Marburger Gespräch und Marburger Artikel* (*Marburg Colloquy and Marburg Articles*) (1529), Aland 452 (AE 38:88). MH

4 *Vom Anbeten des Sakraments des heiligen Leichnams Jesu Christi*, WA 11:431–56 (Aland 664; AE 36:275–305). MH

> On these words rests the matter completely. Every single Christian should and must know them and not allow them to be taken from him by any other teaching, even if it were an angel from heaven. They are a word of life and salvation, so that to him who believes through such faith all sins are forgiven, and he is a child of life, has overcome hell and death. The greatness and power of this word cannot be expressed; *for they are the sum of the entire gospel.* (WA 11:432.19ff.)[5]

Luther was convinced that no one can understand the entire consolation of "given and shed for you" who does not believe "This *is* My body," "This *is* My blood." The question upon which everything depends is whether this is biblical or not.

2

The Holy Scriptures simply teach that church fellowship is altar fellowship.[6] "The cup of blessing which we bless is the *koinonia* of the blood of Christ, the bread which we break is the *koinonia* of the body of Christ" (1 Corinthians 10:16). The apostle connects this participation in the body and blood of the Lord immediately with the assertion that, as the bread is one, so we who are many are one body because we partake of one bread (v. 17). The *Corpus Christi sacramentale* and the *Corpus Christi spirituali sive mysticum* ["the sacramental body of Christ" and "the spiritual or mystical Body of Christ"], *as our dogmaticians say, belong essentially together. Ecclesia*, "church" in the strict sense of the New Testament, is there where the people of God come together at one place and celebrate the Lord's Supper. There the body of Christ in the double sense is reality, though it is of course not only there. From this view of the New Testament—that altar fellowship is church fellowship and church fellowship is altar fellowship—it follows that the boundaries of both coincide. Where does the boundary of altar fellowship in the New Testament lie? It is significant that all our documents concerning the oldest Christian Supper, insofar as they bear a liturgical character, describe a boundary for altar fellowship. "The doors! The doors!" cries the deacon before the Creed yet today in the liturgy of the Eastern Church. With this the liturgy of the "believers" begins, reminiscent of the first Sunday of the Church, when the Lord came to His own behind closed doors (John 20:19). "No catechumen, no hearer, no unbeliever, no heterodox" shall be present at the Supper according to the liturgical cry of the Antiochene liturgy in

---

5 *Vom Anbeten des Sakraments des heiligen Leichnams Jesu Christi* (*Adoration of the Sacrament*) (1523), Aland 664 (AE 36:277). MH

6 So also C. F. W. Walther and the LCMS. "Members of heterodox fellowships are not excommunicated by their non-admission to the celebration of Holy Communion in fellowship with the Lutheran Church, much less are they (declared to be heretics and) condemned, but only suspended until they have reconciled with the orthodox church by leaving the false fellowship in which they stand" ("Communion Fellowship," Thesis XI, in *Essays for the Church*, vol. 1: *1857–1879* [St. Louis: Concordia, 1992], 225). MH

the eighth book of *The Apostolic Constitutions* (ch. 12), and among the believers no one should have anything against another, nor should a hypocrite approach (cf. the text of Brightman, *Liturgies Eastern and Western*, I, p. 13). *Santa sanctis*, "Holy things for holy ones," sounded the warning call before the Communion. And so that no one thereby understood that the Church was a union of Pharisees, the response of the holy people of God sounded: "One is holy, one is the Lord, Jesus Christ, to the honor of God the Father." (Cf. Brightman, p. 24 *et passim*.) The fact that all liturgies of the old Greek Church contain such a cry by which a fence was placed around the Supper points to the fact that this is a very ancient practice. The way in which Justin [ca. 100–165] (*Apology* 1.66) in his account concerning the origin of the Supper emphasizes that Jesus at the institution of the Supper gave bread and wine *to the disciples only*—who else could He have given it to?—shows that the "to them alone" is essential to his understanding of the Supper. The admonitions and warnings of the *Teaching of the Twelve Apostles* [*Didache*] corresponds to this. "No one is to eat or drink from your Eucharist unless they are baptized in the name of the Lord. For concerning this the Lord has said: 'Do not give that which is holy to dogs'" (*Didache* 9.5). Thus follows the "rubric" in the liturgy: "He who is holy, come; he who is not, repent" (10.6). This same writing prescribes Confession and Absolution before the Sunday celebration of the Supper in the same way the later liturgies and church orders do:

> But every Lord's day do gather yourselves together, and break bread, and give thanksgiving after having confessed your transgressions, that your sacrifice may be pure. But let no one who is at variance with his fellow come together with you, until they be reconciled, that your sacrifice may not be profaned. For this is that which was spoken by the Lord.[7]

Here follows the citation from Malachi 1:11 and 14, which in this passage for the first time is applied to the Supper, though not yet in the sense of the later theory of the sacrifice of the Mass. For the "sacrifice" is here still the sacrifice of praise and thanksgiving in the biblical sense, applied to the "Eucharistia" (*Didache* 14). When we look at the New Testament in this light, then we see immediately several passages containing the early Christian concept of the "closed Supper," namely, that the Lord's Supper is celebrated behind closed doors, to the exclusion of those who do not belong at it.

First, it is certain that wherever in the New Testament there is the demand for the holy kiss (Romans 16:16; 1 Corinthians 16:20; 2 Corinthians 13:12; 1 Thessalonians 5:26; 1 Peter 5:14), the "kiss of peace," the later *Pax* which preceded the Communion is in view. The demands for this kiss occur as they do at the conclusion of these letters of Paul because they were read before the gathered *ecclesia*, which then proceeded to celebrate the Supper. Thus the letters conclude with the

---

7 English text cited from ANF 7:381. MH

"apostolic blessing" in its simple form: "The grace of our Lord Jesus Christ be with you," or in the developed Trinitarian form such as we find in 2 Corinthians 13:[14]. Is it mere coincidence that in the Greek (the liturgy of Chrysostom) and in the Syrian (e.g., in the liturgy of Theodore of Mopsuestia [ca. 350–ca. 428]) Churches they do not begin the preface with "The Lord be with you" but with the formula of greeting from 2 Corinthians 13:[14]? The conclusion of the Book of Revelation should also be compared with the Pauline letters. Is it merely coincidental that the "*Maranatha*! The grace of the Lord Jesus Christ be with you!" of 1 Corinthians 16:23 is repeated in Revelation 22:20 with the words: "Come Lord Jesus! The grace of the Lord Jesus be with you all"? Was not Revelation written to be read in the liturgy (1:11; 22:18) as much as the letters of Paul? Even if it is impossible for us to know all the details of the liturgy of the first century (Pliny [the Younger] gives us the responsories for the time immediately before the turn of the century; the *Sanctus* is verified for the first century through Clement of Rome [bishop, 92–101]), the letters of Paul certainly show us this much: besides the Words of Institution, which belong to the celebration of the Lord's Supper, there is the demand for the kiss of peace; and then follows immediately the warning against schismatics and heretics, the anathema (Romans 16:16ff.; 1 Corinthians 16:20, 22); then the ancient petition of the congregation for the coming of the Lord (still spoken in Aramaic in the Pauline congregations); and finally the Benediction. The similarity of the letters of Paul with Revelation and the *Didache* show that these were fixed liturgical usages.

What interests us here is the close connection between the *Pax* and the *Anathema*, the kiss of love and peace, which expressed the unity and fellowship of the Church, and the inflexible exclusion of schismatics and heretics from the Supper and thereby the Church. At the conclusion of 1 Corinthians, which is directed against the divisions in the Church of Corinth, it is the stubborn schismatics to whom the *Anathema* is directed: "If anyone does not love the Lord, let him be anathema" (16:22). For the one who arrogantly splits the congregation, which is the Body of the Lord, cannot love the Lord. In the letter to the Romans, the admonition to greet one another in peace with the kiss of love, and the assurance that the Church of Rome is in this kiss bound together with all churches of Christ, is followed by the express warning over against heretics:

> I appeal to you, brothers, to watch out for those who cause divisions and create obstacles contrary to the doctrine that you have been taught; avoid them. For such persons do not serve our Lord Christ, but their own appetites, and by smooth talk and flattery they deceive the hearts of the naive. [16:17ff.; cf. 1 Corinthians 16:20]

The fellowship of the Church, the deepest and most intimate fellowship which there is, presupposes an inflexible separation from heresy (1 John 4:1–7; 2 John 9ff.; 2 Corinthians 6:14) because it is at the same time both fellowship between believers and fellowship with the triune God (1 John 1:3). And this separation finds its essential expression in who does and who does not receive the Supper (*Abendmahlszucht*). The fundamental axiom of canon law that there can be no *communicatio in sacris cum haereticis* [literally, "no fellowship in holy things with heretics"] comes directly from the Early Church and has its dogmatic basis in the New Testament.

3

Luther's view of church fellowship and altar fellowship can be understood only on this basis. It is not true, as is heard time and again, that Luther no longer correctly understood the fellowship character of the Supper. One need only read his sermons on the Supper to realize that the opposite is the case. The following passage from the work cited above from 1523 shows how deeply the reformer understood the relationship between the sacramental and the spiritual body of Christ:

> Thus it is now true that we Christians are the spiritual body of Christ, and altogether *one* bread, *one* drink, *one* spirit. Christ does all this, who through His body makes us all one spiritual body, and we all alike partake of His body, and so among ourselves are alike and one. Likewise, because we partake of one bread and drink, this also makes us one bread and drink. And as one member serves the other in such common love, he thus also eats and drinks the other, that is, he partakes of him in all things and is indeed the food and drink of the other, so that we thus are pure food and drink for each other, in the same way Christ is for us pure food and drink. With these words, St. Paul has laid out the riches and nature of faith and love. In the same way natural bread and wine also signify as much. For out of many kernels which are ground up, there comes *one* bread, and each one forsakes its form and becomes the flour of another. Also, many berries become *one* wine, and each berry gives up its own form and becomes juice to the other. So also Christ has become everything to us, and so among ourselves each has become everything to the other. This is how we are Christians; what one has, belongs to the other, and if one lacks, this affects the other as though he lacked it himself.[8]

One must have such passages in view in order to understand the "no" with which he denied the hand of brotherhood and the fellowship of the Supper to [Ulrich] Zwingli. This *Anathema*, too, can only be understood against the background of the *Pax* which for Luther belonged to the Sacrament of the Altar. And for him the body of Christ in the Supper is a reality such that he knows that the fellowship of the Church rests upon the participation in this body. The Church is more than a fellowship of the Spirit and spiritual people, as the humanists Zwingli and Calvin thought. It *is* the Body of Christ, because the consecrated bread *is* the body

8 *Vom Anbeten des Sakraments des heiligen Leichnams Jesu Christi* (*Adoration of the Sacrament*), WA 11:440.34ff. (Aland 664; AE 36:286–87). MH

of Christ. "There is one body and one Spirit—just as you were called to the one hope that belongs to your call—one Lord, one faith, one baptism, one God and Father of all . . ." (Ephesians 4:4ff.). This fundamentally important passage of the New Testament on the unity of the Church, upon which also the doctrine of the one Church in *Augustana* VII is based, says with perfect clarity that the Church is not merely what we men call a "spiritual fellowship." As according to 1 Corinthians 6:19 our body is a temple of the Holy Spirit; as our body is baptized and thereby at once on the Last Day will become "like His glorifious body" (Philippians 3:21; cf. Romans 6:4ff.), so the Church is also *one* body (notice that the "one body" precedes the "one Spirit"). We do not know *how* the Church *is* the Body of Christ, just as we do not know how the consecrated bread is the body of Christ. The later theological distinction between the *corpus Christi mysticum* and the *corpus Christi sacramentale* ["the mystical body of Christ" and "the sacramental body of Christ"] is an attempt to formalize [a solution to] this problem. But there is no solution, as the Greek fathers also occasionally designate the sacramental body as the "mystical" body. Thus the Lutheran Church must avoid turning the *est* into *significat* in both cases. Just as we reject every figurative meaning for the Words of Institution, so also we reject as unbiblical every understanding of the Church which sees in the Church only a fellowship of pious souls, a society of believers, who join together in common prayer and for the fostering of their faith. Thus we must also reject the encyclical *Corporis Mystici*[9] and Roman theology which sees in the designation of the Church as "Body of Christ" only an image for the social character of the Church, which is compared to "corporate participation" in one body. Certainly no one can conceive of a comparison which adequately describes the fact that the Church is the Body of Christ, just as indeed reason cannot understand or describe the relationship between the body of Christ in the Supper and the Body of Christ in the Church. For Scripture says nothing of this. What we have to accept in faith is the simple truth of the Bible, that the *ecclesia* is the Body of Christ as certainly as it is the people of God, whatever the relation of the Body of Christ which is the Church to the true body [of Christ] which we receive in the Sacrament.

Accordingly, if a deep correspondence obtains between the Sacrament of the Altar and the Church, then the destruction of this Sacrament must of necessity lead to the destruction of the Church. Here lies the basis for which Zwingli and the other "Sacramentarians" were for Luther destroyers of the Church, with whom there can be no ecclesiastical fellowship. If the apostle only acknowledged that spirit as legitimate which confessed "Jesus Christ come in the flesh" (1 John 4:2), and then treated the denial of the incarnation as a manifestation of the

---

9 This appears to be a reference to Pius XII's *Mystici Corporis Christi* (1943) (Denzinger 2290). MH

Antichrist, then Luther found himself in an entirely similar situation over against the deniers of the flesh and blood in the Supper. For him, incarnation and real presence belonged so closely together that he believed the incarnation was no longer correctly taught where the real presence was denied, and in making this point he called upon the Gospel of St. John, the apostle of the incarnation. In view of the Christological controversy which in the sixteenth century was directly connected to the question of the Supper, it cannot be denied that the doctrinal difference regarding the Supper stretched deep into the Christological [question]. Luther perceived the Reformed denial of the participation of the divine nature of Christ in the attributes of the human, and vice versa, as a destruction of the biblical Christ. When Zwingli called it an *alloeosis* when it was said that the Son of God died for us, because only the human nature could die, Luther called this separation of the person of Christ "the most horrible heresy that has ever existed." And he asked, "What Christian heart can hear or suffer such [teaching]? Indeed, thereby the entire Christian faith and the salvation of all the world [and] all things are taken away and damned. For he who is redeemed by humanity alone is certainly not redeemed." And Luther continues:

> I confess for myself that I regard Zwingli as non-Christian with all his teaching, for he maintains no part of the Christian faith correctly and has become seven times worse than when he was a Papist. . . . I make such a confession in order to be exculpated before God and the whole world, since I have no part in Zwingli's doctrine nor indeed ever will.[10]

This can be understood only when one conceives of the abyss Luther must have glimpsed when he saw behind the theology of Zwingli and [Martin] Bucer (who would become Calvin's teacher) that theology emerging which has effectively conquered modern Protestantism; a theology in which the incarnation is no longer taken seriously. For the incarnation of the eternal Word becomes mere words where the eternal Word remains also outside of the flesh and where the God-man since His exaltation is no longer present with His Church according to His human nature. Where this is the case, the Sacraments fall to the wayside. Baptism, in which the entire man, soul and body (cf. Luther, LC IV), has been buried with Christ into death (Romans 6:4), so that the entire man may rise, body and soul, becomes a symbol of a psychical transaction [*seelischen Vorgangs*]. And the Supper without the real presence of the true body and blood of Christ ceases to be the Sacrament of the New Testament. It becomes a celebration in which nothing else happens than that which according to Matthew 18:20 occurs wherever two or three are gathered in His name. But where the Supper falls away, so also does the Church. Even if it retains its outer organization, still it ceases to be the Church of

10 *Vom Abendmahl Christi* (*Confession concerning Christ's Supper*) (1528), WA26:342.13ff. (Aland 2; AE 37:231). See FC SD VIII 21, 38–45. MH

the New Testament, the people of God, the Body of Christ, and remains only a religious society. Thus it was for Luther, and is for the Lutheran Church of all times, that altar fellowship is church fellowship. And precisely because it rests upon the fellowship of the body and blood of Christ, which is impervious to reason, church fellowship is thus not a fellowship which we men can create, and for this reason neither can we arrange it.

4

Thus if Supper fellowship and church fellowship are essentially one, then it is self-evident that any change in the practice of Supper fellowship demonstrates a change in the concept of Church and in the understanding of the Sacraments. There is absolutely no doubt that the *decline of the Lutheran understanding of the Sacraments*, in particular the Lutheran doctrine of the Sacrament of the Altar, is the deepest reason that so many Lutheran churches have given up the old boundaries over against the Reformed, and thereby Lutheran principles of church fellowship. This happened in the nineteenth century in the form of lawfully constituted unions of various types [*regelrechter Unionen verschiedenen Typs*]. As varied as these may be—there were in Germany some five or six various types of union, which deviated so much from one another that up to the present it has proved impossible to unify these unions—they all had this in common: they all accepted Zwingli's and Bucer's view that altar fellowship and thereby church fellowship is also possible where there are differing doctrines regarding the Supper. The Lord Christ, so it is said, instituted the Supper for His disciples to celebrate in common, not for them to fight over. An Anglican slogan which has been influential in the more recent Ecumenical Movement stated: "Although we may not be united in the definition of the Supper, we can indeed be united in its celebration." Indeed, here we are directly informed that by first experiencing altar fellowship we can be helped to understand correctly the Sacrament. Thus the united celebration of the Supper has even become a means to achieve union. But also in this case the following applies: all this is only possible if the doctrine of Luther and the Lutheran Church are surrendered *de facto*. At the Third (and perhaps last) World Conference for Faith and Order at Lund in August 1952, only an insignificant minority of Lutherans advocated the Lutheran view of closed Communion (indeed, one each from Hanover, Saxony, and the ULC in America). All other Lutheran members of the section which dealt with the question of "inter-Communion" advocated open Communion. Thus one can see how grave is the situation of the Lutheran Church as *Church*, and this all the more since the few who advocated the old Lutheran practice in regard to altar fellowship either were immediately disavowed by members of their own church, or they advocated a law which in their churches obtains only today *de jure*. It has hitherto been impossible to check the movement which has passed through the Protestant world since the beginning of the nineteenth century and which has also brought Zwingli's and Bucer's views on altar and church fellowship to victory even in the Lutheran Church. Even those churches of the Lutheran Confession which have held themselves far distant from the union are themselves influenced by it more than they know or would want. Here lies the deeper reason for why in Germany the EKiD [Evangelical Church in Germany] has become a matter of concern for the "evangelical" populace, while the thought of a "United Evangelical Lutheran Church" gains ground only with great difficulty, and this only among theologians. There is only one thing which can again bring to the Lutheran view of altar and church fellowship recognized validity: the real renewal of the Lutheran understanding of the Sacrament. There is no doubt that this understanding has slowly grown among theologians in recent years. But just how far we still are from a rediscovery of the real presence in the Lutheran sense is shown by the otherwise so influential lecture of Peter Brunner[11] of Heidelberg on "The Nature of the Church's Liturgy" delivered at Hanover. In this paper we first read with joy concerning the Words of Institution (preliminary printing of the manuscript, p. 15):

> They say what the food in this celebration is. The relationship which the word of Jesus establishes between bread and body, wine and blood, is not "a connection by analogy . . . rather a connection by identity" (Lohmeyer). Bread remains bread; wine remains wine. But in the power of the instituting words of Jesus, this bread is His body given up for us, and this wine His blood, shed for us.

But our joy is immediately shattered by the definition of "body" which then follows.

> Jesus' body, which we receive in the Supper, is the embodied *humanity* of Jesus [*leibhaftige Menschsein Jesu*], in which He worked redemption for us. Jesus' *work of salvation*, Jesus' *salvation-suffering*, Jesus' *salvation-victory*, Jesus' entire corporeal *life* lived for us and *death* suffered for us, and the *victory* won for us is in His body and *is His body*, which we receive under the form of the bread in the Supper. Jesus' body is above all His sacrificial body. *This body and His sacrificial death are one.*

Can this really be said? What Brunner goes on to say is indeed correct: "In this sacrificial body we have His sacrificial death. Also in Jesus' blood of the covenant Jesus' covenant-sacrifice for us is present." But this is only the case if we have the essential, the substantial, body [of Christ], as the fathers put it. But do we actually receive the true, essential, substantial body? Or is "body" used here only to designate the true humanity, life, death, and victory of Jesus? This is what the cited passage says plainly enough. Is this not a repetition of what we have seen previously in Paul Althaus, for whom the gift of the Supper can under no

11 Peter Brunner (1900–1981) taught systematics at Heidelberg beginning in 1947. MH

circumstances be the glorified body of the Lord as it is for the Catholic Church, for Luther and indeed—according to his peculiar understanding—for Calvin. Rather, Althaus understands the Words of Institution as though Jesus speaks "of 'body and life' . . . thus as the life as the one dying in the sacrificial death" (*Die Lutherische Abendmahlslehre in der Gegenwart*, 1931, p. 40). We read again in Brunner:

> The duality of bread and wine, of body and blood points to this: that the sacrificed body and the covenant-effecting sacrificial blood of Jesus, and *thereby His sacrifice on the cross* itself, are *present* under the eucharistic food and presented and received through the distributed bread and the distributed cup.

It can certainly be said that where the gifts offered up for sacrifice are, there also the sacrifice itself is present. But can it also be said that the *action of the sacrifice* [*Handlung des Opfers*] is present? This is what we read in Brunner:

> The Supper is the finally fulfilled form of an action of signs [*Zeichenhandlung*] in which Jesus' *salvific deed is rendered present in the power of its eschatological freedom.* That *one-time final salvific happening* which is concentrated in the cross of Jesus *becomes present in the Supper through effective representation.*

Again, there is a deep truth in what is here said. The cross of Christ does in fact have the eschatological meaning which is here ascribed to it. The cross of Christ is a one-time happening (Hebrews 9:12, 26, 28) at the end of the world (Hebrews 1:2), and yet it is a reality which existed already at the beginning of the world (Revelation 13:8), and the Crucified One (*estauromenos* ["the one who has been and remains the crucified"], not only *staurotheis* ["the one who was crucified"] in the New Testament) is a perfect present. But where does the concept of effective representation come from? It does not come from the New Testament, but out of Catholic dogmatics. With the help of this concept, this dogmatics seeks to define the relationship of the one-time sacrifice of Golgotha and the sacrifice offered in the Mass in connection with the doctrine of the Council of Trent on the sacrifice of the Mass as the representation, remembrance, and application of the sacrifice of the cross (Trent, Session 22, ch. 1). The real presence which Peter Brunner teaches is the realization of the death of Jesus on the cross, acquired through effective representation and thereby the realization, representation, [the] actual, sacramental presentation of Jesus Christ, His life, death, [and] victory. But it is indeed no accident, if I understand correctly, that with Brunner there is no mention in the context of Supper of the risen and glorified Lord. It is indeed also no accident that what is said in the brilliant lecture of this profound and honorable theological thinker on the eschatological nature of the celebration of the Supper has been most strongly influenced by Catholic writers such as Erik Peterson

[1890–1960] (*Das Buch von den Engeln*, 1935),[12] but nothing is said of the fact that also for the Lutheran Church the Supper is heaven on earth. It is certainly no accident—rather, intent—that Brunner does not mention the name Luther nor the word *Lutheran*. No one in Heidelberg can accuse him of "confessionalism," and it also has a pedagogical significance if at a session such as that at Hanover, where the word *Lutheran* is on everyone's lips, the point is made that in the Lutheran Church the concern is for the Gospel and not for human or historical recollection. But if one borrows from Catholic theology, then why not borrow from the theology of Luther? And when one speaks before Lutherans of the body and blood of Christ in the Supper, should he not publicly state, in order to avoid misunderstanding, that he does not mean thereby what Luther meant and what the Lutheran Confessions teach? [Should he not state] that he does not mean the glorified body of the Lord, the true body, which participates in the attributes of the divine nature? Why is this distinction kept silent? It sounds indeed like a miraculous rebirth of Lutheranism when suddenly in places where this had hitherto not been the case—the old Heidelberger [theologians] would roll over in their graves if they heard it: that the words "This *is* My body" are again understood in the sense of the *est*. But there will be a lot more water over the dam before we again recognize what *corpus* means here. Perhaps we will also learn this from the Catholics if not from Luther. Much can be learned in this regard, for instance, from [Matthias Joseph] Scheeben's [1835–88] *[Die] Mysterien des Christentums*.[13] The Eastern Church also has something to say about this. Perhaps we will take from there what we no longer believe in Father Luther. Everywhere modern Lutheranism vacillates back and forth between the doctrine of Trent and Calvin, seeking but not yet grasping that which is taught in Luther's catechisms. And thus it is absolutely clear that modern Lutheranism carelessly enters into the various unions and ecumenical conferences and is impressed with the views of altar fellowship of every possible denomination, Protestant and Catholic, but does no longer, or does not yet again, understand what the Lutheran Church teaches on church and altar fellowship.

5

If we Confessional Lutherans firmly hold to the old principle that church fellowship is altar fellowship, and that there can only be a common celebration of the Lord's Supper where there is the "consensus on the doctrine of the Gospel and on the administration of the Sacraments" (the meaning of which for the present we have

---

12 Eric Peterson, *The Angels and the Liturgy*, trans. Ronald Walls (New York: Herder & Herder, 1964). MH

13 Matthias Joseph Scheeben, *The Mysteries of Christianity*, trans. Cyril O. Vollert (St. Louis: Herder, 1946). MH

spoken in our Letter 25, "Concerning the Unity of the Lutheran Church"),[14] then the question is immediately posed to us: "How do you, then, conceive of *the relation of the churches to one another*?" Should they exist as in the sixteenth and seventeenth centuries, every one claiming absolutely to have the pure doctrine, every church hurling the *anathema* against every other church, each seeking to damage the others? Before we answer this question, we should perhaps point out that the Lutheran Church never declared itself to be the only true Church of Christ. This it expressly declared in the Preface to the Book of Concord. The condemnations, that is, "the rejections of godless doctrines, and especially of that which has arisen concerning the Lord's Supper," should in no way mean "that hereby those men who err from a certain simplicity of mind, but are not blasphemers against the truth of the heavenly doctrine, much less, indeed, entire churches, which are either under the Roman Empire of the German nation or elsewhere; nay, rather has it been our intention and disposition in this manner openly to censure and condemn only the fanatical opinions and their obstinate and blasphemous teachers (which we judge should in no way be tolerated in our dominions, churches, and schools)" ([Preface to the Book of Concord 20]). The orthodox fathers constantly made reference to this authoritative explication of the condemnations. The Lutheran Church has never declared that all other churches are sects and no longer churches of Christ. This misunderstanding of the condemnation formulas was held constantly before the enlightened eighteenth and nineteenth centuries, which no longer understood the deep seriousness of the question of truth. This view was taken over by those during the church struggle [at the time of Hitler] who attacked the Lutherans because the latter still took seriously the boundaries of the Supper. Hans Asmussen, for instance, wanted to inform us that according to the Reformation there can be only one Church: either the Church of Christ or Satan's church: "The Word of God knows of no three-quarter church" (*Abendmahlsgemeinschaft? Beiheft 3 zur Ev. Theologie*, 1937, p. 19). Our Church has never denied that the Church of Christ and thus true children of God are found *also in other* denominations *where* the Means of Grace are yet effective. Herein it followed the model of the ancient Church, which in the controversy over the validity of the Baptism of heretics and in the Donatist controversy opposed Cyprian's understanding of "Outside of the church there is no salvation" [*extra ecclesia nulla solus*] (*Epist.* 73.21; the order in which the four words stand expresses: "If the baptism of public confession and blood [i.e., martyrdom] cannot help the heretic himself for salvation because *there is no salvation outside the church*, how much less will it benefit him if he has allowed himself to be sprinkled and polluted with impure water in secret and in a den of thieves. . . . Thus it is impossible for us to have Baptism in

14 [See Hermann Sasse, *Letters to Lutheran Pastors*, vol. 2: *1951–1956*, ed. Matthew C. Harrison (St. Louis: Concordia, 2014), 117–36. MH]

common with heretics"). If one asks which of the confessional churches of the sixteenth and seventeenth centuries in practice exercised the most tolerance, the answer must be the Lutheran Church. It was also the case with the Lutherans that a false teacher was not tolerated, and the "whose rule, his religion" [*cuius regio eius religio*] applied also for Lutheran territories in the same way it applied for the Puritans in America. But there is in Lutheran lands no parallel to the bloody persecutions of the Protestants by French Catholicism or to the equally horrible persecution of the Catholics by the Anglican and Puritan state in England. It is comprehensible from a psychological standpoint that in those lands of the West the fanaticism of religious persecution changed to its complete opposite: a tolerant indifference toward all dogma, whether of religious or enlightenment complexion. But to charge the Lutheran Church with intolerance because it still took the question of truth seriously and thus rejected the union plans of the seventeenth, eighteenth, and nineteenth centuries means to misunderstand fundamentally the intention of the Lutheran Confessions. The problem of how the varying denominations should exist side by side and what their mutual relationship should be was not yet understood and thus could not yet be solved in the sixteenth and seventeenth centuries. This is shown by the historical fact that for the first time only in the second half of the seventeenth century was there general conviction that the division of Western Christianity was final. It was not until the time of Leibniz[15] that the hope of the reunion of the separated confessional churches in the West was finally shattered. The problem of how Christian churches of various confessions can and shall exist side by side has only been defined as such since that time.

6

It is very instructive to see how in the seventeenth century the denominations [*Konfessionen*] began to order their relationships along firmly fixed boundaries. Naturally the Reformed immediately advanced their union plans so as to at least bring together the Lutherans and the various types of the Reformed. But still several more generations were needed until Pietism and Rationalism had so displaced the confessional consciousness of the Lutherans that in wide areas of Germany the accomplishment of the union was possible. Confessionally conscious Lutheranism offered *doctrinal discussion and cooperation in externals* [*cooperatio in externis*] in response to the Reformed plan for union, which declared that the doctrinal differences had to do with unessential matters. It is moving to see how the Lutheran theologians, even after the failure of the religious colloquies of the seventeenth century, did not give up the hope that a union in doctrine on the basis of the correct understanding of the Holy Scriptures would be possible. Valentin Ernst Löscher, whose *Peaceable Address and Admonition to the Reformed Congregations*

15 Gottfried Wilhelm von Leibniz (1646–1716). MH

in Germany (appendix to part three of *Historia Motuum*) is the most humanly stirring document of the voice of late orthodoxy for the unification of Christianity, was the last representative of the "doctrinal discussion" method in the eighteenth century, which method then later was applied to the unification of Lutherans by Ferdinand Walther and the present Missouri Synod.[16] Along with doctrinal discussion as a means toward unification, there arose already in the seventeenth century the fixed and organized *cooperation in externals* between the denominations. The question whether and to what extent Luther would have approved of the denominations working together is falsely posed. In the first place, he was convinced that he lived in the end times, so that even something like calendar reform appeared completely unnecessary to him. Second, he did not yet know of denominations in the later sense—rather, only of the one Church of Christ, which stood in a struggle against the power of Satan and the Antichrist. It was the necessities of life of the seventeenth century which first led to a very remarkable form of cooperation among Lutherans and Catholics and between Lutherans and Reformed. There were cathedral chapters and convents [*Stifte*] in which some of the canons were Catholic and some Lutheran, and nevertheless a fellowship obtained for external reasons which came just short of [*bis zur*] *communicatio in sacris*. The demands of canon law on both sides were reckoned with only later. The most important institution of this nature which the seventeenth century produced was the *Corpus Evangelicorum* at the permanent imperial diet at Regensburg since 1653. It stood until the elimination of the old constitution of the empire in the year 1806 and was the forerunner of all later alliances of larger German Protestantism. It was the first federation of Lutherans and Reformed. Indeed, churches were not allied—there were as yet no independent churches in the age of church government by the princes. Rather, those sent by their rulers as Protestant imperial representatives united to form a standing board. In regular sessions they dealt with problems of concern to all the evangelical churches (such as complaints regarding the violation of the legal rights of the minority), and they represented the interests of Protestantism at the imperial diet, the organ of imperial governance. And so it was inevitable that not only questions of imperial canon law would be dealt with, but even questions which cut deeply into the life of the Church, such as the reform

16 Löscher (1673–1749) lived in the great period of struggle over Pietism. He was the last great proponent of Lutheran orthodoxy in the eighteenth century. As superintendent at Dresden, he led the Saxon Church with tremendous fidelity despite the fact that the royal family had converted to Roman Catholicism. He preached at the cornerstone-laying of the famous Frauenkirche in Dresden, which has been reconstructed. Löscher was also an ancestor of Sasse. See Hans Martin Rotermund, *Orthodoxie und Pietismus: Valentin Ernst Löschers "Timotheus Verinus"in der Auseinandersetzung mit der Schule August Hermann Franckes* (Berlin: Evangelische Verlagsanstalt, n.d.). Paul Schreyer wrote a dissertation under Sasse (which also begs translation): *Valentin Ernst Loescher und die Unionsversuche seiner Zeit* (Schwabach: J. G. Schreyer, 1938). MH

of the Gregorian calendar. At the beginning of the eighteenth century, the *Corpus Evangelicorum* was stormed with the demand from all over that it become the means to bring about the union of both churches. So it was entirely unavoidable that occasionally doctrinal questions arose which the Lutherans did not believe belonged to the sphere of competence of the *Corpus*. None of the theologians of late orthodoxy had taken offense at the establishment of this board, though it was known that "theological matters are smuggled in which are disguised however one wishes" (thus the electoral Saxon delegate who thereby based his case that the board of directors should not be open to the Reformed Palatinate; cited by Ernst Sal. Cyprian, *Abgetrungener Unterricht von kirchlicher Vereinigung der Protestanten,* 2nd ed., 1726, p. 250). Thus the problem of the relationship of the various denominations [*Konfessionskirchen*], which did not yet exist at the time of Luther and which of necessity first emerged in Germany as a result of the splintering of territorial churches, found its first solution. The nineteenth century then further developed this solution: a Lutheran Church can never enter into a union with a church of another confession without surrendering its own confession. It may, however, enter into temporary or permanent federations, if the intent of such federations is only cooperation in externals and ideological discussion.

7

The *ecclesiastical federation* rests upon the acknowledgment that one can believe that the Church of Christ is still found in another church, even though it may be heterodox in essential matters. The Church of Christ is present if and insofar as the Means of Grace, the Word of God, and Holy Baptism, are present. *The* question whether or not in such a church the Sacrament of the Altar is still present was affirmed in the case of the Eastern churches and the Roman Church by Luther and the Lutheran Church. With respect to the Reformed churches, this question cannot be definitely answered. Federation excludes any *communicatio in sacris*, as well as pulpit and altar fellowship. The question of when and under what circumstances joint prayer is possible is difficult to answer. But this much can be said: the solemn prayer of the Church's liturgy as prayer of the Body of Christ has since ancient times belonged to the *communicatio in sacris*, as is shown by the use of the ancient Church in which this prayer as also the corresponding Eucharist was held behind closed doors (which practice was based upon Matthew 6:6). The goal of the federation is first *cooperatio in externis*: for instance, joint dealings with the state on questions of the free exercise of religion [*Fragen der Glaubensfreiheit*], the rights of Christian schools, and the like. But also common churchly tasks may be accomplished through joint effort, such as the way the revision of the Luther Bible in Germany was always a common undertaking by churches, or as in America today the new wording of the Revised Standard Version has been the joint task of various churches. When in the Church external matters and internal matters are not clearly distinct, there naturally always remains a certain lack of surety regarding the competence of an ecclesiastical alliance or an otherwise joint organization such as a Bible society [to deal with the issues involved]. This uncertainty is to be tolerated as long as everyone is clear and unanimous on the principle that everything which is a confessional question for one of the churches concerned can be answered only on the basis of its confession and must be answered by each of the churches on this basis alone. The mistake of the Barmen Theological Declaration lies not in the fact that the evangelical churches spoke a common word against the threat of a totalitarian state, but rather that they said it in the form of a joint confession of doctrine. "No, they confessed at Barmen," responded Karl Barth to a Lutheran territorial bishop when the latter posed this question: "Is it not the case that Barmen was indeed only a theological declaration and not a confession?" A mixed synod, at which one party cannot acknowledge the other as orthodox, can never dogmatically answer questions of doctrine. This has always been the viewpoint of Lutheran canon law. The Reformed have a different view on this matter because for them the Lutherans are erring brothers, but not heretics. So it was in Marburg 1529, so it is today. The tragedy of all modern attempts at union between Lutheran and Reformed churches is explained by these varying understandings of the boundaries of the Church by Lutherans and Reformed. For the Reformed the Lutheran Church is a part (a sort of backward part) of the Reformed Church, which must be helped to complete the Reformation. Where the Lutherans have in view federation, the Reformed have in view union. This is the case with the EKiD; this is the case with the new American church alliance, the NCCCUS [National Council of the Churches of Christ in the United States of America]; this is the case with the Ecumenical Council. At the fervent pleas of the Lutherans, these organizations are called federations, and it is denied that their intent is to be a sort of "super church." The constitutions are "improved" as it happened in America where the United Lutheran Church was downright boastful that they had achieved more than forty changes in the constitution of the National Council of Churches. The most important of these changes was that the goal of the alliance was defined in this: that it should manifest "the common spirit" of the member churches, instead of "essential oneness," as the draft read. The word *devotional* was also dropped from the sentence "to encourage devotional fellowship." Does anyone believe that the Reformed Churches and groups of America consequently changed their concept of church and unity of the church and their understanding of the NCCCUS? Great ecclesiastical structures everywhere in Christendom are arising in this manner. They are called federations, but in reality they are churches. They grant each individual church its private confession, but this confession is relativized in that its claim to speak the truth, bindingly and for all, is taken away. And every one of these great organizations claims to teach and preach the Gospel. But that is the function of the Church, not of the alliance of churches. An alliance of churches cannot evangelize, just as neither can it administer the Sacraments. But that means it can have no joint celebration of the Supper. An alliance of churches can indeed concern itself with doctrine, but only as a forum for serious doctrinal discussion among member churches.

8

These are the basic principles of the Lutheran Church concerning altar fellowship, church fellowship, and ecclesiastical federation. They have universal validity because they are based on the Lutheran Confession. They also apply in the case of the *relationships of Lutheran Churches to each other*. That a church calls itself "Lutheran" (churches such as that of Württemberg, Sweden, and Norway do not call themselves Lutheran, and, indeed, this does not belong to the essence of the Lutheran Church) or that the Lutheran Confession was once in history the real confession of this church may be of great human and historical importance. But it has no theological meaning. These basic principles apply in the case of a federation of Lutheran Churches such as the Lutheran World Federation. It can only be acknowledged as a federation of Lutheran Churches if these churches are truly Lutheran in the sense that the doctrine of the *Unaltered Augsburg Confession* and the catechisms stand *extra controversiam*. If this is not the case, then the Lutheran World Federation is in no way different from any other alliance of churches. One cannot say: "If we Lutherans can join a federation with Reformed or United Churches with the understanding developed above, how much easier can we enter into an alliance with other churches which call themselves Lutheran and also wish to be Lutheran!" In reality it is not easier, but more difficult. With the Reformed and Catholics I can operate together in external matters on the common basis of the ancient ecclesiastical confessions. I can also enter into a doctrinal discussion with them on the basis of the ancient confessions and the Holy Scriptures (e.g., on justification or the Supper). But if I speak with or operate together with Lutherans, then I have to be certain that we are at least unified on these questions.

If the Lutheran World Federation and its possibilities are viewed from this standpoint, the question must be asked: Is it in a position to call upon its member churches to again take the Lutheran Confession seriously? If it can do this, then it has a great task, and we will happily help it in this regard. If it is not in the position to do this, or if it will not do this, then the cooperation of any truly confessional churches is senseless. We trust that within world Lutheranism there are still strong forces which heartily affirm the Lutheran Confession. If they can be advanced in the Lutheran World Federation (hitherto this has been impossible), then they will have our assistance. The decision on this matter will be made in the context of the great *crisis of the Ecumenical Movement* which became evident at the session of the World Conference for Faith and Order in Lund when the Orthodox Churches of the East politely but unmistakably distanced themselves from the Ecumenical Council as it has developed in the last decade. It is understandable that the churches behind the Iron Curtain did not take part. But the fact that anti-Communist churches closely tied to the West from Greece, Alexandria, and the Russian Church in exile were no longer present but allowed themselves to be represented by a small delegation of the ecumenical patriarch cannot be explained on merely political grounds. The true reasons became evident when the London exarch of the ecumenical patriarch delivered a declaration in which he stated that the Orthodox Church maintained the right to decide what is false in the religious sphere and to make known that which agrees with their faith and that which does not. They allow their theologians and representatives at conferences only to make positive and definite statements regarding Orthodox doctrine, but do not allow them to become involved in fruitless discussion or take part in voting on matters of faith, the liturgy, or church government. When this is compared with the address of the late Archbishop Germanos[17] at the beginning of the World Conference of Lausanne in 1927, in which he pointed out the broad areas of doctrine which the Orthodox Churches could discuss because they had not been defined by any of the Ecumenical Councils, then the change the Ecumenical Movement has undergone within the past forty years becomes evident. The simplistic dreams of union have been exhausted. The Ecumenical Council has increasingly become an organization of Reformed and Union Churches together with a portion of Lutheranism which has forsaken the Confession of the fathers. Is it not time, instead of dealing further with the unattainable union of all churches, to work toward that which truly is attainable: the upbuilding of the great confessional churches and the restoration of a Christian relationship among them? Is it not time to be done with ecumenical fanaticism and return to belief in the *Una Sancta*, which exists as a reality in, with, and under the confessional churches, whose unity we cannot see, just as we cannot see the people of God, the Body of Christ, with our earthly eyes? As one who has participated in the Ecumenical Movement for fifty years and worked within it to the extent that a Lutheran who strives to take the Confession of his Church seriously can do so, I see no other possibility for the future. In his great lecture in Lund, Edmund Schlink spoke of the walls which separate the great confessional churches, [walls] which have now become transparent in the apocalyptic events of our century. This is certainly correct. But is the time of the Church not always the end times? Was not the end of all things near when the Lord died on the cross? Did not God's new world already break forth on Easter

17 Archbishop Strenopoulos Germanos is described in the list of "conference participants" as archbishop and metropolitan of Thyatira, representative of the ecumenical patriarch in Western Europe, doctor of theology and philosophy. See Sasse, *Die Weltkonferenz* (1929), 588. MH

morning? Was not the Reformation an eschatological event, and not only because Luther and his followers thought they lived in the end times? Are not the walls between the confessional churches always transparent for those who believe in the Church of God and know that it is holy wherever this Church is? Even there, exactly there where we must speak the *Anathema* over false teaching, there can still be the *Pax*, the peace of God which truly passes all understanding, the peace between children of God, the saints of the entire world, even though they see their unity as little as they perceive their holiness itself!

For the new year I greet you, honored brothers, with the wish that God bless your work in His Church, wherever you may occupy the Office. Let us be certain of this in faith, that no work which is done for God's Church is done in vain, even if our eyes do not see the results. And also that grief which, as I know, many of you bear for the sake of the Church belongs to that which builds the Church in a way that is unimaginable to us, though it means for us, in Luther's words, "the dear, holy cross."

In the bond of the faith I remain,
Hermann Sasse

CHAPTER NINETEEN

SELECTIVE FELLOWSHIP[1]

HERMANN SASSE

THIS ESSAY APPEARS TO HAVE BEEN DIRECTED to a query from the LCMS. In a letter to John W. Behnken of August 12, 1957, Sasse states: "I . . . am just writing a statement on selective fellowship which, as I hope, will be finished today and will be sent to St. Louis." Later in the same letter: "If, as I hope, the paper on selective fellowship will be finished tonight, I shall send it tomorrow to your office. . . . Please excuse this delay."[2] In October of the following year, he writes again to Dr. Behnken:

> The idea of those brethren [Breslau Synod] seems not to be to restore altar and pulpit fellowship with the *Landeskirchen* ["territorial churches"] as such, but to practice a sort of selective fellowship. They have learnt that from the *American Lutheran*.[3] The whole idea comes from America. I have done what I could to counteract this. My article in the *Australian Lutheran Review*[4] of the ELCA, which has caused me much trouble here has been translated by Bro. Bente at Kiel for the *Rundblick*.[5] I do not know whether or not it has been published.

In a period of increased dialogue with other Lutheran churches, particularly with the American Lutheran Church (founded in 1930), the LCMS had

1 This article appeared in *The Australasian Theological Review* 28:3 (September 1957): 45–62.

2 John W. Behnken Collection, Concordia Historical Institute, St. Louis, MO. RF [Annotations in this essay dentifed by "RF" are the work of Ronald Feuerhahn. MH]

3 The *American Lutheran* was published by the American Lutheran Publicity Bureau, a group of laymen and pastors of the LCMS, in New York City (*Lutheran Cyclopedia*, 28–29). RF

4 Sasse is referring to this essay and its publication in the *Australasian Theological Review* 28.3 (September 1957): 45–62. The *ATR* was the theological journal of the Evangelical Lutheran Church of Australia. RF

5 "Selective Fellowship—*Einzelgemeinschaft*," trans. Wilhelm Bente, *Lutherischer Rundblick* 6, no. 3 (1958): 76–88. The *LR* was the theological journal of the *Selbständige Evangelisch-Lutherische Kirche* in Germany. RF

a heightened discussion of fellowship. "Selective fellowship" was a part of that discussion.[6]

In this essay, Sasse asks a very important question: "What has happened during the past thirty years to justify the statement that the various Lutheran churches concerned are no longer separated by doctrinal differences, but by practical issues?" It is a question that addresses a dominant practice among Christian churches today: fellowship before or apart from doctrinal agreement.

The following remarks have been written for circulation among some friends and colleagues in various parts of the world who are deeply interested in the problems of true Lutheran unity. When the editor of this periodical kindly asked for permission to print it, the author could not possibly decline this invitation, especially since the Lutheran churches in Australia are also vitally interested in these problems. The author is writing as a theologian and not as a church politician. It is necessary to emphasize this at a time when theology is in danger of becoming the tool of church politics. When in 1926 Bishop Dibelius[7] published his famous book *Das Jahrhundert der Kirche*,[8] he met with the strong opposition of Lutheran and Reformed theologians. His answer to Karl Barth's *Quousque tandem*, where the mere sociological concept of the church put forward by Dibelius was rejected, was this: "Ich brauche eine Theologie, mit der ich etwas anfangen kann" ["I need a theology with which I can begin something"]. It was the beginning of an era in the history of the Church in Europe when bishops or synods made decisions of far-reaching importance and later called in the theologians to justify all the mistakes which had been made. This disease has spread through the world during the past generation. It threatens the existence of the Church as well as the existence of true theology. Both have to ask not what is opportune, what is useful, but what is true, what is the truth taught by God's Word. In this sense, the following pages are submitted for consideration and discussion.

Hermann Sasse

6 See, for example, William Arndt, "Miscellanea: Selective Fellowship," *Concordia Theological Monthly* 17.6 (June 1946): 455–57. RF

7 From 1925 until his dismissal by the Nazis in 1933, Otto Dibelius (1880–1967) was the general superintendent of the Kurmark of the Old Prussian Union Church. In 1945 he became superintendent (but took rather the title of bishop) of Berlin, and in 1949 he became presiding bishop of the Evangelical Church in Germany (*ODCC*, 478). RF

8 Otto Dibelius, *Das Jahrhundert der Kirche: Geschichte, Betrachtung, Umschau und Ziele* (The Century of the Church) (Berlin: Furche-Verlag, 1926). RF

1

According to the *Lutheran Standard*,[9] the American Lutheran Church has adopted a resolution which reads as follows:

> Wherever congregations and pastors of the ALC find they are mutually agreed in confession and practice with congregations and pastors of other Lutheran Church bodies, they may in good conscience practice fellowship both in worship and work.

The importance of this resolution cannot be overestimated, as is shown by the comment which immediately follows and which must be regarded as an official explanation:

> Since we have reached the place in discussion where *we find no doctrinal differences* between ourselves and the other major Lutheran bodies in America, and since we are agreed that all bear properly the name Lutheran, and since problems arise only in the area of practice, such a declaration is not only possible but practical. It takes into account existing practices within the church. The district presidents have been assigned the task of devising a practical system for implementing the resolution.

There can hardly be any doubt as to the ultimate goal envisaged by the resolution, namely, one Lutheran Church in America which would comprise not only the new church that will come into existence when the impending merger has been completed, but also The Lutheran Church—Missouri Synod, the Augustana Lutheran Church, and the United Lutheran Church.

This is shown by the preceding paragraph, where we read:

> The Union Committee has been instructed to urge the Joint Union Committee—that is, the Union Committee of the merger churches—to maintain the altar and pulpit fellowship which we of the ALC had with the *Augustana Lutheran Church* in the American Lutheran Conference [1930]. The committee has also been instructed to encourage continued negotiations with The Lutheran Church—Missouri Synod and discussions with the Special Commission on Relation to Lutheran *Church Bodies* in America *of the United Lutheran Church.*

The high aim of Lutheran unity in America is to be reached by such negotiations between the church bodies, but at the same time by means of selective fellowship. High-level negotiations are to be supplemented by practicing such fellowship between congregations and pastors of the various churches. The questions which arise out of this plan are as follows:

1. Is it true that there are no *doctrinal differences* between the churches concerned, but only differences of practice, as the authorities of the ALC think?

---

9 *Lutheran Standard* (April 6, 1957): 12. HS

2. Is *selective fellowship*, as suggested by the resolution, a means of overcoming existing disunity?
3. If not, what is the *proper and promising way*?

These questions will be briefly discussed here.

2

Before we try to answer the first of these questions, it should be made clear that every Lutheran pastor, congregation, and church body ought to do whatever they can to further the cause of true Lutheran union. How can the Lutheran churches claim to teach other Christians the great truth about the true unity of the Church as AC VII teaches it on the basis of Ephesians 4 if they themselves are not in fellowship? "Physician, heal thyself" [Luke 4:23 KJV]. But apart from the fact that just this disagreement between those who accept the Book of Concord *magno consensu*[10] and express their consent with a powerful "We believe, teach, and confess"[11] weakens or frustrates the testimony of our churches—we feel this to be the case especially in a country like Australia, where Lutheranism is a small minority of about one percent of the nation—can we face the last judgment with a good conscience in this respect if we have failed to do all in our power to find a real consensus on the basis of Holy Scripture? In eternity only, in the light of God, we shall see how many souls have been lost by the perpetuation of splits which were not necessary. How dare we acquiesce in the divisions between those who claim to be confessors of the doctrine of the Lutheran Reformation? On this, I think we all should be and are agreed.

3

If, from this concern for a true unity among Lutherans, we try to answer the first question, we must in the first place ask: What has happened during the past thirty years to justify the statement that the various Lutheran churches concerned are no longer separated by doctrinal differences, but by practical issues? No one denies that some great differences have disappeared since the linguistic barriers and the varieties caused by the national and cultural backgrounds of the various Lutheran groups in America have disappeared with the integration of the descendants of Lutheran immigrants of various times into the American nation. How far does this concern the question of doctrine? The difference between Walther and Loehe,

10 AC I 1: "*Ecclesiae magno consensu*";"Our churches teach with *great unanimity*"(Tappert, *BC*, 27). RF

11 Formula of Concord, passim. RF

Missouri and Iowa,[12] was most certainly not of a national nature, and the same is true of the difference between these "German" synods and the old General Council.[13] What has happened during the last generation? How can we today make statements like this: "We have reached the place in discussion where we find no doctrinal differences between ourselves and the other major bodies in America" without explaining what we have reached? Three explanations are possible.

It may be that we have come, in the course of our discussions, to see that our fathers erred when they saw such differences, for instance those which have been regarded as dividing issues between Missouri and Iowa, concerning ministry and congregation, chiliasm, *intuitu fidei* ["in view of faith"],[14] and others, to say nothing of the issues between these churches and the synods which now constitute the ULC [United Lutheran Church]. We are not discussing here the wrongs and rights in the controversies in the past. We only ask this: Were our fathers right or wrong when they saw doctrinal differences which made it impossible for them to practice church fellowship? They were conscientious men. Was their conscience an erring one? Is that the discovery we have made?

The second possibility would be that during these years we have reached a consensus on the issues which thus far have divided the Lutheran churches. Have we really? One might say that the "Common Confession"[15] has settled the doctrinal differences between the ALC and Missouri. Is that really the case? Is not this document, important as it may be, understood differently by either side? Is not this borne out by the fact that the ALC could work out this document and, on the other hand, at the same time the "United Testimony"[16] as the basis of the merger with other churches? Both documents are in many respects, for example,

---

12 On the relation of Walther and Loehe (Missouri and Iowa) with regard particularly to office and congregation, see Sasse's essay "Zur Frage nach dem Verhältnis von Amt und Gemeinde" (*Briefe an lutherische Pastoren*, no. 8, 1949). This essay was often reprinted. See, for example, *The Springfielder* 35, no. 3 (December 1971): 176–82, and *We Confess the Church* (St. Louis: Concordia, 1986), 69–83. RF [See "On the Problem of the Relation between the [Office of the] Ministry and the Congregation," trans. E. Reim, in *Letters to Lutheran Pastors*, vol. 1: *1948–1951*, ed. Matthew C. Harrison (St. Louis: Concordia, 2013), 120–34. MH]

13 The General Council was founded in 1867 by Lutheran synods of a more conservative view than the General Synod. RF

14 This is a term that designated the position of the anti-Missouri party in the Election Controversy from 1877 onward. This party held that God elects a person to salvation in view of his faith. RF

15 The Common Confession was accepted by the LCMS and the ALC. See the *Lutheran Cyclopedia*, 189. RF

16 The United Testimony on Faith and Life was approved by the ALC (founded in 1930), the Evangelical Lutheran Church, and the United Evangelical Lutheran Church and helped provide the basis for the merger that formed the (new) ALC in 1960. See the *Lutheran Cyclopedia*, 793. RF

concerning the doctrine on the Church and its unity, contradictory. But even if the "Common Confession" had settled the old issues, how is it possible that the ALC wants to maintain altar and pulpit fellowship with the Augustana Church [Synod], which by its membership in the NCCCUSA[17] practically rejects the doctrine of AC VII on the unity of the Church? For that council wants to express the "oneness" of its member churches, including Baptists, Salvation Army, Disciples, Quakers, and all types of Reformed churches. Since dogmatically altar and pulpit fellowship is the highest expression of church fellowship (*koinonia*, *communio*)[18] this would mean that the ALC (or the future TALC[19]) would be in full communion with Missouri and the Augustana Church. Even communion with the ULC is envisaged. This reminds one of the church policy of Bucer,[20] who first accepted the Wittenberg Concord [1536], thus establishing church fellowship between the Lutheran Church and the former churches of the Tetrapolitana,[21] and then tried to establish fellowship with the churches of Zürich and Basel.[22] This comparison is not meant to question the seriousness and sincerity of the men who have put forward those proposals. It only hints at the dangers looming behind such comprehensive plans unless they are based on a consent that has been reached and is not only hoped for. As long as the doctrinal differences have not been settled by a definite and generally accepted agreement, the second possibility has not yet become a reality.

There is a third possibility. "We find no doctrinal differences." Since we probably do not regard our fathers as having acted carelessly and not conscientiously when they remained separated because they did find doctrinal differences, and

17 This stands for the National Council of the Churches of Christ in the United States of America. See the *Lutheran Cyclopedia*, 566. RF

18 *Koinonia* is Greek and *communio* is Latin for "participation, fellowship, communion." See below. RF

19 In the period right before the merger that would form the American Lutheran Church in 1960, there was an attempt to distinguish it from the older ALC formed in 1930 by designating the new church with the initials TALC (for "The American Lutheran Church"). RF

20 Martin Bucer (1491–1551) was a German Protestant (Reformed) reformer who introduced the Reformation into Strassburg in 1523. He tried to adopt a middle ground in disputes between Luther and Zwingli. One of the chief purposes for Sasse writing *This Is My Body* (1959) was to make available for the American readers a record of the Wittenberg Concord, which represented a debate between Bucer and Luther. See especially "Martin Bucer and the *Wittenberg Concord*" (pp. 244–52). RF

21 The Tetrapolitan Confession was drawn up by Bucer and W. Capito in the name of the four South German cities of Strassburg, Memmingen, Lindau, and Constance and presented at the Diet of Augsburg (1530) (*ODCC*, 1593–94). RF

22 Zürich was where Ulrich Zwingli had brought reform, succeeded by John Bullinger. Basel was represented by Johannes Oecolampadius. The churches in these cities taught essentially Zwingli's theology (see *Lutheran Cyclopedia*, 665). RF

since these differences have not yet been settled, could it be that we have lost sight of the differences and their serious character? Could it be that during the past thirty or more years, our churches have developed in the direction of dogmatic indifference? Such developments have taken place and can take place in any church, the sons no longer understanding the problems of their fathers. Nominally, of course, and most certainly bona fide, the present generation maintains the doctrinal standards of the confessions as they have been inherited from the fathers. But a confession cannot remain a real confession if it is only inherited. It must be confessed. We can confess it only if we are deeply convinced that it is the true interpretation of Scripture. The confession is always the answer of the Church to the Word of God. Christ Himself asked His disciples: "Who do you say that I am?" (Mark 8:29). "What do you think of Christ? Whose son is He?" [Matthew 22:42]. It is our Lord Himself who has provoked the first dogma of the Church: Jesus is the Christ, Jesus Christ is Lord. All later confessions and all the various functions of the confessions have their root in this demand of our Lord not only to follow Him but also to confess our belief. Each generation has to do that again. We do so with the words of the fathers because we find in Scripture the same truth which they found. But we must do so for ourselves. If we cannot convince ourselves of the truth of their statements, then it would be hypocrisy to accept the Confessions. No one wants to be insincere in subscribing to the Book of Concord or the Augsburg Confession (which means the same because we regard the later confessions, as did the Formula of Concord, as the correct interpretation of the AC). But we all should ask ourselves whether we have studied them properly. How many students of theology have even read the Book of Concord from cover to cover? How many of our candidates for ordination have even read the New Testament in Greek from cover to cover, to say nothing of the Old Testament? Our fathers did that. How many Psalms do we know by heart in Hebrew, how many passages of the New Testament in Greek? How many articles of the Augsburg Confession do we know by heart—in Latin of course? If we consider these questions, we might understand the changes that have taken place in the Lutheran churches, and we have to ask ourselves, every one of us: Is this not perhaps the deepest reason why "we *find* no doctrinal differences" any longer where our fathers found them?

4

What does it mean that in these circumstances we favor "selective fellowship" as a means of reaching unity? It means, in the first place, that we, more or less despairing of solving the doctrinal problems on the highest level, push the problem to the lower levels, leaving it to the congregations and the pastors to attain unity. Is not each local congregation "Church of Christ"? Is it not endowed with the Office of the Keys? Has it not, according to Luther's writing of 1523, *Recht und Macht, Lehre zu urteilen?*[23] Of course this is true, as it is also true that the pastor must be able to "judge doctrine." However, the question must be raised and answered in all sincerity whether our present congregations and our present pastors are what they ought to be as Lutheran congregations and pastors. As to the congregations, is a newly established congregation in American or Australian suburbia, brought together by the work of faithful home missionaries, composed perhaps of people who had no Lutheran background, the same as a congregation in the time of Walther? Does such a congregation possess the Christian training, a thorough knowledge of Bible and catechism and the main articles of the Augsburg Confession which we find in the congregations of former generations? This should not be misunderstood. We rejoice over any new congregation, and we do not want to deny their zeal, their serious will to be a true Lutheran congregation. What we question is only their ability to "judge doctrine" as long as they are still in the process of growing into the Lutheran doctrine. This applies in a special way to Australia, where men and means, available to our big American sisters, are in short supply. From our own experience here we can only deplore the hurry in which sometimes a congregation is regarded as mature which still needs indoctrination, education, spiritual nurture in order to become what a Lutheran congregation ought to be if it should be able to make doctrinal decisions on which the eternal salvation of souls may depend. But the same is to be asked concerning older and well-established congregations. We live in turbulent times; we are rushing from place to place; we cannot live the quiet lives of our forefathers. We must make use of all facilities and means of communication, and we are glad that we have them. But every serious pastor knows the dangers of our restless, motorized ways of life. In such an age we must teach our congregations and pastors to be very careful in exercising their rights and powers and to make no decision which may be fateful also for themselves. By no means can we give them the right to make a decision on church fellowship for themselves without taking regard to their synod and church body, as long as they belong to that body. The reasons are the following.

It can be maintained that the local church is a divine institution while synod is only *de jure humano* ["by human law"]—which, however, would not be the view of the ALC, as far as I know. The local church has indeed that character and all the rights and duties which follow from it, but only as long as it remains with the pure doctrine of the Gospel and the right administration of the Sacraments (which includes also the right understanding of the Sacrament, according to Luther). Thus the first concern of every congregation must be to see that the Means of Grace are kept in their purity. For this purpose, it is a member of a synod or church body which looks after the individual congregations, serving them by providing pastors,

---

23 "That a Christian Assembly or Congregation Has the *Right and Power to Judge All Teaching* and to Call, Appoint, and Dismiss Teachers, Established and Proven by Scripture" (1523), AE 39:301–14. The words in italic are quoted by Sasse above in German. RF

visitors,[24] and so on. Without such help a congregation could not remain healthy, especially not in such times as ours. What should our congregations be without the seminaries, to take only this example?

Furthermore, a synod or church body fulfills duties which the individual congregation or the individual pastor could not fulfill if the decision on church fellowship were left to them. Suppose two pastors and their congregations would establish the fellowship envisaged by the resolution of the ALC. Either side would find that no difference in doctrine and practice exists between them. That may be true for the present. Would it also be true some years later? The congregations change rapidly, old members die or move to other places, new members come in. Also the pastors may change. The consensus which existed some years before might no longer exist. Would the fellowship remain? Suppose there is a congregation of the ALC and a congregation of Missouri in one town. They would establish fellowship on the conditions prevailing at the moment. Then a pastor with strong chiliastic opinions would come in, or a man with Romanizing leanings, or a man who no longer believes the doctrine of the real presence, or a man who practices fellowship with other denominations. Whatever changes there would be, some people would favor them, others not. Would the bond of unity be strong enough to keep them together? Would not the desire to maintain at all costs the fellowship established lead to indifference and finally to the loss of that sense of the confessional obligation which always has been one of the outstanding characteristics of the Lutheran Church? As a matter of fact, already now the arbitrary decisions of pastors and congregations to introduce or to abolish liturgical vestments is causing confusion. Certainly these things are adiaphora and do not destroy the unity of the Church. However, we should interpret Article X of the Formula of Concord[25] correctly. The "church of God" to which the right of decision is attributed is by no means always the local congregation, and the translation as found in the *Concordia Triglotta* should be clarified. If a congregation has joined a synod, brotherly love would demand that not only the consciences of the "weak"—whoever these may be in a specific case—should be respected, but that the good order should be maintained without which the synod cannot serve properly the local congregation. If in such adiaphora, arbitrary freedom should be practiced, as for example with the introduction of new liturgies, the adiaphora might soon cease to be adiaphora. The introduction of modern Eucharistic Prayers with Roman or Eastern elements would by all means involve a doctrinal problem. Thus the establishment of new

24 Sasse is referring to theologians who visit churches to help educate the people and, if need be, the pastors, modeled after the visitations conducted in Saxony in the 1520s. On those visitations, see the *Lutheran Cyclopedia*, 802. RF

25 "Concerning Ecclesiastical Practices which Are Called Adiaphora or Indifferent Matters." RF

rites or even of selective fellowship would in the last analysis mean the destruction of synods, the atomization and disintegration of our Lutheran churches.

There is especially one function which a church body of a more or less congregational type cannot fulfill. That is the maintenance of the bond with the Church of the fathers which is so important for the Lutheran Church. Our confession establishes not only the bond between those who now live but also with those who have confessed the true faith throughout the centuries. An agreement between two congregations would express only the *consensus fratrum* ["consensus with brother"], not the consensus with the fathers and the future generations which will confess the truth of the Gospel to the end of the world. The catholicity of the confession in space and time would be destroyed if the church body which confesses *magno consensu* ["with great unanimity"] were atomized and pulverized into a mere aggregation of individuals or small groups. In other words, selective fellowship would not further, but rather destroy, the unity of the church bodies, and this means that measure of unity which had been attained. That has happened in many Reformed churches. Certainly an isolated congregation can exist, as also isolated Christians can remain Christians. Such are cases of emergency.

It should, however, not be forgotten that already in the New Testament we do not find only isolated congregations. The great decision which the church of Antioch had to make regarding Jewish and Gentile Christianity was made in conjunction with the church at Jerusalem as the mother church. Paul writes not only to the church at Corinth, but includes all believers in all Achaia [2 Corinthians 1:1]. For Paul (1 Corinthians 16) as for John (Revelation 1:11), the churches of the province of Asia, though each of them was the church of its city, were one, as probably also the churches of Galatia and Syria, and obviously (Acts 8) the churches of Palestine as daughters of Jerusalem. These higher units were not man-made only. They were the necessary expression of a unity which transcends the local church, because in each of these local churches the one Church of Christ was existing. What bound the churches of the New Testament together was not only a human solidarity, the human desire to help each other, but the strong conviction that they were bound together in the *koinonia ton somatos Christen* ["participation in the body of Christ," 1 Corinthians 10:16], the *soma* ["body"] being not an organization, not an "organism" of which the individual churches were members—according to the New Testament members of the Church are always the believers, not groups or congregations or bodies on a provincial level. Each local church, if it is really Church of Christ, is "Body of Christ." The Church as the mystical Body of Christ is indivisible, just as the sacramental body of Christ is indivisible, each communicant receiving the undivided body, as the Lutheran Church has always taught (compare Luther's last confession[26] and hymns like *Schmücke dich, o liebe Seele*[27]). Thus not only practical considerations, but serious theological reasons, based on the New Testament, make it impossible to separate the fellowship between local churches from the fellowship between the church bodies to which they belong. To put it bluntly: Altar and pulpit fellowship between a congregation of the ALC and a congregation of Missouri or between two congregations in Australia of the UELCA and the ELCA[28] cannot be established unless the church bodies to which they belong have fellowship. Selective fellowship is unbiblical.

5

To understand that better we have to ask what church fellowship is. The English word *fellowship* does not render the deep and unique meaning of the New Testament *koinonia, communio*. This *koinonia* is a divine fact, an article of faith: *Credo . . . sanctorum communionem.*[29] As in the Creed, *sanctorum* has the twofold meaning of "holy person" and "holy things," so the *koinonia* of the Body of Christ (1 Corinthians 10:16–17) has the twofold meaning of the *koinonia* with the sacramental body of Christ, effected by partaking of the one bread (loaf), and with the mystical Body of Christ (see Werner Elert's elaborate investigation of the whole problem in *Abendmahl und Kirchengemeinschaft*).[30] The *koinonia* existing between all true believers cannot be compared with any form of human "fellowship." It is, as 1 John 1 makes clear, always at the same time *koinonia* with the Father and with the Son. It is rooted in the *koinonia* which exists within the blessed Trinity. This is the true "fellowship" which cannot be established by men, not by congregations and church bodies, but which can only be believed. We believe that this fellowship exists wherever the true Church of Christ exists, the Body of Christ, the Bride of Christ, the *ecclesia stricte dicta* ["church strictly speaking"], which is hidden to human eyes, which God alone sees. We believe this hidden Church (*abscondita est ecclesia, latent sancti* ["the Church is hidden, the saints are unknown"], as Luther puts it in *De servo arbitrio*;[31] compare Ap VII/

26 *Short Confession of the Holy Sacrament*, 1544 (AE 38:287–319). RF

27 "Soul, Adorn Yourself with Gladness" (*Lutheran Worship* 239; *The Lutheran Hymnal* 305). RF

28 The United Evangelical Lutheran Church of Australia, of which Sasse was a member, was a member of the Lutheran World Federation and in fellowship with the American Lutheran Church. The Evangelical Lutheran Church of Australia was in fellowship with the LCMS. The two merged in 1966 to form the Lutheran Church of Australia (LCA). RF

29 This is commonly translated in the Apostles' Creed as "I believe in . . . the communion of saints." RF

30 Werner Elert, *Eucharist and Church Fellowship in the First Four Centuries*, trans. Norman E. Nagel (St. Louis: Concordia, 1966). RF

31 *The Bondage of the Will* (1525), WA 18:652.23; AE 33:89. RF

VIII). We know that this *koinonia* is a reality, not only in our church, but in all Christendom wherever true believers are, whom God alone knows. But as this Church—we should avoid speaking of a visible side—must be believed where the *notae ecclesiae* ["marks of the Church"] are present, the pure preaching of the Gospel and the administration of the Sacraments according to Christ's institution, we are bound to recognize the existence of that *koinonia* wherever we find the *notae ecclesiae*, the marks of the true Church. Church fellowship between congregations (for example, within a synod) or church bodies in the sense of intercommunion practiced in the *ecclesia late dicta* ["church in the wider sense"] (*societas externarum rerum ac rituum* ["an association of outward ties and rites"]) is not the divine *koinonia* itself, but rather the recognition that we believe that *koinonia* to be present. The *koinonia proper* is invisible, just as the Body of Christ is invisible. The establishment or practice of the *communicatio in sacris* ["participation in sacred things"] is a human action, the human recognition of the presence of the divine *koinonia* and its practical application.

6

Since the days of the apostles, the practice of the *communicatio in sacris* has been regarded as that which really establishes church fellowship. Altar fellowship is church fellowship (1 Corinthians 10:16–17) and vice versa.[32] Altar and pulpit fellowship is the highest expression of church fellowship, irrespective of organizational consequences. It is one of the most serious misunderstandings of the biblical and Lutheran doctrine on the Church to assume that a merger is the real establishment of church union which may be preceded by the declaration of altar and pulpit fellowship, a misunderstanding born of a mere sociological understanding of the church. How seriously this identity of church fellowship and altar fellowship was taken in the Church of the New Testament is shown by the epistles of Paul, Peter, and John. The greetings at the end of the epistles are not greetings in the ordinary sense, expressing human relationships. They are solemn expressions of the existing unity, declarations or reaffirmations of the *communicatio in sacris*, as the admonition to greet one another with the "holy lass" (Romans 16:16; 1 Corinthians 16:20), the "kiss of charity" (1 Peter 5:14), the *Pax*, as it later was called. This kiss, expressing the full peace and unity of the Church, had its place at the beginning of "Holy Communion" already in the apostolic age, as the fact shows that the formula "The grace of our Lord Jesus Christ be with you" (1 Corinthians 16:23; Revelation 22:21) or its trinitarian form (2 Corinthians 13:14) has remained in the Eastern Church the beginning dialogue leading to the *Preface* and *Sanctus*. The

32 This is a major part of Elert's thesis; see the reference to his book above. RF

Pax is already in the New Testament connected with the "anathema"[33] of those who do not love the Lord (schismatics; 1 Corinthians 16:22) or who "cause divisions and offenses contrary to the doctrine" of the apostles (heretics) and therefore must be avoided (Romans 16:17–18; compare the corresponding warnings in Galatians 1:8; 1 Timothy 6:3–6, 20; Titus 3:10; 1 John 4:1ff.; 2 John 10–11). The heretical doctrines are doctrines that destroy the Gospel, Judaistic confusion of Law and Gospel in the earlier epistles of Paul (Galatians, Colossians), syncretistic Gnosticism in the Pastorals, denial of the true incarnation in John. But any doctrine which contradicts the apostolic teaching and thus is bound to destroy the true Gospel and the Church is such a heresy.

Paul, like every missionary, has great patience with immature Christians who have still to grow into the full understanding of the Gospel. Thus with great patience he argues with the people at Corinth who denied the resurrection of the body—an idea so strange to Greeks, as also Acts 17:32 shows. He refutes the errors existing in Corinth concerning the Lord's Supper. He would have dealt differently with these people had they insisted on their errors and proclaimed them as truth contrary to Paul's doctrine. Even a heretic is to be excommunicated only after the first and second admonition (Titus 3:10). A heretic has to be avoided, as John understood it in the case of the deniers of the incarnation, even in private life. The tradition of John's last admonition—"Little children, love one another"—and of his refusal to be in the same house with Cerinthus[34] is an excellent illustration of the way how, for him, love for Christ and strict rejection of heresy belong together. The strong language which Luther sometimes used when criticizing heretics has often been regarded as deplorable and an unchristian lack of love. He and the great champions of orthodoxy in all ages have followed the example of the apostles (e.g., "serving their belly," Romans 16:18; compare Philippians 3:19, where probably the same heretics are meant as Romans 16:17–18, since Philippians was written in Rome). We do not say that to excuse Luther's expression or similar utterances and ways of speech in dogmatic controversies. We only want to state how abominable to the apostles (as also to the Old Testament prophets) the rejection of God's Word was. "Serving the belly" is, by the way, a very true and not only picturesque description of men for whom theology is a means of satisfying their own desire

---

33 This Greek word literally means "cursed," for example, "let him be accursed" (Galatians 1:8–9; 1 Corinthians 16:22). RF

34 Cerinthus was an early Gnostic teacher (flourished ca. 100). The Church Father Irenaeus wrote: "There are also those who hear [from Polycarp] that John, the disciple of the Lord, went to bathe at Ephesus. But realizing that Cerinthus was within, John rushed out of the bath house without bathing. Instead, he exclaimed, 'Let us fly, lest even the bath house fall down, because Cerinthus, the enemy of the truth, is within' " (*Against Heresies* 3.3.4). Irenaeus further asserted that John wrote his Gospel to refute Cerinthus (*Against Heresies* 3.11.1) (*ODCC*, 314). RF

for fame and an easy life (compare the profound description of sin in its various aspects in 1 John 2:16).

7

If thus the establishment of *communicatio in sacris* and the *excommunicatio haereticorum* ["excommunication of heretics"] belong together as two sides of one and the same thing—see the condemnations of heresies which follow, or are implicitly contained in, every confession of faith—then the establishment or refusal of altar fellowship becomes such a serious issue that such a decision can be made only in view of the last judgment, since every confession of faith and every action based on the confession has consequences which stretch into eternity and involve eternal salvation and eternal condemnation (Matthew 10:32–33). Here lies the deeper reason why the Church has never left this decision to the individual Christian. Already in the New Testament the *communicatio in sacris* is a *communio* of the churches. The churches of Asia are in fellowship with the church of Corinth and the church of Rome. The fellowship which the individual Christians in the various churches have is contained in and derived from the fellowship between the *ecclesiae*. This is evident from Romans 16, where Paul "greets" many individual Christians and groups of Christians (probably in the various house churches of the big city) "in the Lord," that means in the communion of the Church which is the Body of Christ.

Thus these greetings lead up to the admonition to greet one another with that liturgical kiss which expresses and confirms the full unity and peace of the Church. From these biblical facts it must be understood that the Church in all ages up to the seventeenth century always has seen fellowship between Christians as fellowship between the churches to which the individuals belong. There was never such a thing as private practice of intercommunion, never something like "selective fellowship," which is an invention of modern Americans. Elert, in his last book (mentioned above), gives a convincing proof of this for the ancient Church. Many more examples could be added to those collected by him. There have been borderline cases, for example, in that period when the separation between Arianism and orthodoxy took place in a slow development. But as soon as the separation was final, intercommunion ceased. The Visigoth ambassador[35] to the Frankish court at Poitiers before AD 583 attended Sunday service in the Catholic Church. But he never went to Holy Communion. Not the personal conviction of the individual minister or layman decided the question whether or not intercommunion was possible, but solely the membership in a particular church. The schism between East and West developed in a slow process. It could happen that the church of Rome was still in fellowship with the church of Kiev, but not with the church of

35 This man was an Arian. RF

Constantinople. Even in such a period of transition, intercommunion was determined by church membership, not by the views of the individual.

One must never forget that only in the seventeenth century the corporative idea of the Church was slowly being replaced by a religious individualism. Zwingli would never have been able to establish church fellowship with the Anabaptists. He wanted fellowship with the Lutherans because he did not regard the difference concerning the Lord's Supper as church divisive. There was no intercommunion between the churches adhering to the Tetrapolitana and the churches of the Augsburg Confession until 1536 when Bucer and the other delegates of the South German cities accepted the Wittenberg Concord and the Augsburg Confession, not for themselves only, but on behalf of their churches. After this had been done, on the following Sunday Bucer preached and received Holy Communion at Wittenberg. Altar and pulpit fellowship had been established between churches, and this made it possible for the individuals to practice it. When this acceptance of the Augsburg Confession by Strassburg became known at Zürich, the church of Zürich at once advised the students who went to Strassburg no longer to attend Holy Communion at Strassburg.

The principle was abolished only in the seventeenth century in the Reformed churches when, at the Synod of Charenton (1631), they declared that they would admit Lutherans to the Lord's Table. "Syncretism" (*syncretismus* was at the time of the Reformation the technical term for what later was called "union" or "intercommunion") in Lutheran Germany, latitudinarianism in England paved the way for the destruction of the old principles which took place when Pietism and Rationalism destroyed the understanding of the Church and of the Sacraments.

The confessional revival which went through Christendom since 1830 helped to restore, more or less, the idea that altar fellowship is church fellowship and can be practiced only where doctrinal agreement exists. In the national and territorial churches of European—and especially German—Lutheranism, the restoration of the old doctrine and practice was only partly possible after the largest Lutheran Church of the world, the Lutheran Church in Prussia, had accepted the Union. Even where—as in Bavaria at the time of the old Erlangen school and Wilhelm Loehe—the theoretical principle was recognized, it proved to be impossible in the long run to practice what *de jure* was established. While in Europe, Lutheranism, with the exception of the small Free Churches, had to be satisfied with the legal status which could no longer be put into practice, the Lutheran churches in America and Australia had the freedom to establish the old practice, as far as they were desirous to do so. Thus in the nineteenth century, American Lutheranism became the stronghold of the old confessional principle, though also there various views were held as to the application of the generally recognized principle that altar and pulpit fellowship is church fellowship. However, it seems that in our days, our American brethren are losing rapidly what their fathers had learned in that respect from Loehe, Walther, and Krauth. We do not say that by way of an uncharitable criticism, but we must state this historic fact in order to understand the situation of Lutheranism in the world and to think over all possibilities of redeeming this situation, as far as this is in the power of men.

8

One of the most significant events in the history of American Lutheranism was the meeting of the General Council at Galesburg in 1875. Three years before, at Akron, Ohio, the council had accepted a statement of its president, Dr. Krauth, on altar and pulpit fellowship. This has become famous under the name "the Galesburg Rule." The Akron text is an attempt to solve the problem of reconciling the strict confessional principle with the actual situation prevailing in the member synods of the council, and it is worthwhile to have a look at it in order to understand the action which has now been taken by the ALC.

1. The rule is this: *Lutheran pulpits* are *for Lutheran ministers* only; *Lutheran altars* are *for Lutheran communicants* only.
2. The exceptions to the rule belong in the sphere of privilege and not of right.
3. The *determination of the exceptions* is to be made in consonance with these principles by the conscientious judgment of pastors, as the cases arise.

The meeting of Galesburg made an insertion into the first paragraph, the definite form of which was now this: "The rule, *which accords with the Word of God and with the confessions of our church,* is...." This caused a controversy, which went on for years, on the questions whether exceptions according to Scripture and Confessions are possible and who should be regarded as Lutheran in the sense of the rule. The present ALC resolution would seem to be in agreement with the first paragraph, but it leaves the question unanswered who should be regarded as Lutheran. For the statement that all "major Lutheran bodies in America ... bear properly the name Lutheran" leaves the question open whether this applies also to those which do not agree with that paragraph of the Galesburg rule. I know of Lutheran churches in America where everyone who believes in Jesus Christ as Son of God is admitted to the altar, to say nothing of pulpit fellowship. And what about the churches within the Lutheran World Federation which grant the full *right*—not only a privilege, like Sweden, Denmark, Holland—of altar fellowship and even of participation in the government of the church to non-Lutherans, even to Calvinists (for example Brazil and other churches in Latin America, Italy, England, German territorial churches, etc.). Obviously the ALC recognizes also them as Lutheran. In what sense, then, would the ALC still recognize the principle of Galesburg? If the authorities of the ALC or the growing new merger church cannot answer the question, how, then, can they expect the individual pastors and congregations to be able to do that? If the faculties of Capital[36] and Dubuque[37] have no answer, how should their graduates in the ministry have one, let alone the laymen in their congregations? Thus we must say that "selective fellowship" is no solution to the problem of Lutheran unity, least of all to the difficult question of possible "exceptions" from the rule "altar fellowship is church fellowship."

9

Are there exceptions from this rule? We do not ask whether such exceptions have been made. This, of course, has been the case very often. In the seventeenth century it still happened that in monasteries Roman Catholics and Lutherans prayed together the canonical hours for legal and economic reasons, namely, to maintain the endowment and the privileges of such an institution, which actually was no longer a real cloister. The problem is whether the rule that forbids *communicatio in sacris cum schismaticis* and *haeriticis* ["participation in sacred things with schismatics and heretics"] is *de jure divino* ["by divine right"] or only *de jure humano* ["by human law"]. We have shown that it is an apostolic injunction, a doctrine of Holy Scripture, and therefore binding on the Church. If altar fellowship is church fellowship according to the New Testament, then nobody can be admitted to the Lord's Supper who has separated himself from the Church either by schism or by heresy. The tragic situation of our time that many church bodies exist side-by-side, each of which claims to be the Church of Christ, actually prevailed already in the ancient Church since the apostolic age, as the New Testament shows. If we think of the controversy between Paul and the Judaists, we find it even in the very beginnings of the Church. Already at the time of Paul and John, a person who wanted to join the Church had to choose between several bodies—each of which claimed to be the true Church, just as the people in Jerusalem had to make up their minds as to whether Jeremiah or the prophets whom he called liars and false prophets preached the true Word of God. Faith is always a venture. Even the most conscientious decision may come from an erring conscience. A person may decide to make no decision at all. This, however, is still worse. Doubt can never he a substitute for faith, and no man can live without faith, whatever the object of this faith may be (see Luther's explanation of the First Commandment in the Large Catechism). The deepest secret of man's existence is hidden in these facts.

There can be no doubt that the New Testament demands from us that we distinguish between true doctrine and false doctrine, between Church and heresy. It is quite clear that this implies that there is no exception from the rule that altar fellowship is church fellowship. At all times, admission to the Lord's Supper has been

36 This is a reference to the seminary of the ALC at Columbus, Ohio, connected with Capital University. RF

37 Wartburg Theological Seminary of the ALC at Dubuque, Iowa. RF

understood as the "conclusive action" by which a person testifies that he belongs to the church where he receives Holy Communion. In case he did not belong to it thus far, he joins it by partaking in the Sacrament. "Open Communion" is not Communion at all; it may be a fascinating rite, a religious experience, but it is not the Sacrament of the New Testament. There is only one borderline case. That is the immediate danger of death. In the First World War it happened that in desolate prison camps of Siberia a Catholic chaplain, himself a prisoner, gave Holy Communion to dying Protestants who confessed their belief in the real presence. Similar cases are reported from Silesia at the time after the last war when no Protestant minister was available. The borderline in these cases is the borderline between time and eternity. On the battlefield, or in similar cases of emergency when death is imminent, a minister of Christ may decide that he ought not to refuse the Sacrament to a person who believes in Christ as his Savior and wants to receive in faith and penitence that which Christ has sacrificed for him at Calvary, His true body and His true blood, before he passes from this world to the judgment seat of God. The pastor will do that on his own responsibility, and the Church will approve of that, though in this case she has no right of dispensation. We have to ask for Christ's own dispensation, knowing that He will not refuse it. This is no "exception," no "selective fellowship," and cannot be used to abolish the rule.

10

If the rule "Lutheran pulpits for Lutheran ministers only, Lutheran altars for Lutheran communicants only" must be regarded as a correct application of the New Testament doctrine that altar fellowship is church fellowship, it must be accepted—if not verbally, then at least substantially—by all Lutheran churches.

Is that still the case? We have mentioned some examples of churches which claim to be Lutheran, but would no longer accept the first paragraph of the Galesburg rule. Will this process keep going on? Can it be stopped? Can we persuade our fellow Lutherans to reconsider the decisions they have taken in the direction of intercommunion with non-Lutheran churches? Or are perhaps all Lutherans going the same way? It is a remarkable fact that not only men of a younger generation no longer follow their fathers—this could be explained as a natural process—but that even mature men, sometimes old churchmen and theologians who for a lifetime have upheld the confessional standards against unionism, suddenly become champions of what they always had strongly opposed. We who have observed the great revolutions and mass movements of this century in Europe know of such strange phenomena of a revolutionary age when the tremendous changes going on in human society reflect themselves in changes which occur in the depth of an individual soul, transforming it in a way that defies psychological explanation. Also the history of the Church shows such phenomena.

In view of them probably must be understood the apostolic admonitions "to be steadfast, unmovable" (1 Corinthians 15:58) and not to be "children, tossed to and fro, and carried about with every wind of doctrine" (Ephesians 4:14 [KJV]). Sometimes it seems that a profound crisis of the Lutheran faith is hiding behind the astonishing rise of world Lutheranism in its outward appearance. What actually do we mean when calling a person or a church "Lutheran"? The fathers of the Galesburg Declaration still knew what a Lutheran Church was: a church in which the Augsburg Confession was not only nominally recognized, but was really the *norma docendi* ["norm of teaching"] under the Word of God. Also at that time there were differences of opinion as to whether or not in certain cases this norm was adhered to in doctrine and practice. But there was general agreement as to the binding character of the confession. Its great doctrinal decisions, for example as to the real presence, were regarded as being *extra controversiam* ["beyond controversy"]. What has happened now that doctrines which till then were confessed *magno consensu* ["with great unanimity"] have become open questions? What does the word *Lutheran* mean in the documents of the Lutheran World Federation or in the resolution of the ALC?

Thus we are confronted with the great task of rethinking our confessional heritage. We owe it to our own fellow Lutherans and to all Christians to clarify our thoughts. What is a Lutheran Church? What is the unity of Lutheranism which we seek? In what sense do we still not only subscribe to, but actually confess, the Confessions of our fathers? What does the *damnamus*[38] mean which we must speak against every heresy wherever it may appear, even in our own church? For the borderline between truth and error, between Church and heresy goes also right through the churches which call themselves "Lutheran." If we have to reject an error and to warn against a heretical doctrine which is threatening or destroying the Gospel, we can do that only in the spirit of deep humility and self-examination, remembering the heart-searching question: "Is it I?" If we refuse intercommunion, we can do it only with profound sorrow, not [from an arrogant position] as the *beati possidentes* ["the blessed ones possessing (the Sacrament)"], but as poor sinners who are entrusted by the Lord of the Church with the task to preserve, not for ourselves only, but for the whole of Christendom, His Sacrament, as He has instituted it.

11

Thus "selective fellowship" is not the answer to the problem of Lutheran unity. Not only such fellowship but also the term should be avoided. It is misleading and cannot even be justified by the fact that within one-and-the-same church a

38 This Latin word indicates an antithetical statement. It is used, for example, in the confessions where false doctrine is condemned. RF

person may be compelled by his conscience to avoid the Sacrament of a minister whose doctrine is doubtful or even false, as Luther has made it clear in his letter to the Christians at Frankfurt in 1533.[39] How can we lay the grave burden of deciding whether or not *communio in sums* can be practiced with members or congregations of another church body on our pastors and laymen as long as even our bishops, church presidents, and theological scholars cannot tell them what the unity of the Lutheran Church is which we are seeking? And to use the celebration of the Sacrament as a means to create a unity which does not exist—this abuse of the Sacrament in modern Protestantism, which we always have criticized, should be impossible in a Lutheran Church which knows for what purpose the Sacrament of the Altar has been instituted.

What, then, is the proper and promising way which leads to unity? Is it the continued negotiation between the church councils and union committees? Is it theological discussion between faculties, theological committees, and individual scholars? Is it the theological work done either by organizations like the department of theology of the Lutheran World Federation or by free conferences like those of Bad Boll? The answer must be this: all is necessary. We must make use of every possible means and explore all avenues. The work of creating true unity between Lutherans must be the work of the entire Church. Not the presidents and church councils alone can do it, nor the theologians, nor the laymen. The entire Church must set out to work for unity. The apparent failure of so many serious attempts is mainly due to the fact that we are always inclined to expect too much from one part of the Church, be it the bishops or synods, committees, pastors, laymen, theological scholars, women, young people. We must look at the whole. This does not mean that our entire church bodies—from kindergarten to the faculties, from the church councils to the youth societies—should become discussion clubs. It rather means that every member of the Church fulfills his duty at his "station," his *Stand* in Luther's sense. The church leaders must do their share in patient negotiations; the theologians must do their hard work of research, disputation, and teaching. The "station" of the students demands careful studying.

Thus every member of the Church has his station with its particular duties. In a Lutheran Church, the emphasis on the universal priesthood of all believers makes it compulsory for every layman to work for his church, which cannot be done without a careful training, without a serious study of the Bible and the catechism. There is the great duty of parents to teach their children. The solemn promise made at the Baptism of their children does not mean only to allow others to teach them. There is no substitute for the instruction in God's Word and in the catechism by faithful fathers and mothers. Thus every "station" is connected with duties, even the station of those who as aged or sick people can do no more than

39 [See in this book, above. pp. 1–19. MH].

pray—the greatest and hardest work in the Church. God has not yet given us a revival of the Lutheran faith as it was experienced in the first half of the nineteenth century, that great revival from which our churches still live today. Nor can we expect that through a great miracle true unity between Lutherans will suddenly come about.

The unity of the Lutheran Church can come only if our churches return to the diligent use of the Means of Grace, to a serious study of the Word of God and the Confessions of the Reformation. And this must be done in all "stations" of the Church. Our church leaders must become better theologians and—in a time in all Christendom when the burden of administrative work makes it almost impossible to combine administration and scholarship as it was still possible in the nineteenth century—have theological advice. In the Roman Church it is a strict rule that each diocesan chapter must have a *canonicus theologus* ["canonical theologian"]. The professors of theology again must have not only ecclesiastical experience, but must live and work in close contact with the pastors and congregation. Otherwise they will teach an abstract theology which does not help the Church. All great theologians have been able to express, if necessary, the profoundest thoughts in such simple language that the congregation could understand them. The hymns and prayers of Thomas Aquinas are still today used by the people, and Luther's catechisms are masterpieces of a profound theology which can be understood by any Christian, even by children. Just as the church government deteriorates into mere church politics if it is not based on sound and profound theology, so the theologian who loses contact with the real life of the Church becomes a mere theoretical scholar who speaks of God like a shoemaker of his leather, as Luther has characterized that professionalism which is the danger of all theology. The pastors who have no solid theological training and are not studying any longer become mere organizers, and their sermons or "sermonettes" cease to be a preaching of the pure Gospel. The laypeople who do not live up to the divine "stations" which they have by virtue of the universal priesthood may become good business managers in congregation and synod, church council and committee, but what they are building is not a Christian congregation in the sense of the New Testament and the Lutheran Confessions. It is rather a sort of religious society, a society for the furthering of religious interests. They may be well-meaning, pious people, eager to build the "kingdom," but they know neither what the kingdom of God nor what the Church of Christ is. They do not realize that it is *God's* kingdom which *we* cannot build, that it is the Church of *Christ*, who by His Gospel and His Sacraments builds His Church. If these men try to establish Church unity, they can think only in terms of human sociology. They do not know that the unity of the Church is something totally different from the unity existing in a merely human society.

Thus the one and only way to find unity is the rediscovery of the nature of the Church, the transformation, with the help of God, of our secularized churches, synods, and congregations into a true Church which *lives* by the power of the Gospel and of Christ's Sacraments. Everyone of us must return to that "station" which God has given us. Then our lives will be integrated into the life of the true Church, and we shall experience that where the true Church is—in local congregation, synod, or church body—the unity which we seek is given us from above. There is no other way: *Ubi ecclesia, ibi unitas* ["Where there is Church, there is unity"].

CHAPTER TWENTY

Theses on Infant/Toddler Communion

John T. Pless

1. *The question of admission to the Lord's Supper is addressed from the instituting words of the Lord, which also disclose the purpose and beneficial use of the Sacrament.*

Jesus' words tell us what the Sacrament is, His body and blood given Christians to eat and to drink for the forgiveness of their sins. As Luther puts it: "We know, however, that it is the Lord's Supper, and is called thus, not the Christians' supper. For the Lord not only instituted it, but also prepares and administers it himself, and is himself cook, waiter, food and drink."[1] The Sacrament is to be received in "remembrance" of the one who instituted it, that is, in faith trusting in His gracious words, "given and shed for you." The Sacrament itself is the preaching of the Gospel. It is misused when it is turned into an enactment of inclusiveness or thought of as the impartation of a mystical energy through the act of eating and drinking. Arguments for the Communion of infants and toddlers tend to drive a wedge between "take eat, take drink" and trust in "these words, given and shed for you." It is not simply eating and drinking that constitute the salutary use of the Sacrament but eating and drinking accompanied by trust in Christ's words, that is, the explicit promise of His Supper.

2. *The apostolic teaching that a man examine himself (1 Corinthians 11:28) cannot reasonably be interpreted as to exclude the noetic dimension of which infants/toddlers are incapable.*

Paul speaks of self-examination in verse 28 in conjunction with "discerning" (*diakrino*) the body in verse 29. Both BDAG and Kittel demonstrate that this term

1 AE 37:129–30.

means to separate, arrange, make a distinction, differentiate, evaluate, judge.[2] This text cannot be dismissed by limiting its application to the original context of the Corinthian congregation as Wolfhart Pannenberg does when he asserts: "The self-examination that 1 Corinthians 11:28 demands does not relate primarily to the individual moral state but to the breaches of fellowship that ought not exist between members of the body of Christ."[3] While the apostle is certainly addressing and correcting these breaches of fellowship enacted in the way the rich assert their priority over the poor, he does so on the basis that this is no ordinary meal but a communion in the body and blood of the Lord. Communicants are not to eat and drink without the discernment of this reality.[4]

3. *Baptism is an absolute prerequisite for admission to the Lord's Supper, but it does not follow that all the baptized are categorically to be admitted to the altar.*

The slogan "Communion is the birthright of the baptized," sometimes used to assert that all the baptized are entitled to eat and drink in the Lord's Supper, is not only problematic in making admission to the Lord's Supper a "right" rather than a gift, but it also misses the point that for numerous reasons baptized Christians are excluded from the Lord's Table. Those under church discipline are barred from the altar as are those who do not share in the confession of a particular altar. Infants and toddlers who have not yet been taught the faith and examined on the basis of this teaching are not admitted to the Supper. As Werner Elert notes: "Even though a man must first be baptized before he may partake of the Holy Communion, this does not mean that all the baptized may without distinction partake of the Eucharist together."[5] The baptized are to be taught according to the Lord's bidding (see Matthew 28:19–20). This teaching leads to the Sacrament, not vice versa.

4. *Arguments for infant/toddler Communion bypass the truth that in Baptism we receive "victory over death and the devil, forgiveness of sin, God's grace, the entire Christ, and the Holy Spirit with his gifts"*

---

2 See Walter Bauer, William Arndt, Fredrick Danker, and F. Wilbur Gingrich. *A Greek-English Lexicon of the New Testament and Other Early Christian Literature* (Chicago: University of Chicago Press, 2000), 231; and Gerhard Kittel, *Theological Dictionary of the New Testament*, vol. 3, trans. by Geoffrey W. Bromiley (Grand Rapids: Eerdmans, 1965), 946–49.

3 Wolfhart Pannenberg, *Systematic Theology*, trans. Geoffrey W. Bromiley, vol. 3 (Grand Rapids: Eerdmans, 1998), 327.

4 For more here, see Gregory Lockwood, *Concordia Commentary: 1 Corinthians* (St. Louis: Concordia, 2000), 405–8. Also see Jeffrey Gibbs, "An Exegetical Case for Close(d) Communion: 1 Corinthians 10:14–22, 11:17–34," *Concordia Journal* (April 1995): 148–63, which appears below, pp. 445–59.

5 Werner Elert, *Eucharist and Church Fellowship in the First Four Centuries*, trans. Norman E. Nagel (St. Louis: Concordia, 1966), 80.

(LC IV 41–42 [Kolb-Wengert, 461]), as though the promise of Baptism remained unfulfilled without the Lord's Supper. By waiting until children have been instructed, examined, and absolved before admitting them to the Lord's Supper, they are not being deprived of Christ.

In the New Testament and the Lutheran Confessions, Baptism is not an event in a series of "rites of initiation" that is left incomplete without participation in the Sacrament. Instead, Baptism bestows the "entire Christ" and encompasses the whole life of the believer. Not only is it foundational, but it is also enduring in the life of a Christian. The teaching that our Lord attaches to Baptism (see Matthew 28:16–20) surely leads the baptized to eat and drink His body and blood as the Lord bestows His gifts in more than one way, but infants and young children are not deprived of Christ before this teaching has been accomplished. Here note Craig Koester: "The Lord's Supper was instituted 'for the forgiveness of sins' to be received with a discerning faith. Adults and children who recognize their sin and seek forgiveness should be encouraged to partake of the meal. Since infants are not capable of recognizing sin or desiring forgiveness, they should not participate in the Supper. The grace given in Baptism is sufficient for them at this early stage of their lives. It is when they reach the point where they recognize the need for forgiveness for their sins that they should be instructed and encouraged to take, eat, and drink of Christ's body and blood at the Lord's table."[6]

Maxwell E. Johnson, himself an advocate of infant Communion, notes that through a coupling of John 3:5 ("unless one is born of water and the Spirit, he cannot enter into the kingdom") and John 6:53 ("unless you eat the flesh of the Son of Man") into a single *logion* in the *traditio fidei*, both Baptism and the Lord's Supper are made necessary for membership in the Christian community.[7] Unlike Cyprian (and Augustine for that matter), the Lutheran Confessions do not operate with what might be called a "unitive" understanding of the Sacraments. Baptism is the rebirth into the Body of Christ as in it sins are forgiven and the Holy Spirit bestowed. The Lord's Supper is not an additive to Baptism but serves instead to strengthen the Christian in the forgiveness of sins according to the word and promise of Christ to which faith clings.

5. *Faith does not make the Sacrament, but it is only by faith that the benefits of the Sacrament are received. Faith is precisely trust in these words "given and shed for you for the forgiveness of sins" (SC). In the Small Catechism, eating and drinking are joined together with trust in the spoken word "given and shed for you." The Lord's Supper is given*

---

6 Craig Koester, "Infant Communion in Light of the New Testament," *Lutheran Quarterly* (Autumn 1996): 238.

7 Maxwell Johnson, *The Rites of Christian Initiation: The Evolution and Interpretation* (Collegeville: Liturgical Press, 1999), 68–69.

> *precisely to strengthen the faith of those who through the accusation of the Law recognize their sin and whose terrorized consciences acknowledge their need and desire the forgiveness of their sins. "For people are admitted only if they have first had an opportunity to be examined* (explorati*) and heard. The people are also reminded about the dignity and use of the Sacrament—how it offers great consolation to anxious consciences—so that they may learn to believe in God and expect all that is good from God" (AC XXIV 6–7 [Latin, Kolb-Wengert, 68]).*[8]

Eating and drinking the Lord's body and blood *worthily* requires instruction. Admitting the uninstructed and therefore unexamined, whether they are adults or infants, was out of the question for Luther. Already in 1522, Luther provides a descriptive template for the structure of the catechism: "Thus the commandments teach man to recognize his sickness, enabling him to perceive what he must do or refrain from doing, consent to or refuse, and so he will recognize himself a sinful and wicked person. The Creed will teach and show him where to find the medicine—grace—which will help him to become devout and keep the commandments. The Creed points him to God and his mercy, given and made plain to him in Christ. Finally, the Lord's Prayer teaches all this, namely, through the fulfillment of God's commandments everything will be given him. In these three are

---

8 The Augsburg Confession continues the same trajectory set by Luther in 1523 in his *Order of Mass and Communion for the Church at Wittenberg*, where he outlines how those who would commune are to be examined: "But I think it enough for the applicants for communion to be examined or explored once a year. Indeed a man may be so understanding that he needs to be questioned only once in his lifetime or not at all. For, by this practice, we want to guard lest the worthy and unworthy alike rush to the Lord's Supper, as we have hitherto seen done in the Roman church. There they seek only to communicate; but the faith, the comfort, the use and benefit of the Supper are not even mentioned or considered. Nay, they have taken pains to hide the Words of Institution, which are the bread of life itself, and have furiously tried to make the communicants perform a work, supposedly good in itself, instead of letting their faith be nourished and strengthened by the goodness of Christ. Those, therefore, who are not able to answer in the manner described above should be completely excluded and banished from the communion of the Supper, since they are without the wedding garment [Matt. 22:11–12]" AE 53:33. Just a bit later in the same work, Luther continues: "They should request in person to receive the Lord's Supper so that he may be able to know both their names and manner of life. And let him not admit the applicants unless they can give a reason for their faith and can answer questions about what the Lord's Supper is, what its benefits are, and what they expect to derive from it. In other words, they should be able to repeat the Words of Institution from memory and to explain that they are coming because they are troubled by the consciousness of their sin, the fear of death, or some other evil, such as temptation of the flesh, the world, or the devil, and now hunger and thirst to receive the word and sign of grace and salvation from the Lord himself through the ministry of the bishop, so that they may be consoled and comforted; this was Christ's purpose, when he in priceless love gave and instituted this Supper, and said, 'Take and eat,' etc." (34).

the essentials of the entire Bible."[9] Instruction in and confession of these essentials of the Christian faith are a prerequisite for admission to the Lord's Supper. Four years after writing the catechisms in 1533 in his *Open Letter to Those in Frankfurt on the Main*, Luther writes: "It is quite true that wherever the preacher administers only bread and wine for the sacrament, he is not very concerned about to whom he gives it, what they know or believe, or what they receive. . . . However, because we are concerned about nurturing Christians who will still be here after we are gone, and because it is Christ's body and blood that are given out in the sacrament, we will not and cannot give such a sacrament to anyone unless he is first examined regarding what he has learned from the Catechism and whether he intends to forsake the sins which he has again committed. For we do not want to make Christ's church into a pig pen [Matthew 7:6], letting each one come unexamined to the sacrament as a pig to its trough. Such a church we leave to the Enthusiasts!"[10]

Often left out of the discussion of infant/toddler Communion is the aspect of the terrorized conscience, which Luther includes as a dimension of the examination of communicants. Examination includes exploration of why it is that the body and blood are needed. Lutheran practice should be both catechetical (the communicant should have knowledge of the basic texts and how to use them) and diagnostic (the communicant should have an awareness of his/her sin). The communicant should know what the Sacrament is and how the body and blood of the Lord are to be used against the conscience which is afflicted by sin.

6. *The Lutheran Confessions assert that none are to be admitted to the Sacrament who have not been instructed, examined, and absolved. (See LC V 1–3 [Kolb-Wengert, 467]; AC XXV 1–3 [Kolb-Wengert, 73].)*

Arthur Carl Piepkorn summarizes the position of the Lutheran Confessions: "Communicants are to know from memory at least the Decalog, the Creed, the Our Father, and the words of institution of Holy Baptism and the Sacrament of the Altar."[11] Evidence for Piepkorn's assertion may be seen in the Large Catechism where Luther writes: "All this is established from the words Christ used to institute it [the Lord's Supper]. So everyone who wishes to be a Christian and to go to the sacrament should know them. For we do not intend to admit to the sacrament and administer it to those who do not know what they seek or why they come" (LC V 1–2 [Kolb-Wengert, 467]). Near the end of this section of the Large Catechism, Luther does speak of children (not infants!) being instructed in the catechism so that they may come to the Supper: "Therefore let all heads of a household remember

9 Martin Luther, *Personal Prayer Book*, AE 43:14.

10 Martin Luther, "An Open Letter to Those in Frankfurt on the Main," trans. Jon D. Vieker, *Concordia Journal* (October 1990): 343. Cf. above, pp. 1–19.

11 Arthur Carl Piepkorn, *What the Symbolical Books of the Lutheran Church Have to Say about Worship and the Sacraments* (St. Louis: Concordia, 1952), 37.

that it is their duty, by God's injunction and command, to teach their children or have them taught the things that they ought to know. Because they have been baptized and received into the people of Christ, they should also enjoy this fellowship of the sacrament so that they may serve us and be useful" (LC V 87 [Kolb-Wengert, 87]). Article XXV of the Augsburg Confession coheres with the Large Catechism: "For it is not our custom to administer the body of Christ except to those who have been previously examined and absolved" (AC XXV 1 [Kolb-Wengert, 73]).

7. *Lutheran theology does not begin with a generic category of sacraments but works instead from the Lord's mandates for Baptism and the Supper. Each has its own distinctive features. They are not interchangeable. It does not follow that arguments for the Baptism of infants are to be applied for the Communion of infants/toddlers.*

Neither the New Testament nor the Lutheran Confessions operate with a generic definition of "sacrament" but instead begin with the Lord's instituting words for Holy Baptism, the Lord's Supper, and Absolution. What might qualify under the heading of "sacrament" is rather elastic, but it is clear that Baptism and the Lord's Supper are not interchangeable. What applies to one does not necessarily apply to the other. Baptism is administered once for incorporation into the one Body of Christ, while the Lord provides His Supper to be administered time after time to strengthen believers in the forgiveness of sins.

8. *The Lord's Supper is the new testament of the Lord, not the new Passover. Hence it does not follow that because infants/toddlers were included in the Passover meal that they are to be communed.*

Paul G. Bretscher sees the inclusion of infants in the Passover seder as a grounds for their admission to the Lord's Supper. In a paper first presented at the Institute of Liturgical Studies at Valparaiso University in 1963 and subsequently published in *Una Sancta*, Bretscher writes: "Little children, even infants, *were never excluded from the history itself* which worship is designed to relive and recover! In the case of Ancient Israel it is ridiculous even to imagine such a possibility. When that first Passover was celebrated in Egypt, and God commanded all Israel to keep it, did they leave the babies out of the house? Or, when they ate of the roasted lamb and unleavened bread, did they deny this food to their children? When they left the land and crossed the Red Sea and made their way through the wilderness, were the children left behind? It is interesting to note that Pharaoh at one point during the plagues offered to let the men go but not the children (Exodus 10:7–11, 24). The children must be participants in the saving history."[12] Bretscher's desire for

12 Paul G. Bretscher, "First Things First: The Question of Infant Communion," *Una Sancta* (Advent 1963): 37.

inclusivity presses the argument without regard to the obvious, namely, that an infant would choke on such food. On a deeper level, Bretscher operates with a faulty theology of worship as "reliving" a past event.

Following in the wake of Odo Casel, Louis Bouyer asserts in a discussion of Luke 22:19: "Far from needing or not needing to create a new rite for future use, our Lord was only performing again a very ancient rite which, even without him, his disciples would have certainly gone on performing so long as they lived together. What our Lord intended by these words was to give new meaning to this old rite."[13] However, this approach fails to acknowledge the newness of the New Testament in that Christ bestows His body and blood for disciples to eat and to drink. Norman Nagel would often point out that when we line up the Passover as described in Exodus with the narratives of the Lord's Supper's institution in the Synoptics and 1 Corinthians, the first and crucial question is not how they are similar, but how they are different. This is also Luther's approach in the Large Catechism. To paraphrase Sasse, the Lord's Supper renders the old Passover obsolete.[14] Likewise Mark Throntveit writes: "Jesus 'fulfills' the Old Testament Passover, but not by instituting the Lord's Supper in ritual continuity with the Old Testament seder. By dying on the cross, Jesus 'fulfills' the Old Testament Passover in the sense of bringing it to an end, thereby becoming the last paschal lamb, 'the Lamb of God who takes away the sin of the world.' "[15]

The nature of the Passover does not establish a basis for communing infants and toddlers any more than it provides a basis for a yearly celebration of the Lord's Supper or making the appropriate setting of the Sacrament the family dining room rather than the church. Here also see Luther in the Large Catechism where he argues that the Sacrament of the Altar is not like the old Passover, bound to a special time, but frequently where there is "opportunity and need" and not like "the pope (who) perverted it and turned it back into a Jewish feast" (LC V 47–48 [Kolb-Wengert, 471–72]).

---

13 Bouyer, *The Christian Mystery from Pagan Myth to Christian Mystery*, trans. Illtyrd Trethowan (Edinburgh: T&T Clark, 1990), 122–23.

14 Here see Hermann Sasse, "The Lord's Supper in the New Testament," in *We Confess the Sacraments*, trans. Norman E. Nagel (St. Louis: Concordia, 1985), 49–97. Sasse observes that "all the details of the traditional Passover ritual, which Jesus doubtless observed, was irrelevant for the Lord's Supper itself" (64). And again, since Jesus Himself is the Passover Lamb who gives His body and blood to be eaten and drunk, Sasse argues that "there is no analogy to this fellowship, just as there are no parallels to this celebration. The Lord's Supper received this character as something unique, something remarkable from the Words of Institution" (66). Also see Otto Procksch, "Passa und Abenmahl," in *Vom Sakrament des Altars* (Leipzig: Dörffling & Franke, 1941), 11–25.

15 Mark Throntveit, "The Lord's Super as New Testament, Not New Passover," *Lutheran Quarterly* (Autumn 1997): 284.

9. *Evidence for the Communion of infants/toddlers in the Early and Medieval Church is there in some places, but it is not clear that the practice was universal or when it was first practiced. Lutheran liturgical practice is not based on historical precedent but on the Lord's mandates. Not all practices of the Early Church are to be emulated. Infant/toddler Communion is one of those practices.*

That infants were communed in some places in ancient Christianity is not disputed, but to assert that it was a universal practice or that it is normative for historical reasons exceeds the evidence. Marc Kolden writes: "Infant communion was not widely practiced in the early church. Indeed, this practice only became more common later and then for questionable historical reasons. The first mention of it is by Cyprian in about AD 250, but it does not appear to have been well established. Origen, for example, notes that infants were not communed in his church."[16] Likewise, Justin and Cyril of Jerusalem cast doubt on the communing of infants.[17]

The Lutheran Confessions honor the Church Fathers. When their testimony is in agreement with Holy Scripture, they are gratefully cited as confessing the apostolic faith. However, the Confessions also realize that the teachings of the patristic writers are fallible. They can and do disagree with one another. They certainly do not represent an unbroken continuity with the prophetic and apostolic Scriptures, which alone are the rule and norm for church teaching and practice. The fact that one or another or even the majority of patristic writers support the Communion of infants does not establish the practice for Evangelical Lutherans. Unlike the Lutheran Confessions, which are received because they are in agreement with Sacred Scriptures, the Church Fathers are received insofar as they concur with the biblical Word.

10. *Arguments for infant/toddler Communion reveal a problematic hermeneutic of the Lutheran Confessions, which undercuts a* quia *understanding of confessional subscription.*

Given the numerous references in the Book of Concord to the nature and benefit of the Lord's Supper as well as the need for catechetical and diagnostic examination prior to admission to the Lord's Supper, one cannot endorse the Communion of infants/toddlers while maintaining an unqualified subscription to the Lutheran Confessions. To claim otherwise yields a completely ahistorical reading of the Confessions. Such a reading avoids both the meaning of the confessional texts and the actual practices of those who wrote them.

---

16 Marc Kolden, "Infant Communion in Light of Theological and Pastoral Perspectives," *Lutheran Quarterly* (Autumn 1996): 249–50.

17 Mark Tranvik, "Should Infants be Communed? A Lutheran Perspective," *Word & World* (Winter 1995): 86.

11. *Luther may not be cited in support of infant/toddler Communion. He knew of the practice among the Hussites, and while he would not condemn them as heretics (those who deny the fundamental Christological and trinitarian dogma), he did not accept their practice as correct.*

On occasion, Luther's comments recorded in a "table talk" in 1532 are cited in support of infant Communion. Apart from the fact that these comments were made in rather "off the cuff" fashion and that they were recorded by auditors at the table, Luther's words as we have them do not speak of the communing of infants but of children. In response to the question whether the Lord's Supper should be given to children, the reformer replies that "there is no urgency about the sacrament of the altar" and then refers to 1 Corinthians 11: "When in 1 Corinthians [11:28] Paul said that a man should examine himself, he spoke only of adults because he was speaking about those who were quarreling among themselves. However, he doesn't here forbid that the sacrament of the altar be given even to children."[18] Luther notes that contextually the 1 Corinthians 11 pericope is not addressing children but adults. However, given the range of Luther's other statements regarding the need for examination undergirded by teaching, it is quite a jump to conclude from this statement that he endorses the Communion of infants. Children are capable of instruction and examination in a way that infants are not.

Luther was aware that the Bohemian Brethren (Hussites) admitted infants to Holy Communion.[19] While Luther did not condemn them as heretics for this practice, he clearly did not approve of the practice as in the same letter he speaks of communicants being examined and responding concerning their faith.

12. *Infant/toddler Communion is a novel practice in the Lutheran Church. In American Lutheranism, it gained traction only in the 1970s as it was fueled by particular aspects of the liturgical and ecumenical movements.*

Frank Senn has chronicled the move toward infant Communion in the predecessor bodies of the Evangelical Lutheran Church in America, noting the influence of these movements.[20] In regard to the liturgical movement, the work of Eugene Brand, an architect of the *Lutheran Book of Worship* and chief drafter of its baptismal rite, indicates the connection, as can be seen in his essay "Baptism and the

---

18 AE 54:58.

19 Here see Thomas A. Fudge, "Hussite Infant Communion," *Lutheran Quarterly* (Autumn 1996): 176–94.

20 See Frank Senn, "Issues in 'Infant Communion,'" in *A Stewardship of the Mysteries* (New York: Paulist Press, 1999), 155–70.

Communion of Infants: A Lutheran View."[21] Ecumenically, the World Council of Churches consultation at Bad Segeberg in Germany concluded: "If children are incorporated into the body of Christ through baptism, then they belong to the whole body of Christ. As there is no partial belonging to the body of Christ, children must also have a part in the eucharist."[22] The dual trajectories of ritual participation derived from Early Church practices (liturgical movement) and inclusiveness in the one Body of Christ (ecumenical movement) converged in providing a platform for a change in Lutheran practice.

> 13. *The fact that children who have been instructed, examined, and absolved may be admitted to the Sacrament at a younger age than has been the general custom in The Lutheran Church—Missouri Synod is not to be confused with the admitting of infants/toddlers to the altar. Churchly and pastoral concerns for unity in practice are important considerations. But the Communion of infants/toddlers is not an adiaphoron to be left up to individual parents, pastors, or congregations.*

The *Lutheran Service Book: Agenda* makes provision for the admission of children to the Lord's Supper prior to confirmation with this stipulation: "Candidates for admission to the Lord's Supper have learned the Ten Commandments, the Creed, and the Lord's Prayer. They have received careful instruction in the Gospel and sacraments. Confessing their sin and trusting in their Savior, they desire to receive the Lord's Supper for the forgiveness of sins and strengthening of their faith in Christ and their love toward others"; and "Baptized Christians are admitted to the sacrament when they have been examined and absolved by their pastor in accordance with the practice outlined in the Augsburg Confession (AC XXV)" (25). Younger children who have learned these texts, know what the Sacrament is and why they need it, and have been examined by the pastor may be communed prior to the Rite of Confirmation. Concern for unity of practice especially as families move from one place to another would dictate that a common form of instruction and examination be used by pastors within our fellowship. The material in the *Pastoral Care Companion* under "Guidelines for Pastoral Examination of Catechumens—Before the Rite of First Communion" (664–70) provides such an instrument. In congregations where children are admitted to the Lord's Supper prior to confirmation, it is the responsibility of the pastor to see to it that such instruction is given and candidates are examined accordingly.

---

21 Here see Eugene Brand, "Baptism and the Communion of Infants: A Lutheran View," in *Living Water, Sealing Spirit: Readings on Christian Initiation*, ed. Maxwell Johnson (Collegeville: Liturgical Press, 1995), 350–64.

22 Senn, "Issues in 'Infant Communion,'" 164.

CHAPTER TWENTY-ONE

An Exegetical Case for Close(d) Communion

1 Corinthians 10:14–22; 11:17–34

Jeffrey A. Gibbs

The purpose of this essay is to answer the question, "What do the two Pauline texts under consideration (1 Corinthians 10:14–22 and 11:17–34) say about the practice of close[1] Communion?" Two considerations help to explain the approach of the paper, and to justify yet another attempt to show that the practice of close Communion is grounded firmly in biblical soil.

First, whenever possible, one ought to be able to derive doctrine and practice from biblical texts that are actually talking about the topic at hand. That is to say, a discussion of close Communion should be based primarily on the texts which discuss the matter of who should, or should not, commune, and why. It is not to be denied, of course, that other, more remotely related texts are significant and helpful.[2] But the farther away from the actual message of a text one gets, by means of a string of logical deductions, the more chance one runs of actually blurring the message of the text itself. These two texts are the only ones in the New Testament that actually speak in some way about Communion practice. Thus, they should be the basis for as much of one's understanding and policy as possible.

Second, I have attempted to write in such a way as might be convincing, or at least comprehensible, to "outsiders," that is, to non-Lutherans or even to non-Christians. I have attempted to describe the what and the how of Paul's presentation. I've tried not to take too many shortcuts. Consequently, the argument

1 It is of no real significance, in my view, whether we use the term "close" or "closed." Historically, the distinctive uses may be of interest. What is meant, of course, is the theologically based practice of excluding some persons present at worship from participating in the eating and drinking of the Lord's Supper.

2 Such texts would include, among others, those that speak of the larger issues of fellowship among Christians, and the importance of preserving true doctrine.

of the paper hasn't proceeded "as far along" as it might have, theologically. But this is the chosen approach for two reasons. First, it is ultimately to "outsiders" that we as Missouri Synod Lutherans have most often the need to communicate our doctrine and practice of "close Communion." Second, one's own understanding is enhanced when clarity and simplicity are pursued. Theologians and churchmen too quickly resort to shorthand. And shorthand can too quickly become sleight of hand. Only the Spirit of God can bring conviction, faith, and change of heart. But it is our responsibility to be clear.

So with this as introduction, we proceed to the texts. I will briefly describe each text, making comments as are pertinent to the subject at hand. Then, after comments on each, I will offer deductions and implications which appear to flow directly from the material of the texts themselves. 1 Corinthians 11:17–34 will receive the lion's share of attention. It will be helpful, however, to begin with 1 Corinthians 10:14–22 (my translation):

> For this reason, my beloved, always flee from idolatry. (I am speaking as to wise people. You judge what I am saying.) The cup of blessing which we regularly bless, it's the[3] participation in the blood of Christ, isn't it? The bread which we regularly break, it's the participation in the body of Christ, isn't it? Because there is one bread, we many are one body, for we all share from the one bread. Look at "Israel according to the flesh." Those who regularly eat the sacrifices are participants in the altar, aren't they? What, then, am I trying to say? That meat sacrificed to an idol is anything, or that an idol is anything? [No—I am saying] that the things which they regularly sacrifice, they sacrifice to demons, and not to God. And I do not wish you to become participants with demons! You are not able to drink the cup of the Lord and the cup of demons; you are not able to share the table of the Lord and the table of demons. Or are we trying to provoke the Lord to jealousy? We are not stronger than he, are we?

---

3 The noun κοινωνία is anarthrous, and in both occurrences in 10:16, it precedes the linking verb "is." This does not mean, however, that the noun is indefinite, "a participation." It is possible that the qualitative force of "participation" is being emphasized (cf. P. Hamer, "Qualitative Anarthrous Predicate Nouns: Mark 15:39 and John," in *Journal of Biblical Literature* 92 [1973]: 75). This does not fit well with the context, however. Paul does not seem to be stressing "participation, as participation," or something like that.

Rather, following the probabilities offered by Colwell's rule (cf. E. C. Colwell, "A Definite Rule for the Use of the Article in the Greek New Testament," in *Journal of Biblical Literature* 52 [1933]: 12–21), I take "participation" as a definite noun, "the participation." For Paul, the bread and wine of the Lord's Supper are the participation in Christ's body and blood. He could say this of no other act.

Although not in agreement with this choice, A. Robertson & A. Plummer, *Critical and Exegetical Commentary on the First Epistle of St. Paul to the Corinthians*, 2nd ed. (Edinburgh: T. & T. Clark, 1914), 212, call it "justifiable," since κοινωνία is the predicate. For a clear discussion of this and other aspects of the definite article in the Greek New Testament, see Murray Harris, *Jesus as God* (Grand Rapids: Baker, 1992), 301–13.

First, we will make some observations regarding St. Paul's argument in this paragraph. Then will follow what I regard as legitimate "deductions" from Paul's argument.

The first thing to observe is that Paul is not here discussing the Lord's Supper itself. Rather, the issue at hand is that of Christians attending the services of pagan temples at which sacrifices were made to the god of that shrine.[4] The leading sentence of the paragraph defines Paul's main exhortation: Flee idolatry! The paragraph is connected to the preceding promise (10:13) that God will provide the way out of temptations, so that the believers may endure. And, "on account of this," Paul says, "this is the way out—flee idolatry."

In this context, the statements of Paul about the Lord's Supper (as well as those about Israel's sacrifices and those of the idol shrines) are used to validate the command to flee idolatry. Paul's statements assume the realities involved, rather them arguing them.[5]

The realities are these. The cup, from which the Christians drink, is the participation in the very blood of Christ. The bread, broken, from which the Christians eat, is the participation in the very body of Christ. The genitive after the noun "participation," κοινωνία, denotes the "thing" in which there is participation, the κοινόν that two or more share.[6] The dative, denoting those with whom one shares in the genitive object,[7] is not stated. The noun "participation" is understood to be definite, not indefinite; *the* participation rather than *a* participation. The definite article's absence is explained by the predicate noun's position in front of the linking verb. This cup and bread[8] are *the* participation in the blood and body of Christ.

In verse 17, Paul states the necessary implication of that participation: "Because there is one bread, we many are one body, for we all share in the one

---

4 In the following paragraph, 1 Corinthians 10:23–11:1, the specific issue at hand is the eating of meat, possibly meat sacrificed to idols, in private homes—either the home of a Christian, or the home of a pagan in which a Christian is present as a guest.

5 Friedrich Hauck, "κοινός κτλ," in *Theological Dictionary of the New Testament*, vol. 3, ed. Gerhard Kittel, trans. and ed. G. W. Bromiley (Grand Rapids: Eerdmans, 1965), 805, writes, "In terms of the common belief of antiquity it is self-evident for [Paul] that those who partake of the cultic meal become companions of the god."

6 Cf. J. Y. Campbell, "ΚΟΙΝΩΝΙΑ and Its Cognates in the New Testament," in *Journal of Biblical Literature* 51 (1932): 355–56, 375; F. Hauck, pp. 797–98.

7 Campbell, 375.

8 One can ask why Paul here reverses the "normal" order of "bread—cup." It is impossible to be sure, of course. But perhaps by reversing the order given even in Paul's own account of the Last Supper (1 Cor. 11:22–25), Paul can make a smooth transition to the statement of verse 17. He mentions the cup-participation in the blood, and the bread-participation in the body. Then, from "bread-participation," he can move naturally to verse 17, "Because there is one bread, we the many are one body . . ."

bread." The one food of which the communicants eat is the reason; it causes them to be members of one body.[9] To borrow with thanks a colleague's expression, the sacramental body "bodies" together the ecclesiastical "body." The wine which is the blood, and the bread which is the body, are the reason why the many members are one Body, the Church. One should say, of course, that there is no "automatic" sense in which this unity exists, apart from faithful reception on the part of the communicants. Nor is Paul saying that the participation in the blood and body of Christ initially created the unity of the Body. Rather, "for also in one Spirit we all were baptized into one body" (1 Corinthians 12:13; cf. Galatians 3:27).[10] Nor can one deduce that the cup- and bread-participation in Christ's body and blood is the way to overcome divisions in the Church. Quite the opposite perspective is offered by Paul in chapter 11, as shall become apparent below. So, to be specific, one should say that here in 1 Corinthians 10:16–17, Paul is teaching that the Lord's Supper sustains and renews the believers in their identity as one body in Christ.[11] One of the effects and purposes of the Eucharist is the preserving of the unity of the Church. The grammar here is inescapable. There is not one clause with a causal sense, but two—"Because (ὅτι) there is one bread, for (causal γάρ) all share from the one bread, we many are one body."

And this should not be surprising for Paul's readers. They know the parallel practice and reality of the Old Testament sacrifices. The people who ate of those sacrifices were participants in the altar, that is, in the blessings and realities

9 Werner Elert, *The Lord's Supper Today*, trans. Martin Bertram (St. Louis: Concordia, 1973), 25, on verse 17: "Logically this sentence can have no other meaning than that a physical oneness of the communicants is effected through the eaten bread, that is, through each communicant's reception of a part of the broken bread." [See also above, pp. 353–90. MH] F. Hauck, p. 806, writes, "In the interjected statement of verse 17 Paul declares that at the Lord's Supper, as at sacrificial feasts, there is also fellowship between the participants. This is not apart from Christ. It arises out of common union with Him, as Christ is represented by the one loaf." Cf. R. Lenski, *The Interpretation of St. Paul's First and Second Epistle to the Corinthians* (Columbus: Wartburg Press, 1937), 411–12.

10 Gordon Fee, *The First Epistle to the Corinthians* (Grand Rapids: Eerdmans, 1987), 470, creates a false dichotomy. He first states, quite correctly, that Paul is not saying here that the communicants become (for the first time) the Church, the Body of Christ, and he references 1 Corinthians 12:13. Incorrectly, he deduces from that truth that there is no causal sense in the clause, οἵ γὰρ πάντες ἐκ τοῦ ἑνος ἄρτου μετέχομεν, and writes, "Rather, by this meal they affirm what the Spirit has already brought about through the death and resurrection of Christ."

11 Although Paul does not say how this is done in the Eucharist, the most natural explanation would be, "through the forgiveness of sins." That sacramental benefit, which sustains and renews the believer's life in Christ, also sustains and renews the believer's life with other believers in one Body, the Church. Cf. Francis Pieper, *Christian Dogmatics* (St. Louis: Concordia, 1953), 3:379; Werner Elert, *The Structure of Lutheranism* (St. Louis: Concordia, 1962), 316.

mediated through the altar, weren't they?[12] Yes, they were (10:18). This is analogous to the Christian experience of participation in the body and blood of Christ, which makes the communicants into one body.

So then, what does this have to do with eating at idol shrines? Just this. It is not that the meat there sacrificed has any innate power, nor that the statues and images have a true existence (10:19). It is this. Those sacrifices of which those worshipers eat have been offered to demons. That is the reality undergirding that supper. And to eat of that supper is to become participants with demons, and that the Christians cannot do. Two opposing, warring, mutually exclusive realities are mediated through two different meals. To try to combine them in one life is to invite the jealous wrath and power of the Lord (10:21–22). Thus far Paul's argument in 1 Corinthians 10:14–22. What deductions can be drawn from this text for our current issue of close Communion? At least the following deductions seem valid:

1. Christians, characterized by their attendance at the Lord's Supper, cannot and must not participate in non-Christian worship services.
2. By inference, non-Christians must not participate in the celebration of the Christian Lord's Supper.
3. The realities involved in the Eucharist are not created or altered by the attitude and/or faith of those who are eating and drinking. The cup and bread *are* the participation in the blood and body of Christ. In a similar manner, when false gods are invoked, and sacrifice offered to them, the demons with their reality are present, even if an individual Christian is there as participant.
4. To speak of "individuals" communing with their Lord in the Eucharist can lead to a serious misunderstanding. For the participation in Christ's body and blood, through eating and drinking, necessarily involves the individual with those with whom he or she is communing. This Paul explicitly states in verse 17—"Because there is one bread, we the many are one body, for we all share from the one bread."[13]

---

12 F. Hauck, p. 805, writes that, in verse 18, "θυσιαστήριον is obviously used for God." This is not quite as obvious as Hauck asserts. Rather, his own statement, later in the same paragraph, is more likely to be correct: "For Paul the bread and wine are vehicles of the presence of Christ, just as the Jewish altar is a pledge of the presence of God."

13 This necessary connection of the "individual" communicant with the other members of the Body is also implicit in the very term "participation." The element in the construction that remains unexpressed throughout Paul's discussion is that of the dative noun, the other persons with whom one is sharing the reality in the genitive case—the blood and body of Christ.

To move to the second text, 1 Corinthians 11:17–34, I will again describe Paul's argument, and then draw valid deductions for application to the present situation:

> But as I direct this matter, I am not praising [you], because you keep on coming together, not for the better, but for the worse. For first of all, when you come together in the church, I have heard there are divisions among you, and in part I believe it. For even factions among you are necessary, so that those who are approved may be obvious among you. Therefore, although you regularly come together in the same place, it is not for the purpose of eating the *Lord's* Supper,[14] because each one takes *his own* supper beforehand[15] as he eats, and on the one hand, one is hungry, and on the other hand the other is drunk. You have houses for eating and drinking, don't you? Or do you wish to despise God's church, and shame those who don't have [as much as others]? What shall I say to you? Will I praise you? In this matter I will not praise [you].
>
> Because I received from the Lord that which I handed over to you, that the Lord Jesus, on the night when he was being betrayed, took bread, and after giving thanks, he broke [it] and said, "This is my body which is on your behalf; do this for my remembrance." Likewise also [he did with] the cup, after he had eaten, and said, "This cup is the new covenant in my blood; do this, as often as you drink, for my remembrance." For as often as you eat this bread and drink the cup, you are proclaiming the Lord's death until he comes.
>
> Therefore, whoever eats the bread or drinks the cup of the Lord unworthily will be guilty of [sinning against][16] the body and the blood of the Lord. But let a person examine himself, and in this way let him eat from the bread and drink from the cup. Because the person who eats and drinks eats and drinks judgment against himself if he does not discern the body. On account of this, many among you are weak, and sick, and many have died.

---

14 Without explanation or reference, Lenski, *First and Second Epistle to the Corinthians*, 458, writes, ". . . for οὐκ ἔστι with the infinitive means 'it is impossible' to eat, and 'this' cannot be supplied, since coming together and eating are not identical."

15 Peter Lampe, "The Corinthian Eucharistic Dinner Party: Exegesis of a Cultural Context (1 Cor. 11:17–34)," in *Affirmation* 4, no. 2 (1991): 3, claims that the evidence that denies a temporal sense to the prefixed preposition, προ-, is almost nonexistent. Trolls Engberg-Pedersen, "Proclaiming the Lord's Death: 1 Corinthians 11:17–34 and the Forms of Paul's Theological Argument," in *Society of Biblical Literature 1991 Seminar Papers*, ed. Eugene H. Lovering Jr. (Atlanta: Scholars Press, 1991), 598, claims otherwise.

16 Fee, *The First Epistle to the Corinthians*, 560–61, notes that the genitive with ἔνοχος refers to either "the person sinned against or the crime itself." I take it as the former (cf. Robertson & Plummer, *Critical and Exegetical Commentary*, 251). He takes it as the latter: "To 'profane' the meal as they are doing is to place themselves under the same liability as those responsible for that death in the first place. . . . 'to be liable for his death.'" Agreeing with Fee is Engberg-Pedersen, "Proclaiming the Lord's Death," 607.

> But if we were examining/discerning ourselves, we would not be being judged. But if we are being judged, we are being disciplined by the Lord, so that we might not be condemned with the world. So then, my brothers, when you come together to eat, welcome[17] one another. If anyone is hungry, let him eat in [his own] house, so that you may not come together with the result of judgment. And as for the remaining things, when I come, I will arrange [them].

In these paragraphs, Paul deals with a sinful abuse of worship in Corinth. It is apparent that he regards this problem as much more serious than that in the prior paragraph (11:2–16) regarding the proper head-covering of women in worship. With the prior discussion, Paul began gently, with praise (11:2), which he then modified with an adversative, "but" (δὲ, 11:3). Here, by contrast, his opening paragraph (vv. 17–22) is bracketed by, "I am not praising you," and "In this matter I will not praise you."[18] In the earlier material, Paul deals with practices and behaviors that he twice describes as "shameful" (11:4, 6) and contrary to the universal custom of the Church (11:16). Here, it is something much worse.

Verses 17–19 show that, as was so characteristic with the Corinthian congregations, there were divisions (σχίσματα) in the Church. They had divisions over allegiances to different teachers (1:10ff.), divisions manifested through unequal attention and care given to different members of the Body (12:25). These different kinds of divisions should probably be seen as manifestations of a central, deep, cancerous problem—one of arrogance and competitiveness. They were proud that they were wise and strong. They needed to live in line with the countercultural Gospel, which is the foolishness and the weakness of God (1:25).

In verse 20, Paul states that their divisions were effectively turning them away from the very purpose of their gathering together for worship. Verse 20 cannot mean "Your divisions are preventing the Lord's Supper from actually being celebrated," for their sin is against the body and blood of Christ in the Sacrament (v. 27). Rather, by their divisions and sins against one another, they indicate that their "true intention" is really anything but "to eat the Lord's Supper."[19] They are

---

17 Even if προλαμβάνει in verse 21 is translated "eat beforehand," it is not necessary to render ἐκδέχεσθε in verse 33 as "wait for" (cf. Heb. 10:13; 11:10; James 5:7). The meaning "welcome" (1 Cor. 16:11; Acts 17:16) suits the context well enough.

18 Lenski, *First and Second Epistle to the Corinthians*, 461, calls "I am not praising" in verse 17 a "grim irony." Cf. also Engberg-Pederson, "Proclaiming the Lord's Death," 593: "By contrast, in 11:17–34 Paul is *withholding* his praise, and precisely, as the transition from verse 22 to verse 23 makes clear, because the Corinthians have *not* stuck to the tradition which Paul had received from the Lord himself and passed on to them."

19 Fee, *The First Epistle to the Corinthians*, 540, is wrong in writing, "Thus, even though it is *intended* to be the Lord's Supper that they are eating 'in assembly,' their carrying over to this meal the distinctions that divided them sociologically also meant that it turned out to be

more intent, as Paul writes in the next verse with biting irony, on eating "their own supper" (v. 21).

What was the nature of their sinning? It was sinning against fellow members of the Church. The general outline of the situation is this.[20] In the context of public worship and the celebration of the Lord's Supper, a community meal also occurred. During the course of that meal, sinful inequities took place that caused some to have an abundance, even an overabundance of food and drink, while other members of the Church received so little that they remained hungry. This is the situation that has given rise to Paul's admonition and instruction. They were letting culture dictate. The practice within the Church was perpetuating the *divisions* between rich and poor, high status and low in society. They were treating some members of the Church as if they were more important than other members of the same Body. In so doing, they were despising God's Church, and shaming the members who did not have as much (v. 22).

---

not the Lord's Supper you eat." Fee has it backward. It was the Lord's Supper, and that's why their sins were so grievous.

20 The specific setting and procedures are difficult, if not impossible, to nail down. It might be that the drunkenness and hunger is caused purely by inequitable consumption of the elements set aside for the Lord's Supper itself. This strikes me as being highly unlikely.

A setting which envisions the Eucharist in conjunction with a community meal is more likely. Several authors cite striking parallels from Greco-Roman social practice of community meals. Wayne Meeks, *The First Urban Christians: The Social World of the Apostle Paul* (New Haven & London: Yale University Press, 1983), 159, envisions the homes of wealthy church members, in which the patron supplies the food. The offense is the unequal distribution of food and drink, in accordance with normal social class distinctions (cf. Fee, *The First Epistle to the Corinthians*, 542, n. 55). Lampe,"The Corinthian Eucharistic Dinner Party," 4–5, envisions a common meal to which people brought their own foods, but did not place the food in a common "potluck" fashion (cf. Engberg-Pedersen, "Proclaiming the Lord's Death," 597–98). Both Lampe (p. 5) and Fee (p. 533) mention the possibility of "division" due to the rich eating in the smaller "dining room," with the larger number of poor located in another room. But still, it is the problem of the rich having more than the poor.

On the other hand, it is not possible to determine the relative sequence of a "love feast" or "fellowship meal" that would have been observed in conjunction with the Lord's Supper itself. J. Jeremias, *The Eucharistic Words of Jesus* (Philadelphia: Fortress, 1964), 121, thinks "that the abuse of the celebration, against which Paul struggles in 1 Corinthians 11:17–34, could have gained ground is more readily understandable if the communal meal proper, which was taken less seriously, preceded the sacramental act. Also, the advice of the apostle, in certain circumstances to eat first at home (1 Cor. 11:34; cf. v. 22) is best understood if the meal proper normally preceded the Eucharist." (Cf. Lenski, *First and Second Epistle to the Corinthians*, 458.) Engberg-Pedersen, p. 596, thinks that, because μετὰ τὸ δειπνῆσαι in verse 25 is adverbial to the implied verb, "likewise, [he took] . . . ," "This means that Paul is certainly presupposing, in his rendering of Jesus' words, the following order of Jesus' meal with his disciples: blessing and distribution of bread—δεῖπνον (i.e., the meal proper)—blessing and handing round of the cup." This order of "eucharistic bread," actual meal, and "eucharistic wine" is also advocated by Lampe, pp. 7–8.

But what is the root problem here, in the abuse of Christian eucharistic worship? In Paul's mind, why does he say, with grim irony, "I will not praise you in this"? For Paul, the root problem is connected with the very nature of the Sacrament itself. Accordingly, Paul drives to the heart of the matter by citing the Words of Institution. It is because of what the Words of Institution reveal about the Sacrament. "I will not praise you . . . γάρ (for/because) I received from the Lord that which also I delivered to you . . . ." I will not praise you, because *this* is what the Lord's Supper is, the body of Christ and the blood which establishes the new covenant. Paul reminds them of what they already had learned about the institution and nature of the Lord's Supper. The Lord commanded the Church to "do this," that Jesus and His sacrifice for all might be remembered.[21] When the church receives this gift, this participation, it is at the same time the proclamation of Christ's death, until He comes again.[22]

---

21 I find the discussion of Jeremias, *The Eucharistic Words of Jesus*, 237–55, intriguing. His conclusion that it is God who is to remember Jesus, and not the disciples, corresponds more closely to the Palestinian use of "memorial formulae." In addition, to understand the Lord's Supper as the prayer that God would "remember" Jesus' death as "an eschatological event" (p. 253) provides a strong tie to the phrase, "until he comes."

In direct response to Jeremias' position, see Douglas Jones, "ἀνάμνησις in the LXX and the Interpretation of 1 Cor. xi:25," in *Journal of Theological Studies* n.s. 6 (1955): 183–91. Jones argues, pp. 188 and 191, among other things, that the more natural understanding of Jesus' words "for my remembrance" derives from the Passover setting in which the Last Supper took place. In that setting, the Passover itself was for a "remembrance" (לְזִכָּרוֹן, Ex. 12:14; LXX, μνημόσυνος) by the Israelites. Also in favor of the view that it is the Church that is to "remember" Jesus in the Eucharist, see H. Sasse, *This Is My Body: Luther's Contention for the Real Presence in the Sacrament of the Altar* (Adelaide: Lutheran Publishing House, 1959), 304–10.

22 In our circles, it is common to make this logical move, on the basis of verse 26:

1. The celebration of the Eucharist is proclamation.
2. Proclamation involves confession.
3. Confession needs to flow from agreement.
4. Therefore, we should be in doctrinal agreement with those with whom we commune. Cf. Samuel Nafzger, "Who Is Invited to the Supper of the Lord?" in *The Lutheran Witness* (May 1993): 14: "Moreover, St. Paul specifically says that taking part in this sacramental meal is a proclamation of our Lord's death until he returns. Participation in the sacrament is itself an act of *confession*. We *therefore* should not commune with those with whom we disagree in the confession of the Gospel, lest we say one thing with our words and another with our actions" (my emphases).

I do not deny the logic of this. It is, however, relatively far removed from the actual concerns of this text. In my view, this kind of logic, based on 1 Corinthians 11:26, should be only a secondary support for our doctrine and practice. It is more profitable to work directly from texts that speak of "separation" from false teachers, and then to deduce from that general principle that one should "separate" from such also in the fellowship at the altar. Cf. Pieper 3:385, whose biblical support for this point is Romans 16:17.

Then, Paul goes on to infer the real issue involved. His inference comes in verse 27; οὕτως, "So then . . . ." What is really going on is that you are eating and drinking *the Sacrament* unworthily. And when you do that, you become guilty of sinning against the body and blood of Christ, that is, against the Sacrament itself. And it is for this reason that there has been sickness and death in your midst. Let a person examine himself (v. 28), and in this way, οὕτως, not as you have been doing, but in *this* way let him eat from the bread and drink from the cup. Then, verse 29 repeats the message of verse 27. For the person who eats and drinks, eats and drinks judgment to himself, if he does not discern the body. This is the content of "unworthily." To fail to discern the body is to eat unworthily.[23] To "examine oneself," then, is to "discern the body."

At this point in the argument, two questions inevitably surface for the readers. First, and more obviously, to what does "body" refer in verse 29, "if he does not discern the body." This is important, because it stands parallel to and explicates the meaning of "unworthily." The second, but less obvious question, is this: *Why* does the sinning against one another, the despising and shaming of one another, make them guilty of sinning against the body and the blood of Christ?[24] For the overt "location" of their sin is on the horizontal plane. Paul has not accused them of

---

23 Lenski, *First and Second Epistle to the Corinthians*, 477, is probably right when he says, "The nature of the unworthiness in the case of the Corinthians the context has already made plain and will continue to make still plainer. Paul's statement is general and applies to all forms and all types of unworthiness and therefore should not be restricted to the peculiar type of unworthiness found in Corinth."

Thus, my conclusion that the Corinthians' specific form of "unworthy" communing does not and is not intended to contradict the catechisms of Luther. In the catechisms, Luther is intent on addressing the problem of *infrequent* communing, especially infrequent communing caused by guilt-ridden consciences. In this context, his rightful focus is on the Gospel words, "given and shed for you." But infrequent communing was not the problem at Corinth.

24 Note that Fee, *The First Epistle to the Corinthians*, 533, says that this is the *function* of the Words of Institution: "By their abuse of one another, they were also abusing the One through whose death and resurrection they had been brought to life and formed into this new eschatological fellowship, his body the church. *Thus Paul's need to take them all the way back—to the actual words of institution—so that they will restore the meaning of the food to its rightful place in their meal*" (my emphasis).

Thus, we can agree with Fee (a charismatic Protestant) on the function of the Words of Institution in Paul's argument here, and disagree with him on the meaning of the Words of Institution themselves. Lenski, *First and Second Epistle to the Corinthians*, 462, "The first and most important corrective, then, is that the Corinthians remember what Paul had delivered to them from the Lord concerning the Sacrament." Similarly, Lampe, "The Corinthian Eucharistic Dinner Party," 8, calls the Words of Institution "the starting point of Paul's theological argumentation," and Engberg-Pedersen, "Proclaiming the Lord's Death," 599, calls the logical connection between the problem in Corinth and the citation of the Words of Institution "the textual issue."

anything, any sin, other than that on the horizontal plane. In fact, his final exhortation to them in verse 33 returns to the horizontal plane—again, ὥστε, "So then, my brothers and sisters, when you come together to eat, welcome one another. If anyone is hungry, let him eat at home, so that you may not come together resulting in judgment." Why, then, in response to this sin against one another, does Paul bring in the Words of Institution, and then accuse them of being guilty of sinning against the very body and blood of Christ?

The first question first. What is the "body" that they must discern, make a distinction concerning, judge correctly? In context,[25] "the body" has to be a reference to the body of Christ, that is, to the bread of the Lord's Supper. The whole emphasis at this point in the argument is on "eating and drinking," and upon the exhortation not to do so "unworthily." Paul warns them that a judgment from God will follow should they continue to eat and drink the Sacrament without discerning Christ's very body present in it, and the benefits and purposes of that sacramental body.[26]

Why does he not say, "discerning the body and the blood"? Perhaps it is in order to reinforce the answer to the second question. That question, restated, is,

---

25 Note that "church" is never the referent of "body," σῶμα, in chapter 11. Rather, in 11:24 and 11:27, it refers to the body of Christ truly present in the Eucharist. There is no textual marker to indicate a shift at 11:29, away from "body" as "sacramental body." The parallel occurrence of διακρίνειν (v. 29, "because he does not discern the body"; and v. 31, "if we examined ourselves . . .") is not sufficient cause to overturn the view that "body" in 11:29 refers to the sacramental body of Christ. Rather, context shows that διακρίνειν has a slightly different nuance of meaning in verse 29 and verse 31. The sense of verse 31 ("If we examined ourselves") is directly parallel in meaning to verse 28, δοκιμαζέτω, "Let a person examine himself . . . " and not to verse 29.

This is not to deny the closest possible connection between the body of Christ in the Sacrament and the Body of Christ, the Church. Indeed, that connection is the very reason why Paul adduces the Words of Institution as the solution to the problems with the "Body" of the Church. The participation in the blood and body of Christ in the Eucharist has (as one of its effects) the purpose of maintaining the members of the Church as "one Body," 10:17.

However, recall that Paul's analysis of the root problem in the Corinthian situation has caused him to remind them of the Words of Institution. The issue revolves around the question, "What is the Lord's Supper, and what are its implications for your relationships with one another?"

26 Elert, *The Lord's Supper Today*, 25, writes, "The danger of becoming guilty is explained by the fact that the unworthy communicant fails to 'discern the body,' that is, that he eats the bread as though he were thereby not receiving the body of Christ. The point is that he becomes guilty by eating and drinking (verse 29)."

Engberg-Pedersen, pp. 604–5, somewhat reluctantly comes to a similar understanding. He first denies that "this is my body" locates "an infusion of power" in the elements themselves, "independently of the whole ritualized setting to which the bread and the cup belong." He goes on to say, though, that "When the whole ritualized setting is introduced, however, one may well locate 'in' the 'elements' (or the acts performed in relation to them) the power that is being activated . . ."

"Why is sin on the horizontal plane really, most deeply, sin against the body and blood of Christ in the Sacrament?" Once again, this is a bit of a guess. But it is plausible, indeed likely, that Paul is content to refer to "the body," because of the logical connection he has already made between sin against the brother, and sin against the Sacrament. Unfortunately, here in this text Paul does not explicitly explain the connection. He simply joins the Words of Institution to the issue and problem of their sinning against one another with the inferential γὰρ, "For, I received from the Lord . . ." (v. 23). So the readers are left to infer the precise connection implicit in his argument. What is it?

Reasonably enough, the answer lies in the only other place that Paul uses the doctrine of the Lord's Supper to support an argument, 10:16–17.[27] There, it is the participation in the blood, and in the body, that keeps and sustains the Christians as members of one Body, the Church. "Because there is one bread, we the many are one body, for we all share from the one bread." The body of Christ was given for you, for you *all*. It is the true body that makes them and keeps them as one Body. Here in this text, in chapter 11, to participate in the blood and body of Christ while tolerating and even *causing* divisions by sinning against one another is not just sinning against one another. It is becoming guilty of sinning against the body and the blood of Christ. Why? Because that sacramental food has as one of its purposes and effects the uniting of the many members into one Body.

This means that it is the very nature of the Sacrament itself that should prevent us from speaking of "the individual" communing with his or her Lord. It can't be done. For the body and blood are not only "for me." They are "for us." The personal pronouns are plural—for you all. This the Corinthians were effectively denying, by their shaming and despising of one another. They were not discerning the true nature of the Sacrament. The result was God's judgment against them. To avoid such judgment, and, most crucially, to avoid being condemned along with the world, the

---

27 My matrixing of 10:16–17 with 11:27–29 is the "bridge" to explain Paul's logical connection between sinning against fellow Christians and sinning against the Sacrament. Other writers recognize the need to "matrix" other Pauline material to make sense of the argument, but they tend to go somewhat far afield in their question. Cf. Lampe, "The Corinthian Eucharistic Dinner Party," 9–11.

The reasons why I think 10:16–17 serves to explain the mind of Paul in connecting sin against the fellow Christian in worship, and sin against the Sacrament itself, are the following. First, the passage in 1 Corinthians 10 is also addressing the same two "dimensions," the vertical (the Eucharist is "participation" in the blood and body of Christ) and horizontal (the Eucharist is the cause for the unity of the Christians in one Body). Second, in 1 Corinthians 10:16–17, Paul "plays" with the meaning of "body." In verse 16, it refers to the bread of the Eucharist. In verse 17, it refers to the Church, of which the many are all members. Third, as stated above, this is the only other passage, also in relatively close context, where Paul reveals his mind concerning the Lord's Supper. These three reasons make the use of 1 Corinthians 10:16–17 as explanation for the implicit Pauline logic at 1 Corinthians 11:23 an eminently reasonable choice.

Corinthians are to examine themselves. They must by faith grasp again the deepest nature of the Sacrament. They must repent of their sinning against one another. They are to welcome one another, and put an end to their shaming of the poor.[28]

We will now summarize these observations of the text and its argument. The overt sinning in the congregation was on the horizontal plane; they were causing divisions, despising the Church, as the rich shamed the poor.[29] Paul's refusal to praise them is explained by the Words of Institution. In Paul's mind, the deepest offense is against the body and the blood of the Lord, because they are not discerning the body. Why is this so? Because the Sacrament which they eat together is the very blood and body of Christ. That eating and drinking is for the purpose of sustaining the Church as the one Body of Christ,[30] and they are causing divisions in that very Body. They are *not* to continue eating and drinking, in the hope that that will cause their divisions to go away. They must examine themselves, and discern the true nature of the Sacrament. They must examine themselves, and repent of their sins on the horizontal plane, and welcome each other at their meals, and cease to sin against one another and against the Sacrament.

What deductions for the present situation, and with reference to the practice of close Communion, can we draw from this exegesis? At least the following are valid:

1. The attitude and actions of the individual communicants in no way invalidates the Sacrament. The reality remains; the body and blood are present.
2. In this text, Paul teaches that to commune unworthily means three things. First, unworthy communing takes place when Christians commune while abusing the horizontal relationship between Christians, or when that abuse is ignored and tolerated. Second, unworthy communing takes place when the Sacrament's very purpose—to sustain the unity of the members of the one body—is also ignored. Third, unworthy communing occurs when the reality of Christ's body and blood in the Sacrament are overtly or implicitly denied. There are other ways to commune "unworthily." But these emerge from this text.
3. The text does not speak of anyone "excluding" anyone else from the Sacrament. Rather, Paul simply commands them to change. It is, however, a permissible logical step to move from "before you continue communing

28 That the explicit, "surface" problem in worship was an ungodly fracturing of the fellowship fits well, of course, into the entire context of 1 Corinthians, where divisions and fragmentation of the Church were rife.

29 A similar problem, of course, is addressed by James 2:1–7.

30 Sasse, *This Is My Body*, 318, wonders, "Maybe the Pauline idea of the Church as the Body of Christ was first conceived by the apostle at the Table of the Lord."

change these sinful divisions among you" to "don't commune if these divisions still exist."[31]

4. The concrete application that comes first to mind is not that of our relationship as Missouri Synod Lutherans with Christians of different and/or erring confessions. Rather, it is our relationship with one another, especially in the setting of the local Missouri Synod congregation. There are periods in the life of a congregation which are free from marked conflict between members. My own decade of parish ministry was mercifully free from major conflict. But sadly, this is not always so. When bitter church fights are taking place, when resentful words and deeds are being hurled throughout a congregation and echoing round a sanctuary, what shall the believers and their pastor do? Shall they continue blissfully to commune together, leaving the divisions among them to wreak their spiritual havoc, and thus invite the judgment of God? Should the pastor not rather, in deep love and sorrow, propose that the factions refrain from participating in the Sacrament, until the differences and divisions be removed through repentance and mutual forgiveness?
5. However, it is the question of our relationships with Christians of other confessions which is the one at hand for us. Let it be said that the text does not directly address this issue. But the text does say this: Examine yourselves, and do not let divisions among you, whereby you sin against one another, remain. Remove the division before you commune together. Quickly, then, this question presents itself: Do the divisions between church bodies really matter? Are they the occasion of sin against one another? Does it matter that the ELCA seems to have (or, at least, to allow) a different doctrine of Scripture, or church fellowship, of the Office of the Ministry, to mention only some of the most obvious differences between us? Does it matter when another church body denies the saving power of Baptism? Do they matter, these divisions among us? Should they prevent us from communing with one another, until the divisions be removed? The answer seems relatively clear. They mattered to Paul. They must matter to us.

The task of implementing the practice of close Communion is accompanied by an intimidating array of nightmarish problems and complexities. For every easy scenario, there are two difficult ones. What of inactive members, who suddenly appear, perhaps on a whim, after an absence from the Lord's Supper of several years? What of those extraordinary circumstances, to which recent synodical resolutions make reference? The church gatherings in Corinth were probably small,

31 As Engberg-Pedersen, "Proclaiming the Lord's Death," 608, rightly paraphrases the words of 11:28, "Let everyone test himself . . . and then (only then!) eat from the bread and drink from the cup."

perhaps a maximum of sixty persons, spread throughout two rooms. How can one draw precise analogies to gatherings of five hundred or one thousand worshipers? What of the doctrinal divisions between our churches and other Christians? If these divisions are serious cause for sin, is our church urgently putting forth its best efforts in dialogue with other traditions, to communicate our understandings of the Gospel, and of the implications of the Gospel? And what of American individualism, which views with hostility and incomprehension the classic insistence that a Christian joins a church because of the church's confession, and is viewed by us in that way? Every reader of these words knows full well that people join congregations, switch denominations, for many reasons other than faithful allegiance to the official doctrine of that church. Does this individualism render our position incomprehensible to the majority of American Christians? What must be done to overcome these obstacles, and to communicate?

In light of these and so many factors, it is apparent to all that the situation is not always an easy one to address. During my own years as a parish pastor, I was often not sure, in specific situations, what the God-pleasing choice was. I know that I erred on both sides of this issue. At the very least, we must work much, much harder at making sure we are being heard, and understood as we intend to be. At the very least, we must learn to be more eloquent, more winsome, more patient and compassionate in speaking to "outsiders," as well as to one another. The goal, of course, is not to avoid something that the world finds offensive; it is in this epistle that Paul names the Gospel itself as foolishness, and a stumbling block (1 Corinthians 1:23). Rather, the goal is to avoid what will *unnecessarily* confuse or offend others. It is an intimidating task to carry out the practice of closed Communion.

But it must be done. That conviction flows from the way that the apostle Paul reasons here in 1 Corinthians. For the mind of Paul is the mind of Christ (1 Corinthians 2:16). The bread and wine in the Lord's Supper really are the body and the blood of Christ. Through the opening door of the forgiveness of sins, God's power and blessing are really there, to sustain the many members in the one Body of Christ. But it cannot be that sinful divisions be ignored among us, for in so doing, we would effectively deny, and thus sin against, the very Sacrament itself.

CHAPTER TWENTY-TWO

Who Is to Be Admitted to the Lord's Supper

Francis Pieper, Christian Dogmatics[1]

Christian congregations, and their public servants, are only the administrants and not the lords of the Sacrament. The Lord's Supper is not their institution, but Christ's. Therefore they must follow Christ's instructions in administering the Sacrament. On the one hand, they are not permitted [to practice] "Open Communion;" on the other hand, they must guard against denying the Sacrament to those Christians for whom Christ has appointed it. [Johann] Gerhard [1582–1637] and [Abraham] Calov [1612–86] are justified in discussing the *finis cui* or the *objectum* [final purpose or object] of the Lord's Supper also in [their] dogmatics [texts].[2]

It is common knowledge that "Open Communion"[3] is commended and practiced not only in Reformed churches, but also in church bodies calling themselves Lutheran.[4] A Christian congregation, however, should consider well that

1 Francis Pieper, *Christian Dogmatics*, electronic ed., vol. 3 (St. Louis: Concordia, 1953), 381–91. [This document has been included in this collection because of its normative significance for the LCMS. Pieper's text has been used continuously to train pastors for the better part of a century. The full English text was produced in the 1950s. The use of "close" instead of Pieper's original English "closed" had already appeared in J. T. Mueller's 1934 one-volume English condensation of Pieper! See the note below. We have noted and corrected the English text where Pieper's original German in fact used the words "closed Communion." It's very clear that while Mueller for some reason thought "close" the better term, he faithfully rendered the text, which repeatedly states that "close/closed" Communion means also not communing those who remain part of an erring church body. Thus there is no justification for current lax practice. I have restored the bold emphasis in the original and here and there restored Pieper's original where Mueller added or subtracted partial or whole sentences from the original. MH]

2 See Gerhard, *Loci*, "*De coena s.*" § 221f. Calov, *Syst.*, IX, 195ff.

3 [Pieper's German original has "open Communion" in English. 3:444. MH]

4 Regarding American Lutheran circles, see A. L. Graebner, "Zur Geschichte der vier Punkte," in *Lehre und Wehre* (1888): 257ff., 302ff.; *RE*, 3d ed., 1:68.

the Lord's Supper is not intended for all men, but only for **Christians**. Here a difference obtains between the preaching of the Gospel and the Lord's Supper. The Gospel is intended for all men, believers and unbelievers alike. The Lord's Table, however, is appointed only for the people who have already come to faith in Christ.

This we learn from the normative example of Christ. Christ preached the Gospel to the Jewish people generally and for that purpose went from place to place (Matthew 9:35ff.). But the first celebration of His Supper He held in the closed circle [*geschlossenen Kreise*] of His disciples (Luke 22:11, 14; Matthew 26:18, 20). The apostolic Church practiced not "open" Communion, but rather "closed Communion"[5] (1 Corinthians 11:20; 10:17). Luther says: "Thus Christ did; He delivered His sermons to the multitude for everybody, as the apostles later did, so that every person heard them, believers and unbelievers; whoever caught it, caught it. We must do the same. But the Sacrament we are not to cast among a crowd. When I preach the Gospel, I do not know upon whom it takes effect; but here I must be convinced that it has taken effect upon those who come to the Sacrament. Here I must not act in doubt, but be[6] sure that the one to whom I give the Sacrament has laid hold of the Gospel and has true [*rechtschaffen*] faith."[7]

---

5 [The English translation here omitted "closed communion." The orginal reads: "*Auch die apostilische Kirche praktizierte nicht* 'open', *sondern* 'closed Communion'" (*Dogmatik* 3:443). The German condensation of Pieper by J. T. Mueller, published in 1946, likewise changed Pieper's original "closed" to "close." See Franz Pieper, *Christliche Dogmatik*, ed. J. T. Mueller (St. Louis: Concordia, 1946). Earlier still, the 1934 edition of *Christian Dogmatics: A Handbook of Doctrinal Theology for Pastors, Teachers, and Laymen* by J. T. Mueller (St. Louis: Concordia, 1934)—also a recension of Pieper—likewise replaces "closed" with "close" (p. 537). Mueller retained: "The sacrament must be withheld from all who are connected with erring churches and unchristian or antichristian cults, Eph. 4:1–6; 5:7–11; 2 Cor. 6:14–18" (p. 538). It is also noteworthy that Walter Albrecht's translation of the full three volumes of Pieper retained "closed" at this point, both in its first (1939) and second (1942) editions. See Walter Albrecht, trans., *Christian Dogmatics*, vol. 3 (Springfield, IL: Concordia [Seminary] Mimeographing Co., 1939 and 1942). MH]

6 [The English translation inserted "[reasonably]" here in Luther's text. Pieper's original had this footnote here: "Namely so far as one man can know from the words and deeds of another." MH]

7 Walther, *Pastorale*, 144: "The case of the Lord's Supper is quite different from that of the preaching of the divine Word. [The English translation here replaced "divine Word" with "the gospel." MH] The Word is not merely given to sustain the believer in faith, but also initially to awake man from his sleep of sin, to bring him to a knowledge of his sin and to faith; yes, without the Word all this is simply impossible. No one may, therefore, be barred from the preaching of God's Word; for that would mean locking the one door to grace for him. The case is different with the Lord's Supper; by this a man is not to be given the first beginning of repentance and faith, but his existing repentance and faith is to be intensified; by it man is not for the first time to obtain grace and become a Christian, but the grace previously obtained through the Word is thereby to be confirmed to him and he to be preserved, sustained, and furthered in his Christian faith; by this food a man is not for the first time to be quickened unto the life that is of God, but, after having become spiritually alive,

However, not even all Christians are to be admitted to the Lord's Table.[8] To be admitted are:

1. Only[9] such as have been **baptized**. On this order of sequence in the use of the two New Testament Sacraments see p. 292.[10]
2. Only such as are **able to examine themselves**. Scripture expressly declares spiritual self-examination necessary for a salutary use of the Holy Supper: "Let a person examine himself [δοκιμαζέτω δὲ ἄνθρωπος ἑαυτόν], then, and *so* [οὕτως] eat of the bread and drink of the cup" (1 Corinthians 11:28). Excluded therefore are children, the sleeping, the unconscious, the dying

---

to be nourished and refreshed. He, therefore, who would receive the Lord's Supper worthily and for his eternal benefit must previously have come to repentance and faith, must previously have obtained grace and have become a true Christian. Partaking of the Lord's Supper is in and by itself not beneficial; rather the benefit depends on how one partakes. It does not work *ex opere operato*. It is not like a medicine which one need merely swallow to have the benefit. It is rather like a treasure house whose treasures can be taken, grasped, and held only with the hand of faith. He who partakes without faith indeed also receives the genuine and entire Sacrament; for he receives not merely bread and wine, but in, with, and under these elements he with his mouth really and truly receives the body and blood of Jesus Christ as a precious pledge of grace and forgiveness; however, he gets nothing of the blessing contained in it for the salvation of his soul; for what can an ever so precious and costly pledge help a man, and how can it serve to assure him of a fact, if he does not believe that it is so precious and costly a pledge? Moreover, whoever partakes of the Lord's Supper without the right faith, and therefore unworthily, not only loses the grace contained in it, but draws from it wrath instead of grace, death instead of life, curse instead of blessing; he becomes, as St. Paul writes, 'guilty of the body and blood of the Lord; he eats and drinks damnation unto himself, not discerning the Lord's body.' Dreadful therefore is the sin committed by him who partakes unworthily of the Holy Supper; and those who say: 'Still one ought to be glad that the people still come to the Lord's Supper,' thereby reveal how pitiful their knowledge of this holy Sacrament is."

The objection has been advanced that it might occur during the administration of the Sacrament that an unbeliever, hearing the powerful and perfectly clear Words of Institution ("This is My body, which is given for you; this is My blood, which is shed for you"), would be brought to faith in the essence of the Lord's Supper (the real presence) as well as faith in the purpose of the Supper (the remission of sins). This possibility must be granted. The early Christian Church reports how a pagan actor came to faith when in mockery of Christianity he was given Holy Baptism on the stage. But this possibility is none of our concern. What the practice of the Church is to be is established by the divine ordinance. And this reads: "Let a person examine himself, then, and so eat of the bread and drink of the cup. For anyone who eats and drinks without discerning the body eats and drinks judgment on himself" (1 Cor. 11:28–29). The divine order is that in the Lord's Supper, as Luther expresses it, "we should know with whom it takes effect."

8 Gerhard, *L. de coena s.*, par. 222. [Omitted in the English translation. MH]

9 ["Only" is omitted in the English in this and the following statements. MH]

10 [Pieper's original has a footnote referencing Gerhard, *Loci de coena, sac.*, § 222. Pieper's cross-reference to p. 292 references the beginning of the section of the Lord's Supper, titled in English "On the Divine Institution of the Lord's Supper. MH]

deprived of the use of their senses, the insane and possessed while not in their right mind, etc.[11]

3. Only such as believe the **Words of Institution**, hence believe both that they receive the true body and blood of Christ in the Lord's Supper and that Christ gives them this priceless gift for the remission of their sins. This provision excludes the Christians in Reformed denominations [*Gemeinschaften*, fellowships]. There certainly are children of God among the Reformed who still preach Christ's *satisfactio vicaria* [vicarious satisfaction]. Since, however, they lack the right understanding of, and therefore faith in, the **Words of Institution**, they are **not in condition** to use the Lord's Supper to their benefit. Paul **expressly** disqualified all who do not believe the real presence [*Realpraesenz*], since they do not discern the Lord's body (διακρίνειν τὸ σῶμα τοῦ Κυρίου), 1 Corinthians 11:29. With their denial of the real presence they also lose the *finis cuius* [i.e., the final purpose] of the Lord's Supper, namely, that Christ's body and blood is given us in the Sacrament for the remission of sins. This applies, of course, also to such Lutherans as are afflicted with grave doubts as to the real presence of Christ's body and blood,[12] or who, though they confess the real presence,

11 Walther, *Pastorale*, 190: "Since according to God's Word everyone who would approach the Lord's Table should first examine himself and discern the Lord's body, it will not do to give the Lord's Supper to children incapable of examining themselves. It was a manifest abuse when this practice, as the examples of even Cyprian and Augustine prove, was quite general from the third to the fifth century, with the sanction also of Innocent I, through a misinterpretation of John 6:53 as referring to sacramental eating and drinking. This misuse was prevalent also among the Bohemian Hussites and is canon law even today in the Eastern Church. Luther writes: 'I cannot side with the Bohemians in distributing the Lord's Supper to children, even though I would not call them heretics on that account. Furthermore, those who cannot examine themselves and therefore are not to be admitted to the Lord's Supper include also those asleep, or unconscious, those in the throes of death who are already deprived of the use of their senses, deranged people, and the like." Walther, as we saw, points to the fact that the Lord's Supper does not, like bodily medication, work physically, but presupposes consciousness of the essence and faith in the purpose of the Lord's Supper. Further particulars, e.g., the question whether lunatics, raving madmen, yes, also the bodily possessed, may be communed when they have lucid intervals ("*lichte Zwischenzeiten*") belong to casuistry. See Walther, *Pastorale*, 192.

12 When some began to doubt the real presence because of the preaching of Carlstadt and the "enthusiasts," Luther ([Walch] 20:201) gave the advice: "If someone was too weak to take the blow, so that he now has his doubts as to the Sacrament, let him take my advice to do without the Sacrament for the present and to exercise himself without it in God's Word, in faith and love, letting those take the Sacrament who feel safe in their conscience. You are not damned if you do without the Sacrament." The same thought: 20:734.

are not seeking the forgiveness of sins in the Sacrament, but ascribe to it a salutary effect *ex opere operato* [i.e., merely by the act of participating].[13]

4. Such as must **not first remove a public offense that has been given**. The particulars are discussed in *Pastoral Theology*. The course in Dogmatics must point out that this practice—removing a public offense before partaking of Communion—does not rest on human arbitrariness or legalism, but is demanded by the essence and purpose of the Lord's Supper. Because the Lord's Supper is not intended for believers and unbelievers, but only for **Christians**, everyone who has made his Christianity doubtful for the congregation must, before he communes again, enable the congregation to become convinced that by God's grace he has risen from his fall. Scripture therefore expressly prohibits us to treat as brothers in the faith those who live in gross, offensive sins, that is, to act toward them as though nothing had occurred. 1 Corinthians 5:11: "But now I am writing to you not to associate with anyone who bears the name of brother if he is guilty of sexual immorality, or greed, or an idolater, reviler, drunkard, or swindler—not even to eat with such a one."[14] If the grave offense of a person has become known to the congregation, also his repentance must be made known to the congregation before he again communes with the congregation. From the essence and purpose of the Lord's Supper it further follows that persons living in the sin of **being unwilling to be reconciled** must be suspended from partaking of the Sacrament. For the Lord's Supper is distribution of the forgiveness of sins; only he therefore makes the right use of it who there seeks the forgiveness of **his** sins. But in any case there can be a true desire for God's forgiveness only in the heart of him who on his part, too, is ready to forgive the trespasses of his neighbor, or, if he was in the wrong, to seek reconciliation by asking the neighbor's forgiveness.[15]

---

13 Luther, StL 20:748ff.: "It is not sufficient to know what the Sacrament is, viz., that Christ's body and blood actually is there, but it is necessary also to know ***why*** it is there and why and for what end it is given us to eat. . . . This, then, we call the right use; not this, that it is simply performed and obedience rendered to the Church. The point is not the performance of a work, but the strengthening of your heart, as the words say, 'Which is given for you, which is shed for you.'"

14 The συνεσθίειν prohibits any Table fellowship in general. "We are not to have him at our table, nor are we to be found at his table" (Meyer). This applies first precisely to fellowship in the Lord's Supper [***Abendmahlsgemeinschaft***].

15 Cf. Walther, *Pastorale*, 194ff. [Fritz, *Pastoral Theology*, 151]. Luther: "God will not be gracious and forgive a man's sin unless he also forgives his neighbor. Besides, a man's faith cannot be sincere unless it bears this fruit, that he, too, forgives his neighbor and asks his forgiveness; otherwise man may not appear before God. If this fruit is missing, his faith and his first confession [his confession "before God"] is also not sincere" (StL 11:585).

Furthermore, since Christians are forbidden to adhere to teachers who deviate from the apostolic doctrine (Romans 16:17: "Avoid them"; English Revised Version: "turn away from them"), it is self-evident that members of heterodox churches [*irrgläuben Gemeinschaft*] must have severed their connection with the heterodox body and have declared their acceptance of the true doctrine before they may commune with the congregation. Fellowship in the Lord's Supper certainly is fellowship in faith or church fellowship [*Abendmahlsgemeinschaft ist sicherlich glaubensbruederliche Gemeinschaft oder 'Kirchengemeinschaft.'*] (Fritz:[16] "*Abendmahlsgemeinschaft ist Glaubensgemeinschaft,*" altar fellowship is confessional fellowship, *Pastoral Theology*, 154 [Walther, *Pastorale*, 145]). It must also not be overlooked that the Lord's Supper is **private absolution**. God's will, however, is that we give private absolution to him only who, as far as we are able to judge, sincerely repents. To the unrepentant we are not to say: "You shall surely live," but are to give him the ringing warning: "You shall surely die!" (Ezekiel 3:17–18). Therefore **Walther** (*Pastorale*, 146ff.) is right in holding that by practicing "open Communion" [*offenen Kommunion*] a pastor becomes "an unfaithful, careless, and unscrupulous shepherd." **Luther**, too, warns against this soul-destroying mingling of Law and Gospel by saying, as we heard above: "When I preach the Gospel, I do not know with whom it takes effect; but here I should be convinced that it takes effect with him who comes to the Sacrament" (StL 11:615). He expresses this thought somewhat more drastically in pointing out what a faithful pastor must tell an impenitent sinner when he applies God's Word to him individually: "Repent, and that honestly! If not, you can just as well go to the devil by yourself, without me and my absolution, as go doubly to the devil with my absolution and besides by your guilt drag me along without my guilt. Nay, man; I say: You go to the devil, I shall stay here; I am not pastor to go to the devil with everybody, but to bring everybody with me to God" (StL 10:882).

In vain is **love** appealed to in defense of "open Communion" [*offene Kommunion*]. The fact is that this practice is contrary both to love of God and love of the neighbor. For it ignores **God's** order which we find in Scripture regarding the use of the Supper, and it leads the neighbor to sin by partaking unworthily of the Sacrament. And what has been said of "open Communion" applies also to the admission of Reformed to Lutheran altars "**as guests**."[17]

Accordingly, if a Christian congregation is to prove itself conscientious in the administration of the Lord's Supper, it must have the custom of **announcing for**

16 [Of course, Pieper's original does not reference Fritz's revision of Walther's *Pastoral Theology*. MH]

17 This "admission as guests" involves a self-contradiction. When Lutheran synods in America indeed wanted to cling to the **rule** "Lutheran altars for Lutheran communicants only," but then wanted **exceptions** to the rule granted, they were again making admission to the Lord's Supper a matter of **human caprice** and were thus in fact dropping the **divine rule**.

Communion (announcing one's intention to partake to the pastor).[18] Obviously, only through such registration can the pastor limit Communion attendance to those eligible for the Lord's Supper. Of course, he should explore only those persons with whose faith and life he is **unfamiliar**. Pertinent is **Walther's** remark that this exploration before admission to the Lord's Table rests not on a law, but solely on the need of the souls. Exploration not only **may**, but **should** be omitted in all cases where the pastor is dealing with good Christians well-known to him. To explore in such cases would be a needless burdening both of the pastor and of those registering. This is also Luther's opinion. "A person," he says, "may be so knowledgeable that he need be explored but once in his life or not at all" (StL 10:2248).[19]

Both pastor and congregation must most carefully guard against denying the Lord's Supper to anyone to whom Christ wants it to be given. In his day Luther had to warn not only against laxity in practice, but also against legalism and unnecessary rigor. He writes to Balthazar Thüring in Koburg: "I have written the pastor not to torture the ignorant with long examinations when they announce for Communion, but also not to refrain entirely from exploring and examining them. To let them partake without any examination is no good. We censure our opponents for being belly-servers; but our men are stern and inclined to severity. I pray you therefore, for God's sake, to endeavor most earnestly to teach the Gospel in all humility" (Walch 21:1348). To keep the pastor from denying the Lord's Supper to those weak in Christian knowledge, or frightening timid souls away, **Walther** gives directions as to what the pastor ought to ascertain and how he ought to explore when people with whose spiritual condition he is unfamiliar desire Communion. The person registering should not be subjected to a "rigorous examination," but be induced by way of a friendly interview to reveal the state of his Christianity and to tell what the Lord's Supper is and why he desires to partake.

---

18 [The English here is a translation of "*gewoehnlich 'Beichtanmeldung' genannt*" or "commonly called announcing for confession." MH]

19 Walther, *Pastorale*, 152. It would be contrary to Luther's intention if we applied everything Luther said about the necessary "exploration" before admission to the Lord's Supper without further ado to present-day conditions. We today have congregations to which only those belong "who are earnestly minded to be Christians," a condition Luther strove for, but never attained. Among us, therefore, the pastor usually is personally well acquainted with the spiritual life of his members, and for that reason an exploration is unnecessary.—Also the following reminder is here in place: If the pastor as shepherd must reprove some member of his congregation, he should not wait until the next registration for Communion, lest the day of registration become a general day of judgment in his congregation—a thing that is good neither for the pastor nor the congregation. Walther therefore was wont to give the advice to attend to any case requiring special attention before the day of registration, even though it be the day before.

But even apart from the cases where the pastor is seeking to discover the spiritual state of practical strangers, there is danger—and the pastor must not lose sight of this fact—that particularly in regard to the use of Holy Communion the **inherent** *opinio legis* is apt to assert itself in the communicants, perhaps also in the pastor himself. It takes this form: Since one receives Christ's body and blood in the Lord's Supper, a salutary use of the Sacrament presupposes a **special degree of sanctity** and a **strong** faith. Because of this thought particularly earnest Christians, who feel their infirmity more than others, are prone to **postpone** receiving the Sacrament until they feel greater fervency of spirit, have waxed strong in faith, and show a progress in sanctification that satisfies them personally. But these are mistaken notions, a result of forgetting that the Lord's Supper **character is a Means of Grace**. In the Lord's Supper we indeed receive Christ's body and blood. But this wonderful gift is given us for the very purpose of transmitting and pledging to us the **free** grace of God, based entirely on Christ's *satisfactio vicaria*[20] and demanding no worthiness of our own at all. That Christ receives **sinners**—this He wants to stress and bring out, as in all Means of Grace, **so particularly** by His Supper. Luther says: "The Sacrament is instituted for this very purpose of ministering comfort and strength to us. Therefore let nothing keep you from the Communion. If you feel your weakness, good, for you must feel your unworthiness" (StL 11:660). And earlier: "You must not make of Christ a tyrant, but accept Him for what He in truth **is** and **let Him** be unto you nothing but rich, abounding grace. If you feel in your heart that you have not reached this point and do not have such faith, and yet **would like** to believe, you must, after all, not despair and shun the Sacrament, but seek your help right there, so that your faith may burst into flame and increase. For though some have been terribly punished for partaking of the Sacrament unworthily and without faith, they are only those whom we described above, namely, the hardened, wicked hearts. You should proceed and think thus: Lord, see, there is Thy Word, and here is my illness and failing. Thou Thyself hast said, 'Come to Me, all who labor and are heavy laden, and I will give you rest' (Matthew 11:28). Do you think He said that to those who are already fervid and strong in faith? His kingdom is not established to the end of furthering the righteous (Matthew 9:13), but of helping sinners and making them righteous (1 Timothy 1:15). Hence he who is weak and feels it should go to Communion and let God help him" (StL 11:653ff.). Luther also adduces **his own example**: "It has often happened to me that I hesitated and thus only widened the breach, until I saw that this was no help; so I had to partake. Thus you, too, will find that it is a fraud of Satan, to draw people away from the Sacrament, so that the more they are afraid and want to wait until they feel faith in their hearts, the farther they drift away. And at last, if they continue in this state, all desire and impulse, both toward

20 [That is, vicarious satisfaction of the requirements of the Law. MH]

the Word and the Sacrament, dies out in them, and they never come. Therefore you must thrust aside your thoughts and fears, and partake, and ask God to help you. If you do this often, you will feel how you are gaining more and more desire for it, an increase you would not have gained otherwise. To this end I wish you would follow my example and that the number of those might increase who go to the Sacrament in order that their desire for it might grow and they become stronger and stronger. Otherwise, if you do not partake, you will always remain cold and only grow colder and colder."

To keep a pastor from unjustly refusing Communion, and at the same time to save the pastor unnecessary scruples of conscience, the reminder is in place "that a pastor need not be sure of a **living** faith in those desiring the Holy Supper from him—for who but God could be?—he must merely be certain that if they are not Christians, this is not manifest or provable. To act according to his moral convictions in admitting or turning away people from the Lord's Table is an inexcusable tyranny over the consciences" (Walther, *Pastorale*, 192). This verdict is not too severe. Suppose a pastor, because of his "moral convictions," turned communicants away from the Lord's Supper, though he cannot **prove** his conviction to be correct, would he not subject the congregation as well as those desiring to partake of the Sacrament to his caprice?

The Pastor's Right of Suspension. The pastor's right of suspension has been discussed much in times past and present. Here the old Lutheran theologians were not entirely of one voice.[21] (Cf. Walther, *Pastorale*, 163ff.) The thing that must be maintained is that the pastor is **personally** and **directly** responsible not only to the congregation, but also to God, with regard to the persons he admits to the Lord's Supper. Therefore the pastor has both the right and the duty to suspend in all cases those whose admission to the Sacrament would be contrary to God's will and ordinance. **Walther** specifies: "A pastor, though without authority to excommunicate a member of his congregation, must suspend a member from Communion when he has committed or lives in a manifest mortal sin and will not repent; has committed a theft and will not return the stolen goods; has insulted or offended someone or a whole congregation, or has been offended by someone, and in either case will not be reconciled, Matthew 5:23–25; 18:28ff.; Luke 17:3; etc. In such a situation it becomes necessary to suspend from the Holy Supper, that is to say, the pastor refuses to commune such a member until his offense has been removed, or demands that the member postpone his Communion until he gives evidence of repentance, or of readiness to be reconciled, and the like. A pastor may not and must not become partaker of other men's sins, 1 Timothy 5:22. Certainly he must, then, have the right of suspension from the Holy Supper in all cases where he by admittance to the Lord's Table would knowingly assist in the commission

21 [The translation omitted reference to the old Lutheran theologians. MH]

of a grievous sin and thus become partaker of other men's sin. As emphatically, therefore, as our old orthodox theologians deny the right of pastors to excommunicate without the congregation, so emphatically they defend the pastor's right to suspend from the Supper." It must, however, be kept in mind that the pastor by suspending does not excommunicate, as many mistakenly have claimed, but he merely demands **postponement** of the person's use of the Supper until the person in question shows signs of repentance and removes whatever obstacles, according to the Word of God, forbid his going to Communion.

Of course, the suspended person always retains the right of **appeal** to the congregation from the verdict of the pastor, and this for two reasons: (1) the administration of the Lord's Supper is entrusted originally to the congregation and the pastor has suspended as the servant [*Diener*; minister] of the congregation (*minister ecclesiae*); (2) the suspension temporarily affects the relation of the suspended to the congregation. But in the meantime the suspension stands. Should there be a **case of conflict** between pastor and congregations, and the conflict cannot be overcome also through deliberate deadlines on the matter,[22] the pastor must nevertheless rather suffer removal from office than give the Lord's Supper to a person to whom, according to God's Word, he must deny it. Under our church polity [*kirchlichen verhaeltnissen*] we have rarely experienced such conflicts. In most cases the pastor succeeded in convincing the congregation of the propriety of the suspension. Now and then the pastor was convinced by his congregation, or by other advisers called in, that the suspension was unjustifiable. At our theological schools a number of typical cases in which suspension ought not to be applied might well be discussed at length.[23]

---

22 [The sentence up to this point was creatively rendered by Mueller as follows: "If it should happen that the pastor justly suspended a person, but the congregation condemned and annulled the suspension, and despite proper instruction and a thorough review of the case, perhaps even by synodical officials, refuses to change its mind . . . ." MH]

23 Walther, *Pastorale*, 152ff., 190ff. [Fritz, *Pastoral Theology*, 134] lists these cases: When an "evil rumor" circulates concerning one desiring Communion; when he is directly accused of having committed a grievous sin, but his accuser can bring no witnesses or proof; when the pastor alone knows about his guilt; when a Christian is involved in a lawsuit; etc. The many quotations Walther offers show that even the earlier Lutheran theologians are not entirely dependable guides in this matter because they lived under state church conditions and in the exercise of Christian discipline sometimes confused civil and ecclesiastical discipline. It is a correct axiom: *De occultis non iudicat ecclesia* ["The Church does not render judgment concerning things unknown." MH] And this includes that it is not the business of the Church to **ferret out secret sins**. In quoting the earlier theologians Walther repeatedly refers to his note on page 154 of his *Pastorale*, in which he says: "The confession of particular sins before men is not necessary unless by silence an innocent person is made to suffer. Unless this is the case, or unless the member is unburdening his heart to his pastor, the pastor should not **ask** whether or not he has committed a certain sin, lest the pastor thus press him to reveal a hidden sin or to tell a lie." Also during private confession interrogation is, according to Walther, to be limited, but a mild ***suggestion*** may be made to confess

The combination of *confession* [*Beichte*] and the Lord's Supper is a laudable churchly, but not a divine order [*Ordnung*]. This statement holds true both of private confession and of the so-called "confessional service," with its confessional address, general confession of sins, and general Absolution. Walther (*Pastorale*, 168) quotes from the "Instruction for the Visitors" of 1538 (StL 10:1655): "If the pastor, who daily is occupied with it, desires to go to the Sacrament without a confession or questioning, he may do so. The same thing is true of other well-informed persons who know well how to examine themselves, in order that this confession, which should and must remain a free act, does not again develop into a new papistic coercion and indispensable rite. And I, Dr. Martin, once in a while go to the Lord's Table without having confessed, in order that I may keep from feeling bound in my conscience to observe this custom as necessary; then again I use the confession and would not be without it; above all, because of the absolution, that is, the Word of God."[24]

---

a particular sin if the pastor notices that the penitent remains troubled in his conscience despite all instruction and consolation (*Pastorale*, 290). Walther quotes approvingly from Hartmann's *Pastorale evangelicum*, 791: "It is a wrong assumption that a clear and express confession of every single sin, particularly of those sins of which one is accused on the basis of a rumor or a strong suspicion, is necessary, for there is no commandment to that effect in Scripture. It is no less false that '**one is not truly sorry for sins committed, who has not expressly confessed them before the father confessor**.'" That express confession is necessary is the well-known horrible doctrine of Rome (*Trid.*, Sess. XIV, can. 4–8), which makes the Church a spy and eavesdropper among men, makes the forgiveness pronounced uncertain, strengthens the priests' shameful tyranny, and exerts a demoralizing influence, particularly on women. When souls in their trials reveal a desire to unburden themselves, the pastor certainly should meet them halfway. But just as earnestly he must guard against **ferreting out** secret sins. Walther (*Pastorale*, 159) says that it is "contrary to a pastor's office [*Amt*] curiously to hunt for secret sins," and quotes from the Saxon church regulations: "The servants of the Church are not to **ask** of the penitents what these do not confess of themselves." If a pastor blunders here, he has no cause to be offended if his member tells him: "Pastor, that is not your business," and should not regard such an answer as a sign of impenitence.

24 See Luther's classic words on confession in his "Sermon on Confession and the Sacrament" (StL 11:585–90; see p. 210, footnote 107). Here he distinguishes three kinds of confession, of which the first two (the confession of sin before God and confessing to the offended neighbor) are divinely enjoined, but not so the third. "The third kind is the one commanded by the pope, which is confessed privately into the ears of the priest. This one is not commanded by God. . . . Still it is advisable and good. . . . For it is deplorable when the conscience is burdened and in fear and knows of no escape or consolation. For that reason, too, it is a noble, fine deed when two come together and the one gives advice, help, and consolation to the other, and things proceed most brotherly and lovely; the one uncovers his ailment, the other heals his wounds for him. On that account I for one would not do without this private confession for all the treasures of the world. Still it should not be taught as **commanded**, in order not to bind the consciences, as though one **had to** go to confession before going to the Sacrament" (StL 11:590).

CHAPTER TWENTY-THREE

THESES ON THE GALESBURG DECLARATION ON PULPIT AND ALTAR FELLOWSHIP

PREPARED BY ORDER OF THE GENERAL COUNCIL

PART II

44. The Lutheran Church *owes her being* to the conviction that her Confessions depart in no respect from the faith taught in God's Word; that she teaches the Gospel in its complete purity; that all her doctrines are divine; that she is the most perfectly homogeneous portion of that Church visible, of which the Church catholic is the soul; that in a supreme and unique degree she has the marks of the true Church, to wit, the pure Word of God and the right Sacraments. Any communion which does not claim so much for itself, is on its own admission, in some measure, a sect.

45. In maintaining this claim, the Lutheran Church of necessity implies that to the degree, and in the respects in which other parts of Christendom depart from the faith and truth confessed by the Lutheran Church, they depart from the faith and truth of God's Word; that in any case they are less homogeneous portions of the Church whose soul is the Church catholic, and that the distinctive testimony of the Lutheran Church, that which distinguishes her in various degrees from all particular churches, involves not mere points of opinion, but subjects of divine truth, and hence of transcendent importance, which dare not in any measure be imperiled; and this holds true over against Rome, against heresy, against schisms, and against the divergent forms of belief which have assumed the common name of Protestant.

46. The Augsburg Confession lays down the fundamental postulates of that faith which is essential to a complete unity of a church as over against all heresies, perversions, mutilations, and ignoring of divine truth.

47. That Confession means by its very existence, and the Church means by her very existence under it, that the pulpit, which is the organ of a pure Word, and the altar, which represents the true Sacraments, are to be sacredly guarded as at once the witnesses and conservators of her true unity and of her genuine catholicity.

48. There are three general ways in which the sense of unity in the Church can be officially expressed. One is by profession of the same creed, the second by admission to public teaching, the third is by reception at the altar.

49. In every case in which the first—the confession of the common faith—is neither given nor purposed, but is, on the contrary, either in terms or virtually rejected, there can be no ground for the form of the second or third. No church should admit to her pulpits or altars those who publicly deny, either officially or personally, the truth of God's Word as that church officially confesses it.

50. If the present divisions of Christendom can be justified, if the so-called denominationalism is to stand before the judgment bar of God, it must be able to show a ground of supreme necessity for its existence. Unless a denomination has a divine warrant for its separate existence, it is simply a sect. If it claims no divine warrant, but alleges mere human convenience or preference for its existence, it is a self-convicted sect. If its supporters are to be absolved even of the crime of conscious, deliberate wrongdoing, they must be able to show, at least, that they sincerely believe that the necessity for its existence is real and urgent, not a thing of human convenience or preference, but a divinely directed need. Nothing but the proof of necessity can justify it, nothing short of the conviction, at the very least, a mistaken but sincere conviction, of the divinely imposed necessity of its existence, can absolve the men who form it from the charge of criminal trifling with the most sacred principles of Christianity, the most solemn commands of our Lord. The denominationalism of convenience is simply what the New Testament styles schism.

51. When a church holds and confesses the very truth of God in all its parts, and has the pure Sacraments, no man has a right to leave it because of any human defects which may exist in its actual state. He must labor and pray to correct them; must apply the church's own principles to remove her own evils, must reform within the church. A man who remains within a particular church is thereby pledged to its officially confessed faith, and what that faith really involves, but not to anything beyond. If a church has the pure Word and Sacraments, it has the essential means of correcting its actual defects; and the forming of a new denomination, simply as an easier mode of securing any human ends, however important, is schismatic.

52. On whatever else thoughtful Christians may differ they should agree on this, that the awful levity with which sects are originated in Protestantism is a crime against God and His Church, and that a rule shown to be necessary to purify the judgments of men in regard to the sacredness of truth, and of unity in the truth, so

that they shall refuse every possible compromise of these great principles, is a rule which accords with God's Word and with every pure confession of God's Church.

53. That Rule of the Pulpit alone accords with the divine Word, which does not simply demand freedom for the pulpit, permission to teach the truth, if a man happens to know it, or sees fit to preach it, but which insists on an absolute aiming at the whole truth, and nothing but the truth, and this truth a confessing Church maintains to be in whole and in each part the truth to which she witnesses. The teaching she admits to her pulpits must be guaranteed as truth, not by an untested presumption, but by her own careful testing, in the fixed modes involved by a fixed principle.

54. As the Word of God and the Confessions of the Church teach the inviolable sacredness and supremacy of truth, and the obligation of the utmost simplicity and directness in asserting and defending it, that Rule for the Altar alone accords with both, which withholds from coming to our altars those who deny any part of the divine truth, those who are voluntarily ignorant of it, and who neither desire nor would permit us to teach it to them, who have never examined and do not mean to examine the grounds on which we rest our Confession of it, who either know nothing and care nothing about it, or regard it as false, or look upon it as too unimportant even for contempt—those who are in, and intend to remain in, communions which owe their existence to a denial of the very truths which gave our Church her full distinctive being, and to the assertion of which our fathers witnessed by their Confession, their toils, their sacrifices, and, when need was, by their blood—those who, mistaking or abusing the name of charity, and converting what they call love into a foe to the truth, no longer a love by which faith works, but a love which works without faith against faith, those who sink the Communion of our Lord's broken body and shed blood to the sphere of mere social courtesy.

55. We are Lutherans because we believe "that the doctrine of our Confession is drawn from Holy Scripture and the pure Word of God,"[1] and is "in conformity with the pure Word of God and Christian truth," and "clearly grounded in Holy Scripture."[2] We are Lutherans because we believe that in "the summary of doctrine which is in our churches, there is nothing which conflicts with the Scriptures,"[3] that "touching the Articles of Faith, nothing is taught in our churches in conflict with Holy Scriptures."[4] "Nothing is received among us contrary to Scripture,"[5] that "no new and ungodly doctrine has crept into our Churches,"[6] and that because

1 AC *Preface* 8.

2 AC *A Summary Statement* (after AC XXI) 1.

3 AC XXI 5.

4 AC *A Review of the Various Abuses That Have Been Corrected (before AC XXII) 1.*

5 AC *Conclusion 5.*

6 AC *Conclusion 5.*

of all this, "our Confession is of God, and Christian," and that it is our duty as Augustine teaches, and as the Confession quotes him with approval for teaching, "not to be in accord," even with the ministers of the Word, "when they teach anything in conflict with Holy Scripture,"[7] and that the themes of the doctrinal parts of the Confession are "Articles of faith and doctrine," "Chief articles of faith," which are "necessary"[8] to show the accord of our doctrine with the Word.

56. But in asserting this we have already asserted that the doctrine of other Confessions, so far as it conflicts with ours, is not drawn from Holy Scripture, is not in conformity with the pure Word of God, and with Christian truth, and is not grounded in the Word. We have, beyond all possibility of denial, already implied that in the summary of doctrine among them, if it be at war with ours, there is something which conflicts with the Scriptures, a something which touches the articles of faith; and that hence, whatever virtues may be claimed for them in other respects, so far they are not of God, and not Christian; their doctrine is new and not godly. The inference is already involved that we may not be in any such accord with them as weakens our testimony that they do teach something in conflict with Holy Scripture. To make these solemn expressions of the Confession a dead letter by lack of practical conformity with them is to do dishonor to the Confession and the Word, and to be inconsistent with ourselves, who accept the Word itself as an absolute rule of faith and life, and the Confession as a true exponent of the sense of the Word. In giving effect, therefore, to these our solemn convictions, we must stand fast by the rule, that those who by their vows as ministers are bound to systems which in whole or in part conflict with God's Word cannot be admitted to our pulpits. We must not even seem to accord with them, for their churches owe their separate being in part to a forsaking of portions of God's Word. Nor can we without a snare to conscience, both to the inviters and the invited, open our altars to those who are members, and mean to remain members, of churches which rest in whole or in part on unscriptural foundations.

57. It is a wrong to the truth, to Him who has entrusted it to our keeping, to ourselves with our solemn endowments of privilege and responsibility; a wrong to those whom we help to lull in their ignorance of the truth or indifference to it, when we give them our solemn attestation that we recognize them as in full unity with us in the reception of God's Word—that attestation which is involved in inviting them to our Communion. There is no more facile, no more fatal way of telling men that their errors are venial, of bringing faith to the level of opinion and notion, than to throw open to them the most hallowed place in which truth is taught, the most sacred shrine at which truth is confessed, without even asking, Do you know the truth? Are you willing to learn it? nay, rather, knowing perfectly

7 AC XXVIII 28.

8 AC *Conclusion 5.*

that they would resent such questions, as a gross violation of that "courtesy" on which the whole loose practice so largely rests.

58. It is a principle of the New Testament universally recognized in the Church, that the reception of the Lord's Supper in a particular congregation or particular communion has, as one of its objects, the confession of the pure faith as against the false or mingled, the complete as against the imperfect, the sound doctrine as against the corrupt or dubious, the true Church as against the spurious or doubtful. It is the most solemn mode of marking church conjunction, and of witnessing for a particular communion as over against all communions in any way arrayed against it, or officially separate from its fellowship. It is "that we may testify that we approve the doctrine which sounds forth in that Church in which, together with others, we eat the same eucharistic bread, and drink from one cup." "The Lord's Supper not only separates believers, or the Christian people, from unbelievers, but also distinguishes between Christians themselves who have wandered from the purity of the faith, and those of a purer church sincerely professing and defending the sound faith."[9]

59. Hence it is in the highest degree inconsistent and self-stultifying to have a common Communion with sects or denominations which have arisen by divergence from the faith or fellowship of a pure church.

60. The Augsburg Confession declares that the people of our churches are admitted to the Sacrament "if they are fit for it," and that this fitness is to be officially tested, "for none are admitted unless they have been before examined and absolved," and "with the greatest diligence frequently instructed in regard to the Holy Sacrament, whereunto it is instituted, and how it is to be used; and instruction is further given against other doctrines concerning the Sacrament, doctrines which are false."[10] "In this examination the less mature were questioned, and were repeatedly instructed in regard to the entire Christian doctrine."[11] This usage involves a fundamental principle incapable of harmony with interdenominational Communion.

61. If a principle is seen to be evil, the evil should be openly confessed, and openly renounced and abandoned, not glossed over and palliated. The power of a false principle is perpetuated by all attempts to hide its real nature, or to soften its practical mischiefs. Nothing so certainly and speedily awakens aversion to a bad law or bad principle as to insist that those who are committed to it shall strictly carry it out. If the denominational principle be evil, its character will soonest

9 Melanchthon, *Repititio August. Conf., De Coena Domini; Loci* (Corpus Lisiae, 1563), pp. 547–68. Gerhard (Cotta), ch. X, p. 371. Carpzov in *Libr. Symb.*, 405.

10 AC *Of Abuse*, Art. 111, Latin and German.

11 *Repetitio*, AC.

be seen if men are held responsible for strict fidelity to it, till they formally and unequivocally renounce it.

62. No man remaining in a denomination whose confessed faith is wrong has any moral right to the benefit of a mere private disclaimer that for his own part he rejects its errors. Denominations are properly responsible for the faith of their Confessions, and the official relation of our Church to them is to be determined by that faith, and not by the unauthorized statements of the personal views of particular ministers or members.

63. It is a principle of the New Testament, and of all pure churches, that the privileges of the Church are not to be separated from its tests, its duties, and subjection to its discipline. No man has a right to enter the pulpit, or approach the altar of the Church, who has not conformed to the Church's solemnly appointed mode of previous testing, and who is not subject to her divine law of duty, and to her discipline in case of a neglect of duty, or of manifest sin.

64. One communion has no right to decide who shall occupy the pulpits or come to the altars of another.

65. One communion cannot consistently allow another to decide for it, who are the proper persons to occupy its pulpits and come to its altars. It is itself responsible before God for the proper guarding of both, and has no right to exist if it does not accept and act on this responsibility.

66. That which is wrong in principle if constant is wrong in principle if occasional. Expediency, in its proper sphere, may allow of the occasional as over against the constant, but principle does not.

67. The terms of occasional admission to pulpit or altar must be the same in principle as those of constant admission; the terms of admission to either once must be the same in principle as those of admission to either always.

68. Because the Gospel must bring Christ to us, in the divine meaning of His life, sufferings, office, and work, the Word of God attaches importance of the highest kind to doctrine. The substitution of man's notions for the divine doctrine nullifies every act, however beautiful, or proper, or acceptable it would otherwise be.

69. "God's name is hallowed when both our doctrine and our life are divine and Christian. God's name is profaned when men preach, teach, and speak under the name of God what is false and misleading, so that His name is made to cover and give currency to what is false. This is the very highest of all profanations and dishonorings of the divine name."[12] The smooth plausibilities of a loose popular sermon may, according to this, do more real dishonor to God's name than the open profanities of the wicked; the profanities horrify men, the smooth perversions seduce them. There are no profanities like the profanities of a perverted pulpit. Nor are these always smooth. They are coarse enough at times. People will

12 LC III 41.

run to hear, and newspapers will hasten to report a sort of preaching with which is mingled such burlesquing of sacred names and things as once would have been visited by the penalties of the law against blasphemy.

70. It is one of the greatest sins and calamities of the Church of our day that there is widespread and utter carelessness in regard to doctrine, or a fixed aversion to it; in some a contempt for it, in many ignorance or an ignoring of it. Men sometimes array the Gospel against itself by urging that they "want the Gospel," they "don't want doctrine"; as if there could be any real Gospel which is not doctrine, or any Gospel in its totality, which does not embrace all the doctrine of the Gospel. It is as if they said: "We want nourishment; we don't want food"; "We want warmth; but none of your fuel and clothes for us."

71. Whether the laxity of the time helps men toward the extreme pseudo-ecclesiasticism or the extreme of unionistic sectarianism, the beginning of the healing must be a Bible estimate of the indispensable nature of Bible doctrine. Our Church, once chosen of God to lead His people back to the pure faith, must realize that none can take her vocation from her. The front of the host is still her place, if she is faithful to the Captain of her salvation, and she can do now no work more characteristic of her, and more worthy of her great name and responsibility, than to help in awakening the mind of Christendom to a consciousness of the disastrous tendency of the time.

CHAPTER TWENTY-FOUR

Guidelines for Congregational, District, and Synodical Communion Statements

The President of the Synod requested the Commission on Theology and Church Relations (CTCR) to prepare guidelines for Communion statements for congregational, district, and synodical use. The request came to the CTCR after the president made numerous visits to District Conventions and congregations and witnessed a wide variety (and no small disparity) in statements addressing admission to the Lord's Supper.

The challenge of a godly, biblical Communion practice is great. Francis Pieper noted two potential errors of practice: "On the one hand they [churches and pastors] are not permitted to introduce 'Open Communion'; on the other hand, they must guard against denying the Sacrament to those Christians for whom Christ has appointed it."[1] "Open Communion," the admission of individuals to the Sacrament with minimal or no concern for Baptism, repentance, faith, self-examination, or unity of confession, is intolerable for any who take seriously that our Lord gave the Supper only to his disciples (Matt 26:20), Paul's plea that a church be of one mind or judgment and without division (1 Cor 1:10), and his insistence on self-examination and discerning the Lord's body (1 Cor 11:27–28). Just as intolerable is any approach to the Lord's Table which discourages repentant, confessing Christians from receiving the gifts of Christ or implies that only a select few Lutheran Christians are worthy and well-prepared to commune, as if reception is a reward for doctrinal orthodoxy or denominational affiliation. Recognizing such opposing errors, however, does not in itself resolve the practical, pastoral questions about how to administer Christ's Holy Supper faithfully or to communicate

1 *Christian Dogmatics*, vol. 3 (St. Louis: Concordia Publishing House, 1953), 381.

to both members and visitors biblical truths and concerns about proper, God-pleasing participation in the Lord's Supper.

The CTCR first issued guidelines for Communion statements in 1993. In the CTCR's letter to pastors dated February 22, 1993, the CTCR provided a "Model Communion Statement" consistent with its 1983 report, *Theology and Practice of the Lord's Supper*, and with 1986 Resolution 3-08 "To Maintain Practice of Close Communion." The letter accompanying the "Model Communion Statement" of 1993 stated, "The Commission hopes that you will find it helpful as you evaluate and/or develop your own announcements concerning admission to Holy Communion." This 1993 statement was officially "recommended to the member congregations of the Synod for guidance" by the Synod in convention 1995 Res. 3-08 "To Reaffirm the Practice of Close[d] Communion." We may also mention the CTCR 1999 report *Admission to the Lord's Supper: Basics of Biblical and Confessional Teaching.*[2] Such documents and resolutions reflect the underlying respect for and concern with a theology and practice that is part of the long historic tradition of the church.[3]

The 1993 CTCR "Model Communion Statement" was intended to serve as an aid to congregations and pastors "as you evaluate and/or develop *your own announcements*" (emphasis added). Thus, although it has been used "as is" by some LCMS pastors and congregations, the model statement was certainly not intended to be considered either a final word on Communion statements for the LCMS or a perfect statement. However, it may continue to serve as a widely acceptable starting point in the development of guidelines for other additional Communion statements and for consideration of the matter of admission policies.

MODEL COMMUNION CARD STATEMENT

The Lord's Supper is celebrated at this congregation in the confession and glad confidence that, as he says, our Lord gives into our mouths not only bread and wine but his very body and blood to eat and to drink for the forgiveness of sins and to strengthen our union with him and with one another. Our Lord invites to his table those who trust his words, repent of all sin, and set aside any refusal to forgive and love as he forgives and loves us, that they may show forth his death until he comes.

Because those who eat and drink our Lord's body and blood unworthily do so to their great harm and because Holy Communion is a confession of the faith which is confessed at this altar, any who are not yet instructed, in doubt, or who hold a confession differing from that of this congregation

2 The report is available in hard copy from Concordia Publishing House or in electronic format at http://www.lcms.org/Document.fdoc?src=lcm&id=411.

3 See Werner Elert, *Eucharist and Church Fellowship in the First Four Centuries*, Norman E. Nagel, trans. (St. Louis: Concordia Publishing House, 1966).

and The Lutheran Church—Missouri Synod, and yet desire to receive the sacrament, are asked first to speak with the pastor or an usher.

For further study, see Matthew 5:23f.; 10:32f.; 18:15–35; 26:26–29; 1 Cor. 11:17–34.

It may be helpful to identify the significant emphases of this statement. A couple of general observations are important before looking at specifics, however. First, we note that the purpose of the statement is to facilitate a right and blessed receiving of the Sacrament. It attempts to do so by providing an unmistakable confession of the nature of the Supper and, then, who does and does not receive the Supper's intended blessing. This means, second, that the model is by no means relevant only to the "visitor," but to all who would commune. Third, the passages listed at the conclusion are not exhaustive of scriptural teaching on the matter of the Supper and right reception.

In more specific terms, we note the three major components of the statement. It addresses the nature of the Supper, then reception of it by individuals, and also considers the Supper as a confession of faith by a church. Under the heading of individual reception, both a blessed and a harmful reception are recognized and delineated.

THEOLOGICAL COMPONENTS FOR LUTHERAN COMMUNION PRACTICE

1. The Nature of the Lord's Supper ("our Lord gives into our mouths not only bread and wine but his very body and blood to eat and to drink")
    a. The Sacrament is Christ's body and blood, given orally together with bread and wine, for the forgiveness of sins.[4]
    b. Christ's body and blood is intended to benefit the communicant and

4 The term "real presence" has come into common use among Lutherans to describe what is distinctive about Lutheran teaching on the Lord's Supper. We should recognize, however, that while there is a Lutheran understanding of Christ's real presence—namely, his bodily sacramental presence in the bread and wine—other Christians also refer to the "real presence" of Christ in the Sacrament but mean something different. As an Anglican theologian quipped recently: "A spiritual presence is still a real presence." This document therefore avoids that term. See Albert B. Collver, "'Real Presence:' An Overview and History of the Term," *Concordia Journal* (2002): 142–159. "Everyone seems to affirm some kind of doctrine of the real presence. Luther taught the real presence. Calvin taught the real presence. The Reformed Church teaches the real presence. The Roman Catholic Church teaches the real presence. The Anglican Church teaches the real presence. The great accomplishment of the ecumenical discussions in the twentieth century was the recognition that, despite whatever has been the historical teaching of a particular confession of the Lord's Supper, everyone in fact confesses the real presence. This is made clear in the Baptism, Eucharist, Ministry (B.E.M.) document of 1982. All Christian churches that accept the B.E.M. document indeed confess the real presence. What then is the real presence? B.E.M. does not

the church, but it may be received to the harm of both individual and church.

2. The Sacrament's Benefit (or Harm) to Individuals ("for the forgiveness of sins and to strengthen our union with him and with one another")
    a. Faith in Christ and his word is necessary for a blessed reception.
        i. Faith in Christ and his word implies both baptism in the Triune Name and trust (faith) in Christ as Savior.[5]
            i. The communicant is then also called to believe Jesus' clear words that the Sacrament is his body and blood.[6]
            ii. The repentant communicant has faith in the Lord's promise that in the Sacrament his or her sins are forgiven.[7]
            iii. In trusting Christ's word, the believing communicant receives the promised forgiveness and is reaffirmed and strengthened in his or her union with Christ and other Christians.[8]
    b. The source of harmful reception is unbelief or doubt in Christ's word.
        i. The unbaptized and uninstructed person who does not yet know or believe in Christ and his promises is unprepared and should not commune.[9]
        ii. The unrepentant person who does not seek Christ's forgiveness for sins—either general or particular—or refuses to forgive someone is unprepared and should not commune.[10]

---

provide us with an answer, but simply assures us that everyone confesses the real presence. This assurance of the real presence suggests that there are no remaining obstacles (or at least no insurmountable obstacles) which hinder Eucharistic fellowship among the church bodies." (Collver 143.)

5 It should be noted that while the Model Communion Statement does not make explicit mention of Holy Baptism, our Lord's clear words that to be his disciple one is to be baptized "in the name of the Father and of the Son and of the Holy Spirit" (Matt 28:19) and his promise, "Whoever believes and is baptized shall be saved" (Mark 16:16) remind us that the Supper he gives is for those who through baptismal faith are his disciples.

6 Mt 26:26–28; Mk 14:22–24; Lk 22:19–20; 1 Co 10:16; 11:23–25.

7 Note the sacrificial atonement emphasized in our Lord's words about the Supper as they are preserved by the various NT authors: Mt 26:28b "poured out for many for the forgiveness of sins"; Mk 14:24 "poured out for many"; Lk 22:19 "my body, which is given for you" and Lk 22:20 "This cup that is poured out for you"; 1 Co 11:24b "for you."

8 Here as always faith alone receives God's gracious promises (Rom 4:13–17; Gal 3:22).

9 Although the language sounds harsh to our ears, those who are not baptized and believing disciples of our Lord Jesus Christ are idolaters, having some god other than the one true God. Paul's warning in 1 Co 10:14–22 then applies. See also Hb 13:10, the passages in endnote 3, and the discussion in endnote 10.

10 1 Co 5:6–13. See also the discussion in endnote 11.

iii. The doubting person who denies or is unconvinced of what Jesus says of his bodily presence in the sacrament or its promised forgiveness is unprepared and should not commune.[11]

3. Communion, Communicant, and Church ("Holy Communion is a confession of the faith")

   a. The church confesses its faith in Christ and the Gospel as it worships and as it communes.[12]

   b. The person whose life is contrary to the teachings of the communing assembly introduces harmful division if he or she communes.[13]

   c. The person whose confession of faith (his or her personal beliefs and/or the public confession made through his or her affiliation with a particular church body) is contrary to the communing assembly ("to the faith which is confessed at this altar") introduces the possibility of doubt, confusion, and potentially harmful division if he or she communes.[14]

---

11 1 Co 11:27–32. Although this passage never says, in so many words, "you should not commune," the unavoidable implication of these verses is to call a halt to unworthy communing. Note that Paul is writing to fellow Christians ("brothers" 11:33) with deep pastoral concern, seeking to show them what is wrong and to correct them. They are under judgment and discipline (11:29–32). Yet, the purpose is not so much that they would not commune, but that they would commune worthily, examining and judging themselves (11:28, 30) "so that we may not be condemned along with the world" (11:32). Thus he distinguishes between judgment and condemnation: (v. 29) ὁ γὰρ ἐσθίων και πίνων <u>κρίμα</u> ἑαυτῷ ἐσθίει και πίνει μὴ διακρίνων τὸ σῶμα; (v. 32) κρινόμενοι δὲ ὑπὸ [τοῦ] κυρίου παιδευόμεθα, ἵνα μὴ σὺν τῷ κόσμῳ <u>κατακριθῶμεν</u>. Not irrelevant to Paul's warning is the one from Hebrews 10:28–31. There the writer warns of spurning the Son of God and profaning his blood. This risks the fearful reality of condemnation: "fall[ing] into the hands of the living God."

12 1 Co 11:26.

13 1 Co 11:17–34. Jeffrey Gibbs shows that the "overt sin" in Corinth was moral in nature. Paul condemns those guilty of the overt sin of a loveless attitude toward others, turning the Supper into a gluttonous, drunken gathering while providing nothing for the poor who come later to the table. The underlying concern of Paul, however, is to address the primary issue—the problem that these Corinthians are not discerning the Supper's reality as Christ's bodily presence. See Gibbs, "'The Body for the Body': 1 Cor 11:17–34 and Pastoral Practice in the Local Congregation" (unpublished paper presented at "Common Ground" Forum, Pacific Southwest District, Jan 14–15, 1997, p. 8) [Cf. the article above, pp. 445–59. MH]. On file in the office of the Commission on Theology and Church Relations.

14 1 Co 11:26. See also 1 Co 1:10; Eph 4:1–3; Phil 1:27. Doubt or confusion are significant dangers of failing to address the confessional aspect of the Supper "For we do not intend to admit to the sacrament and administer it to those who do not know what they seek or why they come" (LC VI:2). "However, a person who does not believe these words or doubts them is unworthy and unprepared, because the words 'for you' require truly believing hearts" (SC VI:9–10). See pages 32–38 and 41–46 of the CTCR's report *Admission to the Lord's Supper* for a more extensive discussion of "communion as confession."

d. As "the steward of the mysteries of God," the pastor is called by God through the congregation to ensure faithful administration of the Supper.

A final observation is in order about the Model Communion Statement. The statement is obviously intended to inform individuals who may wish to commune about the congregation's understanding of the Sacrament and to help them decide whether to come to receive it. As such, it fits fully into the scriptural admonition, "Let a person examine himself, then, and so eat of the bread and drink of the cup" (1 Co 11:28). This individual self-examination is paramount for right preparation and a blessed reception of the Sacrament. Such personal responsibility should not be misunderstood, however. There is also a responsibility for the congregation, acting especially through its pastor, in the matter of admission to the Supper. This responsibility flows especially out of love for the individual who might commune to his or her harm.[15] For that reason the model urges that in any uncertainties about Communion, individuals should "speak with the pastor or an usher" (with the presumption that the latter would direct the person to the pastor) before partaking.

The preceding comments and the specific points identified within the components are intended to be of further help in the original goal of the Model Communion Statement, to aid in the evaluation and crafting of Communion announcements or statements.

SAMPLE STATEMENTS

In that regard, we are providing a sampling of Communion statements that are representative of some of those in use in the LCMS. Each statement is followed by brief comments in light of the preceding discussion.[16]

---

15 The harm caused by unworthy eating of the body and blood of Christ described by Saint Paul includes, not only, judgment (κρίμα; v. 29) but also weakness (ἀσθενής; v. 30), illness (ἄρρωστος; v. 30), and, in some cases, death (κοιμάομαι; v. 30). One of the reasons partakers of the Lord's Supper are instructed first is so that they do not sin against the body and blood of Christ in ignorance and thereby receive judgment that may include weakness, illness, and death instead of "forgiveness of sins, life, and salvation" (see SC 5). Therefore, when a person does not recognize or denies that the body and blood of Christ is given in the Lord's Supper, the pastor as a "steward of the mysteries of God" has a responsibility to prevent the person from receiving the body and blood of Jesus to his judgment and harm.

16 Some of these statements were shared in whole or in part with CTCR staff members. Others appeared in various online discussions. Still others are from congregational visits. All have been modified to some extent in order to avoid the names of pastors or congregations, to correct grammar, and to remove extraneous matters (e.g., references to the manner of distribution, to the use of individual cups versus the chalice, to availability of low/no alcohol wine, and so forth).

STATEMENT 1

Admission to Holy Communion is by invitation of the Lord, presented through the Church to those who are baptized. Visitors who are baptized and who trust that Christ is truly present in this sacrament are welcome to join us at the Lord's Table.

Comments: This statement is welcoming, but unhelpfully brief. It says almost nothing about the nature of the Sacrament, without any reference to Christ's body and blood. It also fails to say anything of either the benefit of the Sacrament (forgiveness) or of the possibility of receiving the body and blood to one's judgment. Baptism is required as is trust in Christ's presence, but that presence is unclear. Where is Christ not present? Thus, faith in Christ or his words is only vaguely implied. This statement also fails to address the confessional aspect of the Supper.

STATEMENT 2

If you have never communed at this altar, please introduce yourself to our pastor so that he may hear your faith before we share Communion with you. We follow the biblical and apostolic practice of closed Communion. This practice respects Communion as an expression of full unity in doctrine and practice of all who partake. It also assures that no one receives Communion to their condemnation. Only members in good standing of congregations of The Lutheran Church—Missouri Synod (LCMS) which also practice closed Communion are welcome to receive Communion at this altar.

Comments: This statement takes to heart the importance of preventing harmful reception of the Sacrament. Its tone is one of stern warning addressed only to visitors with no guidance for members. No mention is made of the nature of the Sacrament as Christ's body and blood or of his promise of forgiveness or the opportunity of strengthening one's faith. Communion participation is seemingly based entirely on being a member of an LCMS congregation—and only some of them (those that practice closed Communion in the manner that this congregation practices it). Since no attention is given to repentant self-examination or to faith in Christ's words of promise, this statement may actually foster unworthy communing.

STATEMENT 3

The Communion Confession

I believe that I am a sinner. I repent of my sin and ask God's forgiveness. With his help I will amend my sinful life. I believe that Jesus Christ is my only Lord and Savior from sin, Satan, and death. I believe that the risen Christ is really present in the Sacrament and, under the form of the bread and the wine, I receive his true body and blood for the forgiveness of my sin and the strengthening of my faith and life. I resolve to dedicate my life to the service of my Lord by regular group worship, sacrificial giving, thankful living, and sharing the Gospel with others.[17]

Comments: This statement invites thoughtful self-examination. It addresses the nature of the Sacrament and speaks of its benefit, the forgiveness of sins. While personal faith is emphasized, there is no mention of being baptized. Unaddressed as well is the matter of the Sacrament as confession of faith and thus, its churchly character and its intent toward unity. While thoroughly individual in nature, the statement also misses important individual needs. It leaves unanswered the questions or concerns of an individual with a troubled conscience too weak to make bold resolutions or fearful that he can give sacrificially enough, be thankful enough, or share the Gospel often enough. It may then keep such persons away from an acknowledged source of strengthened "faith and life." Similarly, the individual with uncertain beliefs or doubts is left without any guidance or invitation to seek the aid and counsel of a pastor. Lastly, individuals whose beliefs are inconsistent with or contrary to the congregation's confession in areas other than the Supper—Baptism, for instance—are left to assume that such differences pose no obstacle to the unity of the altar.

STATEMENT 4

The Lord's Supper: God's Word teaches the real presence of Christ's body and blood invisibly in, with and under the bread and wine for the forgiveness of sins. We take seriously the spiritual care of those who commune at our altar. The Word of God states that no one offend against Christ and His Word by denying His true presence and its promise and seal of forgiveness. Because those who eat and drink our Lord's body and blood unworthily do so to their great harm (see 1 Cor. 11:27–29), and because Holy Communion is a confession of what is taught and believed at this altar (1 Cor. 11:26), any who are not yet instructed, in doubt, or who hold a confession (beliefs) differing from that of this congregation (that is, belong to another church body or denomination) and yet desire to receive the sacrament, will want to first speak with the pastor before communing. As a courtesy, guests from sister congregations of the LCMS or from congregations of the American Association of Lutheran Churches (AALC) are also asked to introduce themselves to the pastor before communing.

Comments: This statement speaks about the nature of the Sacrament, its benefits, and its churchly character as a confession of faith by the assembly. While indicating the benefit of the Sacrament, it gives greatest attention to the potential that the Supper can be received to the harm of individuals. It asks all those who

17 This is an example of a very common statement which is often presented in the form of several questions. The questions ask for a Yes or No response and those who answer all the questions with a Yes are then welcomed to the Table.

are visiting to speak with the pastor, identifying those who share the same beliefs as the congregation and urging pastoral counsel for the uninstructed, doubtful, or those with other beliefs. While referring to all "who commune at our altar," it does not directly address the importance of repentant faith for every communicant.

STATEMENT 5[18]

A Christmas Communion Statement: The coming of Christ in the flesh at Bethlehem was a concrete outward act of God in humble means that was despised by the world. The flesh and blood coming of Christ in the sacrament is also a concrete outward act of God in humble means that can be despised. Rather than despise it, however, God would have us delight in it! With deep thankfulness for His gifts to us here we also express our deep desire to celebrate it according to God's Will. As this includes oneness in the faith we confess (doctrine), guests who desire to commune are asked to speak with the pastor before the service.

Comments: This seasonal announcement addresses the nature of the Supper with a beautiful link between the Incarnation and the Sacrament. The statement is helpful for members and guests alike. Little further teaching about the Lord's Supper or its benefit is provided, but unity of confession is emphasized together with the need for guests to speak to the pastor before communing.

STATEMENT 6

An Easter Communion Statement: In the Lord's Supper, the Risen Christ is at once the Giver and the Gift! By His promise His very body and blood are really present; and thereby we come into immediate contact with the exalted Christ! As we do so, witness is also given to oneness in doctrine by those who receive the Sacrament together. For this reason, we practice close(d) Communion and kindly ask guests to speak with the pastor before the service.

Comments: Once again a seasonal connection to the Sacrament is made that is helpful for all who read it. The presence of Christ's body and blood in the Supper is affirmed, but without specific mention of the benefit of forgiveness. Oneness in doctrine is emphasized and guests are again asked to speak to the pastor.

CONCLUSION

The foregoing examples and comments are not provided to point fingers, chide, or be picayune. The purpose is to illustrate how theological components underlying

18 Statements 5 and 6 are from a helpful booklet that provides both Communion announcements and artwork that is seasonal in nature, *Lord May Your Body and Your Blood Be for My Soul the Highest Good* by Rev. Kenneth Wieting (originally published in 1990, now available from Luther Memorial Chapel and University Center, 3833 N Maryland Ave., Shorewood, WI 53211).

the CTCR's model statement can be used for evaluative purposes. Moreover, the Model Communion Statement itself is by no means perfect. It neglects to mention Baptism. Further, it could have clarified "who hold[s] a confession different from the congregation and LCMS" by mentioning membership in a different church body. It could also clarify those "not yet instructed" as those who have not been confirmed or admitted to communion at their home congregations.

In addition, the Model Communion Statement is most directly pointed toward the visitor and is seemingly less helpful for the self-examination of member communicants. The CTCR recognizes that the focus of Communion statements tends overwhelmingly to be toward non-member guests or visitors. We acknowledge that this tendency is perfectly understandable, given the fact that there is so much variety among Christians and also within the LCMS on the question of who should be invited to commune. Nevertheless, the matter of admission to the Supper should not be so heavily focused on one particular problem (a problem that is by definition going to involve only a small number of visitors) that it may neglect the weightier reality that *all* who commune are called to be worthy and well-prepared.

It is the CTCR's hope that the guidelines provided here will help our pastors and congregations toward the goal of unity in our understanding of the Lord's Supper and in local practices that are in keeping with that teaching. This indeed would mean that Communion statements should be carefully considered and crafted in a way that is consistent with our theology. But the CTCR also emphasizes that as helpful as a well-crafted, doctrinally sound Communion statement may be, it cannot replace pastoral care. Indeed, perhaps the single most helpful "Communion message" for guests that is consistent with Lutheran teaching and practice is that they should speak with the pastor before communing. (Of course, this means that the pastor needs to find ways to make himself available for this important responsibility.) In that way the pastor can, on a personal level, exercise his responsibility as a steward of Christ's mysteries (1 Cor 4:1) to provide the sort of spiritual care implied by the confessional term, "examination." The pastor is called to care for the soul. In gentle, loving interaction with visitors who inquire about participation in the Supper, he can provide spiritual care to them. Yet, this care for souls is not for visitors alone. Ongoing teaching and preaching about the Sacrament—its nature, benefits, and confessing character—is far more important than any written announcement. Such proclamation is pastoral care for a church's members and will not only help them rightly to commune, it will also help them to assist in spiritual care for others as they invite guests to worship, explain Lutheran convictions and beliefs to their visiting family members and friends, and encourage them to take Communion and confession to heart.

Adopted December 11, 2014
Commission on Theology and Church Relations
The Lutheran Church—Missouri Synod

CHAPTER TWENTY-FIVE

Concerning the Preparation Which Is to Be Exercised in Order That One May Receive the Holy Eucharist Worthily

Martin Chemnitz
Translated by Fred Kramer

Chapter VII

If it is not seemly that a person should approach any sacred function at all except in a holy manner, then surely, the more a Christian man is informed with respect to the holiness and divine quality of this Sacrament, the more he should diligently take heed not to approach this Sacrament without great reverence and holiness, particularly since we read with the apostle these words full of awe: "Whoever eats and drinks unworthily, eats and drinks judgment to himself, not discerning the Lord's body."

Therefore he who would communicate is to be reminded of the precept: "Let a man examine himself." The custom of the Church declares that this examination is necessary so that no one who is conscious of having committed a mortal sin, no matter how contrite he may seem to himself, ought to approach the holy Eucharist without prior sacramental confession. This holy synod has decreed that this should be observed in perpetuity by all Christians, also by the priests on whom it is incumbent by virtue of their office to celebrate, provided there is no lack of a confessor. But if, in case of urgent necessity, he celebrates without prior confession, let him confess as soon as possible.

CANON XI

If anyone says that faith alone is sufficient preparation for receiving the most holy Sacrament of the Eucharist, let him be anathema. And lest so great a sacrament be received unworthily, and therefore for death and condemnation, this holy synod decrees and declares that, in the case of those whose conscience is burdened with mortal sin, sacramental confession must of necessity go before, no matter how contrite they consider themselves, provided a confessor can be had. But if anyone shall presume to teach, preach, or stubbornly assert, or even in a public disputation to defend the contrary, he is by that very act excommunicated.

EXAMINATION

1. I shall explain first of all in a few words what is the teaching and understanding of our churches concerning this preparation on the basis of the Word of God. After that it will not be obscure what it is that the papalists want to condemn in this our teaching. The antithesis will also show the errors in the papalist teaching concerning this preparation.

2. First of all, so far as the question whether there is such a preparation is concerned, there is no doubt or controversy. For Paul clearly asserts that not all receive the Eucharist worthily, but many unworthily. Neither does he want unworthy reception to be something about which one does not trouble oneself, as if it either did not matter or were some infirmity which clearly did not harm one's salvation, even if one did eat and drink unworthily at the Lord's Supper. Rather, he thunders with great vehemence against such levity and security, and affirms that those who eat unworthily eat judgment to themselves, so that they become guilty of violating the body and blood of Christ. And indeed he adds that God often shows this judgment on those who eat unworthily already in this life with external punishments. Therefore he demands that whoever is about to approach this table should first examine himself, and so eat of that bread and drink of that cup. Therefore Paul does not preach concerning this examination and preparation in a casual or cold manner, but earnestly and with true apostolic fervor, lest someone partake of the Eucharist unworthily.

There is also no doubt that it is incumbent on all ministers of the Church that they diligently and earnestly admonish their parishioners, and indeed set before them the very grave threats of guilt and divine judgment, lest they approach the Lord's Supper without making the prior examination or preparation of which Paul speaks. And if those sin who from ignorance or thoughtlessness eat unworthily, the sin of those will be much more grievous who, although they owe it from the nature of their office, yet do not instruct them by reproving, admonishing, exhorting, and teaching that and in what way they should examine themselves, or what preparation they should make, lest they eat and drink unworthily to their judgment, but may worthily receive the Eucharist together with its fruits and effects. These things are diligently and earnestly taught and transmitted among us. This I wanted to show briefly, lest someone should suspect that there is a controversy over this matter, as if we held and taught that no examination or preparation at all should be made in order that a person may receive the Eucharist worthily.

3. But this must chiefly be asked, what and what manner of preparation is to be made, or what the Pauline examination is and in what it consists, in order that we may be able to eat and drink worthily in the Lord's Supper, so that we may be partakers of all the good things or benefits which are offered in the Supper. This is truly a difficult question, and of the greatest importance. Therefore it is not to be explained either by our own private thoughts, or by the opinions of other men, no matter who they may be, but it must be explained according to the teaching of the Word of God. Moreover, we must here understand worthiness, not merit, nor yet a comparison or analogy of excellence in the recipient with the excellence of the food, namely, the body and blood of Christ. For so the ancients piously used the words of the centurion: "Lord, I am not worthy to have You come under my roof," and what Jacob says: "I am not worthy of the least of all the steadfast love and all the faithfulness which Thou hast shown to Thy servant." David also says: "Who am I, and what is my father's house?" Likewise: "What is man, that Thou art mindful of him?"

But to eat worthily is to use the Eucharist in the manner and for the purpose for which it was instituted by the Son of God Himself. For so Ambrose correctly understands and explains this worthiness. Paul indeed embraces this whole teaching in the one word *dokimazein*, which means to think about, consider, and investigate whatever we are examining. Thus Romans 12:2: The godly, commanded to institute the new obedience, ought to prove what is the good will of God. Ephesians 5:17: They understand what pleases God. 1 John 4:1: We are commanded to "test the spirits to see whether they are of God." 1 Thessalonians 5:21: "Test everything; hold fast what is good." And Romans 1:28: A *nous adokimos*, "base mind," is one which orders life in such a way that it neither considers nor cares, even though the things it does are condemned by God and man and by its own conscience.

Therefore that man may be said to examine himself in preparation for the Lord's Supper who in a certain way and according to a certain rule looks attentively at himself and examines and investigates whether he approaches the Sacrament with the kind of heart and disposition of mind which the institution of the Lord's Supper prescribes and requires. For St. Paul says thus (2 Corinthians 13:5): "Examine yourselves, to see whether you are holding to your faith," and he immediately explains the word *examine*, namely, "that you may know that Christ is in you." Therefore the interpretation of the word *dokimazein* shows that he who is about to approach the Lord's table ought to regard attentively, explore, and examine his mind, heart, conscience, and his whole self, whether he is able to use the Lord's Supper, not to judgment but worthily and with profit.

Now there needs to be some sure norm and rule for this consideration, examination, and exploration, so that anyone who disagrees with it and fights against it is judged to eat unworthily. If, however, the mind is informed and disposed according to this rule, then we may be certain that we are not eating and drinking unworthily to judgment in the Lord's Supper, but worthily and with profit. However, the simplest, surest, and safest norm and rule is the institution of the Lord's Supper itself. For also Paul shows (1 Corinthians 11:23–34) from the rule of the institution that some among the Corinthians were eating unworthily. And when he wants to show how they could eat the Lord's Supper worthily and with profit, he sets before them the institution itself as he had received it from the Lord.

4. For the sake of teaching, this instruction about the eating of the unworthy and the examination or preparation of the worthy can be divided into three parts:

I. That the mind, from the Words of Institution, understands, believes with firm assent, and in the use of the Lord's Supper reverently ponders what this Sacrament is, what its use is, and what the nature of this whole action is—that here the Son of God, God and man, is Himself present, offering and imparting through the ministry to those who eat, together with the bread and wine, His body and blood, in order that by means of this most precious testimony and pledge He may unite Himself with us and apply, seal, and confirm to us the New Testament covenant of grace. And this faith, resting on the Words of Institution, excites and shapes reverence and devotion of mind as this Sacrament is used.

Even as the institution itself shows that this is necessary and required for worthy eating, it is seen also from Paul, who says that those among the Corinthians were eating unworthily who thought no more reverently of the Lord's Supper than about some ordinary supping together, came to it with no greater reverence and devotion, and thus did not discern the body of the Lord, that is, they did not consider how immeasurably more precious and worthy is the food of the Lord's Supper than in other, ordinary suppers, where the gifts of God are also present. Therefore those persons eat unworthily who approach the Lord's Supper filled with perverse, wicked, or worldly opinions concerning this Sacrament; likewise those who approach either with stupid or with studied ignorance, or with irreligious thoughtlessness with respect to the teaching and faith of the Eucharist, so that they plainly either do not understand or do not at all consider what manner of action is there instituted by the Son of God Himself, and so they bring no devotion of mind or reverence toward this action of the Son of God. Ambrose calls it receiving the body of the Lord thoughtlessly and negligently. Here also belong those who either pervert the action of the institution or invent other uses and purposes for it, outside of or against the institution.

II. Those eat unworthily who come without repentance, that is, those who do not consider their sins in such a way that they may grieve over them. These are not greatly terrified by a consideration of the wrath of God, but persevere in transgressions against conscience, yield to evil lusts, and do not lay aside the purpose to do evil. For Christ says: "Do this in remembrance of Me." Paul interprets this as referring to proclaiming the death of Christ. Now consideration of the death of Christ is at the same time also a forcible reminder of the abominable nature of sin, and of the fierce wrath of God against our sins. Since the virtues or merits neither of any men nor angels were able to placate this wrath, it was necessary that it should be placated by the death of the Son Himself.

Now the Son of God did not institute His Supper in order that we might learn to think lightly of sin, and by its use be strengthened in the purpose to sin, as though we received there the privilege of being base, without the fear of God, without contrition and conversion, and could securely persevere and continue in sins against conscience or return to them. Therefore anyone who approaches the Lord's Supper with such a purpose and with this mind by this very fact treats the body of Christ with contempt and heaps up new sins on top of his prior sins by this even sadder offense.

Therefore he who would eat worthily at the Lord's Supper ought to examine himself that he may bring to it repentance or the fear of God. Now repentance embraces at the same time also a good purpose. Thus Paul says that those Corinthians were eating unworthily who came together not for better but for worse, who nourished dissension, shamed the poor, and despised the Church of God at the very celebration of the Lord's Supper.

III. To worthy or salutary eating at the Lord's Supper faith is above all things necessary. For in the action of the Lord's Supper the Son of God, by the imparting of His body and blood, offers, applies, and seals the remission of sins and the whole benefit of the New Testament. Now this promise calls for faith; not merely that you say in a general way that these things are true which God promises about His grace on account of the merit of the Mediator, but that in the Supper the Son of God by a special action testifies that He wants to receive into the fellowship of His body and blood everyone who eats, that by the impartation of His body and blood He wants to communicate, give, apply, and seal to each one the benefits of the New Testament. Therefore faith is called for, seeking and accepting with thanksgiving the blessings there offered and given, so that all may confess that this promise pertains also to them, that it is communicated, applied, and sealed to them, and that this is done by the imparting of a most precious pledge—the body and blood of Christ. Yes, it is for this reason that we come to the Lord's Supper, that this faith may be kindled and strengthened in us. For this is the true remembrance of Christ. And in the Words of Institution Christ says to everyone who eats: "Take, this is My body, which is given for you; take, this is the New Testament in My blood, which is shed for you for the remission of sins."

Ambrose testifies that in former times the Eucharist was given with these words. To these words all who ate added the confession of their faith by answering, "Amen." This formula pleases me exceedingly, because it applies the very Words of Institution to everyone who eats, in harmony with the true nature of the Sacrament. Therefore those do not do rightly who, though they are truly penitent over former sins, flee the use of the Sacrament because they are conscious of sins and are weak in faith. For this glorious pledge is offered to us in order that, reconciled to God, we may be restored to the covenant of grace of the New Testament from which we had fallen and be confirmed in it, and that, by means of its use, faith may be kindled and strengthened.

5. The antithesis will show who those are who eat unworthily, because they do not bring true faith to it, namely, those who imagine that the eating profits *ex opere operato*, without a good impulse in the user, who as they eat rely for its salutary use on their own worthiness and purity, as though they were worthy of this heavenly food, or who imagine that by the act of eating they merit remission of sins. For in His Supper Christ does not want to distribute the merits and rewards of our works, but even as He offers His merits gratis there, so He wants them accepted by faith. Likewise, those who teach that men neither should nor can assert that in the use of the Supper the benefits of the New Testament are certainly given and applied to them, but should always be carried to and fro in uncertain doubting, even though the sealing is made by the offering of the body and blood of Christ—surely these make the Son of God Himself a liar in the institution of the Supper.

Also those eat unworthily who come without faith in this sense, that they give no thought to what they seek and receive there; likewise those who come with an Epicurean persuasion, as though the privilege of turpitude were given there, so that they might be able further to persevere freely and with impunity in crimes, continue in them or return to them. For true faith does not ask and seek that sins may remain and be increased; it asks and seeks remission of sins and liberation from sins. And this faith is afterward the mother of the good intention to avoid sins in the future and to obey God according to His Commandments.

6. There is no doubt that this is the true examination or preparation, for it agrees with the norm or rule of the institution of the Lord's Supper. Moreover there is preserved in our churches the godly practice that all who are about to partake of the Supper are first examined, to ascertain what they understand concerning the Sacrament. They are admonished to examine themselves, as has been said, lest they eat unworthily; the more unlearned are instructed how they should and can examine themselves.

Moreover, because the Lord's Supper was instituted so that by its use faith in the reconciliation with God may be confirmed and sealed, a godly person will not neglect but will with thanksgiving use all those means by which God has proposed to faith that it should seek and receive grace or reconciliation, such as the proclamation and hearing of the Gospel promise, either in public preaching or in private absolution. Afterward there follows the confirmation and sealing of this application in participation in the Lord's Supper. For these reasons and in this manner the practice of confession before Communion is devoutly observed in our churches.

7. This examination and preparation is not, however, prescribed and demanded in such a way that it is wholly perfect, without any infirmity and weakness, so that it lacks nothing. For Christ instituted His Supper for this purpose, that repentance may be kindled and increased in us by the remembrance of His death, in order that faith may be strengthened and invigorated by the giving and sealing of the New Testament in the use of the Supper. He knows our frame, that we are flesh; therefore He joins Himself to us by the bestowal of His most holy body and blood, that the body of sin may be mortified, the old leaven more and more purged out, and the newness which has been begun may grow and increase. Therefore the preparation is not required that we may, by our own worthiness and purity, render ourselves worthy of this food so that it may be salutary for us because we are worthy of it on account of our own cleanness. For this persuasion truly makes men unworthy. But Paul demands an examination in order that we may become hungry and thirsty for this food and drink, which is set before us for our salvation in this Supper, and that, knowing our weakness, we may know that we have need of the medicine and remedy of this physician, who provides this Supper for us, and in what way it must be received and used in a salutary manner for our healing.

8. This is the simple and true teaching, drawn from and constructed on the basis of the Words of Institution, about the examination or preparation which a person should employ in order that he may receive the Sacrament worthily. For it is on this basis that Paul preaches to the Corinthians about the eating of the unworthy.

So also the ancients speak about the preparation. Hesychius says that that person receives the Eucharist unworthily, through ignorance, who does not know its power and greatness. Augustine says: "This Sacrament looks for the hunger of the inner man"; therefore whoever does not feel his sin and infirmity is not fit to partake of this Sacrament. The judgment of Chrysostom is: "Because those who are well do not need a physician, but those who are ill, therefore that person is shut out from the power of this Sacrament who, proud of himself, approaches resolutely but with disgust." The same man says: "Let no one commune unless he is a disciple of Christ; otherwise he eats and drinks judgment to himself." Augustine frequently argues thus: "Whoever believes in Christ eats Him in order that He may both remain in Christ and also have Christ remaining in him. But whoever comes to the Eucharist devoid of this faith indeed eats outwardly but not inwardly. He lays hold with his teeth but does not grasp with his mind." It is as Gregory says: "He receives the body and blood of Christ according to its substance but not according to its saving power. He receives the Sacrament, but the life of Christ he does not receive." Very beautiful is the statement of Augustine in which he says of his mother, Monica, that she bound her soul with the chain of faith to that sacrifice which is dispensed in the Lord's Supper so that neither lion nor dragon could tear it away.

9. Now that these things have been thus set forth, the manner of our examination of the seventh chapter and the eleventh canon will be neither difficult nor unclear.

I. They say they condemn those who hold that faith alone is sufficient preparation for taking the Eucharist. The words are, however, put in such a way that they seem to ascribe to us this opinion: Even if a person perseveres in crimes without repentance and holds fast to the purpose to do evil, so long only as he holds the historical faith concerning the essence of the Sacrament, or holds the Epicurean persuasion that impenitence is not punishable, he is sufficiently prepared for worthy eating of the Lord's Supper. But that this is falsely attributed to our churches is clear from what we have said concerning the true examination.

II. Let us consider why they use this trick. The reader will discover that in this whole chapter, where they specifically undertook an explanation of the teaching about preparation for taking the Eucharist, no mention is made by so much as even one syllable of faith, which seeks, apprehends, and accepts the promise of the New Testament, which the Son of God offers, communicates, and seals by the giving of His body and blood in the use of the Sacrament to each and every one who eats. For this faith, applying as it does the forgiveness of sins to individuals, since indeed it is sealed and strengthened by partaking of Christ's body and blood, is diametrically opposed to the teaching of the papalists concerning uncertainty. It is for this reason that they are unwilling to concede any place to this faith in the preparation for the salutary reception of the Eucharist. Nevertheless they have not dared to banish faith simply and clearly from this preparation. Therefore they set faith alone in opposition to repentance or contrition, and condemn anyone who says that faith alone is sufficient preparation. If this is understood of the opinion of ungodly persons, who imagine that they can continue without repentance in the purpose to do evil, I willingly grant this. But it is a far different thing, as I will now show, which they have undertaken to condemn in this canon.

III. We must observe in what sense Luther, in *De captivitate Babylonica*, says that worthy preparation is nothing else than faith that trusts the divine promise set forth and offered in the Lord's Supper. For it is from there that the men of Trent picked something in the eleventh canon. Luther does not, however, exclude the acknowledging of our sins, and contrition or repentance, but is fighting against the papalists, who themselves have and teach others many and varied preparatory works. They think that when they have performed these they are sufficiently worthily prepared to attend or hear Mass, and also for the Communion itself, with the result that they are not concerned about faith, which asks, seeks, apprehends, and accepts the promise of the New Testament in the Supper. They also demand penitence in order that they may ascribe worthy preparation to its works and merit, so that salutary eating may rest on our preparatory works by virtue of our worthiness and purity.

Against these opinions Luther teaches that the Lord's Supper was instituted by Christ not that we may there confer something on God and thus procure salvation for ourselves in the Lord's Supper by our works; but what the Son of God earned by offering up His body and shedding His blood, that, His gratuitous mercy coming before any merit on our part, He offers to us in the promise of the Gospel, to which He adds as pledge and seal the gift of His body and blood under the bread and wine. Now the gratuitous promise of the Gospel is apprehended and accepted, not by our works and merits but by faith (Romans 4 and 11). And this is the task solely of faith, without which the promise is of no use to us, as we have shown in the first part of the *Examination* about faith.

In addition the contrast between our unworthiness and the divine excellence of the food and drink in the Eucharist disturbs and terrifies the conscience. From this temptation we cannot escape if we place our confidence in our contrition, confession, satisfaction, preparatory works, and our own worthiness, purity, and capability. Therefore we must look at the promise of the New Testament which is set before us in the Lord's Supper and freely offers to us the body and blood of Christ, and with them all the benefits of the New Testament. For their acceptance it does not demand our merits and worthiness but only that we acknowledge our poverty, weakness, and unworthiness, and hunger and thirst for this grace and so accept by faith the things which, because of the merit of Christ, are offered to us in the Lord's Supper. Surely these things, flowing as they do from the nature of the gratuitous promise of the Gospel and from the mutual relation between the promise and faith, are most certain and true. It is in this sense that Luther says that faith alone is the true and sufficient preparation for receiving the Eucharist. He specifically states: "Upon this faith there will follow at once of its own accord the sweetest mood of the heart, that is, love." He also teaches that this faith is manifest in repentance.

This is the teaching which Canon XI condemns in order that it may uphold the contrary dogma about trust in our contrition, confession, satisfaction, worthiness, and purity through preparatory works, in order that they may teach that salutary eating in the Lord's Supper depends on these. But in this way the enjoyment of the Lord's Supper is rendered either useless or hollow to us, or certainly doubtful and uncertain. For the scholastics teach that there is a certain preparation which is sufficient and true. Bonaventura says that this consists in the expulsion of all sin, in reverence and love. Those who come so prepared, they say, attain the benefit of the

Eucharist. They say that another preparation is that of probability, when a person does what he can, and believes in the judgment of his own conscience that he is prepared. But this preparation is often not truly sufficient. Here they agree that whoever comes thus does not receive the effects of this Sacrament. They argue, however, over whether such a one eats unworthily and involves himself in a new mortal sin by communing thus. And since it is uncertain when we have a truly sufficient preparation, and when of probability only, the conscience will always remain uncertain whether one eats worthily or unworthily. Thus the necessary consolation which is set before us by Christ in the use of the Lord's Supper will always be wrenched away. This truly is, briefly put, the way by which they scare people away from more frequent use of the Lord's Supper, in order that they may the more avidly follow and embrace the trafficking in private Masses, which is said to be meritorious without peril to wipe out any and all mortal sins. The reader should know that all these things are wrapped up in this eleventh canon, which are not easily noticed at first glance, unless the debates from which this canon was plucked are looked into and considered.

IV. This also must be carefully weighed, that Chapter VII says that one should not go to the Eucharist without great holiness, lest we eat judgment. Now the apostles quite commonly use the phrase which calls believers or disciples of Christ saints, to whom also God Himself says: "You shall be holy, because I am holy." However, even as this word *qadosh* signifies what has been separated from common and worldly use for sacred use, and is applied to either divine service or cult, so people are called saints not because they are so perfectly pure and clean and cleansed of all filth that they either can or should stand before God relying on their own purity; but those are called saints both by way of imputation and by way of a beginning who have turned from sin by repentance and have by faith been implanted in Christ, who is our sanctification, and have begun to be renewed by the Holy Spirit, even though they confess with Paul (Romans 7:7–25) and with Isaiah (64:6) that they are still contaminated with much wrongdoing and uncleanness. They are called saints in Christ Jesus. Thus therefore the ancient Church rightly cried out before the Communion: "Holy things for the saints." For Communion is given to none but the baptized, whom Christ has sanctified, cleansing them by the washing of water with the Word (Ephesians 5:26). And certainly, as has been said, those who would come to Communion worthily ought to bring repentance, which according to the Hebrew way of speaking is sanctification, that is, a turning from sin or uncleanness. They ought also to bring faith in the promise of the Gospel. Truly, the Word is the truth in which those who believe are sanctified (John 17:17), for by faith the hearts are purified. (Acts 15:9)

We do not deny that one must come to the Eucharist with this kind of holiness, lest we eat judgment to ourselves. For whoever perseveres in sin without repentance, and holds fast to the purpose of doing evil, is truly unclean and unworthy.

In this sense Augustine says, *In Johannem homilia*, 88: "He who comes ought to be filled with holiness, and spotless." Thus also Hesychius, bk. 6, ch. 22, *Levitici*, says that the defiled are not to be admitted, nor the pure to be kept away. And he adds the explanation: "If a person who examines himself is conscious of sin in himself and feels that his soul is polluted, he is undoubtedly penitent, and after repentance is able to eat of the bread and to drink of the holy and unstained cup." Also he says, bk. 7, ch. 26, that this is proof that with a pure heart and conscience, intent upon repentance for those things in which he once sinned, he participates with the saints for ablution of their sins. This is the intent also of the saying of Augustine: "Let him who wishes to receive life change his life. For if he does not change his life, he will receive life to judgment and will be corrupted by it rather than healed, killed rather than made alive." *De ecclesiasticis dogmatibus*, ch. 53. "I say that whoever still has the will to sin is burdened even more, rather than purified, by reception of the Sacrament."

This is also the purpose of the custom of the ancient Church, which dismissed from the assembly the catechumens, and those on whom public penitence had been imposed on account of known crimes, when the time had come to partake of the Sacrament. Then the priest, about to offer the Eucharist to the people, said with a loud voice: "Holy things for the saints," in order that everyone might examine himself. If what Chapter VII says is understood in this sense, that one must come to the Eucharist with great reverence and holiness, I do not oppose it, for we also teach the same thing. But I see that the papalists interpret holiness to mean that we should by our own works and satisfactions, before communing, acquire for ourselves the highest purity and innocence of soul (for so Andrada says), so that it is not necessary in receiving the Sacrament to seek and receive either the application or the sealing of the remission of sins but that our purity is already worthy that Christ should join and communicate Himself to it with His body and all His benefits. For with this one argument Andrada proves that remission of sins is not received in the use of the Lord's Supper. This audacity conflicts with the very institution of the Lord's Supper and either makes proud Pharisees or frightens terrified consciences away from the use of the Lord's Supper.

V. They say that this examination is necessary in order that sacramental confession may of necessity precede Communion. I have indicated above in a few words for what use confession is preserved in our churches as useful for a true examination. But the men of Trent place the preparation in the work of confession itself, in the enumeration of all transgressions, and especially in the works of satisfaction which are imposed at confession. This examination they want to set down as necessary. But we shall have to speak of sacramental confession later, under the topic of penitence. For the present I only wanted to show what kind of preparation the papalists dispute about after they have buried faith.

ACKNOWLEDGMENTS

Chapter 1. "An Open Letter to Those in Frankfurt on the Main, 1533" by Martin Luther. Translated by Jon D. Vieker. Originally published in *Concordia Journal*, vol. 16, October 1990. Used by permission.

Chapter 2. "Theses on Communion Fellowship with Those Who Believe Differently" used by permission of translator Laurence White.

Chapter 3. "Closed Communion: In the Way of the Gospel; In the Way of the Law" by Norman Nagel. Originally published in *Concordia Journal*, vol. 17, January 1991. Used by permission.

Chapter 5. "Loehe Correspondence on Unionistic Communion Practice in the Bavarian Church" used by permission of translator Roland Ziegler.

Chapter 6. "Fellowship in the Lord's Supper and Church Fellowship in the Ancient Church" used by permission of translator Wolf Dietrich Knappe.

Chapter 7. "Opinion Concerning Communion Fellowship" used by permission of translator Wolf Dietrich Knappe.

Chapter 8. "Regarding the Question of Fellowship in the Lord's Supper" used by permission of translator Wolf Dietrich Knappe.

Chapter 11. "Church Fellowship and Telling the Good News about Jesus" used by permission of Carl C. Fickensher II.

Chapter 12. "Studies in Holy Communion" used by permission of the Lutheran Church of Australia, SA District.

Chapter 13. "The Confessional Principle" used by permission of Georg Hardt.

Chapter 14. "C. F. W. Walther on Admission to the Lord's Supper" is from *Walther's Works: Pastoral Theology* © Concordia Publishing House. Used with permission. www.cph.org.

Chapter 15. "1 Corinthians 11:29—'Discerning the Body'" originally published in *LOGIA: A Journal of Lutheran Theology*, vol. 3, no. 1, Epiphany 1994. Reprinted by permission of *LOGIA*, which retains the copyright to the article.

Chapter 16. "Step Up to the Altar" used by permission of Joel D. Biermann.

Chapter 17. "The Lord's Supper Today" is from *The Lord's Supper Today* © Concordia Publishing House, 1973. All rights reserved. www.cph.org.

Chapter 18. "Altar Fellowship, Church Fellowship, and Ecclesiastical Federation" is from *Letters to Lutheran Pastors*, vol. 2 © Concordia Publishing House, 2014. Used with permission. www.cph.org.

Chapter 19. "Selective Fellowship" is from *The Lonely Way: Selected Essays and Letters*, vol. 2 © Concordia Publishing House, 2002. All rights reserved. www.cph.org.

Chapter 21. "An Exegetical Case for Close(d) Communion" by Jeffrey A. Gibbs. Originally published in *Concordia Journal*, vol. 17, January 1991. Used by permission.

Chapter 22. "Who Is to Be Admitted to the Lord's Supper" is from *Christian Dogmatics*, vol. 3 © Concordia Publishing House, 1953. All rights reserved. www.cph.org.

Chapter 24. "Guidelines for Congregational, District, and Synodical Communion Statements" used by permission of The Lutheran Church—Missouri Synod.

Chapter 25. "Concerning the Preparation Which Is to Be Exercised in Order That One May Receive the Holy Eucharist Worthily" is from *Examination of the Council of Trent*, Part II © Concordia Publishing House, 2007. All rights reserved. www.cph.org.